Special Edition

USING VBSCRIPT

Special Edition

Using VBScript

Written by Ron Schwarz and Ibrahim Malluf with

William Beem • Yusuf Malluf • Michael Marchuk • Tom Tessier

Special Edition Using VBScript

Library of Congress Catalog No.: 96-68981

ISBN: 0-7897-0809-4

98 97 96   6 5 4 3 2 1

Interpretation of the printing code: the rightmost double-digit number is the year of the book's printing; the rightmost single-digit number, the number of the book's printing. For example, a printing code of 96-1 shows that the first printing of the book occurred in 1996.

Screen reproductions in this book were created using Collage Plus from Inner Media, Inc., Hollis, NH.

Credits

PRESIDENT
Roland Elgey

PUBLISHER
Joseph B. Wikert

EDITORIAL SERVICES DIRECTOR
Elizabeth Keaffaber

MANAGING EDITOR
Sandy Doell

DIRECTOR OF MARKETING
Lynn E. Zingraf

PUBLISHING MANAGER
Bryan Gambrel

ACQUISITIONS EDITOR
Angela C. Kozlowski

PRODUCT DIRECTOR
Russ Jacobs

PRODUCTION EDITOR
Susan Ross Moore

EDITORS
Kelli M. Brooks
Katherine Givens
Sydney Jones
Patrick Kanouse
Jeanne Terheide Lemen
Midge Stocker

PRODUCT MARKETING MANAGER
Kim Margolius

ASSISTANT PRODUCT MARKETING MANAGER
Christy M. Miller

TECHNICAL EDITOR
Tim Schuback

ACQUISITIONS COORDINATOR
Carmen Krikorian

SOFTWARE RELATIONS COORDINATOR
Patricia J. Brooks

EDITORIAL ASSISTANT
Andrea Duvall

BOOK DESIGNERS
Ruth Harvey
Kim Scott

COVER DESIGNER
Dan Armstrong

PRODUCTION TEAM
Stephen Adams
Debra Bolhuis
Jason R. Carr
Erin M. Danielson
Bryan Flores
DiMonique Ford
Jessica Ford
Trey Frank
Jason Hand
Daniel Harris
Daryl Kessler
Casey Price
Laura Robbins
Bobbi Satterfield
Sossity Smith

INDEXER
Andrew McDaniel

Composed in *Century Old Style* and *Franklin Gothic* by Que Corporation.

This book is dedicated to Susan Yeager, whose love and support saw me through many trying times during its creation.

Ron Schwarz

Subhanna Hu'a Ta Allah.

Ibrahim Malluf

About the Authors

Ron Schwarz is a software developer in Mt. Pleasant, Michigan. He has written the CD Tutor presentation program used in Que's *Delphi 2 Tutor* (featured in the August 1996 issue of *Visual Basic Programmer's Journal* "Basic Heroes" column), and is currently writing a Que book covering a future version of Visual Basic. He wrote Performance Track (a Web chart creation and management system, used in the automotive industry and education), and Launch Control, (a DOS and Windows shell). He has been involved in software development since the late 1970s, and has worked with Visual Basic since version 1.0 was released. His programming philosophy is based on the idea that ease of use and power are not mutually exclusive concepts. His WWW home page is available at **http://www.nethawk.com/~rs**, and his e-mail address is **ron.schwarz@nethawk.com**.

Ibrahim Malluf (Malluf Consulting Services, 505-832-6187) is a systems consultant to a variety of industries. He is the principle partner and founder of CyberLex Software, which produces multimedia CD catalogs for industry. His primary focus is on relational database development and MS Office/BackOffice solutions that include the Internet/Intranet. He is also a Microsoft MVP, section leader of the *Visual Basic Programmer's Journal*'s Science & Industrial section CompuServe forum, the sysop of the VBScript Development and Intranet Development forums on the Developer's Exchange (**http:\\www.windx.com**), and writes a regular VBScript column for *Avatar Magazine* (**http:\\www.avatarmag.com**). He also is a founding member of the Albuquerque Visual Basic Users' Group. During his spare time (yeah, right!), he sleeps. He can be reached at **iymalluf@rt66.com**.

William Beem is a systems engineer in Orlando, Florida. He frequently contributes to books on programming and networking issues. When not working or writing, he spends his time throwing tennis balls that his golden retriever ignores, but his pomeranian dutifully retrieves. Any remaining moments, which are too few, find him playing blues guitar.

Yusuf Malluf is a 17 year-old student currently attending Moriarty High School. He has been productively using computers for over nine years. Yusuf has also been a participant in the New Mexico Super Computer Challenge sponsored by the Los Alamos National Laboratories and New Mexico TechNet. He has knowledge of several programming languages including C, Fortran, and Visual Basic, and several scripting languages including VBScript, JavaScript, and HTML. He is also an employee (slave) of Malluf Consulting Services owned by his father, Ibrahim Malluf.

Michael Marchuk has been involved with the computing industry for over 17 years. Michael currently manages the development research department for a mid-sized software development firm while consulting for small businesses and writing leading-edge books for Que Publishing. Along with his bachelor's degree in finance from the University of Illinois, he has received certification as a Netware CNE and a Compaq Advanced Systems Engineer.

Tom Tessier is the president of Solstar Media Technologies, an interactive entertainment and Web page design company. He has written articles on interactive Internet programming for *Dr. Dobbs' Journal* and *Sys Admin Magazine*. Tom holds an advanced degree in engineering physics from the University of Alberta and is a member of IEEE. He can be reached at **tessier@ualberta.ca**.

Acknowledgments

I'd like to thank the many kind folks at Que, including my editors on this project (Angela Kozlowski and Steve Miller) who went the extra mile when dealing with the rapidly changing VBS/Internet situation. Finally, I thank my friend and coauthor Ibrahim Malluf, who has been a constant source of inspiration and knowledge.

Ron Schwarz

Where do I begin? Let me start out with Angela Kozlowski, who must have felt that the production of this book was a plot to drive her insane. Every time she thought she had a handle on it, Ron and I would be calling to tell her that things had changed again. Thank you, Angela, for the always-pleasant patience. Ron, my coauthor on this book, is a close friend. We traveled together up and down on the everchanging face of Visual Basic Script during one of the wildest betas I've ever been on. This book would not have been completed without his persistant drive to keep it going. The editing staff, led by Susan Moore, was faced with working on text that changed even as they were editing it. They also had to put up with two tired and cranky old men (me & Ron) who acted like they believed the editorial staff of Que was a plot to drive authors insane. They did a wonderful job.

Then there is my wife, Jameela. I am almost certain that she had something to do with the food that would miraculously appear at the right corner of my desk and the constant flow of coffee into the wee hours of the night. Those men and women who are married to programming fanatics are the most patient and angelic people on earth. Jameela had an extra ounce of patience because along with her husband, she also had to put up with her 17 year-old son who was also writing chapters for this book. She had to act as referee between the both of us when we disagreed or contradicted each other on the finer points of HTML or Visual Basic Script. This was in addition to the normal ego conflicts between a father and his teenage son. Speaking of Yusuf (my son), with all of the horror stories you read about in the paper or see on TV about teenage violence and crime, I have to count myself among the most fortunate people on Earth. (Yes, I'm bragging.) At 17, he has developed a personal responsibility that far surpasses his age and has been a tremendous asset to this book. For all of these people who have added much to the quality of this experience and to my life, I give thanks to Allah.

Ibrahim Malluf

on a beautiful Monday morning, August 5, 1996

We'd Like to Hear from You!

As part of our continuing effort to produce books of the highest possible quality, Que would like to hear your comments. To stay competitive, we *really* want you, as a computer book reader and user, to let us know what you like or dislike most about this book or other Que products.

You can mail comments, ideas, or suggestions for improving future editions to the address below, or send us a fax at (317) 581-4663. For the online inclined, Macmillan Computer Publishing has a forum on CompuServe (type **GO QUEBOOKS** at any prompt) through which our staff and authors are available for questions and comments. The address of our Internet site is **http://www.mcp.com** (World Wide Web).

In addition to exploring our forum, please feel free to contact me personally to discuss your opinions of this book: I'm **75703,3504** on CompuServe, and I'm **akozlowski@que.mcp.com** on the Internet.

Thanks in advance—your comments will help us to continue publishing the best books available on computer topics in today's market.

Angela C. Kozlowski
Acquisitions Editor
Que Corporation
201 W. 103rd Street
Indianapolis, Indiana 46290
USA

Contents at a Glance

VI Appendixes

Table of Contents

Introduction

As this book is being written, the Internet is in a tremendous state of flux. It's likely this constant transformation will continue for at least the next few months, as Microsoft continues to bombard us with more and more fantastic tools and protocols. While this hectic rate of change makes for a wild ride, it's good to keep the ultimate goal in mind: a limitless vista of programming opportunity, balanced by a set of development tools of unprecedented power, flexibility, and ease of use.

This book is constructed of five sections that provide a logical framework for learning to get around in this new realm. The first three parts provide a foundation to enable you to learning VBScript in-depth. Part 1, "Microsoft, The Internet, and You," is an overview of where the Internet is today, where it's headed, and how you'll be able to capitalize on it using VBScript. Part 2, "Visual Basic Scripting Edition: Active Intelligence for Internet Browsers," is a group of chapters demonstrating the types of solutions that lend themselves to VBScript programming, and a glimpse into the types of things that can be done. Part 3, "VBScript Programming Overview," reveals the essentials of VBScript—how scripts are created, and the low-down of melding

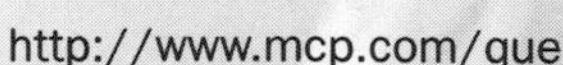

them to Web pages, mixing with HTML elements, using the VB language as implemented in VBScript, and how it differs from "full" Visual Basic.

Part 4, "Doing Real Work with VBScript," is where you'll dig in and learn the nitty-gritty details. Part 5, "Advanced Techniques, Tactics, and Pitfalls," recognizes that VBScript, due to the environment in which it's used, is fraught with subtlety. At times, it can be maddening, as the authors of this book can readily attest. Part 5 steers you around some of the craters and helps you get the skills to find others on your own. It also covers several advanced topics, such as sending information to and from the server and VRML 3-D.

Finally, a series of appendixes will help fill in the gaps by providing a brief history of the Internet, references to HTML, VBScript coding conventions, and tips on porting VB applications over to VBScript.

Writing this book has been a real adventure. In addition to the Internet being in a state of flux, we've had to wrestle with a series of early release versions of the Internet Explorer 3.0, VBScript, and the ActiveX Layout Pad. We watched in horror as the specifications changed—repeatedly—before our eyes. The language evolved *as* we documented it; we spent at least as much time staying on top of changes, and rewriting what we'd already written, as we did writing the original manuscript.

As we thought we were nearing completion of the book, Microsoft quietly dropped a bombshell, without any advance warning. The sudden, unexpected appearance of the ActiveX Control Pad, with its accompanying HTML Layout Page control, completely changed everything—not only for us but for you, too, as well as anyone using the Web. Suddenly, we had a tool that would allow the creation of *real* programs in the context of a browser, with precise, completely discretionary placement and sizing of controls at any position on a form.

We expect the new Layout Page features to make "traditional" HTML virtually obsolete very quickly. A great many of the convoluted and arcane (and voluminous) details of HTML syntax have evolved as workarounds—people wanted to create pages that looked the way they wanted them to look, but HTML wanted to take a stream of text and flow it in from the upper left to the lower right. From that conflict arose scads of HTML "features."

Now, with the ActiveX Control Pad, anything can be placed anywhere, in any shape, size, or format, with nothing more than a few mouse clicks. And, it does it all *without* generating miles of underlying HTML; the new syntax is truly elegant.

So, where are things headed from here? Here's what one Microsoft developer stated on its public newsgroup:

```
"Nashville" has been a code name for the set of technologies that
integrate the Windows shell with Internet Explorer. We're currently
```

```
planning to do an "Internet Explorer 4.0" release that includes these
technologies — ie, integrates internet browsing with the shell — and it
will be free.
```

That's right—the Internet and the desktop will merge; you'll be able to browse files on your local machine, on your local network (in other words, "intranet"), and on the Internet, with total transparency. Not only that, but the document-centric philosophy will be taken to new heights, as applications end up performing more as operating system extensions than as stand-alone programs.

Things are changing. You're in the midst of change, and we hope that what we've written in this book will help you navigate the changes, and succeed.

PART I

Microsoft, the Internet, and You

CHAPTER 1

VBScript and the World Wide Web

by Ron Schwarz

This chapter provides an overview of where we—VBS programmers—fit into the scheme of things vis-a-vis the Internet, and where it's all headed. The Internet continues to grow like Topsy, and it's easy to get overwhelmed. After a look at the plethora of "stuff" coming down the pike in ever-increasing volume and speed, it's tempting to suggest Poe's "A Descent into the Maelstrom" as background material. Instead, we'll try to examine the big picture, separate the wheat from the chaff, and by so doing be able to have an advantage over others who choose to simply dive in, blindly hoping for the best. ■

Where the Internet is today

It's everywhere, and it's more than any one person can grasp. Learn *where* to focus, and how.

What Microsoft is doing on the Net

An abundance of powerful tools and capabilities is being released, many of them free for the downloading. Learn what they are, and how they fit into the big picture.

Where you fit in

The changes occurring on the Net bide well with programmers, especially VB programmers. Find out what some of the opportunities are, and how to implement them.

Globalizing Information

What began as a nuclear-hardened network of military computers (see Appendix A, "History of the Internet") has overnight become the most prominent aspect of personal computing. The Internet is on the brink of fulfilling the promises of the past two decades of desktop computing. What we thought the CD-ROM and online services would eventually bring is now available to anyone with an inexpensive computer and modem, at a fraction of the cost.

Within the next few years, Internet access is expected to be as universal as telephone and television access is today. Right now, traditional media, such as telephone, cable TV, and major broadcast outfits, as well as software companies like Microsoft are in the process of developing the software, delivery and access systems, and content that will be used for the "set-top boxes" that are being planned. No one can say exactly when, or how it will all shape up, but one thing is clear: it *will* happen. And, when it happens, one key ingredient will be active content. And tools like VBScript will be what empowers it.

In the Land of the Blind, the One-Eyed Man Is King

In the old days, it was easy to know nearly everything about any particular aspect of programming. Now, it sometimes seems amazing that anyone knows *anything* at all. Hardly a week passes that we are not inundated with new, powerful, and complex resources and tools. By the time you learn a task, it's been superseded; users, developers, and publishers are swamped by the increasing pace of growth in this field.

In the old hierarchical model, you were either a specialist or a generalist. Generalists filtered up to management, administration, and design positions, and specialists did the dirty work in the trenches. When the right mix of people and personalities were combined, things worked.

Success now, however, requires a new model. You need to be a jack of *most* trades and master of *some*. You need a lot of broad knowledge about quite a few things, and you need some strongly-focused, in-depth expertise in some key subjects. The trick is to decide *which* ones to learn, which ones to master, and which ones to ignore. This book will try to guide you through that process—at least so far as interactive web page development using VBScript is concerned—and leave you with the resources to continue riding the wave. As software development matures, only the savvy will succeed. And as the wealth of new technologies continues to increase in volume, "savvyness" will become a scarce commodity. This is the time to stake your claim, and the way you'll do that is by learning *how* to learn, and *what* to learn. When you've done that, you'll be nicely positioned for what's just starting to happen now.

The Internet is a global network of networks, overflowing with a mix of information ranging from the indispensable to the trite to the obscene. "The Internet" is not a company. You can't "contact the management" to deal with problems or provide solutions, because in a very real sense, there *isn't* any "management." Each system on the Internet, whether it's a large corporate network, or a kid with a Net link in his parents' basement, has its own administration, with corresponding degrees of ability and accountability. There is no "central authority." The Net has become a seething ocean of information *and* noise, and it's becoming increasingly difficult to find and use what's needed.

Chaos Brings Opportunity

The Internet holds an embarrassment of riches, to the extent that large numbers of users have become information junkies, while others burn out on information overload. Just as Microsoft Windows applications provide the ability to control more information by highly abstracting the interface, the vast resources of the Internet will also need to be effectively harnessed. We won't be able to get by with *more* tools—what we need are *better* tools. You may not need power steering on a two-seat sportscar, but you'd find it essential if you're controlling massive earth-moving, logging, or mining equipment. You need a way to leverage your time, effort, and knowledge proportionate to the quantity of raw material you're managing.

The Web in the Window

Windows-based applications don't provide their power and ease of use by means of linear-increase in functionality over their earlier non-GUI-based predecessors. Instead, they offer a higher degree of management and control by virtue of providing newer *ways* of doing things.

Certainly, part of the process does consist of making existing tasks easier. Instead of having to learn numerous commands, control-keys, function keys, and layer after layer of text menus, the user can work with pulldown menus, toolbars, context menus, checkboxes, and other elements of modern GUI interface design. Time and effort previously wasted dealing with the mechanics of the task (and endless rote memorization of command sequences) can now be devoted to the work at hand. And, fewer distractions and lower stress levels lead to more efficient, effective, and contented users.

As impressive as these improvements may be, the real power lies in features such as OLE automation, in-place activation, linked and embedded applications, compound documents, and doc objects, which make it possible to do things that were hitherto impossible. And what is the focus of these "things?" They provide a higher level of abstraction (and by implication, control) over *content*. They provide leverage. The basic interface elements aid productivity; they allow users to do the same things differently. OLE and related functionality leapfrog this, however, and provide the ability to multiply the effectiveness of the user, to the point that work that used to require days of effort by a team of experts can now be done in hours, (or minutes) by one person reasonably proficient in the use of a set of tools.

Developing for Windows requires a different philosophy than developing for earlier non-GUI platforms. To succeed, you must learn to think differently. This same philosophy is mandatory if effective Internet development is to be anything beyond a pipe dream. "More" knowledge just can't cut it. There's just too much to learn. The most important action is focus, and the most important process is determining what to focus on. Learn how to learn, then learn what to learn. Then amaze everyone with your incredible insights!

The greatest area of growth in Internet use has been occurring with the World Wide Web. To many, if not most, recent users, the WWW is "the Net." (Thankfully, such awkward neologisms as "The Information Superhighway" are dying a merciful and rapid death.) While the majority of users can safely exhibit this level of naiveté, we as developers are afforded no such luxury. "The Web" is but one facet of the Internet; however, its prominence is not unwarranted, and as more and more traffic, as well as more *kinds* of traffic, is carried, it's only natural to expect expanded capabilities and tools to appear.

The current high level of chaos is a result of the volume of information, the sheer numbers of users, and the diversity of tools used to manage and access the web. Whoever brings order out of chaos will stand to directly benefit. This is a *good* time to know Visual Basic, and a *good* time to be writing code.

You've probably heard the phrase "Active Content." While it covers a lot of territory, the most important things to keep in mind right now are that it's real, it's probably the most significant new factor in Internet programming, and VBScript falls smack dab in the middle of it all. If you're coming from a traditional HTML programming background, you'll find exciting new possibilities for interactive web pages. If you're a long time VB hack, you'll be able to quickly put your skills to work.

The Internet, and Intranets

Just when the world is learning what the Internet is, along comes another buzzword: "Intranets." Essentially, Intranets are kid brothers to the Internet, and present exciting new opportunities for developers. What the Internet is to the world, Intranets are to organizations. Although different types of content are generally involved, methodologies are identical, and the benefits are significant.

NOTE *Intranet* is more than a buzzword for network or LAN. An intranet is a *type* of LAN, the significant point being the fact that intranets use Internet style tools and applications to manage and present content. ■

One key element of Intranets is exclusivity. Whereas the Internet is an open, global network, Intranets are proprietary to the organizations that create and administer them. This opens a world of exciting development opportunities, as each organization's needs are different.

The World on the Desktop

The next generation of Windows will provide seamless integration of the Internet and your local computer. The Windows Explorer will provide access to the Internet and access to other machines in an organization's Intranet, too. Documents will be accessible the same way whether they are on your local hard drive, on another machine in your local network, or anywhere in the world on the Internet. All this will be accomplished using the same metaphor—no longer will users have to learn three different ways of working.

As Intranets proliferate and supersede traditional networking approaches, a "grand unification" of sorts will occur—*where* information is located will essentially cease to be an issue; instead, users can concentrate on *what* they need to do with it. Users can focus on *tasks*, letting the system deal with *processes*.

A Fractal Microcosm

To get an idea of what an Intranet is, take a look at the Internet, then view it in the context of your naval meditating on *you*. It's a bit counterintuitive at first, if not downright retrograde. What the Internet is to the world, an Intranet is to your local organization. In a sense, it's a miniature walled-off alternate universe clone of the Internet. So what's the big deal anyway? The same productivity and comfort payoffs that the Internet provides for global information are available locally with an Intranet. In fact, the same tools are used, and the same skills are used.

While many people perceive LAN applications to be stagnant, difficult to learn, painful to use, and downright obtuse, Internet software has become incredibly powerful, and (from the users' perspective, at least) extremely easy to learn and use. Probably the main reason for this is simple economics of scale. The very large base of Internet users has created an attractive target for application developers.

The result of all this is a proliferation of "mini-Internets" (quickly termed *Intranets*) that breathe new life into LAN technology, and, create a burgeoning new market for application developers. And, as new tools like VBScript make it easy to create web pages that move beyond the realm of "virtual television," whole new markets will quickly appear.

Corporate information systems will no longer be limited to whatever access an overworked "priesthood" can provide. Support staff will have to be able to get information they need, when they need it, without having to tackle any learning curves other than that required for basic operation of Windows.

The Microsoft Vision: Information at Your Fingertips

As large corporations go, Microsoft is unique. Generally, the rule is that the bigger they are, the slower they move, and the more inertia-bound they become, until they reach a point at which they are overtaken by a team of garage operators with that lean and hungry look. 'Taint so in Redmond. The folks there have learned how to be big, and how to be nimble at the same time. They rigorously apply a set of principles that ensure steady, continuous progress, and real growth.

Fortunately, there's no big secret involved here—the rules are pretty straightforward, as we'll see, and we can apply them with similar results (albeit on a less-grandiose scale) to our own operations.

Broken Paradoxes

Microsoft is not perfect. They make mistakes. They head off in wrong directions, they make strategic blunders, and they develop software that people don't use or like.

In that regard, they're just like everyone else.

However, Microsoft learns from its mistakes. You *won't* see them make the same mistake twice. Other companies seem to run into the same brick walls over and over again, as if mindless repetition has some merit in and of itself. While the largest corporations may have the resources (by virtue of sheer mass, if nothing else) to survive such pigheadedness for a while, countless smaller outfits wash in and out with the tides.

Microsoft, in spite of all this, has become the de-facto leader in its field, and only the sour-grapes crowd seriously attributes it to their size. The fact is, they are darn good at what they do, and a great deal of what they do consists of analyzing where things are headed.

So, even though they are subject to the same limitations as any other group of people working in this industry, they manage to make steady progress. They work hard, *and* they work smart. And when they commit to something with the fervor they've dedicated to the Internet, you should ignore them at your own peril.

Having it All, and Using it All

The tools are available. The market is available. After you read this book, you'll have the skills required. What's missing? Direction. Without a vision of where *you* fit in to the scheme of things, you'll be like someone at the airport, bags packed, ready to go, but with no destination.

You can bet that a lot of your competition will simply try to reinvent the wheel, only on a grander scale. Let's face it: what separates a great programmer from a competent programmer is not so much coding skills as much as it is the ability to think. Too many programmers spend too much time writing code, and too little time thinking about what they are writing.

The inclination, of course, is to subconsciously view time spent thinking as time wasted, since nothing tangible results from it. Nothing could be further from the truth. Diving in before you have a clear idea of where you're going is simply one more variation on the "haste makes waste" theme. When you're running around in circles, shifting into high gear does not translate into progress.

Time spent reading, studying, learning, and above all, *thinking*, is anything but wasted. Just as we should not be afraid to learn from the failures of others, we ought to take a look at their successes, too. Microsoft is a prime example—it's clear from the breadth and depth of their present Internet offerings that a fantastic amount of thought and planning has gone into the process.

We can benefit from this in two ways. First, we can ride their coattails. The less industrious will merely grab the latest tools, and hope that this alone will be sufficient to keep them in business. The rest of us, however, will want to take the time and effort to determine where Microsoft is headed, and anticipate how we can fit into things. Granted, they (understandably) play things close to the vest—it's not in *their* interest to tip their hand to the competition. Even so, there's more than enough solid info available in press releases, online notes, SDK documentation, published interviews, and books like this, to give us what we need to get an idea of what's going on. Keeping an ear to the ground is a good way to avoid the plight of buggy-whip manufacturers in Henry Ford's time.

The second way we stand to gain from this is by emulating their methods. Study, think, plan, test, and review. Above all, review your *failures*. When something goes wrong, find out what went wrong, why it went wrong, and how to avoid it in the future. Too many developers focus on their successes, but quickly distance themselves from their failures. Never underestimate the value of an intensive postmortem.

Looking Over the Next Hill

One lesson American corporations are finally learning from the Japanese is the false economy of short-sighted planning. While we were basing long-term decisions on quarterly payoffs, they were willing to accept short-term losses as part of long-term strategy. It's really nothing more than avoiding missing the forest for the trees. When you're driving your car, you know to "drive long," and watch the road more than one car-length ahead. It's the same when writing software, and this becomes even more of a consideration when beginning to use a new environment, such as VBScript.

To be sure, you *will* be applying many of your existing skills. But, whether you're coming from an HTML background, or a VB background, you're going to have to learn to think differently. *You* don't want to be one more wheel-reinventor, right?

For a while now, a type of web interactivity *has* existed. We've all seen sites that allow searches, selection of options, and fill-in-the-blanks form entry. Of course, it's been fairly crude, since all the logic was contained at the server end, and was further restricted by CGI limitations.

So, you can expect to see a proliferation of VBScript pages that are little more than direct translations of older CGI style interactive pages, with perhaps a few cosmetic bells and whistles tacked on, reminiscent of the "ransom note" effect—mixed fonts, sizes, and styles, all on the same page—that earmarked the initial efforts of neophytes when desktop publishing software became widely available.

This same type of thinking (or more correctly, lack of thought) thwarted the efforts of numerous DOS programmers when they made the initial transition to Windows programming. Direct "translations" of old-style applications to the new environment were common.

New platforms require new ways of thinking. Those who are the first to realize this, *and* the first to learn the new ways, will be the ones who position themselves to benefit the most from the technology. Those who persist in trying to do new things using old methods will be doomed to years of hard work for little return.

We're entering an era where pretty much everything will be new to everyone. Yes, it's a bit intimidating. But it's also rife with opportunity. After all, when everyone is at the starting gate at the same time, we all have an equal chance of success. Bill Gates got his start as a teenager by writing the first decent BASIC interpreter for 8-bit microcomputers. He didn't have much of an advantage over his contemporaries, other than the foresight to take the available resources, and be the first to use them to that end.

Opportunities like this don't come along very often, and the astute reader will realize this, and capitalize on it.

So, we've decided that we have the tools we need, we are dedicated to using them thoughtfully, and we are going to be anything other than one more me-too hack slaving away at painfully tedious work. After all, we want to excel at what we're doing, but we want to enjoy our work too! So, what to do?

The first step is to look at what's being done now *without* tools like VBScript. (If you don't want to intentionally reinvent the wheel, you certainly don't want to inadvertently do so!)

Examine different web sites that offer old-style HTML interactivity. (Remember to do your testing on systems that are connected to the Internet via modem links—if you're using a super-fast direct connection, you will not get a feeling for the frustration the vast majority of users face when using server-bound HTML interactivity.) Pay attention to look and feel, capabilities and limitations. Pay particular attention to things that are slow, cumbersome, and awkward. Ask yourself if the things you don't like are due to programmer failings, or reflect basic shortcomings of the HTML-way of doing things.

At this point, the immediate temptation will be to think of ways to work around these problems with VBScript. As with most temptations, though, the rewards are largely illusory. Remember, we're out to avoid reinventing the wheel. The reason we're examining the way things are done now is *not* so that we can do the same things, only better. Instead, we want to familiarize ourselves with the limitations inherent in the current platform, and use the new technology to leapfrog the competition.

By realizing the restrictions built into the current HTML world, we can begin to see to what extent look-and-feel is shaped by the environment in which it exists. By making a "gripe list" of things we don't like, we can get a sense of just how low the ceiling is. Eventually, we'll form an instinctive disgust for the innate restrictions of HTML, and lose any and all interest in emulating them.

When you reach that point, you'll be chomping at the bit to see what VBScript can do for you, and your users. And, you'll have zero inclination to reinvent the wheel.

The next step is to familiarize yourself with the tools. Learn what they are, how they interact, and how to use them. Find other people using the same tool sets, and form strategic alliances. (Cutthroat competition may be fine for used-car sales, but chances are, you don't even have a tacky plaid suit…)

The Tools

VBScript is one part of Microsoft's Internet strategy. So are the Internet Explorer (IE), Internet Information Server (IIS), VRML, SQL Server 6.5, dbWeb, ActiveX SDK (and controls), the Internet Control Pack (ICP), FrontPage, Jakarta, Java, and on and on. The offerings are so extensive that it's impossible to pay more than lip service to them all in any one book. One thing to remember, though, is that Microsoft is literally the "House that Basic Built," and we can see that this versatile language is being given a place of prominence in the realm of Internet development.

Internet Explorer

In most cases (at least until other vendors get on the bandwagon and add VBScript compliance to their browsers), you and your users will be using the Internet Explorer. The IE will be fully integrated into the next versions of Windows and will be able to be included with applications you develop using Visual Basic and other full-fledged development languages. It is important to remember that net exploring will be a seamless part of the operating system.

Internet Information Server (IIS)

The IIS will also be used by more providers. It's likely that this will initially manifest itself in a groundswell of Intranet installations, since the server version of Windows NT will come with a free copy of IIS and new installations don't have to cope with inertia issues (existing Internet providers may for a while be loath to change from their existing web servers, until sufficient user and market demand forces them to upgrade).

Fortunately, even though VBScript and IIS dovetail nicely, IIS is not necessary for VBScript page use. Any web server can dish up working VBS-enabled web pages, so long as you avoid any IIS-specific functionality.

SQL Server 6.5

SQL Server 6.5 provides Internet-specific hooks and is designed to work with IIS, as is dbWeb. These tools allow you to easily publish databases on the Internet (or, Intranets). Applications like online order-entry, data reference, and other data-centric systems can become truly practical over the web for the first time.

FrontPage

FrontPage, and other page development systems, provides a means to develop and publish web content without having to immerse oneself in the arcana of HTML programming.

VRML

VRML will allow real-time 3-D graphic applications to be run over the web. Uses for this run the gamut from games to medical diagnosis.

ActiveX SDK

ActiveX development is a very broad area—so extensive, that the initial beta version of the SDK was made available as a 12 megabyte—*compressed*—file, and the shipping version commanded a CD of its own. The part we'll be paying particular attention to here is ActiveX controls (formerly called "OCX controls"). These custom controls provide a capability to embed virtually anything on a web page, and VBScript is the language that manages them.

The ICP is a set of very useful ActiveX controls that can be used to add anything from e-mail to web browsing to any application written in any language that can use ActiveX controls. By merely setting some properties, and writing a few lines of code, you can add e-mail (sending and receiving), news reading, FTP, HTTP, or nearly any Winsock function required to your applications.

Other facets of Microsoft's Internet strategy provide compliance with Java and JavaScript, secure information transfer, merchant services, multimedia broadcast, and so much more as to beg comprehension, let alone description in one book. The list *is* expected to grow significantly, too!

The Applications

It's often said in this industry that you can always tell who the real pioneers are—they're the ones with the arrows in their backs. Starting out now, you'll be working in largely uncharted territory with early-generation tools, and most every step you take will take you somewhere you've never been before. In a way, it's no exaggeration to assert that this *is* the birth of the Internet; yes, it's been around a while, but until now, its growth was largely horizontal. It got bigger and bigger, but it really didn't change all that much, and what change occurred was slow.

Now, it's poised to take off, and you're in the pilot's seat. So, where do you take it?

Remember, the most important thing is *focus*. It's easy to succumb to the kid-in-a-candy-store syndrome. All roads lead everywhere, and you're in the middle.

The first thing you'll need to bring into focus is the main fork in the road. This is the intersection that leads in one direction to Internet applications, and to Intranet applications in the other. Having found this, you are immediately placed at the head of the pack, since you can safely rely on most of your competitors to frantically dither from one "wow" topic to another.

Cabbages and Kings

Internet and intranet apps are developed using the same tools, and the same skills as each other. But, the targeted users are completely different, and the types of applications are consequently different, too.

Intranets will be used by organizations of every stripe. The most immediately visible type will be the corporate organization. But don't forget to consider the wide scope of groups that will be setting up Intranets—educational organizations (universities, public schools, private schools, charter schools, "distance learning" schools, school districts), unions, churches, units of local, state, and federal government (including branches of the above), libraries, insurance companies, law firms, medical groups, and fraternal organizations are just a few of the types of outfits that will be able to make real use of a private, Internet-style network.

Internet applications, on the other hand, are for the most part "open to the public." While intranet applications are by nature restricted to those who have physical access to the specific intranet in question, Internet apps that need restricted access (due to content, security, or other considerations) will have to take extra precautions to make sure that only members of the intended audience can gain entry. Security issues are discussed in Chapter 8, "Security."

We can examine some typical examples of VBScript applications (in fact, we'll be doing that in the chapters that follow) but trying to list all possible (or even all likely) uses for VBScript-enabled active content web pages would be an exercise in sheer folly, as well as a serious disservice to you. We can no more reasonably ask "What applications are suited to VBS?" than we could inquire as to which types of programs can be developed in ***any*** programming language. While it's true that each language, and each platform, has its own set of features and shortcomings, the fact remains that the scope of possibilities is endless.

Just as early predictions of a total worldwide demand of only five or six computers are now seen as absurd, anyone thinking they have a handle on just what types of apps can and cannot be developed with a particular set of tools is going to be astonished at the fruits of

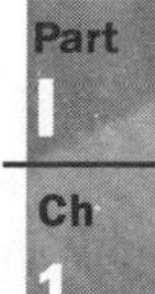

the labors of those who refuse to wear a similar set of blinders.

With this in mind, let's look at a few representative uses for this technology. Again, it cannot be sufficiently emphasized that this list is non-inclusive.

Some typical Internet uses include:

- Online Catalogs
- Order Entry
- Subscription Information Services
- Pay-Per-Access Information Services
- "Smart" Content Retrieval and Collating
- "Virtual Community" Creation
- Games

Naturally, some of these things are already being done now, using earlier technology (server-side CGI scripts, for example). However, their implementations are by nature typically crude, cumbersome, and non-intuitive. By using current (such as VBS) tools to re-implement (as opposed to duplicating) these applications, you'll be able to offer your clients (or employer, as the case may be) a powerful competitive advantage.

The real power of active content web programming, however, will be evidenced in new applications—applications that are simply too complex and powerful to even consider attempting in "pure" HTML with its, bandwidth-bound, limited intrinsic controls, and complete lack of client-side logic.

Although Internet applications will frequently differ in type from Intranet applications, the same abstract reasoning skills are required for development. We'll discuss these considerations after we look at a few typical applications for Intranet installations:

- Data Entry/Maintenance/Reporting
- Confidential Information Publishing
- "Virtual Community" Creation
- Organizational News Reporting
- On-site and Remote Education
- Testing and Automated Scoring
- Online Classes
- Group Scheduling
- "Smart" Content Retrieval and Collating

As you can see, there is some overlap, even in the few examples we've provided. Some applications, such as content retrieval, are near-universal in scope, even though actual implementations will vary widely, based on content and context requirements.

Both the Internet, and Intranet lists above represent only a smattering of potential applications. You'll easily be able to come up with several others after a few minutes of brainstorming, and even more after discussing possibilities with others.

Implementation

It's a simple word; most of us in this business probably use it at least once or twice a day. This might be a good time to review it, since we're about to experience a tsunami-like event that will affect us all. Whether we accept it with open arms, or are dragged into it kicking and screaming, we *will* be confronted with, and have to deal with, Internet/Intranet programming issues.

Events of these proportions do not happen that frequently. Probably the last time our industry faced similar changes was when Windows 3.0 was released. The last time prior to that was when DOS killed the future of CP/M.

In each of these past events, there were two groups of people: those who said "It'll never fly" (the buggy-whip manufacturers), and, those who realized that they'd better get with the program regardless of their own feelings on the matter.

It's no different now. And, while no change is entirely pleasant, we have certain benefits that were unavailable to earlier "pioneers." For one thing, we've seen this happen before. They didn't—at least not to the extent that we have. If *we* choose to play the "it can't happen here" game, we've only ourselves to blame when we find ourselves out in the cold in the not-too-distant future.

Another factor giving us an advantage over our predecessors is the fact that the industry as a whole has matured, platforms and standards are well-established, and fantastic tools are available to implement new solutions.

With all this in mind, let's take a brief look at just what makes *implementation* such an important concept.

At one time or another, you've probably found yourself in a situation in which you were being asked to take an existing system, (either paper-based, or running on an earlier non-Windows operating system) and "make a Windows version of it."

It's not only large bureaucracies that are subject to inertia. Everyone is resistant to change to one degree or another. This isn't always bad, and is frequently good. However, when it manifests itself in the desire to *duplicate* an existing system, rather than *implementing* it in the new environment, there's really nothing at all to be said in its defense.

An existing system reflects the limitations of the context for which it was initially developed. It also reflects the constraints imposed by whatever development tools were available when it was created.

Attempting to create a "straight port" of the system may indeed be possible, but if you do so, you are doing your client no favor, even if he claims it works and is what he wants. It's not just a matter of cosmetics. Consider the earlier transition from character-based DOS programs to GUI-based Windows applications. There were plenty of straight ports. One language vendor (not, by the way, Microsoft) even developed a library that made it easy—it emulated the character-based DOS "interactive" (as opposed to event-driven) interface in a window!

When you *implement* a solution, you have to focus, think, and learn. The goal of this is to be able to intelligently and accurately determine the characteristics of the task to be implemented, and devise a solution offering the most effective combination of ease of use, power, and utilization of the feature set provided by the environment in which you're working.

For example, having 400 small "fill-in-the-blank" fields may be o.k. on a form printed on a sheet of legal-size paper. Trying to duplicate that monster in a window, however, is nothing short of an exercise in futility.

If you can understand that explaining to the client that there is a better way is *not* "an excuse" for your inability to create a workable (and identical) duplicate of the existing system, you grasp the principle involved. If, on the other hand, when presented with a situation of this type, your practice is to first try to create an exact duplicate of the existing system, and then try to make excuses for the inevitable problems that ensue, you need to seriously examine the principles we've explored in this chapter.

Why is this *so* important now?

The Internet, and the WWW in particular, have overnight become household terms. People who never used a computer before are now running heavy-duty iron, and the only program many of them ever use is their web browser. The user base is there—the demand is there—and the existing systems, ready for implementation—are there.

There is no way to accurately predict the ground-swell of demand for "computerization." The only thing we can be sure of is that it will be immense. If this next generation of applications is tackled intelligently, thoughtfully, and carefully, we will all benefit greatly. If we jump in and flail away at anything that moves, we'll end up shooting ourselves in the feet.

For the first time, we are going to be dealing with mass quantities of people who have existing systems that they will want ported to the net. The keys to bringing about one successful port after another are understanding of the properties of the "new" Internet, and succinctly communicating this to the client.

Master what we've covered in this chapter, learn the mechanics of VBScript as presented in this book, and with the right attitude, you'll be one of those who are able to write their own ticket.

Extending HTML

After spending the better part of this chapter with our heads in the virtual-clouds, this topic may seem an odd way to wrap up. But, for better or worse, HTML is currently the Lingua Franca of the Internet, and until the WWW is replaced with something completely different, nearly everything we've discussed in this chapter will have its realization expressed in the form of HTML statements, and scripts contained within HTML blocks.

So, let's take a minute or two to get our feet back on the ground, and prepare to segue into the nitty-gritty of VBScript development.

HTML extensions come in two main forms: those that affect appearance, and those that affect behavior. Cosmetic changes are the most visible, but active content is where it's at, and that's where the focus of this book will take you. As you read on, you'll learn how to use VBScript to manage active content, and "glue" together the elements required to move the net beyond "virtual-TV."

So go brew a bucket of coffee, get a *big* box (and clear off the top of your desk into it), fire up Notepad and Internet Explorer, and dig in!

From Here...

- See Chapter 2, "Review of HTML," for information on HTML language issues.
- See Chapters 3 and 6 for coverage of the ActiveX Control Pad.
- See Chapter 5, "Internet Explorer," for a discussion of issues surrounding web browser selection.
- See Chapter 7, "ActiveX Objects," for information on using ActiveX objects.
- See Chapters 11-14 for coverage of VBScript programming issues.
- See Chapters 15-20 for intensive VBScript language coverage.

CHAPTER 2

A Review of HTML

by Yusuf Malluf

When using Visual Basic Script as one of your Internet authoring tools on the Web, it is necessary to know the medium upon which VBScript rests: Hypertext Markup Language, or HTML. HTML is the standard by which World Wide Web documents are served. VBScript and the ActiveX controls provide a greater degree of interaction inside HTML documents. To become more proficient with Visual Basic Script, it is necessary to understand some key components of HTML and how it works, conceptually.

There are two components to creating a hypertext document. The layout or design of the page and the general syntax of Hypertext Markup Language. This chapter primarily deals with the syntax of HTML and the elements that are useful to Visual Basic Script. All of the examples presented in this chapter are created with the use of Microsoft Internet Explorer 3.0 in mind. Many of the HTML elements presented, such as style sheets and marquees, are currently supported by Internet Explorer only. ■

The basics of HTML

General HTML terminology, elements of HTML such as hyperlinking, multimedia and forms, and the logic of HTML.

The extensions made to HTML

This includes frames, tables, objects, and other proposals to the Hypertext Markup Language that have been implemented but not standardized.

The future standards of HTML

This includes a discussion of proposals to HTML that are still being drafted, such the HTML 3.0 DTD and style sheets.

A brief overview of Internet servers and Web browsers

Look here for an explanation of the relationship between servers and browsers, and a brief comparison between the leading MS Windows browsers and servers available.

Understanding Core HTML Components

The Hypertext Markup Language is a simple language that was designated as the language for hypertext communication across the Internet. Its initial advantages were its simplicity and its multi-platform flexibility. Today this phenomena is more than just simple text and graphics rendering, it has become the reality of Cyberspace.

There is a standards committee, the World Wide Web Consortium (W3C) which is responsible for establishing standards for HTML and general standards for Internet communication.

HTML Terminology and the Logic of HTML

If you have ever seen HTML or have ever heard it mentioned before, some of the terms that may come to mind are *elements, attributes, tags,* and *values*. These are all, indeed, simple to understand; but to gain a better understanding of them you must understand the structure of an HTML document. An HTML document consists of two parts: a header and a body. A header is used in specifying the title of the document, the document's owner, and other miscellaneous information dealing with the document. The body portion of the document is where all the displayable content goes. In an HTML document, the header and the body are specified similarly to what is shown in Listing 2.1. You can also get this listing off the CD-ROM in the file FIRSTHTML.HTM.

Listing 2.1 FIRSTHTML.HTM—A Simple HTML Document Demonstrating Basic Usage

```
<HTML>
<HEAD>
<TITLE>The title goes here</TITLE>
</HEAD>
<BODY BGCOLOR="#FFFFFF">
<P>Just a test - where the body goes</P>
</BODY>
</HTML>
```

The words surrounded by the < and > brackets are called *elements* or *keywords*, whereas the entire keyword including the brackets is called a *tag*. These tags usually come in pairs, encapsulate a portion of the document, and define what is to happen inside that portion. The `<HEAD>` and `</HEAD>` tags naturally specify the header of the document, and the `<BODY>` and `</BODY>` pair specifies the body of the document. The tag examples you see in Listing 2.1 consist of a `<Name_of_Tag>`, which begins the tag, and `</Name_of_Tag>`, which ends the tag. Everything encapsulated by these tags is affected by it. Tags can be nested, which means certain tags can be within other tags. The `<P>` and `</P>` tags, which are used to specify a new paragraph block, are nested between the <BODY> tags. The <HEAD> and <BODY> tags are both nested in the <HTML> and </HTML> tags (which specify that this is an HTML document).

CAUTION

Remember! You can nest or encapsulate tags in other tags but you cannot overlap tags. For instance, the following is not acceptable and is considered bad form:

```
<I><B>This is just a test</I></B>
```

The first tag pair, <I></I> which indicates that the text is placed in italics and the second pair, and <B></B> which renders text as bold, are overlapping. In general, tags overlap when a nested tag is closed outside of the tag pair it is nested in.

CAUTION

Many tags cannot be nested. Tags that are permitted in the header section are usually not permitted in the body, and vice versa. Check Appendix B, "HTML Reference," to see which tags are allowed in the header and body of an HTML document.

Let's examine Listing 2.1 a little closer. The tag that begins the body of the document, the <BODY> tag, has this within the brackets: BGCOLOR="#FFFFFF". The BGCOLOR part of the <BODY> tag is called an *attribute*. The information to the right of the equal sign is called a *value*. In this case, the attribute, BGCOLOR, is used to specify the background color of the document. ùÙs value, "#FFFFFF", is the hexadecimal value for the color white. An attribute is an additional keyword to an HTML tag that modifies the tag in some manner. In this case, the BGCOLOR attribute specifies what the background color should be. All attributes for a particular tag are specified when the beginning tag is used (notice there are no attributes for the </BODY> tag in Listing 2.1).

It is always a good idea to surround your values with double quotation marks (" "), so the browser recognizes all the information passed as a value as one block.

NOTE Microsoft Internet Explorer also uses names for major colors, so you can use the value of "white" for the BGCOLOR attribute instead of "#FFFFFF", which is the hexadecimal value for the color white. Over 100 color names are supported in Internet Explorer 3.0 and these can be found in Appendix B. Additionally, you can specify collapsed hexadecimal color values as well (for example, the value "#F0C" is really "#FF00CC"). The singular value specified for the red, blue, or green section (in the form of #RRBBGG) is duplicated into the other R, B, or G slot (for example, the "F" value in "#F0C" is expanded to "FF", and so forth, so the entire value looks like: "#FF00CC"). ■

You now have a foundation for an understanding of how HTML works. Many tags follow the "encapsulation" rule where an opening tag and a closing tag encapsulate some text or other tags. However, there are several tags in HTML that have their exceptions and they will be dealt with in their respective sections.

Linking

Linking is the process of connecting different hypertext documents and other resources on the Internet (or lately, intranets as well). This is easily done with HTML, but, again, some basic terminology must be understood first. The following list acquaints you with some of these terms.

- *Anchor:* Used to indicate a place that references or is referenced by other resources or URLs
- *URL:* A Uniform Resource Locater is the standard method of accessing resources by an Anchor
- *Hyperlink:* Refers to any clickable object in an HTML page that requests another URL

The tag used for anchoring is the `<A>` tag, but it has some required attributes. These required attributes are listed in Table 2.1.

Table 2.1 Required Attributes for the *<A>* Tag

Attribute	Purpose
HREF	Used to reference another URL when the text, pictures, or other objects encapsulated in the `<A>...</A>` tags is clicked.
NAME	Used to identify an anchor. This name can be called by other URL's tags with a # appended to the name (for instance, if an `<A>` tag has NAME="test", then another `<A>` tag in the document can reference that anchor by `<A HREF="#test">...</A>` [reference meaning you will go to the place where the named anchor is in the document when clicked]. If the anchor is in another document, then it can be referenced by appending the name, with the preceding number sign to the URL: HREF="http://www.test.com/test1.html#test" would go an anchor with the name "test" in the file test1.htm at the location of www.test.com.

There are also more attributes that are used with anchor tags, but they are specific to elements like frame sets. The `HREF` attribute points to some URL, another anchor in the local file, or another anchor in a different URL. The `NAME` attribute can specify a unique identity for each tag in the current or on other HTML documents. Listing 2.2 illustrates how this is done. This listing can also be accessed on the accompanying CD.

NOTE The NAME attribute and its new replacement, the ID attribute, have the same function. However, certain tags cannot work with the ID attribute (like frames) and some tags will not work with the NAME attribute (like objects).

Listing 2.2 SCNDHTML.HTM—A Simple HTML Document that Shows How Linking Works

```
<HTML>
<HEAD>
<TITLE>A Test demonstrating the anchor tag</TITLE>
</HEAD>
<BODY>
<A HREF="http://www.nm.org">
      This Anchor goes to the url http://www.nm.org</A>
<A HREF="#bottom" NAME="top">
      This tag is called top and references bottom</A>
...
<A HREF="#top" NAME="bottom">
      This tag is called bottom and is referenced by top</A>
</BODY></HTML>
```

This is all there is to hyperlinking, but also keep in mind that you can put many things in an anchor, including pictures, which become clickable images. Other HTML tags that rely on (or are indirectly used by) anchors are image maps, frames, and forms. In Visual Basic Script, the NAME attribute is used extensively throughout documents that contain those scripts because Visual Basic Script has the capability to use those names to make HTML more interactive. You may find, though, that Visual Basic Script is used extensively with forms and input boxes, which are discussed later in this chapter.

Images and Multimedia

Images and multimedia also help to make hypertext documents more interesting. When dealing with graphics, the major HTML tag associated with multimedia is the <IMG> tag. With the <IMG> tag, you can specify what picture to display, and the dimensions of the picture. Also, with an <IMG> tag you can display different animation clips to play. The Microsoft Internet Explorer supports inline AVI animation clips. Listing 2.3 is an example that stresses the major features of the image tag. This example is illustrated in Figure 2.1. Listing 2.3 may also be found on the CD that accompanies the book. Notice that the clickable image has a border around it. Images that are clickable usually are surrounded by a border indicating that it is a link. The attributes for controlling borders and clickable images are covered fully in Appendix B.

Listing 2.3 PICSDEMO.HTM—The Different Ways to Use the *<IMG>* Tag

```
<HTML>
<HEAD>
<TITLE>This page stresses the major features of the IMG tag.</TITLE>
</HEAD>
<BODY>
<IMG SRC="test.gif" HEIGHT="100" WIDTH="100" ALIGN="left">
This is an image that will be rendered 100x100 pixels <BR CLEAR="left">
<A HREF="test.html"><IMG SRC="test.gif" WIDTH="100" HEIGHT="100">
</A>This image is clickable
<BR CLEAR="left">
<IMG DYNSRC="test,avi" LOOP="infinite" START="mouseover"
WIDTH="100" HEIGHT="100" ALIGN="CENTER">
This a centered picture of an AVI file. Move the mouse over it.
</BODY></HTML>
```

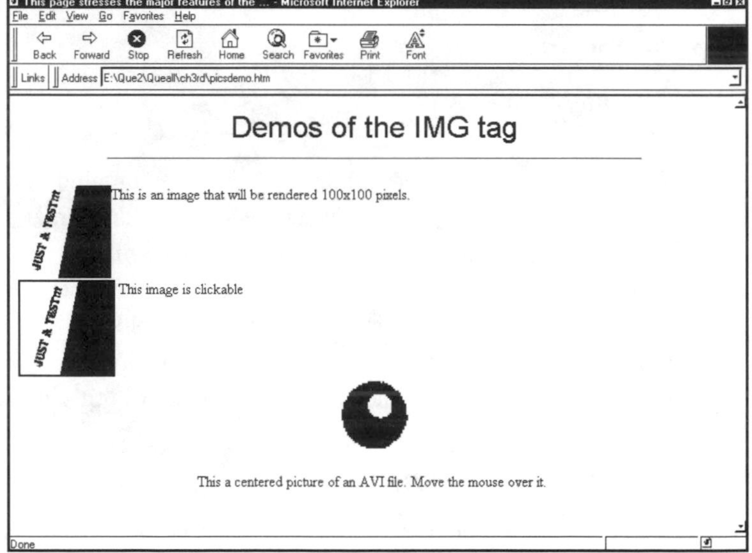

FIG. 2.1
This figure demonstrates the different uses of the <IMG> tag.

This example displays three different ways to use the <IMG> tag. The first example displays a normal image that is left aligned, 100 pixels long, and 100 pixels wide. The next is a clickable image, which you can tell because it is encapsulated by the <A></A> tags. The final example shows how to display an AVI animation which plays infinitely (specified by the LOOP attribute) and only plays when the mouse is moved over the animation (specified by the START attribute). One other interesting HTML addition is the MARQUEE tag. With this tag, you can make text and other objects encapsulated in the marquee scroll across the screen. Graphics and multimedia are very useful for Visual Basic Script and the ActiveX environment because it obviously enhances the interaction capability of the page by providing interactive animations and even games. More information on both these tags can be found in Appendix B at the end of the book.

Forms and Their Interaction with Visual Basic Script

HTML forms are where Visual Basic Scripts can be very handy and helpful to use. Originally, forms were usually processed and validated by the Common Gateway Interface (CGI). With the CGI method, a third source was involved in processing and validating all the information provided by forms and other interactive programs. This was usually implemented by the Web server that hosted these pages. With the introduction of scripting languages, such as Microsoft's Visual Basic Script and Sun's Java, everything has changed. With the inline scripting capabilities provided by these script languages, most of the processing is done at the client's side, or on your computer. As a matter of fact, many tasks involving scripting can be done on the client's side.

In this section, forms are covered in depth, since they are one of the major applications of Visual Basic Script. Forms are fairly simple, but there are several more HTML elements that make forms what they are. A pair of `<FORM>` tags encapsulate everything that is related to the form, and everything that is submitted in that form. The form's controls can include input boxes for entering text, radio buttons for specifying one choice out of several, select boxes, which are drop-down menus of different selections, and buttons, which can reset, submit, or perform other tasks with the form. According to the HTML specification, the general syntax for specifying a form is:

```
<FORM ACTION="POST/GET" METHOD="URL"> ... </FORM>
```

The ACTION attribute specifies what URL to go to for processing data. The METHOD attribute specifies what method the data should be given for processing by the URL specified by ACTION. However, the ACTION and the METHOD attributes are not necessarily needed for use in Visual Basic Script. Since the script is being used internally, it is redundant to specify what URL is needed to process the form. The following example shows how Visual Basic Script uses a form. You don't need to understand all the specifics of the form now, because they are fully covered later in this chapter or in subsequent ones. Listing 2.4, FORMDEMO.HTM is a simple form. This listing is illustrated in Figure 2.2 and can be found on the CD under the file name FORMDEMO.HTM.

Listing 2.4 FORMDEMO.HTM—A Simple HTML Document that Demonstrates How a Form Works with VBScript

```
<HTML>
<HEAD>
<TITLE>This is a page which demonstrates how vbscript functions with
forms</TITLE>
</HEAD>
<BODY BGCOLOR="#DDFFFF">
<CENTER><FONT FACE="Arial" SIZE="4" COLOR="blue">
How to use forms with VB Script</FONT></CENTER>
<HR>
<PRE><FORM NAME="me">
The text typed here                    :
<INPUT TYPE="text" VALUE="Default" NAME="test1" SIZE="50">
Will go here when the button is pressed:
<INPUT TYPE="text" VALUE="Hello" NAME="test2" SIZE="50">
<CENTER><INPUT TYPE="BUTTON" NAME="but1" VALUE="Push Me"></CENTER>
</PRE>
</FORM>
<SCRIPT LANGUAGE="VBS">
Sub but1_OnClick
          Set Form=document.me
          Form.test2.Value = Form.test1.Value
     End Sub
</SCRIPT>
```

When viewed with Internet Explorer 3.0, the first text box has the text "Default" and the second text box has the text "Hello." When you click the button, the text in the first box replaces that in the second, producing "Default" in both boxes. This example is shown in Figure 2.2.

FIG. 2.2
An example of a form created with VBScript. This is a pretty simple form with some Visual Basic Script capabilities.

There are a few new tags to consider in this document. The tags such as <FONT> and <PRE> are for cosmetic purposes only. The substance of this document lies in the <FORM> and <SCRIPT> tags. The form and its controls (for example, input boxes, radio buttons, and so on) are just HTML tags, and everything inside the <SCRIPT> tags is Visual Basic Script used for manipulating those tags.

Let's consider a few things inside the form. First, we assign the form a name, "me", and this is the name used by the script. Next, we have a few <INPUT> tags with no </INPUT> because they do not encapsulate any text, but define a control to use, the control's name, and any values associated with it. Finally, we have a button control, and that is the end of the form. The <INPUT> tags both have a NAME, TYPE, and VALUE attribute. The TYPE attribute in each tag is set to "text," which is a text input box with a size of 50 characters. The NAME is the input box's unique identifier and the VALUE is the default value that is first seen in the box when the page is viewed. Table 2.2 shows the different form controls, specified by the TYPE attribute and used in the <INPUT> tag.

Table 2.2 Values of Form Controls Used by the *TYPE* Attribute of the *<INPUT>* Tag

TYPE Value	Function
"text"	Specifies a one-line text box.
"password"	Similar to the "text" value, except the characters are not seen and are usually replaced by one similar character.
"radio"	Can specify a series of buttons with the same value for the NAME attribute, but only one of the buttons can be chosen.
"checkbox"	Specifies individual text boxes with different values for NAME; additionally, the VALUE attribute must have a value of TRUE or FALSE (TRUE means it is initially checked and FALSE means it is not initially checked).
"hidden"	Specifies a hidden field, which should contain a VALUE attribute. This control is not seen by the user.
"submit"	Creates a button that submits the form to the URL specified by the ACTION attribute of the FORM tag.
"reset"	Creates a button that clears all the entries on the form.
"button"	Creates a button that can be referenced by Visual Basic Script; a name can be given to the button (and all buttons) by giving a value to the NAME attribute. A name that is displayed on the button can be given by assigning a value to the VALUE attribute of the button.
"image"	Instantly submits the form when clicked, with the coordinates of the position of the mouse-click on that image.
"textarea"	Specifies several lines of input text similar to the one-line text box control.

NOTE The image control requires the additional attribute, SRC to specify a graphic to use. All input types should have a NAME or ID tag to be manipulated by Visual Basic Script. The size allotted to the text control is lengthwise, for example, `<INPUT...SIZE="50">`, whereas the textarea control's size is given by length and height, respectively—for example, `<INPUT...SIZE="50,50">`.

In addition to the input tag, there are also a few other controls, such as combo boxes and drop-down lists, that can be used in forms and manipulated by Visual Basic Script. These additional tags are shown in Table 2.3.

Table 2.3 Additional Form Tags

Control Tag	Function
`<SELECT>`	Can specify a drop-down list or a list box depending on whether the attribute `MULTIPLE` (has no value) is present. If `MULTIPLE` is present, then it is a scrollable list box, which allows the user to select more than one option from the list.
`<OPTION>`	Is encapsulated inside the `<SELECT>` tags and specifies the name and values for the various list options of that combo box or drop-down box with the `NAME` and `VALUE` attributes.

NOTE The `SELECT` tag, unlike the `INPUT` tag, has a closing tag (for example, `<SELECT>...</SELECT>`). The `NAME` and `VALUE` attributes associated with the `OPTION` tag deal with the data that is submitted when that option is selected, and not with the text that is displayed when the form is viewed. The text which describes the option on the screen immediately follows the `<OPTION>` tag (for example, `<OPTION>Displayed text here`). The `<OPTION>` tag does not have a closing tag.

This wraps up forms and their usage. For a more elaborate example that uses all the `FORM` controls, refer to FORMCOMP.HTM (on the CD), which has output as shown in Figure 2.3. The other major tag mentioned, the `SCRIPT` tag, is used to specify a scripting language to use. In this book, the script language is exclusively Visual Basic Script. The `LANGUAGE` attribute of the `SCRIPT` tag defines what language the script is interpreted in. The value for this language, "VBScript", specifies Visual Basic Script. The `SCRIPT` tag also has a closing tag.

CAUTION

Make sure you include the closing tag, `</SCRIPT>`, at the end of your Visual Basic Script; otherwise it does not execute.

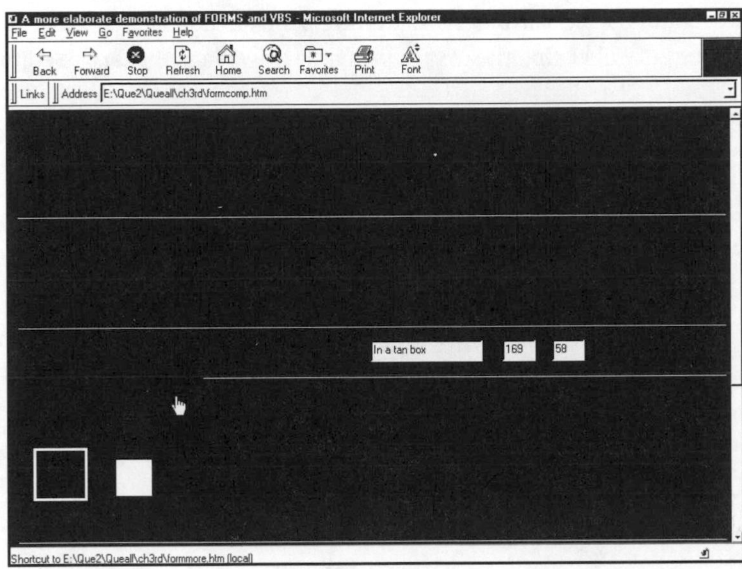

FIG. 2.3
A more complete demonstration of forms.

It may be helpful to surround your entire Visual Basic Script with a comment so the script is not displayed on browsers that do not support it.

Using Extensions

To this point we have discussed HTML entities that will more or less remain the same, with minor additions now and then. In this section, many of the important extensions made to HTML are covered. It is fair to say that Netscape Communications, Inc. was the first company to implement several extensions to the HTML language, including background colors, the ability to center text, frames, and so on. Microsoft and its product, the Internet Explorer, have also made many contributions to HTML including client-side image maps, marquees, smoother support for tables and frames, objects, and, of course, the ActiveX controls. Many of these entities such as objects and the ActiveX controls are very useful to Visual Basic Script—some of which were demonstrated in Figure 2.3. As previously stated, the tags and entities dealt with in this section have great potential for change, as the standards have not yet been decided on by the HTML standards committee at the World Wide Web Consortium (W3C).

Base Attributes

A system of base attributes, which are intrinsic to every tag, has been proposed and is largely implemented in Internet Explorer's implementation of HTML. Table 2.4 lists some of the base attributes which have been already implemented and a brief explanation. Also remember that these tags primarily affect tags that are used to render text.

Table 2.4 Supported Base Attributes

Attribute name	Purpose
CLASS	Commonly groups a tag or set of tags. This base attribute is used mostly with Style Sheets to specify rendering properties for different classes (groups) of tags.
ID and NAME	Identifies other tags besides the anchor tag. These tags are also used with style sheets to set certain styles to tags that have styles for the name they use in the style section of a document (see the style section). In future versions of Internet Explorer 3.0 however, there might be support for the <A> to access other tags with NAME and ID attributes in the same manner as it would access other <A> tags with the NAME/ID attribute.

Extensions of HTML

In addition to entire tags extending the HTML language, there have been several minor extensions to existing tags, some of which were demonstrated in prior sections. These are covered here, briefly.

To begin with, the `<IMG>` tag has the attribute extension, `DYNSRC`, which allows the author to embed inline AVI animations. The `DYNSRC attribute` specifies which animation to play and has several additional attributes that enable you to customize the way the AVI animation looks and plays. When you encapsulate an image tag with an anchor, you can allow a Visual Basic Script to utilize this image from within the script (demonstrated in fig. 2.3).

The `<input>` tag that is used inside the form to specify form controls also has the new button control, which allows you to specify other buttons on the form instead of your every day submit and reset buttons. The `ALIGN` attribute works with most of the HTML tags, which affect text in some manner. The `ALIGN` attribute is used to specify where the text or other object should be displayed—usually with the values “left” and “right”; although “center” is used, it has not been implemented on all tags.

HTML Tables

The introduction of tables into the HTML language has vastly improved the way data is handled and content is served. Tables provide an efficient way to handle and organize data and Web pages, which formerly would have been accomplished by images and pre-formatted text tags! This section discusses the table’s basic usage, the various types of tables supported, and a couple of methods for implementing different tables.

Figure 2.4 is an example of a basic HTML table, which has several rows and columns and a caption.

The code for this table is in Listing 2.5, which can be found on the CD in the file TABLE1.HTM.

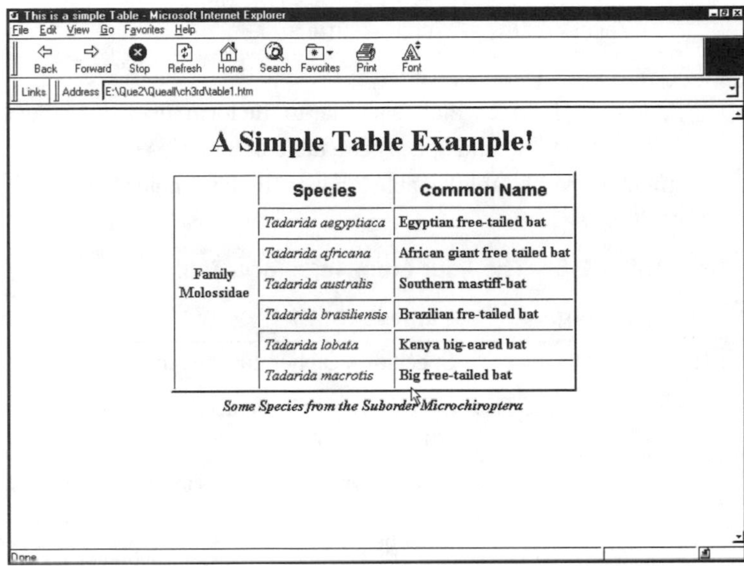

FIG. 2.4
A sample HTML table. This table demonstrates several of the basic tags used in tables.

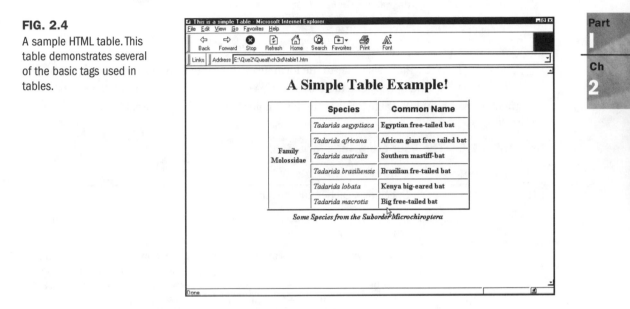

Listing 2.5 TABLE1.HTM—A Brief Example of Tables in HTML

```
<HTML><HEAD>
<TITLE>This is a simple Table</TITLE>
</HEAD>
<BODY BGCOLOR="ALICEBLUE">
<H1 ALIGN="CENTER">A Simple Table Example!</H1>
<CENTER>
<TABLE CELLPADDING="5" CELLSPACING="2" BORDER="2" BGCOLOR="#CDCDCD">
<CAPTION ALIGN="BOTTOM">
<B><I>Some Species from the Suborder Microchiroptera</I></B></CAPTION>
<TR>
<TH ROWSPAN="7" BGCOLOR="LIME">Family<BR>Molossidae</TH>
<TH><FONT SIZE="4" FACE="ARIAL" COLOR="RED">Species</FONT></TH>
<TH><FONT SIZE="4" FACE="ARIAL" COLOR="BLUE">Common Name</FONT></TH>
</TR>
<TR><TD><I>Tadarida aegyptiaca</I></TD>
<TD><B>Egyptian free-tailed bat</B></TD></TR>
<TR><TD><I>Tadarida africana</I></TD>
<TD><B>African giant free tailed bat</B></TD></TR>
<TR><TD><I>Tadarida australis</I></TD>
<TD><B>Southern mastiff-bat</B></TD></TR>
```

continues

Listing 2.5 Continued

```
<TR><TD><I>Tadarida brasiliensis</I></TD>
<TD><B>Brazilian fre-tailed bat</B></TD></TR>
<TR><TD><I>Tadarida lobata</I></TD>
<TD><B>Kenya big-eared bat</B></TD></TR>
<TR><TD><I>Tadarida macrotis</I></TD>
<TD><B>Big free-tailed bat</B></TD></TR>
</TABLE></CENTER></BODY></HTML>
```

A table in HTML, which is similar to the form, uses the <TABLE> and </TABLE> tags, which initiate the table and specify the table boundaries (everything inside the <TABLE> tags is affected by the table). Table 2.5 lists the four major tags used inside a table.

Table 2.5 The Four Main Tags for a Table

Table Tag	Purpose
<CAPTION>	Specifies a caption for the table.
<TR>	Specifies a row to be used in the table. This should be the first tag used when actually constructing a table.
<TH>	Any test or HTML that is inside the <TH> tags is considered the heading of the table. Each instance of the <TH> tag denotes a cell in the table that must be encapsulated in the <TR> tag. All cells that are in a <TR> tag are arranged horizontally—for example: <TR><TH>Header 1</TH> <TH>Header 2</TH></TR> would be a row with two columns; the first column has "Header 1" as its text and the second "Header 2" as its text. By default, all text encapsulated in the <TH> tags is centered and rendered in bold.
<TD>	Specifies table data in the form of cells that functions the same as a <TH> tag does. All instances of <TD> nested in a <TR> tag are placed horizontally in columns.

The four major tags listed in Table 2.5 were used in Listing 2.5. There are also attributes to each of these tags. The attributes listed in Table 2.6 will work with the <TR>, <TH>, <TD>, and <TABLE> tags. The <TR>, <TH>, <TD>, and <TABLE> tags work by inheritance. *Inheritance*, in terms of HTML, means that whatever attributes are specified by a tag are used by tags that are encapsulated by it. However, if these child tags (tags that are encapsulated by the parent tag) have their own attributes defined, then these are used instead for tables.

Table 2.6 Attributes for <TABLE> Tags

Attribute	Function
ALIGN	Specifies the alignment of the table or text in the table. Values of "left" and "right" are supported.
BGCOLOR	Specifies the background color of the table, which uses either Internet Explorer colors or colors given by hexadecimal RBG.
BACKGROUND	Specifies an image to use as a background of table cells. The image is tiled.
BORDERCOLOR	Specifies the color of the border of the table. Works similarly to BGCOLOR.
VALIGN	Specifies where the text is to be vertically aligned in each cell. Values for this attribute are "top", "bottom", "middle", and "baseline".
COLSPAN	Specifies how many columns a particular cell should span across (used with <TD> and <TH> only).
ROWSPAN	Specifies how many rows a particular cell should span across (used with <TD> and <TH> only).
WIDTH	Similar to COLSPAN, except that pixels or a percentage of the screen are used for the span value.
HEIGHT	Similar to ROWSPAN, except that pixels or a percentage of the screen are used for the span value.

Additionally, there are other, minor attributes dealing with detail in border color and spacing that are not covered here. A full review of table styles can be found in Appendix B, "HTML Reference," of this book. For extensive coverage on the HTML language, check out Que's *Special Edition Using HTML.*

There are also different styles for tables. Some tables can be defined in terms of header, body, and footer, and some can be defined in terms of columns instead of rows, according to the HTML 3.0 Standard. Borderless tables can be used to make a page look very stylish by using them to set different areas of the page with different background colors or images in the table's cells. Listing 2.6 shows how to use borderless tables with different background colors and images to make a page look interesting. You can find the listing on the CD-ROM in the file TABLE2.HTM.

Listing 2.6 TABLE2.HTM—Some Techniques for Creating an Interesting Page with Tables

```
<HTML><HEAD>
<TITLE>This is table demo 2 - how to use tables for page layout...
</TITLE></HEAD>
<BODY BGCOLOR="BLACK" TEXT="#FFFFFF">
<TABLE>
<TR><TD BGCOLOR="BLACK" WIDTH="150" HEIGHT="50">
<FONT FACE="MS Sans Serif" SIZE="3" COLOR="RED">
<CENTER>MALLUF Travel Agency</CENTER></FONT>
</TD>
<TD WIDTH=500" ><FONT FACE="WINGDINGS" SIZE="20" COLOR="ORANGE">
<MARQUEE DIRECTION="RIGHT">Q</MARQUEE>
</TD>
<TD WIDTH="100" HEIGHT="100">
<IMG DYNSRC="TheEarth.avi" HEIGHT="100" WIDTH="100" LOOP="INFINITE">
</TD></TR></TABLE>
<TABLE CELLSPACING="20" CELLPADDING="10">
<TR><TD VALIGN="TOP" WIDTH="600" HEIGHT="350" BGCOLOR="RED">
<H2>Tours to Earth Special</H2>
We are offering a 50% discount for a 2 passenger flight to Earth!
What a deal! Get away from those orbiting atrocities and have
a taste of reality.
<HR><H2>Universal Discount</H2>
That's right! For the month of April, we are offering universal discounts,
for free flights to Mars, Jupiter, Earth and Venus.
<HR>A Service of MCS. Your ONLY universal affiliate.</TD>
<TD WIDTH="625" VALIGN="TOP" BGCOLOR="BLACK" ALIGN="RIGHT"><CENTER>
<IMG SRC="bigm.jpg"></CENTER>
</TD></TR></TABLE></BODY></HTML>
```

Consider Listing 2.6; two tables were used in this example. There are several interesting ways tables are used here. First, the lengths and widths of each of the table's cells are not uniformly positioned, which causes different areas covered by these widths to contain different colors and styles. Also notice the Marquee that is nested in the `<TD>` tag with a width of 500 pixels, which spans across the screen to the cell that contains the AVI of the Earth spinning. The airplane, and other icons shown, can be displayed in this manner by using the Wingdings or Dingbats fonts (the `<FONT>` tag should surround the marquee, but not vice versa). The example in Listing 2.6 demonstrates a basic method of page layout. Other alternatives include style sheets (which are covered in this chapter) and ActiveX controls (which are covered in depth in Chapter 11, "Designing VBScript Applications").

HTML Frame Sets

This section discusses one of the more recent extensions to the HTML language, which allows the existence of multiple HTML documents or other resources on one page. Frame sets are an efficient, neat, and effective way to organize and present information in an HTML document. Frame sets are a group of frames in an HTML document, each of which display a different resource (an HTML file, for instance).

A frame set is relatively simple to understand. Frame sets are used within the <BODY> tag and replace any content that would otherwise exist inside the body of a document. There are two parts to a frame set. The general tag for specifying a frame set and the properties of all frames in the frame set (this tag is the <FRAMESET> tag) and the tag which is used to indicate the frames (the <FRAME> tag). The general syntax is expressed in the following syntax section. A simple demonstration of a frame set is shown in Figure 2.5. The code to this figure is in Listing 2.7.

Listing 2.7 MAINFRAME.HTM—The HTML File that Specifies All the Other Frames and Files to Use

```
<HTML><HEAD>
<TITLE>This Document Demonstrates Frames</TITLE></HEAD>
<FRAMESET COLS="50%,*">
     <FRAME SRC="frmfile1.htm" SCROLLING="no" NAME="frame1" FRAMEBORDER="1">
     <FRAMESET ROWS="40%,*">
          <FRAME SRC="frmfile2.htm" SCROLLING="yes" NAME="frame2"
➥ FRAMEBORDER-"yes">
          <FRAME SRC="http://www.rt66.com/iymalluf" SCROLLING="yes"
➥ NAME="frame3">
           FRAMEBORDER="yes">
     </FRAMESET>
</FRAMESET>
```

Notice that there are a few new tags introduced with frame sets. The first tag, the <FRAMESET> tag, is used to define the length of the frames, how many there are, and how they are to be rendered. Next, we have the <FRAME> tag which is used for specifying the actual content of the frame which was defined by the <FRAMESET> tag (see Listing 2.8). The SRC attribute of the <FRAME> tag is used to specify the URL of the file it is to display. These files follow.

FIG. 2.5
This figure illustrates some basic uses of frames.

Listing 2.8 FRMFILE1.HTM—First File Used with Frames

```
<BODY BGCOLOR="LIME" TEXT="PURPLE">
<CENTER>
<FONT SIZE="5" FACE="Matura MT Script Capitals" COLOR="PURPLE">
My File</FONT></CENTER>
<HR>
This is the daily chatter column; anything goes here, except
you shouldn't be overly rude or excessively fastidious. Here
is the first frame, hope you enjoy!!
<HR>
</BODY>
```

This is the first file used with the first frame defined in the previous code example. The files displayed in frames are nothing but individual HTML documents, so whatever you can do in an HTML document is valid content for a frame. Listing 2.9 illustrates another use of frames.

Listing 2.9 FRMFILE2.HTM—Second File Used with Frames

```
<BODY BGCOLOR="BLUE" TEXT="LIME">
Here are some quick facts about physics:
<OL>
     <LI>It's the study of matter</LI>
     <LI>It involves the study of Quantum mechanics wave theory</LI>
```

```
    <LI>Facts are subject to change at any time</LI>
    <LI>Most general equations were derived with ide00al situations in mind</LI>
</OL>
</BODY>
```

This is the second file which is used with the second frame. It is also another HTML document. Since you can use any HTML document for content for a frame, you can also add background colors or images to the frames.

Syntax of Frames and Frame Sets The tag used to specify a frame set is the <FRAMESET> tag and it has a closing tag, </FRAMESET>. Contrast this to the <FRAME> tag that has just one tag specifying what is to be in a frame. Some attributes for the <FRAMESET> tag are in Table 2.7 and the general syntax is below:

```
<FRAMESET>
      <FRAME>
      ...
</FRAMESET>
```

There are also a few required attributes for the <FRAMESET> and the <FRAME> tags and they are listed in Tables 2.7 and 2.8. Figure 2.6 illustrates a simple layout of a frame set. The files MAINFRAME.HTM, FRMFILE1.HTM, and FRMFILE2.HTM are used for this example and can also be found on the accompanying CD.

Table 2.7 Required Attributes for the *<FRAMESET>* Tag

Attribute	Function
COLS	Used to specify the number of columns in a frame set and their width. The number of columns in a frame set is specified by how many comma separated values exist for this attribute (the values represent the columns width).
ROWS	Used to specify the number of rows and each row's height in a frame set. The number of rows in a frame set is specified by how many comma-separated values exist (these values specify the length of each row).

In the <FRAMESET> tag, either the ROWS attribute or the COLS attribute can be used, but not both. The ROWS and COLS attributes are used in specifying how many frames are to exist in a frame set, their width or height, and how they should be displayed (as rows or columns, based on which attribute is used). The number of frames that are to exist and their length are both specified at once. The number of frames is specified by how many comma-separated values exist in the ROWS or COLS attributes. These comma-separated values specify the length of each frame. So if you have 3 lengths specified for the ROWS or COLS attributes, then you use three frames, or other nested <FRAMESET> tags. For example, if one wanted a frame set that consists of two columns, one that is 300 pixels and the other which takes up the remainder of the space, they would do the following:

```
<FRAMESET COLS="300,*">
      <FRAME SRC="somefile.htm">
      <FRAME SRC="somefile2.htm">
</FRAMESET>
```

Note that two <FRAME> tags are used. There are two <FRAME> tags since there are two values specified. The <FRAME> tags correspond to the lengths specified by the <FRAMESET> tag in the same order that they are specified. So the first value of 300 in the COLS attribute is assigned to the first frame specified, and so on. There are three ways to specify a length for the COLS and ROWS attributes. These valid values are in the following list.

- *Pixels:* When you wish to use pixels to specify a length, then you use any integer up to the maximum width or height of the browser. For example: COLS="300,200" specifies two columns in a frame set, the first is 300 pixels wide and the second is 200 pixels wide.
- *Percentage of screen:* Lengths are specified as a percentage of the screen. Valid values are a number (up to 100) with a % sign appended to the end representing how much of the available screen space to use. For example, ROWS="10%,90%" would create two rows. The first row uses 10% of the height of the screen and the second uses 90 percent (or the rest) of the screens height.
- *Relative size:* Using relative values, you specify how much space to use based on how much the other frames have used. Relative values are specifed by a * or a number with the * appended to represent a relative proportion to other relative values. For example: ROWS="3*,*" would create two rows. The first uses 3 parts (3/4) of the screen and the second uses one part (1/4). These frames are relative to each other, so if the size of the browser window changes, their lengths will remain in this proportion.
- *A combination of lengths:* You can use one or more of the previously mentioned methods for specifying lengths of frames. For instance: COLS="100,20%,*" would specify three columns. The first column is 100 pixels wide, the second uses 20 percent of the remaining screen and the final column uses the remainder of the screen's width.

The attributes for <FRAME> are in Table 2.8.

Table 2.8 Attributes for the *<FRAME>* Tag

Attribute	Function
SRC	Specifies what URL the frame should point to
NAME	Gives an identification to the frame, so other links can manipulate the frame
SCROLLING	Specifies if the frame is capable of scrolling (valid values are "Yes" and "No")
NORESIZE	Is an attribute with no value. It is inserted into the <FRAME> tag if the person designing the frames does not want the user to resize the frame
FRAMEBORDER	Specifies if the frame has a border (valid values are "Yes" or "No")
FRAMESPACING	Makes the spacing between frames larger

Again, note that these are not all the attributes that are available for the <FRAME> tag. There are other attributes; however, they are for cosmetic purposes. These minor attributes are covered fully in Appendix B, "HTML Reference."

NOTE For browsers that do not currently support frames, you can add the tag <NOFRAMES> to the very end of your document and treat the content encapsulated in the <NOFRAME> tags like the content in a normal HTML document, which has <BODY> tags.

Manipulating Frames As previously mentioned, you can manipulate frames in HTML with anchor tags and anything else that can reference another URL. To do this, you must include the TARGET attribute in your anchor tag. Whatever URL the anchor is pointing to is displayed in the frame specified by the TARGET attribute when that anchor is clicked. The TARGET attribute is used to specify the name of the frame to put the resource in. If you have a frame named "test1," to access that frame through a link, you would have to put TARGET="test1" as an attribute in the anchor tag. Refer to Listings 2.10–2.13 for a full example. This example covers the basic uses of frames that we have already discussed. These listings can also be found on the accompanying CD under their respective file names. Figure 2.6 illustrates this basic example.

Listing 2.10 FRAME2.HTM—An Example of Frames and the *TARGET* Attribute

```
<HTML>
<HEAD><TITLE>This is a frame page demonstrating the TARGET attribute
</TITLE></HEAD>
<FRAMESET ROWS="25%,*">
     <FRAME SRC="links.htm" SCROLL="no" FRAMEBORDER="yes" FRAMESPACING="4">
     <FRAME NAME="linktarget" SRC="blank.htm" SCROLL="yes" FRAMEBORDER="yes"
➥ FRAMESPACING="4">
</FRAMESET>
```

Listing 2.11 LINKS.HTM—This is the First Frame of the Frame Set

```
<BODY BGCOLOR="WHITE">
<CENTER>
<FONT FACE="COMIC SANS MS" SIZE="+1" COLOR="BLUE">
Click-a-link!</FONT><BR>
<TABLE CELLSPACING="2">
<TR>
<TD>
<A TARGET="linktarget" HREF="http://www.nm.org/~chfaq">Supercomputer Challenge
➥</A>
</TD>
<TD><A TARGET="linktarget" HREF="http://tesuque.cs.sandia.gov/">
Adventures in Supercomputing</A></TD>
</TR>
<TR><TD><A TARGET="linktarget" HREF="http://www.mcp.com/que">QUE
➥ Corporation</TD>
<TD><A TARGET="linktarget" HREF="http://www.rt66.com/iymalluf">Malluf
➥ Consulting Services</A></TD></TR>
<TR><TD><A TARGET="linktarget" HREF="http://www.microsoft.com/">
➥ Microsoft Website</A></TD>
<TD>
<A TARGET="linktarget" HREF="http://www.yahoo.com">YAHOO</A></TD></TR>
</TABLE></CENTER></BODY>
```

Listing 2.12 BLANK.HTM—This Is a Blank File Used by the Second Frame

```
<BODY BGCOLOR="#000000">
</BODY>
```

This is a simple frame set demonstration that allows content specified by links in the first frame to be placed in the second frame when clicked. The TARGET attribute also has several special values that are listed under the "Frames" section of Appendix B.

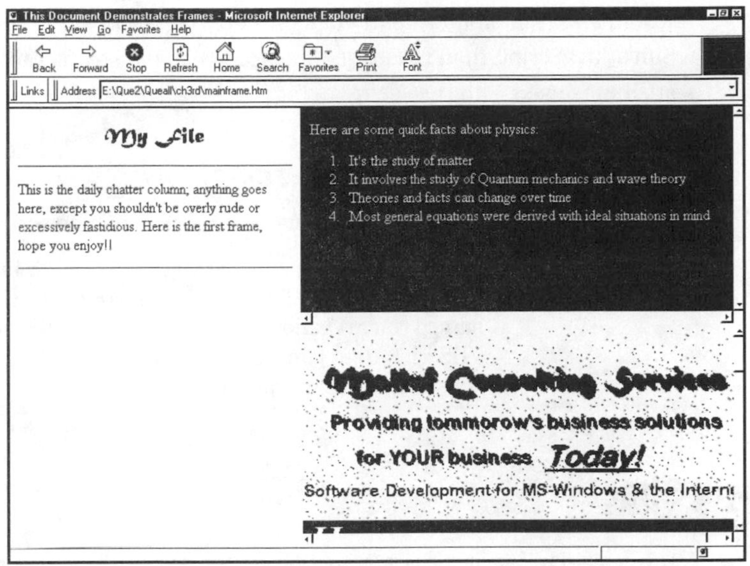

FIG. 2.6
An example of frames and the `TARGET` attribute.

Using Frames with Visual Basic Script When using frame sets and Visual Basic Script together, you are providing a higher level of interactive HTML documents and Web pages. With Visual Basic Script and frame sets, you can make interactive games, more advanced ordering systems, and electronic catalogs. You can use Visual Basic Script inside each frame and scripts that are used in other frames in the frame set can be accessed using the frames collection of Visual Basic Script (refer to Chapter 11 for a description of the frames collection under the Internet Explorer 3.0 Object Model section).

This section basically covers frame sets and their usage. Next we'll look at some very recent components of HTML that work very nicely with Visual Basic Script.

Scripts in HTML Documents

Scripts are the whole basis for Visual Basic Script and other inline scripting languages. Scripts are used for a number of things in an HTML page. Some of these tasks have already been mentioned, such as a validation tool for forms, games, and electronic magazines (E-zines).

▶ **See** "Using VBScript for Designing Web Applications," **p. 184**

The `<SCRIPT>` tag specifies what scripting language to use in the HTML document. There are also several attributes that make the `<SCRIPT>` tag as advanced or as simple as you want. For most purposes, though, only the `LANGUAGE` attribute needs to be used. This attribute specifies which language to use. If the language is Visual Basic Script, then you would insert the following in your `<SCRIPT>` tag: `LANGUAGE="VBScript"`. If the language is Sun's JavaScript, then `LANGUAGE="Javascript"`, and so on. Table 2.9 shows the different attributes used with the `<SCRIPT>` tag.

Table 2.9 Attributes for the *<SCRIPT>* Tag

`LANGUAGE`	Specifies the language the corresponding script uses
`IN`	Specifies what the script should "bind" to, as in a form or some other group of elements that fall under one NAME or ID. For example, if a form was named "form1" and you wanted to access the controls in that form with VBScript, then you would use: in="form1", which specifies that this script is used for the controls in this form.

Style Sheets

NOTE If you are not familiar with HTML beyond what you have read in this chapter, it is recommended that you review Appendix B, "HTML Reference," to understand the tags discussed in this section, which are not mentioned in this chapter.

Style sheets are the newest introduction to the HTML Language. Style sheets allow a user to have a collection of HTML documents or an entire Web site use one or several formats of style, which was formerly accomplished by the tedious task of inserting many `<FONT>` tags, graphics and other miscellany into an HTML document. Microsoft Internet Explorer is the first browser to implement style sheets to a useable level. Formerly, the UNIX based browser Arena had some style sheet support but lacked support in many areas; Microsoft Internet Explorer hosts several additional features to its style sheet implementation. This section covers the concept of style sheets, how to use style sheets, and their integration with HTML.

How Style Sheets Work This section describes the concept behind style sheets and how they work. A style sheet does not only apply to the page's style in general, but also to the tags used on that page. For instance, if one wanted all `<H1>` headers in a page to be rendered as a size 14 pt. and the face of the font to be Arial, he or she could use style sheets to change all those headers. If one only wanted specific `<H1>` headers to be 14 pt. and Arial, and others 16 pt. and Matura, he or she could use the CLASS base attribute to assign certain headers to be of the former style and other headers to be the latter style.

How to Use Style Sheets This section covers the syntax of style sheets, how and when to use them. The syntax for style sheets is a little different from the syntax of HTML but it is almost as simple. There are three major ways to use style sheets with an HTML document and they are in the following list.

- *Pre-defined styles in a separate file:* You can predefine styles in a file to use on a page. This is most efficient when there are several pages that need to comply to the same style. The syntax will be covered in the syntax section.
- *Inline-defined styles:* You can define styles for different tags within the document as well. With the current implementation of Internet Explorer, however, if there is a file-specified style format, it will override any inline styles. This will be changed in a future release.
- *Tag-specified styles:* There are a series of HTML tags for style sheets that you can use in the body of your document to change the style of text and other entities. These tags allow you to change the style the same way as inline styles and styles stored in a separate file.

Syntax This section covers the general syntax for defining styles for different elements in HTML. When specifying a series of styles that are located in a file you have to use the `<LINK>` tag in this format:

```
<LINK REL="STYLE" TYPE="text/css" SRC="URL">
```

The `<LINK>` tag is used to specify files that are related to the document with that link tag. The attributes in this link tag are described in Table 2.10.

Table 2.10 Attributes of the *<Link>* Tags for Style Sheets

Attribute	Function
REL	Specifies a relationship for the `<LINK>` tag. In this case, the file specified in the `<LINK>` tag has the relationship "style" which, of course, indicates that the corresponding file is a style sheet.
TYPE	Specifies a MIME type that states that the text in the file specified is a style sheet. The value "text/css" is used to indicate that the file is a style sheet.
SRC	Specifies the name of the file to use. This can either be the name of the file (I.E. style.css) or the URL to that file (**http://www.somewhere.org/styles/style.css**).

NOTE The file method for specifying a style sheet works across a server only, which means that this method will not work on your machine alone. The file must be requested across the server. The server must have the MIME type: text/css for the extension .css for this method to work across a server. ■

NOTE You should always name your files that contain style information with the extension .css, so it is recognizable by the server as a style sheet file. ■

When you specify inline style information, you have to use the <STYLE> tag, which should be used outside of the body of an HTML document (preferably inside the header of the document). The <STYLE> tag also has a closing tag </STYLE> and all the defined styles are to be encapsulated in the <STYLE> tags. Each defined element can have a series of styles; the syntax is listed below:

```
TAGNAME {style1: value1; style2: value2; ...}
```

NOTE When you use style definitions that are on a separate file, you use the syntax in this section, without the <STYLE> tags. Any number of style definitions can exist in this file.

TAGNAME is a pseudonym for any text-rendering HTML element. Following this tag is a pair of curly braces ({ and }) in which are all the style properties for that element's corresponding tag (the element with the "<" and ">" brackets); *style1* and *style2* ... are pseudonyms for the different style properties for that element. Note how this varies from attributes and values in HTML. A property and its value, in style sheet syntax, are separated by a colon instead of the equal sign.

For instance:

```
A {text-decoration: none}
```

is used to specify no additives to the <A> (anchor) tag (like underlines and strikethrough). Text-decoration is a property of the <A> tag which is set to the value none, which means no text decoration. All tags share the same set of properties listed in Table 2.11.

Table 2.11 Style Properties for Use with Different HTML Elements

Property Name	Function and Allowed Values
font-family	Specifies the fonts used with the specified element. Any font name is allowed (as long as the font is on the user's system—see the appendix under the <FONT> tag for some common fonts. Fonts can be separated by commas to indicate different fonts to use (for example: ...{font-family: Arial, Times}). If the first font in the list is not available, the browser checks to see if the next is available, and so on until it finds a font that is on the user's system; if none of the specified fonts exist, the default font (Times New Roman) is used. Any number of fonts can be specified.
font-size	Specifies the size of the font using several different measurements, listed in Table 2.12. Valid values for font sizes are a number with one of the abbreviations listed in Table 2.12 appended to it.
font-weight	Specifies the weight of the font. Valid values are bold and normal (such as ...{font-weight: bold; ...} sets the font-weight for the specified element to bold).

Property Name	Function and Allowed Values
font-style	Sets the style of the font. Only the value of italic is supported currently (for example: ...{font-style:italic;...}) would set the style of the corresponding element to italics.
text-decoration	Specifies some additional text decoration to the corresponding element. Values allowed are: none (this removes all text decoration), line-through (this draws a line through the text), and underline (underlines the text).
line-height	Specifies a height of a line for an element. There are several possible measurement values you can use, listed in Table 2.6 (for example: ...{line-height: 5cm; ...} makes the height of each line for the specified element 5 centimeters). Extra spacing (unused spacing) is placed before lines.
background	Specifies a background color or image. There are a few ways to specify background colors and images. You can specify a color name (for example: {...background: forestgreen...}); you can specify a color using a hexadecimal value (for example:{...background: #FF00CC...}) or you can specify a URL to an image (for example: {...background URL(http://myimage.com/imag.gif)...}). Note that the location of the image is surrounded in brackets. You can specify multiple values for this property. For instance, if the specified background does not exist, then you can use a background color (...{background: url(http://www.grfics.com/pic.gif) seagreen} specifies to use the background image pic.gif and use the background color seagreen).
margin-left	Specifies the length of the left margin for the specified element. The value in the length can be any of the measurements listed in table 2.12 (for example: ...{margin-left: 10in;...} sets the left margin at 10 inches).
margin-right	Specifies the length of the right margin for the specified element. The value in the length can be any of the measurements listed in Table 2.12 (for example: ...{margin-right: 10in;...} sets the right margin at 10 inches).
text-indent	Sets the indentation for each paragraph for the specified element, when the specified element's tag is used in the document to begin a paragraph block.
text-align	Sets the alignment for the specified element. Valid values are: "left," "center," and "right."
color	Specifies the color of the text that is encapsulated by the element's tag. The color can be a color name or a hexadecimal #RRGGBB value (see Appendix B for a valid list of color names); values are specified in the same manner as the background property.

The abbreviations in Table 2.12 are appended to the end of a size specified for several of the properties of Table 2.11. For instance, the property margin-right can use any of the measurements listed below; all that is needed is the length with the abbreviation appended to the end of the length (for example, magin-left: 5in would be 5 inches for the left margin).

Table 2.12 Measurement Sizes Used with Different Properties of Style Sheets

Measurement Name	Abbreviation	Description
Points	pt	Points are a measurement of font size. The default font on a web page is 10pt–12pt.
Pixels	px	Pixels are a measurement of screen pixels. Pixels are relatively small compared to the other units.
Centimeters	cm	Centimeters are 1/100 of a meter (.39 of an inch).
Inches	in	Inches are a United States standard measurement (1/12 of a foot, 2.5 centimeters).

In addition to the properties listed in Table 2.12, there is also the font property that is used for specifying several properties for a font at once. The general syntax for specifying many different values of style for the font property is:

```
...{font: italic bold font size/line height fonts; ...}
```

The values font and italic for this property are literal. You use them to specify whether the font is italic, bold, or both (if both are specified). The "font size" section is used in specifying the size of the font in the same way as the font-size property and the "line height" section is used in specifying the height of each line, exactly like the line-height property (the "/" in the syntax does separate the two values; for example: 12pt/14pt specifies a font size of 12 pt and a line height of 14pt). The "fonts" section is used in specifying a font to use and alternative fonts to use, the same way as the font-family property (multiple fonts are separated by columns and should be in quotations: for example: "Arial, Times, Symbol"). These properties should be used in the same order as indicated in the syntax or the current implementation of this property may exhibit some strange behavior (like add additional line spacing).

Here's a full example:

```
P {font: bold italic 12tp/18pt Times}
```

In this example, we used the font property for the P element. We set both the bold and italic attributes, we made the font size 12pt and the line height 18pt. We specified one font: Times.

Style Sheets and Base Attributes A brief mention of base attributes was made in a prior section. One of their major applications, besides Visual Basic Script, is style sheets. For complex documents that required many different fonts and styles (an E-zine, for instance) you can use the system of classes in an HTML document to conveniently use multiple styles for a tag specified in the `<STYLE>` section. Additionally, you can use the ID/NAME tag to reference different styles you have defined. The method for accomplishing both of these are listed in the next sections.

Using Style Sheets and the CLASS attribute You understand that the CLASS attribute is used inside an HTML tag; now, how do you use this attribute to have many defined styles for the same tag? The method is simple. You append a . with a class name of your choosing to the end of the TAGNAME portion of a style definition for an element. Now, using the corresponding tag in an HTML document, you can use the style you specified for that tag if you set the CLASS attribute of that tag equal to the name you chose (without the .).

For example:

```
<HEAD>
...
<STYLE>
A.weird {text.decoration: none; color: navajowhite}
</STYLE>
</HEAD>
<BODY>
<A HREF="http://www.someplacefaraway.com/" CLASS="weird">
...
</BODY>
```

In this example, we chose to give the A element a certain style. We also assigned this style definition a class: weird. When we want to use the style defined by the weird class for the A element, we just call that class name from the corresponding tag in the body portion of the document.

NOTE Remember: a tag is an element with the "<" and ">" brackets surrounding it.

CAUTION

When you are using the CLASS attribute with HTML for style sheets, you must have a class specified for the tag you are using (for example, if you had the element B which was part of the class "test", you could not use this class with the <A> tag unless you had a style specified for the A element in the "test" class). Now, to use different defined styles for the same tag, you just append a different class name to the element in the <STYLE> section and call that class from your respective tag in the body of your document.

For example:

```
...
<HEAD>
...
<STYLE>
A.foo {text-decoration:none;
        color: hotpink}
A.bar {color: gray;
        font-size: 14pt}
</STYLE>
</HEAD>
<BODY>
<A CLASS="foo" HREF="http://www.rt66.com/iymalluf/">Go to the MCS
➥ Web site</A><BR>
<A CLASS="bar" HREF="http://www.microsoft.com">The Microsoft Web
➥ site</A><BR>
<A HREF="http://www.farawayforgottenland.ffl">This goes nowhere</A>
➥ <BR>...
```

Note in this code snippet that there are two classes used in the style section: "foo" and "bar". The A element is used in both these classes and the first two <A> tags in the body reference those classes. Note that with the third <A> tag there is no class specified. It uses the default style. If there was a style specified for just the <A> tag then that style would be used if the tag did not use any class.

The A element, when used in style sheets, has two "pseudo-classes" which are used to set the different styles of a visited link and unvisited link. These are: A:link and A:vlink and all the properties for each "pseudo-class" are specified in the same manner as the normal syntax (for example: a:link {color: red} and A:vlink {font-size:12in}).

Using the ID/NAME Attributes and Style Sheets You can also use the ID/NAME attribute with HTML tags to use a particular style you have defined. Normally, you would define styles with an element preceding a set of curly braces, which contain all the properties to that element. Now, instead of specifying a style for a specific element, you can specify these styles for a name that you choose (the name must be preceded by the # sign). You then reference this name from your tags with the ID attribute. This tag then has all the styles that you specified for that name in the <STYLE> section.

For instance:

```
...
<STYLE>
#mystyle {color:pink; background: aliceblue; font-size: 4in}
...
</STYLE>
...
<BODY>
<P ID="mystyle"> Hi!! I should have a pink background and I should be
➥ pretty large</P>
...
```


In this example, we chose the name: mystyle and gave it a few properties as shown. Then, from the body of the document, we used the <P> tag to call this style. We set the ID attribute of the <P> tag to "mystyle" which is where we have defined our styles for this particular name. When calling the name from your tags, you do not use the number sign. You can use this method for any element, but it would not be a good idea to use it with the <A> tag or other tags that need the ID attribute. For their case, it is safer to use classes or just define styles for those tags.

HTML Tags Used with Style Sheets This section covers two tags and an additional attribute which change the style of HTML tags in a different document. There are two tags: the <DIV> and <SPAN> tags which allow one to encapsulate a block of text or other tags and apply a style to them. The STYLE attribute, which can be used in any tag is also capable of setting different styles for the text that tag encapsulates (effective in tags which render text somehow).

The STYLE Attribute The STYLE attribute, as previously mentioned, is capable of setting many style properties for the tag that it is used in. The text that tag encapsulates then receives those styles. The values for the STYLE attribute are the different style properties mentioned in Table 2.12 and their values with each property separated by a semicolon (for example: STYLE="color: blue; font-size: 30px; ..."). The STYLE attribute is a simple way to give bits and pieces of your text different styles if you want explicit styles to exist, or if you feel no need for defining multiple styles for several elements.

The <DIV> and <SPAN> Tags The <DIV> and <SPAN> tags, which are very similar to each other, are used to encapsulate blocks of text and tags and apply a style to them. This could be tediously accomplished with the STYLE tag, but these tags make it easier.

The <DIV> Tag

The <DIV> tag is used to divide sections of the document and apply a style to that section. Consider the use for this tag. Maybe you have a set of pre-defined styles in the page. Maybe you are quoting someone's work as reference and you want that section of your document to be italicized and also have an inch more of margin space on the right and left sides. All you would have to do is simply encapsulate the entire cited text with the <DIV>

and </DIV> tags. Then you use the STYLE attribute and set the properties for spacing and italics:

```
...
<DIV STYLE="
     left-margin: 1.0in;
     right margin: 1.0in;
     font-style: italics
">
...This is my reference material ...
</DIV>
```

In this example, we set the left-margin, right-margin, and font-style attributes. Whatever text that is encapsulated by this tag *inherits* the properties specified by this tag. Style sheets also work by inheritance (refer to the Nesting and Inheritance section for more information). The <DIV> tag can also use classes and the ID attribute for defining its own style in the style section as well. You would put the DIV element in a class the same way you would any other element: append the name of a class you choose (with the .) to the end of the DIV element in the style section with the properties you specify.

```
DIV.ref {line-height: 12pt; background: moccasin}
```

The previous example uses the class "ref" for the DIV element. To use the styles specified for this element, all you would do is add the attribute CLASS="ref" in the <DIV> tag you want. The ID attribute also works the same as for other tags.

The *<SPAN>* Tag

There is virtually no difference between the <SPAN> tag and the <DIV> tag. Their syntax is the same and more of a logical difference exists. The <DIV> tag is used to divide sections and render them with different styles, whereas the <SPAN> tag is used to span portions of text and render them different styles. As in the <DIV> tag, you can also use the STYLE, CLASS and ID attributes in the same manner.

Inheritance and Nesting with Style Sheets Inheritance is also allowed with style sheets, and inheritance for frame sets and tables functions the same as style sheets. You can also control the styles of nested tags with style sheets.

Inheritance When tags are nested in other tags which have a style specified, these nested tags also inherit that style. For instance:

```
...
P {font-size: 3in}
...
</STYLE>
<BODY>
...
<P>This text is 4 inches tall.
<A HREF="http://www.nm.org">This is a link to somewhere
```

```
</A></P>
...
```

In this example, we gave a style to the P element, and in the body we put an anchor (<A>) tag inside the <P> tag. Notice in Figure 2.7 that the text in the anchor is the same size as the rest of the text but is still blue and underlined. Why? No properties were specified for color and text-decoration so the tag retains them. This rule holds true for all elements.

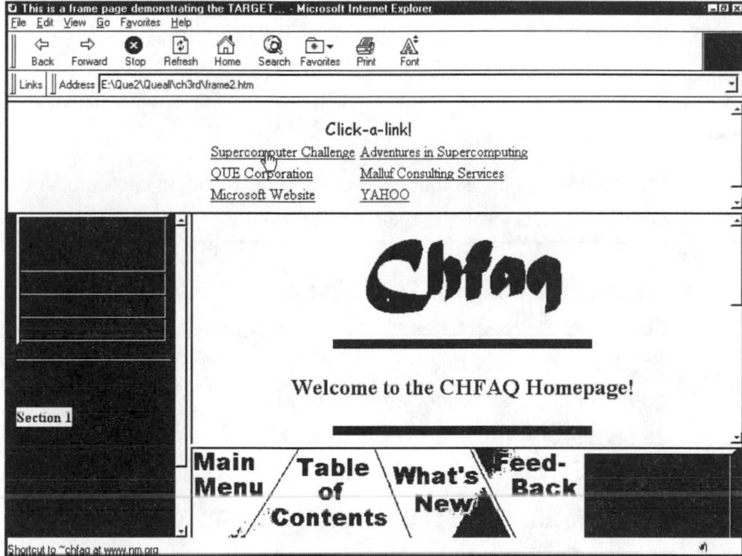

FIG. 2.7
This figure demonstrates how nested tags are affected by styles assigned to their parent tag (or the tag that encapsulates the nested tag).

Styles for Nested Tags It is possible to specify styles for different instances of nested tags. For instance, if you have an <A> tag nested inside an <H3> tag, you can set the properties for the A element when that "nesting" occurs. The syntax is quite simple. All one does is place the element that is to be nested after the element it is to be nested in (these elements should be separated by a space). When the nested tag specified is nested, then it will use the styles defined by it in the style section of your document.

For example:

```
<STYLE>
...
H3 {color: forestgreen}
H3 A {color: #00CC00}
...
</STYLE>
</HEAD>
<BODY>
...
<A HREF="http://none.com">This is a normal link</A>
<H3> Some text in a level-3 head,
```

```
<A HREF="http://www.where.com">A link, that is a different color because
➥ it is nested.
</A></H3>
...
```

We specified styles (a color) for the H3 element in the style section. Right after the style definition for the H3 element, we defined a style for the A tag if it is nested in the `<H3>` element. So when one uses this style, all the `<A>` tags nested (or encapsulated) inside `<H3>` tags will be rendered in a dark-medium blue. All other `<A>` tags will be rendered normal unless they are encapsulated in other tags that have different default or defined styles.

Many elements can be nested when specifying different styles. For example:

```
UL UL A {color: red}
```

This example indicates that an anchor tag nested in an unordered list which is nested in another unordered list is given the color red.

An Example Usage of Style Sheets In this section, an example of style sheets will be demonstrated. All the style properties and the methods for implementing them will be used to creatively design a page. Note how the styles are used to create an interesting page. The file stylescool.htm is in Listing 2.13 and can be found on the accompanying CD as stylescool.htm. Figure 2.8 illustrates this listing.

Listing 2.13 STYLESCOOL.HTM—An Elaborate Usage of Style Sheets

```
<HTML><HEAD><TITLE>
      A neato demonstration using style sheets...
      It's cooler than you</TITLE>
<STYLE>
BODY         {
               background: wheat
             }
TABLE.forest {
               background: URL(new33.gif) gold;
                     color: lime;
                     text-align: center;
               margin-left: 0in;
               margin-right: 0in
             }
TD.firstb    {
               background: goldenrod;
               text-align: left;
               color: black
             }
#newhead     {
               color: blue;
               font-size: 18pt
             }
#small             {
```

```
              font-size:8pt;
              color: blue;
              font-family: Helvetica;
              text-align: right;
              line-height: 8pt
            }
P.subhead   {
              margin-left: 20px;
              text-align: left;
              background: forestgreen
             }
SPAN.head1   {
              font-family: Arial Black;
              color: midnightblue;
              font-size: 14pt
            }
P           {
              text-indent: 0.25in;
              margin-right: 1.0in;
              margin-left: 5px;
             line-height: 0.20in
            }
EM          {
              color: red;
              font-style: none;
              font-weight: bold
            }
STRONG            {
              font-family: script;
              font-weight: normal;
              color: green;
              font-size: 18pt;
              text-align: right;
              line-height: 18in;
            }
UL LI       {
              color: blue;
              margin-left: 0.25in;
            }
UL UL LI      {
              color: slateblue;
            }
DFN            {
              font-style: normal;
              background: lime;
              font-style: none
            }
A:link            {
              color: honeydew;
              text-decoration: none
            }

</STYLE>
```

continues

Listing 2.13 Continued

```
</HEAD>
<BODY TOPMARGIN="0" LEFTMARGIN="0">

<TABLE CLASS="forest" WIDTH="100%" HEIGHT="65%">
<TR><TD COLSPAN=2>
<HR>
<P ID="small">WELCOME TO. . .</P>
<NOBR>
<SPAN STYLE="color:#00FF00; font-size:100px">F</SPAN>
<SPAN STYLE="color:#00EE00; font-size:99px">O</SPAN>
<SPAN STYLE="color:#00DD00; font-size:98px">R</SPAN>
<SPAN STYLE="color:#00CC00; font-size:96px">E</SPAN>
<SPAN STYLE="color:#00BB00; font-size:97px">S</SPAN>
<SPAN STYLE="color:#00AA00; font-size:95px">T</SPAN>
<SPAN STYLE="color:#00BB00; font-size:100px">G</SPAN>
<SPAN STYLE="color:#00CC00; font-size:100px">R</SPAN>
<SPAN STYLE="color:#00DD00; font-size:100px">E</SPAN>
<SPAN STYLE="color:#00EE00; font-size:100px">E</SPAN>
<SPAN STYLE="color:#00FF00; font-size:100px">N</SPAN></NOBR>
<HR>
<P CLASS="subhead">An electronic magazine for everybody, including vindictive
➥ vegetable heads and mucky meatball morsels.</P>
</TD></TR>
<TR>
<TD WIDTH="100%" CLASS="firstb">
<SPAN CLASS="head1">Our first issue!</SPAN><BR>
<P>
Welcome to our premiere edition of FG. We are proud to have it up.
We are sad to say, however, that our feature article will not be
available because we have nothing to say. So we are writing this apology,
hoping you will read our news letter next week. We will have 2 times as much
next week. We <EM>PROMISE</EM>!
<BR>
-<STRONG>The Editorial Staff</STRONG></P>
<P>Actually, this is just a demonstration on how to use style sheets,
and some of the many different elements involved in making style sheets.
You can add nice headings without a whole bunch of font tags, you can also
<DFN>highlight</DFN> certain portions of your text by assigning a background
property to an element you choose in the stylesection and then using the
corresponding tag (the element you chose with the &quot;&lt;&quot;
and &quot;&gt;&quot; brackets).</P>
<P>Below is a link:<BR>
<A HREF="http://www.microsoft.com"> When you click on this link,
you will go some where</A>. It is not underlined.
This is done with style sheets as well.</P>
<HR>
<SPAN CLASS="head1">New Garden Tips</SPAN><BR>
<P>Peter Planter divulges some of his best gardening tips, some of these
➥ tips are:
<UL>
  <LI>Never water your plants when it is raining</LI>
  <LI>Don't put turtles in your garden.</LI>
  <UL>
```

```
    <LI>This is <EM>never</EM> a good Idea!</LI>
    <LI>Really, take it from experience!</LI>
  </UL>
  <LI>Nature controls how your garden turns out</LI>
</UL>
</P>
<HR>
<SPAN CLASS="head1">More Stuff Soon!</SPAN>
</TD></TR></TABLE></BODY></HTML>
```


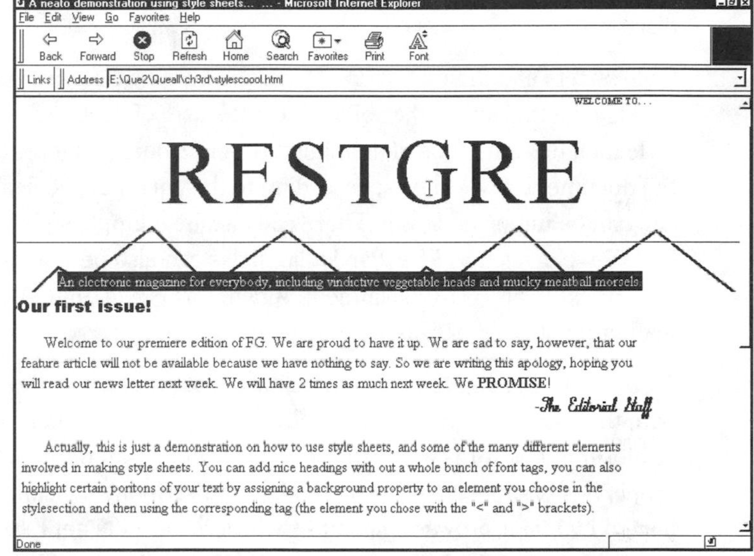

FIG. 2.8
This figure illustrates Listing 2.13. It shows an extensive use of style sheets. Most of the entities of style sheets mentioned are used in Listing 2.13.

It is not necessary to have all the properties for an element immediately follow one another when specifying multiple properties for an element in the styles section of a document. It might be more helpful to organize them (as shown in the previous listing). With this method, you put each of your properties on a separate line and place them after the curly braces to indicate that these properties belong to the specified element; the properties are more organized and you can clearly spot errors when this method is used.

Emerging HTML Standards

HTML is a continually evolving language, not only because the standards committees often introduce new drafts and ideas, but because the commercial producers also extend with their own proprietary extensions that are sometimes incorporated into HTML. The HTML 2.0 Document Definition Type, or DTD, is currently in the phase of final review and should become a standard pretty soon. While this final review is going on, it seems as if the standard for the HTML 3.0 DTD is swiftly on its way, but there are several tags and elements that are still under heated discussion.

The new entities of HTML that are in the spotlight now are, of course, client-side scripting capabilities, the usage and standards of objects, client-side image maps, ways to represent mathematical expressions and equations, client-drawn figures, and style sheets. Some of these HTML components are pretty stable and only minor syntax is being discussed. However, other tags and elements of the HTML language are still in the midst of intense discussions.

Style sheets and their usage in HTML will be very effective once fully implemented. Style sheets give the author the ability to create a set of documents using a certain style. This style includes a method of defining different colors and fonts to form a particular feel for the document. Style sheets, according to the current specification, can be separate files and can be imported at will. There can also be multiple style sheets based on different MIME types such as RTF. Particular styles can also be spanned to affect a specified portion of text in an HTML document. Again, this is still under heavy discussion so the information mentioned here is likely to change.

As you can see, objects and scripting are more mature, in development and implementation, than style sheets. Of course, the first implementation of style sheets with Internet Explorer 3.0 beta 1 is pretty impressive, even though only a handful of the proposed properties is supported. Object models and scripting capabilities have already been supported by major browsers such as the Microsoft Internet Explorer and Netscape Navigator, but Internet Explorer can boast one of the more complete implementations of style sheets. Mathematical representation and client-drawn figures are still in the early stages of development, and will probably make significant progress in the second or third quarter of 1996. We have talked about the emerging standards of HTML and how they will affect future versions of HTML, but now let's examine and compare what makes it possible for us to utilize HTML: the Web servers and browsers.

ON THE WEB

The W3C (World Wide Web Consortium) has practically all the documentation available for standards and works in progress on HTML, objects, MIME types, and other standards related to HTML. Their Web site is located at **http://www.w3.org/**.

Internet Browsers and Servers

This section contains a brief comparison of the leading browsers and servers, and their advantages and disadvantages. This comparison involves Microsoft-based operating systems, since that is the only place where Visual Basic Script is implemented. First, we compare Web browsers in functionality and performance, then we compare Web servers in the same fields. This is not a benchmark comparison or any formal comparison, but more of a general comparison based on use and preference.

The three major browsers, it is fair to say, are the Microsoft Internet Explorer, Mosaic (and all variations), and Netscape Navigator. Internet Explorer is easily the latter of the three, but still it has many advantages. Also, it ties in with both JavaScript and Visual Basic Script, has support for tables and frames, works well with the ActiveX controls, and is free. Plus, Microsoft's Web site is easy to navigate through and is very simple to find information for the consumer and the author. Netscape has very good support for JavaScript and most of the HTML support previously mentioned, but there seems to be no direct support for ActiveX or Visual Basic Script. Also, it is not free. The pioneer Web browser, Mosaic, was developed primarily by the National Center for Supercomputing Applications (NCSA) at the University of Urbana-Champaign in Illinois. This browser does support some HTML 3.0 and has a nice Hotlist feature, but it lacks many of the newer functions including objects, frames, and script support. If you're for die-hard standards, then Mosaic is for you!

ON THE WEB

There is a Netscape plug-in available which will allow you to use Visual Basic Script in Netscape. You can get this add-on at **http://www.ncompasslabs.com/**.

The status of Web servers is similar to that of browsers. There are several free Web servers that are based on the UNIX NCSA or CERN models. These are somewhat powerful, easy to use, and provide pretty good support for CGI programs. Netscape Enterprise is a very powerful, yet very expensive, Web server that offers full support for Java and CGI programs; Netscape communications also has FastTrack server, which is more of a "desktop" server that can be used by individuals with small connections. Microsoft has the Internet Information Server (ISS), which is free and comes with Windows NT v4.0 Server, and is also available freely for Windows NT. It supports much of what Netscape supports, except JavaScript. IIS supports Visual Basic and works very smoothly with SQL databases. It's an excellent deal for the price. Microsoft also has Vermeer Front Page, which is its counterpart to Netscape's FastTrack server. Vermeer has a fairly decent editor and an excellent organizer, plus it allows extensions to many popular UNIX and PC servers.

FrontPage, which is still a beta product, consists of an editor, an organizer, and a Web server, which can run on Windows 95 or NT Server/Workstation.

From Here...

In this chapter you have learned the fundamental workings of HTML. HTML is an unsophisticated "mark-up" language which is the primary method for communicating hypertext documents across the World Wide Web. Visual Basic Script is an "inline" scripting language which allows you to amplify the interactive content of your web pages. This chapter has helped you understand some of the basic concepts crucial to the use of Visual Basic Script, such as forms and other entities which complement Visual Basic Script's ability to create truly dynamic web pages. Some of these complementary elements are tables, frame sets, and style sheets.

Also covered in this chapter is a brief discussion on the future of HTML and a brief overview of the leading Internet browsers and Web servers. In subsequent chapters, you learn the different functions and methods of Visual Basic Script. Check out the following chapters:

- Chapter 3, "Introducing the ActiveX Control Pad," provides an excellent overview of how to use the ActiveX control pad: a tool for making your documents very interactive.
- Chapter 12, "A Sample VBScript Page," takes close look at other entities which are crucial to designing Visual Basic Script applications such as the ActiveX controls, the Internet Explorer 3.0 object model, and the ActiveX control Pad.
- For a general explanation of VBScript and examples, see Chapter 13, "Comparing VBScript, VBA, and Visual Basic."
- The different data types, structures, and variables VBScript supports are covered in Chapter 15, "VBScript Data Types and Variables."

CHAPTER 3

Introducing the ActiveX Control Pad

by Ibrahim Malluf

When the ActiveX Control Pad was released, almost no one in the development community knew it was coming. We all knew that the VBScript development tools at the time were limited to NotePad or some other text editor. Ron and I were even working on the beginnings of a limited IDE to include with the book. The ActiveX Control Pad completely changed all of that. Enthusiastic? You bet !

Exactly what the ActiveX Control Pad is

ActiveX Control Pad is a complete VBScript or JavaScript editor, as well as an ActiveX Control editing tool.

ActiveX Control Pad as an editing environment

ActiveX Control Pad is an excellent tool for learning VBScript and the Explorer object model.

The ActiveX Control Pad's use of the Layout Form

ActiveX Control Pad's central theme, the Layout Form, gives incredible drop-in-place capabilities for HTML document development.

Animated Demonstration

Build an animated demonstration of the ActiveX Chart control using the Layout control as the container.

The ActiveX Control Pad's IDE

The first impression you get of the ActiveX Control Pad is that it is a really cool environment for placing ActiveX controls on a form, visually aligning them, and manipulating their properties. As you dig deeper and play with the Script Wizard, you find that you have access to all of the Explorer's object properties and methods, access to all of the added control properties and methods, and, finally, the ability to add and edit user-defined procedures and variables—all within the Script Wizard. You come to the realization that the ActiveX Control Pad is actually a complete VBScript or JavaScript editor, as well as an ActiveX Control editing tool. Some serious limitations and a few bugs exist in the beta product we are writing about here, but expect the ActiveX Control Pad to be much more robust and stable by the time you read this book.

The MDI Interface

The first thing that greets you when you load the ActiveX Control Pad is a Multiple Document Interface (MDI) setup with the usual menu bar, tool bar, and status bar (see fig. 3.1). The right mouse button calls a pop-up menu that gives access to the ActiveX Control Pad's features, depending on your current context. The ActiveX Control Pad adheres to the Windows 95 standard interface for MDI applications.

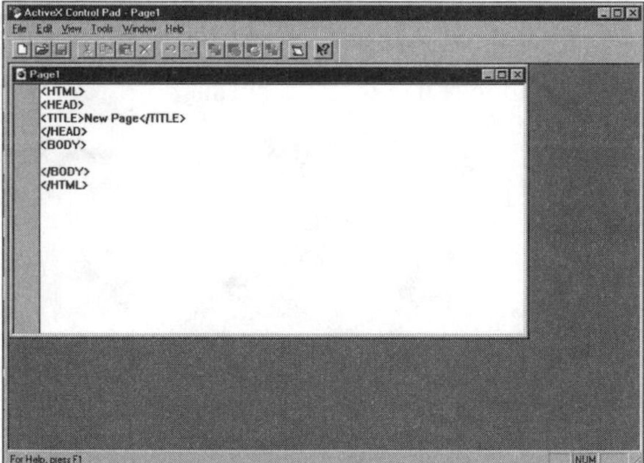

FIG. 3.1
Open the ActiveX Control Pad for the first time.

The Document Window

A child form containing a document window titled Page1 is open waiting for your input. This document window is a direct edit window for HTML documents, complete with a skeletal outline of HTML tags (refer to fig. 3.1). You can load any HTML page into ActiveX

Control Pad and begin editing it. Down the left side of the edit window a gray vertical bar serves as a container for mini-icons that indicate the placement of Controls, Script, and Layout Forms (see fig. 3.2).

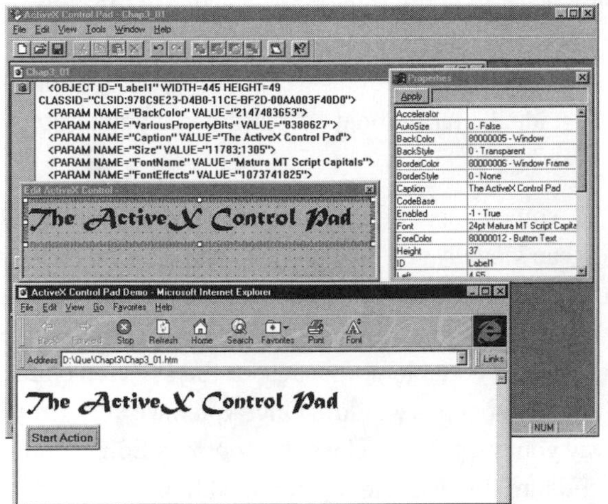

FIG. 3.2
Look at the mini-icons in the Document Window.

These icons will bring up the appropriate object editor when you click the left mouse button on them. Clicking the script icon brings up the Script Wizard; clicking the control icon brings up the ActiveX control editor. Figure 3.3 shows the ActiveX Control Pad with the label control in edit mode and the resulting Web page with that label in an Explorer 3.0 window.

Direct Placement of ActiveX Controls

Limited Placement

The placement of ActiveX controls directly on a Web page is limited to the peculiarities of the Web design. You cannot exactly place a control in terms of its Top or Left properties but are limited to the Right, Center, Left type of placement commands that HTML provides. You can create tables and place controls within those tables for a greater degree of control over where they will appear, but the placement limitations are still there.

Ideal Editing Environment for Controls

Prior to the availability of the ActiveX Control Pad, placing ActiveX controls in your document involved getting the CLSID of the object from the Registry, placing it into the Object Tag, remembering all of the relevant properties of the control that you needed to modify, and finally remembering or otherwise finding out what event or methods were available for the control. It was very tedious work. The ActiveX Control Pad puts all of this behind with an almost ideal environment for placing and editing ActiveX controls in your document.

In Figure 3.3, you can see the Edit Control window in the upper left. In the Edit Control window, you can visually size your control and directly edit some properties; in the label's case, you can edit the caption property. On the left side of Figure 3.3 is the Properties window. If you have ever worked with Visual Basic, this window is quite familiar. It provides a list of all the editable properties for the selected control. You can edit those properties right in the Properties window. Once you have your properties set and the control sized the way you want it, you close the control's Edit window and the resultant HTML code is placed into the document you are editing.

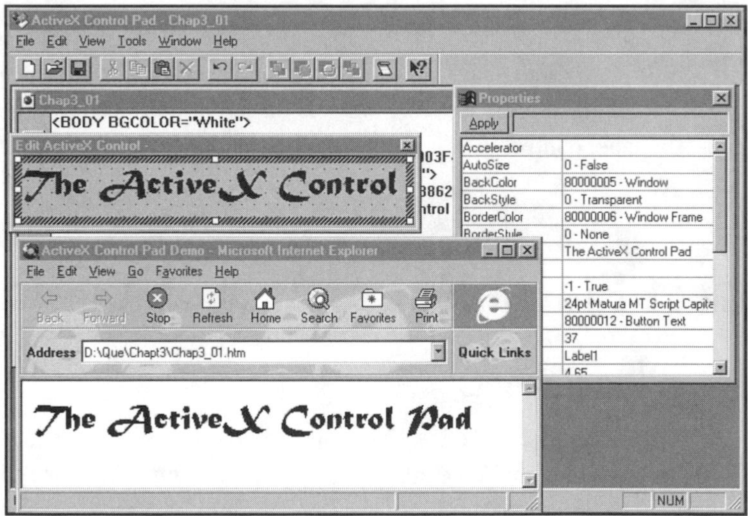

FIG. 3.3
Edit an ActiveX label control with the ActiveX Control Pad.

The code that the ActiveX Control Pad inserted into our document for our example label is shown in Listing 3.1. As mentioned earlier, in the beta version of Explorer 3.0, the only way to insert an ActiveX object into the document was to extract the CLSID number from the Windows registry by looking it up with a utility like Regedit. The ActiveX Control Pad eliminates this entirely.

On the CD

Listing 3.1 CHAPER3_1.HTML—The ActiveX Control HTML Code Inserted by the ActiveX Control Pad

```
<OBJECT ID="Label1" WIDTH=445 HEIGHT=49
 CLASSID="CLSID:978C9E23-D4B0-11CE-BF2D-00AA003F40D0">
    <PARAM NAME="BackColor" VALUE="2147483653">
    <PARAM NAME="VariousPropertyBits" VALUE="8388627">
    <PARAM NAME="Caption" VALUE="The ActiveX Control Pad">
    <PARAM NAME="Size" VALUE="11783;1305">
    <PARAM NAME="FontName" VALUE="Matura MT Script Capitals">
    <PARAM NAME="FontEffects" VALUE="1073741825">
    <PARAM NAME="FontHeight" VALUE="480">
    <PARAM NAME="FontCharSet" VALUE="0">
    <PARAM NAME="FontPitchAndFamily" VALUE="2">
    <PARAM NAME="FontWeight" VALUE="700">
</OBJECT>
```


When directly working with ActiveX controls on the HTML document as shown in this chapter, you simply choose the Insert ActiveX Control from the edit menu or from the pop-up menu when right-clicking the mouse button. A dialog box, as shown in Figure 3.4, pops up and lets you select from a list of all available ActiveX controls on your system. Just click the desired control and it is automatically inserted into your document including the required CLSID number.

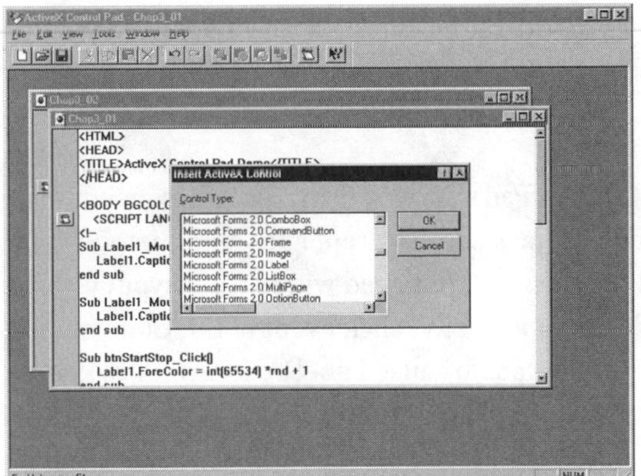

FIG. 3.4
Select an ActiveX Control to insert directly into an HTML document.

CAUTION

At the time of writing this book, Explorer 3.0 Beta 1 did not have the licensing mechanism in place. Many ActiveX controls, while functional in a development environment would not work in a Web page. Only the controls that actually shipped with ActiveX Control Pad were guaranteed to work. Microsoft said that this issue would be resolved by the time Explorer 3.0 is a shipping product. Part of this solution will include a limitation on what controls you can use based upon those licensing requirements.

In Figure 3.4, you can see that a command button is about to be selected from the controls list dialog. The command button will be used to add some user interaction to the demo page. The command button is added to the project by having its name property changed to btnStartStop. After going through the drill of setting properties, sizing the button, and so on, the edit window is closed and the script behind the button is entered into the button's click event.

Limited Script Editing Environment

By right-clicking the mouse in the HTML document on the desired insertion point, the pop-up menu enables the selection of the Script Wizard as shown in Figure 3.5.

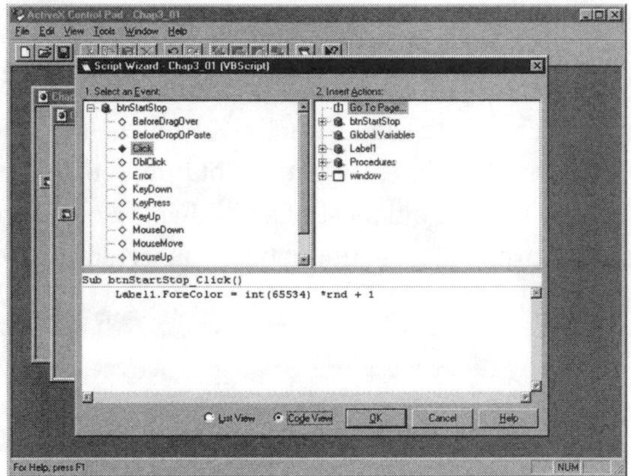

FIG. 3.5
The Script Wizard opened to the *btnStartStop* Command button's click event procedure.

The ActiveX Control Pad's Script Wizard provides an editing environment that gives easy access to all events, procedures, properties, and methods of the Layout control and all other controls and scripts contained within the Layout Control. Figure 3.5 shows the Script Edit window open to the click event of the Command button that was added to the HTML document. I want to cause Label1's forecolor to change every time the button is clicked to a randomly selected color. Looking again at Figure 3.5, in the right side list box labeled *2. Insert Actions*, select the Label1's forecolor property by double-clicking it. It will be automatically inserted into the button's click event script. Complete the script by adding the code in Listing 3.2 to generate a random number. Finally, finish by closing the Script Wizard's window. The VBScript code is automatically inserted into the HTML document.

On the CD

Listing 3.2 CHAP3_01.HTM—The Click Event Code Is Inserted by the Script Wizard

```
Sub btnStartStop_Click()
     Label1.ForeColor = int(65534) *rnd + 1
end sub
```

The Script Wizard can work with either VBScript or JavaScript. But the Wizard, as it stands now, cannot work with a document that is using both. It's a one-or-the-other proposition. The Script Wizard's List View provides an alternative method to writing VBScript. By selecting List View, you can have the Script Wizard insert code into events for you using dialog boxes based on the action you select from the Insert Actions list.

As an example, let's have Label1's caption change to *This is a Test* when clicking the mouse button on it it and have the caption return to *ActiveX Control Pad* when letting the mouse button back up. To do this select the MouseDown event in the Event window as the event where the code will be inserted. Select Label1.Caption in the Select Action window. The dialog shown in Figure 3.6 illustrates how to add the changed caption to the MouseDown event. The Script Wizard will present any one of a number of different dialogs based on the action selected. In this case, selecting the caption action means that I want to add a different text to the caption, so a text entry dialog is presented.

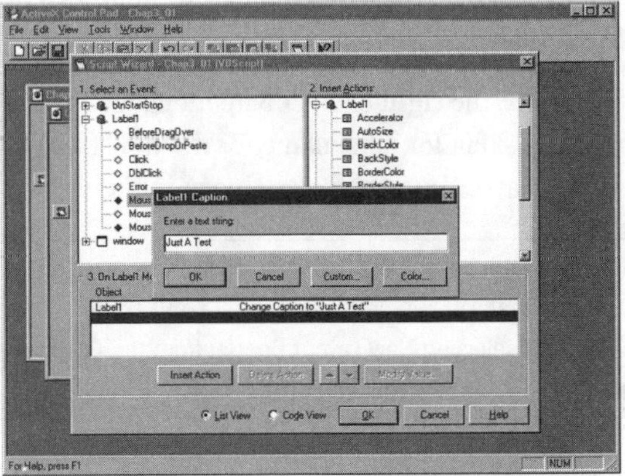

FIG. 3.6
Use the Script Wizard in List View Mode to add code to the MouseDown event of a label.

The Script Wizard is a great aid to writing event driven script that holds your hand when needed and easily gets out of the way when you want to do things your way.

Since the ActiveX Control Pad is an MDI application, you can have several Web page documents open at one time. You can have several Layout Forms open as well. What are Layout Forms, you ask? Just continue reading to find out about one of the most innovative improvements to HTML Web pages to come down the information highway.

The Layout Form: An Object to Contain Your Objects

The HTML document, as it stands today, allows you to place many different types of objects on a browser's screen but imposes a very strict set of placement rules that can make designing Web pages very frustrating at times. How often have you wanted to be able to precisely place a graphic, input box, or even text in an exact spot on your page, or have the ability to place overlapping graphics and controls? Well this ability, along with a few other eye-opening advancements, is now available through the auspices of the ActiveX Layout Control. (For Visual Basic programmers, the closest analogy to the Layout Control is a Visual Basic Form's client area. You have this sizable form that enables you to place your text and controls precisely where you want them with none of the restrictions imposed by HTML pages.)

From the File menu or the right-click pop-up menu, select Insert New Layout Control. A dialog box pops up, asking for a file name for the new Layout control. Enter **Chap3_02** for the name of the Layout control file as shown in Figure 3.7.

While the example that I am developing here is specifically intended for insertion into a particular page, I should mention that you can create or edit a Layout control without making it part of a Web page document. By selecting New Layout Control from the File menu, you can set up a new Layout control without any associated Web Pages.

Continuing on with this example, you can see in Figure 3.8, a Layout Control open in edit mode, along with a Toolbar containing available ActiveX controls. As mentioned earlier, the Layout Control appears exactly like a Visual Basic form, but unlike a Visual Basic form, only the client area of the form is visible when displayed on a Web page document.

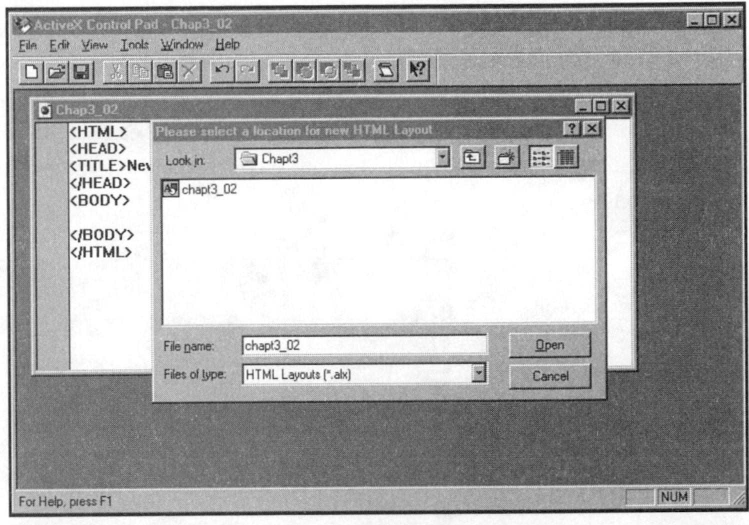

FIG. 3.7
Insert a new Layout control into a Web page.

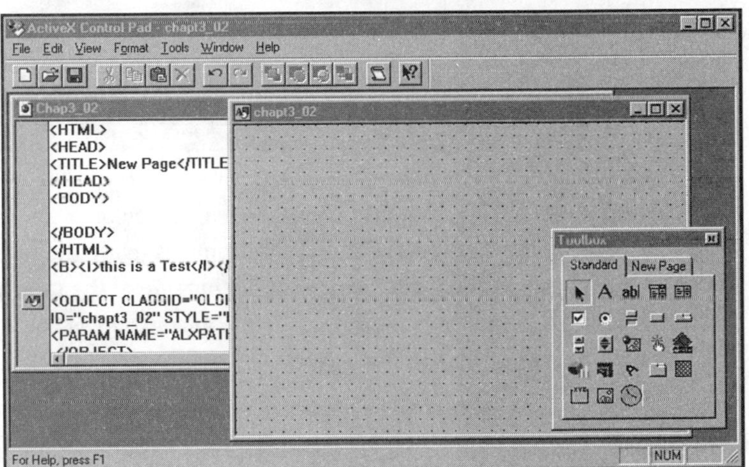

FIG. 3.8
The Layout control and toolbar are ready for editing.

Modifying the Toolbar

The Toolbar gives you a selection of ActiveX controls that you easily can add to your Layout Control. Select an ActiveX control on the Toolbar by left-clicking the ActiveX control desired. You can then draw the control on the form by moving the mouse pointer to

Layout Control's client area and drawing the control while holding down the left mouse button. The list of available ActiveX controls can be easily added to by right-clicking the Toolbar; a dialog (as shown in fig. 3.9) pops up allowing you to choose the controls to add to your toolbar. In fact the toolbar is a fascinating expansion of the original Visual Basic toolbar. The ActiveX control toolbar enables you to arrange groups of controls on different pages.

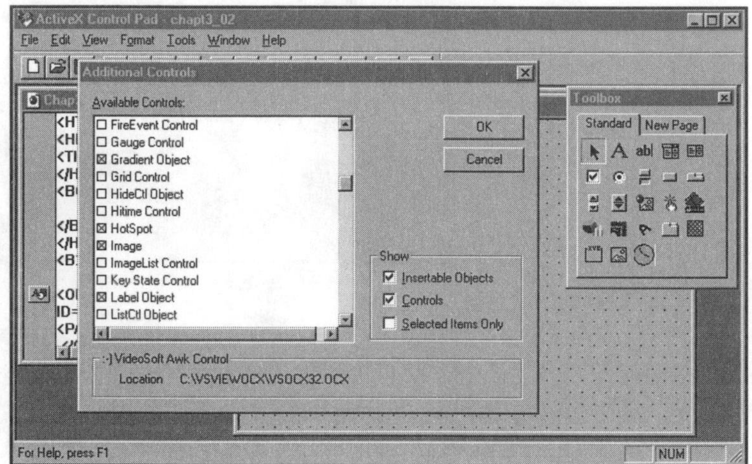

FIG. 3.9 Use this dialog window for adding ActiveX controls to the toolbar.

To add controls to or delete controls from a particular page, make the page the active one, right-click that page, then add or delete controls using the pop-up menu's selections. You can add pages to the toolbar by right-clicking one of the tabs to get a pop-up menu enabling you to add or delete pages. The menu also allows you to rename the page's tabs or change the order of the tabs.

But here's the real kicker: you can export or import toolbar pages! Imagine having a set of custom controls relevant to a particular project assembled on one toolbar page. Now if you have several of these pages, you can load or unload depending on what is needed for the project you are working on.

Adding Controls

Going back to the project at hand, I can begin to add some controls and then add some VBScript to round out the example project for this chapter. Let's say that the assignment is to create a demonstration of the Chart ActiveX control that can be dropped on any HTML document. The Chart ActiveX control has several different chart types that should have a method that makes it easy to switch back and forth between the different types. In this case a TabStrip is used as an easy way to select the viewing of the different chart types. After adding the TabStrip, add several tabs, one for each chart type that is going to be displayed using the pop-up menu shown in Figure 3.10. To get to this menu, you have to get the tab strip to change into Tabselect mode by left-clicking a tab. When the tab you are clicking gets the focus (noticeable by the tab's caption being outlined), right-click the mouse and the pop-up menu in Figure 3.10 appears.

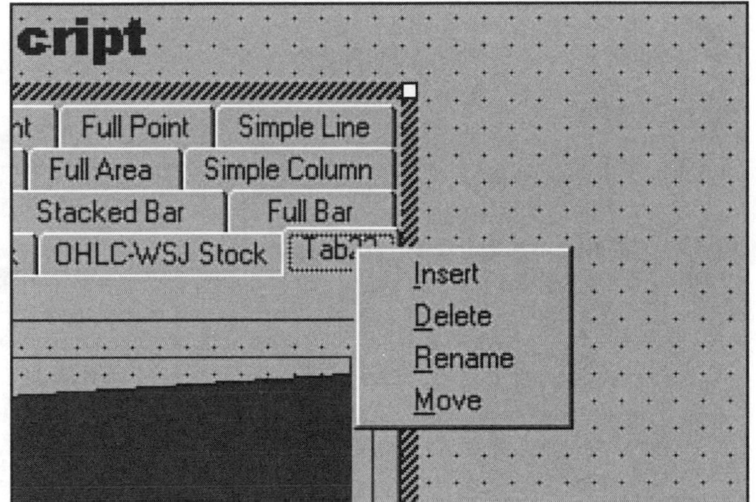

FIG. 3.10
Here's the pop-up menu for adding tabs to the TabStrip.

CAUTION

I had trouble getting this to work consistently and attribute it to the still shaky interface code of the Beta product. I expect that it will have improved responsiveness by the time this book is printed. If you are still working with the Beta release, be patient with some of these interface problems and retry some of these things until they do work for you.

In this example, 21 tabs were added to the control. For each tab, select Rename from the tab's pop-up menu and add the Chart type name to the tab that corresponds to the Chart control's Chart type (such as Tab 0 = 0-Simple Pie Chart, Tab 1 = 1-Special Pie chart, and so on), until all of the chart types are entered into the tab control. Then put an ActiveX Chart control into the layout as shown in Figure 3.11. and add an ActiveX IELabel control to the Layout Form to complete the example layout. Later in the chapter I will flesh out the example Layout Control with some code.

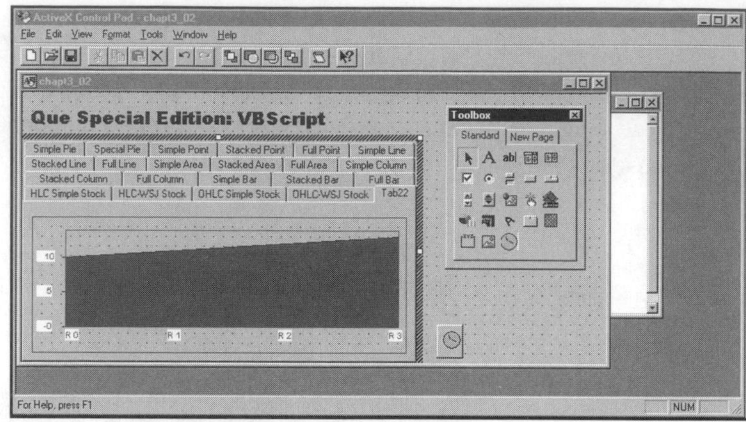

FIG. 3.11
Here's the Layout control with the Chart control and Label control added to it.

Creating Drop-in-Place Interfaces

The Layout Control (at the time of writing this book) was a separate item that had to be downloaded by the IE30 Beta 1 browser. According to Microsoft, the release version of Internet Explorer 3.0 will incorporate the Layout Control so that it will not have to be downloaded. The code for the Layout Control is presently contained in a separate .ALX file that is downloaded by your Web document during runtime. My understanding is that as soon as the W3C approves and adopts the new initiatives presented by Microsoft, the Layout Control's code will be able to be within the Web document itself. In any case, the Layout Control lends itself to the development of drop-in-place interface elements such as navigational bars, data input forms, data display, and other operations that can be easily encapsulated.

Building a Layout Control Application

The application developed in this section demonstrates the different capabilities of ActiveX Chart Control, which comes with the ActiveX Control Pad. In this section we'll use the Script Wizard to build the underlying code that will control the ActiveX Chart control demo.

Selecting Different Chart Views Using the Tab Strip

In this example the tab strip has 21 tabs, each named after a chart type in the Chart control's properties. Conveniently, the chart types are designated by numbers, so each tab can correspond to a chart type number. Right-clicking to bring up the Script Wizard as shown in Figure 3.12, choose the change event of the tab strip (ID=tab-Chart) and add the code shown in Listing 3.3.

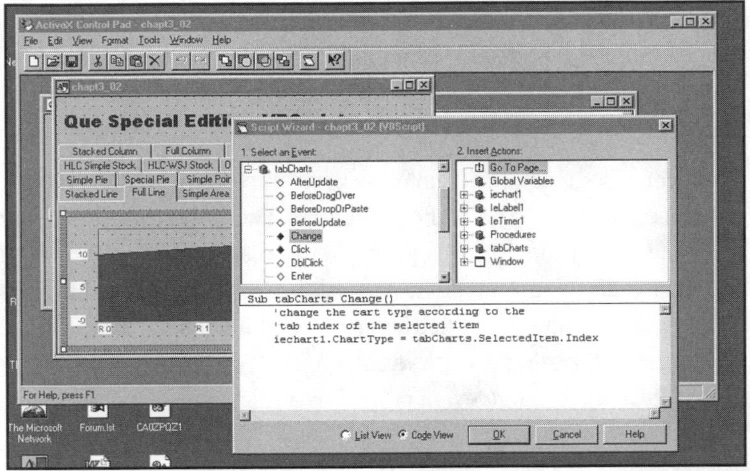

FIG. 3.12
Select the Change Event of the TabStrip from the Script Wizard.

Listing 3.3 CHAP3_02.ALX—Changing the Chart Type Displayed According to the Selected Tab Index

```
Sub tabCharts_Change()
   'change the chart type according to the
   'tab index of the selected item
   iechart1.ChartType = tabCharts.SelectedItem.Index
End Sub
```

This single line of code in the tabCharts_Change event causes the chart types to change with each change of a tab.

NOTE If you are considering using the the click event instead of the change event, I should warn you that in a multi-row tab control the click event will not show a change to the tab you clicked if there was a row change. Even though the focus ring in the tab changes to the tab you clicked, the actual focus will not change. You have to click the tab a second time to cause an actual shift of focus to the desired tab. Using the change event avoids this problem.

With this much completed, save the Layout Control and call up the page containing it in Explorer. The user should be able to go through each chart type, as shown in Figure 3.13. You could leave it at that and have the demo completed, but many of the different chart views will not be showing their best view with the default data contained in the chart control. There might also be a desire to have a different look every time tabs are changed.

Let's start by adding a procedure that will add a random number of rows and columns. Calling up the Script Wizard, right-click the mouse pointer on Procedures in the Insert Actions list, and a pop-up menu enables you to select New Procedure. The procedure window shows a sub named Procedure1. Since the procedure is supposed to return a value, a function procedure is wanted instead of the Sub type procedure. Change the sub to function while also changing the name of the procedure to RandomNumber. In this edit window, note that the procedure declaration area is entered by clicking the declaration line.

You also need to click into the procedure body area to edit the script after you have edited the name and type of the procedure. There were no shortcut keys that I could find to let me jump from one area to another in the editor. The Tab key didn't work either. Going through the prototype help file also didn't reveal any shortcuts. Perhaps by the time the ActiveX Control pad has been released from beta, issues like this will have been addressed. Listing 3.4 shows the RandomNumber function along with the modified tabChart_Change event procedure utilizing the function.

Listing 3.4 CHAP3_02.ALX—The RandomNumber Function and the tabChart_Change Event Procedure Modified to Use the Function

```
<SCRIPT LANGUAGE="VBScript">
<!--
Function RandomNumber(MyLimit)
  'first make sure a number was passed
  If IsNumeric(MyLimit) Then
    'returns random numbers
    RandomNumber= int(MyLimit)*rnd + 1
  Else
    'if a non-numeric value then return
    'a random number based on a fixed limit
    'No need to have a code failure here
    RandomNumber = int(10)*rnd + 1
  End If
end function
Sub tabCharts_Change()
   'change the chart type according to the
   'tab index of the selected item
   iechart1.ChartType = tabCharts.SelectedItem.Index
   iechart1.Columns=RandomNumber(15)
   iechart1.Rows = RandomNumber(10)
end sub
-->
</SCRIPT>
```

The function takes a numeric argument that determines the upper range of the random number to be generated. First check the argument for being a numeric value with the IsNumeric() function. If it is not a numeric value, then the argument is ignored and a random number is generated that would be safe for all circumstances in this application. In this instance, keeping the script operational is more important than confronting the user with an error condition. When the user selects a chart type, it will present the chart in a different configuration every time.

Animating the Chart Demo

Am I satisfied yet? Not at all! I want the chart to have some timer-driven animation, so let's add an ieTimer object to the Layout Control and set its Interval property to 3000, as shown in Figure 3.13.

Create a procedure using the Script Wizard that iterates through all of the rows and columns of the chart control, setting each row/column DataItem property to a new random value. This subprocedure will be called by the timer at the end of each interval. Listing 3.5 shows the code.

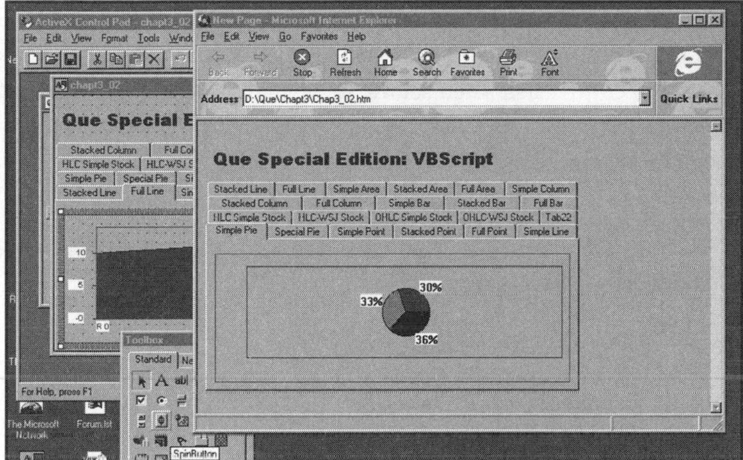

FIG. 3.13
Add a timer control to the chart demo Project.

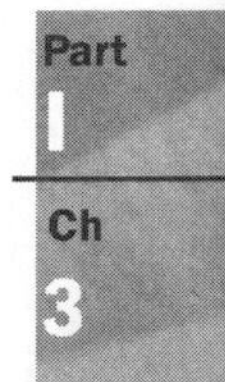

Listing 3.5 CHAP3_02.ALX—The ieTimer_Timer Event Calling the ColumnValues Procedure

```
Sub IeTimer1_Timer()
   call ColumnValues()
end sub
Sub ColumnValues()
  Dim lngColCount
  Dim lngRowCount
  'iterate through each row and column
  'changing values
  For lngRowCount = 0 to iechart1.Rows -1
    iechart1.RowIndex = lngRowCount
    For lngColCount = 0 to iechart1.Columns -1
    iechart1.columnIndex = lngColCount
    iechart1.DataItem = RandomNumber(100)
    Next '
  Next '
end sub
```

The ColumnValues subprocedure changes all the DataItem values in the chart control every time it is called, using two simple nested `For...Next` loops.

Accessing the Properties and Methods of the Layout Control from an HTML Document

Let's continue with this example program and write some VBScript in the HTML document that will manipulate the chart demo. Suppose I wanted the demo to automatically change the chart types after a given period of inactivity. The way to do this would be to place a timer in the document that would count down a set period of inactivity and change the current tab in the Layout Control if it hasn't been changed by the user within that period of time. Right-click the Chap3_02.HTML Document and select the ieTimerCTRL from the control list. Then set the Interval to 3000 and Enabled to true and close the edit window for the control. After opening the Script Wizard, add four global variables and the code shown in Listing 3.6.

Listing 3.6 CHAP3_02.HTM—The Timer Event Code Used to Change the Displayed Chart Type

```
<SCRIPT LANGUAGE="VBScript" On Load="InitALX">
<!--
dim lngCurrentTab
dim lngCountInterval
dim lngLastTab
dim lngCountDown

Sub IeTimer1_Timer()
   lngCountInterval = 5
   lngCurrentTab=ChartDemo.tabCharts.SelectedItem.Index
   'check to see if the tab has changed
   'since the last timer event
   If lngLastTab <> lngCurrentTab Then
    'if it has changed then restart
    'the countdown
    lngLastTab = lngCurrentTab
    lngCountDown = lngCountInterval
   Else
    'if no changes then count down
    lngCountDown = lngCountDown - 1
   End If
   If lngCountDown < 0 then
    'move to the next tab
    if ingCurrentTab = _
    ChartDemo.tabCharts.Tabs.Count -1 then
      'we are at the last tab so
      'start over
```

```
      lngLastTab=0
    Else
      'move to the next tab
      lngLastTab = lngCurrentTab + 1
    End If
    'here is where the tab is actually moved
    ChartDemo.tabCharts.SelectedItem.index _
    =lngLastTab
    'start the countdown over
    lngCountDown = lngCountInterval
  End If
  status = lngCountDown
end sub
-->
```


The code presented in Listing 3.6 is fairly straightforward. It first checks to see if the current tab index is different from what it was in the previous timer event. If it is, then it restarts the countdown. If not, then it decrements the count contained in lngCountDown. When lngCountDown falls below 0, the tab is moved to the next available tab. If the last tab has been reached, it restarts at tab 0 and the whole process starts over again.

CAUTION

The Beta version of the Layout Control is usually loaded after the VBScript in the HTML document is parsed. This results in your VBScript code's references to the Layout Control to always fail. Microsoft's original position on this was that you would not be able to reference the properties and methods of the Layout Control from your HTML document. But someone on the VBScript newslist discovered that by adding the OnLoad="InitALX" to the VBScript declaration tag you could indeed reference the Layout Control's properties and methods. Microsoft says that this won't be an issue in the released product. This caution is included just in case this is still a problem and you find yourself in the above described situation.

From Here...

The Chap_03.alx file can be dropped on any Web page document. The most convenient way to do this is to load your HTML document into the ActiveX Control Pad and select the Add Layout Control menu item from the Files menu or from the right-click pop-up menu. In subsequent chapters there will be more examples of using the ActiveX Control Pad with ActiveX controls and VBScript to produce some useful applications.

This chapter introduces the ActiveX Control pad as the tool de jour for creating VBScript HTML pages. The Layout Control is also introduced here because of its close relationship to the ActiveX Control pad. The Layout Control is not an integral part of the ActiveX Control Pad; but an independent ActiveX Control that will be distributed as part of the ActiveX controls distributed with the Internet Explorer 3.0 browser. The Active X Control Pad and the Layout Control are used throughout this book to develop various approaches to Web page development. These chapters include:

- Chapter 11, "Designing VBScript Applications."
- Chapter 12, "A Simple VBScript Page."

PART II

Visual Basic Scripting Edition: Active Intelligence for Internet Browsers

CHAPTER 4

Creating a Standard HTML Page

by Ron Schwarz

This chapter covers the creation of "standard" HTML pages, using the ActiveX Control Pad. The word "standard" is in quotation marks, because even though these Web pages only make use of script- and control-enabled HTML (as opposed to HTML Layout Page features), the ActiveX Control Pad provides the opportunity to create pages that are anything but "standard" in appearance and function. And the ease with which these pages can be managed will enable you to focus on the task at hand, rather than get bogged down in the minutia of HTML.

In this chapter, you use the ActiveX Control Pad to create a simple page, add a control, and enable it with a script. Throughout the example, you'll see references to objects, properties, code, and other programming language elements. Don't try to understand the guts of the language at this point—they're fully described elsewhere in this book (check the "From Here" section at the end of this chapter for references to other chapters)—the purpose of this chapter is to show you how to create a script-enabled HTML page using ActiveX controls, in a concise, step-by-step manner. ■

Essential HTML with the ActiveX Control Pad

Use the ActiveX Control Pad to manage the creation of standard HTML pages.

An environment for code creation

Use the features of the ActiveX Control Pad to go beyond simple text editing.

Control management

Insert and manage controls with a mini-IDE.

Event code management

Automatically create event code skeletons.

Script management

Automatically insert method and property calls; add non-event procedures.

Using the ActiveX Control Pad

The ActiveX Control Pad is sometimes called (in jest) *Visual Notepad.* If anything, it's Notepad on steroids. Its appearance is deceptively simple. When you first run it, you see what appears to be little more than a text editor. As with all decent software, its real power is under the hood. You're never more than a few mouse clicks away from features that will literally shave hours from the development time of any significant project. This little program is not to be underestimated, nor should the fact that Microsoft is giving it away at no cost be misconstrued to imply that it's of limited usefulness.

Starting the ActiveX Control Pad

Start the ActiveX Control Pad (see fig. 4.1), either by finding it in your Start Menu, or by navigating to it via Explorer or "My Computer."

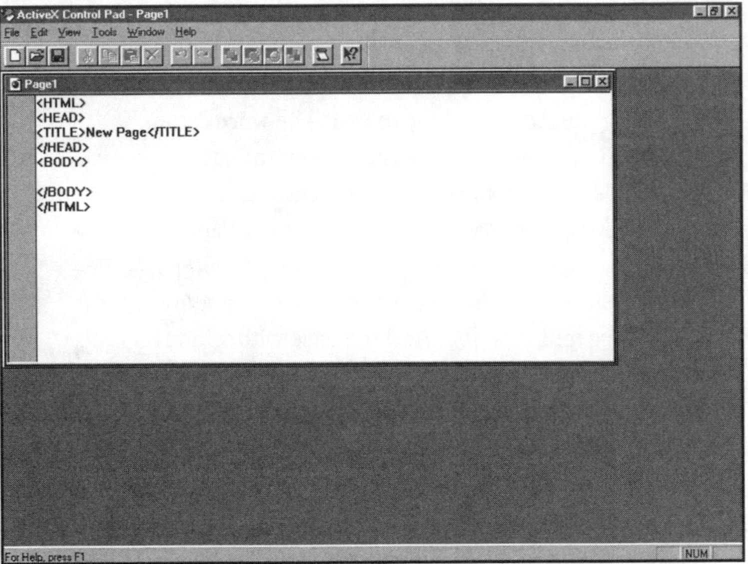

FIG. 4.1
This is the ActiveX Control Pad.

Figure 4.1 shows the ActiveX Control Pad as it first appears when run. As you can see, it automatically creates a skeleton for your project, consisting of `<HTML>`, `<HEAD>`, `<TITLE>`, and `<BODY>` blocks. (The blank line in the `<BODY>` block is where you'll put your content.) It also creates a default filename of "*Page1*," and a default Title of "*New Page.*"

So far, so good. Now, for the good part. Let's say you want to put a command button on the page, and have it take the user to **www.microsoft.com** when it's clicked. You can do it the hard way, with lots of HTML, or, you can do it the easy way with an ActiveX control. The ActiveX Control Pad makes it extremely simple.

Inserting a Control

The first thing you need to do is insert the button. To do this, bring up the context menu by clicking the mouse on the blank line. This puts the cursor at the position you want the control to appear. Now, move the mouse over the vertical gray area to the left of the editing area, and click its *right* button once. You'll then see a context menu like the one in Figure 4.2.

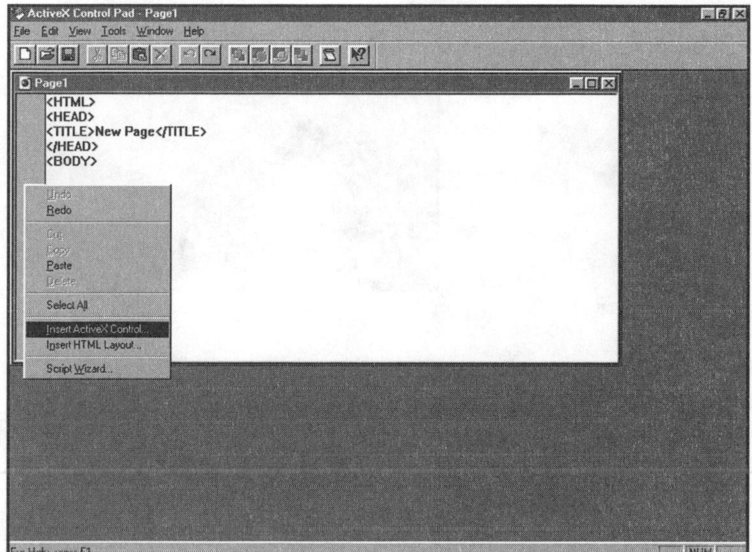

FIG. 4.2
ActiveX Control Pad context menu.

In Figure 4.2, the Insert ActiveX Control menu item is selected. Select it on your machine, and click. In a few seconds, you'll see the Insert ActiveX Control dialog box. Find the entry for Microsoft Forms 2.0 CommandButton, as shown in Figure 4.3.

Once you've selected the CommandButton, either double-click its entry or click the OK button. Once you do that, you'll see two new windows floating over the Control Pad—"Edit ActiveX Control," and "Properties," shown in Figure 4.4. If you've used VB before, things may be starting to appear familiar.

Setting Control Properties

The "Edit ActiveX Control" window contains what appears to be a small VB-style form, containing a single button control. It's not *really* a form, however. It's just a container to hold the prototype of the control, to provide a context for editing purposes. When you're done editing, the control itself will be placed into the HTML on the page, without any trace of the "form."

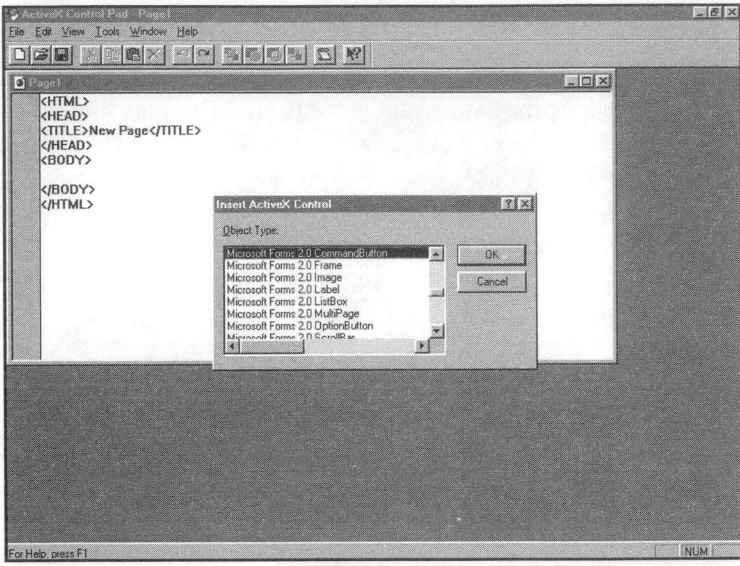

FIG. 4.3
Insert ActiveX Control dialog box.

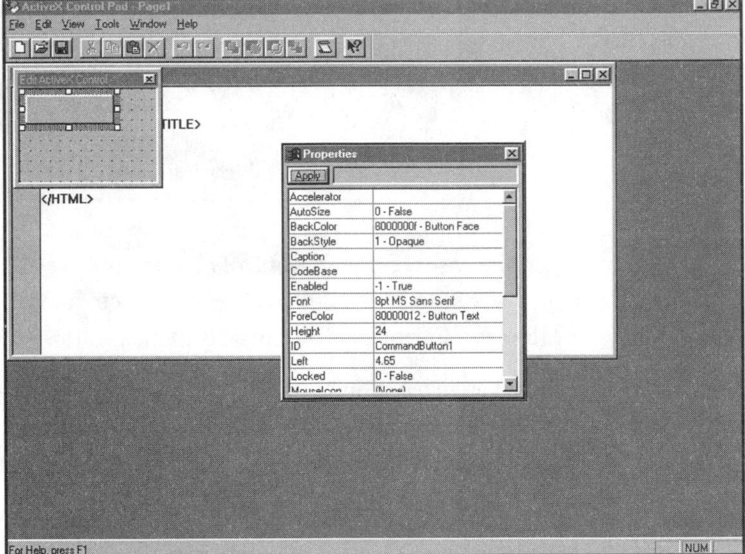

FIG. 4.4
Control editing is accomplished by way of the Properties window.

The other window (the "Properties" window) contains a list of properties and settings that apply to the control. From here, you can set starting properties that will determine the condition of the control when the page first loads.

One advantage many of the ActiveX controls hold over their earlier VB counterparts is the ability to edit Caption and Text properties in-place. What this means is that you can type

Button and Label captions right on the buttons, and TextBox text can be typed into the text. Other controls feature drag-and-drop capability too.

To assign a caption to the button in this example, you can either locate its Caption property in the Properties window, or, you can enter it directly on the button. To enter it directly, click one time on the button to bring the focus to the control. Then, wait a second or two. Then, click one more time. (The reason for the delay between clicks is to avoid sending a double-click.)

As soon as you click the second time, you'll see a cursor appear in the center of the button. Type **Go West!**. As you type, the letters will appear one by one on the button. Because button captions are centered, the text will move to the left and right as you enter it, maintaining its centering.

After you've finished entering the caption, your screen should look like the example in Figure 4.5.

FIG. 4.5
Entering a caption.

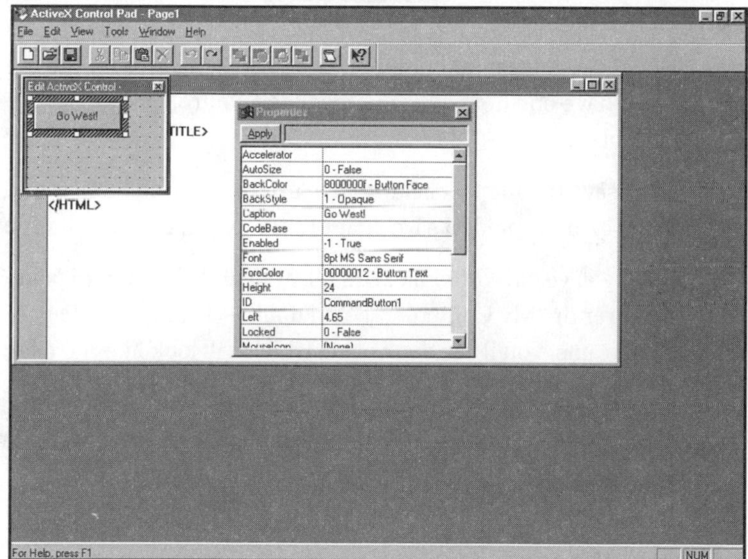

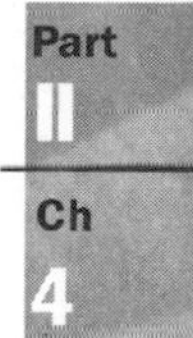

Trying the Example

Click the Close button on the "Edit ActiveX Control" editing window (the small "x" in the upper-right-hand corner of the window). This will return you to the ActiveX Control Pad's main HTML editing window, with the declaration for the button placed into the <BODY> block, as shown in Figure 4.6.

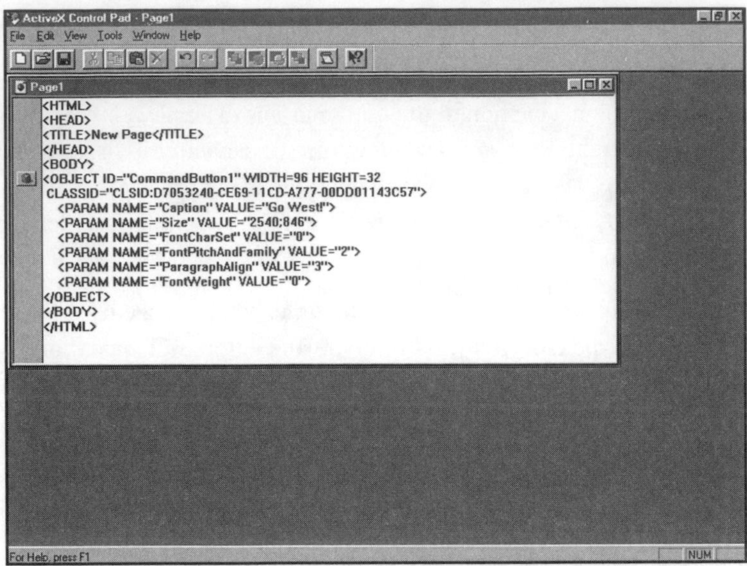

FIG. 4.6
Viewing the updated HTML code.

Notice the button that now appears in the gray area on the left of the editing window. You'll have one next to each embedded control on the page; it's used for editing the control.

Now, save the file by clicking the Save button (the toolbar button with a floppy disk icon). You'll be prompted to save "Page1.htm". Click the Save button to save the file.

Once you've saved the file, run it by opening the folder it's in (or, browsing there with Explorer or "My Computer"), and double-clicking the "Page1" icon. After Internet Explorer runs, you'll see your page, which will look like the example in Figure 4.7.

Although you have a button on the page, if you click it, nothing will happen; you can't *do* anything with it until you add some code, which is explained in "Adding Event Code" later in this chapter.

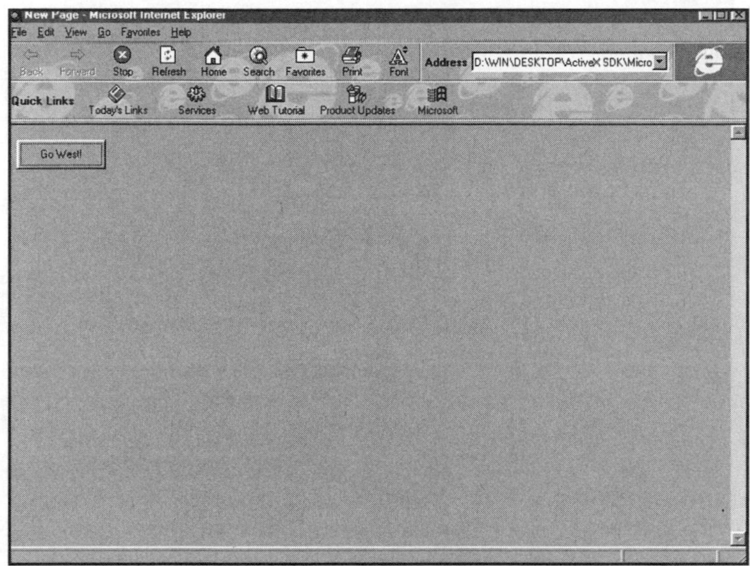

FIG. 4.7
Command button example in Internet Explorer.

Editing a Control

You've got a button on a page, but it's a bit large for its text, so, go back into the ActiveX Control panel, and click the button to the left of the Control declaration. You'll be taken back into control editing mode, which means you'll again have the control visible in its editing window, and the Properties window shown on the right.

To resize the button, you can either edit its Height and Width properties in the Properties window, or, you can simply "grab" it with the mouse, and resize it. To do this, point the mouse at one of the "sizing handles" (the white squares on the sides and corners of the control). You'll see the mouse pointer change to a diagonal dual-headed arrow, which indicates that when you resize from here, you'll be changing both width and height. (If you move the mouse over the top or side border, the mouse pointer will be either vertical or horizontal, indicating the ability to change either height or width; moving anywhere else over the control results in a pointer with four arrows, which allows you to move the control. However, because positioning a control's XY coordinates has no effect in a standard HTML page, it should be disregarded.)

To do the actual resizing, hold down the left mouse button, then drag the mouse toward the center of the control. You'll see a rectangle composed of a dotted-line following the mouse, indicating the new size, as shown in Figure 4.8.

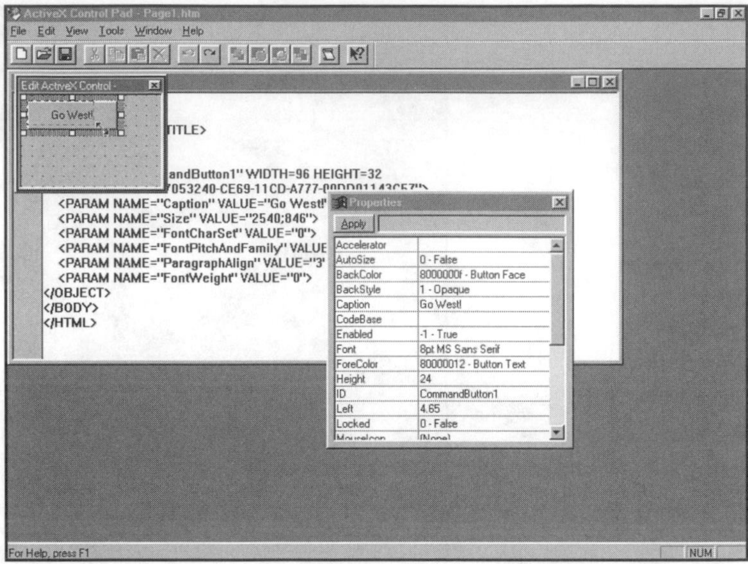

FIG. 4.8
Resizing a control.

When you release the button, the control will resize to the new size, as shown in Figure 4.9. After you've resized the control, click the Close button in the upper right-hand corner of the "Edit ActiveX Control" window to save the changed properties back to your HTML page.

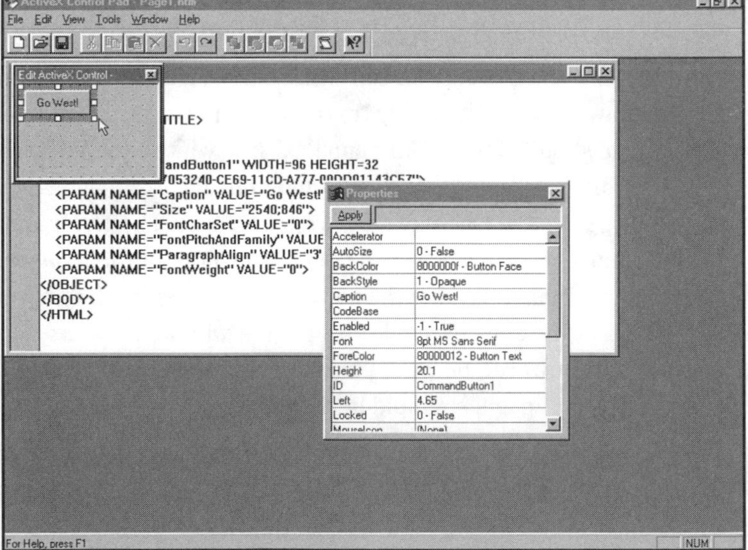

FIG. 4.9
The control after resizing.

Adding Event Code

Before you can do anything with the button, you'll need to add some event code in a script to intercept mouse clicks. The easiest way to do this is to use the Script Wizard that's built into the ActiveX Control Pad. To bring up the Script Wizard, point the mouse anywhere over the gray area to the left of the editing window (other than over a control button) and click the right button. This will display the context menu, as shown in Figure 4.10. Select Script Wizard, and click.

NOTE As this book goes to press, Microsoft is suggesting placing scripts in the <HEAD> section in some of their documentation, and at the end of the <BODY> section in other writings. The execution of scripts is unaffected by placement, and the pre-release version of the Script Wizard currently available for testing places scripts in the <BODY> section. This may change in future releases of the Control Pad.

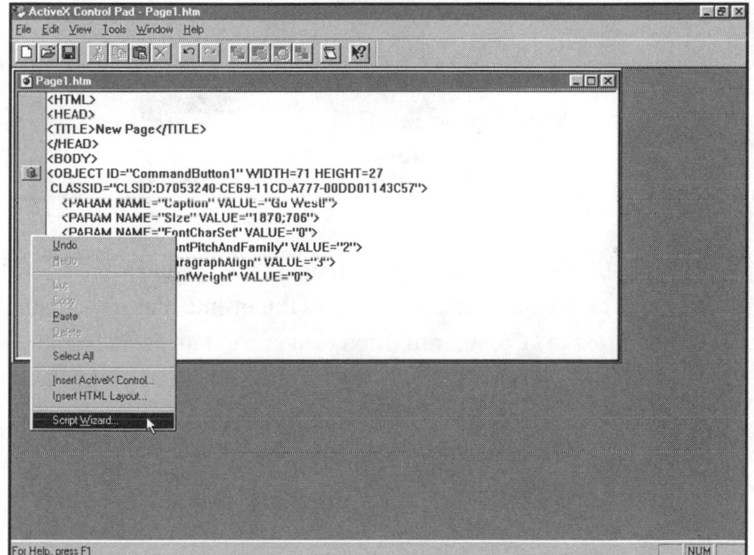

FIG. 4.10
Selecting the Script Wizard.

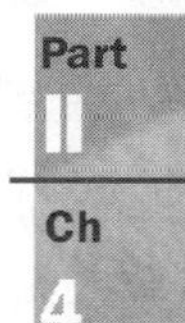

The Script Wizard, shown in Figure 4.11, provides a convenient platform for creating event code and procedures and, an easy way to insert property settings and invoke methods for controls and objects.

The Script Wizard consists of three main areas: two tree lists, and one code window. The code window has two modes—it can be used in "List View," or "Code View." (Figure 4.11 shows List View.) In List View, it displays a list of actions taken when events occur. These actions are generated automatically according to selections you make. In Code View, the

Script Wizard creates event code headers, and property and method code skeletons for you, and lets you write any code you want.

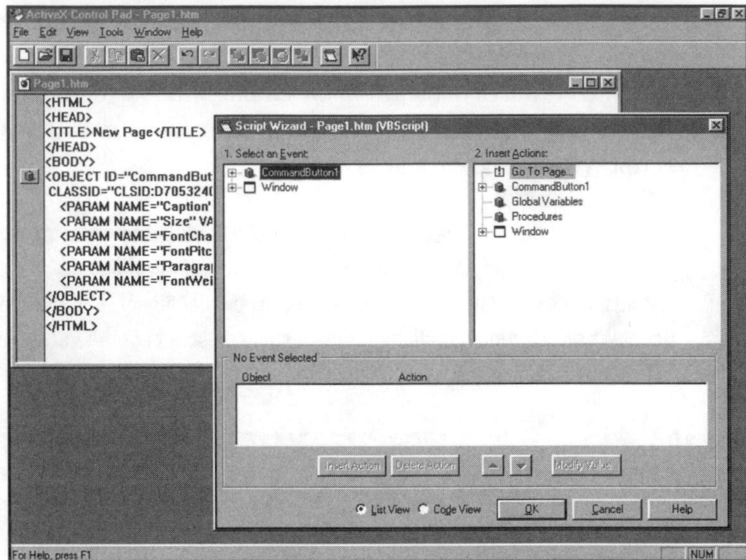

FIG. 4.11
The Script Wizard in Code View.

List View

The outline list on the left is captioned Select an Event. It contains a list of objects on the page, and, when expanded, shows the events that each object exposes. Click the plus (+) sign next to "CommandButton1" to expand its list of events, and click "Click." You'll then see "On CommandButton1 Click Perform the following Actions:" in the bottom pane, as shown in Figure 4.12, indicating that the Script Wizard has created an Event Procedure for the button's Click event.

Now, it's necessary to place some code into the routine. (When the user clicks the button, any code residing in its Click procedure (or "routine") will be automatically executed.) The Script Wizard makes this easy. In the outline list on the right (Insert Actions), click the plus sign next to "Window" to expand the properties belonging to the Window object. You'll then see a number of entries (shown in fig. 4.13), several of which also show plus signs—the Window object consists of a hierarchy nested several layers deep.

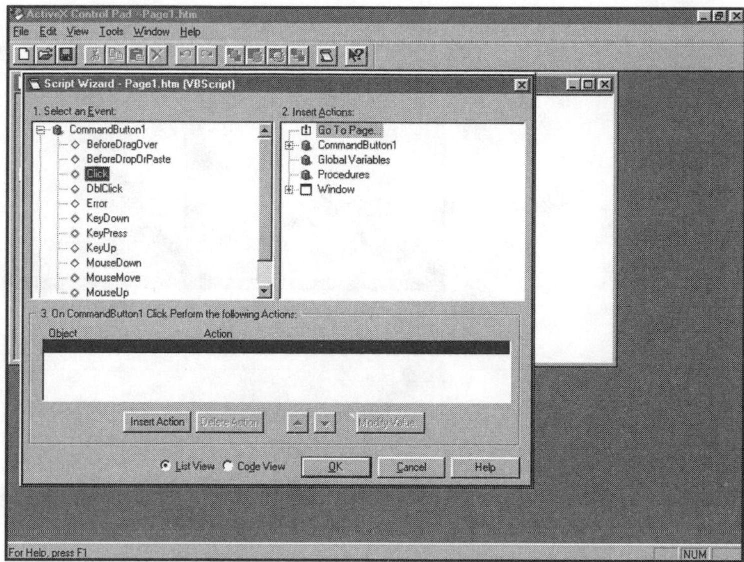

FIG. 4.12
Creating an event procedure.

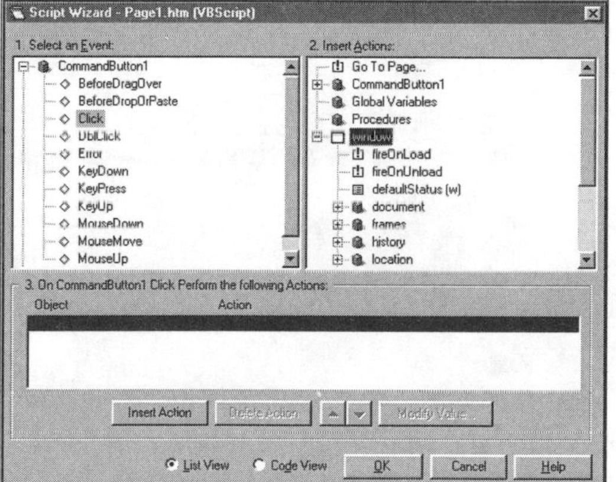

FIG. 4.13
The window Object Hierarchy.

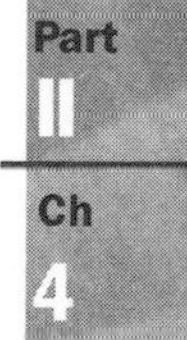

Find the entry for "location," and click its plus sign to expand it, then click href, as in Figure 4.14.

At this point, it's time to tell the Script Wizard what to do with the href property. So, double-click "href," and a dialog captioned "Change Window.location href" appears. It will contain a textbox, with a caption saying, "Please enter a string constant value." Type **http://www.microsoft.com**, as shown in Figure 4.15, then click the OK button.

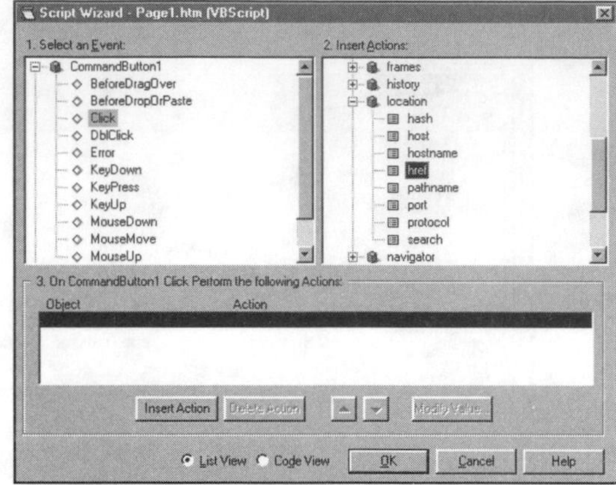

FIG. 4.14
Expanded view of window.location.

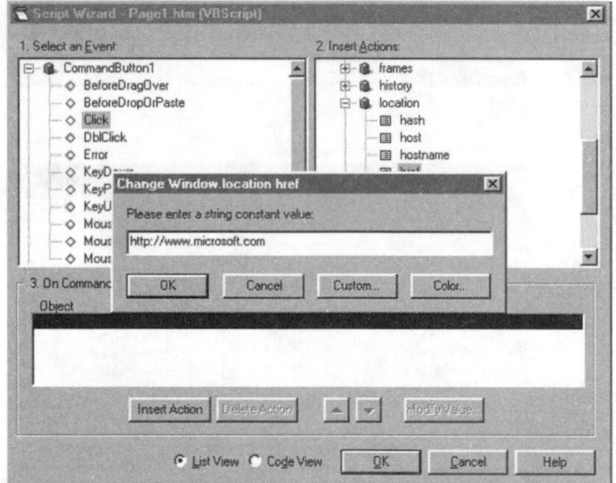

FIG. 4.15
Change Window.location href dialog box.

After you click OK, the bottom panel will contain an entry saying `Go To Page "http://www.microsoft.com"` as shown in Figure 4.16. Click the Script Wizard's OK button to return to the HTML editing window, and the script it just created will be inserted into the `<BODY>` section, shown in Figure 4.17. You're now ready to save the updated file, and run it. (If you've still got the previous version of Page1.htm loaded in Internet Explorer, just click the "Refresh" button on its toolbar to have it load the new version.)

When you run the example, it will *appear* exactly as it did in Figure 4.7, before you added the script. To demonstrate the fact that it's changed, click the button. This time, instead of nothing happening, as it did before, you'll be transferred to the Microsoft home page. (To return to the page you just created, click the "Back" button on Internet Explorer's toolbar.)

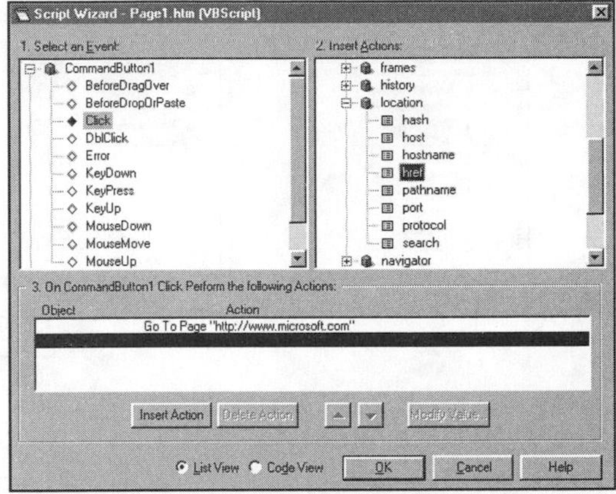

FIG. 4.16
Event entry created by Script Wizard.

```
Page1.htm
<HTML>
<HEAD>
<TITLE>New Page</TITLE>
</HEAD>
<BODY>
    <SCRIPT LANGUAGE="VBScript">
<!--
Sub CommandButton1_Click()
Window.location.href = "http://www.microsoft.com"
end sub

-->
    </SCRIPT>
    <OBJECT ID="CommandButton1" WIDTH=96 HEIGHT=32
     CLASSID="CLSID:D7053240-CE69-11CD-A777-00DD01143C57">
        <PARAM NAME="Caption" VALUE="Go West!">
        <PARAM NAME="Size" VALUE="2540;846">
        <PARAM NAME="FontCharSet" VALUE="0">
        <PARAM NAME="FontPitchAndFamily" VALUE="2">
        <PARAM NAME="ParagraphAlign" VALUE="3">
        <PARAM NAME="FontWeight" VALUE="0">
    </OBJECT>
</BODY>
</HTML>
```

FIG. 4.17
Script inserted into HTML.

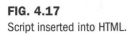

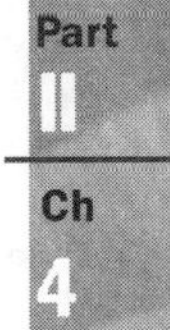

Code View

In the gray area to the left of the editing window in Figure 4.17, you can see a button next to the script that the Script Wizard inserted. Just as controls have buttons to bring up the control editing windows, scripts have buttons to bring up the Script Wizard. You use the Script Wizard for editing existing scripts, as well as for creating new ones.

Click the button, and you'll be back in the Script Wizard. Now, click the "Code View" option button, and you'll see that the bottom panel now shows the actual code created by the Wizard, shown in Figure 4.18.

The event code consists of two lines:

```
Sub CommandButton1_Click()
Window.location.href = "http://www.microsoft.com"
```

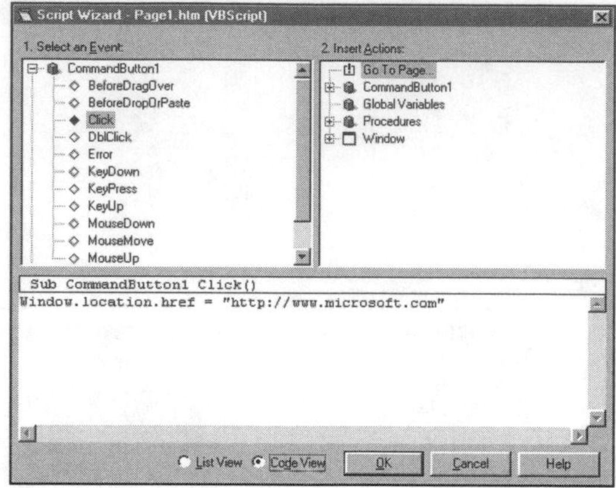

FIG. 4.18
Event code in Script Wizard.

The first line is the procedure declaration. It's in a section by itself, and you can't edit it. (Actually, you *can* edit it, but to do so you need to right-click over it, and select the "Edit Procedure Prototype" option.) The second line is the actual code, and, you *can* edit its section. Change it by adding one line above it and one below it, and indent the original line, as shown below and in Figure 4.19. Then click the OK button to return to the HTML editor.

```
If MsgBox("Really Go West?", 4) = 6 Then
     Window.location.href = "http://www.microsoft.com"
End If
```

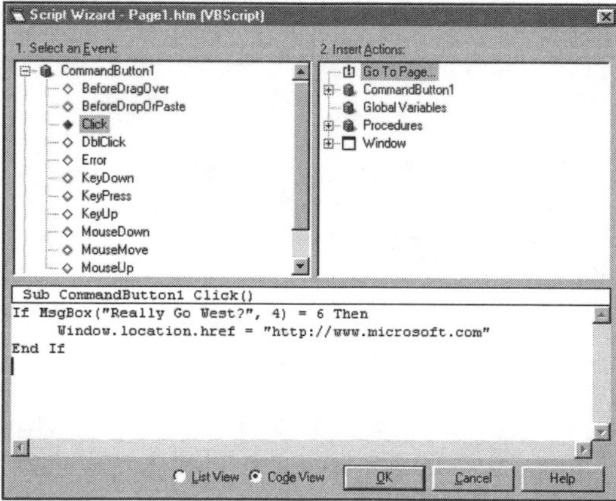

FIG. 4.19
Script code after editing.

When you're back in the HTML editor, save the file, reload it into Internet Explorer, then run it again by clicking the "Go West!" button. You'll see a message box asking "Really Go West?" that has two buttons: "Yes," and "No," and is shown in Figure 4.20.

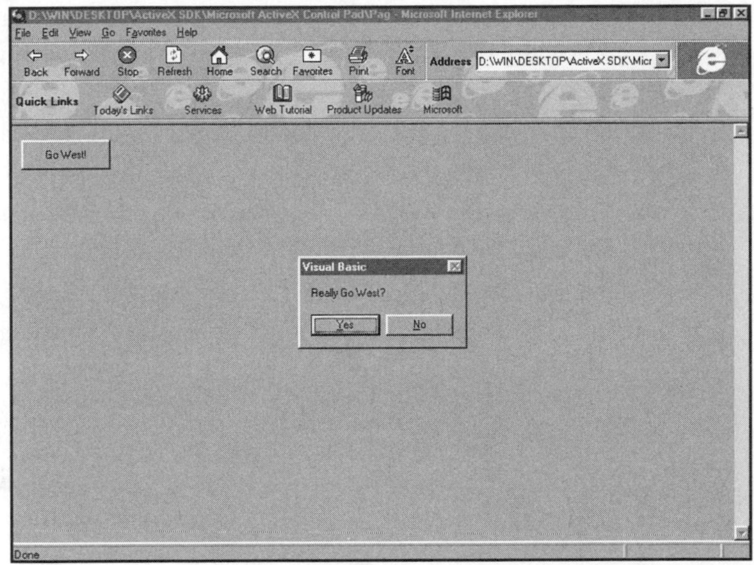

FIG. 4.20
Message box in Internet Explorer.

If you click the "No" button, nothing will happen; if you click the "Yes" button, you'll be taken to the Microsoft Web site.

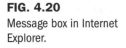

Although this example used the href property to change to a new URL, it's *such* a common operation that the Script Wizard offers an easy way to automate it. Just right-click over the lower panel of the Wizard, and you'll see a context menu that offers you a shortcut to insert "go to page" code. It makes it *really* easy to use controls for creating links to other pages, without writing a single line of code. You'll find this especially useful when you use the ActiveX Control Pad in HTML Layout Page mode, which is covered in Chapter 6, "Creating an HTML Layout Page."

From Here...

In this chapter, you learned how to use the ActiveX Control Pad to create standard HTML pages. You discovered how to insert and edit ActiveX controls, and work with scripts.

- See Chapter 6, "Creating an HTML Layout Page," to learn how to use the ActiveX Control Pad to create powerful VB-style pages.
- See Chapter 11, "Designing VBScript Applications," to see how to use the language elements to create script-enabled pages.
- See Chapter 15, "VBScript Data Types and Variables," for information on variant subtype issues.

- See Chapter 16, "VBScript Operators," for more information on declarations and procedures and for coverage of Arithmetic, String, Comparison, and Logical operators.
- See Chapter 17, "VBScript Control of Flow and Error Handling," which delves into the looping and testing structures, and the Error Object.
- See Que's *Special Edition Using Visual Basic 4* and *Visual Basic 4 Expert Solutions* for extensive information on the Visual Basic language.
- Refer to the *Microsoft Visual Basic Scripting Edition Language Reference*, for exhaustive syntax descriptions and requirements of all statements, functions, and methods.

CHAPTER 5

Internet Explorer

by Ron Schwarz

This short chapter provides you with a brief synopsis of what browsers are, what they do, and what *you* can do using the functionality they provide. Chances are you've been using a browser for a while, and, there's a good chance it's a version of Netscape. Don't be surprised if you find yourself quickly moving to Internet Explorer. Microsoft is in the process of standing the browser world on its ear, and you're right in the middle of it. Whatever browser you've *been* using, it appears very likely that you'll be surfing the Net with Internet Explorer before too long. ■

Browsers and the World Wide Web

A quick overview of what the WWW is, and the job browsers perform.

Three generations of browsers

Internet Explorer 3.0, the newest version, has a long and colorful history.

Current art

What browsers can do today.

The future

Where browser technology is headed.

First Generation Browsers

The first widely available graphical browser for the WWW was NCSA Mosaic (see fig. 5.1). Lynx, a character-based browser (still popular with UNIX users) allowed connection to Web sites, reading text, and downloading files. Although the early browsers were crude by today's standards, they were revolutionary—they enabled fast, easy, hypertext access to information on computers located all over the world.

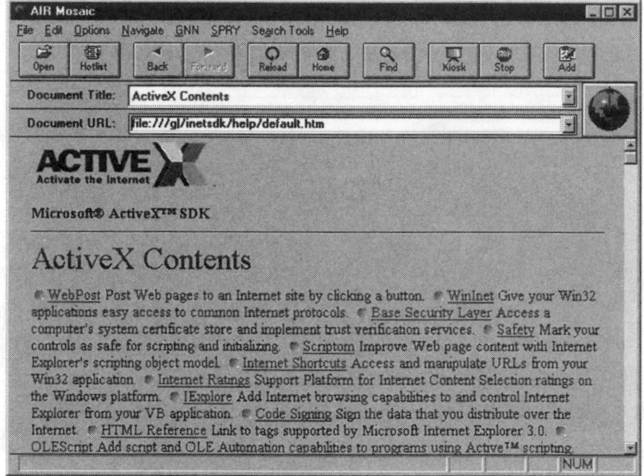

FIG. 5.1
A view of Mosaic, a first generation browser.

At this time (the early '90s), the Internet was still somewhat unknown outside of academia and government, and Web traffic was a small percentage of the overall volume of data moving over the Net. Most information traveling over the Internet consisted of e-mail, remote Telnet sessions, and FTP file transfers. The available bandwidth was sufficient for the traffic.

Second Generation Browsers

After the success of Mosaic, Netscape Navigator was released by Netscape Communications Corporation (see fig. 5.2). It offered better graphics, better formatting, and more features. Eventually, it provided the ability to use plug-ins and Java applets (programs that run within the browser), which provided a means for enhancing and expanding the basic operation of Netscape Navigator.

FIG. 5.2
Netscape Navigator, a second generation browser.

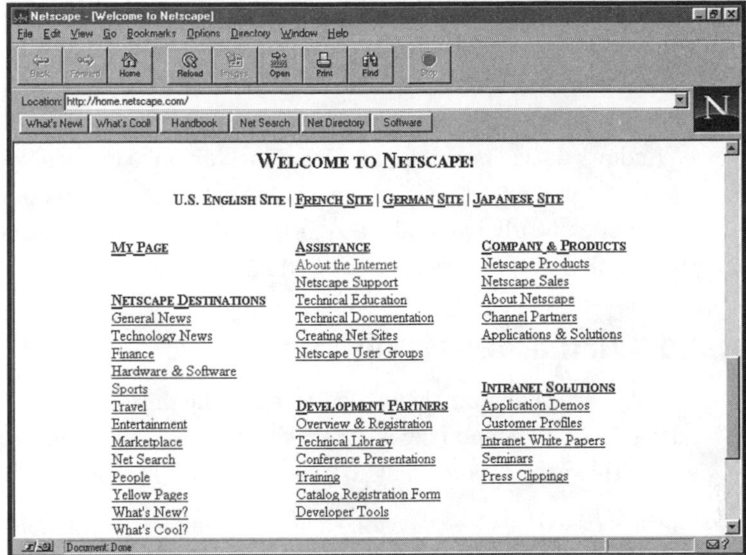

Third Generation Browsers

The end of the second generation of browser technology is marked by a user base consisting of incredible numbers of people in all walks of life, as well as a somewhat discouraging reality. For all its potential, the Internet (widely and incorrectly considered synonymous with the WWW) has become the moral equivalent of television.

The More Things Change...

The Internet has become television for the nineties. The remote control has been replaced by the mouse; rather than waving their clickers at the tube, users slide their mouses over their desks, in click-o-ramic ecstasy, viewing, viewing, and viewing. Instead of changing channels, they surf the Web. Instead of poring through their local television listings, they pull down their Favorites menus.

The interactivity of the Web has developed in a way that is heavily weighted in one direction. Web site construction has been a labor-intensive endeavor, requiring a significant measure of skill, and a non-trivial level of physical infrastructure in terms of server hardware, server OS, high-speed Internet connection, and ongoing maintenance. The *consumer* end of the equation, however, has become embarrassingly simple. *Point-and-Shoot* interfaces have never been more ubiquitous (with the possible exception of the age of Samuel Colt), and *The Web* is an inescapable facet of contemporary life.

Apart from the difficulties that have accompanied the creation of Web content, the fact remains that browsers, for all their utility, have essentially been little more than hypertext formatting and display engines. Actually, traditional WWW content has been little different in concept from the common WinHelp files that have been used all along by every Windows user. The difference is that in addition to being able to link to "pages" within the same "document," they can also link to content on other computers. Other than that, they have been nearly identical—text formatted to fit any size window, highlighted hot-links, hotspotted graphics, and a Back button.

Beyond "Virtual Television"

Things are changing, though, as we enter the third generation of browser technology. Java, JavaScript, and Plug-ins created the possibility for interactivity *beyond* mere "clicking." However, it's one thing to have potential—it's another thing entirely to actualize it.

Java is based on C++, and while a bit less complex, is still not for the faint of heart. Plug-ins are a proprietary solution that require special programming techniques that are not portable to environments other than supporting browsers.

Just as Windows did not *really* take off so long as all programming had to be done using the complex Windows SDK (Software Development Kit) and the C language, truly widespread interactive applications over the Web have not proliferated.

At the same time as all this growth has occurred on the Internet, Microsoft has been quietly creating the tools to use the Internet (and Intranets) to completely revolutionize the way people use computers.

Opportunities for the Taking

The Microsoft Internet Explorer 3.0 represents state-of-the-art browser technology (see fig. 5.3). In addition to supporting Java and JavaScript (as this book goes to press, Plug-in compatibility is expected, but not yet implemented, in the available beta of IE 3.0), Internet Explorer 3.0 provides ActiveX and VBScript compatibility.

ActiveX technology is perhaps the most widely-accepted standard for component-level programming. It's used as the basis for Visual Basic 4.0, the most popular programming language in history, and it's also used by numerous other programming languages and major applications. By making it the foundation of Internet Explorer, Microsoft has cleared the path for a genuinely monumental change in what the Web is, who uses it, and how it's used.

This is a *good* time to be a Visual Basic programmer.

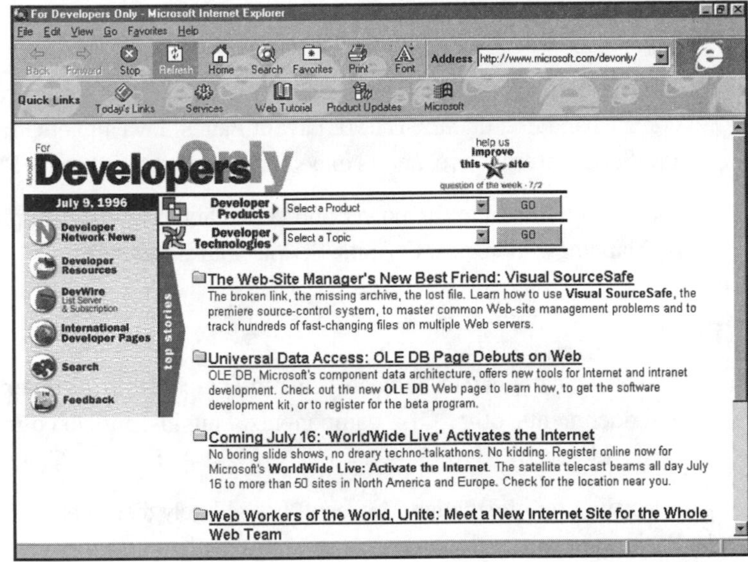

FIG. 5.3
Internet Explorer 3.0.

Internet Explorer versus Netscape Navigator

It's really difficult to predict the future of Netscape Navigator. After all, at this time, it *is* the most popular browser. However, it seems to be headed in a direction different from that chosen by the designers of Internet Explorer.

It's entirely likely that Internet Explorer will become the predominant Web browser; not only is it bundled with Windows, and available for free download for other OSs, but future versions will be fully integrated with Windows (see "Browser Extensibility" in this chapter) and be part of the OS.

While Netscape seems less than enthralled with the idea of building in ActiveX compliance, at least one third-party vendor has announced a Plug-in designed to support ActiveX components within Netscape. Whether this type of solution will be viable for the majority of Netscape users (particularly in light of the momentum Internet Explorer is generating), remains to be seen.

One thing does seem clear: you won't go wrong supporting Internet Explorer.

There is more than a bit of irony in all this: Netscape Navigator swept the market out from under Mosaic, by offering a better, easier to use, and more capable browser.

Now, it appears that the mantle may be passing back, after a fashion. Internet Explorer is based in large part on Mosaic, licensed by Microsoft. "What goes around" *could* be about to "come around."

Browser Extensibility

Internet Explorer 3.0 is the most highly-extensible browser available. It supports ActiveX controls and documents, HTML Layout Pages, Java applets, has built-in VBScript and JavaScript interpreters, and is expected to support Netscape Plug-ins when released.

Elements that add to the power and versatility of Internet Explorer fall into a group of overlapping categories: Objects, Scripts, and Containers.

Objects

The broad category of "Objects" currently includes such diverse items as ActiveX controls and documents, other OLE components, Plug-ins, and, of course, the Internet Explorer object hierarchy.

According to information Microsoft has publicly disclosed, the next version of Visual Basic will provide the means to create ActiveX controls. This means that in the not-too-distant future, any competent VB programmer will be able to create virtually any type of Web automation required. Just as the first release of Visual Basic made it possible for thousands of Windows applications to be created by people other than hard-core C programmers, it will soon be possible for these same people to create stunning Internet applications.

Scripts

Scripting languages such as VBScript provide a "glue" to connect the objects. If you're familiar with Visual Basic, you know that a VB application consists of controls placed on forms, with VB code tying it all together. Properties, events, and methods interact with objects to create full-featured applications. VBScript performs the same function in the context of Web pages. ActiveX objects are enabled by virtue of scripts that hook into their exposed properties, events, and methods.

Containers

One of the drawbacks inherent in the nature of HTML browsers is the fact that HTML was designed to be a simple hypertext formatting language. Text flows in from the upper-left corner of the page, and is "fitted" to the current dimensions of the browser. If you resize the browser, the text reformats.

This is fine, as far as it goes. And, for content that is primarily comprised of text, with a few images tossed in for good measure, it is perfectly sufficient. Unfortunately, that's not what happened. The Web was pressed into service for a wide variety of presentation purposes, and the ability to create and display visually attractive pages became very necessary, and very difficult.

Various "hacks" were mixed into the HTML language. Things like *tables* allow a bit more control over positioning, but even then, items within table cells are *still* cursed by their Upper-Left-Lower-Right flow-of-text HTML heritage.

As the language grew, it became more convoluted, difficult to master, and proprietary.

The root of the problem lied in the inability of HTML to place an element at a particular XY coordinate. The very notion of fixed-placement of objects runs counter to the "stream" method HTML uses to fill a page with text.

HTML Layout Pages address the problem head-on, and provide an elegant solution. By placing an HTML Layout Page on your Web page, you give yourself the ability to use a tool like the ActiveX Control Pad to visually, interactively place and size controls on a window that looks remarkably similar to a typical Visual Basic form. Because the Layout Page provides a "non-HTMLish" context, you can create everything from beautifully formatted Web pages with rich content, to sophisticated programs that depend on a fixed-positioning of their controls.

It should not surprise anyone if HTML Layout Pages become the *de facto* standard, displacing traditional HTML for all but the most trivial of Web pages, just as Windows has edged DOS off the desktops of millions of computer users.

Just Over the Horizon

As exciting as things are now, it's important to remember that we're in the midst of a transitional phase. So, where *are* things headed? You've probably heard the code name "Nashville" mentioned recently. You might have heard that it's the next version of Windows. Maybe you've heard it's the next version of Internet Explorer. Or, perhaps you've heard that it's a major add-on to Windows 95.

Like the proverbial blind men analyzing an elephant, all of the above is true. Nashville (currently being called *Internet Explorer 4.0*) combines Windows 95 and Internet Explorer into an integrated environment providing seamless continuity between documents on your local computer, other computers on your local Intranet, and other computers on the Internet. Although Microsoft has not released too many details of what the Nashville upgrade will possess, they've dropped enough tantalizing tidbits to make any programmer's mouth water.

Desktop as Browser, Browser as Desktop

As the desktop metaphor is merged with browser technology, it will complete the transformation to *document-centric* computing. Users will work with documents, regardless of where they reside, regardless of which application they belong to. In fact, most major applications will become nearly invisible as they work behind the scenes to service their documents. As users browse from document to document (or document embedded within document), the appropriate applications will quietly take over in the background.

OLE 2.0 provided a great deal of the required capability, but users still needed to run applications to work with documents. Even when double-clicking a document's icon, the OS *still* had to present the user with an application to run. Double-click a Word document, and a few seconds later, you'll be in Word, ready to view, edit, or print that document.

In the near future, everything will be done in a browser window; you'll work with all kinds of documents *within* that window, and the actual applications will become, in essence, extensions to the operating system.

Documents themselves will change too; while documents are currently based on the paper metaphor, and by nature static, ActiveX technology will enable the creation of dynamic documents, containing a mix of content and logic. What's really happening is a blurring of the lines of demarcation between code and content.

Code, content, and location are being mixed together into a potent brew. Those who see what's happening now, and where it's headed in the near future, will be in a position to ride the waves with aplomb, and chart their own course.

From Here...

- See Chapters 3, "Introducing the ActiveX Control Pad," and 6, "Creating an HTML Layout Page," to understand features of the new HTML Layout Pages.
- See Chapter 11, "Designing VBScript Applications," to learn how to integrate the new browser capabilities into your Web applications.
- See Que's *Special Edition Using HTML, Second Edition*, for information on HTML.
- See Que's *JavaScript by Example*, for information on JavaScript.

CHAPTER 6

Creating an HTML Layout Page

by Ibrahim Malluf

- **Rules and benefits of 2-D layouts**

  This includes excerpts of a White Paper presented by Microsoft.

- **Creating and populating layouts by using the ActiveX Control Pad**

  You will see how to design and place your layout.

- **Code management**

  You learn to use the Script Wizard to manage your code development.

- **Creating a project called the Navigator**

  This is a project that creates a Layout control based drop-in-place navigational tool.

In Chapter 3, "Introducing the ActiveX Control Pad," we talked about the mechanics of the ActiveX Control Pad and its features. The Layout control was introduced along with an example Layout Control project that demonstrated the ActiveX Chart control. Here I present a little more detail on the Layout control. The Layout control will be distributed as part of the Internet Explorer 3.0 release version. It is an ActiveX Control that can be distributed to any browser that supports ActiveX controls. In the case of Netscape, ActiveX is not directly supported, but there is at least one add-on available that gives Netscape ActiveX compatibility, and thus Layout Control capability.

The ActiveX Layout control gives you full two-dimensional layout capability for your Web pages. Within this control's area, you can place items wherever you desire using pixel granularity. It should be mentioned here that the Layout control is envisioned by Microsoft as an interim application of a preliminary specification approved by the World Wide Web Consortium(W3C). This new specification will include HTML extensions that will radically extend layout capabilities within your documents.

For now though, the Layout Control is the tool for providing 2-D layout in HTML pages. As currently implemented, the Layout Control requires that you place your 2-D layout information in a separate file with an .ALX extension. This file is a text file that contains the layout information formatted in the W3C's preliminary syntax.

In this chapter, you learn about the benefits of true two-dimensional layout and design capabilities provided by the Layout control. You also see how to use the Script Wizard to manage VBScript development within this Layout Control. Finally, there is an application project that provides an example of using the Layout control and how to work around some of its limitations. ■

Preliminary 2-D Layout Rules and Benefits

- 2-D regions must be defined in a separate file. This file must be given an .ALX extension and is defined as part of the HTML Layout control object tag within the HTML stream. (Please note that after the W3C 2-D layout specification is finalized, Microsoft will support 2-D-style layout definitions directly within the HTML document, rather than in a separate file.)
- Objects defined within the 2-D region must be ActiveX-compliant objects.
- The 2-D region must be enclosed within `<DIV>` tags as follows:
  `<DIV STYLE="LAYOUT:FIXED; HEIGHT value WIDTH value">...</DIV>`

According to Microsoft, they are committed to supporting the final specification natively within the Microsoft Internet Explorer after the W3C standard is formalized. Microsoft also says that they will ensure that the HTML Layout Control format is compatible with future 2-D layout support, which will be incorporated directly into future releases of the Microsoft Internet Explorer. The advantages of this new specification include the following:

- *Exact 2-D placement:* Controls are placed exactly where the author intended them to be placed within the 2-D region.
- *Overlapping regions:* The author can also specify the exact z-order of each control on the page.
- *Transparency:* Graphics, labels, and other controls that support transparency can be placed over each other, giving an attractive layered look.
- *Scripting:* The HTML Layout control also fully supports scripting, including both Visual Basic Scripting Edition (VBScript) and JavaScript.

Creating and Populating the Layout

To use a Layout Control in your Web page document, you need to declare it as you would any other ActiveX control. Listing 6.1 shows a sample declaration of an ActiveX Layout control in a Web page document.

Listing 6.1 CHAPT6_01.HTM—Sample Declaration of an ActiveX Layout Control in a Web Page

```
<HTML>
<HEAD>
<TITLE>Navigator Demo</TITLE>
</HEAD>
<BODY>

<OBJECT CLASSID="CLSID:812AE312-8B8E-11CF-93C8-00AA00C08FDF"
ID="Navigator" STYLE="LEFT:0;TOP:0">
<PARAM NAME="ALXPATH" REF VALUE="Navigator.alx">
 </OBJECT>

</BODY>
</HTML>
```

Within the ALX file itself you will also find plain text describing the different items to be contained within the Layout control. All of the ActiveX controls that you place within a Layout control have their object declarations placed with a set of `<DIV>...</DIV>` tags. Listing 6.2 illustrates the code required to place a TabStrip control within an ActiveX Layout control.

Listing 6.2 NAVIGATOR.ALX—The 2-D Layout Code within an ALX File Specifying a TabStrip Control's Placement

```
<DIV STYLE="LAYOUT:FIXED;WIDTH:134pt;HEIGHT:144pt;">
  <OBJECT ID="tabNavigator"
   CLASSID="CLSID:EAE50EB0-4A62-11CE-BED6-00AA00611080"
   STYLE="TOP:0pt;LEFT:0pt;WIDTH:124pt;HEIGHT:132pt;TABINDEX:0;ZINDEX:0;">
    <PARAM NAME="ListIndex" VALUE="1">
    <PARAM NAME="Size" VALUE="4374;4657">
    <PARAM NAME="Items" VALUE="Tab1;Tab2;">
    <PARAM NAME="TabOrientation" VALUE="2">
    <PARAM NAME="TipStrings" VALUE=";;">
    <PARAM NAME="Names" VALUE="Tab1;Tab2;">
    <PARAM NAME="NewVersion" VALUE="-1">
    <PARAM NAME="TabsAllocated" VALUE="2">
    <PARAM NAME="Tags" VALUE=";;">
    <PARAM NAME="TabData" VALUE="2">
    <PARAM NAME="Accelerator" VALUE=";;">
    <PARAM NAME="FontCharSet" VALUE="0">
```

continues

Listing 6.2 Continued

```
    <PARAM NAME="FontPitchAndFamily" VALUE="2">
    <PARAM NAME="FontWeight" VALUE="0">
    <PARAM NAME="TabState" VALUE="3;3">
  </OBJECT>
</DIV>
```

Parts of a Layout Control Page

The <DIV> tag syntax is :

```
<DIV [ID=name] STYLE = "layout-style-attributes">
  object-blocks
</DIV>
```

The ID part of the tag is an optional attribute that specifies the name given to that particular Layout control and is used by scripting to identify it. The style tag specifies the style attributes for a given Layout Control and are defined in Table 6.1.

Table 6.1 Style Attributes for *<DIV>* Tag

Attribute	Description
LAYOUT	Must be defined as FIXED for a 2-D region
HEIGHT	Specifies the height of the layout region in pixels
WIDTH	Specifies the width of the layout region in pixels
BACKGROUND	Specifies the background color of the layout region in HEX digits

You can include any ActiveX control within your ALX file. This includes but is not limited to controls that implement the ActiveX Control '96 specification for windowless, transparent controls.

NOTE One thing I should note, however, is that with some ActiveX controls, you will have to have a developer's license for you to include and distribute them through your Web documents. The beta version of Internet Explorer that I am working with right now does not have the licensing mechanism in place and does not indicate which controls require a license. This should be corrected by the time you are reading this book.

How to Start a New Project

Fortunately, you do not have to hand edit these ALX files. You can produce them through the ActiveX Control Pad described in Chapter 3, "Introducing the ActiveX Control Pad." To create a new Layout control, you need merely select the New Layout Control from the Files menu of the ActiveX control menu as shown in Figure 6.1. This brings up a new ActiveX Layout control that is ready for your editing.

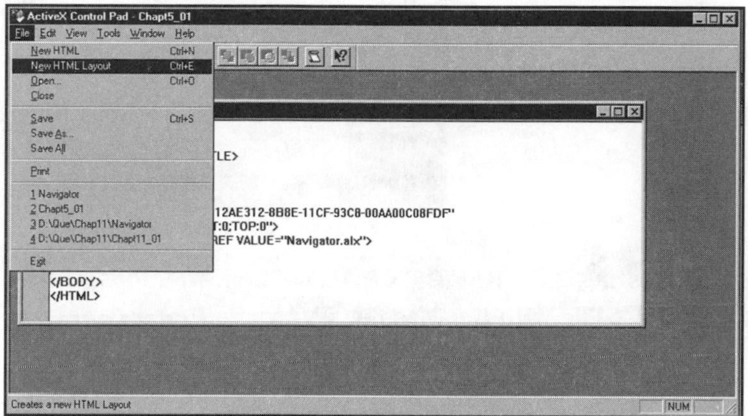

FIG. 6.1
Select a New HTML Layout control from the menu of the ActiveX Control Pad.

Let us create a navigator tool that can act as a drop-in-place navigational object that is fully modifiable based on a given page context. The idea being presented here uses a Layout control that contains a TabStrip control and an ieLabel control. The number of displayed tabs will differ depending upon the modifications made by external sources such as the parent Web page, or even a Web page in another frame.

First, we'll begin by creating the new Layout Control, adding a tab control and ieLabel control, and arranging them as shown in Figure 6.2. The TabStrip is named tabNavigator, and the label is simply named ieLabel. The TabStrip's TabOrientation property is set to left, and the ielabel's angle property is set to 90 degrees. Finally, add an ieTimer control that will drive some animation effects to be added later. Save the control with the name of Navigator.alx.

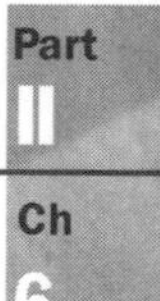

So altogether there are three controls on the Layout Pad. The ieLabel control in this beta version of the ActiveX Control Pad would not permit changing the FontName property from the Properties Edit Window. This is a bug that might or might not get fixed before you get an opportunity to read this book. The workaround for this and many similar problems is to directly edit the properties using the "View Source Code" selection from the right button click's pop-up menu. This produces a NotePad-based edit window that enables you to do direct editing. Listing 6.3 shows the HTML code as presented by the View Source Code menu selection. Note that I changed the ieLabel's FontName to Brush Script MT.

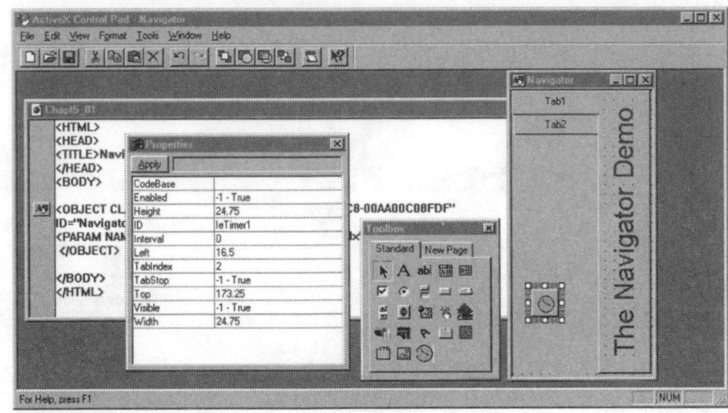

FIG. 6.2 Begin the Navigator Demo project within the ActiveX Control Pad.

On the CD

Listing 6.3 NAVIGATOR.ALX—The Navigator's *<DIV>* Code Section in the ALX File with the Modified FontName Property of ieLabel

```
<DIV STYLE="LAYOUT:FIXED;WIDTH:125pt;HEIGHT:250pt;">
    <OBJECT ID="tabNavigator"
     CLASSID="CLSID:EAE50EB0-4A62-11CE-BED6-00AA00611080"
     STYLE="TOP:0pt;LEFT:0pt;WIDTH:124pt;
     HEIGHT:248pt;TABINDEX:0;ZINDEX:0;">
        <PARAM NAME="ListIndex" VALUE="0">
        <PARAM NAME="Size" VALUE="4374;8749">
        <PARAM NAME="Items" VALUE="Tab1;Tab2;">
        <PARAM NAME="TabOrientation" VALUE="2">
        <PARAM NAME="TabFixedWidth" VALUE="2646">
        <PARAM NAME="TipStrings" VALUE=";;">
        <PARAM NAME="Names" VALUE="Tab1;Tab2;">
        <PARAM NAME="NewVersion" VALUE="-1">
        <PARAM NAME="TabsAllocated" VALUE="2">
        <PARAM NAME="Tags" VALUE=";;">
        <PARAM NAME="TabData" VALUE="2">
        <PARAM NAME="Accelerator" VALUE=";;">
        <PARAM NAME="FontCharSet" VALUE="0">
        <PARAM NAME="FontPitchAndFamily" VALUE="2">
        <PARAM NAME="FontWeight" VALUE="0">
        <PARAM NAME="TabState" VALUE="3;3">
    </OBJECT>
    <OBJECT ID="IeBanner"
     CLASSID="CLSID:99B42120-6EC7-11CF-A6C7-00AA00A47DD2"
     STYLE="TOP:8pt;LEFT:83pt;WIDTH:33pt;
     HEIGHT:231pt;TABINDEX:1;ZINDEX:1;">
        <PARAM NAME="_ExtentX" VALUE="1164">
        <PARAM NAME="_ExtentY" VALUE="8149">
        <PARAM NAME="Caption" VALUE="The Navigator Demo">
        <PARAM NAME="Angle" VALUE="90">
        <PARAM NAME="Alignment" VALUE="4">
```

```
        <PARAM NAME="Mode" VALUE="1">
        <PARAM NAME="FillStyle" VALUE="0">
        <PARAM NAME="FillStyle" VALUE="0">
        <PARAM NAME="ForeColor" VALUE="#612238">
        <PARAM NAME="BackColor" VALUE="#C0C0C0">
        <PARAM NAME="FontName" VALUE="Brush Script MT">
        <PARAM NAME="FontSize" VALUE="32">
        <PARAM NAME="FontItalic" VALUE="0">
        <PARAM NAME="FontBold" VALUE="0">
        <PARAM NAME="FontUnderline" VALUE="0">
        <PARAM NAME="FontStrikeout" VALUE="0">
        <PARAM NAME="TopPoints" VALUE="0">
        <PARAM NAME="BotPoints" VALUE="0">
    </OBJECT>
    <OBJECT ID="IeTimer1"
     CLASSID="CLSID:59CCB4A0-727D-11CF-AC36-00AA00A47DD2"
     STYLE="TOP:173pt;LEFT:17pt;WIDTH:25pt;
     HEIGHT:25pt;TABINDEX:2;ZINDEX:2;">
        <PARAM NAME="_ExtentX" VALUE="873">
        <PARAM NAME="_ExtentY" VALUE="873">
    </OBJECT></DIV>
```

So if you are working with an ActiveX control that is giving you trouble modifying a property value, you can try using the text editor to manually modify that value. One thing I should warn you about: Some properties that are not recognized, or other text like comments that are manually typed in by you between the `<DIV>` and `</DIV>` tags will be removed by the ActiveX Control Pad the next time it reads in the ALX file.

Code Management

The Script Wizard gives you very good control over the editing environment within a Layout control. All of the event code for your controls can be written through the Script Wizard using the Select Event and Insert Actions tree views. You can even add non-event procedures and Global variables through the Script Wizard as well.

Figure 6.3 shows the pop-up menu that appears when right-clicking the Procedures node in the Insert Actions tree view. When selecting a New Procedure from this menu, the Script Wizard opens a Code window to that procedure with the default name of Sub Procedure1. In this situation a Function is desired instead of a subprocedure. Left-click the mouse button into the area where the procedure name is and edit the text there to say "Function NewColor." This function will be used to return a number representing a randomly generated color. It will be called by the ieTimer_Timer event to provide a little bit of animation.

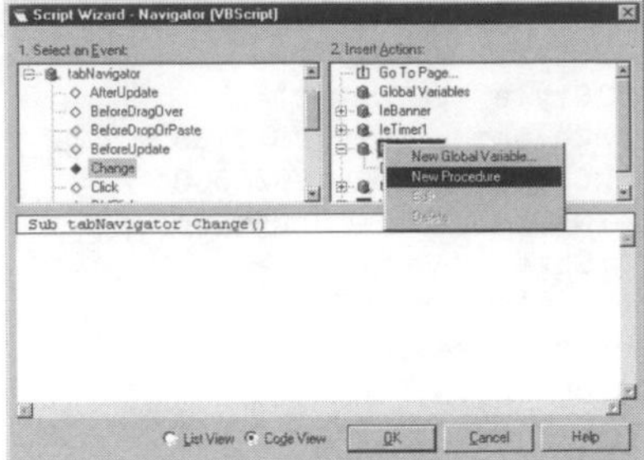

FIG. 6.3
Add code to the Change event of the tabNavigator tabstrip.

To add functionality to a control's event procedure, just select the correct event from a control node in the Select Event window of the Script Wizard. Figure 6.4 shows the tabNavigator_Change event selected and the appropriate code being added to the event.

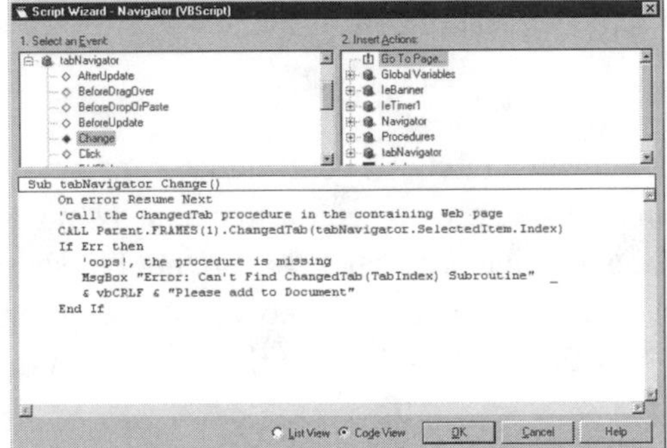

FIG. 6.4
Edit the code in a Procedure through the Script Wizard.

Let's get down to the code required to build this drop-in-place Navigator tool. Listing 6.4 includes three event procedures and one utility procedure. The utility procedure is a function that returns a randomly generated number. The ieTimer_Timer event calls a function that randomly generates a new number for the ieBanner label's text. The tabNavigator_Change event calls a ChangedTab procedure in the parent document.

Listing 6.4 NAVIGATOR.ALX—The VBScript Code within the HTML Layout Control for the Events and Methods of the Navigator.ALX Demo

```
<SCRIPT LANGUAGE="VBScript">
<!--
'====================================
'          Global Variables
'====================================
dim blnLoaded

'====================================
'          Event Procedures
'====================================
```

```
Sub Navigator_OnLoad()
     rem:'to prevent the double load
     rem:'bug use a global flag that
     rem:'indicates a prior pass through
     rem:'the OnLoad event.
     If blnLoaded Then

      Exit Sub
     Else
        'first time through
        blnLoaded = true
        'make sure the MyTabs value is numeric
        If IsNumeric(PARENT.FRAMES(1).MYTABS.Value) Then
            For lngTabCount = 1 To PARENT.FRAMES(1).MYTABS.Value
                call tabNavigator.Tabs.Add()
            Next
        Else
            MsgBox "ERROR: MyTabs hidden value not found or"  _
            & vbCRLF & " contains non-numeric value on parent"
       End If
       rem:'call the function that provides the names and locations
       rem:'of the navigator's tabs.
       rem:'if the procedure is missing then
       rem:'let the user know
       On Error resume next
       If Err then
           MsgBox "The NameTabs Procedure was not found on Parent"
       End If

    End If

end sub

Sub IeTimer1_Timer()
     if Navigator.tabNavigator.Tabs(0).Caption = "LoadTabs" then
       Parent.Frames(1).NameTabs
     End if
     rem:'get a randomly generated color for the text
     ieBanner.ForeColor = NewNumber(&HFFFFFF)
end sub

Sub tabNavigator_Change()
     rem:'call the action specified in the parent's ChangedTab procedure
     On Error Resume Next
     CALL Parent.FRAMES(1).ChangedTab(tabNavigator.SelectedItem.Index)
     if err then msgBox Err.Description
end sub

'===========================================
'          Utility Procedures
'===========================================
Function NewNumber(lngLimit)
          Dim lngNumber
          rem:'make sure that the argument
          rem:'is a numeric value
```

Part II Ch 6

continues

Listing 6.4 Continued

```
          If Not IsNumeric(lngLimit) Then
              lngNumber = &HFFFF
          Else
              lngNumber = lngLimit
          End If
          NewNumber = int(rnd * lngNumber) + 1
End Function

-->
</SCRIPT>
```

The Navigator_OnLoad event contains special code to deal with some vagaries of the relationship between a parent document and the ALX file. There are some very tricky timing issues involved with the Layout Control and the parent document's VBScript. In the case of this Navigator project I wanted to be able to have the parent document determine how many tabs would be needed, what those tabs' titles would be, and finally what would happen when those tabs where selected.

The problem here had to do with the way the VBScript would be parsed by Explorer. In order to have the parent document's VBScript recognize the Navigator Layout control I had to use the OnLoad ="InitALX" event in the VBScript of the parent document. This will cause the Navigator to get loaded before the VBScript is parsed thus avoiding parsing errors when the parser came upon references to the navigator. The caveat here was that none of the Parent Document's VBScript code could be run outside of a procedure or a parser error would occur anyway. So I had to have a way to invoke the parent document's VBScript code that would populate the tabstrip with data. The Navigator's OnLoad event did the trick. Since the ALX code apparently gets parsed while loading, and this particular event wouldn't occur until the Navigator was loaded, all the timing issues of the parser were resolved.

The OnLoad event of the Navigator called back to the parent document's VBScript procedure that loaded the tabstrip with the data. This problem is purely an initialization problem. Once the parent document has completed loading, the Navigator's data can be manipulated from other frames as needed.

Saving and Running

The Navigator Demo created here has a set of requirements in order to run. They are:

- A Hidden Control named MyTabs that specifies the initial number of tabs to display
- A Subroutine named "NameTabs()" that provides the Tab names and related URLS

- A Subroutine named "ChangedTab(MyTab)" that takes a numeric argument and acts upon the tab number provided to it by the Navigator
- The Navigator Demo must reside in Frame 1 of a three frame project.

You can modify the Navigator to have different requirements depending upon your needs but as it is presented here these are the things it needs to work. To build and test your Layout Controls you need to have one or more Web page documents to create the environment needed for your layout control project. In my case, here I needed three documents:

- *Chapt6_00.htm:* The document that creates the three frames
- *MyBanner.htm:* The document that creates a title at the top of the window
- *Chapt6_01.htm:* The document that contains the Navigator and related code

The code for Chapt6_00.htm includes the definition of three frames that have no borders and are not sizable. Listing 6.5 shows the code for this page. You won't find any rocket science there.

Listing 6.5 CHAPT6_00.HTM—The Layout HTML for the Required Frames

```
<HTML>
<HEAD>
<TITLE>MainFrame</TITLE>
</HEAD>
<BODY>
<FRAMESET ROWS="55,*" FRAMEBORDER=NO>
       <FRAME SRC="MyBanner.htm"
       NAME="MyBanner" SCROLLING=NO
       NORESIZE>
       <FRAMESET COLS="180,*">
            <FRAME SRC="Chapt5_01.HTM"
            NORESIZE
            SCROLLING=NO
            NAME="MCSMENU">
           <FRAME SRC="Blank.HTM" NAME="MCSMAIN">
      </FRAMESET>
</FRAMESET>
</BODY>
</HTML>
```

The next page is the MyBanner.htm. While not exactly relevant to the topic of this chapter I am including it to show some of the things you can do with VBScript. Listing 6.6 provides the code.

Listing 6.6 MYBANNER.HTM—A Fancy Banner to Fill Frame 0 in the Navigator Demo

```
<HTML>
<HEAD>
<TITLE>New Page</TITLE>

</HEAD>
<BODY BGCOLOR="navy" TopMargin=0>
<SCRIPT LANGUAGE="VBSCRIPT">
Dim strTitle
Dim lngCount
Dim lngColor
Dim lngRate
lngColor = &H0000FF
Dim strLetter
strTitle="VBScript: The HTML Layout Control"
lngRate= &H0001FF\hex(len(strTitle))
For lngCount = 1 to len(strTitle)
   strLetter = mid(strTitle, lngCount, 1)
   Document.Write "<SPAN STYLE=color:" & hex(lngColor) _
   & ";font-size=0.5in>" & strLetter & "</SPAN>"
    If lngColor > &H20 then
       lngColor= lngColor - lngRate
    Else
        lngColor =&H0000FF
    End If
Next
</SCRIPT>
</BODY>
</HTML>
```

And now we come to the actual page that contains the navigator. The first part of this page contains the page's layout information including the required hidden control mentioned above and the object declaration for the layout control. This is all in Listing 6.7.

Listing 6.7 CHAPT6_01.HTM—The Layout HTML Code for the Navigator Page

```
<HTML>
<HEAD>
<TITLE>Navigator Demo</TITLE>
</HEAD>
<BODY TOPMARGIN=0 LEFTMARGIN=0>
  <INPUT TYPE=HIDDEN VALUE="4" ID="MYTABS">
  <OBJECT ID="Navigator"
   CLASSID="CLSID:812AE312-8B8E-11CF-93C8-00AA00C08FDF">
    <PARAM NAME="ALXPATH" REF VALUE="Navigator.alx">
  </OBJECT>
```

As you can see, the Layout Control is declared like any other ActiveX object. The remaining code is VBScript Code that directly works with the Navigator Layout Control. The first procedure loads the navigator's TabStrip with titles for the tabs and puts a URL into the corresponding tab's ControlTipText property. Listing 6.8 shows that procedure.

Listing 6.8 CHAPT6_01.HTM—The Procedures for Setting Up and Responding to the Navigator Layout Control

```
<SCRIPT LANGUAGE="VBSCRIPT" OnLoad="initALX">
Sub NameTabs
       Navigator.tabNavigator.Tabs(0).Caption="HOME PAGE"
       Navigator.tabNavigator.tabs(0).controltiptext  _
        = "http://www.mcp.com/que"
       Navigator.tabNavigator.tabs(1).Caption = "Microsoft"
       Navigator.tabNavigator.tabs(1).controltiptext  _
       = "http://www.microsoft.com"
       Navigator.tabNavigator.tabs(2).Caption="Internet Explorer "
       Navigator.tabNavigator.tabs(2).controltiptext  _
       = "http://www.microsoft.com/ie"
       Navigator.tabNavigator.tabs(3).Caption="Avatar"
       Navigator.tabNavigator.tabs(3).controltiptext  _
       = "http://www.avatarmag.com/"
       Navigator.tabNavigator.tabs(4).Caption="MS Int. Dev."
       Navigator.tabNavigator.tabs(4).controltiptext  _
       = "http://www.microsoft.com/intdev/"
       Navigator.tabNavigator.tabs(5).Caption="Change Menu"
       Navigator.tabNavigator.tabs(5).controltiptext  _
       = "NewMenu.htm"
              ChangedTab 0
End sub
Sub ChangedTab( MyTab)
      Status = "Getting " & Navigator.tabNavigator.tabs(mytab).controltiptext
            PARENT.FRAMES(2).Navigate
Navigator.tabNavigator.tabs(mytab).controltiptext
End Sub
</SCRIPT>
</BODY>
</HTML>
```


With all of this in place, you can load the Chapt6_00.htm and start out with the window shown in Figure 6.5.

By clicking any of the tabs of the Navigator control you can cause the indicated Web page to be loaded into the main window of the frameset. Customizing this navigator during runtime is accomplished through the modification of the value in the MyTabs hidden value and the values in the NameTabs Sub procedure to match your location titles and URLs.

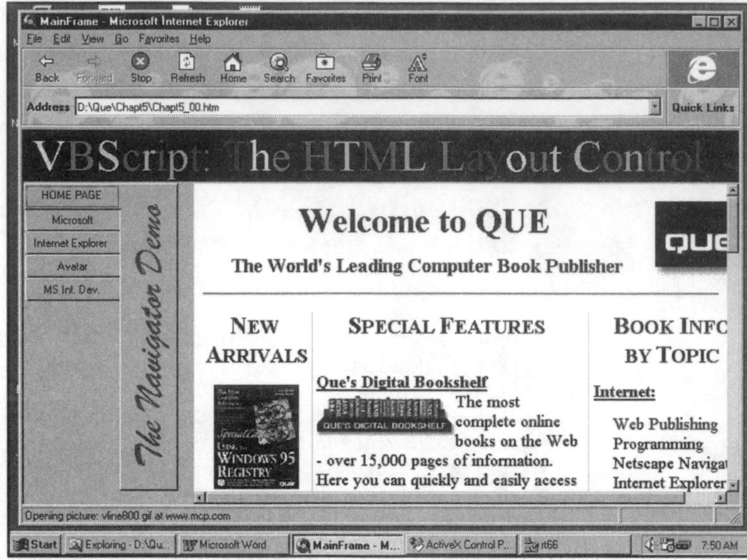

FIG. 6.5
Here's the Navigator Layout control in action.

From Here...

Try experimenting with the Navigator concept such as having pages that are loaded into the main frame dynamically change the Navigator's tabs and locations data.

For more information on developing with the Layout Control using the ActiveX control Pad see Chapter 3, "Introducing the ActiveX Control Pad."

CHAPTER 7

ActiveX Objects

by Michael Marchuk

If you haven't read Chapter 9, "An Introduction to Distributed Objects," you may want to go back and at least browse through the information contained there. This chapter will assume you have an understanding of the basics behind distributed application development that were covered in Chapter 9.

This chapter focuses on explaining the core ActiveX objects which are included with Microsoft's Internet Explorer 3.0. By understanding these components, you will be able to see how ActiveX objects can fit into your own distributed applications. By now you're probably eager to begin learning how specific ActiveX objects will be able to meet the needs of your interactive Web pages or distributed applications. ■

Describing the standard ActiveX

This chapter outlines and discusses the Active X objects included with Internet Explorer 3.0.

Installing and using ActiveX objects

ActiveX objects don't install the way other software does. You'll find out how to get ActiveX objects up and running on your system.

Finding ActiveX objects

Find out where to look for ActiveX objects to enhance your distributed applications.

An overview of ActiveX object development

ActiveX object development is not for the faint of heart, but you will find out the general method of how an ActiveX object is created.

Understanding ActiveX Objects

ActiveX objects will become much more real to you after you have read this section. Until now, the discussion of ActiveX objects has been conceptual. Now, you can be exposed to some of the real aspects of installing, using, and programming with ActiveX objects. As you read through the discussions of the various objects, let your mind wander to the Web pages that you have developed and to the applications which you've been waiting to move on to the Internet. These controls, and the many others which are currently available, will enable your plans for an interactive Internet application to become reality with VBScript.

Installing ActiveX Objects

Chapter 9 mentioned the concept of installing objects using a trust arrangement with a Certificate Authority (CA). Since the ActiveX controls are signed with a digital fingerprint that is verified by a CA, the users which download the objects will feel more confident about the distributed applications they are running. Additionally, you will feel better about the objects that you incorporate into your distributed applications, knowing that they are sealed with a tamper-evident digital signature.

You learn how to incorporate ActiveX objects into your Web pages later in Chapter 11, "Designing VBScript Applications," so for now, assume that you have successfully implemented the object within your HTML document. Since this is a distributed environment, the user who downloads your Web page may not already have the ActiveX component that you have used. In this case, the browser will have to retrieve and install the object before your application runs. Figure 7.1 shows a page which contains an object which is not available locally and must be downloaded. Note the status bar on the bottom of the Internet Explorer window which indicates that the objects are being installed locally.

After an ActiveX object has been downloaded from an archive, the object must be installed on the user's system. Recall that the digital signature which accompanies the object must be checked with the Certificate Authority which issued the signature. After the signature has been authenticated, the user is presented with a verification dialog like the one shown in Figure 7.2.

The user is allowed two options on the dialog box. The first option allows the user to place full trust in the software developer who wrote the object so that when another object by the same vendor is required, the browser will automatically trust the authenticated digital signature and install the software. The second option indicates that any object which is signed by this particular Certificate Authority will be trusted, no matter who the vendor is.

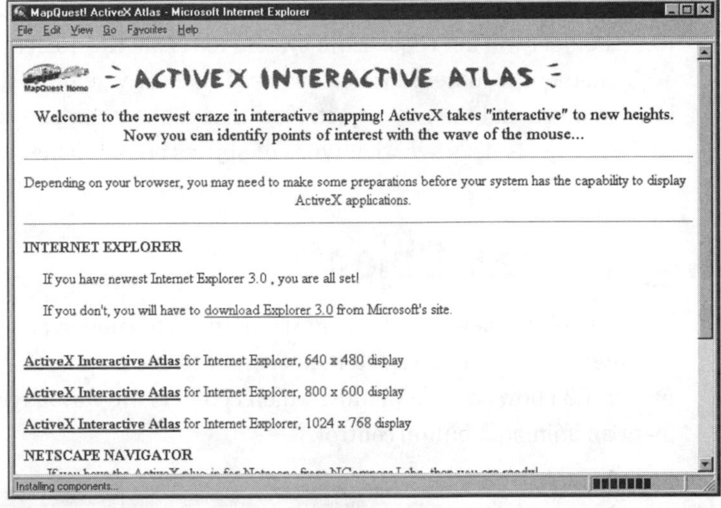

FIG. 7.1
ActiveX objects must be available locally to be used by a distributed application or interactive Web page.

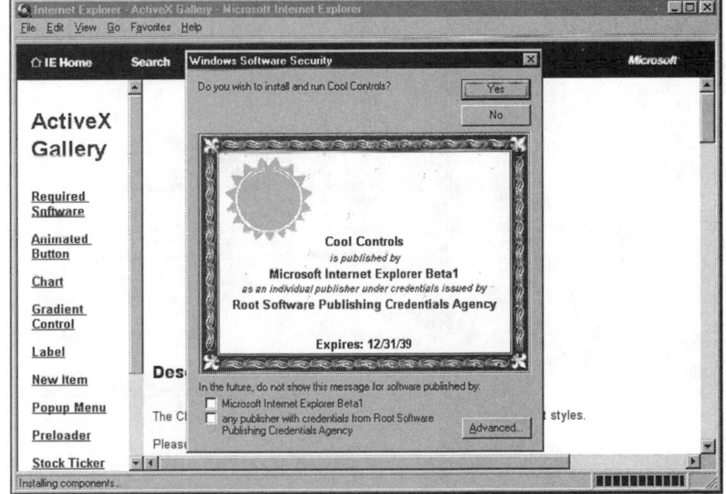

FIG. 7.2
ActiveX object installation requires the user to accept the validated digital signature from the Certificate Authority that issued it.

CAUTION

You will have to decide how much trust to place on the various vendors and Certificate Authorities before you answer these questions. It may be wise to leave the automatic acceptance selections unchecked until you feel more comfortable about the vendor or the Certificate Authority.

After an object has been successfully installed on the user's system, any future references to that object will not require the system to reload the object from an archive. If a future Web page is encountered which requires a newer version of the object, the browser will have to download the new object. Now that you've been exposed to the installation of ActiveX objects, let's see what types of objects are available.

Using ActiveX Objects

The ActiveX framework allows an HTML page to contain an OBJECT identifier tag that specifies the various parameters necessary to use a particular object. For example, Figure 7.3 shows a code window which contains the various pieces required to implement an animated button control.

FIG. 7.3
ActiveX objects can be added to an HTML page using simple code that describes the operation of the object.

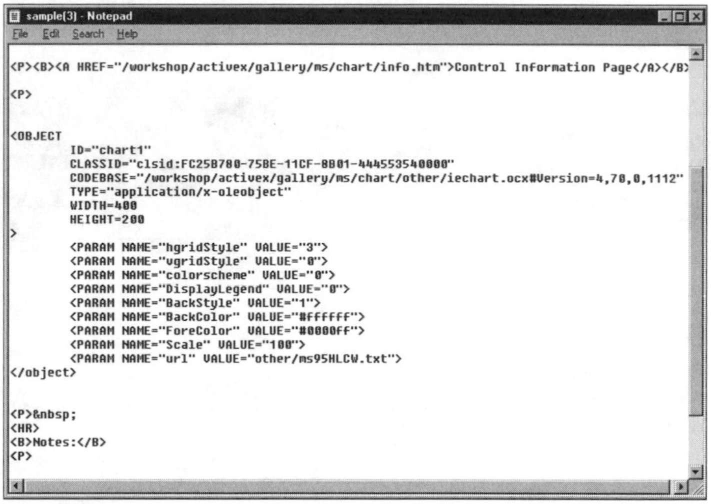

sample(3) - Notepad

File Edit Search Help

```
<P><B><A HREF="/workshop/activex/gallery/ms/chart/info.htm">Control Information Page</A></B>

<P>

<OBJECT
        ID="chart1"
        CLASSID="clsid:FC25B780-75BE-11CF-8B01-444553540000"
        CODEBASE="/workshop/activex/gallery/ms/chart/other/iechart.ocx#Version=4,70,0,1112"
        TYPE="application/x-oleobject"
        WIDTH=400
        HEIGHT=200
>
        <PARAM NAME="hgridStyle" VALUE="3">
        <PARAM NAME="vgridStyle" VALUE="0">
        <PARAM NAME="colorscheme" VALUE="0">
        <PARAM NAME="DisplayLegend" VALUE="0">
        <PARAM NAME="BackStyle" VALUE="1">
        <PARAM NAME="BackColor" VALUE="#ffffff">
        <PARAM NAME="ForeColor" VALUE="#0000ff">
        <PARAM NAME="Scale" VALUE="100">
        <PARAM NAME="url" VALUE="other/ms95HLCW.txt">
</object>


<P> 
<HR>
<B>Notes:</B>
<P>
```

As a VBScript developer, you can add any number of ActiveX components to your HTML page to create the environment you need. The OBJECT tag indicates that the information contained within the brackets pertains to a particular object. The information contained within this OBJECT tag will be provided to you by the ActiveX vendor that supplied the component. Typically, a vendor-supplied component would be installed on your system using a standard setup application under Windows. A component can be supplied on a floppy or downloaded from a vendor's Internet server. Once that component has been installed, you need to make the runtime version of that component (if it is different than the developer's version) available on your Web server for others to download when they use your distributed application.

The ActiveX properties are assigned using the PARAM tags. Each PARAM tag has a NAME and a VALUE which identify which property is being set and to what value. For example, if a particular ActiveX control included a property for changing the size of the font on the control, you might include a line like the one in the following example.

```
<PARAM NAME="FontSize" VALUE="12">
```

Since some ActiveX controls will have more properties than others you may add as many PARAM tags as necessary. Most controls will assume a default value if you do not specify a particular property value using the PARAM tag. While this is not bad, it may produce unwanted results. You might be better off explicitly setting each property value to ensure that your application runs and looks the way you want it to.

Now that you've seen how the ActiveX controls are added into your HTML pages, let's take a look at some of the default ActiveX controls which the Internet Explorer 3.0 uses.

Animated Button Object

Windows software has been using animated buttons for years. Animated buttons are button controls which allow a series of images to be repeated on top of a button either continuously or when the button changes states. For example, you may have a Web page which includes a search function for your Web site. The animated button you use could have a rotating magnifying glass which scans over pages flying by when the button is pushed.

Animated buttons require a certain flair for creativity and graphical art talent, but then you probably already have some of that in you if you've been designing HTML pages. The animated button control provides five events that activate the various animations associated with you control. These events are:

- ButtonEvent_Click
- ButtonEvent_DblClick
- ButtonEvent_Focus
- ButtonEvent_Enter
- ButtonEvent_Leave

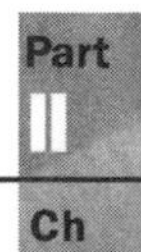

Additionally, you may obtain various properties from the button control. Notice that the properties correspond closely to the events listed above. The properties are:

- *URL:* Specifies the location of the AVI file to display
- *DefaultFrStart:* Specifies the starting frame in the default state
- *DefaultFrEnd:* Specifies the ending from in the default state

- *MouseoverFrStart:* Specifies the starting frame in the mouseover state
- *MouseoverFrEnd:* Specifies the ending from in the mouseover state
- *FocusFrStart:* Specifies the starting frame in the focus state
- *FocusFrEnd:* Specifies the ending from in the focus state
- *DownFrStart:* Specifies the starting frame in the down state
- *DownFrEnd:* Specifies the ending from in the down state

The animated button has four states. These states are:

- *Default:* No other events are occurring
- *Down:* The button is pressed
- *Focus:* The button control has the focus
- *Mouseover:* The mouse cursor is currently over the button control

NOTE While a button may actually be in multiple states at once, like when the button has the focus and the mouse cursor moves over the button, only one event will trigger at a time. To handle these types of conditions, there are certain states that take precedence over other states. For example, the Mouseover event will trigger when the button has focus. The Down event will trigger even if the button has focus and the mouse cursor is over the control.

Chart Object

Creating colorful charts is easily accomplished using the chart control object. The chart control supports seven basic types of charts:

- Area chart
- Bar chart
- Column chart
- Line chart
- Pie chart
- Point chart
- Stocks chart

Each of these chart types supports properties (see Table 7.1) that allow you to control the number of rows and columns, grid lines, color schemes, transparency of the background, the scale of the chart, and whether a legend should be included. Additionally, each of the basic chart types may support variations such as simple, stacked, or full. Figure 7.4 shows an example of a chart created by this object.

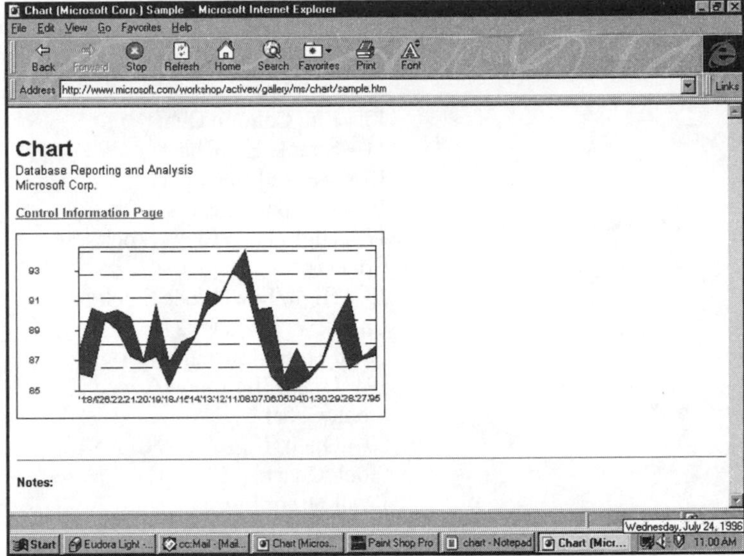

FIG. 7.4
The chart object can create great-looking charts with little effort.

Table 7.1 Chart Object Properties

Property	Value Description	Example
Columns, Rows	Specifies the number of columns or rows in the data set.	<PARAM NAME="COLUMNS" VALUE="2"> <PARAM NAME="ROWS" VALUE="18">
ChartType	Specifies which style of chart to create using the data set provided. The values for ChartType are: 0 = Simple Pie Chart 1 = Pie with wedge out 2 = Simple Point Chart 3 = Stacked Point Chart 4 = Full Point Chart 5 = Simple Line Chart 6 = Stacked Line Chart 7 = Full Line Chart 8 = Simple Area Chart 9 = Stacked Area Chart 10 = Full Area Chart 11 = Simple Column Chart 12 = Stacked Column Chart	<PARAM NAME="CHARTTYPE" VALUE="3">

continues

Table 7.1 Continued

Property	Value Description	Example
	13 = Full Column Chart 14 = Simple Bar Chart 15 = Stacked Bar Chart 16 = Full Bar Chart 17 = High/Low/Close Stock Chart 18 = High/Low/Close Stock Chart (Wall Street Journal style) 19 = Open/High/Low/Close Stock Chart 20 = Open/High/Low/Close Stock Chart (Wall Street Journal style)	
ColorScheme	Specifies which of three predefined color sets to use when creating the chart.	<PARAM NAME="COLORSCHEME" VALUE="2"
ColumnIndex, RowIndex, DataItem	Used together to specify a particular data cell within the data set. The example for these properties shows how the value for the data cell at column 2, and row 3, is set to the value of 8.	<PARAM NAME="COLUMNINDEX" VALUE="2"> <PARAM NAME="ROWINDEX" VALUE="3"> <PARAM NAME="DATAITEM" VALUE="8">
ColumnName, RowName	Used for displaying legends. These properties also require the ColumnIndex or RowIndex properties to be set when assigning a value. The example for these properties shows column 2 being assigned the name "February".	<PARAM NAME="COLUMNINDEX" VALUE="2"> <PARAM NAME="COLUMNNAME" VALUE="February">
DisplayLegend	This property specifies whether or not a legend is displayed for the chart. The values are: 0 = Do not display legend 1 = Display legend	<PARAM NAME="DISPLAYLEGEND" VALUE="1">
Scale	The Scale property size indicates the relative	<PARAM NAME="SCALE" VALUE="80">

Property	Value Description	Example
	percentage to which the chart is to be scaled when it is displayed. The default value is "100", which means that the chart will not be re-scaled. Values between 1 and 100 are valid. The example for this property will scale the chart to 80% of its default.	
HorizontalGrid, VerticalGrid	These properties will specify whether or not a horizontal or vertical grid pattern will be shown on the chart that is created. The values for these properties are: 0 = No grid is shown 1 = Display grid	<PARAM NAME="HORIZONTALGRID" VALUE="1">
BackStyle	Specifies whether the chart background is transparent. The values are: 0 = Transparent 1 = Opaque	<PARAM NAME="BACKSTYLE" VALUE="1">
GridPlacement	Specifies how the grid lines are to be drawn on the chart. The values are: 0 = Grid lines are drawn behind the chart 1 = Grid line are drawn over the chart	<PARAM NAME="GRIDPLACEMENT" VALUE="0">

Gradient Control Object

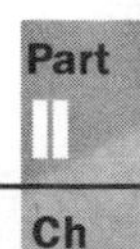

The gradient control object allows an area to be filled with a color which transitions to another color across the area. For example, the installation screens for most Windows applications use a blue to black gradient as a backdrop. The gradient control has few properties (see Table 7.2) that are needed to create this effect. Figure 7.5 shows an example of the gradient object.

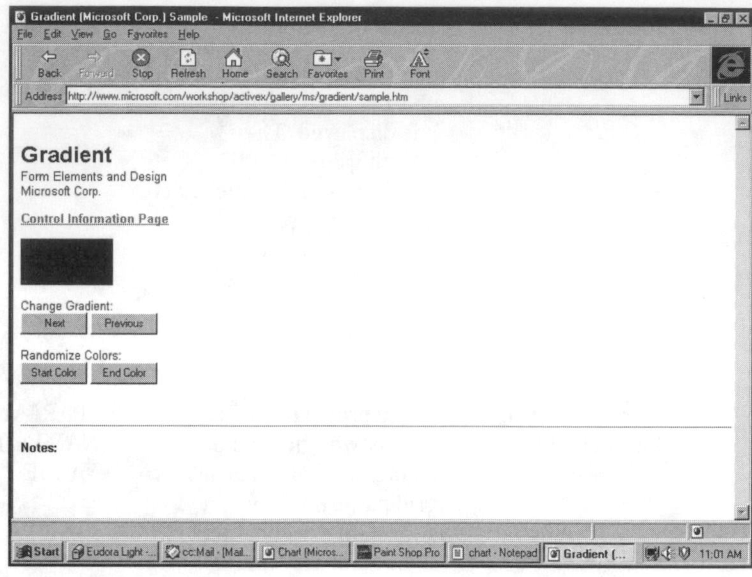

FIG. 7.5 The gradient object can be used to create interesting effects.

Table 7.2 Gradient Control Object Properties

Property	Value Description	Example
StartColor, EndColor	Define the two colors which will be used in the transition. Note that the color is defined by using the standard hexadecimal HTML color codes.	<PARAM NAME="STARTCOLOR" VALUE="#FFFFFF">
StartPoint, EndPoint	Define the coordinates (x,y) within the HTML page which will be filled using the specified gradient.	<PARAM NAME="STARTPOINT" VALUE="25,25"> <PARAM NAME="ENDPOINT" VALUE="575,75">
Direction	Defines the gradient effect which will be used with the colors specified. The values are: 0 = Horizontal (start at left) 1 = Vertical (start at top) 2 = Towards center 3 = Towards corner 4 = Diagonal down (start at left)	<PARAM NAME="DIRECTION" VALUE="1">

Property	Value Description	Example
	5 = Diagonal up (start at left) 6 = Around the "StartPoint" coordinate 7 = Across the line between "StartPoint" and "EndPoint"	

Label Object

The label object allows text to be displayed at an angle on the page using a particular font, color, and style. You may wonder why you would want to use a label rather than just a standard HTML tag such as `<FONTSIZE = 7>`. The power of the label object comes from two factors: the ability to rotate the text to any angle, and the ability to use the events triggered by the control. The label object supports several events including:

- Click
- Change
- MouseDown
- MouseOver
- MouseUp

These events will give you the freedom to create interactive text which may spin or change colors as the user moves the mouse over the label's text. Figure 7.6 shows how this object can be used. Table 7.3 lists the properties for this object.

Table 7.3 Label Object Properties

Property	Value Description	Example
Angle	Specifies the angle, in counter-clockwise degrees, to which the text should be rotated.	<PARAM NAME="ANGLE" VALUE="90">
Alignment	Controls how the text is aligned within the boundaries of the control. The values are: 0 = Align to top-left 1 = Center to top 2 = Align to top-right 3 = Align to middle-left	<PARAM NAME="ALIGNMENT" VALUE="4">

continues

Table 7.3 Continued

Property	Value Description	Example
	4 = Centered horizontally and vertically 5 = Align to middle-right 6 = Align to bottom-left 7 = Center to bottom 8 = Align to bottom-right	
BackStyle	Specifies whether or not the text's background is transparent. The values are: 0 = Transparent 1 = Opaque	<PARAM NAME="BACKSTYLE" VALUE="0">
Caption	Specifies the text that the label control will display.	<PARAM NAME="CAPTION" VALUE="Welcome!">
FontName	Specifies the name of a TrueType font which will be used when the text is displayed.	<PARAM NAME="FONTNAME" VALUE="Arial">
FontSize	Determines the size (in picas) of the text to be displayed. Note that this is different from the HTML tag which uses arbitrary font sizes.	<PARAM NAME="FONTSIZE" VALUE="12"> <FONTSIZE>
FontItalic, FontBold, FontUnderline, FontStrikeout	Specify whether the font has the characteristics of italics or bolding.The values are: 0 = Turn off effect 1 = Turn on effect	<PARAM NAME="FONTBOLD" VALUE="1">
Mode		<PARAM NAME="MODE" VALUE="1">
TopPoints, TopXY, TopIndex, BotPoints, BotXY, BotIndex	Allow the text to be skewed and stretched along a top and bottom line. You may want to experiment with these properties to see how they can be used to create some very interesting text displays. The basic usage is to define a number of transition points across the top and assign this value to the TopPoints property.	<PARAM NAME="TOPPOINTS" VALUE="2"> <PARAM NAME="TOPINDEX" VALUE="1"> <PARAM NAME="TOPXY" VALUE="0,0">

Property	Value Description	Example
	Then for each point, assign the TopIndex value and a TopXY coordinate. Do the same for each bottom line point and assign these values to the BotPoints, BotIndex, and BotXY values. The lines on the top and bottom will then serve as guides when the text is rendered.	

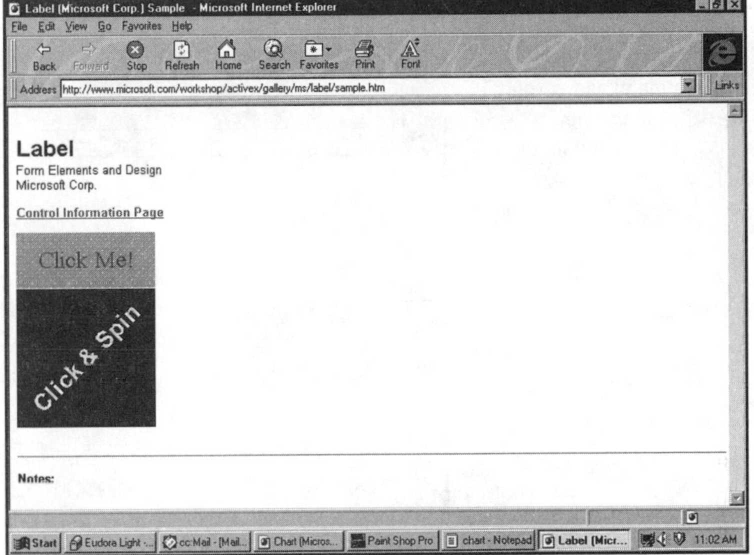

FIG. 7.6 The label object gives you more freedom when placing text on an HTML page.

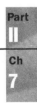

New Item Object

There may be times when you want to highlight new items on a particular HTML page. The New Item object handles this by displaying an image until a particular date. After that date, another image may be shown, if desired. Table 7.4 outlines the properties available from the new item object.

You most commonly use this object when you add headlines or sections to an HTML to which you would like to draw attention when they've been added. The date parameter also allows you to manage when the added item is no longer considered new.

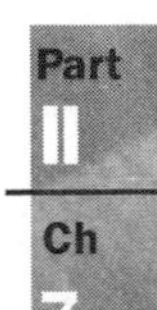

Table 7.4 New Item Object Properties

Property	Value	Example
Date	Specifies the date until which the specified graphic will be shown.	<PARAM NAME=“DATE” VALUE=“10/31/96”>
Image	Specifies the URL to which the image will be displayed.	<PARAM NAME=“IMAGE” VALUE=“http://www.xyz.com/images/new.gif”>

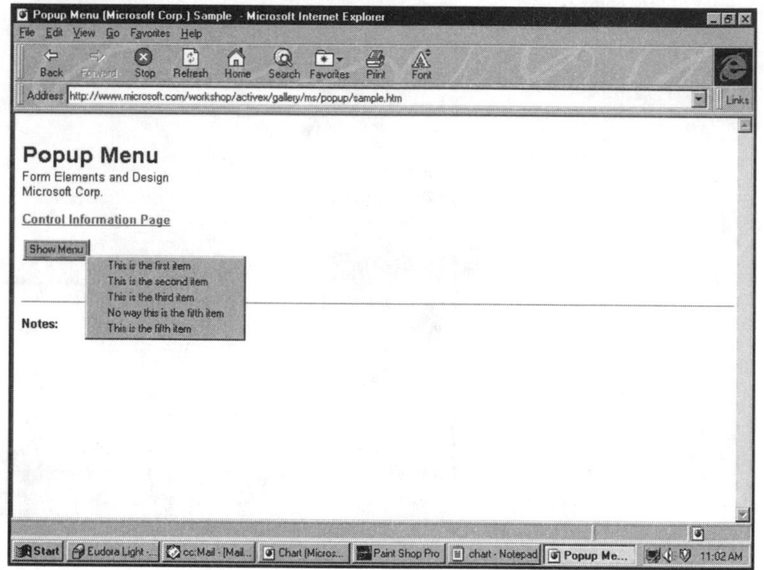

FIG. 7.7
The popup menu allows your HTML pages to use new means of gathering data or linking to other pages.

Popup Menu Object

You may have a need to use a popup menu within your distributed application. The Popup Menu object allows your HTML page to contain an image or button which causes the menu to appear. The items on the menu are created when the object is loaded. The menu items themselves are activated when the user clicks on the menu item (see fig. 7.7). This action fires the IEPop_Click() subroutine and passes the items list index value. The only property for the popup menu object is listed in Table 7.5. Note that the property may be repeated for multiple items.

Table 7.5 Popup Menu Object Property

Property	Value	Example
Menuitem[]	Specifies the item in the popup menu array.	<PARAM NAME="MENUITEM[1]" VALUE="First Item"> <PARAM NAME="MENUITEM[2]" VALUE="Second Item">

Preloader Object

Your application may make use of some performance enhancements through the preloader object. This object will begin downloading pages in the background while a user is still reading the current page. By doing so, the user will experience a much faster load of the next page since the images and text will already be loaded into the browser's cache directory.

It is possible to overuse the preloader object and download everything at once. This is an unnecessary waste of bandwidth and disk storage since the user may not go to the next page. However, you may have a set of Web pages that would benefit from the preloader object. The properties for the preloader object are shown in Table 7.6.

Table 7.6 Preloader Object Properties

Property	Value Description	Example
CacheFile	The name of the local file contained in the browser's cache. This property is read-only.	(within VBScript) CacheFileName= ieprld.CacheFile
Data	The contents of the file which was read in. This property is read-only.	(within VBScript) DataDownloaded=ieprld.Data
Enable	This property switches the control on and off: 0 = Disabled 1 = Enabled	<PARAM NAME="ENABLE" VALUE="1">
URL	This property specifies which file to download when the control is enabled.	<PARAM NAME="URL" VALUE="http:// www.xyz.com/pricing.html">

Stock Ticker Object

Your distributed application may call for a constant display of information at the bottom of the screen or within a frame. The stock ticker object can handle this sort of constant update display by downloading an XRT file which handles real-time data. The stock ticker object scrolls the data from right to left as it is loaded. The file which is loaded is refreshed using a periodic interval. The file format of the data follows the XRT format. This format is as follows:

```
XRT file format
XRT
DataName1<TAB>DataValue1<TAB>DataValue2...<CR><LF>
DataName2<TAB>DataValue1<TAB>DataValue2...<CR><LF>
```

The XRT file contains data records which use a tab character to separate the data within the record. The data record may include any number of data values separated by tabs. The record is terminated by a carriage return and a line feed character. For example, an XRT file which contains sports scores might look like this:

```
XRT
Cubs/Mets<TAB>10<TAB>3<TAB>Bottom of Ninth<CR><LF>
Sox/Expos<TAB>5<TAB>2<TAB>Top of Third<CR><LF>
```

An XRT file can contain as many data elements as necessary, but the display of this data is limited to the stock ticker format. The properties of the stock ticker object are shown in Table 7.7.

Table 7.7 Stock Ticker Object Properties

Property	Value Description	Example
BackColor, ForeColor	These properties specify the color scheme for the background and the foreground. The colors are indicated using the standard HTML color coding.	<PARAM NAME= "BACKCOLOR" VALUE="#FFFFFF">
DataObjectName	Indicates the data source. This can be a URL or an OLE object that generates the XRT data stream.	<PARAM NAME= "DATAOBJECTNAME" VALUE="http:// www.xyz.com/ RealTime/Baseball/ ALWest.XRT">
DataObjectActive	This property is used to toggle the data refreshing.	<PARAM NAME= "DATAOBJECTACTIVE" VALUE="1">

Property	Value Description	Example
	0 = Data source is inactive 1 = Data source is active	
ScrollWidth	Specifies how much data is scrolled during each scroll interval.	<PARAM NAME= "SCROLLWIDTH" VALUE="10">
ScrollSpeed	Specifies the interval (in seconds) in which the display is scrolled.	<PARAM NAME= "ScrollSpeed" VALUE="1">
ReloadInterval	Specifies the interval (in seconds) between the XRT file reloading. This interval is also used to refresh the data stream from an OLE server which is providing the data.	<PARAM NAME= "RELOADINTERVAL" VALUE="10">
OffsetValues	Specifies that the data element will be offset from the name element by the indicated number of vertical pixels. This gives the appearance of superscript or subscript text.	<PARAM NAME= "OFFSETVALUES" VALUE="-20">

Timer Object

The timer object will enable your distributed application or HTML page to animate text, change colors of objects, or trigger some other event at a periodic interval. The timer control has only a few properties and one event. The properties for the timer object are shown in Table 7.8.

Table 7.8 Timer Object Properties

Property	Value	Example
Enabled	The timer control object can be enabled or disabled by setting this property to the following values:	<PARAM NAME="ENABLED" VALUE="TRUE">

continues

Table 7.8 Continued

Property	Value	Example
	True = Timer enabled False = Timer disabled	
Interval	This property specifies the interval (in milliseconds) between event triggers. When set to zero or a negative number the timer will act as though it was in a disabled state.	<PARAM NAME="INTERVAL" VALUE="1000">

Other Available ActiveX Objects

Many more ActiveX controls are available which can provide the display or processing power which you desire in your distributed application. Currently, Microsoft is maintaining a list of the vendors which are producing ActiveX controls. This list can be found at **http://www.microsoft.com/activex/controls/**.

Developing ActiveX Objects

The ActiveX software development kit is currently available only for the Visual C++ environment; however, Microsoft has mentioned that a Visual Basic environment is in the works. This will provide the ability of creating your own ActiveX components to be used on your own or others HTML pages.

Developing ActiveX components is beyond the scope of this book, but it should be mentioned that the process and tools for these components are evolving quickly. By the time this book is published, some of the more difficult development tasks surrounding ActiveX object development may be automated by the advancing tools used to create them. But for now, the development of ActiveX objects requires a relatively involved development environment including Microsoft's Visual C++.

ON THE WEB

http://www.microsoft.com/intdev/sdk/ For more information on developing ActiveX objects, see Microsoft's Web site.

From Here...

Now that you've had a taste of the ActiveX controls you can use, you're probably ready to start trying them out in some sample VBScript enabled pages. Check out the following chapters to see how these controls are used within VBScript:

- Chapter 11, "Designing VBScript Applications," guides you through the process of properly designing distributed applications using VBScript.
- Chapter 12, "A Simple VBScript Page," presents a simple example of how to put it all together and produce a functional VBScript page.
- Chapter 18, "VBScript Event Programming," teaches you about event programming and the how-to's of using VBScript events.
- Chapter 19, "VBScript Procedures," focuses on defining subroutines and functions for use in your distributed applications.

CHAPTER 8

Security

by William R. Beem

The concept of Internet security is almost an oxymoron. The purpose behind the Internet is to provide an open communication platform among a cooperative collection of users. The Internet's designers' main purpose was not to protect or conceal information, but rather to publish and share it. No regulating body or government has absolute control over who can access the Internet. Anyone can enter it as a user or provider. Any computer attached to the Internet is almost an open invitation for visitors to peek inside.

This model of universal, unrestricted access served Internet users well for many years. The fairly recent commercialization of the Internet brings forth an entirely new set of users with different objectives, concerns, and strategies. Their entry also brings forth a heightened sense of overcrowding, and with it, a need for privacy. The increasing number of personal computer users brings, unfortunately, increasing occurrences of computer crime. Given this increase of criminal activity, it's only natural that commercial entities on the Internet want to protect their assets.

What types of security are available on the Internet

Use different types of security to protect your information assets.

How encryption protects documents and files

Using encryption is like putting your data in a sealed envelope with a heavy-duty lock. Discover how protection works and why you should use it.

Why security is essential to electronic commerce

Nobody wants to send unprotected money across a public network. Learn why security and commerce go hand in hand.

The difference between security specifications and their implementations

The Internet abounds with specifications for various topics, and security is no different. As with many other things in life, the difference between theory and practice isn't always what you expect.

What security proposals are forthcoming on the Internet

More security techniques will appear in the future. The increasing amount of financial traffic and commerce on the Internet will continually demand protection. Learn about it before it happens.

These users see the Internet as a place to gather and exchange information, and also as a new way to purchase products and services. By using current Internet technology, a company can provide information about its specific products to any consumer at any time. Current credit card transaction technology makes it possible for users to send their credit card numbers over the Internet and receive their purchase almost immediately. Attracted by advertising and the ease of buying items with a credit card, consumers are easily lured into making immediate, impulsive purchases. The immediacy of electronic communication thus becomes a strong enticement to buy a product now! Some software publishers are already using this technology to sell and distribute their products and upgrades. Others will surely follow the trend and create a new distribution channel.

Though it sounds nice, this online marketplace has the same dangers as the real world. A criminal who knows that you have money will feel compelled to relieve you of its burden. Consider this scenario. The mechanism that sends your money to a vendor is like a robot. It knows that its job is to carry an amount of money from your account to a vendor. It's feasible for a criminal to create a robot of his own that either disguises itself to look like the vendor, or just plain beats up your robot. Either way, it takes your money. ■

Why Bother with Security?

Commerce is fast becoming the driving force for Internet programmers and Web page designers. Organizations interested in protecting their assets hire programmers who understand the needs of commercial enterprises and how to protect them with security techniques. As a VBScript programmer, make sure you understand this concept. Your purpose is to serve the motivating interests of your employer. Most likely, that interest is commerce. Show your employers, or prospective employers, that you know how to conduct business in a safe and secure manner.

Suppose that a computer vendor posts a Web page that enables consumers to custom tailor their new computers with specific peripherals, software, and other accessories. To a customer, this idea is intriguing. Now, add security to the Web page and the concept changes from intriguing to a viable incentive for the customer to place an immediate order with a credit card transaction. Adding security helps assuage a customer's fears of some unscrupulous person stealing a credit card number as it travels across the Internet. By eliminating the customer's fear of compromising credit card security, you help the vendor establish an impulse buying center for a several thousand dollar computer system. As this concept becomes more accepted in online commerce, the number of vendors seeking developers capable of implementing secure transactions will rise.

Two types of people have an interest in Internet security: those who must protect information and those who want to get it. You can probably learn more valid security information from the criminal hackers than from security professionals. After all, the hacker likes to disseminate information, whereas the security professionals prefer to conceal information. Keep this in mind when browsing the Internet for additional information about security. This chapter provides information on the prevalent Internet security topics in action today, and those in the design stages for tomorrow.

Transaction Security

A *transaction* is the process of conducting business. In most cases, such a transaction involves moving something of importance from one location to another. The amount of security that you choose depends on how much value is attached to the items involved in the transaction. If you're sending a message to someone else, the value that you place on the message determines whether you send an open postcard, a letter in a sealed envelope, or perhaps a package with a dedicated courier service. The degree and type of transaction security that you use for sending data over the Internet is much the same as sending a letter.

Most electronic mail (e-mail) is much like a postcard. It travels from one location to the next, stopping at various points along the path. Any network administrator could read your message without any resistance or any way for you to detect that it is being read. Should such indiscriminate access to data be unacceptable to you or those to whom you send the data, you might find yourself in need of transaction security.

Before deciding on a method of transaction security, it helps to define the elements necessary to secure a transaction. The following list may help you decide what's best for your situation:

- *Transactions must remain confidential*

  Your transaction should remain private and unavailable to others as it travels the Internet. Encryption is the best way to ensure that your transactions remain confidential.

- *The transaction must retain integrity*

  This means that your transaction arrives in the same state that you sent it. Nothing along the path should alter or affect the contents of your transaction. If you send $10 in a financial transaction, you don't want it to arrive with a zero cash balance. Encryption helps retain integrity. Installing some form of authentication, such as a checksum or digital signature, is also wise.

- *Both the sender and receiver must be accountable*

  Both parties should agree on the transaction and offer some form of acknowledgment when sending or receiving the transaction.

- *Both parties must be authenticated*

  Some communication protocols use a series of Acknowledgment and Negative Acknowledgment codes to communicate the status of a transaction. The codes verify whether the transaction made it in one piece, but don't verify that the right person is sending or receiving the transaction. Authentication ensures that each party is who they say they are.

The following sections in this chapter discuss how encryption technology helps you achieve these goals in your own applications.

Encryption

Encryption is the process of transforming a message so that only the intended receiver can restore the message to its original, readable form. A random pattern can easily scramble a message. However, the problem with random patterns is that because of the unpredictable nature of the scrambling process, nobody, not even the message's originator, knows how to unscramble the message so that the receiver can use it again. A valid scheme must use a regular pattern to encrypt the message so that the receiver can decrypt it. However, such a scheme must retain some secrecy so that others cannot decrypt the message.

Regular encryption patterns are called *keys.* The size and type of a key determines how difficult it is for someone to crack the encryption code and reassemble the message. Keys are bit codes. A computer can easily perform a repetitive search until it finds the correct key to decode the encrypted message. The longer the bit code, the more difficult and time-consuming it is to crack it. The shorter the bit code, the easier it is to crack, especially with the assistance of modern computer technology. Many Internet servers use only 40-bit keys that, although difficult to decipher, are still vulnerable to decoding. A larger bit code increases the number of possible bit combinations and therefore greatly diminishes the likelihood of unauthorized access. Some products use a 128-bit key to make unauthorized decryption practically impossible.

NOTE To calculate the number of possible bit combinations in a given set of bits, raise 2 to a power *X*, where *X* is the number of bits in the set. For example, a 2-bit set has four possible combinations because $2^2 = 4$. The possible combinations are (in binary notation) `00 01 10 11`. An 8-bit set has 256 possible combinations because $2^8 = 256$. A 40-bit set has 1,099,511,627,776 possible combinations because $2^{40} = 1,099,511,627,776$.

CAUTION

The United States government considers encryption schemes to be a form of munitions. Therefore, the exporting of encryption-capable applications falls under heavy scrutiny. The government allows as much as 40-bit key encryption for export. Any key using an encryption over a 40-bit code must remain within the United States. Violation of this policy is subject to criminal penalty.

There are two types of keys: symmetric and asymmetric. A *symmetric key* is one in which the sender and receiver use the same key to encrypt and decrypt a message. Using only a single key is the major weakness of symmetric key encryption schemes. In a symmetric key encryption scheme, the key code must travel unencrypted so that the receiver can use it to decrypt the message. If an attacker gets this key code, he can decrypt your messages, regardless of how many bits you have used to encrypt them.

The United States government defined and endorses the Data Encryption Standard (DES), which is a symmetric, secret-key encryption scheme. Both the sender and receiver must know the same secret key code to encrypt and decrypt messages with DES. The DES standard operates on 64-bit blocks with a 56-bit key. DES operates rather quickly and works well for encrypting large data sets. So far, no one has ever broken into a DES-encrypted file, although many researchers have tried. A pair of researchers proposed a theory that could break the DES encryption scheme, but they still consider DES a secure standard due to the resources and time required to crack a DES-encrypted file. One of these researchers, Adi Shamir, is also one of the creators of the RSA public-key encryption system. The section "RSA Encryption," later in this chapter, covers that encryption system.

Asymmetric key encryption schemes use a public and a private key. Anyone who wants to receive an encrypted message must have both keys. The receiver provides the public key, and the sender then uses it to encrypt the message. The only way to decrypt the message is with a combination of the receiver's public and private key. Even the sender can't decrypt the message, because the sender doesn't know the receiver's private key. Asymmetric encryption schemes soon turn into a web of public keys. In small groups, this process is reasonable, but it becomes unmanageable in large environments with many users.

Imagine you're in a group with five users. Each has a public key. To exchange encrypted documents, you need to have the public key of every user. That draws a line from you to user 1, another to user 2, and so on. Now, each of those other users has exactly the same situation, drawing lines from themselves to other users. One user ends up holding multiple keys, and must know which one to use when sending an encrypted document to someone else. Now, multiply that by a 5,000 user corporation and imagine the chaos.

Secure Electronic Transactions

If you have any doubt that electronic commerce drives the need for Internet security, this section should open your eyes. The Secure Electronic Transactions (SET) protocol is a combined development—including Visa, MasterCard, Netscape Communications, IBM, VeriSign, SAIC, Terisa Systems, GTE, and Microsoft—that provides a method to secure bankcard transactions over open networks such as the Internet. Previously, these organizations were working on separate technologies to perform the same basic task. You may find old references to Secure Transaction Technology (STT) or Secure Electronic Payment Protocol. Many of the overview details seem similar, but the implementations varied. Fortunately, for both developers and consumers, these groups decided to pool their talents to create a single technology designed to secure transactions conducted on public networks.

NOTE Visa and Microsoft developed STT as an open specification for the industry. Meanwhile, MasterCard, IBM, and others worked on another open specification for the industry: Secure Electronic Payment Protocol (SEPP).

On February 1, 1996, MasterCard International and Visa International joined together to announce a technical standard for safeguarding payment-card purchases made over the Internet. They call the new specification Secure Electronic Transactions (SET), which combines both efforts. ■

Earlier sections of this chapter discussed the growing trend of electronic commerce and the need for secure financial transactions. Breaking into an encrypted file is a daunting task, and people always take the path of least resistance. Cracking an encrypted transaction is the modern equivalent of blowing up the bank to steal its money. To say the least, it's not subtle. A criminal must decide if the contents are worth the effort. If the prize inside an encrypted file is nothing more than a collection of movies in AVI format, it's probably not worth the effort required to crack the file. If the prize is a financial transaction, the criminal may decide to expend some time and effort to steal money or credit card numbers.

Suppose that an attacker wants to steal your funds. Instead of attacking your secure file, he may instead set up a Web server that claims to represent a legitimate business. With a little creative programming, the attacker's site can let you browse an electronic catalog of goods. After you decide to make a purchase, you engage your super-secret encryption scheme and send off a payment to the server. After a nice run of collecting credit card numbers, the server closes down. You're left anxiously awaiting a package that never arrives. As you wait, the attacker is trashing your credit history. This kind of nightmare is exactly what bankcard holders want to avoid. They already spend millions of dollars to combat credit card fraud.

With the aim of fighting such scams, SET has the following objectives:

- Ensuring confidentiality of payment information
- Authenticating cardholders and merchants
- Preserving the integrity of payment data

Bankcard providers certainly want to encourage commerce on the Internet. An analysis of past mail order and telephone order transactions shows that customers strongly prefer paying with bankcards rather than with checks, wire transfers, or any other type of payment. Credit cards fit better with the nature of electronic communications than any other payment medium.

The SET protocol specifications, like other security specifications, can address only a portion of the protocols necessary for electronic commerce. Standard Internet protocols (such as TCP/IP and HTTP) already exist to provide the transport mechanism, communication services, and application interface necessary for commerce. STT differs from the protocols previously discussed in this chapter in that it concentrates exclusively on the security aspects that pertain to bankcard transactions. The following aspects of bankcard transactions are within the scope of the SET protocol:

- The application of cryptographic algorithms, like RSA and DES
- Credential messages and object formats
- Purchase messages and object formats
- Authorization messages and object formats
- Message protocols between client and server

Clearing and settlement is the process by which a merchant receives payment for a transaction using a bankcard. The merchant authorizes the transaction and then later requests payment from the cardholder's financial institution. Merchants who use the Internet for commerce are subject to the same credit card fraud dangers that occur in other purchase sources, such as telephone orders.

The clearing and settlement process differs depending on the card used and the relationship defined between the merchant and the financial institution. As such, SET does not modify the clearing and settlement process. The merchant is responsible for clearing and settling electronic commerce transactions in the same manner in which it processes other transactions. The clearing terms depend upon the merchant's agreement with its bank.

SET brings forth a new application of digital signatures by requiring dual signatures. Electronic commerce requires two sets of authorizations. Suppose that you want to send an offer to a vendor to buy an item. You include a digital signature to authenticate yourself as a customer and otherwise validate the message. The same time that you send your message to the vendor, you send another message to your financial institution that authorizes it to release the funds that you specify if the vendor accepts your offer. You need not disclose the details of the offer to the financial institution. All the financial institution needs is your instruction to release funds if it meets a specified condition.

To process the offer automatically, the vendor sends a request for payment, including your digital signature, to your financial institution. The financial institution matches signatures. If it verifies that both are the same, it transfers the funds to your vendor. The transaction, from a financial perspective, is then complete.

A dual signature concatenates the message digests from your letters to the vendor and the financial institution. SET then computes another message digest from the concatenated result and encrypts it with the signer's private signature key.

One key element necessary for authorization is a credential for cardholders and merchants alike. The financial institution provides a credential for cardholders. In theory, you cannot alter these credentials and only the financial institution can generate them. Likewise, the merchant's financial institution issues the merchant's credential.

NOTE A *credential* in this case is a binary file that acts as the bank's seal of approval for financial transactions. The binary file is actually a digital signature like those discussed earlier in the chapter.

RSA Asymmetric Keys

RSA is an algorithm for asymmetric encryption. It is named after its inventors Ron Rivest, Adi Shamir, and Leonard Adleman. The algorithm, owned by Public Key Partners (PKP) of Sunnyvale, California, received a patent in 1983. RSA's use is subject to the approval, and possible license, of its owners. Anyone in North America must obtain a royalty-based license from PKP to use the RSA algorithm in a commercial endeavor. Fortunately, PKP usually allows free non-commercial use of RSA for personal, academic, or intellectual reasons, with written permission. The United States government can use RSA without a license, because the algorithm was developed at the Massachusetts Institute of Technology (MIT) with some government funding. The patent does not apply outside North America.

RSA is well established as a *de facto* standard. As the most widely implemented public-key encryption system, it is a safe choice for implementing encryption schemes in applications. RSA's common use makes it easier to exchange digital signatures. This standard is entrenched in the financial transaction protocols being developed for electronic commerce. This endorsement alone confirms that RSA carries much weight as a secure standard.

RSA and DES

RSA is a complement to, rather than a replacement for, DES encryption. Each scheme has benefits that the other lacks. DES is a fast encryption scheme and works well for bulk encryption. Although RSA is fine for encrypting small messages, DES is a better choice for larger files because of its speed. RSA provides digital signatures and secure key exchange without requiring a prior exchange of secret codes.

A single user protecting files for personal use probably doesn't need RSA. For such use, a single-key encryption scheme like DES usually suffices because there's no danger involved in passing the key to anyone else. RSA becomes important when you must share messages with others.

Combining the two encryption schemes is like sending a coded message in a secure envelope. A typical RSA digital envelope transaction with another party might operate as follows:

1. Encrypt the message with a random DES key.
2. Encrypt the DES key with RSA.
3. Send the combined DES/RSA encrypted document through the Internet.

As mentioned before, RSA also creates digital signatures. When authentication is as important as concealment, you must use RSA in place of or in conjunction with DES encryption.

How Does RSA Work?

RSA starts with two large primes: p and q. The product of p and q is n, the modulus. You might find some documentation pertaining to RSA that recommends choosing a key pair with strong prime numbers. A ***strong prime*** is one with properties that make the product (n) hard to factor with certain methods.

NOTE A *modulus* is the mathematical process of dividing two operands and returning the remainder. ■

NOTE *Factoring* is the process of splitting an integer into a small set of integers (*factors*) which, when multiplied, yields the original integer. Prime factorization requires splitting an integer into factors that are prime numbers. Multiplying two prime integers is easy, but factoring the product is much more difficult. That's why prime integers are such prize candidates for encryption schemes. Reversing the process of multiplication using prime numbers is extremely difficult. This is called a *one-way function,* one that is easy to perform in the forward direction, but far more difficult to compute in the inverse direction. ■

Due to new factoring methods, the common knowledge method of choosing strong primes is no longer an advantage. The new methods have just as much success on strong primes as with the weak ones.

Another concern with choosing your primes is the size of modulus that you want. There's a bit of a trade-off: a larger modulus creates a more secure encryption scheme, but also slows the encryption process. Choose your modulus length based on your security needs, or perhaps based on the resources that an attacker may use to crack your encrypted message. Here's some research trivia to help guide your decision: Rivest's estimates suggest that an attacker can factor a 512-bit modulus with an $8.2 million effort. If you require a 512-bit modulus, each of your primes should be approximately 256 bits long.

Next, choose a number, called e, that is less than the value of n and also relatively prime to (p-1)(q-1). Next, find its inverse value, d, (mod(p-1)(q-1)). That means that (ed = 1 mod(p-1)(q-1)).

The variables e and d are, respectively, the public and private exponents. The public key pair is (n,e). The private key is d. You should keep factors p and q confidential, or else destroy them.

Before you start writing your own code, pay attention to this next part, because it reveals the Achilles heel of RSA encryption.

Trying to determine the private key (d) from the public key combination (n,e) is practically impossible. Now look at those variables (p and q) that you want to hide or destroy. If you factor n into p and q, you can discover the private key (d).

The following list shows you how the RSA encryption algorithm flows step by step:

1. Create two variables, P and Q. Create another variable, N.
2. Choose two large prime numbers and assign one to P and the other to Q.

3. N is the modulus of P and Q (n := P mod Q)
4. Create a variable, E.
5. Choose a number to assign to E that is less than the value of N and also relatively prime to the results of the formula ((P-1) (Q-1)).
6. Create a variable, D.
7. Find the inverse value of E with the formula (mod(P-1) (Q-1)). Assign that value to variable D.

Keeping in mind how much an attacker would love to have your p and q primes, carefully consider which method to use to generate primes. If you select a predictable pattern, an attacker might duplicate it and render your machinations useless. It's best to obtain random numbers from a physical process, although some computers use dedicated peripheral cards just for this purpose. One example is the FedWire II system used by many U.S. banks. FedWire II is an encrypted communication network that performs monetary wire transfers between banks and the Federal Reserve. You probably want a less expensive solution. Try timing some of the various input devices connected to your computer (such as your mouse, keyboard, or serial device) and use the time difference between inputs as a random number generator. If you choose an algorithm based on a random seed, try to select a seed that isn't obvious to someone who can duplicate your efforts, or at least select a seed that is truly random.

RSA Authentication

RSA authentication is a specific method for creating a digital signature. A digital signature holds a unique advantage over a handwritten signature. With a handwritten signature, you can alter a document's contents without invalidating the signature. You cannot do this with a digital signature, because the document's contents comprise the digital signature itself.

NOTE A digital signature failure doesn't always mean that someone tampered with your document. If you are transmitting the document over the Internet or other network lines, a digital signature failure may also suggest a corrupted file transfer.

You obtain your digital signature from a message digest. A message digest is the result of a hash function. A hash function is a mathematical algorithm that reads some input data source, usually a message or some kind of document, and returns a compact binary output that represents the source. Some other types of programs, like databases, use hash functions as an index to the data source for quick searches.

NOTE A hash function uses a variable-size input and returns a fixed-size string, called the *hash value.*

Hash functions that are difficult to invert are specifically useful for creating message digests. A *message digest* is a concise representation of the message used to create the digest. Any change in the message itself yields a different message digest string, thus making it useful as a digital signature.

Several well-known message digest functions are in use, but MD5 is perhaps the best function to implement as a digital signature. MD5 is secure, reasonably fast, and publicly available for unrestricted use.

ON THE WEB

http://ds.internic.net/ds/dspg0intdoc.html For more details on the MD5 function, see RFC 1321 at this Web site.

One significant issue with digital signatures is a legal matter rather than a technical one. Digital signatures may not have the same legal status as a handwritten signature. No one has yet challenged the validity of a digital signature in court, so there is no legal precedent. The National Institute of Standards and Technology (NIST) has, however, requested an opinion from the United States General Accounting Office (GAO) regarding the legal status of digital signatures. The GAO opinion is that digital signatures meet the legal standards of handwritten signatures.

Authentication

Authentication is a process that assures a document's recipient of the sender's validity and the document's integrity. The authentication process verifies that a transaction is original and unmodified. The process yields a digital signature created from a *message digest,* which is a unique string of bits based on the message's contents. A *signature* is an unforgeable data string that testifies that a specific person created or agreed with the document's contents. A sender creates the message digest and encrypts it with a private key. The message digest accompanies the message. The receiver decrypts the message digest and compares it to the message. If the two agree, the authentication process is valid. You can encrypt and sign a message at the same time.

Another authentication process relies on digital certificates. These digital certificates contain the following:

- A public key

- A *distinguished name* (name and address information)
- Issue data and expiration data
- The digital signature of a certifying authority (CA)

The CA is a trusted authority, such as VeriSign, that creates digital certificates. The CA generally charges for this service. A CA publishes its public key and distinguished name for other people to add to Web browsers or servers as part of their trusted root. Users who want to authenticate a digital certificate use the CA's public key to verify the CA's signature in the certificate.

Microsoft CryptoAPI

As Microsoft started providing Internet development tools, it realized that programmers creating sophisticated communications software needed an application programming interface (API) to provide encryption and secure communications. The result is CryptoAPI, an API that allows Win32 developers to include cryptography technology in their applications. Its goal was to create an API that made cryptographic application development functional, flexible, usable, and exportable for Windows developers.

The CryptoAPI uses a modular approach. The actual cryptographic operations are performed by replaceable components known as cryptographic service providers (CSPs). CSPs are dynamic link libraries with associated cryptographic signatures authorizing it for use by the CryptoAPI. Each CSP contains the cryptographic algorithm, but is developed independently of the application. This means your applications can run with many different CSPs, allowing you to choose a CSP that fits the level of security you need without having to modify your application code.

The CryptoAPI provides the following services:

- Digital signatures
- Store-and-forward encryption
- Online encryption

CryptoAPI provides 24 function calls contained under five categories, as follows:

- Context management
- Key generation/management
- Key exchange
- Data encryption/decryption
- Hashing/signature functions

Context management functions connect an application to a CSP. The functions let your applications choose a specific CSP by name, or choose a CSP with a specific functional class.

Key generation functions let your applications generate and customize cryptographic keys. You can randomly generate keys or derive them from a password. The functions include support for changing initialization vectors, chaining modes, and other encryption features.

Key exchange functions allow your applications to exchange or transmit keys. Encryption keys transmitted outside the CSP are themselves encrypted with the user's public key. They remain so encrypted until they reach the destination user's application. This allows you to transmit keys without compromising them as a security breach to your own encryption techniques. You can use these key exchange functions to implement Private Communication Technology (PCT) or Secure Sockets Layers (SSL) technologies in your own applications.

The Data encryption and decryption do much as the titles suggest; they allow you to encrypt and decrypt data. The functions also include support to simultaneously encrypt and hash data.

The Hashing and Signature functions allow your applications to compute cryptographically secure message digests based upon data. They also enable you to include digital signatures based upon those message digests. Once signed, anyone possessing the signer's public key can easily verify the signer's identity, or whether something modified the data file.

Microsoft licensed its cryptographic technology from RSA Data Security to create the default CSP that will ship with its Win32 operating systems. This CSP supports both public-key and symmetric cryptography. The first version should ship with the Windows NT 4.0 operating system, and then later with a future version of Windows 95. You can find the Microsoft CryptoAPI on Microsoft's Internet Development Toolbox Web site.

From Here...

Encryption is an age-old technology that still works quite well. Its application in electronic commerce is still in its infancy, however. Each of the Internet security specifications discussed in this chapter is still under revision. Some products, particularly those from Netscape and Microsoft, already implement the concepts, even though the specifications are nothing more than working drafts. Perhaps that's why people still don't trust their cards to these schemes.

Nevertheless, the market for such technology continues to grow. If you're a programmer who works as an independent contractor, this is an excellent field to enter on the ground floor. With billions of dollars in purchasing power at stake, vendors clamor for space on the Internet. As this happens, they spend a lot of money on developers who can ensure the safety of their dollars, as well as that of their customers.

In the meantime, here are some Web sites that may help you find more information:

- RSA Data Security at **http://www.rsa.com/**
- Microsoft at **http://www.microsoft.com**
- Netscape Communications at **http://www.netscape.com**
- The Internet Spec List at **http://www.graphcomp.com/info/specs/**
- InterNIC Specifications at **http://ds.internic.net/ds/dspg0intdoc.html**
- Raptor Systems Security at **http://www.raptor.com/./library/library.html**
- Stardust Technologies at **http://www.stardust.com/wsresource/wsresrce.html**
- WinSock Development Info at **http://www.sockets.com/**
- MasterCard at **http://www.mastercard.com**
- Visa at **http://www.visa.com**
- VeriSign at **http://www.verisign.com**

In this chapter, we took a bird's eye view of Internet security concepts and techniques. You can browse some of the Web pages listed previously for more information on security topics. After that, perhaps you'll want to try your hand at implementing security in some of the protocols discussed in other chapters of this book.

CHAPTER 9

An Introduction to Distributed Objects

by Michael Marchuk

- The meaning behind distributed objects
- The basic models used to implement distributed object applications
- The security implications of distributing application objects
- The mechanisms that are used to prevent object code tampering or object viruses

Software composed of distributed objects is one of the newest genres of application development. Software developers are making use of the ability to add application "components" as they need them through distributed object development models. This chapter exposes you to the basics behind the distributed object models and their uses in Internet application development.

Distributed object software development makes use of technologies such as Java, JavaScript, ActiveX, and VBScript, which have all been recently introduced as key Internet components. Both Netscape and Microsoft have committed to the distributed object direction by including these technologies into their Internet browsers. ■

Understanding Application Objects

Application objects have been used for a long time. These objects may take the form of reusable code segments, subroutines, DLL code segments, and OLE controls. The more common view from a Windows perspective is that of the Object Linking and Embedding (OLE) controls. An OLE control is a self-contained application that provides specific functionality when called by another application.

OLE controls allow various properties and methods by which the data is stored and used between the main application and the OLE control. This type of functionality enables developers to reuse the OLE controls in other applications easily. Some examples of OLE controls include the multimedia control interface (MCI32.OCX) used to manage the interface between an application and a CD-ROM drive or an AVI movie file and the grid control (GRID32.OCX), which is used to handle the spreadsheet-like interface managing cells and their contents.

If you have used Visual Basic or VBA to write applications, you may be very familiar with OLE controls. These control objects provide the functionality from which the application can extend their own usefulness without re-creating application code (see fig. 9.1). Because the functionality exists within the OLE control, the developer simply needs to call the functions within the control with the proper parameters to make use of the embedded functions.

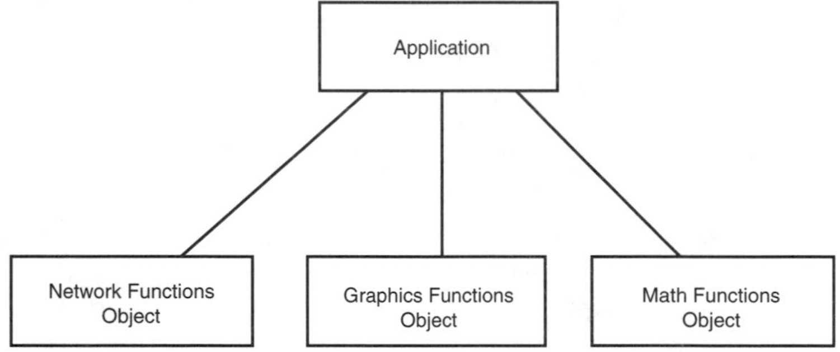

FIG. 9.1
Applications written to use OLE control objects can make use of the object's functionality easily.

The benefits of using controls become apparent when the focus of the development effort is directed away from the controls themselves and onto the functionality that the controls provide. Not only will the developer save time and effort from avoiding the duplication of rewriting control code, but the developer can significantly increase the functionality of the application by making use of properties that might not be essential to the operation of the application but are available through the control object they are calling. For example, a developer may not necessarily build a subroutine to handle interpreting all of the tags in an HTML 3.0 document when the only tag that needs to be used is the title. But if a control object can fit into the application to provide complete HTML decoding, the developer might be inclined to use the other features simply because there is no additional coding required.

Control objects are becoming an easy way to develop complex applications in a relatively short amount of time, because the objects provide the framework around which your application can be written. The popularity of control objects is evident with the increase in usage of programming environments like Visual Basic that use control objects to a great extent. The Internet extends this type of object usage through VBScript and JavaScript, which utilize standard control objects as well as custom controls to create distributed applications.

Understanding Object Distribution Models

Control objects supplied on diskette with applications make use of the traditional transportation mechanism for distributing programs. However, the Internet is challenging that method by introducing on-demand object distribution and application loading. Web pages sprinkled with scripts add functionality to the static content of an HTML page. The added functionality helps to distribute application logic to the end-user and ease the processing burden on the server.

But on-demand control object distribution has its own set of issues. For example, when an object is requested from a distributed application, the application must know where to get the object if it does not exist on the user's workstation. Additionally, because distributed objects are likely to be upgraded or modified periodically, applications that use these objects will need to be able to request the correct version of an object to ensure that the proper functionality is present for the program to operate.

This section briefly explains a few distributed object models and how they work. The next section, "Securing Distributed Objects," covers some of the details associated with guaranteeing that a particular object has not been infected with a virus or that the object comes from an unknown source.

COM/DCOM

Microsoft initiated the Component Object Model (COM) specification to cover the Object Linking and Embedding programming interface, which stresses an open usage of software objects. The object components are distributed and called by an application to perform a particular function.

Vendors who supply COM-compliant application objects enable applications that are COM-compliant to make use of the functions within the object. The COM specification permits a handshaking between the application and the objects, which enables the application to utilize the most functionality available in the particular version of the object. The COM specification also requires location transparency for the execution of the object. In other words, an object may be running on the local workstation, or on a server across the Intranet. The application only needs to know how to access the features that the object is presenting and the object only needs to present its functions for the applications to use. The underlying functions within the object may be accomplished in any fashion, as long as they are consistent with the services the object is providing.

Microsoft recently introduced the Distributed Component Object Model (DCOM) to the Internet Engineering Task Force, which manages Internet standards. The DCOM-proposed standard establishes a uniform mechanism for building application-level protocols between servers and clients in a distributed environment.

ON THE WEB

The Distributed Component Object Model Request for Comment Internet standards draft is available at **http://ds1.internic.net/internet-drafts/draft-brown-dcom-v1-spec-00.txt**.

CORBA

The Common Object Request Broker Architecture (CORBA) is an industry standard distributed object model that is maintained by the Object Management Group (OMG). The OMG established CORBA as a standard in 1991 to enable client applications to find the proper server objects for a particular request.

An ORB (Object Request Broker) is the middleware that establishes the client-server connections between distributed objects. Using an ORB, a client application can use a function on a server object, which can be local or over a network. The ORB manages the request and finds an object that can fulfill the request (see fig. 9.2). The client application does not have to know where the object is located, what programming language it uses, which operating system it is running on, or anything else that is not part of an object's application programming interface. This enables the ORB to provide cohesion between applications on different machines in distributed environments.

Java/JavaScript

The recent popularity of Java and JavaScript has brought the theory of distributed applications to a new generation of programmers. The basic concept behind the Java operating environment is the compiled "byte-code," which is executed on a remote client within a virtual machine environment. The remote client does not need to have any permanent storage facilities, because the application is downloaded from the server each time it is run. For example, if you want to display fancy marquee-style moving lights around a picture on an HTML page, you could embed the Java application that manages the marquee lights when the page is loaded.

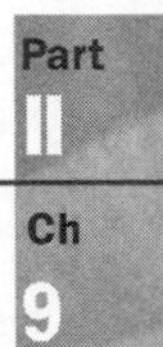

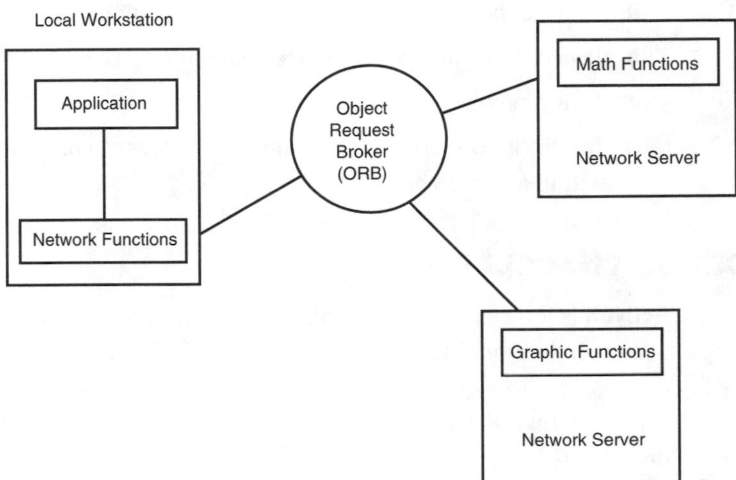

FIG. 9.2
The ORB facilitates the process of fulfilling an application's object request.

This model of getting the code for the application every time it is run allows the code to remain up-to-date and does not require the client to manage any storage space to hold the marquee light application. In addition, the client running a Java application may not be a workstation or PC, but could be an appliance such as a telephone, because the application is running within the standard Java virtual machine environment within the real system environment of the hardware. The virtual machine concept is discussed later in this chapter in the section titled "Virtual Machines."

Java applications can be very large, depending on their complexity. Additionally, a large application requires a fast network or a lot of patience on a slow network connection. Because the application must be downloaded each time before it runs, a slow modem connection may cause large delays when using Java applications.

JavaScript, on the other hand, is a scripting language that requires the client workstation to have the base JavaScript classes from which the applications may use the various functions. For example, a JavaScript application might make use of an equation that calculates a mortgage payment schedule. The JavaScript application would use the math functions that are part of the JavaScript base classes that exist on the client workstation's hard drive.

JavaScript applications are relatively small and read much like Visual Basic source code. Because the application is really a script that draws from the functions already available on the client workstation, the download times and sizes are much smaller than Java applications.

To summarize the advantages of Java and JavaScript:

- Java can be used to create complex applications.
- Java can be compiled into byte-code for fast execution.
- Java can be used on many different operating systems and hardware platforms.
- JavaScript can provide quick and easy access to pre-built Java components that exist within a client's browser.

ActiveX/VBScript

ActiveX is a recent technology offering by Microsoft that extends the OLE control concept a step further into the Internet realm. The ActiveX architecture is designed around the concept that the applications that are downloaded should be installed on the client workstation so that they may be used at a later time without requiring the application to be downloaded again. This mechanism saves download time and increases the application's speed because the object that is downloaded is a natively compiled application.

VBScript is a subset of Visual Basic for Applications, which allows ActiveX controls to be called like the OLE controls (OCX) are called from within Visual Basic. This type of mechanism opens up the ability to create interactive Web pages to millions of Visual Basic programmers and Microsoft Office users who have created Visual Basic applications. The VBScript source code is embedded into the HTML page like JavaScript, and uses functions from within the VBScript base classes and from within the ActiveX controls, which may be downloaded.

To summarize the advantages of ActiveX and VBScript:

- ActiveX objects are natively compiled for a particular platform, allowing them to run faster and provide more functionality than a Java application.
- ActiveX objects are stored locally after they are downloaded, which makes them available for future usage without the need to re-download them.
- ActiveX objects are created much like OLE objects, so Visual C++ programmers will be familiar with the development efforts.
- VBScript uses very familiar Visual Basic coding, which allows millions of Visual Basic programmers the ability to start producing VBScript code.

Securing Distributed Objects

Using distributed objects makes a lot of sense when you begin thinking of how the Internet works. The applications that are being written and downloaded by clients do not need a formal installation routine and can be used when the need arises. However, like the virus threat that began in the 1980s and is still very prevalent, there is a healthy concern about the security aspects of downloading programs on-the-fly.

Security of distributed objects is based on two concepts: trust and isolation. For example, if your friend wrote an application and gave it to you, you would probably feel fairly confident that the application would not contain any malicious code. The same feeling applies to applications that you may purchase from a local retailer or via mail order. There is a certain level of trust that you have put into the sources from which you've obtained the software.

This next section covers the various methods that are used to ensure some level of security when a user runs a distributed application.

Trusting Distributed Objects

The ActiveX method of maintaining security through the distributed objects that are used is by assigning a digital "fingerprint" to create a verified object when it is released. A verified object is one from which a registration number has been obtained through a third-party like VeriSign. That registration is embedded into the object to allow you to trace the author of the object.

For example, let's assume a programmer writes an object that can display various obscure graphic image types. In order for others to use this object within their distributed applications, the object must be placed into a location from which it can be accessed. The programmer chooses to place the object into an archive on a server that holds other distributed objects. In order for that object to be accepted, however, the programmer must register the object and provide detailed information like a street address, e-mail address, and phone number by which the programmer can be reached. This registration process provides some assurance that a malicious object, or an object with a serious bug, can be traced back to its author. This also provides a level of comfort to the user downloading the object that the author is responsible for the actions of their code. Now, this registration process will probably not stop the hardened criminal from bypassing these safeguards, but it will curb the flow of amateurs who might see this as an easy way to get noticed. See "Code Signing" for more information on the mechanisms involved with this type of security.

Code Signing

The mechanism for maintaining a trust relationship between distributed object developers and end users is by using a mutually trusted third-party. This is done through the use of authoritative digital signatures that are assigned to a registered developer. A certificate authority (CA) holds information that positively identifies the developer and holds the developer responsible for not releasing intentionally malicious programs. After a developer has signed a legal document that promises to abide by the CA's rules, the developer will receive a digital certificate that can be used to cryptographically "sign" all of the programs that are released from that developer.

The cryptographic signing will ensure that the code is from a particular developer and that the code has not been tampered with since it left the developer's hands. This allows end users to accept code that has been signed by particular CAs with whom the end user is familiar and trusts. The digital signature also provides the end user with the knowledge that the developer who signed the code has taken steps to ensure their reputation.

ON THE WEB

For more information on obtaining a digital ID signature through a certificate authority, check VeriSign's Web site at **http://digitalid.verisign.com/**.

Isolating Distributed Objects

When an anonymous distributed object is called from an application you are running from within a Web page, you should have a certain level of paranoia regarding the functionality of the application. This is where the second concept of securing distributed objects comes in. By running an application in a contained environment, the objects will not be allowed to run rampant on your workstation and destroy your data. Instead, misbehaved applications may cause the browser to fail or possibly cause the application that was calling the object to self-destruct. Sealing off these unknown applications and distributed objects allows the system to protect itself from the virus-like activities that might be built into the distributed objects. The most common method of creating a contained environment, known as a virtual machine, is explained in the next section, "Virtual Machines."

Obviously, the security of any system depends on the strength of the mechanisms involved. For instance, the Netscape Navigator version 2.01 contained a bug that could have been used to create a Java "virus" application. Netscape released version 2.02 to correct this fault, but the same type of problem can occur with any browser or operating system.

The only way to completely prevent malicious distributed objects from causing damage is by shutting off any distributed application usage. This will obviously remove all the benefits of using distributed applications. Two methods of preventing damage caused by distributed objects is to enable all the error-checking and monitoring switches on your current browser and by maintaining the most current browser release that will include fixes for known security holes.

Virtual Machines

A *virtual machine* is an environment in which applications may run with restricted access to real system resources. For example, a Java virtual machine includes the ability to allocate memory resources dynamically, but restricts the ability to write to the system's hard drive or to communicate with another process on the system. These types of restrictions allow the end users a sense of well-being when they run an application that operates within a virtual machine. The user will not need to worry about a virus infection or a malicious application, because no damage can be done outside of the virtual machine.

An additional advantage that a virtual machine carries is the ability to create an environment within any operating system on any platform. A virtual machine is just that: a virtual operating environment that can work the same on every platform. This powerful advantage allows developers the ability to create applications that can literally be run within virtual machines on every platform that is supported. For example, an application written for a virtual machine environment may be run on a computer with DOS or Windows, a Macintosh computer, or even a mainframe. As long as the virtual machine environment is consistent from platform to platform, the application can make the same function calls and operate the same way.

The main disadvantage of using a virtual machine is that the code that is created to run within the virtual machine environment is a compiled "byte-code," which must be interpreted when the program is run. This causes the applications to perform more slowly than natively compiled applications. It is unlikely that the objects running in a virtual machine will be used for computationally complex applications in which the user would notice much of a difference between a native application and one running on a virtual machine.

From Here...

Now that you've had a brief tour of distributed objects and their usage, you'll want to move forward and start to learn about how VBScript can make use of these distributed objects to produce a robust distributed application. You may want to check out these chapters next:

- Chapter 7, "ActiveX Objects," outlines the various ActiveX components that are available by default within the VBScript environment.
- Chapter 11, "Designing VBScript Applications," describes the Visual Basic scripting syntax from within an HTML page.

CHAPTER 10

Embedding Internet Explorer in Your Application

by Ibrahim Malluf

Control Internet Explorer 3.0

You'll be prepared to use Internet Explorer as an application object.

Build your own browser

After you've read this chapter, you'll be ready to construct your own Web browser.

While Internet Explorer is a complete stand-alone application, it is also an OLE Automation Server and a COM object. This means that you can use the Internet Explorer as an object in your programs from which you can instantiate and manipulate through its automation interface. If you are a VB or C++ programmer, you can also utilize the WebBrowser object contained within the shdocvw.dll as the foundation for your own customized browser. ■

Controlling the Internet Explorer 3.0 Application as an Application Object

While you could use the VB Shell command to call up the Internet Explorer as a separate application, controlling the Internet Explorer application through OLE automation is a more appropriate approach that gives you direct access to many properties and methods of the InternetExplorer object. In this chapter, Visual Basic 4 will be used to present a very easy example of automating the Internet Explorer through a Visual Basic application.

To lay out the form, do the following:

1. Start a new Visual Basic project and save it with the name IEControl.vbj.
2. Add a text box and an array of eight command button controls with the name cmdBrowser for the command controls. Arrange them as shown in Figure 10.1.

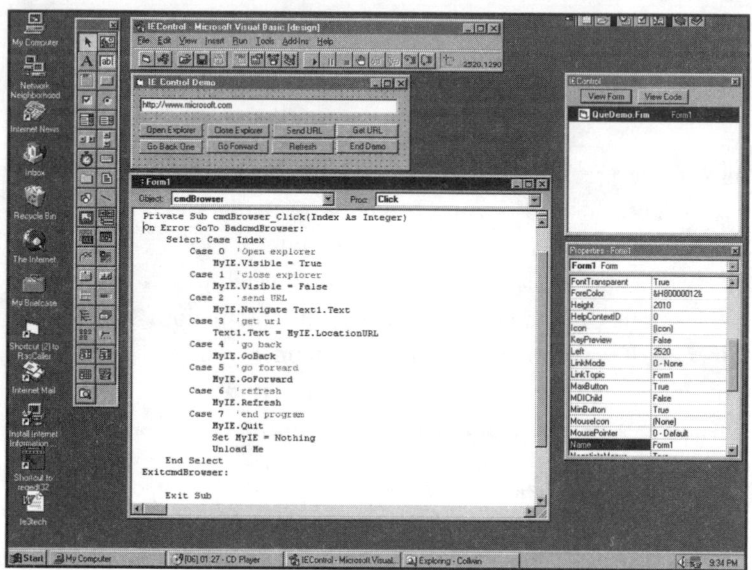

FIG. 10.1
This Internet Explorer automation project is being created in Visual Basic 4.

3. From the tools menu of the Visual Basic menu, select the Custom Controls menu item.
4. From the list of custom controls, select the Microsoft Internet and Shell controls.
5. In the General Declarations area of the QueDemo form, add the declaration of the automation server, "Private MyIE as New InternetExplorer." This creates an instance of the Internet Explorer as an OLE automation server within your project. To complete this example, enter the code in Listing 10.1

Listing 10.1 quedemo.frm—Programming the Methods and Properties of the Internet Explorer

```
Option Explicit
Dim MyIE As New InternetExplorer

Private Sub cmdBrowser_Click(Index As Integer)
On Error GoTo BadcmdBrowser:
Select Case Index
Case 0 'Open explorer
MyIE.Visible = True
Case 1 'close explorer
MyIE.Visible = False
Case 2 'send URL
MyIE.Navigate Text1.Text
Case 3 'get url
Text1.Text = MyIE.LocationURL
Case 4 'go back
MyIE.GoBack
Case 5 'go forward
MyIE.GoForward
Case 6 'refresh
MyIE.Refresh
Case 7 'end program
MyIE.Quit
Set MyIE = Nothing
Unload Me
End Select
ExitcmdBrowser:

Exit Sub
BadcmdBrowser:
MsgBox Err.Description
Resume ExitcmdBrowser
End Sub
```

When the project is run, the QueDemo form is displayed, giving the user eight actions to select. By clicking the Open Explorer button, a fully operational instance of the Internet Explorer will be displayed. The user can manipulate the Explorer from either the Internet Explorer itself or from the project form. If the user ends the Internet Explorer from the Explorer's interface, an automation error occurs. You will also get an automation error when trying to go back or forward when there are no pages to go back or forward to. Using this method to provide Internet browsing to your applications is very limited but allows quick implementation. If you are looking for something a little more robust, read on.

Building Your Own Browser

The shdocvw.dll exposes a control called the WebBrowser that can be dropped on your application's form and provides a set of events, properties, and methods that gives you almost complete control over your Web browsing. In this section, we'll build the shell of a browser application that can be easily customized to meet organizational requirements for functionality, security, and so on. Table 10.1 is a table of controls to be placed on the form.

Table 10.1 Controls to Place on the Project Form

Control	Name	Description
ToolBar	MyTools	A Win95 common controls toolbar
TextBox	txtAddress	A text box control with the caption "Address:"
ComboBox	cmbAddress	A style 0 combo box
CommonDlg	cdgFileBox	A common dialog box
PictureBox	WebContainer	A picture control with background set to black
WebBrowser	MyWeb	The WebBrowser control
StatusBar	Status	A status bar control

Arrange the controls on the frmBrowser.frm as shown in Figure 10.2. In the case of the WebBrowser control, make it a child of the WebContainer picture box control by first selecting the picture box and then drawing the WebBrowser control into it. The txtAddress and cmbAddress controls can be placed anywhere since they will be sized and moved into place by program code anyway. The status bar should have three panels with the last two panels having their Styles set to Date and Time respectively.

For the ToolBar control, set the button properties as shown in Table 10.2.

Table 10.2 The Button Property Settings for the MyTools ToolBar

Button	Property	Setting
1	Key	'GetFile'
1	ToolTipText	'Get an HTML Document from disk'
2	Key	'TextPlace'
2	Style	4-PlaceHolder
2	Width	1400
3	Key	'ComboPlace'

Button	Property	Setting
3	Style	4-PlaceHolder
4	Key	'Quit'
4	ToolTipText	'Close the browser application'
5	Key	'GoBack'
5	ToolTipText	'Go back to previous page'
6	Key	'Refresh'
6	ToolTipText	'Refresh the current page'
7	Key	'GoForward'
7	ToolTipText	'Go forward to next page'
8	Key	'GoHome'
8	ToolTipText	'Go to home page'

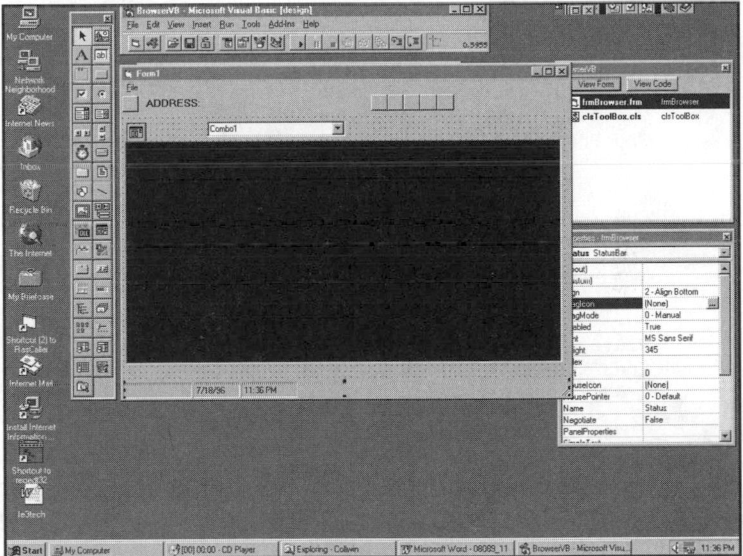

FIG. 10.2
Where do the browser project controls go?

At this point, there should be a form with all of the required controls with properties set up properly. I should make it clear here that when this project has been completed, you will have a working browser, but it is not anywhere near complete enough for distribution and is only a vehicle to demonstrate what can be accomplished. You will have to flesh this project out with appropriate error handling, user interface, and other enhancements by yourself. Included on the CD is a file called clsToolBox.cls that contains some utility procedures that the project requires. Add this file to the project now.

There are two public properties exposed by this form, the Location and ShowStatus properties as shown in Listing 10.2. While not used anywhere in this project, they are included so that you can easily add this form and its supporting clsToolBox class to another project. You can also add other public properties and methods as needed. By setting the Location property to a valid URL, you can cause the results of that URL to be displayed in this form. The ShowStatus properties allow you to read and write to the form's status bar.

Listing 10.2 frmbrowser.frm—The General Declarations and Property Procedures of the frmBrowser Form

```
Option Explicit
'class contains required utility procedures
Private clstools As New clsToolBox
'contains the name of the file returned by
'the GetDocumentFile procedure
Private strFilePath As String

'==============Begin Property Procedures=============
Public Property Get Location() As String
Location = MyWeb.Location
End Property

Public Property Let Location(strNewValue As String)
MyWeb.Navigate strNewValue
End Property


Public Property Get ShowStatus() As String
ShowStatus = Status.Panels(1).Text
End Property

Public Property Let ShowStatus(strNewValue As String)
Status.Panels(1).Text = strNewValue
End Property
```

The next group of procedures are general procedures that provide supporting code to the events triggered by the user or by the browser. The first procedure in Listing 10.3 is the GetDocumentFile() function that returns a Boolean True if the user selected a file and a False if the user cancels. If the function returns a True, then the file path is returned through the function's strFileName argument. The ResizeAll sub procedure maintains the sizing of all of the controls as the user resizes the form or as the WebBrowser control changes size due to URL parameters. We call this procedure from the form's Resize event and from the WebBrowser's MyWeb_OnDownloadBegin() event. This gives the WebBrowser an ugly flicker when a given URL is acted upon, but it was the only solution available with the beta release Internet Explorer 3.0. The final release of Internet Explorer 3.0 is supposed to include an OnWindowResized event that shows some interesting possibilities, but it was not functional as this book went to press.

On the CD

Listing 10.3 frmbrowser.frm—The General Procedures Code

```
'=================Begin General Procedures====================
Private Function GetDocumentFile(strFilename) As Boolean
On Error GoTo BadGetDocumentFile
'assume success
GetDocumentFile = True
cdgFileBox.Filter = "HTML Documents *.htm¦*.htm¦All Files *.*¦*.*"
cdgFileBox.ShowOpen
strFilename = cdgFileBox.filename

ExitGetDocumentFile:

Exit Function
BadGetDocumentFile:
GetDocumentFile = False
Resume ExitGetDocumentFile
End Function
Private Sub ResizeAll()
'============================================
'resizes all visible components to fit form
'============================================
Dim MyHeight As Long
Dim MyWidth As Long
Dim MyTop As Long
Dim MyLeft As Long
'----Basic Dimensions----
MyHeight = Me.ScaleHeight
MyWidth = Me.ScaleWidth

'----Calculated Dimensions------
If MyTools.Visible Then MyTop = MyTools.Height
'----------Resizing--------
MyTools.Top = MyTop
mywebcontainer.Move 0, MyTop, MyWidth, _
MyHeight - (150 + (MyTop + Status.Height))
If MyWeb.Visible = True Then
mywebcontainer.Visible = False
MyWeb.Move 0, 0, _
mywebcontainer.Width - 110, _
mywebcontainer.Height - 110
MyWeb.Container.Visible = True
End If
Status.Panels(1).Width = MyWidth - 2200
txtAddress.Left = MyTools.Buttons(2).Left
txtAddress.Top = MyTools.Buttons(2).Top
cmbAddress.Top = MyTools.Buttons(3).Top
cmbAddress.Left = MyTools.Buttons(3).Left
cmbAddress.Width = MyTools.Buttons(3).Width
txtAddress.ZOrder
cmbAddress.ZOrder
End Sub
Public Sub AddToList(MyCombo As ComboBox)
Dim MyText As String
MyText = MyCombo.Text
```

continues

Listing 10.3 Continued

```
If Not clstools.IsExactComboMatch(MyCombo) Then
If MyCombo.ListCount > 20 Then
MyCombo.RemoveItem 1
End If
If Len(MyText) > 7 And InStr(MyText, "www.") > 0 Then
If Left(MyText, 7) <> "http://" Then
MyText = "http://" & MyText
End If
Else

End If
MyCombo.AddItem MyText
MyCombo.ListIndex = MyCombo.NewIndex
Else



End If
End Sub
```

The last procedure in Listing 10.3 is the AddToList() subroutine. Its purpose is to check the URLs contained in the ComboBox passed as an argument to it for duplicates. If there are no duplicates, it adds the URL to the list. Also, if the list has exceeded 20 entries, it removes an entry from the list to keep it at the maximum 20 entries. The subroutine calls a utility procedure from the clsTools object called IsExactComboMatch().

Listing 10.4 contains the event code for the form. The Load Event of the frmBrowser sets the form's caption, adds a URL to the cmbAddress ComboBox, and displays the browser's home page as determined by Internet Explorer's system settings.

Listing 10.4 frmbrowser.frm—The From Events Code for the frmBrowser

```
'==============Begin Event Procedures======================
Private Sub Form_Load()
Me.Show
Me.Caption = "Que Special Edition Web Browser"
cmbAddress.AddItem "http://www.rt66.com"
cmbAddress.ListIndex = cmbAddress.NewIndex
MyWeb.Visible = True
MyWeb.GoHome
ResizeAll
End Sub

Private Sub Form_Resize()
If Me.WindowState <> vbMinimized Then ResizeAll
End Sub

Private Sub Form_Unload(Cancel As Integer)
Set clsTools = Nothing
End Sub
```

The form's Resize event calls the ResizeAll() procedure as long as the form's window state is not transitioning to the minimized state. If the ResizeAll() procedure was called with a minimized window, then invalid property errors occur. Finally, being a hopeless paranoid and knowing the OS is out to get me, I make sure that I terminate the clsTools object by setting the object reference to nothing.

Moving on to the cmbAddress and MyTools events, we have Listing 10.5.

Listing 10.5 frmbrowser.frm—The Event Procedures for the cmbAddress and MyTools Controls

```
Private Sub cmbAddress_KeyPress(KeyAscii As Integer)
Select Case KeyAscii

Case 13
AddToList cmbAddress
MyWeb.Navigate cmbAddress.Text
End Select
End Sub


Private Sub MyTools_ButtonClick(ByVal Button As Button)
On Error GoTo BadMyTools_ButtonClick
Select Case Button.Key
Case "GetFile"
'go get an HTML file from a local drive
If GetDocumentFile(strFilePath) Then
MyWeb.Navigate strFilePath
End If
Case "GoHome"
MyWeb.GoHome
Case "GoBack"
MyWeb.GoBack
Case "GoForward"
MyWeb.GoForward
Case "Refresh"
MyWeb.Refresh
Case "Test"
MsgBox MyWeb.Location
End Select
ExitMyTools_ButtonClick:

Exit Sub
BadMyTools_ButtonClick:
MsgBox Err.Description
Resume ExitMyTools_ButtonClick
End Sub
```

The cmbAddress KeyPress() event checks for a carriage return signaling the end of input and the desire to activate the URL and load the Web browser. The MyTools_ButtonClick event provides the navigational tools that allow you to go back, forward, home, or refresh the HTML document displayed. If you attempt to navigate to a page that doesn't exist (no next or previous page), an error is generated. Those errors are trapped here and displayed in a message box. They are not fatal errors and merely need to be trapped to prevent program crashes.

Now we can get to the WebBrowser's events. In the beta version of the Internet Explorer, several of the events were not yet functional, but enough were working that I could make a substantial browser application. Listing 10.6 provides the event code for the WebBrowser control.

Listing 10.6 frmbrowser.frm—The Event Code for the WebBrowser Control

```
Private Sub MyWeb_OnDownloadBegin()
ResizeAll
End Sub

Private Sub MyWeb_OnDownloadComplete()
Screen.MousePointer = vbDefault
End Sub

Private Sub MyWeb_OnNavigate(ByVal URL As String,  _
ByVal Flags As Long, ByVal TargetFrameName As String,  _
PostData As Variant, ByVal Headers As String,  _
ByVal Referrer As String)
Screen.MousePointer = vbHourglass
End Sub

Private Sub MyWeb_OnStatusTextChange(ByVal bstrText As String)
Status.Panels(1).Text = bstrText
End Sub
```

In the MyWeb_OnDownloadBegin() event, the ResizeAll procedure is called to counteract the fact that loading a new URL causes the WebBrowser control to be resized to accommodate the size of the HTML document. The ResizeAll procedure provides the mechanism to pull the WebBrowser's size back into conformity with the size of its container, the PictureBox control. In the MyWeb_OnNavigate() and MyWeb_OnDownloadComplete() events, the mouse pointer is manipulated to let the user know that something is happening. In the MyWeb_OnStatusTextChange() event, the user is notified of the WebBrowser's status through the status bar control.

One limitation here is that the WebBrowser control does not return any text indicating when the mouse pointer is positioned over a link. All the code is now in place to run the WebBrowser project. Press F5 to run the project. It should look like Figure 10.3.

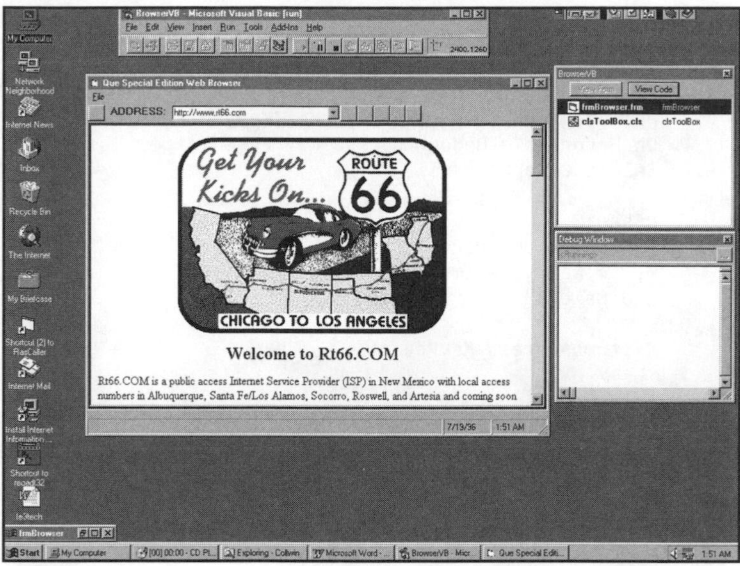

FIG. 10.3
Here's the WebBrowser project running.

We have created a minimal Web browser. What can be done with it? Let's take a situation where we only want the users within our organization to have limited access to the Internet. We want to limit this access to the Microsoft.com site for the purposes of research. We don't want anyone cruising the net for entertainment on our time. So built into our organization's browser is code that allows free navigation within Microsoft's environment, but not anywhere else. Listing 10.7 adds this functionality.

On the CD

Listing 10.7 frmbrowser.frm—Limiting the Browser's Internet Scope

```
Private Sub MyWeb_OnBeginNavigate(ByVal URL As String, _
ByVal Flags As Long, ByVal TargetFrameName As String, _
PostData As Variant, ByVal Headers As String, _
ByVal Referrer As String, Cancel As Boolean)

If InStr(URL, "microsoft.com") < 1 Then Cancel = True

End Sub
```

All I am doing here is checking the URL for microsoft.com and canceling the navigation event if not found. This is a very simplistic example and should be fleshed out with a little more sophistication that reflects your needs. When the navigation is canceled in this manner, the Web browser generates an error event in the procedure that called the navigate method. You will have to add error-handling code to address this error. Listing 10.8 shows the two relevant procedures in this project modified to handle this error.

Listing 10.8 frmbrowser.frm—Adding Error Code to Compensate for the Navigation Method Being Canceled

```
Private Sub cmbAddress_KeyPress(KeyAscii As Integer)
On Error GoTo BadcmbAddress_KeyPress
Select Case KeyAscii

Case 13
AddToList cmbAddress
MyWeb.Navigate cmbAddress.Text
End Select

ExitcmbAddress_KeyPress:

Exit Sub
BadcmbAddress_KeyPress:
'trapping fopr the canceled
'navigate method
If Err.Number = 287 Then
MsgBox "This URL Not Allowed"
Else
MsgBox Err.Description
End If
Resume ExitcmbAddress_KeyPress

End Sub

Private Sub MyTools_ButtonClick(ByVal Button As Button)
On Error GoTo BadMyTools_ButtonClick
Select Case Button.Key
Case "GetFile"
'go get an HTML file from a local drive
If GetDocumentFile(strFilePath) Then
MyWeb.Navigate strFilePath
End If
Case "GoHome"
MyWeb.GoHome
Case "GoBack"
MyWeb.GoBack
Case "GoForward"
MyWeb.GoForward
Case "Refresh"
MyWeb.Refresh
Case "Test"
MsgBox MyWeb.Location
End Select
ExitMyTools_ButtonClick:

Exit Sub
BadMyTools_ButtonClick:
'trapping fopr the canceled
'navigate method
If Err.Number = 287 Then
MsgBox "This URL Not Allowed"
```

```
Else
MsgBox Err.Description
End If
Resume ExitMyTools_ButtonClick
End Sub
```

From Here...

In the release version of the Internet Explorer, there will be more Events wired in and working to give you greater control of the WebBrowser control. Internet Explorer gives you the ability to create custom browsers that fit the exacting needs of an organization's environment—from the corporate intranet to Internet access for students in high-school classrooms. We did not show examples of VBScript and Visual Basic interacting with each other here because the Document Object was not functional at the time of this writing. Be sure to watch the Web site related to this book for examples.

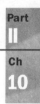

PART III

VBScript Programming Overview

CHAPTER 11

Designing VBScript Applications

by Yusuf Malluf

From this point, if you have followed the chapters sequentially, you have a pretty good understanding of the concepts of Visual Basic Script. In this case, you have a pretty good understanding of the ActiveX control pad. You have also seen some usage of the ActiveX controls and you have seen many of the principle functions of Visual Basic Script, not to mention several examples. Now the question is, how can I put this all together to design an excellent application for my Web site? This chapter introduces you to the Internet Explorer 3.0 Object model, which is basically what you use to control different objects of the browser, such as the window object, the document object and several others. A brief explanation on objects is provided too, in case you haven't had much experience with them. ■

Using Visual Basic Script for designing Web applications

You can use Visual Basic Script for designing applications inside your Web pages. These applications can be anything from games to displaying today's date and time.

Using Dynamic Web Content

Static Web pages are a thing of the past. With the introduction of scripting and object capable browsers, one can design highly interactive pages on the Internet without using several mix-and-match alternatives.

The Internet Explorer 3.0 Object Model

The Internet Explorer Object model is one of the entities which is most important to designing your applications. This chapter gives coverage to the object model.

Using the ActiveX Controls and the ActiveX Control Pad

The ActiveX controls are the other entities which are important to designing your Visual Basic Script based HTML applications. We will cover the intrinsic ActiveX controls as well as some ActiveX controls included in the ActiveX control pad.

Moving From Static to Dynamic HTML Pages

It is possible that you were using the Internet in the time when browsers served very static and unchanging content. These first-generation browsers had a handful of HTML commands for different styles of text and inserting pictures. This was an extraordinary improvement over other Internet information systems at the time, such as Gopher. Next came HTML 2.0 and the second-generation browsers that supported forms and the common gateway interface (CGI). CGI was used to process and store the data of the forms that the new model of HTML offered, with the addition to proprietary tags instituted by different browsers.

Today, the expansion of HTML 3.0 and third-generation browsers is unbelievable. Many different companies are rolling out their own browsers; these browsers have the capability to serve truly dynamic web content. With scripting capabilities and the ability to insert a plethora of objects into your pages, you can now have more creative control over how your Web pages are presented. Let's move on to how to create these killer applications.

Using VBScript for Designing Web Applications

Before you can understand how to create these Visual Basic Script applications, you must understand a few concepts that you use to design those applications. The most important concept that you may need to understand is how objects work. Understanding how objects are used is a prerequisite to understanding how the Internet Explorer 3.0 object model works, to understanding the ActiveX controls, and understanding how to integrate these two with elements of an HTML page. You also need to have a pretty good working knowledge of Visual Basic itself—specifically, how events and procedures work. These topics are discussed in this section as well. Remember, objects and Visual Basic Script are closely knit; you must think of designing your applications on a level that considers them both.

Understanding the Basics of Objects

An *object* is simply an interactive entity that you can control by its methods, properties and events. A *method* is a procedure, or rather, a set of instructions which tells the object to perform a certain task. A *property* is some sort of attribute of an object. An *event* is some sort of action that happens to the object. Let's take a human for our example object. A human has methods, properties, and events. A method might be eating, digestion, gestation, or a number of other processes. A property might be eye color, skin pigmentation or a number of things which describe the human object. An event for a human might be when the human is pushed.

Now, in terms of computers, let's take an ActiveX control for an example object. We will use the label object (object and control virtually mean the same thing). The label control consists primarily of properties and has one method. Some of the label control's properties include its caption, its background color, its foreground color, its size and its font. Its method is the About Box method which displays an about box with information about the control when called. An event for the label control is when the mouse pointer is moved over that control. There is a specific tag for inserting objects in an HTML page and this tag is the <OBJECT> tag. This will be covered in the next section.

Using the *<OBJECT>* Tag

The <OBJECT> tag, as you already know, is used to insert objects of various types in your Web page, but we will primarily focus on the ActiveX objects. The general syntax for an object tag is:

```
<OBJECT>
        <PARAM>
        ...
</OBJECT>
```


There are two tags used in this syntax: the <OBJECT> tag and the <PARAM> tag. The <OBJECT> tag is used to define what the object is and any other general attributes related to the object that are called or defined with the <OBJECT> tag. The <PARAM> tag is used to set the different properties of the object specified by the <OBJECT> tag those <PARAM> tags are nested in. The attributes for the <OBJECT> tag are listed in Table 11.1 and the attributes for the <PARAM> tag are listed in Table 11.2.

Table 11.1 The Attributes of the *<OBJECT>* Tag

Attribute	Function
ID	Specifies the name of this object in the document.
CLASSID	Specifies which class the object belongs to. Can be a uuid (unique universal identifier) or another group of classes such as Java. For ActiveX controls, this is the classid given of that ActiveX object in your system's registry (which is generally the same for all machines which use ActiveX objects).
DATA	Specifies where the object should get its data from, could also include data for specifying all the classes properties.
CODEBASE	Specifies where the code for implementing the object is.
TYPE	Specifies what Internet MIME type to use (example: application/ x-oleobject would specify an OLE object to be used as code)
HEIGHT	Specifies how much vertical space to allot to the object's field.
WIDTH	Specifies how much horizontal space to allot to the object's field.

Table 11.2 Attributes for the *<PARAM>* Tag

Attribute	Function
NAME	Specifies which property of the Object to utilize
VALUE	Specifies a value to give to the Object property specified by NAME

NOTE There are other attributes which are used with the <OBJECT> and the <PARAM> according to the specification, but these attributes are all one needs to use ActiveX and other objects in a page.

Now that we know what attributes are used by an ActiveX control, let's look at an example control. The code in Listing 11.1 is an example of the ActiveX label control. Figure 11.1 illustrates this listing. FIRSTEXAMP.HTM can be found on the CD that accompanies this book.

Listing 11.1 FIRSTEXAMP.HTM—This Is a Simple Demonstration of an ActiveX Object

```
<HTML>
<HEAD>
<TITLE>The first listing for chapter 12 demonstrates
      a simple ActiveX control</TITLE>
</HEAD>
<BODY BGCOLOR="steelblue">
<OBJECT ID="mylabel" WIDTH="100" HEIGHT="51"
 CLASSID="CLSID:99B42120-6EC7-11CF-A6C7-00AA00A47DD2">
    <PARAM NAME="_ExtentX" VALUE="2646">
    <PARAM NAME="_ExtentY" VALUE="1349">
    <PARAM NAME="Caption" VALUE="This is label 1">
    <PARAM NAME="Angle" VALUE="0">
    <PARAM NAME="Alignment" VALUE="4">
    <PARAM NAME="Mode" VALUE="1">
    <PARAM NAME="FillStyle" VALUE="0">
    <PARAM NAME="FillStyle" VALUE="0">
    <PARAM NAME="ForeColor" VALUE="#000000">
    <PARAM NAME="BackColor" VALUE="#C0C0C0">
    <PARAM NAME="FontName" VALUE="Arial">
    <PARAM NAME="FontSize" VALUE="12">
    <PARAM NAME="FontItalic" VALUE="0">
    <PARAM NAME="FontBold" VALUE="0">
    <PARAM NAME="FontUnderline" VALUE="0">
    <PARAM NAME="FontStrikeout" VALUE="0">
    <PARAM NAME="TopPoints" VALUE="0">
    <PARAM NAME="BotPoints" VALUE="0">
</OBJECT>
</BODY>
</HTML>
```

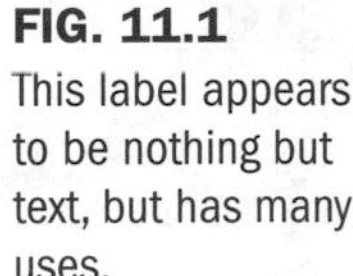

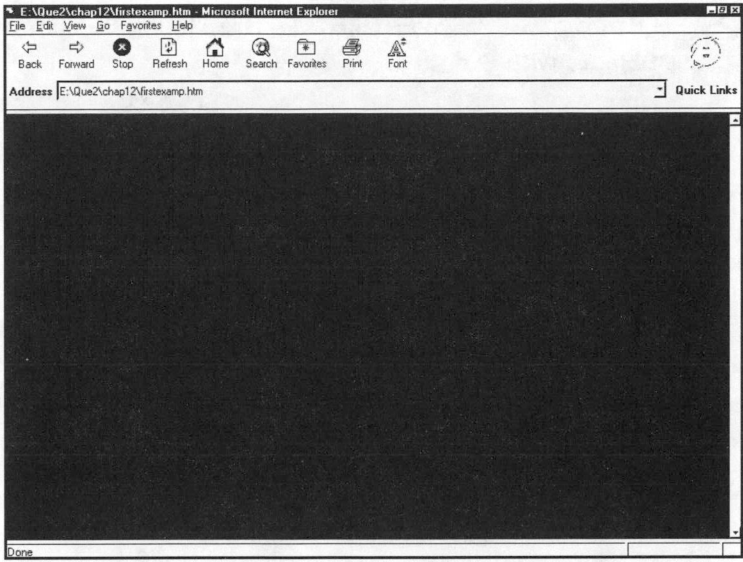

FIG. 11.1
This label appears to be nothing but text, but has many uses.

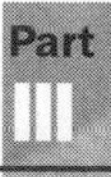

Consider Listing 11.1 for a moment. Several attributes are defined for the <OBJECT> tag which gives useful information about the object being used. First the object is named "mylabel," then the width and height properties for the tag are defined, then the control is specified with the CLASSID attribute. The value "CLSID:99B42120-6EC7-11CF-A6C7-00AA00A47DD2" is what identifies the object on your system, through your registry. The nested <PARAM> tags contain the properties of the label object. As you already know, the NAME attribute is used to specify which property to use and the VALUE attribute is used to assign a value to that property. This entire process is automated, as you have read, with the ActiveX control pad which was covered fully in Chapter 3, "Introducing the ActiveX Control Pad." There is a properties window in the control pad editor which allows you to adjust the properties of any control.

Looking Closer at Scripting and the *<SCRIPT>* Tag

The <SCRIPT> tag was mentioned briefly in Chapter 2, "Review of HTML." The <SCRIPT> tag is where all Visual Basic Script statements go. Several tags (primarily form input controls) and ActiveX controls can access certain procedures (subroutines) of your script based on an event. An *event*, as mentioned earlier, is when the user triggers some action related to an object. A mouse-pointer moving over a button is an example of an event. Events can be called from the <A>, <BODY>, <INPUT>, and <OBJECT> tags. There are several ways to control the events of these tags. One method of doing this is by using the event as an attribute; another method is using that method in a subroutine. Examine Listing 11.2 (OBEVENTS.HTM can also be accessed off the accompanying CD). Figure 11.2 illustrates this listing.

Listing 11.2 OBEVENTS.HTM—This Listing Demonstrates the Usage of Objects with Events

```
<HTML>
<HEAD>
<TITLE>This is the 2nd demo, with more
functionality</TITLE>
</HEAD>
<BODY BGCOLOR="slateblue"><BR>
<CENTER>
<OBJECT ID="MyLabel" WIDTH=215 HEIGHT=93
 CLASSID="CLSID:99B42120-6EC7-11CF-A6C7-00AA00A47DD2">
    <PARAM NAME="_ExtentX" VALUE="5689">
    <PARAM NAME="_ExtentY" VALUE="2461">
    <PARAM NAME="Caption" VALUE="Watch me change!!">
    <PARAM NAME="Angle" VALUE="0">
    <PARAM NAME="Alignment" VALUE="4">
    <PARAM NAME="BackStyle" VALUE="1">
    <PARAM NAME="Mode" VALUE="1">
    <PARAM NAME="FillStyle" VALUE="0">
    <PARAM NAME="FillStyle" VALUE="1">
    <PARAM NAME="ForeColor" VALUE="#00FF00">
    <PARAM NAME="BackColor" VALUE="#DDAADD">
    <PARAM NAME="FontName" VALUE="Comic Sans MS">
    <PARAM NAME="FontSize" VALUE="12">
    <PARAM NAME="FontItalic" VALUE="0">
    <PARAM NAME="FontBold" VALUE="0">
    <PARAM NAME="FontUnderline" VALUE="0">
    <PARAM NAME="FontStrikeout" VALUE="0">
    <PARAM NAME="TopPoints" VALUE="0">
    <PARAM NAME="BotPoints" VALUE="0">
</OBJECT></CENTER><BR><BR><CENTER>
<INPUT TYPE="button" value="click ME to change"
onclick="changes" Language="VBScript"></CENTER>
<SCRIPT>
      sub changes

            MyLabel.Caption="See. . . I TOLD YOU!"
            MyLabel.ForeColor = "6316128"
            MyLabel.BackColor = "167111680"
            MyLabel.FontName = "Arial"
      end sub
      sub MyLabel_Click
            MyLabel.Caption="Watch me change!!"
            MyLabel.ForeColor = "65280"
            MyLabel.BackColor = "14527197"
            MyLabel.FontName = "Comic Sans MS"
       end sub
</SCRIPT>
</BODY>
</HTML>
```

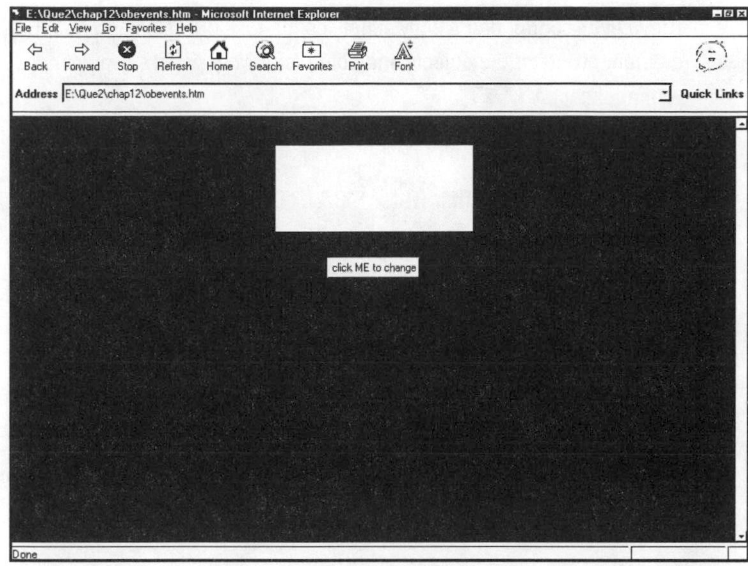

FIG. 11.2
The ActiveX label control is changed by the button control and by itself through the use of events.

In this example, an ActiveX label object is used, but some scripting features and some events have been added. First, an ActiveX label control is defined, then a button control is added using the `<INPUT>` tag; some events with the scripts have also been used. When the user clicks the button, the label changes. When the user clicks the label after the button has been pressed, the original label returns. Both of these actions are events. When a user clicks the button, an event occurred which caused the label to change. The OnClick attribute in the `<INPUT>` tag caused that event to trigger. The OnClick attribute itself is an event and its value calls a Visual Basic Script procedure which causes the label to change.

The contents of the label are changed back by just using a script and additional attributes to the `<OBJECT>` tag of the label are not included. In the script used in this page, there are two subroutines. The first subroutine is used by the button control, and the second subroutine is used by the label object to change its contents back. As you notice in the second subroutine, the name of the label object (MyLabel) is followed by an underscore and the name of an event. This means, that when the OnClick event is true (when the event occurs) for the object named, then the statements contained in this subroutine are to be evaluated.

With form controls, objects and other entities, you can use their events as attributes if the controls you are using them with supports that event. You can also use the event in a subroutine as well. Table 11.3 lists some attributes to the `<SCRIPT>` tag. The next section will cover the syntax for using events, methods, and properties of objects in Visual Basic Script.

The ActiveX control pad greatly simplifies the task of assigning Visual Basic commands for different events of the objects and controls on your page, so you can focus more on the design of your application.

Table 11.3 Additional *<SCRIPT>* Tag Attributes

Attribute	Function
EVENT	Specifies the event (for the object or control specified by FOR) used to invoke the following code encapsulated in the `<SCRIPT>` tag with these attributes.
FOR	Specifies which object or control on the page to use the following script for, if the event specified by the EVENT attribute occurs.
LANGUAGE	Specifies which language should be used. The value for this is always "VBScript" for Visual Basic Script or "JavaScript" for Javascript.
EventName	A pseudonym for an event. Any event for a specified object or control can be used as an attribute for one of the four mentioned tags (`<BODY>`, `<INPUT>`, `<OBJECT>`, and `<A>`). The value for this event is always a subroutine in both Visual Basic Script and Javascript. You must use the LANGUAGE attribute and whatever event attribute you specify together in the same tag. Some event names that can be used as attributes are listed in Table 11.4. Note that the compatibility of these attributes vary with different objects and controls. Also, this method may not work with some ActiveX controls.

Table 11.4 A Sample Table of Some Events Used for Different Objects by VBScript

EventName	Function
OnClick	Triggered when the user clicks the corresponding control or object.
MouseOver	Triggered when the user positions the mouse pointer over the corresponding control or object.
DblClick	Occurs when the user double-clicks the corresponding object or control.
OnLoad	Occurs when a document object or other controls are loaded in the current page.

Visual Basic Scripting

This section's main goal is to familiarize you with some of the elements of Visual Basic Script that you need to know in order to understand how Visual Basic Script works with objects and controls on a page. To that end, this section focuses on the syntax of how to call methods, how events are triggered, and how to set properties for different objects and controls.

Setting Properties for Controls and Objects Setting properties for different objects in a page is perhaps one of the simplest tasks to do in Visual Basic Script. The general syntax for doing this is:

```
<SCRIPT>
...
ObjectName.property = value
...
</SCRIPT>
```

ObjectName is the name or identity of your object specified by the ID or NAME attribute, *property* is a specific property for the object named by ObjectName, and *value* is the value that property is set to. Consider this piece of code from Listing 11.2:

```
...
            MyLabel.Caption="Watch me change!!"
            MyLabel.ForeColor = "65280"
            MyLabel.BackColor = "14527197"
            MyLabel.FontName = "Comic Sans MS"
...
```

NOTE It is always possible (especially in the Internet Explorer 3.0 Object model) for child objects (nested objects) to exist. If a specific property is needed of a child object, append a . (period) followed by the name of the child object after ObjectName, then specify the property in the same manner as shown in the syntax (for example: `object.child1.value = "some stuff here"`. `object` is the name of the object, `child1` is the name of the child object and `value` is a property of the object `child1`). This method holds true for any number of nested objects, should they exist.

The preceding section of code illustrates several properties used by Visual Basic Script for the object named MyLabel, which is a text label. The first property is the Caption property, set to the value of "Watch me change!!" Next, the properties of ForeColor (foreground color of the text) and of BackColor (background color of the text) are set, and finally, the FontName property is set to Comic Sans MS. This is how you set properties for any object or control on the page. The properties for ActiveX controls vary from control to control, and the properties for controls specified by the `<INPUT>` tag are the attributes used in that tag (such as VALUE and NAME). Other tags on the page have properties too, including the document itself, anchors, and other objects described in the Internet Explorer 3.0 object model section.

Triggering Events Visual Basic Script is known as an event-driven language. Everything in Visual Basic Script operates by events. Some of the events listed in Table 11.4 work with many controls and objects. There are a few ways for specifying what happens in a script when an event occurs. The following list shows the syntax of three ways for specifying what happens when a certain event is triggered:

- *Specifying events as attributes:* You can specify an event as an attribute of a tag for an object or control on a page. The value of this attribute should be a subroutine which you have already defined inside a Visual Basic Script tag. The LANGUAGE attribute (see the attributes of the <SCRIPT> tag in Table 11.3) must be included as an additional attribute to this tag, if the specified subroutine is to be used. The general syntax is:

  ```
  <... EventName="method" LANGUAGE="VBScript" ...>
  ```

  where EventName is any valid event for the corresponding object or control and method is the name of the subroutine that is evaluated when the specified event occurs. The LANGUAGE attribute is used to specify which language to use and must be included when an event is specified on a page.

- *Specifying events for an element in a script tag:* Using the attributes described in Table 11.3, you can specify, in the <SCRIPT> tag what event of what object to use the following code for. This is useful if you have multiple subroutines and statements outside of subroutines that need to exist in your script. The syntax for doing this is:

  ```
  <SCRIPT LANGUAGE="VBSCRIPT" FOR="ObjectName" EVENT="EventName">
  ➥... </SCRIPT>
  ```

  The LANGUAGE attribute is used to specify which language to use (Visual Basic Script, of course), the FOR attribute is used to specify the name of the control or object to use the following code for, and the EVENT attribute specifies what event causes the following code to be invoked.

- *Specifying an event by using a subroutine:* This may well be the simplest method of triggering an event and executing some code after the event has occurred. This method uses a subroutine with the same name as the object or control you intend to use with an underscore and the name of the event appended to it. The general syntax follows:

  ```
  <SCRIPT LANGUAGE="VBScript">
  ...
  sub ObjectName_ObjectEvent
  ...
  end sub
  ...
  </SCRIPT>
  ```

  The actual subroutine consists of two parts: ObjectName, which is the name of the object you wish to use the event for, specified by EventName. When the event specified by EventName occurs for the object specified by ObjectName the statements in the subroutine are evaluated. A subroutine is always the procedure involved when events are used for different objects and controls. However, other procedures and functions can be called from within that subroutine.

The following listing fragments illustrate two of the aforementioned methods in Listing 11.2. Events are specified as attributes, and are also used as subroutines inside the code. Re-examine this listing again:

First, look at the button control, specified by the `<INPUT>` tag. It has the attribute OnClick, which is an event that calls the subroutine *changes* in the `<SCRIPT>` section. This event, obviously, is when the user clicks the button. In the subroutine *changes* several properties of the label named MyLabel are changed, as you can see.

```
...
<INPUT TYPE="button" value="click ME to change"
onclick="changes" Language="VBScript"></CENTER>
<SCRIPT>
      sub changes

            MyLabel.Caption="See. . . I TOLD YOU!"
            MyLabel.ForeColor = "6316128"
            MyLabel.BackColor = "167111680"
            MyLabel.FontName = "Arial"
      end sub
...
```


Now, examine the second subroutine in the script. Its name is MyLabel_Click. From this, you know that this subroutine is called when the Click event for the object named MyLabel occurs. When this happens, a set of properties for MyLabel are changed. This is the whole logic behind this program.

```
...
<OBJECT ID="MyLabel" WIDTH=215 HEIGHT=93
 CLASSID="CLSID:99B42120-6EC7-11CF-A6C7-00AA00A47DD2">
    <PARAM NAME="_ExtentX" VALUE="5689">
    <PARAM NAME="_ExtentY" VALUE="2461">
    <PARAM NAME="Caption" VALUE="Watch me change!!">
    <PARAM NAME="Angle" VALUE="0">
    <PARAM NAME="Alignment" VALUE="4">
    <PARAM NAME="BackStyle" VALUE="1">
    <PARAM NAME="Mode" VALUE="1">
    <PARAM NAME="FillStyle" VALUE="0">
    <PARAM NAME="FillStyle" VALUE="1">
    <PARAM NAME="ForeColor" VALUE="#00FF00">
    <PARAM NAME="BackColor" VALUE="#DDAADD">
    <PARAM NAME="FontName" VALUE="Comic Sans MS">
    <PARAM NAME="FontSize" VALUE="12">
    <PARAM NAME="FontItalic" VALUE="0">
    <PARAM NAME="FontBold" VALUE="0">
```

```
    <PARAM NAME="FontUnderline" VALUE="0">
    <PARAM NAME="FontStrikeout" VALUE="0">
    <PARAM NAME="TopPoints" VALUE="0">
    <PARAM NAME="BotPoints" VALUE="0">
</OBJECT></CENTER><BR><BR><CENTER>
...
sub MyLabel_Click
            MyLabel.Caption="Watch me change!!"
            MyLabel.ForeColor = "65280"
            MyLabel.BackColor = "14527197"
            MyLabel.FontName = "Comic Sans MS"
      end sub
</SCRIPT>
</BODY>
</HTML>
```

All events have pneumonic names, so it is easy to tell what an event does. For example, the DblClick event is the double-click event.

Calling Methods In this section, you will learn how to call methods from your scripts. This section does not examine procedures in detail; it illustrates general syntax and how to call procedures of objects and procedures you create yourself. A procedure is always a function or a subroutine. To call a subroutine from within your script, use the following syntax:

```
call ProcedureName(arguments)
```

ProcedureName is the name of the method you are calling, and *arguments* (surrounded in brackets) are any values that are passed to that procedure (arguments for a procedure are not required, unless that specific subroutine or function requires them). As previously mentioned, you always use the subroutine method when events happen to objects. For example:

```
<SCRIPT>
...
sub MyObject_Click()
alert "This is a subroutine which is called _
when the Click event happens for the MyObject object."
end sub
...
</SCRIPT>
```

The statements in the subroutine are evaluated when the Click event for MyObject occurs. This would not work for a function, because a function is a procedure which returns a value. Subroutines can return values as well, but the function itself is returned as a value. For example:

```
<SCRIPT>
...
y = 2
x = GiveValue(y)
alert x
...
function GiveValue(a)
      GiveValue = a +4
end function
...
</SCRIPT>
```

However, different objects do have methods which are functions as well as subroutines.

Remember, you can also use the same general syntax expressed previously for calling methods of an Object or a control. Listing 11.3 shows an example of a subroutine and a function call in a script, as well as calling a method from the ActiveX Label Object. Figure 11.3 illustrates Listing 11.3. The file, ACTVX12.HTM can be found on the CD that comes with this book.

Listing 11.3 ACTVX12.HTM—This Listing Demonstrates the Use of Procedures in VBScript

```
<HTML>
<HEAD>
<TITLE>An HTML Document Using ActiveX controls and procedures</TITLE>
</HEAD>
<BODY BGCOLOR="mistyrose">
<OBJECT ID="IeLabel1" WIDTH=170 HEIGHT=93
 CLASSID="CLSID:99B42120-6EC7-11CF-A6C7-00AA00A47DD2">
    <PARAM NAME="_ExtentX" VALUE="3625">
    <PARAM NAME="_ExtentY" VALUE="2461">
    <PARAM NAME="Caption" VALUE="Click Me">
    <PARAM NAME="Angle" VALUE="0">
    <PARAM NAME="Alignment" VALUE="4">
    <PARAM NAME="Mode" VALUE="1">
    <PARAM NAME="FillStyle" VALUE="0">
    <PARAM NAME="FillStyle" VALUE="1">
    <PARAM NAME="ForeColor" VALUE="#FF0000">
    <PARAM NAME="BackColor" VALUE="#373737">
    <PARAM NAME="BackStyle" VALUE="1">
    <PARAM NAME="FontName" VALUE="Matura MT Script Capitals">
    <PARAM NAME="FontSize" VALUE="24">
    <PARAM NAME="FontItalic" VALUE="0">
    <PARAM NAME="FontBold" VALUE="0">
    <PARAM NAME="FontUnderline" VALUE="0">
    <PARAM NAME="FontStrikeout" VALUE="0">
    <PARAM NAME="TopPoints" VALUE="0">
    <PARAM NAME="BotPoints" VALUE="0">
</OBJECT><BR CLEAR="ALL">
<INPUT TYPE="button" NAME="button1" VALUE="Get Value">
```

continues

Listing 11.3 Continued

```
Enter Angle:
<INPUT TYPE="text" NAME="AngleInpt" VALUE="0" SIZE="10" MAXLENGTH="10">
The Sine is:
<INPUT TYPE="text" NAME="SineInpt" VALUE="0" SIZE="10" MAXLENGTH="10">

<SCRIPT LANGUAGE="VBScript">
      dim pi
      pi = 4 * atn(1.0)
      sub button1_OnClick
            dim angle, sinangle
            angle = AngleInpt.value
            sinangle = getsin(angle)
            SineInpt.value = sinangle
      end sub
      function getsin(angle)
            getsin = sin((pi * angle)/180)
      end function
      sub ieLabel1_Click
            call ieLabel1.AboutBox
      end sub
</SCRIPT>
</BODY>
</HTML>
```

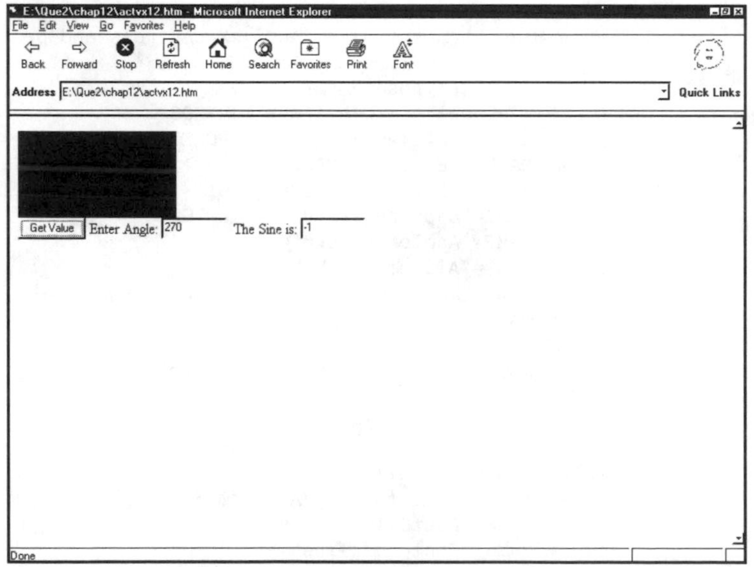

FIG. 11.3
This figure illustrates two controls. When the label is clicked the About Box method is called. The input boxes are used to calculate the sine of a given angle (in degrees).

Basically how this program works is: When the user clicks on the label, the About Box of that label is shown. When the user enters a number in the first input box which is preceeded by the text “Enter Angle” and clicks the button, the number is then converted into radians and the sine for that angle is calculated and displayed.

There are several methods used in the code; this section discusses them as they appear in the <SCRIPT> tag. The first procedure is called when the user clicks on the button named button1; this happens to be the only button on the page. When this event occurs, a series of methods is called.

First, all the variables you are going to use for this program are declared. Next, the value that the user specifies in the input box named AngleInpt is retrieved. Next, a function is called that passes an *argument* which is the value specified by AngleInpt. This function converts the angle from degrees to radians, then calculates the sine of that angle (radians are the base angle measure for trigonometric intrinsic functions of Visual Basic Script). That value is assigned to the name of the function (getsin) which then returns the value to the variable we specified it to return to. Finally, this value is displayed in the text box named SineInpt. Simply, the two methods involved in this entire process are the button1_OnClick subroutine (which, if you remember, is called when the user clicks the button) and the function `getsin(angle)` (`angle` is the argument which is used to convert the angle measure into radians).

The methods used with the ActiveX label control are very unsophisticated. Basically, there are two methods involved: the one that is called when the label is clicked on (ieLabel1_Click), and the method that is called inside that method (ieLabel.AboutBox(). Methods are usually called from various objects using the following syntax:

```
call ObjectName.MethodName()
```

Remember the *call* keyword from the former syntax section; its purpose is to call the specified method. ObjectName is the name of the object you wish to call the method for, and MethodName() is the name of the method for that object you are calling. The object name and the called method are separated by a . (period). Also, the brackets immediately following MethodName are not required for a method so long as no arguments are used with the method.

Using the Internet Explorer 3.0 Object Model

This section briefly discusses the Internet Explorer 3.0 Object Model and the various objects associated with it. This section highlights the main portions of the Internet Explorer 3.0 Object model, which includes the Window Object, the Document Object, the Frames Object and a few others. Figure 11.4 shows the hierarchy of the objects used in the Internet Explorer 3.0.

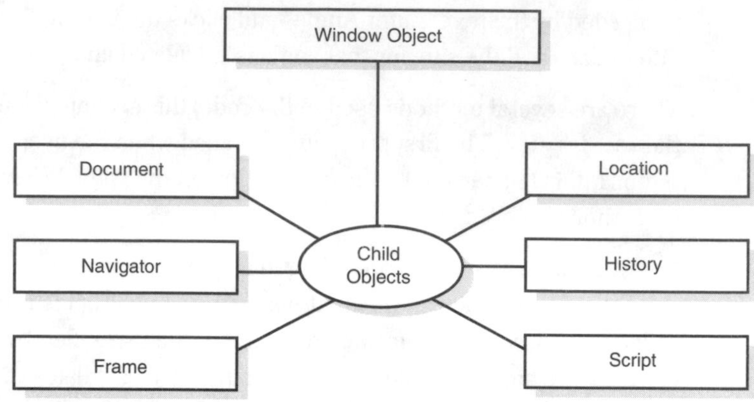

FIG. 11.4
This figure illustrates how all the objects of the Internet Explorer 3.0 Object Model are related. The six objects shown are child objects of the document object at the top of the figure.

In Figure 11.4, all the objects are child objects of the Window Object. The Window Object represents Internet Explorer and its methods, properties, and events, as well as the six following objects in their entirety. The Window Object has several methods, properties, and events. Some of these key methods, properties, and events are listed in Tables 11.5–11.7. The Window object is the default object; you do not have to append any of its properties or child objects to it in Visual Basic Script. For example, instead of:

```
window.name
```

you could just use:

```
name
```

Table 11.5 The Properties of the Window Object

Property Name	Purpose
Frames	Used when there is a frame set in the current document. This property is an array representing the frames on the page. This will be covered in the frames section.
Location	Specifies the location of the current window. This is identical to the location object which is covered later.
Name	Indicates the name of the window the property is in. If it is in a frame, the name assigned to that frame is used. If there are no frames, then this property does not have a value unless you assign it one.
Parent	Indicates the parent frame or window this property is in. If there is no frame, then this property refers to the browser window.

Table 11.6 Some Key Methods of the Window Object

Method	Purpose
Open	Opens or closes a document inside the current window or another specified window. It has two arguements: the name of the file you want to open and the name of the window you wish to open it in in the form of: window.open(*filename,windowname*) where *filename* is the name of the file and *windowname* is the name of the window you want to put it in. Both arguments are required.
Prompt	Specifies a pop-up prompt that the user can enter data into. It also has two arguments: the text that describes the prompt and any default text which goes in the prompt in the form of: window.prompt(ExpString,DftString) where ExpString is the text that describes the prompt and DftString is the default text in the prompt. Both arguments are optional. If this method is assigned to a variable (such as x = prompt("stuff","more stuff")) then the variable assigned the prompt will receive any data that was entered in the prompt unless cancel was pressed.
Close	Closes the window.
Navigate	Navigates the window to another URL in the form of: window.navigate(URL). Where URL is the name of the URL to go to.

Table 11.7 Some Key Events of the Window Object Model

Event	Purpose
OnLoad	This event is triggered when the page containing this event is *loaded.* This is used in the `<BODY>` tag as an attribute to call a procedure.
OnUnLoad	This event is triggered when the page containing this event is *closed.* This is used in the `<BODY>` tag as an attribute to call a procedure.

Using the Document Object

The Document object primarily deals with the body of an HTML page. It has three child objects: the Link, Anchor, and Form object. Each of these objects are an indexed array of the number of links, anchors, and forms found on a document. The Form object further contains the Element object, which is an indexed array of all the objects and controls on the page. Some key properties and methods are listed in Tables 11.8 and 11.9; no events exist for the document object.

Table 11.8 Some Key Procedures of the Document Object

Procedure	Purpose
BgColor	Sets the background color of the current document. This color can be a #rrggbb hexadecimal number or a valid color name (see Appendix B for details on color names).
FgColor	Sets the foreground (text) color of the document, in the same manner as the BgColor property.
Referrer	Indicates the URL of the document that referred to the page the user is currently on. For example, if someone accessed http://www.nm.org/welcome.htm from http://www.someplace.com then the referrer property would be http://www.someplace.com, if this property was in the page of the former location. If there is no prior referrer, then the string returned is a NULL.
LastModified	Indicates the date when this document was last modified.

Table 11.9 Some Key Methods of the Document Object

Methods	Purpose
Open	Opens the document for purposes of writing additional lines of HTML. Its general format is: document.open().
Write	Writes text and HTML to the current document and should be called when the document is opened for writing. Its general format is: document.write(*somestring*) where *somestring* can be one string, a variable, or several concatenated strings formatted in HTML which are written to the screen.
Close	Closes the document after any document.writes have taken place. The general format is: document.close(). Remember, the ()s do not have to exist after the method if no arguments exist.

Using the Frame Object

The Frame Object is an indexed array of the number of frames on a page. The first frame of the index corresponds to the frame in the uppermost left-hand corner of the browser. You can use this object to set or get different URLS of the different frames that are on the page. The frame array is similar to the window object in that it can use the other objects in the same manner. For example, you can use the location object to get or set the location of the corresponding frame, and you can use the history object to navigate through that frame's history.

Using the History Object

The History Object's main purpose is to access the history list of the browser. This history list lists all the places you have visited during your Internet sessions with this version of Internet Explorer 3.0 (beta 2). There are a few properties for this tag, and three methods which are used to navigate through the history folder. Some key properties, and methods are listed in Tables 11.10 and 11.11. The history object has no events.

Table 11.10 Some Key Properties of the History Object

Property	Function
Length	Specifies the length or the total number of URLs visited in this sessions history. Currently, the only number that is returned is 0. This will be fixed in future versions.

Table 11.11 Some Key Methods of the History Object

Method	Purpose
Go	Specifies how many times the browser should go forward in the history list, in the format of: history.go*(n)* where *n* is the number of the history file to jump to.
Forward	Specifies how many times the browser should go forward in the history, in the format of: history.forward*(n)* where *n* is the number of times to go forward.
Back	Specifies how many times the browser should go back in the current history of your browser, in the format of: history.back*(n)* where *n* is the number of times back the browser should go.

Using the Location Object

The Location Object is used to provide information about the current location of Internet Explorer. Some key properties are listed in Table 11.12. There are no events or methods for the Location Object.

Table 11.12 Key Properties of the Location Object

Property	Purpose
Href	Gets the URL of the current window, or to give the current window a new URL.
Protocol	Retrieves or sets the Protocol type (such as FTP or HTTP) of the current document. What is returned or set is the protocol type followed by the colon (the URL "ftp://ftp.nowhere.org" would return "ftp:" using this property).
Host	Retrieves or sets the host portion of the URL of the current document along with the port number being used.
Hostname	Retrieves or sets the hostname portion of the URL. This is exactly the same as the host property, except the port number is not included.

Using the Navigator Object

The Navigator Object is used to provide application information about the browser. Some of this information includes the code name of the application, the user agent of the application, the name and version of the application. Some key properties are listed in Table 11.13.

Table 11.13 Some Key Properties of the Navigator Object

Property	Purpose
appCodeName	Indicates the code name of the current browser.
AppName	Returns the name of the application.
appVersion	Indicates the version number of the current browser.
UserAgent	Returns the name of the UA (user agent) of the browser.

Using the Script Object

The Script Object was covered fully under the "Looking Closer at the `<SCRIPT>` Tag" section earlier in this chapter.

Using ActiveX Controls and the ActiveX Control Pad

This section describes some of the ActiveX controls you can use with your application and briefly overviews the ActiveX control pad and its usefulness in designing an Application for your Web Page. There are several ActiveX controls which are included with the ActiveX control pad which are dysfunctional or behave in an unusual manner. You can find information about all the ActiveX control's properties, methods and events with the extensive help provided with the control pad. The script wizard also enables you to easily embed scripts in your HTML document that enable you to seamlessly interact with the ActiveX controls or other elements you have defined for a page. The following list describes some ActiveX controls and their usefulness in designing a Visual Basic Script Application:

- *The Label Control:* The Label Control is a pretty interesting control. Not only can you set different values to font sizes, captions, foreground and background colors, but you can also set values for different points on the label which gives the text an irregular "twisted" effect.
- *The Tab Control:* By using the Tab Control, you can easily set and present numerous options with a slick "tab" interface as seen with many applications.
- *The Image Control:* The Image control is used to specify an image to be put on the page or layout.
- *The Text Box Control:* The text box control is virtually the same control as the one specified by the `<INPUT>` tag.
- *The Button Control:* The button control is virtually the same control as the one specified by the `<INPUT>` tag.
- *The Combo/Drop-down List Controls:* The Combo/Drop-down List Controls can contain a list from which you can select multiple entries, or a drop-down menu from which the user can choose options. These controls are similar to the controls specified by the `<SELECT>` tag.
- *The ActiveX Layout Control:* This control is the most important control for designing your Visual Basic Script applications on your Web page. With it, you have absolute control over the layout of your page. Formerly, all blank space beyond two spaces in HTML was considered "white space" and was collapsed accordingly. This ActiveX control actually references a file with all the ActiveX controls on this layout and any code associated with them.

From Here...

In this chapter, you have learned the bare essentials of designing a Visual Basic Script application. You now have an understanding of how objects and their events, methods and properties work. You now know how to use Visual Basic Script to call procedures based on different events that occur for an object, and you are familiar with how to call and define procedures. You've also learned about a few ActiveX controls which can help you design your application. Remember, there are many more ActiveX controls in the ActiveX control pad than are mentioned here, but some are defunct due to licensing problems with Internet Explorer 3.0 beta 1, which will be resolved in the next release. There are over 2,500 commercially-available ActiveX controls.

In the chapters that follow, you will be provided with an extensive overview of the syntactical elements of the Visual Basic Script language, and a comparison to other Visual Basic family languages and Java script. Some of these chapters include:

- Chapter 14, "Comparing Scripting Languages," discusses the differences between Visual Basic Script (VBScript), Visual Basic for Applications (VBA) and Visual Basic (VB).
- Chapter 15, "VBScript Data Types and Variables," begins the long chain of chapters that explain the different elements of Visual Basic Script, including Variants and Data types, Procedures, Operators, and other elements of the Visual Basic Scripting language.
- Later chapters in Part 5 cover the multimedia aspects of the Internet, such as Active VRML and serving multimedia content across Web servers.

CHAPTER 12

A Simple VBScript Page

by Ron Schwarz

When you complete this chapter, you'll have a good grasp of what VBS is, and how to use it. You'll have the foundation required to grasp the information provided in the rest of this book. At that point, you should have a "feel" for VBS, and be able to rapidly pick up the more weighty information that follows.

Although you will create some working VBS pages in this chapter, you will not find HTML covered to any great extent. HTML is covered in greater depth in Chapter 2, "Review of HTML." This chapter is a full-immersion in VBS, and VBS alone. ■

Visual Basic Basics

Visual Basic (VB), and Visual Basic Scripting Edition (VBS, or VBScript) are very similar, but there are some key differences. In this chapter you learn some rudiments to bring you up to speed.

Script-Enabled Web Pages

Several elements come into play when you create a VBS-enabled Web page. This chapter brings them together.

HTML and Controls

Learn how to insert HTML and ActiveX controls onto a simple page, and add scripting to tie them together.

Creating a Working Page

Once you know the basics, it's easy to create a script-enabled page, and understand how and why it works.

Coming Up to Speed with Visual Basic

If you're familiar with Visual Basic, you may want to skip ahead to the next section, "Identifying the Important Differences Between VB and VBScript." If, however, you're new to VB, take a moment here to bone up on VB essentials. This short primer will help you understand a few important VB principles.

Visual Basic is a programming language that features a visual IDE (Integrated Development Environment) which is used to create Windows applications. In VB, you create "Forms," which contain "Controls," and associated code. A VB Form is a window. (A VB form is related in name only to an HTML form.)

When you write a VB program, you begin by placing controls, such as Labels, TextBoxes, and Command Buttons on a Form. Form creation is interactive, and very easy. You select controls from a toolbox, and place them on the form. You use the mouse to position and size them, and set their properties from the Properties window, which is a list of properties and values.

After you create an object (a form or a control) you set its Properties, and enter event code, and non-event program code. (Simply double-clicking a form or control will bring up the editor, with the cursor positioned in an automatically created procedure skeleton for the selected object.)

At this point, it might be good to remind yourself that we're discussing VB, and *not* VBS. The reason for this will become apparent when we begin to discuss VBS.

Properties, Events, and Methods

In Visual Basic, most objects (such as Forms and Controls) have three key features: Properties, Events, and Methods. A *Property* controls a characteristic, such as size, color, contents, or position. *Events* are things that occur while the program is running. Examples are mouse clicks, keystrokes, and form resizing. *Event Procedures* are blocks of code that are automatically executed when the associated event happens. For example, when the mouse is clicked over a form named Form1, the Form1_Click procedure will be executed.

You can also have Sub procedures and Functions that are *not* associated with events. These routines must be accessed by other code–they will not execute automatically.

Methods are instructions to objects. When you invoke a method, you are telling the object to execute a specific set of instructions. Examples of Methods are Print, Refresh, Show, and Hide.

These principles all carry over to VBS, even though their actual implementation is quite different.

Visual Basic code is located in either the General or Events sections of a Form. (Code Modules are similar to Forms, but contain only a General section, and have no visual interface.)

The General section consists of two parts. The first part is the Declarations section, which contains non-executable code, such as variable and API call declarations. The rest of the General section contains procedures that are not attached to events. An example of a procedure in the General section would be a routine that centers your form on the screen. Such a procedure could be called from anywhere, and is not directly attached to any one specific event.

The Events section of a Form contains Sub procedures that *are* connected to events. When you click a Command Button, for example, any code in its Click event (such as Command1_Click) will execute.

Identifying the Important Differences Between VB and VBScript

There are three main areas in which VBS differs from VB. These are the development environment, the instruction set, and the user interface.

At this time, it might be good to point out that VBS is not a new version of VB, nor is it a general purpose programming language. While you may be able to port certain routines from a VB app to a VBS script, you will *not* generally be able to port most entire applications to VBS, barring superhuman effort far beyond the point at which the law of diminishing returns has been invoked.

VBS is designed to make Web pages interactive and intelligent. By leveraging your VB skills, you'll be able to get up to speed quickly. Although you may have to make a conscious effort to remember that a VBS-enabled Web page is not a VB application, you'll find the possibilities, especially when using VBS in conjunction with the powerful new HTML Layout features, to be endless.

Development Environment

When Microsoft first announced VBScript, it had no IDE. All coding, control creation and placement—*everything*—had to be done in code, and all code had to be created with an ASCII text editor, such as Notepad. Now, the ActiveX Control Pad makes creation and maintenance of VBS pages nearly painless. Like "real" VB, VBS pages can be designed interactively and visually. The IDE provided with the ActiveX Control Pad is *very* similar to the one in VB, and you'll have no problem transitioning to it if you're at all familiar with VB.

Still, there are differences. Perhaps the most notable are the lack of a Run Mode, and the lack of a Debugger. (Remember, you're not creating programs, *per se*, but Web pages, and the "run environment" of a Web page is a Web browser—so, the final product of your efforts, for all its amazing power and flexibility, is not a program in the literal sense; it requires a specialized environment—such as the Internet Explorer—in order to run.)

▶ **See** "Understanding Core HTML Components," **p. 24**

In HTML, you're working with a document, rather than a VB-style "form." The browser receives the page as a stream of data, and formats it as it displays it. If you change the width of the browser window, in most cases, you'll also be reformatting the contents of the page.

As a result of this inherent difference from the VB form model, on-screen control placement is essentially determined by control declaration context. Where you "create" your controls determines where they will be placed in the document when it's displayed.

As limiting and restrictive as this sounds, you can do quite a bit by carefully constructing your HTML and using advanced features, such as frames. When you are script-enabling existing HTML pages, this is probably what you'll find yourself doing most of the time. However, when creating new pages, you will be wise to consider doing most, if not all, of your development within HTML Layout Style Pages.

▶ **See** "Introducing the ActiveX Control Pad," **p. 63**

▶ **See** "Creating a Standard HTML Page," **p. 83**

▶ **See** "Creating an HTML Layout Page," **p. 107**

HTML Layout Style Pages provide a very close approximation of the Visual Basic Form model—you can place, position, and size ActiveX controls on a page anywhere you choose, without any regard for HTML stream-of-text issues. And, you can set properties by using a Properties window, just as you can in VB. Finally, you can use a powerful Script Wizard to manage event code and method insertion.

Instruction Set

VBS is a subset of the Visual Basic language. Many statements, features, and functions you may be accustomed to using in VB are not available. Some are missing due to security considerations (you wouldn't want to have critical files on your local machine corrupted or deleted simply by clicking a link on a Web page, for instance), and others are unimplemented to keep the "footprint" small. You can work around some of the differences (for example, you can use the `ElseIf` keyword to compensate for the lack of a `Select Case` structure, and you can use multiple arrays instead of using typed record variables), but others may very well present impenetrable barriers. There is, for example, no direct file I/O available. This means you won't be able to use any sequential, binary, or random file I/O in your scripts. The specific differences in instruction sets are covered in greater detail in later chapters. For now, be aware that there *are* differences, many of which are non-trivial.

User Interface

VBS provides a high degree of flexibility and functionality. However, unless you are using HTML Layout Style Pages, it is important to keep in mind the fact that the underlying container is still an HTML Web page, and is *not* a VB form. Much of the "look and feel" of a VBS-enabled page is determined by (and, limited by) HTML factors. Elements such as toolbars, menus, MDI forms, multiple windows, and standard graphics methods are for the time being beyond the province of VBS scripting. (However, it is possible to implement many of these features by using ActiveX controls—by keeping a watchful eye on the market, you will quite likely to find controls appropriate to the task at hand, as new ones are constantly being developed and released.)

As HTML Layout Style Pages become more of a standard, you can expect demand for (and proficiency in) "traditional" HTML pages to rapidly diminish. Still, it's good to learn as much as you can, because they will be with us in one form or another for some time, even as they are superseded by the newer standard.

Users who have used a variety of Windows apps, and are familiar with existing Web browsers, will have little difficulty making the transition to VBS-enabled pages. Users who are new to Web browsers, and users whose exposure to Windows apps is limited to Web browsers (of which there are quite a few) can expect to experience a bit of a learning curve. This *will* be ameliorated by virtue of the ease of use these pages provide.

Creating a VBS-Enabled Page

A VBS-enabled page consists of a mix of HTML blocks and/or HTML Layout declarations, Control declarations, and VBS scripts. (Strictly speaking, Control and Script blocks are also HTML, but we are now examining the differences between HTML code and VBS code.) HTML is a fairly crude language (it is essentially a top-down text formatter), and one advantage you have over a "pure" HTML programmer is the fact that much of the HTML functionality can be done more simply in VBS. Still, you'll need to learn some HTML basics, and this section will give you what you need to get started. HTML itself is covered in greater detail in Chapter 2, "Review of HTML."

HTML Syntax and Statements

If you've used WordPerfect in the past, you're probably already familiar with the most noticeable characteristic of HTML tags—paired commands. Most HTML commands are used in pairs. For instance, if you wanted to center a line of text, you'd precede it with a `<Center>` command (or "tag") and place a `</Center>` command at the end. (The "`/`" in the second command designates it as the closing half of a command pair.) Everything inside the block is centered, even if it requires multiple lines of text.

Because HTML is designed to be formatted on-the-fly by the browser, whitespace generally is meaningless. Carriage returns, tabs, and spaces are "eaten" by the browser, in the absence of specific formatting commands. (This affects control, as well as text placement.) Therefore, this block:

```
<Center>Simple HTML Command Demo</Center>
```

is functionally identical to this block:

```
<Center>
Simple                                   HTML

Command
Demo
</Center>
```

Next, we'll examine a few HTML statements.

<HTML> The `<HTML>` statement is used at the beginning and end (as `</HTML>`) of a page. It tells the browser that everything in the resultant block is HTML code and text.

<Head> The `<Head></Head>` section exists primarily for purposes of source code organization. As a rule, you should place non-displayed parts of your HTML page in the `<Head>` section. This includes VBS scripts, but not control declarations.

<Body> The `<Body></Body>` block is the counterpart to the `<Head></Head>` block. Place your displaying elements here, such as text, links, and controls.

<Title> The `<Title></Title>` block defines a block of text, which is placed in the title bar of the browser. It is similar to a VB form's Caption property.

<Hn> The `<Hn></Hn>` block defines a text style used for headers. `<H1>` is the largest, `<H2>` is the next smallest, and so on. (`<H6>` is the smallest.)

<Script...> `<Script...>` and `</Script>` tags are used to mark off your VBS scripts. Their use is discussed further on in this chapter in the section labeled "Script Blocks."

<Input...> The `<Input...>` tag is used to declare HTML controls. Its usage is explained later on in this chapter in the section titled "Buttons."

<Object...> The `<Object...></Object>` pair is used to declare ActiveX controls, and is described later on in this chapter in the "Declaring the Controls" section.

<!...> Prefacing any HTML tag with a "!" changes it into a comment, similar to Rem or "'" in VB.

<!-- ... --> You can mark several lines with the Extended Comment tags. These are open-ended (no closing ">") at the start, and close-ended at the end. All lines in between will be converted to comments, if your browser cannot execute them. This can be used to hide your `<Script>` blocks from displaying as text on browsers that cannot execute them. They will still not execute, but they will at least not show up on the users' screens.

NOTE The tag for comments and extended comments is the same: `<!... >`. (Note the exclamation point.) The dashes (`--`) are not required but do add readability. Hence, the following listings are syntactically identical:

```
<! This is a single line comment >

<!-- And so is this -- >

<! This is an extended (multi-line) comment. Some browsers improperly
interpret comments that span more than one line, so this form should
be avoided. >
```

<A HREF=...></A> The `<A>` (Anchor) tag is generally used to designate a link to another URL. The format is:

```
<A HREF="http://url.address"></A>
```

<P> `<P>` is the Paragraph command. When you want to insert a carriage return in the flow of text (which also determines control placement), insert a `<P>` command. This command is different from most HTML statements in that it is not part of a command pair. There is no closing `</P>` statement, because `<P>` does not create a block; it merely inserts a line break wherever it appears.

<Center> `<Center>` and `</Center>` create a block of centered text. All text between them is centered. Placing `<P>` paragraph markers inside a centered block will insert line breaks, but will not turn off centering. The same applies for other HTML formatting command pairs, which are covered in more detail in other chapters.

Control Declarations

As discussed earlier, there is no visual "drag and drop" means for placing controls on Web pages when using VBS. Instead, controls are embedded in pages by means of declaration statement blocks. There are two types of controls: HTML controls, and ActiveX controls. Each type is declared using its own syntax, which we will examine in this section.

HTML Intrinsic Controls HTML has a number of built-in controls, including equivalents to the Command Button, OptionButton, CheckBox, ComboBox, and TextBox that are used in VB programming.

Although they offer similar functionality, there are differences in usage.

ActiveX Controls ActiveX is the name that Microsoft has given to 32-bit custom controls contained in .OCX files. They are the successors to the venerable .VBX controls, which were designed for earlier (16-bit) versions of Visual Basic.

A wide selection of ActiveX controls are available, providing nearly limitless potential. We'll examine two (Label and Timer) that are primarily intended for use with the Internet Explorer. Once you learn the techniques involved in embedding them in HTML, you'll be able to make use of others as the need arises.

Script Blocks

All VBS code is contained in Script blocks. These are HTML blocks beginning with `<Script>` (see following code segment), and ending with `</Script>`. You can have more than one block; however, at least the first one must specify VBS as the language you're using, as in:

The `LANGUAGE=` clause tells the browser that this script contains VBScript code (as opposed to another scripting language, such as JavaScript). Following scripts on the same page can simply begin with `<Script>`. The `<Script>` tag has other options; we'll examine some of them later on.

Code contained in a VBS script falls into one of three categories: initialization code, event code, and non-event code.

Initialization Code Initialization code is code that executes when the Web page loads, without requiring any action on the user's part. If you're familiar with VB, you're familiar with the Form_Load event, which executes when a form is loaded into memory, and the Sub Main procedure, which will execute automatically when a program is loaded (if the project has the "Use Sub Main" option selected). VBS initialization code is similar; however, it actually hearkens back to pre-VB days. Earlier versions of BASIC, such as

QuickBasic and PDS 7.x were (like VBS) non-window-oriented languages. Although they had Sub procedures and Functions (like VB), they also had the ability to place executable code outside of any named procedures. In VB, only non-executable code, such as variable and API declarations, can be placed outside of named procedures.

VBS will allow you to place executable code there; however, there are a few caveats, and doing so is not encouraged unless you have a specific reason, and are prepared for some extra work. You may find, for instance, that when you set properties of ActiveX controls in your initialization code, not all of them are in fact assigned, yet no errors are generated.

Event Code Just as in "regular" VB, objects used with VBS can generate events. And, like VB, event code will automatically execute when the associated events occur.

The ActiveX Control Pad can, like the regular VB IDE, create event headers for you.

Non-Event Procedures In addition to writing procedures that execute automatically when objects generate events, you can also create procedures that can only be invoked by code. The format is the same as that used with event procedures, with the following exceptions: you can create Functions, as well as Sub procedures (Functions return a value in their name, and are invoked on the right side of the equal sign), and, you can declare your own parameter lists.

Before you can create your first page, you will need to have an understanding of data types, and controls. The next two sections cover this material.

Introducing Data Types

VB has a variety of data types, including user-defined typed structures. VBS, however, has only one data type: the Variant. Fortunately, a variable of Variant type can contain nearly any type of data, and treat it as a subtype. So, you can store strings, numeric values, dates, and so forth. You can use the `VarType` function to determine what subtype is in use in a particular variable, and there are several conversion functions built into VBS that make it possible to convert data from one subtype to another. These features are described more fully in Chapter 15, "VBScript Data Types and Variables."

A short summary of several common data types follows:

Type	Description
Boolean	Either returns True or False
Byte	Unsigned Integer limited to a range of 0 – 255
Integer	Signed integer, range is –32,768 – 32,767

continues

continued

Single	Single-precision floating-point subtype; can hold negative values from –3.402823E38 to –1.401298E-45, and positive values from 1.401298E-45 to 3.402823E38
Double	Double-precision floating point subtype; can hold very large (or small) values
Date	Value contains a numeric representation of a date
String	Can hold a string up to about 2 billion characters; fixed-length strings are not supported

Introducing Controls and Events

Now that we've had an overview of controls and events, let's dig in and actually create some pages that use them. We'll begin with a simple page that demonstrates the use of HTML intrinsic controls, and then we'll create another page that uses ActiveX custom controls. We'll also have a chance to see how both event and non-event code are created and used.

Creating Your First VBS-Enabled Page

In this example, we'll use the Button and Text HTML intrinsic controls. We'll also take a sneak peek at the underlying IE (Internet Explorer) object architecture, which provides access to and control of many of the built-in features of the IE.

▶ **See** "Using the Internet Explorer 3.0 Object Model," **p. 197**

The first example is only slightly more ambitious than a "Hello World" first effort; it uses a few lines of HTML and a short script to determine the current URL, and, accepts input for a new one. Then, it changes to the new location when a Button control is clicked. Here's the full listing:

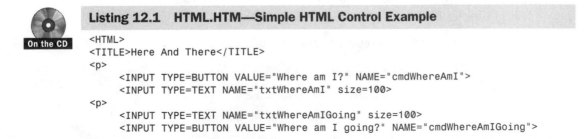

Listing 12.1 HTML.HTM—Simple HTML Control Example

```
<HTML>
<TITLE>Here And There</TITLE>
<p>
     <INPUT TYPE=BUTTON VALUE="Where am I?" NAME="cmdWhereAmI">
     <INPUT TYPE=TEXT NAME="txtWhereAmI" size=100>
<p>
     <INPUT TYPE=TEXT NAME="txtWhereAmIGoing" size=100>
     <INPUT TYPE=BUTTON VALUE="Where am I going?" NAME="cmdWhereAmIGoing">
```

```
<SCRIPT LANGUAGE="VBScript">
     Sub cmdWhereAmI_OnClick    'Event generated when Button is clicked
          txtWhereAmI.Value = Location.href
                                'Load Text control with current location
     End Sub                    'End of event procedure

     Sub cmdWhereAmIGoing_OnClick    'Event generated when Button is clicked
          Location.href = txtWhereAmIGoing.Value
                                'Set new location, from Text control contents
     End Sub                    'End of event procedure
</SCRIPT>
</HTML>
```

Startup This example begins with three simple HTML statements:

```
<HTML>
<TITLE>Here And There</TITLE>
<P>
```

The first line is the standard HTML opener—it tells the browser that what follows (up to the closing `</HTML>` at the end of the page) is HTML code. (Even though VBS Scripts are not strictly speaking HTML code, they are contained within `<Script>` blocks, which *are* HTML.)

The next line creates a Title which will be displayed in the browser's Title bar. (In Visual Basic, the corresponding element is a form's Caption property.)

The third line marks a new paragraph. This causes an empty carriage return to be inserted, to leave a little whitespace at the top of the page.

Controls The next few statements include several `<Input...>` tags. The `<Input...>` tag does not have a closing tag; this is because the declaration information is contained *within* the actual tag, and no closing tag is required.

`<Input...>` is used to declare an HTML Intrinsic control that is used to interact with the page. The TYPE= parameter declares which control (for example, Text or Button) will be used.

Remember, this is HTML, not VB (or even VBS), so *where* we declare the control determines its actual physical placement on the page. If you declare it at the top of the page, it appears at the top; if you declare it in the middle, it appears in the middle. (Using the HTML Layout Page features provides a powerful mechanism for dealing with this, and once you gain proficiency with VBS, you'll probably want to use it, and the ActiveX Control Pad, for most serious development.)

▶ **See** Chapters 3-5, which cover these topics in depth.

The first control declaration line creates a Button control, and assigns it a Name and Value.

```
<INPUT TYPE=BUTTON VALUE="Where am I?" NAME="cmdWhereAmI">
```

After we declare the TYPE= as BUTTON, we need to assign two other properties: VALUE, and NAME. VALUE is the same as the Caption property in Visual Basic. Whatever you assign as the VALUE of a Button control will appear on the button. In this case, the button will say "Where am I?"

The NAME property is identical to the Name property in Visual Basic. It assigns a name to the control. Whenever you reference a control in code, you refer to it by its NAME property.

In addition to this fairly straightforward declaration, it is possible to use more complex declarations. This is described in detail in Chapters 9, "An Introduction to Distributed Objects," and 20, "VBScript Forms, Controls, and Managing Transactions."

NOTE The HTML Button control is the HTML equivalent for the Visual Basic CommandButton control, which is itself simply the standard Windows command button.

The next line creates a Text control, and assigns it a Name and Size.

```
<INPUT TYPE=TEXT NAME="txtWhereAmI" SIZE=100>
```

Like the Button control, the Text control has a NAME property, which is used to reference the control in code. The Text control also has a SIZE property, which is used to assign a width for the control when it's created in the browser. HTML controls use a simplified series of properties when compared to Visual Basic. If you're a VB user, you may be surprised at the lack of Height and Width properties. The height is determined automatically, and the width is expressed in the maximum number of characters you want to allow in the control. In this case, we assign 100 characters as the maximum.

Text controls also have a VALUE property, which corresponds to the Text property in a Visual Basic TextBox control. If you assign any text to the VALUE when you declare the control, it will appear in the control when the control is created in the browser. Likewise, any time you assign text or a string to the VALUE in code, it will replace any existing contents with the new text. To determine what text the control contains, you read the VALUE property.

NOTE The HTML Text control is similar to the TextBox control used with Visual Basic. It's a window that the user can type in, and it can also be pre-loaded with text. Unlike its Visual Basic counterpart, it has no MultiLine property—this means that it can accept only a single line of text. (For MultiLine text entry requirements, you can use the TextArea HTML Intrinsic control.)

▶ **See** "Understanding Core HTML Components," **p. 24**

The next three lines add another <P> paragraph break (to provide some more whitespace, and to assure that the next two controls start on a new line) and two more controls—another Text control and another Button control.

At this point, the HTML part of the page is complete (with the exception, of course, of the closing </HTML> tag at the very end of the page). If you placed the </HTML> tag after the control declarations, you'd see the page in all its glory, just as it will appear after you add the Script to enable it. However, it will be brain-dead; you'll be able to type in the Text controls, and click the Buttons, but since there is no code to deal with those properties and events, nothing will happen. The next section details the simple script that enables this sample to actually do something.

Code The actual script is contained in a block of matching HTML tags. The `<SCRIPT LANGUAGE="VBScript">` tag marks the beginning of the script, and the `</SCRIPT>` closes it. Everything between these tags is VB, *not* HTML.

Listing 12.2 HTML.HTM—Event Code for HTML Control Example

```
<SCRIPT LANGUAGE="VBScript">

     Sub cmdWhereAmI_OnClick     'Event generated when Button is clicked
          txtWhereAmI.Value = Location.href
                    'Load Text control with current location
     End Sub        'End of event procedure

     Sub cmdWhereAmIGoing_OnClick     'Event generated when Button is clicked
          Location.href = txtWhereAmIGoing.Value
                    'Set new location, from Text control contents
     End Sub        'End of event procedure

</SCRIPT>
```


The code in Listing 12.2 contains two event procedures. The `cmdWhereAmI_OnClick Sub` procedure is automatically executed when the button named `cmdWhereAmI` is clicked by the user. (Similar behavior rules apply to the `cmdWhereAmIGoing_OnClick` procedure.)

The first procedure sets the `Value` property of the `txtWhereAmI` Text control to the current value of the `href` property of the `Location` object. This results in the Text control displaying the URL for the current page.

▶ **See** "Using the Internet Explorer 3.0 Object Model," **p. 197**

The second procedure changes `Location.href` to the contents of `txtWhereAmIGoing.Value`, which causes the browser to load the page at the URL contained in the Text control.

To try out the example, load the CD that accompanies this book, and navigate to the icon for HTML.HTM, then double-click it. (You will need Internet Explorer 3.0 or higher installed on your machine; if you haven't already installed it, do so before trying any of the examples in this book.)

Figure 12.1 shows what you'll see when you run the program contained in Listing 12.2, and click the button captioned "Where Am I?"

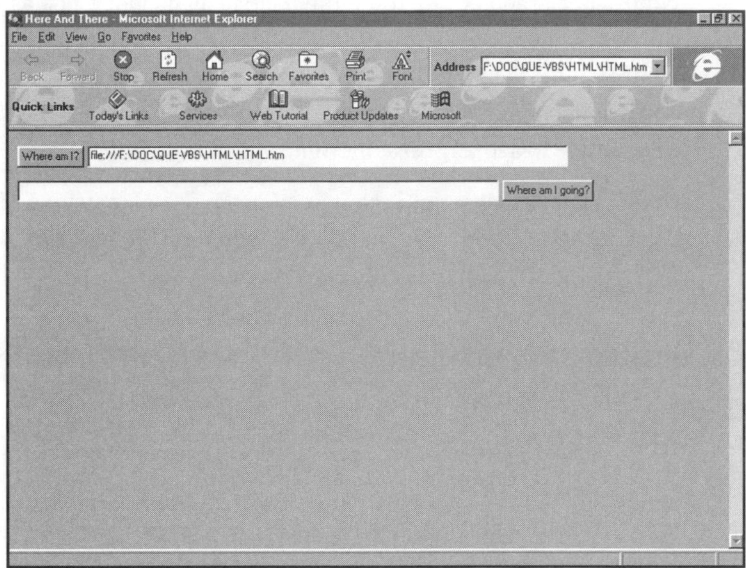

FIG. 12.1
Here and There (HTML.HTM).

Using ActiveX Controls

From an implementation perspective, the same general rules that apply to HTML controls apply to ActiveX controls. The main difference is declaration style. ActiveX controls are more powerful and flexible than intrinsic HTML controls, and their declaration is more complex, too.

NOTE It is important to remember that ActiveX control declarations take place in "HTML space," rather than inside a `<Script>` block. As a result of their mixed heritage, they require setting a combination of HTML properties and ActiveX properties. Because it is possible for properties from one context to have names similar to different properties in the other context (such as the properties relating to size and alignment characteristics), it is necessary to keep track of which is which when assigning values to them.

In the ActiveX control example that follows next in this chapter, you'll use two controls—a Timer and a Label. At the time this book went to press, the Internet Explorer 3.0, as well as development tools such as the ActiveX Control Pad, were still in pre-release form. It's likely that you'll have these controls automatically installed by either of them, or you can get them from the ActiveX Gallery at:

http://www.microsoft.com/ie/appdev/controls/

You'll also find several other useful ActiveX controls available at that URL.

Using the Timer Control The inTimer (Internet Explorer Timer) control is similar to the standard Timer control that is used in VB. It provides an Interval property, and has a Timer event. The setting in the Interval property tells the Timer how often to fire its Timer event. You enter the number of milliseconds you want to time, and when that time has elapsed, the Timer event occurs. (If you enter 1000, the event will fire once every second.)

If you set the Interval to 0, the event will never occur. (The Timer control also has an Enabled property. If you set it to False, it will have the same effect as setting the Interval to 0.)

Using the IeLabel Control The IeLabel (Internet Explorer Label) control is similar to the standard Label control that is used in VB. There are two principal differences: first, the IeLabel control is an ActiveX control (rather than a built-in control, as is the case in VB). Second, the IeLabel control can be set to display its text at any angle (for example, it can display text diagonally, vertically, upside down, or anywhere in between), whereas the VB label control can display its caption only at 0 degrees—horizontal. It is important to note that the IeLabel control itself does not change angle—it is only the text *within* the control that is rotatable. Therefore, the control needs to be set to a sufficient height to contain the full length of the text it contains, at whatever angle is used.

The display angle is set with the `Angle` property. 0 degrees results in standard, horizontal display of text, the same as a standard label control. The control's display moves counter-clockwise according to the value placed in the `Angle` property. So a setting of 90 degrees causes the text to run vertically, starting at the bottom.

Figure 12.2 shows the Angle property setting in the ActiveX Control Pad (described in Chapters 3-5). In this figure, the Angle property is set to 45, and the control can be seen to have its text display set to a 45-degree angle.

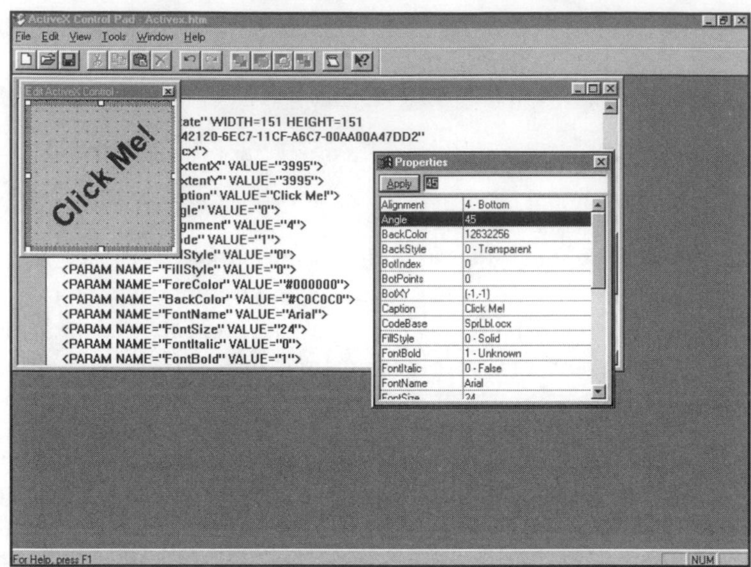

FIG. 12.2
Setting the Angle property.

The IeLabel control has several other properties, including:

Property	**Description**
Caption	Text that is displayed in the control
FontName	Name of font used to display text
Alignment	Aligns text within the control
Height	Height of the control in pixels
Width	Width of the control in pixels
ID	Name by which you refer to the control in code (same as Name property in VB)

NOTE The ActiveX Control Pad, when installed, provides another label control, which although unable to rotate text, *does* provide the unique ability to enter text directly into the control. (When you install the ActiveX Control Pad, you will have a wide selection of controls available, including a TextBox that also allows direct text entry.) Being able to insert text directly into a control when you are designing a form makes it very easy to place content on pages.

Creating Your First ActiveX Page

This example demonstrates the basic elements required in a VBS-enabled Web page using ActiveX controls. You'll create a page that contains the Timer and Label controls, and uses event and non-event procedures.

The complete source for the ActiveX example appears in Listing 12.3, and is contained on the CD accompanying this book in the ACTIVEX.HTM file.

Listing 12.3 ACTIVEX.HTM—The Complete ActiveX Example

```
<HTML>
<HEAD>
<Center><h2>ActiveX Controls Example</h2><Center>
    <SCRIPT LANGUAGE="VBScript">
      Dim Direction

      sub lblRotate_Click
            PrepareRotation "Wheee!"   'call procedure that gets it started
      end sub

      Sub tmrTimer_Timer
            If Direction then
                  lblRotate.Angle=lblRotate.Angle-10
            Else
                  lblRotate.Angle=lblRotate.Angle+10
            End If

            If lblRotate.Angle=0 then   'when horizontal, left to right
                  tmrTimer.Interval=0   'shut off timer
                  lblRotate.Caption="Click Me!"  'restore label
            End If
      End Sub

      Sub PrepareRotation (CaptionText)
            lblRotate.Caption=CaptionText    'set label
            Direction=Not Direction          'reverse direction
            tmrTimer.Interval=18             'start timer
      End Sub
    </SCRIPT>
</HEAD>
<P>
<BODY>
<Center>

----¦
    <OBJECT ID="lblRotate" WIDTH=151 HEIGHT=151 ALIGN=CENTER
 CLASSID="CLSID:99B42120-6EC7-11CF-A6C7-00AA00A47DD2"
 CODEBASE="ielabel.ocx">
    <PARAM NAME="Caption" VALUE="Click Me!">
    <PARAM NAME="Angle" VALUE="0">
    <PARAM NAME="ForeColor" VALUE="#000000">
```

continues

Listing 12.3 Continued

```
    <PARAM NAME="FontSize" VALUE="24">
    <PARAM NAME="FontBold" VALUE="1">
</OBJECT>
¦----

</Center>
    <OBJECT ID="tmrTimer" WIDTH=60 HEIGHT=49
     CLASSID="CLSID:59CCB4A0-727D-11CF-AC36-00AA00A47DD2"
     CODEBASE="inTimer.ocx">    </OBJECT>
</BODY>
</HTML>
```

As with the previous example in this chapter (HTML.HTM, under "Creating Your First VBS-Enabled Page"), this example begins with a standard `<HTML>` tag. This time, however, we're including a `<Head>` tag, so as to better conform with coding standards, which suggest placing all scripts in the `<Head>` section of the page, and all displayed elements in the `<Body>` section. Note that for modern browsers, these conventions will have no effect on display or execution of scripts. Still, HTML is far from a readable language, looking in its raw form more like ancient GWBASIC code than a modern programming language like Visual Basic, so, anything that enhances your ability to understand code *after* it's been written should be utilized. And, segregating VBScript code from the page proper is a good first step.

Here are the first three lines of the example:

```
<HTML>
<HEAD>
<Center><h2>ActiveX Controls Example</h2><Center>
```

The `<H2>` (fairly large heading) line is also placed in the `<Head>` section as per standard practice. (See Chapter 2, "Review of HTML," and Appendix B, "HTML Reference," for more on HTML.)

Having said all this, we're now going to (apparently) break with this pattern, and examine the example in a seemingly random pattern. There is a method to the madness, however; it's called HTML. It's *because* of the vagaries of HTML, which require declarations to be placed as a hodgepodge scattered throughout the document, that we have to examine it this way. (Scripts are placed ahead of content, and controls are embedded in content. Before you can understand scripts, you need to understand controls.)

Designing the Layout

After creating the HTML skeleton, the first stage in creating a page is layout design. Remember, we're not in VB anymore, so it's not a simple process of dragging controls around on a form. All positioning is determined by placement in the text (and to a lesser degree by factors such as <Center> tags and Align attributes), and size is determined by setting properties in HTML code. (Of course, when you're using HTML Layout Pages—discussed in Chapters 3–5—you are free of HTML limitations, and you *can* work in a manner nearly identical to VB.)

Declaring the Controls

Declaration of ActiveX controls is handled differently from declaration of HTML intrinsic controls. However, they are still declared using HTML tags; they are *not* declared inside of VBS scripts. And, unless you're using the ActiveX Control Pad to create HTML Layout Pages, they are also subject to the rules concerning positioning on the page: where they are declared in code determines where they appear when the page is displayed.

Here's the first declaration encountered in the ACTIVEX.HTM example. It creates an instance of the IeLabel (Internet Explorer Label) control:

```
<OBJECT ID="lblRotate" WIDTH=151 HEIGHT=151 ALIGN=CENTER
 CLASSID="CLSID:99B42120-6EC7-11CF-A6C7-00AA00A47DD2"
 CODEBASE="ielabel.ocx">
    <PARAM NAME="Caption" VALUE="Click Me!">
    <PARAM NAME="ForeColor" VALUE="#000000">
    <PARAM NAME="FontSize" VALUE="24">
    <PARAM NAME="FontBold" VALUE="1">
</OBJECT>
```


The IeLabel control is used to place text on an HTML form. It also accepts mouse events, and can display its output at any angle.

The first thing you may notice in this section of the example is the <Object...> open-ended tag. HTML intrinsic controls are declared with the <Input...> open-ended tag, followed by their type, and other HTML properties. ActiveX controls, on the other hand, are declared as Objects, and require additional information. The IeLabel control declared here contains a mix of HTML and ActiveX properties.

HTML properties are defined with a simple assignment statement. The property name is to the left of an equal sign, and the value is on the right. It is important to place them inside the opening <Object...> tag. Note the > after the ALIGN=CENTER assignment. The HTML part of the declaration, including setting of HTML properties, takes place within the opening <Object...> tag itself. The ActiveX properties are placed *after* the <Object...>, but *before* the </Object> closing tag (see Table 12.1). Confused yet? Here's the format:

```
<Object HTML Declarations [HTML Property Assignments]> ActiveX Property
Assignments </Object>
```

Because this declaration is all HTML code, it can be placed on a single line or broken into multiple lines at your discretion.

The HTML part of the declaration contains entries for CODEBASE, CLASSID, ID, WIDTH, HEIGHT, and ALIGN properties. Other controls (or this control in other applications) require additional properties; however, the ones used here are fairly universal.

Table 12.1 ActiveX Properties

Part	Description
`CODEBASE="IeLabel.ocx"`	Points to the filename of the .OCX containing this control (This info is buried deep in your Windows Registry, and can be retrieved, and pasted into an HTML or HTML Layout Page document with the ActiveX Control Pad (described in Chapters 3 – 5). This property is also used to point to a URL containing a control that can be automatically downloaded to the user's machine. See "Using Objects in HTML Pages," in Chapter 11, "Designing VBScript Applications."
`CLASSID="CLSID:99…D2"`	Must point to this control's ClassID in the Registry—the ClassID can be retrieved, and pasted into an HTML or HTML Layout Page document with the ActiveX Control Pad (described in Chapters 3 – 5).
`ID=lblRotate`	The name you'll use for this control in your scripts
`WIDTH=100`	This control's width in pixels in the browser
`HEIGHT=100`	This control's height in pixels in the browser
`ALIGN=CENTER`	This control's alignment on the text line in the browser

The other thing you've probably noticed is that the ActiveX property assignments are a bit more complex then their HTML counterparts. The `<Param...>` tag is used to hold all information for a single declaration. This tag is similar to the `<Object...>` tag in that it contains declaration information *within* the tag, but it is different in that it has no counterpart to the `</Object>` tag.

The assignment is in the format `name="`*`PropertyName`*`" value="`*`Property Contents`*`"`. Note that the property name must be delimited by quotation marks.

The timer control (inTimer) is declared similarly to the the label control; being a different type of control, it uses different properties, but the format is the same, as it is for all ActiveX controls. Here's the relevant section of ACTIVEX.HTM:

```
<OBJECT ID="tmrTimer" WIDTH=0 HEIGHT=0
     CLASSID="CLSID:59CCB4A0-727D-11CF-AC36-00AA00A47DD2"
     CODEBASE="inTimer.ocx">    </OBJECT>
```

This declaration only contains HTML property assignments. We set its ActiveX Interval property in VBS code in the "Writing Event Handlers" section of this chapter. We set its Width and Height to 0, since it's an invisible control, and we don't want it to consume any more HTML space than necessary.

Script Block Declaration

```
<SCRIPT LANGUAGE="VBScript">
     Dim Direction
```

Here, we declare the beginning of our Script block. We also create a script-level variable with the `Dim Direction` statement. This variable is available to all procedures in our script. (Scoping issues are discussed in the next section of this chapter, "Writing Event Handlers.")

Writing Event Handlers

Event handlers are contained inside a `<Script>` block. (Event handlers are Sub procedures that automatically execute whenever the specified event occurs. They are covered more extensively in Chapter 18, "VBScript Event Programming.")

The first event handler in the script deals with the Click event of the Label control. Because the ID of the control was set to `lblRotate`, the event handler Sub procedure is named `lblRotate_Click`. (Event handlers begin with the name of the control, and use an underscore to attach it to the name of the event.) This is the actual event code from ACTIVEX.HTM:

```
sub lblRotate_Click
     PrepareRotation "Wheee!"  'call procedure that gets it started
end sub
```

This procedure contains the `Click` event for the `lblRotate` control. In this case, we simply use it to call the `PrepareRotation` non-event procedure, which is discussed later on in this section. This code executes when you click on the label control, and starts the process that makes the label rotate on screen.

Here's the code that executes after it's called by the click event:

```
Sub PrepareRotation (CaptionText)
      lblRotate.Caption=CaptionText    'set label
      Direction=Not Direction          'reverse direction
      tmrTimer.Interval=18             'start timer
End Sub
```

The `PrepareRotation` `Sub` is called from the `lblRotate` Click event, which also passes it the `CaptionText` parameter. Although the call that invokes this routine passes a string literal (text contained in quotation marks), here it is converted to the `CaptionText` variable, because it's declared as a parameter in the `Sub` declaration.

This routine also uses the `Direction` variable, which is available because it was declared at the Script level, rather than declared inside another procedure. (A variable's scope is generally determined by where it is declared. If it is declared inside a script, but outside any procedure in that script, it is available to all procedures in all scripts. If it is declared inside a procedure, it exists only within that procedure.)

This is the place where we set the timer control's `Interval` property, which tells the control to begin its countdown to firing its `Time` event. We have set it to 18 milliseconds. (When it is set to 0, which is its default, the event never fires.)

Next, the event handler for the Time event of the Timer control (inTimer) is added. Here's the complete event routine:

```
Sub tmrTimer_Timer
      If Direction then
            lblRotate.Angle=lblRotate.Angle-10
      Else
            lblRotate.Angle=lblRotate.Angle+10
      End If

      If lblRotate.Angle=0 then    'when horizontal, left to right
            tmrTimer.Interval=0    'shut off timer
            lblRotate.Caption="Click Me!"  'restore label
      End If
End Sub
```

The `tmrTimer` event procedure fires each time the interval assigned to the timer control's `Interval` property transpires. The code in this event procedure does a fair amount of work. It contains two If/Then blocks (described in Chapter 17, "VBScript Control of Flow and Error Handling"). The first one tests for the direction of rotation. If it's True, it decreases the value of the Angle property of the label control by ten degrees; otherwise, it increases it by ten degrees:

```
If Direction then
     lblRotate.Angle=lblRotate.Angle-10
Else
     lblRotate.Angle=lblRotate.Angle+10
End If
```

The second If/Then block determines when to stop moving:

```
If lblRotate.Angle=0 then    'when horizontal, left to right
     tmrTimer.Interval=0     'shut off timer
     lblRotate.Caption="Click Me!"  'restore label
End If
```

When the Angle property of the label control equals 0 (indicating that the text is at a horizontal, left-to-right orientation), it shuts off the timer by setting its Timer property to 0, and restores the label's caption to its original contents.

Listing 12.4 contains the complete ActiveX example page. Locate the ACTIVEX.HTM example on the CD, then double-click its icon to load it into your browser. You'll see a label captioned "Click Me!" When you click the label, its caption changes, and it begins to rotate in a clockwise direction. When it has completed 360 degrees, it stops, and its caption is restored. If you click it again, it rotates again in the opposite direction. If you click it while it is rotating, it immediately reverses direction.

Here's how it will look after you load it (see fig. 12.3):

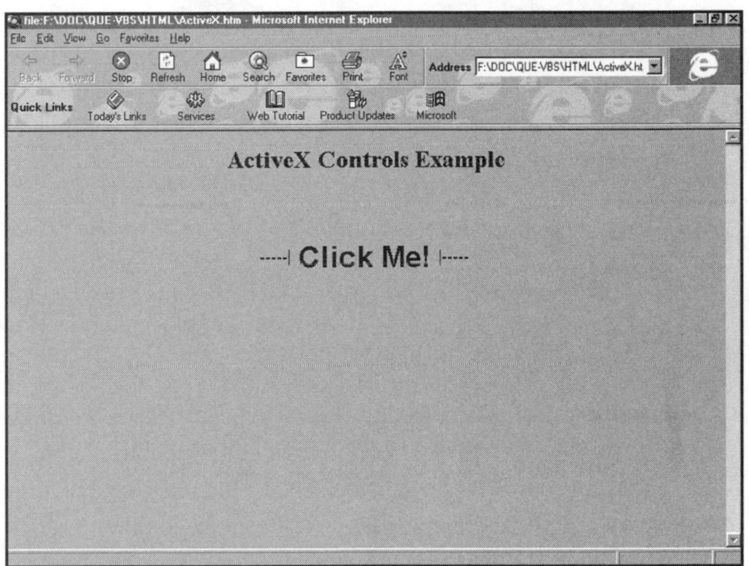

FIG. 12.3
ACTIVEX.HTM example.

And here's how it will appear right after you click the label (see fig. 12.4):

While this demonstration doesn't accomplish any real work, it does demonstrate how just a few lines of VBS code, combined with a couple of control declarations, and a handful of HTML code, can automate a Web page.

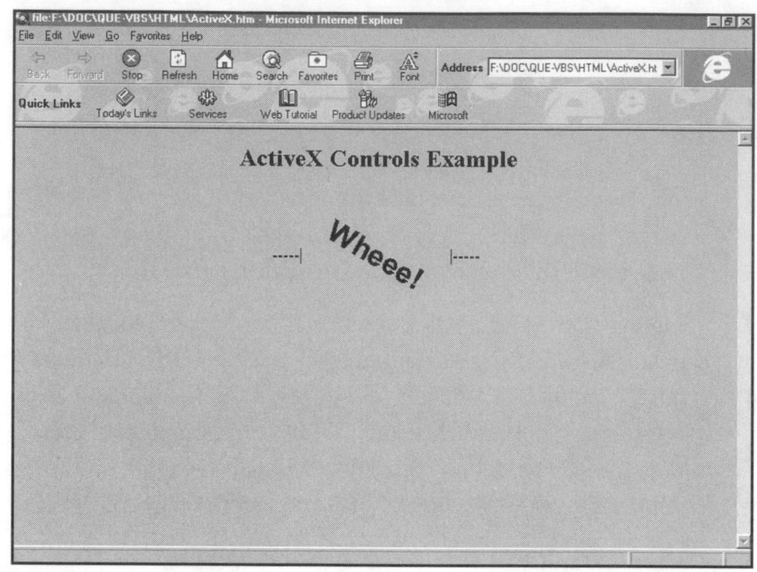

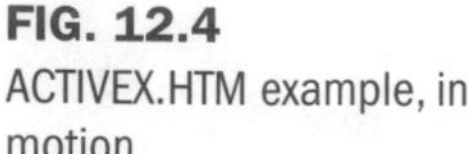
FIG. 12.4
ACTIVEX.HTM example, in motion.

We've placed the VBS script code in the `<Head>` block, although it will work fine in the `<Body>` too. By placing it all in the `<Head>` section, we free up the `<Body>` for control declarations (remember, where we declare them determines where they appear), and text. This makes formatting the actual page much simpler, as the HTML source will more closely resemble the final output in the browser.

Testing the Page

Before a page is published it needs to be tested. You'll probably want to do most of your initial testing locally (rather than over the Internet, or on your Intranet server) unless you have a high-speed network connection and tools to make the upload relatively transparent.

Local Testing Local testing is fairly painless, since it essentially consists of saving the HTML file with your text editor, then either double-clicking its icon, or clicking the Reload button in your browser (if it's currently loaded from a previous test). There are a few caveats, however. If your page includes links to other pages or files, you have to make sure that the links are either absolute links (fully qualified URLs), or, if relative links, are duplicated on both systems (your local machine and the remote host on which the page will ultimately reside) in the exact same structure.

NOTE Relative links are links that point to a file in a directory that is relative to the current URL. Absolute links point to a complete URL.

This is a relative link:

```
<A HREF="/pages/page1.htm"><B>First Page</A></B>
```

And this is an absolute link:

```
<A HREF="http://www.nethawk.com/~rs><B>Home Page</A></B>
```

Note that the relative link doesn't include a host name—it only includes a path and file name.

Relative links are generally preferred because it is easier to port a page from one machine or path to another, but you *must* make sure to port *all* files that are referenced, and keep them in the same path relative to the original. If you keep all related files in the same directory as your page, you're set—just copy them all together. If you include them in a tree inside your working directory, it's fairly trivial to duplicate the tree on the target machine. If, however, you are referencing lateral branches and facing the task of duplicating massive or complex directory structures on other machines, you may want to consider editing your page to use a more concise structure.

▶ **See** "Understanding Core HTML Components," **p. 24**

As with most programming issues, there are tradeoffs, and no two situations are exactly alike. If you are aware of the considerations from the outset, you can craft your pages in such a way as to minimize porting headaches later on.

Remote Testing Unless you are developing your pages on the same machine that will serve as their HTTP server, you need to transfer them before they can be accessed by Internet or Intranet users. As flawlessly as they may perform after extensive local testing, you still need to run them through their paces after you place them on the server. Subtle errors, usually related to link names, frequently fail to be detected during local testing.

From Here...

For more information on HTML programming, check out *A Beginner's Guide to HTML*, at the following URL:

http://www.ncsa.uiuc.edu/General/Internet/WWW/HTMLPrimer.html

Also, check out these other chapters for additional information:

- See Chapter 2, "Review of HTML," for a discussion of general HTML programming issues.

- See Chapters 3-5 for information on the ActiveX Control Pad and HTML Layout Pages.
- See Chapter 12, "Designing VBScript Applications," to learn details of script and object integration.
- See Chapters 16-21 for extensive information on the essentials of the VBScript language.
- Refer to Que's *Special Edition Using HTML* for an exhaustive study of HTML.

CHAPTER 13

Comparing VBScript, VBA, and Visual Basic

by Ron Schwarz

This chapter addresses the differences you'll encounter when coming to VBScript from a background in one of the "traditional" VB dialects (VB/VBA). ■

VBScript for VB programmers

Find out the VB features that are not supported, or behave differently in VBScript.

Syntax differences

Learn how to deal with Declaration and Language constraints.

Design interface issues

The ActiveX Control Pad is an excellent tool for developing VBScript Web page applications and content, but it's different from the VB IDE. Find out how this impacts your coding efforts.

User interface issues

VBScript does not create stand-alone applications. Well-designed script-enabled pages can help alleviate the differences. Find out how in this chapter.

Overview

Because VBS is a subset of VB, the bulk of the information provided in here consists of differences—mainly differences of omission—as documented by Microsoft at the time this book goes to press. (Some of this may change eventually—the VBS specifications have changed more than once since work began on this book, but are expected to stabilize shortly.)

Syntactical differences, covered in Table 13.1, *Declaration Issues*, and Table 13.2, *Language Issues*, are only part of the picture. If you're going to excel in what you're doing, you need to learn the nuances of the platform and accommodate yourself to it.

Trying to "force-fit" either existing code or existing skills to a new environment is tantamount to the backwoods axiom that advises, "Don't force it, use a bigger hammer!" Even if you *do* succeed in fitting the square peg to the round hole, neither you nor your users are apt to be particularly satisfied with the results.

Therefore, it's an absolute necessity that you gear yourself to the language (VBScript), the development tools at hand (ActiveX Control Pad), and the presentation medium (Internet Explorer).

If you're a VB programmer, you can probably remember muddling through the documentation, the IDE, and the language, making small headway until things suddenly "clicked," and it started making sense. This event marked the beginning of your ability to "think in VB," and you can expect a similar illumination after playing with VBS and the Control Pad for a while.

Naturally, you *will* be able to leverage a considerable measure of your existing skills and language. But, it will quickly become apparent that VBS has its own gestalt. It's not too different from situations that occur with spoken language: Cantonese and Mandarin are both "Chinese," but fluency in one does not equate to fluency in the other. So it is with VBS and the other dialects of VB.

You'll find some of the differences maddening at first, but the frustration will diminish as you begin to work instinctively.

There are two main reasons for omitted functionality. The first consideration is security (it would be poor form to make it easy for unscrupulous individuals to harm users who stumble upon their websites), and "weight" (because of issues such as download time and memory footprint, VBS is designed to be a "lightweight" implementation of the language).

Declaration Comparison

Table 13.1 covers the declaration changes documented by Microsoft. If you're experienced with one of the other dialects of VB (VB or VBA) you should take the time to familiarize yourself with the differences now, to avoid frustration later on.

Table 13.1 Declaration Issues

Declaration	Issues
Declare	DLL API calls are not implemented due to security considerations, and because VBScript is intended to be a cross-platform language. (Windows-specific API calls would fail on a browser running on a non-Windows OS.)
Property Get	Not applicable due to absence of Class creation support in VBS.
Property Let	Not applicable due to absence of Class creation support in VBS.
Property Set	Not applicable due to absence of Class creation support in VBS.
Public (variables)	Not currently supported—conflicting information available. *May* be implemented in final release.
Private (variables)	Not currently supported—conflicting information available. *May* be implemented in final release.
Static	Use global variables when you need to retain contents between invocations of a procedure.
ParamArray	Optional arguments not legal.
Optional	Optional arguments not legal.
New	Not possible to create new objects. Only legal to create aliases to existing instances of objects.
Array function	Not supported. Use explicit assignments of each element of an array to load with values.
Option Base	Not supported. All arrays have starting subscript of 0.
Private (procedures)	Not currently supported—conflicting information available. May be implemented in final release.
Public (procedures)	Not currently supported—conflicting information available. May be implemented in final release.
Dim (arrays)	You cannot use the Dim Array(LowerBound To HigherBound) form of the Dim statement. All arrays begin with a 0 subscript. You can create a multi-dimensional array, but all dimensions must begin with an implied element 0.

continues

Table 13.1 Continued

Declaration	Issues
Const	Constants are not supported in VBScript. Use variables, and for convenience, make their names all uppercase, with words separated by an underscore, in other words, MAX_USER_COUNT. Note that this will not make a variable into a constant—you will not be protected from inadvertently changing the value of the variable. It is strictly a means for identifying variables that are being used as ersatz constants.
Built-in Constants	The only built-in constants currently implemented in VBScript are `True` and `False`.
Dim *X* As	The `As` keyword is not supported because in VBScript all variables are of Variant type. It is likewise illegal to append a type-declaration character (such as !, @, #, $, %, &) to a variable or literal. Hence, both VehicleYear% and 1967% are illegal.

While not all VB funtionality is supported in VBScript, implemented features are fortunately highly compatible with their VB counterparts. This behavior carries over to most language elements, covered in the next section, "Language Comparison."

Language Comparison

Table 13.2 lists the changes in language elements at the time this book goes to press. There are significant differences between VB/VBA and VBScript. The changes are essentially changes of ommission—while you will need to learn what to avoid, you won't have to relearn any implemented features, since syntax remains consistent.

Table 13.2 Language Issues

Term	Explanation
Add	User-defined collections are not supported in VBScript.
Count	User-defined collections are not supported in VBScript.
Item	User-defined collections are not supported in VBScript.
Remove	User-defined collections are not supported in VBScript.
! (for Collections)	User-defined collections are not supported in VBScript.
#Const, #If ... Then ... #Else	Conditionals are not supported in VBScript.
DoEvents	Not supported.

Term	Explanation
For Each ... Next	Not supported. Determine actual quantity being counted (such as array UBound), and use a For ... Next loop structure instead.
GoSub ... Return	Not supported—line labels are not supported in VBScript.
GoTo	Not supported—line labels are not supported in VBScript.
On Error GoTo	Not supported—line labels are not supported in VBScript.
On ... GoSub	Not supported—line labels are not supported in VBScript.
On ... GoTo	Not supported—line labels are not supported in VBScript.
Line Numbers, Labels	Not supported in VBScript. (Line Labels are not to be confused with Label controls, which are implemented via ActiveX controls.)
With ... End With	Not supported—use fully-qualified Object.Property names instead.
CCur	Not supported (Currency subtype not implemented in VBScript).
CVar	Not supported, all variables are Variant in VBScript.
CVDate	Not required because there is a built-in Date subtype in VBScript. Was only included in VB4 for backward-compatibility reasons.
Format	Not supported. Use String manipulation functions to build formatted strings as a workaround.
Str	Not implemented in VBScript.
Val	Not implemented in VBScript.
Type ... End Type	Typed records are not implemented in VBScript.
Date Statement	The Date *function* is implemented in VBScript, but the Date *statement* is not. (The function *returns* the current date; the statement *sets* the system clock.)
Time Statement	The Time *function* is implemented in VBScript, but the Time *statement* is not. (The function *returns* the current time; the statement *sets* the system clock.)
Timer	The Timer function is not implemented in VBScript. This should not be confused with the Timer control, which *is* implemented (via an ActiveX control). The Timer function returns the number of seconds that have elapsed since midnight; equivalent functionality can be derived by using the date/time math functions for whatever purpose the Timer function would have produced (as in start/end time logging).

continues

Table 13.2 Continued

Term	Explanation
LinkExecute	Not implemented—VBScript does not offer DDE support.
LinkPoke	Not implemented—VBScript does not offer DDE support.
LinkRequest	Not implemented—VBScript does not offer DDE support.
LinkSend	Not implemented—VBScript does not offer DDE support.
Debug.Print	The Debug object is not implemented in VBScript because there is no means to execute a script within an IDE. (The ActiveX Control Pad provides a development environment, but it does not support *running* scripts within itself.)
End	Not implemented in VBScript. Inapplicable in non-standalone (as in browser-hosted) applications.
Stop	Not implemented, because there is no debug object in VBScript. There is no means to execute a script within an IDE. (The ActiveX Control Pad provides a development environment, but it does not support *running* scripts within itself.)
Erl	Not implemented in VBScript; line numbers are not supported in VBScript.
Error	Old-style error-handling keyword is not implemented in VBScript. Use the Error object's `Raise` method instead.
On Error ... Resume	Not implemented in VBScript. `On Error Resume Next` is the only error-recovery structure available in VBScript (besides the Error object).
Resume	Not implemented in VBScript. `On Error Resume Next` is only error-recovery structure available in VBScript (besides the Error object).
Resume Next	Not implemented in VBScript. `On Error Resume Next` is the only error-recovery structure available in VBScript (besides the Error object).
Open ... Close	No file I/O statements or functions are implemented in VBScript due to security considerations.
Get/Put	No file I/O statements or functions are implemented in VBScript due to security considerations.
Input #	No file I/O statements or functions are implemented in VBScript due to security considerations.
Print #	No file I/O statements or functions are implemented in VBScript due to security considerations.

Term	Explanation
Write #	No file I/O statements or functions are implemented in VBScript due to security considerations.
Financial Functions	No financial functions are implemented in VBScript.
GetObject	Not implemented in VBScript due to security considerations.
TypeOf	Not implemented in VBScript. Use `Is`*`Type`* when necessary to test against specific subtypes.
Clipboard	Not implemented in VBScript due to security considerations.
Collection	Not implemented in VBScript.
Like (Operators)	
Def*type*	Not implemented in VBScript—all variables are of Variant type.
Option Base	Not implemented in VBScript—all arrays begin with a subscript of 0.
Option Compare	Not implemented in VBScript. Use `StrComp` options as a workaround.
Option Private Module	Not supported. (No modules in VBScript.)
Fixed-length strings	Not supported in VBScript. If absolutely required, use standard (variable-length) strings, and pad with spaces to desired length using `Space()`.
Lset	Not supported in VBScript.
Rset	Not supported in VBScript.
Mid Statement	Not supported in VBScript. Do not confuse the `Mid` *statement* with the `Mid` *function*. The function form of `Mid` is used to read characters within a string; the (currently unsupported) statement form is used to insert characters into a string.
StrConv	Not implemented in VBScript—LCase and UCase can be used to provide vbLowerCase and vbUpperCase functionality.
TypeName	Not implemented in VBScript—all variables are of Variant type.

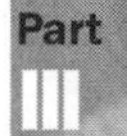

As you can see from Table 13.2, there are quite a few VB features that are unimplemented in VBScript. The reasons are threefold: VBScript is designed to be a *lightweight* language for performance and resource reasons, it's necessary to prevent potential for damage via "dangerous" functions, and, the Web page platform has different characteristics than a VB program. The next section, "Style Differences," shows you how to accommodate yourself to the differences covered so far in this chapter.

Style Differences

Just as VB programming requires a change in philosophy from non-GUI programming, creating script-enabled Web pages hosted in a WWW browser mandates a new way of thinking and coding. To further complicate matters, the Internet is undergoing a series of concurrent—and major—transformations. If change indeed brings opportunity, the Internet is likewise what might be termed a "target-rich environment." It has lots of potential, and it has lots of risk. *Surfing the Web* is more accurate an aphorism than it might seem; the trick is to stay on *top* of the wave.

If you come from a traditional HTML programming background, your head is probably spinning about now. It'll pass. The Web will remain content-heavy, but the fantastic array of ActiveX controls, combined with HTML Layout Page functionality will provide the ability to do more than ever before, and to do it easier than you ever imagined. You'll have to learn to think in new ways, and at first, you'll need to resist the temptation to do things the old way. As long as the traditional HTML methods are more familiar to you than the new ActiveX features, you'll have to discipline yourself to work with the new capabilities, but it will be worth it in the long run, and besides, it won't take *that* long.

VB programmers, on the other hand, will probably feel like they're back in the training-wheel stage. To an extent, it's an accurate perception: VBS *is* rather limited when compared to VB 4.0. But, unlike traditional VB programming, where the program is the totality of your efforts, or even VBA development, where you have freedom from language and security restrictions, VBScript applications are *documents*, and the code itself takes a role subservient to the end product.The changes of style affect you, as a developer, and, they affect the people who use what you write. Whether you're creating Internet pages, used by anyone who stumbles onto your site, or vertical-market intranet systems, you'll have to conform yourself to the realities and requirements of the medium, and the needs and expectations of the users.The following sections focus on the issues you'll need to keep in mind when working with VBScript.

Development Environment

The ActiveX Control Pad (covered in detail in Chapters 3–5) provides an excellent platform for creating script-enabled Web pages. However, convenient and powerful as it may be, it is not a full-featured IDE. In addition to the features that are available in VB, but are not present in the Control Pad, you'll have to deal with the "look and feel" differences, and limitations imposed by the target platform.

Error Control The area that is perhaps most notable in its absence is any type of debugging facility. Because scripts are only one part of a page, it may be some time before there's much debugging capability built-in to VBS development tools. (When you reflect on the complexity of the Internet Explorer, and consider that any debugger worth its salt would have to emulate the IE, in addition to being able to interpret VBScript with the level of detail offered by VB—breakpoints, single-step, expression watches, and so on—it becomes apparent that the undertaking would be monumental.)

This being acknowledged, you *do* still have to deal with debugging issues, and the onus is entirely on you at this stage of the game. What to do? First and foremost, read Appendix C, "VBScript Coding Conventions," and take its message to heart. By rigorously adhering to a set of standards, your code will be readable and understandable, and as a result, you'll be better prepared to comprehend it later on.

Use Option Explicit to help prevent errors caused by typos. Yes, even with Option Explicit turned on, you won't find undeclared variables until you're running your page in Internet Explorer, but at least you *will* find them.

Layout Management When you're first learning VBScript, you'll probably experiment with Notepad, or an equivalent ASCII text editor. It's a fast, easy way to enter a few lines of code and save them to a file. However, once you begin to gain an understanding of ActiveX "stuff" (of which VBScript is but one part), you'll need to make the transition to the ActiveX Control Pad.

While it's true that anything the Control Pad can do interactively, you can do manually in Notepad, it's also true that you can walk from New York to California. This is especially important to remember if you're *really* good in HTML, because you will have to consciously depart from familiar territory to something completely new and alien.

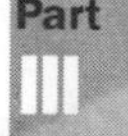

It's likely that HTML as we know it is dead. It may not know it's dead, and maybe a lot of HTML-oriented folks don't know it's dead either. But, that doesn't change the reality that the new Layout Page flexibility has been needed for some time, and is finally available. HTML will remain as the underlying container, but the old-style flow-of-text formatting is gone, gone, gone, once ActiveX takes hold.

Why is this *such* a big deal?

Consider for a moment the confusion that surrounds HTML. The proliferation of new, proprietary formatting codes—everything from special font handling commands to table codes (and everything in between) exists to provide a measure of control over the appearance of the final product. The fact that it's possible at all, given the underlying formatting model, is a testament to the ability of the people writing browser software.

But, it's resulted in language-bloat of gargantuan proportion. It's hard to believe that *anyone* is proficient in the near-countless codes, let alone the variations between one browser and another.

The "big deal" is this: HTML Layout Pages provide a simple, elegant, and workable solution to the problems of placing, sizing, and formatting content and active elements in a web page. They sweep away the need for the vast majority of HTML arcana, and render much of it functionally obsolete. If it was a movie, it would be called, "Buggy-whip manufacturers versus the Model T Redux."

The moral is, don't be so attached to the old way of doing things that you miss out on the opportunity that the new technology presents. It can become a personal issue, especially if you are proficient in the existing system, but don't make the same mistake that so many have before during times of change. Remember the countless programmers who stayed with CP/M, because they thought, "MS–DOS will never make it," or, the ones who stayed too long at the C: prompt, because "Windows? Who needs it!"

It's good to learn from your mistakes. It's better to learn from the mistakes of others. Remember: the trick is to stay on *top* of the wave.

User Environment

When desktop publishing software first became widely available, there was a wave of what were snickeringly referred to as "Ransom Notes"—documents with numerous typefaces and sizes all on one sheet. People went wild playing with fonts, pitches, attributes, and formatting. Everyone became an instant typesetter. People who should have been managing operations instead spent their time playing at "publishing," and simple memos turned into major productions, replete with grammatical and spelling errors galore.

Marshall McCluhan said, "The medium is the message." The sad fact is, people naturally tend to get wrapped up in the glitz and trappings of something new, especially when that something is a graphical presentation system.

While this book can't cover everything you'll ever need to know about style, layout, and presentation, it can at least give you some pointers, and aim you in the right direction.

The first bit of advice is simple. Simple, as in "Keep It Simple." Resist the temptation to do everything, everywhere, every time. You don't *really* have to use every last feature offered by ActiveX and VBS in *each* project you create. To be sure, the temptation will be there—when it's easy to drop a group of controls into a tabbed container, and surround it with buttons and pictures and... You get the idea. Present the users with what *needs* to be presented, in a visually attractive manner, without overwhelming them. Sensory overload is not a pretty sight.

One of the best sources of design insight is available to you immediately. Take a look at the different types of web pages that are posted on the net. As of late, Microsoft seems to be paying particular attention to design issues, and, they seem to be doing a good job of it. Their pages are logical, relatively fast loading, and contain quite a bit of content without appearing "busy" or confusing.

Other sites go to the opposite extreme. You've probably landed at one time or another on a page that took fifteen minutes to load, and consisted of miles of links and random bitmaps all arranged in an incredibly long single column down one drawn-out page.

Some general, and near universal, rules are easy to follow: avoid clutter—don't cram large numbers of controls on one page. If it's really necessary to have a lot of controls, use a tabbed container, and place the controls on tabs according to logical considerations. Try to put yourself in the place of the users. Remember that having thought up, written, debugged, and tested your project, you are intimately familiar with it in its entirety, but, a user dealing with it for the first time will find it all new, and no matter how well-designed it is, a bit intimidating.

The fallacy in our field is the notion that as software becomes increasingly powerful, it becomes increasingly difficult to use. The best illustration of the falsehood of this statement is the new change that is taking over Web programming. It's changing from something of finite capability and incredible complexity, to something of limitless potential, and less and less effort.

From Here...

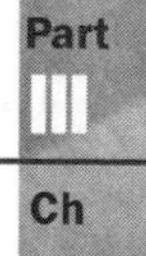

For all the similarities between VB and VBScript, it *is* truly a *major* new approach to programming. The following resources will prove very valuable.

- See Chapters 3–5 for information on using the ActiveX Control Pad.
- See Chapters 15-20 for details on the VBScript language implementation.
- See Appendix C, "VBScript Coding Conventions," for hints on making your code maintainable by imposing consistent structure.
- See Que's *Special Edition, Using VB 4*, and *Visual Basic 4 Expert Solutions*, for extensive information on the Visual Basic language.
- Refer to the *Microsoft Visual Basic Scripting Edition Language Reference*, for exhaustive syntax descriptions and requirements of all statements, functions, and methods.

CHAPTER 14

Comparing Scripting Languages

by Tom Tessier

In this chapter, you learn about Microsoft's implementation of the JavaScript language. It should be noted that JavaScript is *not* Java. While Java is a scaleable, platform-independent language requiring a Java compiler, JavaScript is a scripting language interpreted on-the-fly by a Web browser in much the same manner as VBScript. Developed by Netscape Communications Corporation, JavaScript (known as LiveScript during development) requires no compiler or development kits. In an attempt at compatibility with Netscape's browser, Microsoft has included a JavaScript interpreter within Internet Explorer 3.0. ■

How JavaScript variables and operators work

JavaScript operators and variable data type literals are very similar to their VBScript counterparts, both in usage and in declaration.

How JavaScript execution flow works

JavaScript execution flow and function calling is easily understood when compared to the corresponding VBScript equivalents.

How to use JavaScript objects

Learn how to use the built-in JavaScript objects and how to create your own objects. Examine which VBScript functions equate to the given JavaScript methods.

How JavaScript event programming is used

Thanks to the `onEvent` HTML definition, JavaScript event programming is identical to VBScript event programming.

Real-world example

Examine a real-world example of JavaScript in action, and then view the same page done in VBScript.

NOTE JavaScript is *not* Java. Although JavaScript has syntax and operators exactly the same as that of Java, the concept and capabilities of JavaScript are very different. A Web browser interprets JavaScript on-the-fly upon contact with a page containing the `<SCRIPT LANGUAGE="JavaScript">` tag, whereas Java is first precompiled using the Java SDK and then the resulting bytecodes are placed on a Web server and referenced on a page via the `<APP>` HTML command. When a browser encounters this tag, it loads in the precompiled bytecodes and interprets these on-the-fly.

In essence, Java is half a compiled language and half an interpreted language, whereas JavaScript is entirely interpreted. Both JavaScript and Java resemble C++, without C++'s nuisances such as memory leaks. Java is a distributed language, of considerably more power than JavaScript or even VBScript. Java is comparable to Visual Basic for Applications (OLE creator for use on Web pages) in power.

ON THE WEB

http://java.sun.com If you are interested in Java programming, download the latest free Java SDK from this site.

An Overview of JavaScript

If you've done any Java or C++ programming, you'll be at home with JavaScript. Unlike C++, it is not necessary to include a ; symbol at the end of each code line, but for consistency with Java it is recommended. The C++ comments `// comment text` and `/* comment text */` also pass over to JavaScript. To wrap a section of code down to the next line in JavaScript, use the backslash (\) character. Refer to Table 14.1 for a summary of these very basic JavaScript syntax commands and their VBScript counterparts.

Table 14.1 Comparison of JavaScript and VBScript Basic Syntax

Operation	JavaScript Syntax	VBScript Syntax
Comment	// comment text	' comment text or /* comment text */
Wrap down to next line to continue a section of code	\	_ (underscore)
Code line terminator (optional)	;	N/A

As with VBScript, a JavaScript session is initiated via the `<SCRIPT>` command. However, instead of `"VBS"` the `Language` parameter is set to either `"LiveScript"` or `"JavaScript"`

(LiveScript was the previous name of JavaScript). The following JavaScript code demonstrates how to use the <SCRIPT> tag:

```
<SCRIPT Language="JavaScript">
{
        JavaScript code body here
}
</SCRIPT>
```

It should be noted that both JavaScript and VBScript are *case-sensitive*. This means that the case of letters composing a name or object is important—a variable named `Myvar` is entirely different than one written as `myvar`.

JavaScript Variables and Operators

As you probably know by now, some of the most basic instructions of any programming language are variable declarations and operators. These are used to set up numbers and text strings as well as to perform actions and comparisons that determine the outcome of a given program.

Variables Variables are used to set up numbers and text strings for use later in a program. Variables in JavaScript are assigned exactly the same way as in VBScript. The variable name is on the left, and the corresponding data type literal is on the right. For example, to define an integer, a floating-point literal, a string, and a Boolean, one would write the following JavaScript program:

```
myint = 10;
mystring = "Joe Moe";
myfloat = 50.99;
myboolean = false;
```

The `var` command must be employed if you want to reuse a variable name inside of a function. For example, this JavaScript code changes the original value of the variable `life` to 299:

```
function lifetime()
{
     life = 100;
     changelife();                // call the changelife function
     document.write (life+" "); // write the life variable to the page
}
function changelife()
{
     life = 299;                  // change life variable to 299
                                  // (changes the original variable)
     document.write (life);       // write the life variable
}
```

Part III Ch 14

The page output is `299 299` (`document.write` is a built-in object that places text directly onto the HTML page—see the "JavaScript Objects" section for more information). Now, let's look at the same JavaScript example, this time using var to create a new instance of the `life` variable:

```
function lifetime()
{
     life = 100;
     changelife();                   // call the changelife function
     document.write (life+" "); // write the life variable to the page..will
                                     // be unchanged
}
function changelife()
{
     var life = 299;                 // create a new instance of the life variable
                                     // and initialize it to 299
     document.write (life);          // write this new life variable
}
```

The page output is `299 100`. By using `var`, `life` is redeclared, hiding the previous definition in the code body. When the `changelife` function ends, the second `life` variable is destroyed and the original restored.

Variable and function names must begin with a letter or underscore character. The remaining characters can include digits (0–9) and upper- or lowercase letters. Remember, the case of such variable names is important (in both VBScript and JavaScript)—a function named `MyFunction99` is entirely different from one called `myfuncTion99` (see "JavaScript Execution Flow and Functions" for more information on `functions`).

The available JavaScript data type literals available for equating to variable names are as follows:

- *Boolean literals:* These literals represent a Boolean type having a value of true or false only.
- *Integer literals:* These include all integer values such as 2, 1000, 999, and 20000, and may be written in JavaScript using decimal base 10 (default), octal base 8 (precede the digits with a 0), or hexadecimal base 16 (precede the digits/letters with a 0X).
- *Floating-point literals:* These represent all values that require a decimal point or exponent. For example, 10.4234435, 4e-16, and 2.35434e23 are all floating-point literals.
- `string` *literals:* These refer to any characters enclosed in quotation marks (`""` or `''`). For example, "Hi peoples!" and 'Good day mates' are string literals. By using special JavaScript control characters inside of these strings, special effects can be achieved—`\n` causes a new line; `\t` represents a tab; `\\` indicates a backslash; `\'` causes a single quotation mark; and `\"` implements a double quotation mark.

When declaring a variable, note that its literal type is automatically determined at runtime by the browser. For example, `n = 100` declares a variable of type integer. If, later on, *n* is assigned a floating-point literal, the browser automatically converts *n* to a floating-point variable.

Operators *Operators* are used to perform actions and comparisons that determine the outcome of a given program section. For example, to add two numbers together, the JavaScript plus (+) operator is used:

```
a = b + c;
```

`a` is assigned the value of `b` plus `c`. To check if `b` is greater than `c`, one of the JavaScript compare (<, <=, >, or >=) operators must be used:

```
if ( b > c )
```

If `b` is greater than `c`, then the code contained in the `if` statement will activate (see "JavaScript Execution Flow and Functions" for more information on `if` statements).

Table 14.2 lists the various JavaScript operators and their corresponding VBScript counterparts.

Table 14.2 Comparison of JavaScript and VBScript Operators

Operation	JavaScript Operator	VBScript Operator
Mathematical Operators		
Addition	+	+
Subtraction	–	–
Multiplication	*	*
Division	/	/
Divide and return an integer value	N/A	\
Exponentiation	N/A	^
Modulus	%	MOD
Negation	–	–
String concatenation	+	+ or &
Left shift	<<	N/A

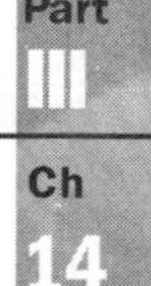

continues

Table 14.2 Continued

Operation	JavaScript Operator	VBScript Operator
Mathematical Operators		
Right shift	>>	N/A
Bitwise AND	&	AND
Bitwise OR	¦	OR
Bitwise XOR	^	XOR
Bitwise complement	~	NOT
Comparison Operators		
Less than	<	<
Greater than	>	>
Less than or equal to	<=	<=
Greater than or equal to	>=	>=
Equal to	==	=
Not equal to	!=	<>
Evaluation AND	&&	AND
Evaluation OR	¦¦	OR
Evaluation XOR	N/A	XOR

All of the preceding operators function exactly the same as their VBScript counterparts. For example, take a look at this JavaScript code:

```
a = b + c;
a = b & c;
```

The VBScript equivalent has the exact same structure:

```
a = b + c
a = b AND c;
```

For examples of JavaScript vs VBScript comparison operators, see the following section, or refer to Chapter 16, "VBScript Operators."

JavaScript Execution Flow and Functions

JavaScript's methods for directing execution flow, via decision and loop statements, are identical to those of C/C++.

Decision Statements These control statements evaluate an expression and then take an action based on whether the expression is true or false.

The `if` command executes one or more lines of code based on whether the *expression* in parentheses after the `if` statement is true. Note that *expression* makes use of the compare operators listed in the previous section, "JavaScript Operators." The following JavaScript program illustrates a typical `if` statement in action:

```
if ( (str == "") && (myval < min) || (myval > max) )
     alert("Str is empty, and either myval is less"+
            " than min or greater than max");
```

The JavaScript alert is only executed if the entire expression from left to right evaluates to true. In other words, the variable string `str` must be empty, and either `myval` less than `min` or `myval` greater than `max` for the expression to evaluate as true. Notice the use of the plus (+) operator to wrap the string over multiple lines.

In VBScript, no parentheses enclose the `if` expression(s). As well, the `Then` command must be placed at the end of the `if` line. Finally, an `end if` is placed at the end of the entire `if` structure (after the executable code). The following presents exactly how the `if` statement is used in VBScript:

```
if str = "" AND myval < min OR myval > max Then
     alert "Str is empty, and either myval is less"+
           " than min or greater than max"
end if
```

More than one line can be included for execution after the `if` statement by enclosing the line in standard C/C++ brackets. The following JavaScript code illustrates this:

```
if (confirm("Proceed?"))
{
     myval = min;
     myval++;
}
```

If the results of the built-in JavaScript function `confirm` (which initiates a `YES/NO` dialog box) are true (`YES` selected), then the two lines enclosed in `{ }` are executed. In VBScript, the brackets must not be used since the interpreter keeps reading in lines of code until an `end if` statement is encountered.

The else and else if commands are placed directly after if statements to select alternate code that executes when the if expression fails. else executes its alternate code every time, whereas the code contained in an else if statement only runs if its expression is true. For example, suppose one needed to perform three different actions, with only one action occurring at any given time based upon the value of certain variables. An if statement would be used to decide whether to perform the first action, an else if command to decide the second, and another else if statement (or simply else if this alternate code is to execute every time) for the third. The following JavaScript code illustrates the if...else concept:

```
if (aint < bint)
     aint = bint;
else if (aint > bint)
{
     aint = cint;
     cint--;
}
else
     aint++;
```

In the preceding example, aint is set to bint only when aint is less than bint, otherwise aint is set to cint if aint is greater than bint. If neither the (aint < bint) or (aint > bint) expressions are true, then aint is incremented. VBScript if...else coding conventions follow exactly the same structure as in JavaScript. The only difference is that VBScript uses elseif to represent JavaScript's else if, and no { } brackets are used (an end if is simply placed at the end of the entire structure in VBScript). The following VBScript code is equivalent to the preceding JavaScript program:

```
if aint < bint Then
     aint = bint
elseif aint > bint Then
     aint = cint
     cint = cint - 1;
else
     aint = aint + 1
end if
```

It should be noted that it is possible to nest if...else statements within other if...else statements, as in the following JavaScript code snippet:

```
if (aint < bint)
{
     if (aint < cint)
     {
          aint = cint;
          cint++;
     }
     else
          aint = bint;
}
```

The preceding example in VBScript follows:

```
if aint < bint Then
     if aint < cint Then
          aint = cint
          cint = cint + 1
     else
          aint = bint
     end if
end if
```

Loop Statements Loop statements repeat an action over and over again until an expression evaluates to true or false.

The `while` loop executes a set of commands as long as the test *expression* in parentheses after the `while` statement evaluates to true. As in JavaScript's `if...else` structure, `{ }` brackets must enclose the repeatable code body of the `while` statement. The `{ }` brackets are optional if the code body is composed of only one line. The following JavaScript program shows the `while` loop in action:

```
while ( aint < cint || aint < bint )
{
     aint++;
     bint--;
}
```

The preceding program executes the two lines over and over until `aint = cint` or `aint = bint`. Literally, while `aint` is less than `cint` or `aint` is less than `bint`, increment `aint` and decrement `bint`. What follows is the VBScript version of the above program:

```
while aint < cint OR aint < bint
     aint = aint + 1
     bint = bint - 1
wend
```

Note that for the `while` loop in VBScript, parentheses are not needed around the conditional expression, no `{ }` are used around the code body, and a `wend` statement terminates the repeatable code segment.

The `for` loop's structure is very similar to that of the `while` loop. Observe the `for` loop in the following JavaScript code:

```
for (var i = 0; i < 10; i++)
{
     aint++;
     bint=bint+10;
}
```

The `for` loop is decomposed as follows:

```
for (expression a; expression b; expression c)
```

`Expression a` is executed when the `for` loop begins. This is usually where one initializes the loop variables. While `Expression b` is true, the statements enclosed in the `{ }` area execute. Upon reaching the last statement enclosed within the `{ }` block, `expression c` runs and the loop repeats until `expression b` becomes true, upon which the loop ends. The equivalent VBScript code for the preceding `for` loop follows:

```
for i = 0 to 10 step 1
     aint = aint + 1
     bint = bint + 10
next
```

Again, no parentheses enclose the expression list in VBScript. As well, a `next` statement is used to indicate the end of the repeatable code body, in place of JavaScript's `{ }` commands. Observe that the `step 1` VBScript keyword is optional in this case, since the step size (amount to increment `i` by) automatically defaults to one. Refer to Chapter 17, "VBScript Control of Flow and Error Handling," for a complete explanation of VBScript's flow control handling.

Table 14.3 contains a summary of the various decision and loop statements versus their VBScript counterparts.

Table 14.3 Comparison of JavaScript and VBScript Execution Flow Methodology

Required Code	JavaScript Version	VBScript Version

if	`if (`*`expression`*`)`
	{
	code to execute if expression is true
	}
		`if `*`expression`*` Then`
		code to execute if expression is true

else if	`else if (`*`expression`*`)`
	{
	code to execute if this alternative is true
	}
		`elseif `*`expression`*` Then`
		code to execute if this alternative is true

else	`else`
	{
	code to execute if none of the alternatives are true
	}
		`else`
		code to execute if none of the alternatives are true

if terminator	N/A	`end if`

Required Code	JavaScript Version	VBScript Version

while	`while (expression)`
	{
	code to execute while expression is true
	}
		`while`
		code to execute while expression is true
		`wend`

for
`expression b;`
`expression c)`
{
code to execute while expression b is true
}
	`for (expression a;`
	code to execute until expression goes to max. expression automatically incremented by x each time through.
	`next`
		`for expression to max step x`

Functions A *function* is a means of subdividing a program into smaller, easier to read code packets. Functions are also modular, in that they can be reused with ease from program to program. A function is usually passed a list of variables, performs actions based upon these variables, and then returns a value to the calling code. The calling code then performs subsequent actions based upon this returned value. JavaScript functions are defined using the function keyword, as follows:

```
function name(arguments)
{
     code body of function
}
```

`Name` indicates the name of the function to use, while arguments represent the values or variables passed to the function for use in its code body. The `return` statement is used in the function's code body to pass a value back to the calling code. The preceding function is called with the below JavaScript:

```
name(arguments);
```

Or, if the function is returning a needed value via the `return` statement, the function must be called with the equate (=) operator to assign the returned value to a variable. The following JavaScript code illustrates this:

```
function name(arguments)
{
     code body of function
     return value;
}

storevalue = name(arguments);
```

The variable `storevalue` is assigned the `value` returned by the `name` function.

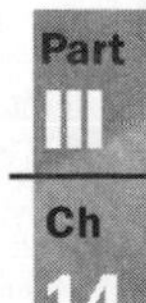

VBScript, in contrast, defines functions using `sub`. Refer to the VBScript function layout that follows:

```
sub name(arguments)
     code body of function
end sub
```

Notice the differences between JavaScript and VBScript. First of all, VBScript employs `sub` in place of JavaScript's `function`. Secondly, VBScript uses `end sub` to terminate the function code body, instead of JavaScript's enclosing `{ }` brackets.

If `function` and `end function` are used in place of `sub` and `end sub`, the VBScript function is allowed to return a value. The below VBScript code illustrates how this is done:

```
function name(arguments)
     code body of function
     return name
end sub
```

Notice that in VBScript, the actual name of the function must be used after the `return` statement.

VBScript functions are called almost exactly the same way as in JavaScript. Refer to this VBScript example:

```
name arguments
```

Notice that no parentheses are used in the VBScript version of the function call. As in JavaScript, if the VBScript function is returning a value, the function must be called with the equate (=) operator to assign the returned value to a variable. The following VBScript shows this:

```
storevalue = name arguments
```

The variable `storevalue` is assigned the `value` returned by the `name` function (note that `name` must be declared using VBScript's `function` and `end function` statements in order to return a value).

See Chapter 19, "VBScript Procedures," for more information on VBScript subroutines and functions.

All functions should be placed between `<HEAD><SCRIPT>` and `</SCRIPT></HEAD>` tags, since the `<HEAD>` tag information is loaded first on a Web page. This ensures that no JavaScript or VBScript code attempts to call a function that has not been loaded yet.

Table 14.4 summarizes function calling between the two scripting languages.

Table 14.4 Comparison of JavaScript and VBScript Function Methodology

Required Code	JavaScript Version	VBScript Version

Define a function	`function name(`*`arguments`*`)`
	`{`
	code body
	`}`
		`sub name(`*`arguments`*`)`
		code body
		`end sub`
		or
		`function name(`*`arguments`*`)`
		code body
		`end function`
		if the function must return a value

Call a function	`name(`*`arguments`*`);`	`name` *`arguments`*

Listing 14.1 and the resulting page shown in Figure 14.1 demonstrate JavaScript control flow and function calling in action. Listing 14.2 is the same program in VBScript. Listing 14.1 can be found on the CD-ROM in file `LST14_1.HTM`.

Listing 14.1 LST14_1.HTM—Sample JavaScript Program Illustrating Control Flow and Function Calling

```
<SCRIPT Language="JavaScript">

function writepage(start_text, number_repetitions)
{
        document.write ("<H1>"+start_text+"</H1><BR>");

        for (j = 0; j < number_repetitions; j=j+2) // increment j by 2 each
                                                   // time through the loop
        {
                document.write ("J = "+j+"<BR>");  // write the value of j
                                                   // to the page

                if (j == 10)
                        document.write ("<H2>Five times through</H2><BR>");
                else if (j == 20)
                        document.write ("<H3>Ten times through</H3><BR>");
        }

} // end of function writepage

  // above function has not been executed up to this point...

        writepage ("Greetings OB1. We meet again at last.",20);
  // call the  writepage function with "Greetings... for the first argument
  // and 20 for the second argument

</SCRIPT>
```

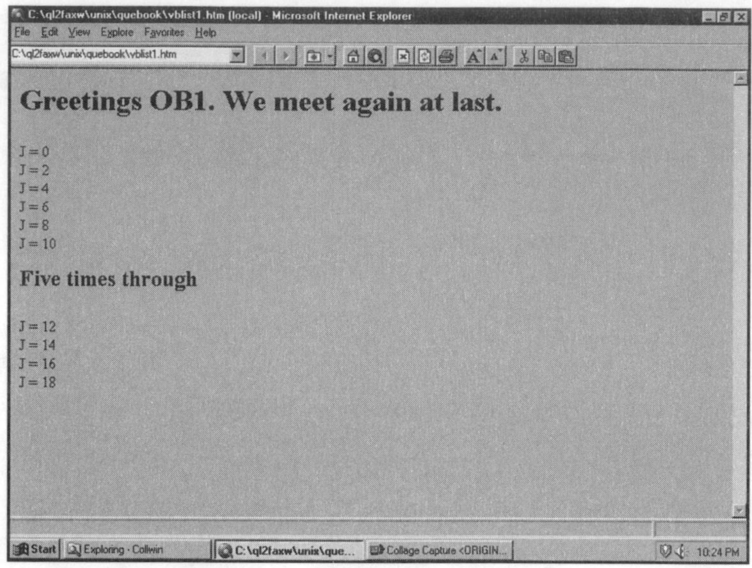

FIG. 14.1
The resulting page generated both by the JavaScript in Listing 14.1 and the VBScript in Listing 14.2.

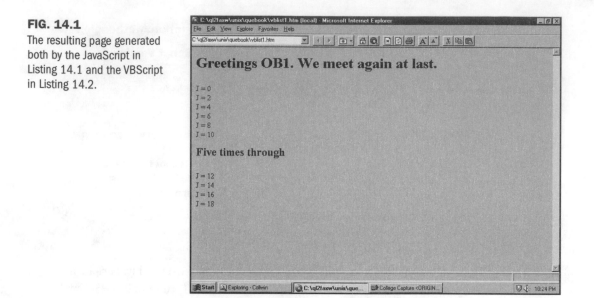

Listing 14.2 can be found on the CD-ROM in file LST14_2.HTM.

Listing 14.2 LST14_2.HTM—VBScript Equivalent of Listing 14.1

```
<SCRIPT Language="VBS">

sub writepage(start_text, number_repetitions)
        document.write "<H1>" & start_text & "</H1><BR>"

        for j = 0 to 18 step 2                        ' increment j by two each
                                                      ' time through the loop

                document.write "J = " & j & "<BR>" ' write the value of J
                                                      ' to the page

                if j = 10 then
                        document.write "<H2>Five times through</H2><BR>"
                elseif j = 20 then
                        document.write "<H3>Ten times through</H3><BR>"
                end if

        next

end sub ' end of function writepage

        ' above function has not been executed up to this point...

        writepage "Greetings OB1. We meet again at last.",20
  ' call the  writepage function with "Greetings... for the first
  ' argument and 20 for the second argument

</SCRIPT>
```

JavaScript Objects

JavaScript does not provide all of the features of a true Object Oriented Programming (OOP) language. Features such as encapsulation, inheritance, and abstraction are missing. It does in fact allow one to create and use objects that have methods (functions associated with an object) and properties (variables or attributes of an object). JavaScript has several built-in objects available for use. Some of these objects are quite similar to VBScript's built-in functions.

Built-In Objects VBScript has *functions*, whereas JavaScript has *objects*. These *objects* in turn have methods (functions associated with the object) and properties (variables associated with the object). Table 14.5 lists some common JavaScript built-in objects alongside their VBScript function equivalents (if any).

Table 14.5 Comparison of Common JavaScript objects versus VBScript Functions

Object	JavaScript Object	VBScript Function
Language-Specific Objects	**String object**	**Properties**
Indicate length of a string	`length`	`len(string)`
Methods		
Return a character in a string at given index	`charAt(index)`	N/A
Search string for first occurrence of a character starting from index	`indexOf(char,ind)`	`instr(str1,str2)`
Search through the string backwards starting from index, looking for a character	`lastindexOf(char,ind)`	`instr(str1,str2)`
Take a substring from i to j inside the string	`substring(i,j)`	N/A
Convert string to all lowercase characters	`toLowerCase()`	`lcase(string)`
Convert string to all uppercase characters	`toUpperCase()`	`ucase(string)`

continues

Table 14.5 Continued

Methods	Math Object	Properties
Value of Euler's constant e: 2.718…	`E`	`exp(1)`
Value of constant PI: 3.14…	`PI`	`3.14159`
Methods		
Return absolute value of a number	`abs(number)`	`abs(number)`
Return the arc cosine	`acos(number)`	N/A
Return arc sine	`asin(number)`	N/A
Return arc tan	`atan(number)`	`atan(number)`
Return cosine	`cos(number)`	`cos(number)`
Return e to the power of number	`exp(number)`	`exp(number)`
Return natural logarithm	`log(number)`	`ln(number)`
Return value of base to the power of exponent	`pow(base,exponent)`	`base^exponent`
Return sine	`sin(number)`	`sin(number)`
Return square root	`sqrt(number)`	`sqr(number)`
Return tangent	`tan(number)`	`tan(number)`
Browser-specific Objects	**Window Object**	**Properties**
Array of frame objects, from 0 to number of frames minus 1	`frames[index]`	N/A
Number of frame objects in the current window	`frames.length`	N/A
Access to status bar at the bottom of the browser	`status`	N/A

Methods		
Create an alert dialog box	`alert(string)`	`alert string`
Close the window	`close()`	N/A
Create a dialog box with two options: OK and CANCEL	`confirm()`	N/A
	Location Object	**Properties**
The current URL	`href`	`href` OBJECT
Methods		
None		
	Document Object	**Properties**
Array of form objects, from 0 to number of form tags minus 1	`forms[index]`	`forms` OBJECT
Number of form tags in the document	`forms.length`	N/A
Methods		
Clear the window	`clear()`	N/A
Write HTML code directly to the page	`write(string)`	`document.write`
Write HTML code directly to the page and include a newline character at the end of the string	`writeln(string)`	`document.writeln`

These JavaScript built-in objects are used very differently than the VBScript built-in functions. First of all, a property is an attribute or variable of an object while a method is a function associated with the object. In JavaScript, for example, one would use the following code to get the length of a string:

```
mystring = "Greetings";
stringlength = mystring.length;
stringlength2 = "Greetings".length;
```

where `stringlength` contains the same value as `stringlength2`. Notice that the string itself is treated as an *object* and the length is simply a *property* of this object. Observe that a period separates the object name on the left from the desired property on the right. The JavaScript convention, borrowed from C/C++ (which Java also uses), is to have the object name on the left, with the desired *method* (function) or *property* (variable) on the right (a dot separates the *object* on the left from the *method* or *property* on the right).

To perform similar actions in VBScript, built-in *functions* must be used. For example, to mimic the earlier JavaScript code that computed the length of a string, the VBScript `len` *function* must be employed as in the below VBScript program sample:

```
mystring = "Greetings"
stringlength = len(mystring)
stringlength2 = len("Greetings")
```

Notice that built-in VBScript *functions* must have parentheses surrounding their arguments (as in `len(mystring)`).

In order to obtain a deeper understanding of the JavaScript objects in Table 14.5, each of them will now be examined in greater detail.

String Object To access the string object, a string variable or literal must be used as the object name on the left, with the desired string object *method* (function) or *property* (variable) on the right (left and right separated by a dot again). For example, observe the `UpperCase()` *method* in the following JavaScript:

```
newstring = oldstring.toUpperCase();
```

`newstring` is filled with the contents of `oldstring` (`oldstring`'s contents are converted to uppercase first). The VBScript equivalent of the preceding line follows:

```
newstring = ucase(oldstring)
```

Properties are accessed the same way, as illustrated by the JavaScript string object example just after Table 14.5.

Math Object In order to use any of the math *properties* and *methods,* the `Math` keyword (note the capital M) must precede all references to the math *object*. Refer to the following JavaScript code:

```
a = Math.cos (Math.PI/4);
b = Math.pow(3,5);
```

When run, the above program gives a = 0.70710678 and b = 243. Alternatively, the special JavaScript keyword `with` can be used to associate ALL references to a *method* or *property* to a given object. For example, using `with` on the `Math` object in the previous code gives the following new JavaScript:

```
with (Math)
{
      a = cos (PI/4);
      b = pow (3,5);
}
```

The VBScript version of the preceding code follows:

```
a = cos (3.14159/4)
b = 3^5
```

Note again that VBScript uses *functions* in place of JavaScript's *objects* (the `cos` function, and the ^ "function").

Window Object The window object represents all properties and methods associated with the browser itself. This object allows access to the status bar, activates pop-up message windows, and so forth. It is not necessary to prefix any of the `window` *object's* properties and methods with the `window` keyword. For example, look at the following JavaScript code:

```
window.alert ("INTRUDER ALERT! INTRUDER ALERT!");
```

Instead of accessing the `alert` *method* (function) via `window.alert`, JavaScript allows `alert` alone to be used (since alert is a *method* of the `window` *object*). The following JavaScript code performs exactly the same function as in the previous example:

```
alert ("INTRUDER ALERT! INTRUDER ALERT!");
```

The VBScript equivalent follows:

```
alert "INTRUDER ALERT! INTRUDER ALERT!"
```

The `window` keyword may also optionally be placed in front of the VBScript `alert` *function,* since the web browser's interpreter automatically removes any `window.` statements on-the-fly while going through the web page.

Location Object The location object represents only the properties associated with the current document location/URL (**http://www.solstar.com** is an example of a URL, or Uniform Resource Locator). Having no methods, the location object is used to access and/or change the current page (URL) the document is pointing to. The JavaScript `location` object's properties must be prefixed with the `location` keyword. Refer to the following JavaScript code:

```
location.href = "http://www.url.com";
```

The preceding example points the current page to http://www.url.com (in other words, the current page is lost, and the new page replaces it). Pointing the `location.href` to itself (`location.href = location.href`) causes the document to reload—however, this only works in Netscape 2.0 and up (although the final release of Internet Explorer 3.0 may in fact support dynamic document reloads like Netscape 2.0). Notice from Table 14.5 that the VBScript equivalent of the JavaScript `location.href` object is exactly the same. The VBScript `location.href` is not actually an object, however. Instead, think of it as a global variable, built into the VBScript language. So the VBScript version of the preceding JavaScript code is exactly the same, as illustrated here:

```
location.href = "http://www.url.com"
```

Document Object The document object represents all of the properties and methods associated with the actual HTML document itself. This object allows write access to the page, lets HTML *form* input areas be examined and/or changed, and so on. The properties and methods of the document object must be prefixed with the `document` keyword. For example, to write directly to the HTML page, use the `write` method (function) as illustrated by the following JavaScript:

```
document.write ("Well good day to you too!!");
```

Note that one cannot use document.write AFTER the page has completely loaded and executed (in an event, for example—see "JavaScript Event Programming").

The VBScript function equivalent operates almost exactly the same way, as shown here:

```
document.write "Well good day to you too!!"
```

`document.write` is not an object in VBScript—think of it as a built-in function. Notice that this `document.write` function is called using standard VBScript function calling practices: no parentheses must enclose the arguments.

When the web browser encounters a form defined in standard HTML code via the `<FORM>` tag, an array table is set up for use by JavaScript or VBScript. For each pair of `<FORM>` and `</FORM>` tags, a separate entry in the `document.forms` array object is created. To access individually named <INPUT> tags in these forms, append the desired <INPUT> item's name and VALUE attribute to the document.forms object, as in the JavaScript in Listing 14.3. The output of Listing 14.3 is shown in Figure 14.2. Listing 14.3 can be found on the CD-ROM in file LST14_3.HTM.

Listing 14.3 LST14_3.HTM—JavaScript Program Illustrating *document.forms[0]* Array Object to Access Form Data

```
<HTML><BODY>
<FORM>
       <INPUT TYPE="text" NAME="accessme">
</FORM>
</BODY></HTML>
<SCRIPT Language="JavaScript">
document.forms[0].accessme.value = "HIYA MON!";
</SCRIPT>
```

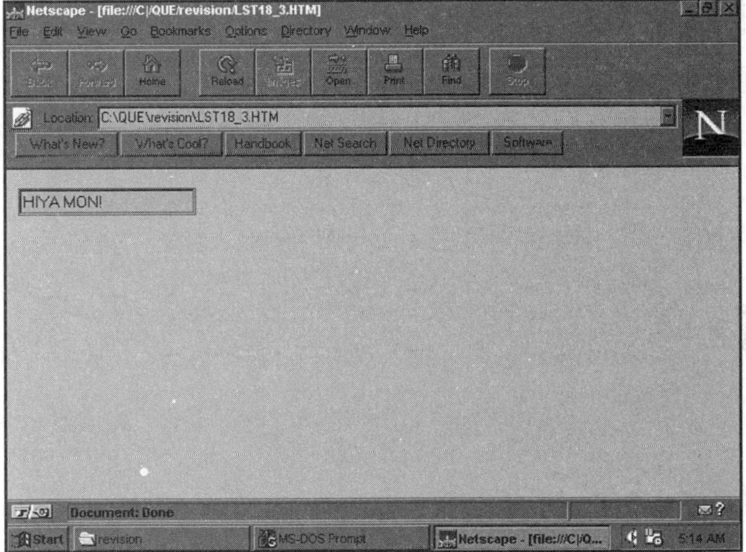

FIG. 14.2
The resulting page generated by the JavaScript in Listing 14.3.

The document.forms[0] array is indexing the first form in the document (form 0). As well, the object is reading the accessme form input and changing its value to the string "HIYA MON!" Notice the code that changes the form input must be placed *after* the definition of the accessme input, since the page is loaded into the browser from the top down. If the JavaScript document.forms[0].accessme.value code is placed above the actual form, no data can be entered into the form input: The <FORM> tag has not even been read in and defined at that point.

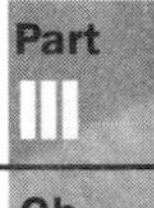

Forms can also be referenced by name instead of by array, as in the JavaScript in Listing 14.4. Listing 14.4 can be found on the CD-ROM in file LST14_4.HTM.

Listing 14.4 LST14_4.HTM—JavaScript Program Demonstrating Form Data Access via Form Names

```
<HTML><BODY>
<FORM NAME="form_name">
      <INPUT TYPE="text" NAME="accessme">
</FORM>
</BODY></HTML>
<SCRIPT Language="JavaScript">
document.form_name.accessme.value = "HIYA MON!";
</SCRIPT>
```

The JavaScript in Listing 14.5 shows that Microsoft's Internet Explorer 3.0 Alpha 1 (4.70.1028) allows one to get away with not using a <FORM> tag in the JavaScript. Listing 14.5 can be found on the CD-ROM in file LST14_5.HTM.

Listing 14.5 LST14_5.HTM—JavaScript Program Showing Internet Explorer 3.0's Capability to Create and Access Form Data without the Need of *<FORM>* Tags

```
<HTML><BODY>
      <INPUT TYPE="text" NAME="accessme">
</BODY></HTML>
<SCRIPT Language="JavaScript">
accessme.value = "HIYA MON!";
</SCRIPT>
```

The preceding JavaScript code is incompatible with the Netscape browser. The Netscape client requires that all input elements be placed within <FORM> and </FORM> tags.

As long as you can get used to treating form inputs as page outputs, the concept of the form object can be easily understood. Unlike the JavaScript in Listing 14.3, the forms [index] array property can*not* be used to access VBScript form data. Instead, the actual form name must be used, as in the VBScript in Listing 14.6. Listing 14.6 can be found on the CD-ROM in file LST14_6.HTM.

Listing 14.6 LST14_6.HTM—VBScript Program Illustrating Form Access via Form Names

```
<HTML><BODY>
<FORM NAME="form_name">
      <INPUT TYPE="text" NAME="accessme">
```

```
</FORM>
</BODY></HTML>
<SCRIPT Language="VBS">
document.form_name.accessme.value = "HIYA MON!"
</SCRIPT>
```

For VBScript in Internet Explorer 3.0 Alpha 1 (4.70.1028), the `<FORM>` tag is not even necessary, as shown in the VBScript in Listing 14.7. Listing 14.7 can be found on the CD-ROM in file `LST14_7.HTM`.

Listing 14.7 LST14_7.HTM—VBScript Program Demonstrating Internet Explorer 3.0's Capability to Create and Access Form Data without the Need of *<FORM>* Tags

```
<HTML><BODY>
        <INPUT TYPE="text" NAME="accessme">
</BODY></HTML>
<SCRIPT Language="VBS">
accessme.value = "HIYA MON!"
</SCRIPT>
```

In general, it is good practice to use the `<FORM>` tag around `<INPUT>` sections. That way the contents of the form can be submitted to a server for post processing, and converting the HTML/VBScript code to Netscape's JavaScript implementation becomes trivial.

Creating Objects In JavaScript, use the C++ `new` command to dynamically create an object. Unlike C++ (and like Java), these dynamically created objects do not need to be destroyed, as the interpreter does all construction and destruction on-the-fly. Although VBScript can assign an object reference to a variable or property (as in `Set formvar = document.form_name`), it can't actually create a new *object* as JavaScript does.

To create an *object*, first define a function for the new object, as illustrated by the following JavaScript code:

```
function myobject(arguments)
{
     methods/properties of function
}
```

Then later in the program, use the `new` command to dynamically create a new instance of the object. The next JavaScript illustrates this:

```
newobject = new myobject(arguments);
```

Creating Properties and Methods for Objects When in an object function, use the keyword `this` to refer to the current object. With `this`, object properties are easily created, as the following JavaScript shows:

```
function myobject(name, number)
{
     this.name = name;
     this.number = number;
}
```

An instance of the object must be created with `new`, as the following JavaScript demonstrates:

```
newobject = new myobject("Morphing Fork",22)
```

The properties of this new object can then be accessed in the usual way (*object* on the left, period, *property* or *method* on the right). For example, to assign values to two variables named `a` and `b`, use the following JavaScript:

```
a = newobject.name;
b = newobject.number;
```

Where `a` = "Morphing Fork" and `b` = 22 (these values were defined when `newobject` was created via the `new` command, shown earlier). To add a method to this object, simply point a property in the object definition to a function, as this JavaScript code illustrates:

```
function myobject(name, number)
{
     this.name = name;
     this.number = number;
     this.method_name = method_name;
}

function method_name()
{
     code body of method
}
```

The methods of this new object are again accessed in the usual way—*object* on the left, period, *method* (function) on the right.

Creating an Array Object As an example of object creation, the following creates an array `object` for use in your JavaScript:

```
function CreateArray(num)
{
     this.length = n;
     for (var i = 1; i <= n; i++)
          {
               this[i] = 0;
          }
     return this
}
```

This creates an array of num entries with a length property indicating the number of entries in the array. The array entries are initialized to zero upon creation. To make an array, use the object in JavaScript as follows:

```
array = new CreateArray(3);
array[1] = 3;
array[2] = 1;
lenarray = array.length;
```

Compared to JavaScript, making arrays in VBScript is easy. For example, the next VBScript uses the Dim statement in conjunction with Array to define an array:

```
Dim A
A = Array(3,1,2)
B = A(2)
lenarray = len(A)
```

JavaScript Event Programming

As in VBScript, JavaScript can be activated by events placed in ordinary HTML tags such as <INPUT> and <FORM>. These event tags work exactly the same as in VBScript, since JavaScript and VBScript share common HTML code. For example, what follows is the JavaScript HTML onChange handler to call a function when a form input named text_area changes:

```
<INPUT TYPE="text" NAME="text_area" onChange="function(arguments)">
```

In VBScript HTML, the function is called without parentheses as shown in this next line of code:

```
<INPUT TYPE="text" NAME="text_area" onChange="function arguments">
```

It is also possible to place JavaScript code directly into the onEvent area, as shown in this line of code:

```
<INPUT TYPE="text" NAME="text_area" onChange="alert('Don\'t touch that
dial!');">
```

Notice the use of the apostrophe (') character within the alert. This serves to prevent the interpreter from confusing the start of the alert text with the end of the onChange event (which must be enclosed in quotation marks). Also, a \' character is used to create the apostrophe for the don't text, since it would be confused with a closing apostrophe otherwise.

VBScript code can also be used in an onEvent, as the following example illustrates:

```
<INPUT TYPE="text" NAME="text_area" onChange="alert 'Don\'t touch that
dial!' ">
```

The browser automatically determines which language (VBScript or JavaScript) to use in onEvent's, based upon what was previously implemented in the same file. Beware of mixing JavaScript and VBScript code within the one file—this crashes Internet Explorer 3.0 (when Explorer 3.0 encounters an `onEvent` containing a language different from what was used before in previous `<SCRIPT>` tags, a runtime error is generated). Table 14.6 summarizes the various HTML events available to JavaScript and VBScript programs.

Table 14.6 List of Events Available for Placement in HTML Tags

Event	Occurs When	Used with Objects
onBlur	The input focus is removed from an object by the user pressing enter, clicking outside of the form input, and so on	text field, text area, selection
onChange	The value stored inside of a form input changes	text field, text area, selection
onClick	The user clicks a radio button, a select button, and so on	checkboxes, links, radio buttons, reset buttons, submit buttons
onFocus	The input focus is transferred to the object by the user clicking on the form input, text area, and so on	text field, text area, selection
onSelect	The user selects text in a text field or text area	text field, text area
`onMouseOver`	The user moves the mouse over a link	link
`onSubmit`	The user submits a form	form

As of this writing, the current version of Internet Explorer 3.0 is Alpha 1 (4.70.1028). This version does not function properly with the `onSelect`, `onMouseOver`, and `onSubmit` event handlers. JavaScript code using these events under Netscape 2.0 or higher works just fine, however. Refer to Chapter 18, "VBScript Event Programming," for more information on using events in VBScript.

Putting It All Together

Using all of the basic techniques learned so far, you now have the ability to create real-world JavaScript applications. At the very least, you should be able to convert existing

VBScript applications to JavaScript (to guarantee your Web page's compatibility with Netscape 2.0 as well as Internet Explorer 3.0). The JavaScript found in Listing 14.8 and the VBScript equivalent in Listing 14.9 (both listings are too large to print entirely here, the full versions can be found on the CD) generate the page shown in Figure 14.3. The complete Listing 14.9 can be found on the CD-ROM in file LST14_9.HTM.

This type of page is the perfect example of a typical real-world JavaScript and VBScript Web page. The program makes use of HTML *tables* extensively to create an order form, and employs all of the concepts I've discussed so far, as well as those mentioned throughout the rest of this book. Refer to Chapter 2, "Review of HTML," for more examples of table usage. The complete Listing 14.8 can be found on the CD-ROM in file LST14_8.HTM.

ON THE WEB

http://java.sun.com/Tutorial/HTML/Tables If you are interested in Java programming, download the latest free Java SDK from this site.

http://microsoft.com/visualj Microsoft's Visual J++ information.

Listing 14.8 LST14_8.HTM—Real World JavaScript Program: Calculates the Total Price Based on User Selections

```
<HTML>
<HEAD>
<SCRIPT Language="JavaScript">

// below variables automatically globalized since they are not defined inside
// any functions - ie: these variables will be remembered each time through
// the updateprice function
old_p_price=0; // initialize variables to 0
old_d_price=0;
old_v_price=0;
old_m_price=0;
old_o_price=0;
old_c_price=0;
subtotal_price=0;

function updateprice (who_called, chosen)
{

// processor price data
p0 = 2000; // P166
p1 = 1800; // P150
p2 = 1500; // P133
p3 = 1300; // P120
p4 = 1100; // P100
```

continues

Table 14.8 Continued

```
p5 = 900;  // P90
p6 = 600;  // P75
p7 = 425;  // P66
p8 = 300;  // P60

.
.
.
        // point to subtotal form input
        form_subtotal = document.computer.subtotal;

        if (who_called == 0)        // clicked on Processor area?
        {
                                    // point to processor price form input
                curItem = document.computer.processor_price;

                if (chosen == 0)                // P166?
                {
                        curItem.value = "$"+p0;
                        new_prev_price = p0;
                }
                else if (chosen == 1)           // P150?
                {
                        curItem.value = "$"+p1;
                        new_prev_price = p1;
                }
                else if (chosen == 2)          // P133?
                {
                        curItem.value = "$"+p2;
                        new_prev_price = p2;
                }
                else if (chosen == 3)          // P120?
                {
                        curItem.value = "$"+p3;
                        new_prev_price = p3;
                }
                else if (chosen == 4)          // P100?
                {
                        curItem.value = "$"+p4;
                        new_prev_price = p4;
                }
                else if (chosen == 5)          // P90?
                {
                        curItem.value = "$"+p5;
                        new_prev_price = p5;
                }
                else if (chosen == 6)          // P75?
                {
                        curItem.value = "$"+p6;
                        new_prev_price = p6;
                }
                else if (chosen == 7)          // P66?
                {
```

```
                curItem.value = "$"+p7;
                new_prev_price = p7;
        }
        else if (chosen == 8)           // P60?
        {
                curItem.value = "$"+p8;
                new_prev_price = p8;
        }


    // subtract the old processor price from the subtotal
        subtotal_price = subtotal_price - old_p_price;

    // and set the old processor price to the newly
    // selected processor price
        old_p_price = new_prev_price;

    // and add the new processor price to the subtotal
        subtotal_price = subtotal_price + new_prev_price;

    // and set the subtotal form input to the subtotal price
        form_subtotal.value = "$"+subtotal_price;

  }

.
.
.

  // compute the shipping value (0.1 * the subtotal_price)
  document.computer.shipping.value = "$"+(0.1 * subtotal_price);

  // and compute the total amount owed (the subtotal_price + the
  // shipping value)
  document.computer.total.value = "$"+
                    (subtotal_price + 0.1 * subtotal_price);

}

</SCRIPT>
</HEAD>
<BODY>
<FORM NAME="computer">

<TABLE BORDER=1 BGCOLOR="#FFFFCC" WIDTH=80 ALIGN=LEFT>
<FONT SIZE=2 COLOR=BLUE>
   <TR><TD BGCOLOR=WHITE ALIGN=CENTER>Processor...</TD></TR></FONT>
     <TR><TD>

<!-- when P166 is clicked on, call updateprice with arguments 0 and 0 -->
       <INPUT TYPE=RADIO NAME=processor onClick="updateprice(0,0)"> P166

     </TD></TR>
     <TR><TD>
```

Part III Ch 14

continues

Listing 14.8 Continued

```
<!-- when P150 is clicked, call updateprice with arguments 0 and 1 -->
       <INPUT TYPE=RADIO NAME=processor onClick="updateprice(0,1)"> P150

     </TD></TR>
     <TR><TD>
       <INPUT TYPE=RADIO NAME=processor onClick="updateprice(0,2)"> P133
     </TD></TR>
     <TR><TD>
       <INPUT TYPE=RADIO NAME=processor onClick="updateprice(0,3)"> P120
     </TD></TR>
     <TR><TD>
       <INPUT TYPE=RADIO NAME=processor onClick="updateprice(0,4)"> P100
     </TD></TR>
     <TR><TD>
       <INPUT TYPE=RADIO NAME=processor onClick="updateprice(0,5)"> P90
     </TD></TR>
     <TR><TD>
       <INPUT TYPE=RADIO NAME=processor onClick="updateprice(0,6)"> P75
     </TD></TR>
     <TR><TD>
       <INPUT TYPE=RADIO NAME=processor onClick="updateprice(0,7)"> P66
     </TD></TR>
     <TR><TD>
       <INPUT TYPE=RADIO NAME=processor onClick="updateprice(0,8)"> P60
     </TD></TR>
     <TR><TD>
       <INPUT TYPE=TEXT NAME=processor_price SIZE=11 VALUE="$0.00">
     </TD></TR>
</TABLE>

 .
 .
 .


<BR><BR><BR><BR><BR><BR><BR><BR><BR><BR><BR>
<TABLE BORDER=1 BGCOLOR="#FFFFCC" WIDTH=530 HEIGHT=90 ALIGN=LEFT>
     <TR><TD>
       Subtotal
     </TD></TR>
     <TR><TD>
       Shipping Charges (please allow 4-6 weeks for delivery)
     </TD></TR>
     <TR><TD>
       Total
     </TD></TR>
</TABLE>

<!-- form inputs whose values are changed by the JavaScript code,
depending on the selections the user has made in regards to
processor type, monitor, memory, and so forth -->
```

```
<TABLE BORDER=1 BGCOLOR="#FFFFCC" WIDTH=70>
     <TR><TD>
       <INPUT TYPE=TEXT NAME=subtotal SIZE=10 VALUE="$0.00">
     </TD></TR>
     <TR><TD>
       <INPUT TYPE=TEXT NAME=shipping SIZE=10 VALUE="$0.00">
     </TD></TR>
     <TR><TD>
       <INPUT TYPE=TEXT NAME=total SIZE=10 VALUE="$0.00">
     </TD></TR>
</TABLE>

<BR>
        <INPUT TYPE=SUBMIT VALUE="Order now">
        <A HREF="index.html">Return to main page</A>
</FORM>

</BODY>
</HTML>
```

The complete Listing 14.9 can be found on the CD-ROM in file `LST14_9.HTM`.

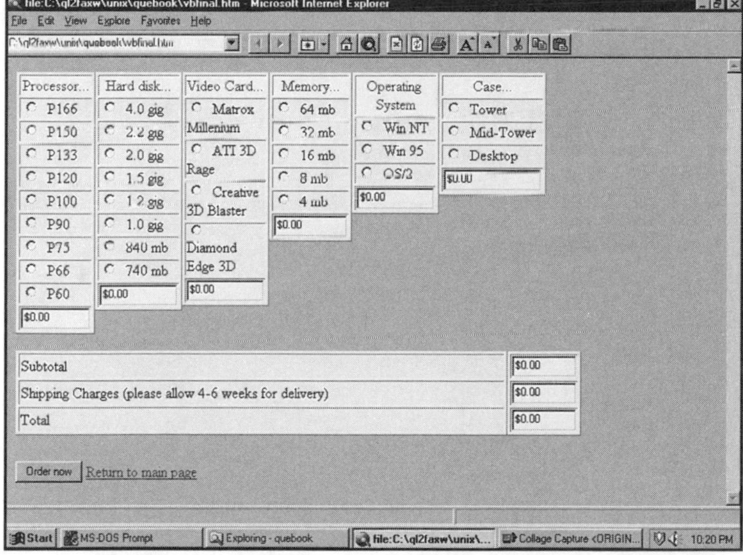

FIG. 14.3
The resulting computer pricing page generated both by the JavaScript in Listing 14.8 and the VBScript in Listing 14.9.

Part III Ch 14

Listing 14.9 LST14_9.HTM—VBScript Equivalent of Listing 14.8

```
<HTML>
<HEAD>
<SCRIPT Language="VBS">

' use Dim to indicate that these variables are to be remember each time
' through the updateprice subroutine - ie: to GLOBALIZE the below variables
```

continues

Listing 14.9 Continued

```
Dim old_p_price     ' old processor price (integer)
Dim old_d_price     ' old drive price (integer)
Dim old_v_price     ' old video price (integer)
Dim old_m_price     ' old memory price (integer)
Dim old_o_price     ' old os price (integer)
Dim old_c_price     ' old case price (integer)

Dim subtotal_price    ' subtotal price (integer)


old_p_price=0  ' initialize variables to 0
old_d_price=0
old_v_price=0
old_m_price=0
old_o_price=0
old_c_price=0
subtotal_price=0


sub updateprice (who_called, chosen)

Dim form_subtotal

Dim curItem


' processor price data
p0 = 2000  ' P166
p1 = 1800  ' P150
p2 = 1500  ' P133
p3 = 1300  ' P120
p4 = 1100  ' P100
p5 = 900   ' P90
p6 = 600   ' P75
p7 = 425   ' P66
p8 = 300   ' P60

.
.
.

        ' point to subtotal form input
        Set form_subtotal = document.computer.subtotal

        if who_called = 0 Then        ' clicked on Processor area?

        ' point to processor price form input
                Set curItem = document.computer.processor_price


                if chosen = 0 Then                 ' P166?
                        curItem.value = "$" & p0
                        new_prev_price = p0
```

```
            elseif chosen = 1 Then              ' P150?
                    curItem.value = "$" & p1
                    new_prev_price = p1
            elseif chosen = 2 Then              ' P133?
                    curItem.value = "$" & p2
                    new_prev_price = p2
            elseif chosen = 3 Then              ' P120?
                    curItem.value = "$" & p3
                    new_prev_price = p3
            elseif chosen = 4 Then              ' P100?
                    curItem.value = "$" & p4
                    new_prev_price = p4
            elseif chosen = 5 Then              ' P90?
                    curItem.value = "$" & p5
                    new_prev_price = p5
            elseif chosen = 6 Then              ' P75?
                    curItem.value = "$" & p6
                    new_prev_price = p6
            elseif chosen = 7 Then              ' P66?
                    curItem.value = "$" & p7
                    new_prev_price = p7
            elseif chosen = 8 Then              ' P60?
                    curItem.value = "$" & p8
                    new_prev_price = p8
            end if

        ' subtract the old processor price from the subtotal
            subtotal_price = subtotal_price - old_p_price

        ' and set the old processor price to the newly
        ' selected processor price
            old_p_price = new_prev_price

        ' and add the new processor price to the subtotal
            subtotal_price = subtotal_price + new_prev_price


        ' and set the subtotal form input to the subtotal price
            form_subtotal.value = "$" & subtotal_price

.
.
.

      ' compute the shipping value (0.1 * the subtotal_price)
      document.computer.shipping.value = "$" & (0.1 * subtotal_price)

      ' and compute the total amount owed (the subtotal_price + the
      ' shipping value)
      document.computer.total.value = "$" &
                        (subtotal_price + 0.1 * subtotal_price)

end sub
```


continues

Listing 14.9 Continued

```
</SCRIPT>
</HEAD>
<BODY>
<FORM NAME="computer">

<TABLE BORDER=1 BGCOLOR="#FFFFCC" WIDTH=80 ALIGN=LEFT>
<FONT SIZE=2 COLOR=BLUE>
   <TR><TD BGCOLOR=WHITE ALIGN=CENTER>Processor...</TD></TR></FONT>
     <TR><TD>

<!-- when P166 is clicked, call updateprice with arguments 0 and 0 -->
       <INPUT TYPE=RADIO NAME=processor onClick="updateprice 0,0"> P166

     </TD></TR>
     <TR><TD>

<!-- when P150 is clicked, call updateprice with arguments 0 and 1 -->
       <INPUT TYPE=RADIO NAME=processor onClick="updateprice 0,1"> P150

     </TD></TR>
     <TR><TD>
       <INPUT TYPE=RADIO NAME=processor onClick="updateprice 0,2"> P133
     </TD></TR>
     <TR><TD>
       <INPUT TYPE=RADIO NAME=processor onClick="updateprice 0,3"> P120
     </TD></TR>
     <TR><TD>
       <INPUT TYPE=RADIO NAME=processor onClick="updateprice 0,4"> P100
     </TD></TR>
     <TR><TD>
       <INPUT TYPE=RADIO NAME=processor onClick="updateprice 0,5"> P90
     </TD></TR>
     <TR><TD>
       <INPUT TYPE=RADIO NAME=processor onClick="updateprice 0,6"> P75
     </TD></TR>
     <TR><TD>
       <INPUT TYPE=RADIO NAME=processor onClick="updateprice 0,7"> P66
     </TD></TR>
     <TR><TD>
       <INPUT TYPE=RADIO NAME=processor onClick="updateprice 0,8"> P60
     </TD></TR>
     <TR><TD>
       <INPUT TYPE=TEXT NAME=processor_price SIZE=11 VALUE="$0.00">
     </TD></TR>
</TABLE>

.
.
.

<BR><BR><BR><BR><BR><BR><BR><BR><BR><BR><BR>
<TABLE BORDER=1 BGCOLOR="#FFFFCC" WIDTH=530 HEIGHT=90 ALIGN=LEFT>
     <TR><TD>
```

```
        Subtotal
      </TD></TR>
      <TR><TD>
        Shipping Charges (please allow 4-6 weeks for delivery)
      </TD></TR>
      <TR><TD>
        Total
      </TD></TR>
</TABLE>

<!-- form inputs who's values are changed by the VBScript code,
depending on the selections the user has made in regards to
processor type, monitor, memory, and so forth -->

<TABLE BORDER=1 BGCOLOR="#FFFFCC" WIDTH=70>
      <TR><TD>
        <INPUT TYPE=TEXT NAME=subtotal SIZE=10 VALUE="$0.00">
      </TD></TR>
      <TR><TD>
        <INPUT TYPE=TEXT NAME=shipping SIZE=10 VALUE="$0.00">
      </TD></TR>
      <TR><TD>
        <INPUT TYPE=TEXT NAME=total SIZE=10 VALUE="$0.00">
      </TD></TR>
</TABLE>

<BR>
        <INPUT TYPE=SUBMIT VALUE="Order now">
        <A HREF="index.html">Return to main page</A>
</FORM>

</BODY>
</HTML>
```

From Here...

This concludes your crash course in JavaScript. Perhaps in a later release, Netscape will include VBScript support in its interpreter. Until then, if you want to create script pages compatible with both Netscape 2.0 and Internet Explorer 3.0, JavaScript is the way to go. VBScript is perhaps inherently more powerful with its capability to dynamically alter the behavior of Java and OLE objects (via the <OBJECT> tag), whereas Netscape 2.0 cannot yet read in a Microsoft OLE object (NetScape works great with Java, however). I wouldn't be surprised if Netscape Communications soon incorporated VBScript into its Netscape browser. So in the end, it probably doesn't really matter which scripting language you use: all browsers will be able to read all scripts.

For more information on JavaScript and VBScript, go to the following sites and chapters.

ON THE WEB

http://home.netscape.com/eng/mozilla/Gold/handbook/javascript/index.html Refer to this site for Netscape's JavaScript Authoring Guide.

http://www.c2.org/~andreww/javascript This site contains an index of various JavaScript pages on the web plus JavaScript source code.

- Refer to Chapter 2, "Review of HTML," for more information on basic HTML and tables.
- Consult Chapter 16, "VBScript Operators," for a description of VBScript Operators.
- Refer to Chapter 17, "VBScript Control of Flow and Error Handling," for a complete explanation of VBScript's flow control handling.
- Refer to Chapter 18, "VBScript Event Programming," for more information on using events in VBScript.
- See Chapter 19, "VBScript Procedures," for more information on VBScript subroutines and functions.

PART IV

Doing Real Work with VBScript

CHAPTER 15

VBScript Data Types and Variables

by Ibrahim Malluf

Learn how Visual Basic Script manages your state data

Introduction to the Visual Basic Variant data type as well as how data is scoped.

Learn about the different data types that are provided

There is a brief description of each data type along with examples of use where appropriate.

Data Typing and Variable naming conventions

How to minimize errors due to mismatched data types and ideas on writing maintainable VBScript code.

Visual Basic Script, in keeping with its lightweight implementation, has limited its data types to only one—the variant. For those unfamiliar with Visual Basic in general, the *variant* is a data type that can contain a representation of almost any other data type. Strings, longs, doubles, dates, and so on are easily contained within a variant. This is what is known as weak data typing and is the opposite of the preferred strong typing of a more robust programming environment like Visual Basic Professional, where you have specific data types to contain your data. Having a weakly-typed language offers the simplicity of the variant in use for the programmer in declaring variable storage and simplicity in Visual Basic Script's implementation since the code library for VBS need only contain the functionality of the variant type. On the other hand, this simplicity also carries the danger of passing the wrong data type to a procedure that can be very hard to debug. VBScript programs can become real monsters to maintain if the programmer doesn't take care to insure some sort of procedural level data typing. It's a tradeoff that seems to work quite well. ■

The Variant's Data Sub-Types

Let's take a more in-depth look at the variant's capabilities. As I mentioned, the variant can contain any of the other data types normally associated with Visual Basic. It also automatically converts between data types where possible. When assigning a value to a variant, Visual Basic fits that value into a type that it assumes is the optimal type. Whole numbers become integer types, numbers with fractional portions become floating point types, and character values become string types without any intervention on your part. For example, if you have two variables, one containing a string and the other a numeric value, you can concatenate them without any explicit type conversions.

The result here is that `MyDisplay` contains the string "The Number is: 1234.5678." In most cases, you do not have to be concerned with the conversions of one data type to another since all conversions are automatic. But you need to be careful in your use of the `+` operator. While it concatenates strings, if you use it to concatenate two numericals or two numeric strings, they are added instead of concatenated. Therefore, always use the `&` operator to concatenate string type variants and the `+` operator to add numeric values. The following listing shows the proper method to use when concatenating a string.

```
MyString = "The Number is: "
MyAnswer = 1234.5678
MyDisplay = MyString & MyAnswer
```

The Boolean Sub-Type

The Boolean sub-type is a 16-bit signed integer, but when accessed can only return a True (–1) or False (0). In Visual Basic Script you can use either the keywords or the numeric representation of True and False. If you coerce a numeric value into a Boolean variant the result is a –1 for any value other than 0. Be aware that VBScript and the browser that's containing it may not always handle Booleans the same. In the example code shown in the following listing, the `Alert` statement of the Explorer browser displays the Boolean as a numeric value while Visual Basic Script's `MsgBox` procedure displays it as a keyword.

```
MyBool = True
Alert MyByte                'displays (-1)
MsgBox MyByte               'displays 'True'
```

The Byte Sub-Type

The Byte sub-type is an 8-bit unsigned integer. It was first included with Visual Basic 4. Its main purpose was to replace the use of strings for containing binary data. Prior to Visual Basic 4, string data was a single byte unsigned integer that represented an ASCII character. This changed to the two byte Unicode system with Visual Basic 4 and made strings unreliable for carrying binary data. The advantage of the Byte sub-type in Visual Basic Script is limited to using it as an unsigned integer value up to 65535, or as a set of eight Boolean flags.

The Currency Sub-Type

The Currency sub-type is optimized for the highly accurate manipulation of currency values or any math that requires accuracy up to 15 whole number places and four decimal places. Internally, it is an 8-byte integer with a 4-digit fixed decimal place. The numeric range of the currency type is –922,337,203,685,477.5808 to 922,337,203,685,477.5807.

The Date Sub-Type

The Date sub-type is a 64-bit floating point number that can represent a date from 1/1/100 to 12/31/9999. The way it works is that each whole number represents a day and the decimal numbers represent time. Negative whole numbers count back from 12/30 1899 and positive whole numbers count forward from that date. Time is represented by the digits to the right of the decimal point with .0 equal to midnight and .5 equal to 12 o'clock noon. Date sub-types recognize input either as strings that represent dates or their numeric equivalents. Listing 15.1 shows a set of date representations and how they are displayed under different circumstances.

Listing 15.1 The Different Ways a Date Value Can Be Handled

```
Myname = 12345.123
Myname = cdate(myname)
alert myname                'displays "10/18/33 2:57:07 AM"
alert cdbl(myname)          'displays 12345.123
Myname = cdate("10-10-10")
alert cdbl(myname)          'displays '3936'
alert cdate(myname)         'displays '10/10/10'
Myname = cdate("April 15, 1996")
Alert Myname                'displays '4/15/96'
Alert cdbl(myname)          'displays '35170'
```

The Double Sub-Type

The Double sub-type is an IEEE 64-bit double precision floating point number that can represent a range from –1.79769313486232E308 to –4.94065645841247E-324 in negative numbers, and 1.79769313486232E308 to 4.94065645841247E-324 in positive numbers.

The Integer Sub-Type

The Integer sub-type is a signed single byte integer value that ranges from –32,768 to 32,767. I would like to point out that there is no longer any speed advantage to using the Integer type over the Long in 32-bit environments and, of course, the Integer type has the disadvantage of a more limited value range.

The Long Sub-Type

The Long sub-type is a signed two-byte integer value. Its numerical range is from –2,147,483,648 to 2,147,483,647. Since Win95 and WinNT are 32-bit operating systems, they naturally do everything in 32-bit chunks. The long integer type no longer incurs a speed penalty over the integer type. I recommend that the Long be used everywhere you might have previously used the integer type.

The Object Sub-Type

The Object sub-type is a 32-bit address pointer reference to an OLE automation object instance. The ActiveX and Java controls are OLE Automation objects. You can set a reference to an object using the following syntax:

```
Set MyObject = New OleObject
```

At present, Visual Basic Script limits you to only the ActiveX and Java objects as OLE automation objects.

The Single Sub-Type

The Single sub-type is a 32-bit IEEE single precision floating point number. It has a numerical range of –3.402823E38 to –1.401298E-45 for negative values, and 3.402823E38 to 1.401298E-45 for positive values. Being a 32-bit number, it can show significant speed improvements over a double precision number in complex repetitive math that does not exceed the range of the single.

The String Sub-Type

The String sub-type is a continuous set of character values. In Visual Basic Script this can be up to two billion characters. Visual Basic Script only supports variable length strings, not the fixed length strings of the full version of Visual Basic. As noted in the Byte sub-type, Visual Basic strings should not be used to manipulate binary data as was done in previous BASICs since the string now utilizes two-byte Unicode characters that could corrupt binary data under the right circumstances.

When designing your Visual Basic Script, consider this: You are writing a script program that is intended for access over the limited bandwidth of the Internet. Your Visual Basic Script program will not be compiled or optimized in any way by the server or the browser. The more raw text that needs to be sent over the network, the longer it takes to load the page. Everything you can do to compact your code's use of text lessens the time to deliver the page to the client. This is not to say that you should write cryptic code, eliminate error trapping, or otherwise compromise the professionalism of your resulting product. I am just suggesting that you attempt to use the most efficient methods and algorithms you can devise to accomplish your task.

Working with Visual Basic Script's Variables

Back to the subject at hand! Besides the limitations of only one data type, Visual Basic Script does not provide for user-defined collection objects and user-defined types. This can be a severe limitation in a normal programming environment. But this is a limited scripting version of Visual Basic optimized for use within an HTML document with the idea of placing as small a load on the network as possible.

There is also the inability to pass data by reference that requires your data variables to be global if you intend to use them from one procedure to another. You cannot pass changes to a procedural argument back to the caller. Of all the constraints in VBScript this is perhaps the greatest concerning the use of variables. It makes it very easy to have one procedure corrupt the data for another procedure. You are going to have to pay close attention when changing data values and you are going to have to validate data for both type and value.

Creating Variables

There are two ways to create variables. You can implicitly create them where needed in a program or explicitly declare them before use. The accepted practice among most professional programmers is to explicitly declare them. In addition to explicitly declaring them, Visual Basic Script also includes the `Option Explicit` statement as an insurance against misspelling variable names. When used, it requires explicit declaration of a variable before attempting to use it. This prevents the programmer from common mistakes such as reusing a variable name or misspelling a variable name only to go insane later on trying to figure out why a given variable always has incorrect results in it. I strongly suggest that you use the `Option Explicit` statement in all of your scripts to help you eliminate as many potential bugs in your programming efforts as possible. The `Option Explicit` statement must be the very first line in your script for it to work properly.

Determining Data Type

If you are in a situation where you need to know the data type of a value in a variant before you use it, Visual Basic Script provides a function that tests the variant for certain data types. The `VarType()` function returns an integer type value that represents the data type of the variant. A set of intrinsic constants within Visual Basic Script is provided so that you can easily write code to determine the data type without having to remember these integer values (see Table 15.1).

Table 15.1 Visual Basic Script Constants for Return Values of the *VarType()* Function

Constant	Value	Description
`vbEmpty`	0	Empty of any value and not initialized
`vbNull`	1	Contains a null value
`vbInteger`	2	Contains an integer value
`vbLong`	3	Contains a long integer
`vbSingle`	4	Contains a single precision floating point value
`vbDouble`	5	Contains a double precision floating point value
`vbCurrency`	6	Contains a currency type floating point value
`vbDate`	7	Contains a date type value
`vbString`	8	Contains a string type value
`vbObject`	9	Contains a reference to an OLE automation object
`vbError`	10	Contains an error
`vbBoolean`	11	Contains a boolean true or false value
`vbVariant`	12	Contains a variant
`vbDataObject`	13	Contains a non-OLE object
`vbByte`	17	Contains a byte value
`vbArray`	8192	Contains an array

Given the information in Table 15.1 you might wonder in what kind of situation you would want to use this `VarType()` function. How about error trapping?

The example shown in Listing 15.2 sends a set of coordinates to a function that checks to see if the coordinates are within a given range of values, and returns a true or false based on that comparison. But it also checks to see if minimal values are being returned and returns an error value if these minimals are not met. Other possible uses include branching logic based on the type of data returned from a query.

Listing 15.2 Passing an Error Value to a Function Result

```
<Script ="VBS">
<!--
Sub Image1_MouseMove(a,b,x,y)
blnSuccess = IsMyArea(x, y)
If VarType(blnSuccess) = vbError Then
     MsgBox "An unknown error has occured"
ElseIf blnSuccess = True then
     Aleret = "Click Here for More Information"
End If
End Sub
Function IsMyArea(x, y)
     If x >0 and y> 0 then
          If x >100 and x <201 then
               IsMyArea = True
          Else
               IsMyArea = False
          End
     Else
          IsMyArea = CVErr(5)
     End If
End function

-->
</Script>
```

In the case of a variant of type Array, the value returned from `VarType()` is a binary combination of `vbArray` and whatever the contained data type is. That is to say that a variant array of string types would return the value `vbArray` plus `vbString` added together. To determine that a variable is a variant array you would use a logical AND. Then, to determine the data type you can use a select case statement to determine the data type of the array as Listing 15.3 does.

Listing 15.3 Detecting Sub-Type of a Variant Array

```
If VarType(MyValue) And vbArray then
     Select Case VarType(MyValue) - vbArray
          Case is vbEmpty
          Case is vbNull
          ...
          Case is vbByte
     End Select
End If
```

Variable Naming Conventions

While using the `VarType()` function in the preceding chapter to ensure data type in your code is an excellent way of protecting individual procedures from fatal errors due to the inadvertant passing of the wrong type, you can also take preventative steps against this and other errors by using a sensible and consistant naming convention in your scripts. Clearly, if every variable is instantly recognized as to type and purpose by its name then misuse of that variable in your code becomes less likely. There are several different naming conventions floating around in the Visual Basic community and all have their merits, and you might even develop your own. What is important is that your VBScript is consistant in those conventions. Table 15.2 provides a suggested set of prefixes for data types.

Table 15.2 Suggested VBScript Variable Naming Conventions

Prefix	Type	Example
bln	Boolean	blnDataValid = True
byt	Byte	bytStateFlags = bytStateFlags And &H10
cur	Currency	curTotal = curSubTotal + curSalesTax
dte	Date	dteNextAppointment = NOW + 14
dbl	Double	dblZPlot = 375.035 * 127.999
int	Integer	For intCount = 1 to intMaximum
lng	Long	For lngCount = 1 to lngMaximum
obj	Object	Set objMyDoc = Document
sng	Single	sngXLocation = sngMyX * 2.5
str	String	strUserName = strFstName & " " & strLstName

In addition to the prefixes that identify the data type, I also recommend that you use names that clearly define the purpose of the data contained in the variable. Looking at Table 16.2 again you can see that the `blnDataValid` is a True/False condition of some state data's validity. If you have a set of data inputs that you validate either during input or during an attempt to submit it, this variable would represent the result of the data having been checked for valid type and range. Seems to be very obvious looking at it, but suppose I had named that same variable bDVal instead. If I had to maintain code with variables named like bDVal I would probably spend a lot of time finding out what each variable is supposed to represent as opposed to the more robust name of blnDataValid which fully describes data type and purpose.

Variable Scope

Variables in Visual Basic Script have three levels of scope: page level scope, script level scope, and procedure level scope. The script level variables are declared right at the beginning of the script and are available to all procedures within that page's script (see Table 15.3). Variables with a procedure level scope are declared in the procedure they are used in and are visible only within the context of that procedure. Outside of procedures, you declare a variable as either Private or Public. The variable that is declared as Private is visible to only the procedures within the script it is declared in. The variable that is declared as Public is visible to all of the scripts on that HTML document (see Listing 15.4).

Table 16.3 Variable Scoping in VBScript

Keyword	Placement	Description of scope
Dim	In Procedure	Limited to the procedure
Dim	Not in Procedure	Visible throughout script
Private	Not in Procedure	Visible throughout script
Public	Not in Procedure	Visible throughout all scripts

Listing 15.4 Examples of Variable Scope

```
<SCRIPT LANGUAGE=VBS>
<!--
Option Explicit
Dim MyName     'Script level variable
     Sub Main (ButtonName)     'ButtonName is Procedure Level
          Myname = ButtonName &"Ibrahim"
     End Sub
     Sub BtnHello_OnClick
          Main "Hello"
          Alert Myname
     End Sub
     Sub BtnGoodBye_OnClick
          Dim MyButton     'Mybutton is procedure level
          MyButton = BtnGoodBye.Value
          Main MyButton
          Alert Myname
     End Sub
-->
</SCRIPT>
```

In the example script shown in Listing 15.4, `MyName` has a script level scope and is visible in both button click events. The `ButtonName` argument to the `Sub Main` procedure is a procedural level variable and is visible only to the `Sub Main` procedure. In the `BtnGoodBye Click` procedure, the `MyButton` variable is also limited in scope to the procedure. It is a commonly accepted programming practice to limit the scope of a variable as much as possible.

With Visual Basic Script, you can pass values only by value. When you pass a variable by value, the procedure that it is passed to cannot pass the changes to the variable back up the call stack. The value is local only to the procedure. To be more specific, when you pass an argument by value, you are only passing the value contained in the variable to the procedure, and the procedure stores the value in a local replica of the variable. When you are passing a variable by reference then you are passing the address of the variable to the procedure, and the procedure directly accesses the passed variable's values. VBScript does not support passing values by reference at this time.

Literals, Constants, Structs

Visual Basic Script does not support constants or structs like the `Type...End Type` as in Visual Basic 4. You can either use literal values or define variables and populate them with values. Most programmers have learned to not use literals in their code due to the difficulty in maintaining such code. Instead, a good practice is to utilize constants to represent literal values throughout your projects. Since Visual Basic Script does not actually allow for constants, you have to use global variables that you initialize during runtime. Not a lot of difference in use from constants, just a slightly different way of doing it. But remember, unlike true constants, you can change the value of these variables during runtime so you should have some sort of naming convention that clearly marks them out as constants as in the example code in Listing 15.5.

Listing 15.5 Pseudo Constants

```
'pseudo constants
Dim cstSunday
Dim cstMonday
Dim cstTuesday
...
cstSunday = 0
cstMonday = 1
cstTuesday = 2
...
Sub WhatDayIsIt
     If DayOfWeek(cstSunday) then
          Alert "Sorry We are closed today"
     Else
          ...Do some code
     End If
End Sub
```

From Here...

You have seen that VBScript uses Visual Basic's Variant data type as a catch-all utility variable for all other data types. The Variant is like a sack that you can drop anything you want into. But you have to be careful that you have a method in place to keep track of what each variable contains as your scripts become more complex and as you attempt to reuse code in other projects. Where this is really going to become a problem is in the use of the ActiveX Layout control in the development of drop in place functionality. You, or someone else, will develop a control for a particular purpose and expose certain properties and methods of that control for use by the main HTML document. Knowing what kind of data type is expected for a given property by just looking at the name of that property will go a long way in helping to write bug-free code.

CHAPTER 16

VBScript Operators

by Ron Schwarz

Operators are keywords and characters that tell the VBScript interpreter to act upon the values contained in variables, literals, and expressions.

This chapter examines arithmetic, string, comparison, and logical operator groups. Each group is discussed in a separate section, and each section contains a short table listing the operators in that group. ■

Unsung heroes

Operators are not particularly glamorous, but used judiciously can save lots of coding effort.

Groups of operators

Different types of operations require different operators. This chapter groups them by category.

What they're for

Find out uses for different types of operators.

Understanding operators

Learn how they work, and things to watch out for.

Using operators

See syntax and result details.

Using Operators

In most cases, you can view operators as behaving identically on expressions, variables, and literals. One important exception is the assignment operator—you can only assign a value to a variable. (You can have a numeric literal or an expression on the left side of an equals sign, but only when performing a test—for example, `If (A + B) = (C + D) Then...`)

Much of your VBS code depends on logical operations. A good understanding of the more commonly used operators is essential. If you come from a background of programming in other languages, you've undoubtedly got a good grasp of the subject, and only need to brush up on VBS syntax. If you're just getting into programming VBS from a background of HTML programming, it's time to dig in and learn the principles of logical testing and bitwise operations.

Operator Precedence

Throughout this chapter, you'll see extensive use of parentheses in example code. While it's frequently possible to rely on Operator Precedence rules (described later), you may find that your code is much more readable and you spend much less time debugging your apps if you are not overly sparing in your use of parentheses.

Parentheses *always* override Operator Precedence rules. And, expressions are evaluated from the inside out, starting with the innermost set(s) of parentheses. Coercing evaluation this way eliminates ambiguity–both to you and to the VBS script execution engine.

If you neglect to use sets of parentheses to force evaluation to take place according to your rules, VBS falls back on its default Operator Precedence rules. According to these built-in rules, the order of evaluation is:

Arithmetic operators (see following)

Comparison operators (evaluated left-to-right)

Logical operators (see following)

Arithmetic and logical operators, unlike comparison operators, are evaluated in specific order. The evaluation order for arithmetic operators is:

Exponentiation

Unary negation

Multiplication

Division

Integer division

Modulo arithmetic

Addition

Subtraction

String Concatenation (not an arithmetic operator, but evaluated in same order sequence)

The evaluation order for logical operators is:

Logical negation

Logical conjunction

Logical disjunction

Logical exclusion

Logical equivalence

Logical implication

Arithmetic Operators

The arithmetic operators are used with numeric variables and literals and expressions. (Since VBS at the moment has no constants, they are not an issue here.) The plus sign (+) can also be used as a string concatenation operator, but this usage is obsolete and should be used sparingly.

The following table lists the Arithmetic Operators:

Operator	Definition
-	Unary negation
*	Multiplication
/	Division
\	Integer division
Mod	Modulo arithmetic
+	Addition
-	Subtraction
^	Exponentiation

In addition to the arithmetic operators discussed in this chapter, VBS offers a rich selection of math functions. These are covered in greater detail in Chapter 22, "VBScript Language Elements."

▶ **See** "Math Functions," **p. 432**, for a discussion of VBScript math features.

Unary Negation

The *Unary Negation* (-) operator designates the negative value of a variable, number, or expression. Please note that the minus character is also used as the subtraction operator and is discussed later in this chapter. The following example returns –10 in B:

```
A = 10
B = -A
```

Multiplication

The *Asterisk* (*) character is used to multiply two values according to the following syntax:

```
Total = Item * Quantity
```

Division

The forward slash (/) is used when dividing one value by another. It returns either an integer or floating point value, as dictated by the actual operation. For coerced integer division, see the integer division operator description.

The *Division Operator* is demonstrated in the following example:

```
UnitPrice = TotalPrice / Quantity
```

Integer Division

The integer division (\) operator is used the same way as the division operator. However, it truncates any remainder, and only returns the integer part of the result.

The following example returns 3:

```
IntResult = 10 \ 3
```

Modulo Arithmetic

The *Modulo Arithmetic* (Mod) operator is used to return the non-integer part of a division operation. The following example returns 1:

```
IntResult = 10 Mod 3
```

Addition

The plus sign (+) is used as the *Addition Operator*. As mentioned earlier, it can also be used as a string concatenation operator, but this usage should be avoided unless there is a specific need for the peculiarities it introduces. (When using the + sign between two variables, the expression can be rendered as either an addition operation or a concatenation operation, depending on the values and types of the two variables. Because of the uncertainties this creates, it's generally best to reserve use of the + sign for addition, and the & for concatenation.)

The following example returns `10` in `A`:

```
A = 5 + 5
```


Subtraction

The minus sign (-) is used as the *Subtraction Operator*. It is important to avoid confusing this with its other use (as a unary negation operator). The following example returns `5` in `A`:

```
A = 10 - 5
```

Exponentiation

The *Exponentiation Operator* (^) is used to raise one value to the power of another. The following example returns `256`:

```
Result = 2 ^ 8
```

Unlike multiplication, you must be careful about where you place exponentiation expressions—reversing the order produces dramatically different results. The following example returns `64`:

```
Result = 8 ^ 2
```

String Operators

There is only one *String Operator*: the & string concatenation operator. Don't think of this as a real limitation, however. Unlike numbers, strings aren't really subject to "operations," *per se*—for example, you don't multiply one word by another. However, there is a rich set of string manipulation functions, and the comparison operators (described later in this chapter) apply to most variable types, including strings.

String Concatenation

The ampersand (&) is used for concatenating strings. *Concatenation* simply consists of joining two strings together. Concatenation does *not* join one string to another—it returns a third string that represents the result of the operation. The original strings are left intact. The following example returns `Ron's Computer`:

```
MyComputer = "Ron's" & " " & "Computer"
```

In the preceding example, we used two concatenation operations in one expression. This is perfectly legal—each operation only works on two strings. The + sign can also be used to concatenate strings but its use is generally discouraged.

▶ **See** "Addition," **p. 296**, for a discussion of the addition operator.

Comparison Operators

The *Comparison Operators*, as show in the following table, are used when testing expressions and variables against each other or against other conditions such as True or False.

Operator	Definition
=	Equality
<>	Inequality
<	Less than
>	Greater than
<=	Less than or equal to
>=	Greater than or equal to
`Is`	Object equivalence

Equality

The equals sign (=) is used as the *Equality Operator*. It is also used as an *Assignment Operator*.

The = Assignment Operator

You may have noticed that there is no section for assignment operators and no entry in any table for the equals sign in its assignment operator mode. This is due to some BASIC arcana—the equals sign is, strictly speaking, part of the `Let` statement. However, use of `Let` is optional in VB, and the only time you're apt to see it in use is when non-VB code (for example, other non-Microsoft dialects of BASIC) is ported over to VBS. In VB and VBS, `X = 10` is functionally identical to (and more readable than) `Let X = 10`.

(The Let X = 10 syntax should not be confused with Property Let settings in VB, which are not implemented in VBScript.)

The equals sign is used when testing one expression against another for equality. As with all comparison operators, the result is an implicit Boolean (True or False) result. `If A = B Then` is equivalent to the following code:

```
If (A = True) And (B = True) Then
EndIf
```


Due to the way VBS handles these tests, you do not have to test for explicit True, and, as demonstrated in the following code snippet, you don't even have to use the equality operator in some cases.

```
If A Then
EndIf
```

In the preceding example, as long as `A` is non-zero (presuming that `A` is a numeric variable) the test succeeds. If you need to test against True (or any other specific value), you need to use the equals sign, as in the following:

```
If A = 25 Then
EndIf
```

Inequality

The < and > characters combine to form the *Inequality Operator*. They function opposite to the equality operator. The following example demonstrates their use:

```
If CreditStatus <> FlaggedAccount Then
EndIf
```

In this example, as long as the two variables are *not* equal, the test passes.

The inequality operator can also be used on strings. It performs a test based on ASCII value, which is case-sensitive. If you need to perform a case-insensitive test, you must use either `Lcase` or `Ucase` to assure that both values are of the same case. If the strings do not match, the result is True.

Less Than

The < character is used as the *Less Than Operator*. If the expression on the left side of the less than operator is less than the expression on the right, the test passes. In the following example, as long as the value in `RPM` is less than the value in `Redline`, the test passes:

```
If RPM < Redline Then
EndIf
```

The less than operator can also be used on strings. It performs a test based on ASCII value, which is case-sensitive. If you need to perform a case-insensitive test, you must use either `Lcase` or `Ucase` to assure that both values are of the same case. Be careful, as differences in length can affect the results. This can be a problem when strings contain numeric values, and different numbers of leading zeros further complicate matters.

Greater Than

The *Greater Than Operator* (>) is the opposite of the less than operator. If the expression on the left side of the > is higher, the test passes. In the following example, as long as `Balance` is higher than `Limit`, the test passes:

```
If Balance > Limit Then
EndIf
```

The greater than operator can also be used on strings. It performs a test based on ASCII value, which is case-sensitive. If you need to perform a case-insensitive test, you must use either `Lcase` or `Ucase` to assure that both values are of the same case. The same concerns mentioned for the less than operator also apply here.

Less Than or Equal To

The *Less Than or Equal to Operator* (<=) can also be used on strings. It performs a test based on ASCII value, which is case-sensitive. If you need to perform a case-insensitive test, you must use either `Lcase` or `Ucase` to assure that both values are of the same case. The same concerns mentioned for the less than operator also apply here.

This example will pass if the value in `Amount` is less than or equal to the amount in `Limit`:

```
If Amount <= Limit Then
EndIf
```

Greater Than or Equal To

The *Greater Than or Equal to Operator* (>=) can also be used on strings. It performs a test based on ASCII value, which is case-sensitive. If you need to perform a case-insensitive test, you must use either `Lcase` or `Ucase` to assure that both values are of the same case. The same concerns mentioned for the less than operator also apply here.

In this example, the test will pass if the value in `Age` is greater than or equal to the value in `Minimum`:

```
If Age >= Minimum Then
Endif
```

Object Equivalence

The *Is* keyword is the *Object Equivalence Operator.* It tests two objects or object variables to see if they are referring to the same object. The following code snippet demonstrates a test of Object Equivalence:

```
Match= Handy Is LongFormName.LongControlName
```

In this test, if `Handy` is an object variable that has been previously `Set` to a reference to `LongFormName.LongControlName`, `Match` will return *True*, otherwise, it will return *False*.

▶ **See** "Assignment," **p. 426**, for a discussion of the Set keyword.

Logical Operators

This table defines the Logical Operators:

Operator	Definition
Not	Logical negation
And	Logical conjunction
Or	Logical disjunction
Xor	Logical exclusion
Eqv	Logical equivalence
Imp	Logical implication

The logical operators apply to Boolean expressions. The elements of a Boolean expression can be of any data type—it's not necessary to build a Boolean expression out of Boolean variables.

NOTE A *Boolean Expression* is an expression that returns either True or False (-1 or 0) as its result.

The *And* and *Or* operators wear two hats: they are used in simple tests of expressions and in bitwise Boolean operations. The differences are noted in the following respective sections.

Each logical operator description contains a truth table that shows the results produced by all possible bit combinations.

NOTE A *Truth Table* is a list of all possible operations and results for a specific operator.

One additional factor comes into play with logical operations. When any value contains `Null`, the result is also Null. Null propagates through the operation. This is not shown in the truth tables, but should be taken into consideration if there is a possibility that any of your values might contain Null.

Logical Negation

Logical Negation (the *Not* keyword) is similar to unary negation, but, like all logical operators, is carried out on the bit level rather than on the value of the expression. It's easy to fall into the trap of using *Not* when testing expressions and finding that things aren't working as they should. *Not* reverses all the bits in a variable, and is generally used against either True or False in Boolean tests.

A common programming error is to look at the *Not* operator in the same context as the *And* and *Or* operators. While we can use *And* and *Or* to build a logical testing expression, we cannot be so cavalier with *Not*.

For example, the following code does not work correctly:

```
If (Balance < Limit) And (Lastname Not "Smith") Then
EndIf
```

For one thing, we can't "NOT" a string. And, even if we use numeric values, we'd still have a large unpredictability factor.

There are some nifty uses for this operator, though. A variable (or a property) that needs to toggle between True and False can be easily managed with one simple line of code. The following line of code toggles the value of the `Direction` variable between True and False. This is *much* simpler than a complex `"If Direction = True Then Direction = False Else..."` block of code.

```
Direction=Not Direction          'reverse direction
```

The reason for this is simple: when we reverse the bits in False (0), we end up with True (–1), and vice versa.

Here is the Logical Negation Operator's truth table:

Expression	**Result**
False	True
True	False

Logical Conjunction

The *And* keyword is used as the *Logical Conjunction Operator* in VBScript. As with the logical disjunction (*Or*) operator, it has dual uses. You can apply any logical test against a clause of one expression *And* another, or you can use *And* to return a value representing a bitwise (*bitwise* means that the two values are tested one bit at a time) "*And*ing" of two values.

The following example passes if both expressions evaluate to an implicit True:

```
If (Total < Limit) And (AccountStatus = Current)Then
EndIf
```

The next example returns `127` in `C`, since the set bits that are common to both `A` and `B` equal `127`:

```
A = 127
B = 255
C = A And B
```

This is the truth table for the Logical Conjunction Operator:

First Expression	Second Expression	Result
False	False	False
False	True	False
True	False	False
True	True	True

Logical Disjunction

Or is used as the *Logical Disjunction Operator*. Like *And*, it is used when testing expressions and also for bitwise Boolean operations.

The comparison test in the following example passes if either of the expressions evaluate to an implicit True:

```
If (Moves > GameLimit) or (GameTime > TimeOut) then
EndIf
```

The next example always returns the lowercase form of whatever (single letter) string literal is passed:

```
LowerCase = Chr(Asc("A") or 32)
```

Here is the Logical Disjunction truth table:

First Expression	Second Expression	Result
False	False	False
False	True	True
True	False	True
True	True	True

Logical Exclusion

The *Xor* (Exclusive Or) keyword is used as the *Logical Exclusion Operator*. The logical exclusion operator is similar to the *Or* operator, with one significant difference. Whereas *Or* evaluates when either or both bits are set (remember, we're comparing values one bit at a time), *Xor* evaluates when *only* one bit is set—hence, its "exclusive" qualification.

The *Xor Logical Exclusion Operator* is frequently used for simple encryption routines, since a byte *Xor*ed by another number produces a number that is restored when *Xor*ed by the same number. By *Xor*ing a string one character at a time against each character of a password string, an encrypted string results. And, when *Xor*ing the encrypted string by the same password, the plaintext string is restored.

It is interesting to note that any value *Xor*ed with itself results in False.

The first routine in Listing 16.1 encrypts the string contained in `PlainText`, and places the encrypted value in `CryptText`.

The second routine reverses the process, and places the decrypted string in `NewText`.

Listing 16.1 Logical Exclusion Example

```
PlainText = "Test Text"
Password = "Swordfish"

For C = 1 To LEenPassword$)
        CryptText = CryptText + Chr(Asc(MIidPlainText, C, 1)) _
           Xor Asc(Mid(Password, C, 1)))
Next

For C = 1 To Len(Password)
        NewText = NewText + Chr(Asc(Mid(CryptText, C, 1)) _
           Xor Asc(Mid(Password, C, 1)))
Next
```

The Logical Exclusion truth table follows:

First Expression	Second Expression	Result
False	False	False
False	True	True
True	False	True
True	True	False

Logical Equivalence

The *Eqv* keyword is used as the *Logical Equivalence Operator*. This operation is similar to *And*, but, in addition to evaluating when both bits are set, it also evaluates when both bits are *not* set. If both bits are the same (either True or False) the expression passes evaluation. Here is the Logical Equivalence Operator truth table:

First Expression	Second Expression	Result
False	False	True
False	True	False
True	False	False
True	True	True

Logical Implication

Imp is used as thc *Logical Implication Operator*. If identical bits in both expressions are True or if bits in the righthand expression are True, the operation evaluates as True. Here's the Logical Implication truth table:

First Expression	Second Expression	Result
False	False	True
False	True	True
True	False	False
True	True	True

From Here...

Operators are used in every aspect of VBScript programming. Check Chapters 11-20 for general coverage of language features. And, specifically, consult these chapters for more information:

- Chapter 15, "VBScript Data Types and Variables," contains valuable information on manipulating data in VBScript.
- See Chapter 19, "VBScript Procedures." Procedures are the central building block for code.
- Chapter 22, "VBScript Language Elements," explains string manipulation functions, math functions, and other useful language features of VBS.

CHAPTER 17

VBScript Control of Flow and Error Handling

by Ibrahim Malluf

Visual Basic Script provides an almost complete set of sequential, looping, and branching structures. VBScript also only allows the 'On Error Resume Next' error handling structure, limiting Visual Basic Script to inline error control. That means Visual Basic programmers who are used to branching to labeled error-handling routines will have to make do with this limited approach. Despite this major limitation on error handling, Visual Basic Script is a very robust programming platform for adding client-side scripting capabilities. Let us review the fundamental structures that comprise the basis of structured programming techniques and how they are implemented in Visual Basic Script. ■

Programming Structures in Visual Basic Script

Here we discuss the building blocks of structured programming available in Visual Basic Script.

Error Handling in Visual Basic Script

A discussion on error-handling techniques available in Visual Basic Script.

Applying Visual Basic Script to HTML

This section quickly gets you into applying Visual Basic Script to an HTML document while also introducing the use of ActiveX controls.

Programming Structures in VBScript

Modern programming techniques revolve around structures. VBScript includes the three main types of structures: sequential, looping, and conditional branching. Different combinations and variations of these three structures are the tools that you'll use to accomplish the programming task at hand. What follows is a description of each structure included in Visual Basic Script.

Sequential Structures

Sequential structures are the simplest of programming structures. They are the lines of code that actually perform the calculations, state changes, printing, input and output, and other required operations. They can also be branching instructions, such as a function or subroutine call. Generally speaking, sequential statements are almost always contained within other more complex structures. Listing 17.1 shows a set of five example sequential structures.

Listing 17.1 Simple Structure Statements

```
Username = "John Doe"
UserID = "ABC123"
MyRate = A * (C1/C2)
MyResult = Myfunction(MyRate)
Call AnySub(Arg1, Arg2, Arg3)
```

Looping Structures

Looping structures cause program execution to repeat in a continuous loop until some condition is met. In Visual Basic Script, there are four different looping structures. They are called looping structures because the one common feature among them is that they repeat the same section of code until something causes the loop to end.

The *Do...Loop* Structure The `Do...Loop` structure continually repeats a block of code until a specified condition is met either before each loop or after each loop. What determines if the loop runs at least once depends on where the structure's conditional is placed and whether that conditional is a `While` or `Until` conditional. Let's take a look at the different ways you can construct a `Do...Loop` along with some example code that shows how the particular style can be used.

The following code shows all of the `Do...Loop` structure's possible syntactical variations. The conditionals that break the loop can be at the beginning, middle, or end of the loop. In the beginning or end of the loop structure you would use the `While` or `Until` keywords to indicate the conditional. In the middle of the loop you can use an `If...Then` structure to break out of the loop with an `Exit Do` statement as part of the `If...Then`'s statements.

```
DO [WHILE¦UNTIL condition]
[statements]
[EXIT DO]
LOOP [WHILE¦UNTIL condition]
```

The following example runs only if the *condition* is met in the beginning and repeats as long as the *condition* is met.

```
DO WHILE condition
[statements]
LOOP
```


An example of this structure is shown in Listing 17.2. Here the statements inside of the `Do...Loop` will execute only if `intPlace` is less than or equal to 8 and repeat until `intPlace` is greater than 8. Also note that the `Do...Loop` will immediately exit if the `intCount` value exceeds the upper bounds of the `strData` array.

Listing 17.2 A *Do While* Example

```
Do While IntPlace =< 8
       If IntCount > Ubound(strData) then Exit Do
       intPlace=instr(strData(intCount),";")
       Call MyProcess(intPlace,intCount)
       IntCount=IntCount + 1
Loop
```

The following runs only if `condition` is not met and repeats as long as the `condition` is not met.

```
DO UNTIL condition
[statements]
LOOP
[statements]
```

An example of this form of the `Do...Loop` structure is shown in Listing 17.3. Note that it is a minor modification of Listing 17.2 that does the exact same thing only using the `Until` keyword instead and will also repeat as long as `intPlace` is less than 8.

Listing 17.3 A *Do Until* Loop

```
Do Until IntPlace > 8
       If IntCount > Ubound(strData) then Exit Do
       intPlace=instr(strData(intCount),";")
       Call MyProcess(intPlace,intCount)
       IntCount=IntCount + 1
Loop
```

The next example's `Do...Loops` always run at least once regardless of the loop's conditional requirements. This is because the conditional is not checked until the end of the loop's statements.

In this example a `While` statement is used for the conditional. In this case the loop will repeat as long as the condition is met.

```
DO
[statements]
LOOP WHILE condition
```

Continuing to use a slight modification of the same sample code, Listing 17.4 shows a `Do...Loop` that will always execute once, and if the condition is met will repeat again.

Listing 17.4 A *Do Loop While* Example

```
Do
        If IntCount > Ubound(strData) then Exit Do
        intPlace=instr(strData(intCount),";")
        Call MyProcess(intPlace,intCount)
        IntCount=IntCount + 1
Loop While IntPlace =< 8
```

Finally, the `Do...Loop Until` structure will repeat as long as the condition is not met.

```
DO
[statements]
LOOP UNTIL condition
```

Listing 17.5 shows the same example code this time using an `Until` condition structure.

Listing 17.5 A *Do Loop Until* Example

```
Do
        If IntCount > Ubound(strData) then Exit Do
        intPlace=instr(strData(intCount),";")
        Call MyProcess(intPlace,intCount)
        IntCount=IntCount + 1
Loop Until IntPlace => 8
```

Figure 17.1 demonstrates the structure of the `Do...Loop` process.

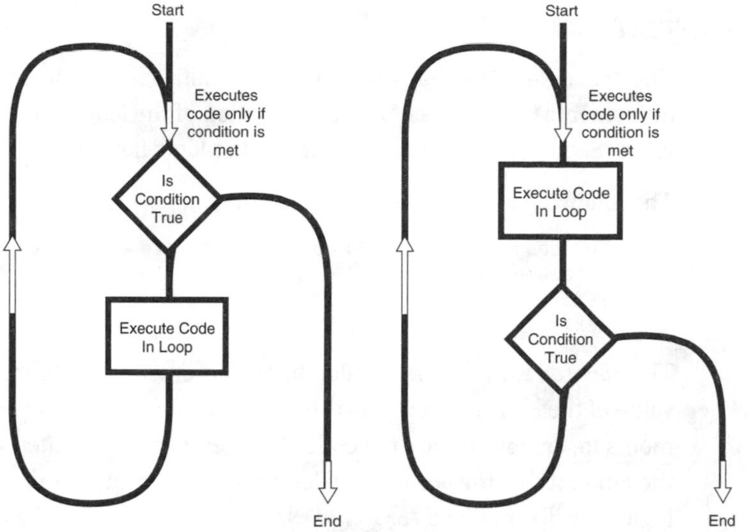

FIG. 17.1
Logic Flow diagram of the `Do...Loop` structure.

> **CAUTION**
>
> Beware The Endless Loop! Make sure your looping structures have an explicit ending condition that must occur! When using a `Do...Loop` or `While...Wend` make sure that these loops have a definite ending condition; otherwise, you could end up locking up the browser from further interaction with the user. VBScript does not have the equivalent of a Visual Basic `DoEvents()` function, so there is no way to break out of a loop or allow other operations outside of the loop to occur.

These looping structures are used to repeat a given set of code based on a certain condition. The condition is usually the result of some calculation or other operation within the loop. It is possible, with multiple threads running in an application, for the condition to be affected from another operation independent of the `Do...Loop` itself, though relying on this can be dangerous. Looping structures must eventually arrive at a condition that allows the loop to end; otherwise, your application could lock up and stop responding to the user. This is especially true in Visual Basic Script because there is no mechanism like a `DoEvents()` function to allow breaking out of a loop through user intervention. Internet Explorer 3.0 will, after a particular operation has been looping for a while, ask if you want to end the script, but don't depend on other browsers to allow for this. Make sure your looping structures have a definite ending condition.

For...Next

The `For...Next` loop has a counter that is initialized to some value and then increments or decrements that counter for every iteration of the loop until it has reached some specified value. See Figure 17.2 for a diagram of the logic flow of a `For...Next` loop.

The following code shows the syntax for `For...Next` loops:

```
FOR counter = start TO finish STEP rate
[statements]
[EXIT FOR]
NEXT
```

The *`counter`* is the numeric value being incremented or decremented, *`start`* is the starting value of the *`counter`*, *`finish`* is the final value that the *`counter`* either increments or decrements to, *`statements`* are the code statements to be executed within the loop, and *`rate`* is the amount that the *`counter`*'s value changes with each interation. Figure 17.2 provides a logic flow diagram of a `For...Next` loop.

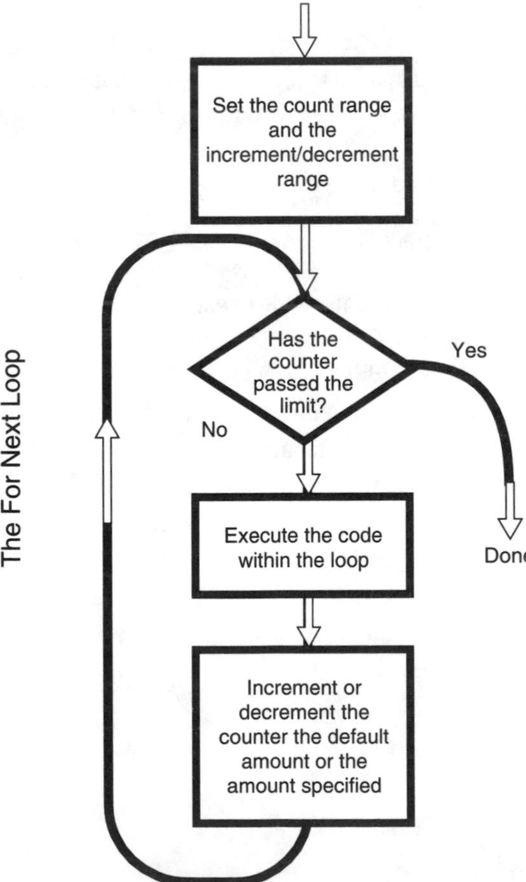

FIG. 17.2
The Logic Flow Diagram of a `For...Next` loop.

The `STEP` *`rate`* argument is optional and is required only if the rate of change is to be other than an increment of 1 per iteration. If you want the value of *`counter`* to increment 5 every interation, you use `STEP 5` as part of the statement. If you want to decrement the count by 5, then use `STEP -5`.

NOTE In Visual Basic the placing of the *counter* name right after the Next statement has been a normal programming practice that actually saved CPU cycles that were noticable in long iterations of a loop. In VBScript this will produce an error because placing the counter after the Next statement is not supported.

While...Wend

`While...Wend` loops through a group of statements as long as a given condition is true. If the condition is True, then the statements between the `While...Wend` execute and return to the `While` statement to check if the condition is still True. If the condition is not True, execution resumes at the first line after the `When` statement. You can nest `While...Wend` statements. The syntax for `While...Wend` is shown in the following code:

```
WHILE condition
[statements]
WEND
```

`condition` is any operation that results in True or False. *`statements`* are the code statements to be executed within the loop. The example code in Listing 17.6 parses a string displaying each set of characters between ampersands. When it reaches the word `"Stop"` the loop ends.

Listing 17.6 Using the *While...Wend* Loop

```
Dim strMyTest
strMyTest = "This&While...Wend&Loop&Will&Now&Stop&test5&test6"
  Sub btnTest_OnClick
        Dim strMyWord
        Dim lngStart
        Dim lngEnd
        Dim lngLength
        lngStart = 1
        While   strMyWord <> "Stop"
                    'find position of separator
                    lngEnd = instr(lngStart, strMyTest, "&")
                    'determine length of word
                    lngLength = lngEnd - lngStart
                    'extract word from string
                     strMyWord = Mid(strMyTest, lngstart, lnglength)
                    'display extracted word
```

continues

Listing 17.6 Continued

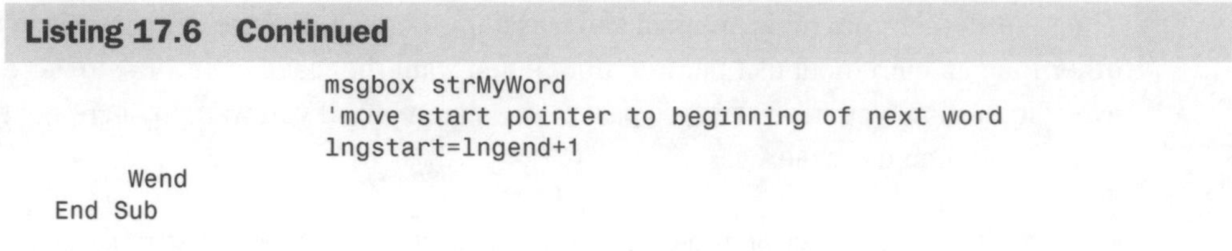

```
                        msgbox strMyWord
                        'move start pointer to beginning of next word
                        lngstart=lngend+1
        Wend
    End Sub
```

Figure 17.3 shows the logic flow diagram of the `While...Wend` statement.

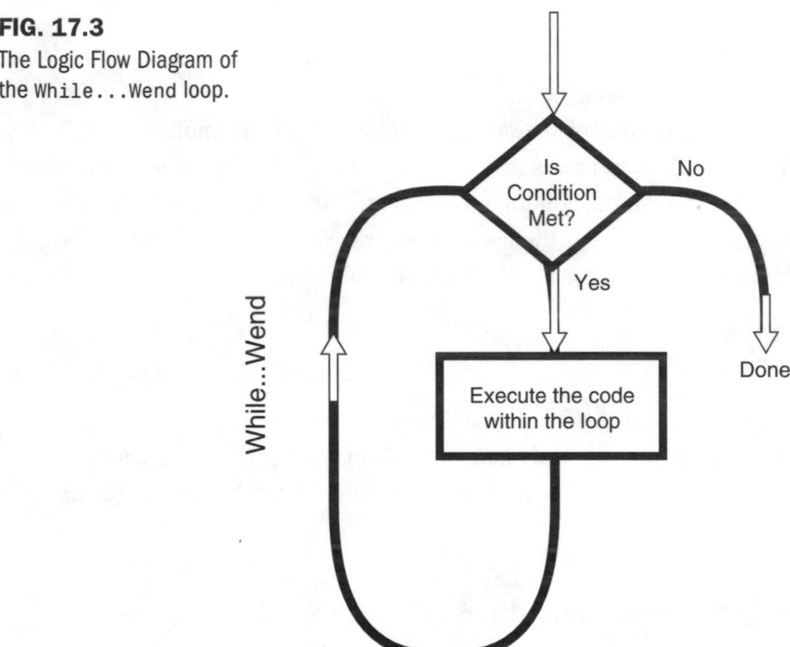

FIG. 17.3
The Logic Flow Diagram of the `While...Wend` loop.

That completes the looping structures for Visual Basic Script. The next structure type is a conditional-branching structure, known as the `IF...THEN...ELSE` structure.

Conditional Branching Structures

Conditional branching structures cause the flow of program logic to change according to a specified set of criteria. In VBScript there are two conditional branching structures, the `If...Then...Else` structure and the `Select Case` structure.

If...Then...Else What an `If...Then...Else` *conditional-branching structure* essentially does is this: if a condition is met, a group of statements executes. If the condition is not met and there is an `ELSEIF` condition that is met, then those statements immediately following the `ELSEIF` execute. There can be multiple `ELSEIF` conditionals within the structure allowing for a cascading set of `If...Then`s until a condition is met. Finally if none of the previously stated conditions are met, you can have an `ELSE` group of statements that executes. The following code shows the syntax for the `If...Then...Else` structure (see fig. 17.4):

```
IF condition THEN
[statements]
[ELSEIF condition THEN]
[statements]
[ELSE]
[statements]
END IF
```

`condition` is any operation that results in True or False. *`statements`* are the code statements to be executed within the branch.

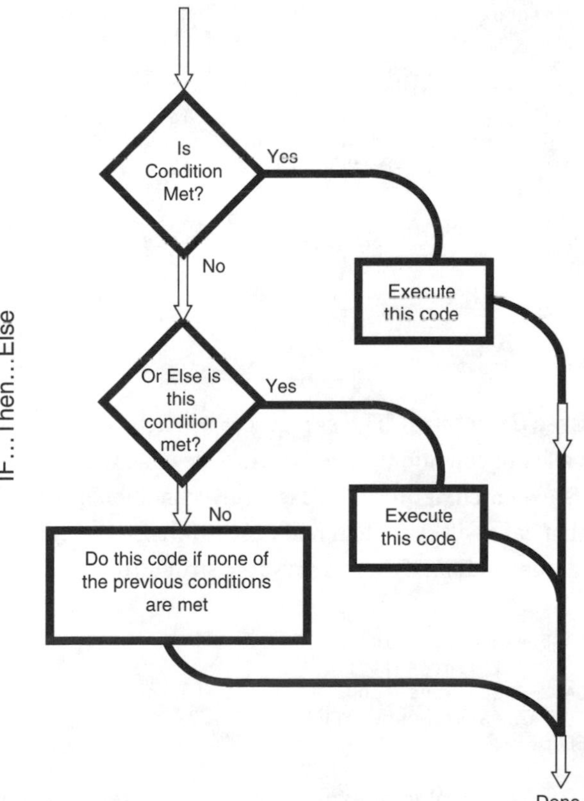

FIG. 17.4
The logic flow of the `If....Then...Else` conditional-branching structure.

You can have as many `Else If...Then` statements as needed in your script logic. You should always try to have an `Else` condition; at least consider the need for one carefully when constructing your logic. I automatically include it in any multiline `If...Then` structure and remove it only after I have positively identified that it is not needed. Listing 17.7 shows an example `If...Then...Else` that includes an `If`, `ElseIf`, and `Else` condition. The purpose of the example is to ensure that a value entered into a textbox is within a valid set of bounds before passing it to the rest of the program through the `lngMLat` variable. If the value entered is not valid then the previous value contained in `lngMLat` replaces the text in `txtMLat`. If the value entered is valid then the entered value replaces the value in `lngMLat`.

Listing 17.7 An Example *If...Then...Else* Structure

```
Sub txtMLat_OnChange
      'make sure latitude is within boundaries
      if txtMLat.Value < 25 then
            msgbox "Latitude is Outside Continental US"
                          'revert to previous value
                          txtMLat.Value= lngMLat
      ElseIf txtMLat.Value > 48 then
                          msgbox "Latitude is Beyond the Contiguous US"
                          'revert to previous value
                          txtMLat.Value= lngMLa
            Else
                         'Valid entry so  post it to lngMlat
                          lngMLat=txtMLat.Value
      End If

End Sub
```

The Select Case Structure The `Select Case` structure takes a Value and compares that value to a list of conditions called `Cases`. The code within the first `Case` that matches the value gets executed. If there is a `Case Else` condition included in the structure then the code in that case will execute if none of the other cases matched the value. Here is the syntactical representation of the `Select Case` structure:

```
SELECT CASE testexpression
    [CASE expressionlist-n
        [statements-n]] . . .
    [CASE ELSE expressionlist-n
        [elsestatements-n]]
END SELECT
```

`Testexpression` is any value or expression that represents the conditional critria. `CASE` is any expression that matches the criteria contained in `testexpression`. `expressionlist` is an expression or value to be compared with the criteria identified in `testexpression` statements is the code to execute for the given expression.

The `Select Case` structure is well suited to situations where there is a large list of possible conditions to match up to. Listing 17.8 shows an example `Select Case` being used in conjunction with a Popup Menu control.

Listing 17.8 Using the *Select* Case Structure

```
sub IeMENU1_Click(ByVal x)

      select case x
            case 1  'zooms the map in by a factor of 10x
                  Parent.Frames(0).MAPTOOL.cmdZOOMIN.Value=True
            case 2  'zooms the map out by a factor of 10x
                  Parent.Frames(0).MapTool.cmdZOOMOUT.Value=True
            case 3  'resets map back to default coordinates
                  Parent.Frames(0).MapTool.txtMLat.Text = 35.02
                  Parent.Frames(0).MapTool.txtMLon.Text = -106.0075
                  Parent.Frames(0).MapTool.cmdShowMap.Value=True
            case 4  'no action here. allows user to close menu
            case else
                    'no else situation
      end select
```


The code shown in Listing 17.8 compares the index of the menu item selected to a set of cases and executes the code where the case matches. Note that in this example I have a `Case Else` with no code to execute but a note saying that no else situation exists. On final review of this code, satisfied that there are no `Else` conditions to account for, I would remove the `Case Else` condition. Putting it there when I first write the skeleton structure reminds me to make sure that there are no possible conditions that I have overlooked and to allow for them if they do indeed exist.

This concludes the text on logic flow control for VBScript. All of the structures shown in this section are the building blocks that you use to construct your program logic. The next section covers the techniques of handling your program logic when errors occur.

Error Handling

Visual Basic Script allows only inline error handling in its present incarnation. What this means is that you must immediately check for an error condition after each statement that might possibly cause an error.

The error handler is invoked in the following manner:

```
On Error Resume Next
[Statement]
```

```
If Err then
     [statements]
Else
     [statements]
End If
```

Now some programmers prefer this style as opposed to using jumps to labels that handle errors. Myself, I prefer to be able to allow for only one place to enter a routine and one place to exit it using the following code structure:

```
Sub MySub ()
On Error Goto BadMySub
[statements]
ExitMySub:
     [exit code statements]
     Exit Sub
BadMySub:
     [error handler statements]
     If fixed THEN
          Resume
     Else
          Resume ExitMySub
     End If
End Sub
```

The advantage of the latter approach is the ability to provide an area for cleanup code that always executes regardless of any other circumstances within the procedure. With the inline method, if the error is fatal then you must exit immediately where you have determined this error to be fatal. If there is cleanup code that has to be included then you must repeat that code everywhere that this kind of error exit occurs. The opportunity for introducing even more errors due to procedural complexity is present. But inline error handling is what is provided in the current incarnation of VBScript.

The `ERR` object provides two methods and five properties, listed in Table 17.1.

Table 17.1 The *ERR* Object's Properties and Methods

Name	Type	Description
`Description`	Property	String containing a description of the error.
`HelpContext`	Property	Long integer pointing to a context in a help file.
`HelpFile`	Property	String containing the path to the relevant help file.
`Number`	Property	Long integer indicating the error number.
`Source`	Property	The name of the object causing the error.
`Raise`	Method	Causes a specified error to occur.
`Clear`	Method	Clears the ERR object of error status.

The `Description` property contains a short description of the error that was generated. You can use this string in a message box or an alert box to inform the user that an error has occurred. The `HelpContext` property provides a jump to a help topic within a specified help file when the user presses F1 or clicks the Help button on a message box. If no context is provided, it defaults to the contents window of the help file. The `HelpFile` property of `ERR` object is a fully qualified path to a help file. If no help file is specified, then the browser's default help file is invoked. The `Number` property corresponds to a Visual Basic error number or a user-defined error number and is specific to the type of error generated. This property is usually checked to determine the error that has occurred, and program logic is usually branched off accordingly. The `Source` property contains the name of the object where the error originated.

The `Raise` method has the following syntax:

```
object.RAISE (number[,source,description,helpcontext,helpfile])
```

`object` is always the `ERR` error object. *`number`* requires a long integer that specifies the error being raised. *`source`* is an optional string naming the object that originated the error. *`description`* is an optional string describing the error. *`helpcontext`* is an optional long integer pointing to a help topic in the specified help file. *`helpfile`* is an optional string specifying the full path to a relevant help file.

The `Raise` method is used to create an error condition in your code. In the context of Visual Basic Script, you can use this method to test and debug your own error handling code. It's original purpose was to generate a user-defined error condition in the Visual Basic environment from an OLE `Automation` object. Since Visual Basic Script does not allow you to create `Automation` objects, the use of the `Raise` method is probably limited to debugging your script code. The `Clear` method clears all of the property settings of the `ERR` object. An example of the Err.Object's use is given in Listing 17.9. This is a rewrite of the code shown in Listing 17.8. The `While...Wend` loop had a major flaw in it. Before going any further, go back to that listing and see if you can determine what that flaw in that `While...Wend` loop was before reading on.

Listing 17.9 ERROBJ1.HTM—Doing Inline Error Handling with the Error Object

```
<SCRIPT LANGUAGE="VBScript">
Dim strMyTest
strMyTest = "This&While...Wend&Loop&Will&Now&Create&An&Error&"
  Sub btnTest_OnClick
        Dim strMyWord
        Dim lngStart
        Dim lngEnd
        Dim lngLength
```

continues

Listing 17.9 Continued

```
        lngStart = 1
        lblDisplay.Caption=""
        While   strMyWord <> "Stop"
                    'provide for possible errors
                     On Error Resume Next
                    'find position of seperator
                    lngEnd = instr(lngStart, strMyTest, "&")
                    'determine length of word
                    lngLength = lngEnd - lngStart
                    'extract word from string
                     strMyWord = Mid(strMyTest, lngstart, lnglength)
                     'check for an error condition in the string parser
                    If lngEnd = 0 then
                          'error 99 is a user defined error
                          Err.Raise 99, "btnTest_Click","No STOP found in string"
              End If
                     'this checks for any error either user defined
                     'or system error
              If Err then
                        'show the user the problem
                        Msgbox Err.Description, 48, Err.Source
                        'end the While...Wend now
                        Exit Sub
                    End If
                    'display extracted word
              msgbox strMyWord
                   lblDisplay.Caption=lblDisplay.Caption & " " & strMyWord
                    'move start pointer to beginning of next word
                    lngstart=lngend+1
        Wend
  End Sub
</SCRIPT>
```

The flaw in Listing 17.8 was that there was the possibility of an endless loop if the `strMyTest` string did not contain a `"Stop"` in it. Or if the string was improperly formatted or empty an endless loop could also occur. So in Listing 17.9, I rewrote the code with an error handler that will catch either of these conditions and log them as an error and exit the subroutine. I created a user defined error using the number 99 and provided a description of the error for later display. I then check for an error condition, display it, and exit the procedure.

The example in Listing 17.9 shows how to use the `Raise` method of the `Err` object for indicating an actual error condition in the code. You could also use the `Raise` method as an error assertion for testing your program's code ability to handle various error by introducing specific errors at strategic places with this method and observe the outcome of that contrived error.

Applying Visual Basic Script to HTML

Now we can get into some Visual Basic Script examples that will give you a taste of what is possible. If you have had any experience with HTML you know that up until recently almost all activity was on the server side of things. HTML has been getting more and more capability added with each revision. But still it lacks the essentials of a good programming language. Visual Basic Script gives your HTML documents the client-side capabilities that HTML doesn't have.

The Rotating Labels Example

To get you started with a quick and impressive example, we will create a Web page with three rotating labels that display the current angles of the labels. We will also have the point size of the label text expand and contract.

The Page Layout for the Rotating Labels Example The first order of things is to place all non-script elements on the page. Using a text editor like Notepad enter the code in Listing 17.10.

On the CD

Listing 17.10 ROTATELABELS.HTM—HTML Portion of an HTML Document that Shows How to Place ActiveX Controls and Other Items on the Document

```
<HTML>
<HEAD>
<TITLE>Rotating Labels</TITLE>
</HEAD>
<BODY BGCOLOR="TEAL">
<OBJECT
      classid="clsid:99B42120-6EC7-11CF-A6C7-00AA00A47DD2"
      id=sprlbl4
            width=650
            height=40
      align=CENTER
>
<param name="_extentX" value="50" >
<param name="_extentY" value="700" >
<param name="angle" value="0" >
<param name="alignment" value="3" >
<param name="BackStyle" value="0" >
<param name="caption" value="ROTATING LABELS EXAMPLE">
<param name="FontName" value="Arial">
<param name="FontSize" value="32">
<param name="FontBold" value="1">
<param name="frcolor" value="2552500">
</OBJECT>
<HR>
<CENTER>
```

continues

Listing 17.10 Continued

```
<INPUT TYPE=BUTTON VALUE="&Change Angle" NAME="BtnchangeAngle">
<INPUT TYPE=TEXT VALUE="Running" NAME="txtBox" SIZE = "30">
<BR><BR><BR>
</CENTER>
<OBJECT
      classid="clsid:99B42120-6EC7-11CF-A6C7-00AA00A47DD2"
      id=sprlbl1
            width=200
            height=200
      align=left
>
<param name="_extentX" value="50" >
<param name="_extentY" value="500" >
<param name="angle" value="0" >
<param name="alignment" value="2" >
<param name="BackStyle" value="0" >
<param name="caption" value="My Label">
<param name="FontName" value="Arial">
<param name="FontSize" value="20">
<param name="FontBold" value="1">
<param name="frcolor" value="16791935">
</OBJECT>

<OBJECT
      classid="clsid:99B42120-6EC7-11CF-A6C7-00AA00A47DD2"
      id=sprlbl2
            width=200
            height=200
      align=left
>
<param name="_extentX" value="50" >
<param name="_extentY" value="700" >
<param name="angle" value="0" >
<param name="alignment" value="2" >
<param name="BackStyle" value="0" >
<param name="caption" value="My Label">
<param name="FontName" value="Arial">
<param name="FontSize" value="20">
<param name="FontBold" value="1">
<param name="frcolor" value="2552500">
</OBJECT>

<OBJECT
      classid="CLSID:99B42120-6EC7-11CF-A6C7-00AA00A47DD2"
      ID=sprlbl3
            width=200
            height=200
      align=left
>
<param name="_extentX" value="50" >
<param name="_extentY" value="700" >
<param name="angle" value="110" >
<param name="alignment" value="2" >
```

```
<param name="BackStyle" value="0" >
<param name="caption" value="My Label">
<param name="FontName" value="Arial">
<param name="FontSize" value="20">
<param name="FontBold" value="1">
<param name="frcolor" value="96711935">
</OBJECT>
<OBJECT
      classid="clsid:59CCB4A0-727D-11CF-AC36-00AA00A47DD2"
      id=timer1
      align=middle
>
<param name="Interval" value="100">
<param name="enabled" value="True">
</OBJECT>
```


The code in Listing 17.10 places several label controls, a button control, and a text box on the form; the background color is set to teal. What we are going to do here is have three of the labels rotate their text in a circular pattern while changing the text to reflect their current angle. Clicking the button control starts and stops the rotation. The text control's text changes to `Running` when the labels rotate and displays the current angle when the rotation stops.

The Visual Basic Script for the Rotating Labels Example The Visual basic Script portion of this example contains two procedures. The first procedure is an `OnClick` event of a button control. It utilizes a single `If...Then...Else` structure to toggle the timer control's `enable` property on and off. The second procedure is a `timer` event that contains a `For...Next` looping structure that iterates through the array of three label controls. Within the `For...Next` loop there are two `If...Then` structures. The first `If...Then` checks to see if the `Icount` property of the `For...Next` loop is an even or odd number and selects the direction of the rotation accordingly. The second `If...Then` loop compares the font size of the label against the maximum 20-point size points and increases or lowers the label's `fontsize` depending on the outcome of that comparison. Listing 17.11 shows the VBScript portion of the document that actually accomplishes these tasks.

Listing 17.11 ROTATELABELS.HTM—VBScript Portion of ROTATELABELS.HTM

```
<SCRIPT Language="VBScript">
<!-- Option Explicit
      Sub BtnchangeAngle_OnClick
            'toggle the timer on and off with
            'each subsequent click of the button
            'and change the textbox's value to
            'reflect the label's condition.
```

Listing 17.11 Continued

```
        If timer1.Enabled   Then
              timer1.Enabled = false
              txtBox.Value ="Stopped at " & sprlbl1.Angle & " Degrees"
        Else
              timer1.Enabled = true
              txtBox.Value ="Running"
        End if


  End Sub
  sub timer1_timer
                    On Error Resume Next
        'create an array of lables and
        'populate the array.
        Dim MyLabels(2)
        Dim Icount
        Set MyLabels(0) = sprlbl1
        Set MyLabels(1) = sprlbl2
        Set MyLabELs(2) = sprlbl3
        'iterate through each label in the array
        For Icount = 0 to 2
          'rotate element 0 and 2 clockwise and
          'rotate element 1 counter clockwise
          IF Icount\2 <> Icount/2 then
                    MyLabels(Icount).Angle = (MyLabels(Icount).Angle + 5)
                      mod 360
          Else
              MyLabels(Icount).Angle = (MyLabels(Icount).Angle - 5) mod 360
          End If
          'change the label text to reflect the current angle
          MyLabels(Icount).Caption = "My Angle Is " & MyLabels(Icount).Angle
          'allow the font size to increase to 20 point
                'then set it back to 6 points and start over
          If MyLabels(Icount).FontSize < 20 then
                MyLabels(Icount).FontSize = MyLabels(Icount).FontSize +2
          Else
                 MyLabels(Icount).FontSize = 8
                      End if
        Next
                    If Err then
                       MsgBox Err.Description
                    End if
  end sub
-->
</SCRIPT>
</BODY>
</HTML>
```

Save the document as ROTATELABELS.HTM and load it into your Internet Exporer 3.0 browser. Click the Change Angle button. The three labels on the bottom should start rotating the text in opposite directions. So this isn't rocket science but I just wanted to get you started with a simple script that utilized a looping structure and a conditional-branching structure. See Figure 17.5 for an idea of what the Web page should look like.

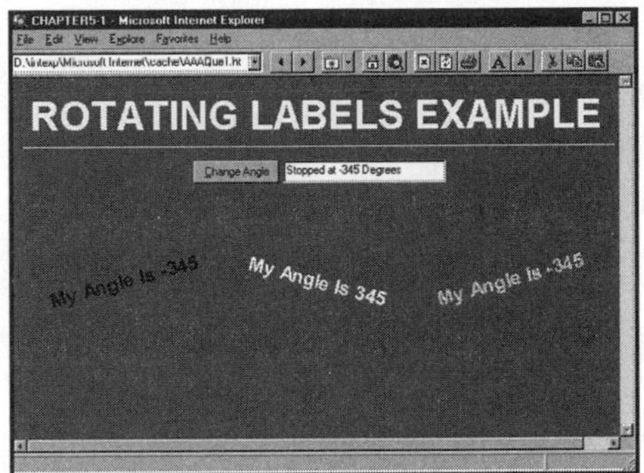

FIG. 17.5
The Rotating Labels from Listing 17.11.

Client-Side Data Validation Example

Now let's move on to a more realistic and practical example of using Visual Basic Script. In the past, when a Web page was used for data entry, the user entered their data and clicked the Submit button. The data was then sent to the Web server; the server submitted the data to a server-side program, such as Perl, or a CGI script. If the data was missing items or improperly submitted, then the server-side script sent an error page back to the server that, in turn, sent the page back to the user informing him that his data was invalid. Given all the traffic on the Internet lately, this procedure could cause a considerable delay—just to find out you forgot to enter something or that there was a typo.

Visual Basic Script gives you the ability to write pages that provide immediate client-side validation of data. When the user clicks that Submit button, your script can immediately validate the data for proscribed format and content. This is the theme of this chapter's next example. I make extensive use of `If...Then` structures in it. I also use a `For...Next` structure to iterate through the characters in a phone number field, formatting and validating it as I go.

The Page Layout of the Client-Side Data Validation Example The HTML code for formatting the document includes two ActiveX label controls, two command buttons, eight text entry controls, and a HTML table. Open a text editor and enter Listing 17.12's code for the body of the page.

On the CD

Listing 17.12 CH17_3.HTM—HTML Code for the Client-Side Validation Page

```
<HTML>
<HEAD>
<TITLE>Client-Side Validation</TITLE>
</HEAD>
<BODY BGCOLOR="TEAL">
<CENTER>
```

continues

Listing 17.12 Continued

```
<OBJECT
      classid="clsid:99B42120-6EC7-11CF-A6C7-00AA00A47DD2"
      id=sprlbl4
        width=700
        height=40
      align=CENTER
>
<param name="_extentX" value="50" >
<param name="_extentY" value="700" >
<param name="angle" value="0" >
<param name="alignment" value="3" >
<param name="BackStyle" value="0" >
<param name="caption" value="Client-Side Data Validation">
<param name="FontName" value="Arial">
<param name="FontSize" value="48">
<param name="FontBold" value="1">
<param name="frcolor" value="2552500">
</OBJECT>
<HR>
<TABLE BGCOLOR="#FFFFCC" WIDTH=565 ALIGN=CENTER>
<TR><TD BGCOLOR=NAVY ALIGN=LEFT>
<FONT COLOR=FFFFCC>PLEASE ENTER YOUR DATA..</TD>
   <TD BGCOLOR=NAVY ALIGN=RIGHT></TD></TR>
   <TR><TD>NAME</TD><TD><INPUT TYPE=TEXT
     VALUE="" NAME="txtBoxName" SIZE = "65"></TD></TR>
<TR><TD>ADDRESS1</TD>
    <TD><INPUT TYPE=TEXT VALUE=""
      NAME="txtBoxAddr1" SIZE = "65"></TD></TR>
<TR><TD>ADDRESS2</TD>
    <TD><INPUT TYPE=TEXT VALUE=""
      NAME="txtBoxAddr2" SIZE = "65"></TD></TR>
<TR><TD>CITY,STATE,ZIP</TD>
    <TD><INPUT TYPE=TEXT VALUE=""
      NAME="txtBoxCity" SIZE = "35">
    <INPUT TYPE=TEXT VALUE=""
      NAME="txtBoxState" SIZE = "5">
    <INPUT TYPE=TEXT VALUE=""
      NAME="txtBoxZip" SIZE = "15"></TD></TR>
<TR><TD>PHONE, FAX</TD>
    <TD><INPUT TYPE=TEXT VALUE=""
      NAME="txtBoxPhone" SIZE = "30">
    <INPUT TYPE=TEXT VALUE=""
      NAME="txtBoxFax" SIZE = "30"></TD></TR>
</TABLE>
<INPUT TYPE=BUTTON VALUE="SUBMIT ENTRY" NAME="BtnSubmit">
<INPUT TYPE=BUTTON VALUE="CANCEL ENTRY" NAME="BtnClear">

<OBJECT
      classid="clsid:99B42120-6EC7-11CF-A6C7-00AA00A47DD2"
      id=sprlbl5
        width=600
        height=30
      align=CENTER
>
```

```
<param name="_extentX" value="50" >
<param name="_extentY" value="700" >
<param name="angle" value="0" >
<param name="alignment" value="3" >
<param name="BackStyle" value="0" >
<param name="caption" value="">
<param name="FontName" value="Arial">
<param name="FontSize" value="18">
<param name="FontBold" value="1">
<param name="frcolor" value="2552500">
</OBJECT>
</CENTER>
```

If you haven't worked with HTML tables before, the code in Listing 17.12 gives you some idea just how easy they are to use. See Appendix B for more detailed information on tables. Figure 17.6 gives you an idea of what the resulting table looks like.

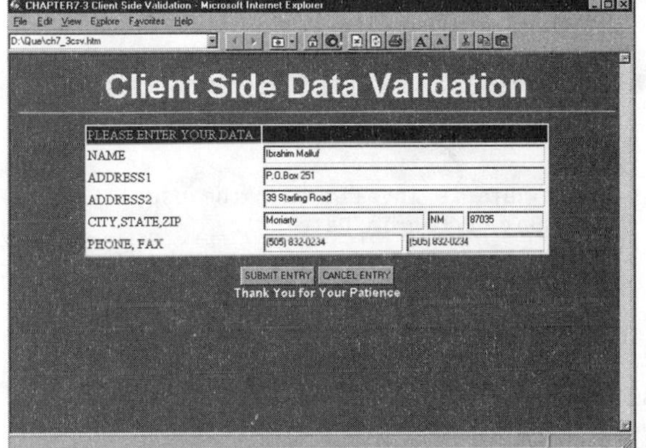

FIG. 17.6 The Client-Side Data Validation page.

The Visual Basic Script for the Client-Side Validation Example The Visual Basic Script is broken into two sections. The first section, Listing 17.13, contains the code underlying the two command buttons. It's short, easy to understand, and knows nothing about the validation functions that it calls. The sole purpose of the Submit button is to call the `CheckAll()` validation function; if it returns a True value, submit the data; and if it returns a False value, alert the user that there is a problem. The Clear button simply calls a routine that clears out all data on the page so that the user can start over with a clear page. What this means is that this first script is entirely independent of the underlying data structures and validation routines. If the data-entry requirements change at a later date, they only have to be changed in the actual validation functions contained in the second script. The more you can encapsulate functionality and limit the scope of data, the more secure your application is from inadvertently introducing errors by changing something in one place that is dependent on something in another.

By encapsulating your code as much as possible you protect yourself from cascading errors in design. Listing 17.13 shows the first script.

Listing 17.13 CH17_3.HTM—Command Button Script for Client-Side Data Validation

```
<SCRIPT LANGUAGE="VBScript">
<!--
'====================================================
'                     Event Code
'====================================================
Dim IsValidData
Dim MyErrorNotes
      'the data is checked for validation
      'when the user attempts to submit the
      'data.
      Sub BtnSubmit_OnClick
         'If CheckAll returns a true
         'you would submit the data
         'to whatever processing is required
         'then clear out the entry fields
         If CheckAll() Then
              MsgBox "Your Data has been accepted"
            ClearAll
         Else
            'if data is invalid warn the user
            MsgBox "Error in Data Entry"
         End if
         'tell exactly what needs to be
         'corrected
         NotifyUser
      End Sub
      'allow the user to clear the
      'entry fields
      Sub BtnClear_OnClick
         ClearAll
      End Sub
-->
</SCRIPT>
```

I know, there's not a lot there. But this is the idea behind encapsulating your code. Notice that the procedure names clearly state their purpose in life. `CheckAll()` means to check all of the data, `ClearAll` means to clear all the data out, and `NotifyUser` notifies the user of the current status. The alerts that are used here are solely for demonstration and should be replaced with code that does something like submitting the data to the server.

The second script is much more involved, though still pretty simple. There are four procedures in the script. I present them in three sections. The first section contains the

ClearAll and NotifyUser procedures. The third and fourth sections each contain one considerably more complex procedure.

The *ClearAll* and *NotifyUser* Procedures The ClearAll procedure is very straightforward, using only sequential statements that set text values and captions to empty strings. The NotifyUser procedure uses a simple If...Then...Else structure to display a message to the user based on the IsDataValid Boolean value. Listing 17.14 shows these two procedures:

Listing 17.14 CH17_3.HTM—The *ClearAll* and *NotifyUser* Procedures of the Client-Side Data Validation Page

```
<script language="VBS">
<!--
'====================================================
'         Data Validation Routines
'====================================================
     'clears all entry fields
     Sub ClearAll
         txtBoxName.Value = ""
         txtBoxAddr1.Value = ""
         txtBoxAddr2.Value = ""
         txtBoxCity.Value = ""
         txtBoxState.Value = ""
         txtBoxZip.Value = ""
         txtBoxPhone.Value = ""
         txtBoxFax.Value = ""
         sprlbl5.Caption =""
     End Sub
     'display status message to user
     Sub NotifyUser
       If IsValidData then
          sprlbl5.Caption = "Thank You for Your Patience"
       Else
          sprlbl5.Caption =  MyErrorNotes
       End If
     End Sub
```


The *CheckAll()* Procedure The CheckAll() function utilizes several If...Then structures to determine whether their respective text fields contain required data. In this example program, I only checked certain fields to make sure that they contain data. The exception to this is the Phone and Fax validation routines. They are If...Then...Else structures that call another function that actually checks each character for proper type and format. The CheckAll() function starts by assuming success and sets the IsDataValid variable to True. If any of the validation routines fail, they will set this value to False. They also set the ErrorNotes variable to contain their particular error message. Listing 17.15 shows the CheckAll() procedure's code.

Listing 17.15 CH17_3.HTM—The *CheckAll()* Function of the Client-Side Data Validation Page

```
'checks all fields for valid data
     Function CheckAll
          'assume valid data to begin with
          'and clear the ErrorNotes.
          Dim MyCheck
          IsValidData = True
          MyErrorNotes=""
          'there are a series of If..then statements
          'that check for valid data in each field
          If Len(txtBoxName.Value) < 1 then
             IsValidData = False
             MyErrorNotes ="Name Field is required data. "
          End If
          If Len(txtBoxAddr1.Value) < 1 then
             IsValidData = False
             MyErrorNotes = "Address1 Field is required data. "
          End If
          If Len(txtBoxCity.Value) < 1 then
             IsValidData = False
             MyErrorNotes = "City Field is required data. " & Newline
          End If
          If Len(txtBoxState.Value) <> 2 then
             IsValidData = False
             MyErrorNotes = "State Abbreviation Field  is required data. "
          End If
          If Len(txtBoxZip.Value) < 5 or _
             Len(txtBoxZip.Value) >10  then
             IsValidData = False
             MyErrorNotes = "Postal Code #####-#### Field is required data. "
          End If
          'Phone & Fax are not required fields so
          'validate them only if there if data is present
          If len(txtBoxPhone.Value) > 0 then
             MyCheck = IsUSPhone(txtBoxPhone.Value)
                If Len(MyCheck) > 0 then
                txtBoxPhone.Value = MyCheck
                Else
                IsValidData = False
                MyErrorNotes = "Phone Number Is Incomplete or wrong Format"
                End If
          End If
          If len(txtBoxFax.Value) > 0 then
             MyCheck = IsUSPhone(txtBoxFax.Value)
                If Len(MyCheck) > 0 then
                txtBoxFax.Value = MyCheck
                Else
                IsValidData = False
                MyErrorNotes = "Fax Number Is Incomplete or wrong Format"
                End If
          End If
          CheckAll = IsValidData
     End Function
```

You'll notice that the `Phone` and `Fax` validation routines differ from the other validation routines in that there is an `If...Then...Else` nested within the `If...Then` structure. The outer conditional first checks to see if there is any data in the fields to begin with. Since in this application the Phone and Fax numbers are not required fields, the outer conditional skips validation if there is no data in the Phone or Fax fields. If there is data, then the outer conditionals will call the `IsUSPhone()` function to ensure that the data entered is both valid and properly formatted.

The `IsUSPhone()` function validates only for North American phone standards, including the area code. Again in the case of the `CheckAll()` function, it is not concerned with how `IsUSPhone()` does its job, it only is concerned with getting a string with data back. If the string returned is empty, then it assumes an error condition and sets `IsValidData` to False. If it does get a non-empty string back it replaces the string in the `Phone` or `Fax` text control and continues on.

You may wonder what happens if the phone number is incomplete. The `CheckAll()` function is unconcerned with the format and flags correct but incomplete data as valid data. Well, I had to break the encapsulation rules here. Visual Basic Script does not support passing data arguments `by reference`; thus, I was not able to pass a modified argument back to the calling routine. The compromise was to use the function value itself to pass back a string if the data was valid in format and content. The problem is that I couldn't pass back the fact that the data was incomplete if it was incomplete.

The answer was to make `IsDataValid` global and change it's value in `IsUSPhone()` if the data was incomplete. Had I been able to pass the string back in a `ByRef` argument, I could have used the `IsUSPhone()` return value as a Boolean True or False value, thus indicating incomplete or invalid data by that value. Listing 17.16 shows the code for the `IsUSPhone()` procedure.

Listing 17.16 CH17_3.HTM—The *IsUSPhone()* Procedure of the Client-Side Data Validation Page

```
'this function formats and validates phone
     'numbers in the US format.
     Function IsUSPhone(MyText)
        Dim Icount
        Dim MyChar
        Dim MyBuffer
           'iterate through all the characters
        'in MyText checking for format and type
        For Icount = 0 to Len(MyText)-1
            MyChar = Mid(MyText,Icount,1)
```

continues

Listing 17.16 Continued

```
            If Icount = 0  then
            If MyChar <> "(" then
                  If IsNumeric(MyChar) then
                    MyBuffer = "(" & MyChar
               Else
                    IsUSPhone = ""
                        Exit Function
                  End If
                   Else
                        MyBuffer = MyChar
             End if
               ElseIf (Icount = 2 and Mid(MyText,0,1) <> "(")  _
                      Or (Icount = 4 and Mid(MyText,0,1) = "(") Then
                   If MyChar <> ")"  then
                         If IsNumeric(MyChar) then
                        MyBuffer = MyBuffer & MyChar & ") "
                  Else
                        IsUSPhone = ""
                              Exit Function
                      End If
                 Else
                   MyBuffer = MyBuffer & MyChar
                 End if
            ElseIf (Mid(MyText,0,1) = "(" and Icount = 9 and MyChar <> "-") Or--
                (Mid(MyText,0,1) <> "(" and Icount = 6 ) then
                If IsNumeric(MyChar) then
                        MyBuffer = MyBuffer & "-" & MyChar
                  Else
                        IsUSPhone = ""
                      Alert "3" & MyChar
                              Exit Function
                      End If
            ElseIf (Mid(MyText,0,1) = "(" and Icount = 9 and MyChar = "-") Then
             MyBuffer = MyBuffer & MyChar
            ElseIf (Mid(MyText,0,1) = "(" And Icount > 13)  _
            Or (Mid(MyText,0,1) <> "(" And Icount > 9) Then
              'Exit For
            ElseIf IsNumeric(MyChar) or MyChar = " " Then
                MyBuffer = MyBuffer & MyChar
            Else
             IsUSPhone = ""
                   Exit Function
            End If
        MyChar=""
        Next
        If Len(MyBuffer) < 13 then
          IsValidData = False
        Else

        End If
```

```
        IsUSPhone = MyBuffer
    End Function

-->
</script>
</body>
</html>
```

The main feature of this function is the `For...Next` looping structure that iterates through each character in the `MyText` value that is passed to it. It checks each character for proper format position and value. If it finds one of the `(`, `)`, or `-` characters missing, it inserts them where they belong and continues on. If it finds characters that are not part of the phone number format or are not numeric where they should be or some other condition it cannot handle, the loop exits the function, returning an empty string. If it does complete its iteration through the string without incident, then the loop checks for proper length, chopping off any extra characters it finds. This validation routine is not the best algorithm I have ever written, but it does give you a strong indication of the possibilities using Visual Basic Script. Refer to Figure 17.6 for an illustration of the client-side validation example.

To add a little more functionality to this example I added a `Timer` control that checks the `Phone` and `Fax` entries to see if they are changed and if they are to run the `IsUSPhone` procedure to format them. Initially I would have thought that the changes in the text would be immediately evaluated, formatting the text as you typed. But it seems that the text is not available until after you leave the text box either by tabbing or clicking somewhere else on the page. Anyway, the code in Listing 17.17 adds the ability to validate the data as the user moves to another area, giving a more immediate response to data entry. Enter this code immediately after the `<Body>` tag on your HTML document.

Listing 17.17 CH17_4CSV.HTM—Adding the *Timer* Control

```
<object
    classid="{59CCB4A0-727D-11CF-AC36-00AA00A47DD2}"
    id=timer1
    align=middle
>
<param name="TimeOut" value="100">
<param name="enable" value="1">
</object>
```

In the second Visual Basic Script module add the `Timer` event code shown in Listing 17.18.

Listing 17.18 CH17_4CSD.HTM—*Timer* Event Code for Immediate Data Validation

```
'validate as we leave the text box
     sub timer1_time
             MyCheck = IsUSPhone(txtBoxPhone.Value)
                If Len(MyCheck) > 0 then
                txtBoxPhone.Value = MyCheck
                Else
                IsValidData = False
                MyErrorNotes = "Fax Number Is Incomplete or wrong Format"
                End If

             MyCheck = IsUSPhone(txtBoxFax.Value)
                If Len(MyCheck) > 0 then
                txtBoxFax.Value = MyCheck
                Else
                IsValidData = False
                MyErrorNotes = "Fax Number Is Incomplete or wrong Format"
                End If
     End Sub
```

Once added, the `Timer` calls the validation routines for the `Phone` and `Fax` entries. The validation effects won't happen until you leave the field you are editing.

I hope this chapter has given you a fair idea of what is possible in Visual Basic Script as well as an idea of what the limitations are as well.

From Here...

The programming structures presented in this chapter are nothing new to most intermediate programmers. They are a set of interlocking building blocks used in constructing programs. In later chapters you will see more complex and advanced application of these structures. VBScript continues to evolve even as I write this chapter and you may find some things altered. The release that I am working with added the `Select...Case` structure only the week before editing this chapter. The `ByRef` keyword was removed from the documentation at the same time. The best approach you can take is to experiment to see what works and what doesn't at the time you are working with VBScript. The ActiveX Control Pad makes an excellant tool for writing structured VBScript code and Chapter 3 takes you through its capabilities.

CHAPTER 18

VBScript Event Programming

by Ron Schwarz

VBScript programming consists largely of designing layouts and writing code that deals with properties, events, and methods. This chapter covers events. It contains a short tutorial on event programming, and a rundown on handling events generated by the Internet Explorer, HTML Intrinsic controls, and a few of the literally thousands of available ActiveX custom controls. ■

Events

Learn what events are, and how they relate to other aspects of VBScript programming.

Event sources

Find out which objects generate events, and what events they generate.

Comparing events

Examine differences between similar events generated by related elements.

Managing events with the ActiveX Control Pad

See how to use the Script Wizard component of the ActiveX Control Pad to easily manage event code.

Using events

Create event-driven scripts using the information learned in this chapter.

Event Programming

An event-driven environment, such as Microsoft Windows, allows the user to interact with applications in a manner entirely different from older procedural systems, which tended to force the user to respond to the software in a highly regimented action/reaction sequence.

When a user clicks or moves the mouse, strikes a key, or opens a document, events are generated. By intercepting these events, and associating program code with them, applications provide a flexible, responsive interface, without the constraints imposed by old style procedural programs.

VBScript (VBS) provides a mechanism for dealing with events as they occur. If you're familiar with Visual Basic, you have a head start on coping with VBS event issues. However, there are some significant differences in how things are handled in VBS. Thanks to the differences between Web pages and VB applications, event handling is a bit more complex with VBS. Fortunately, the ActiveX Control Pad helps ease the bumps, and automates much of the process of declaring and installing objects.

In VB, you have the luxury of the code window and an editor that automatically keeps track of all possible events for all objects in your project. It also automatically creates perfect event procedure headers. When working with VBS, however, you have two choices: you can either work in Notepad or a similar simple editor (this means you have to know which objects generate which events, and how to manually create the appropriate headers for each, as required), or, you can work in the ActiveX Control Pad.

For popping in and out of simple scripts, you may find Notepad sufficient, but for any significant development, you'll definitely want to learn how to use the ActiveX Control Pad. In addition to making it easier to manage complex Web pages, it also provides a visual, interactive "VB-like" IDE (Integrated Development Environment), which facilitates the creation and management of HTML Layout Pages. The HTML Layout Pages are a *very* close approximation of "real" VB programming, right down to the toolbox, mouse-driven control placement and sizing, and Properties window. About the only thing missing is the debugging features.

▶ **See** Chapters 3-5, which cover the ActiveX Control Pad in detail.

VBScript Events

VBS events can originate in the Internet Explorer, HTML Intrinsic controls, or ActiveX custom controls. ActiveX custom control event handling is closest to VB event handling—this is no surprise because ActiveX controls are also used in VB.

HTML Intrinsic controls are not all that different in usage; the main differences are in declaration syntax and event and property naming conventions.

Listing 18.1 gives you a typical VBScript event handler. If you've used VB before, you'll note that it's virtually identical to a VB event handler; the only exceptions are the HTML tags that mark the beginning and end of the script, and the event name (*OnClick*, rather than *Click*). You can, by the way, have many separate routines in a single script.

Listing 18.1 *Typical Event* Header

```
<SCRIPT LANGUAGE="VBScript">
   Sub cmdCalculate_OnClick
      Total = LastMonth + Current
   End Sub
</SCRIPT>
```


You may also want to experiment with alternative control header styles such as the `FOR` syntax, shown in Listing 18.2.

Listing 18.2 *FOR* Style Event Header

```
<SCRIPT LANGUAGE="VBScript" FOR="cmdEvent" EVENT="OnClick">
     Window.Status="Clicked!"
     txtStatus.Value = link1.href
</SCRIPT>
```

This syntax does away with VB-style event sub-procedures. You may notice the absence of either a `Sub` or `End Sub` line in the preceding script block. The code is VBS, but it's not part of a VBS procedure—it is invoked when the object declared with the `FOR` parameter fires the event described in the `EVENT` parameter.

Internet Explorer Events

The Internet Explorer Object Model consists of a hierarchy of objects, most of which provide events (see fig. 18.1). This chapter does not cover aspects of objects that do *not* pertain to events. These topics are covered in "The Internet Explorer Object Model," in Chapter 10, "Embedding Internet Explorer into your Application." (Objects that provide no events are mentioned here in passing, to allow continuity of the Object Model, so you will have a good perspective on where events fit into the general scope of the hierarchy.) The relationships between the different levels of the Object Model (to the extent that they involve event handling issues) are discussed in the following sections.

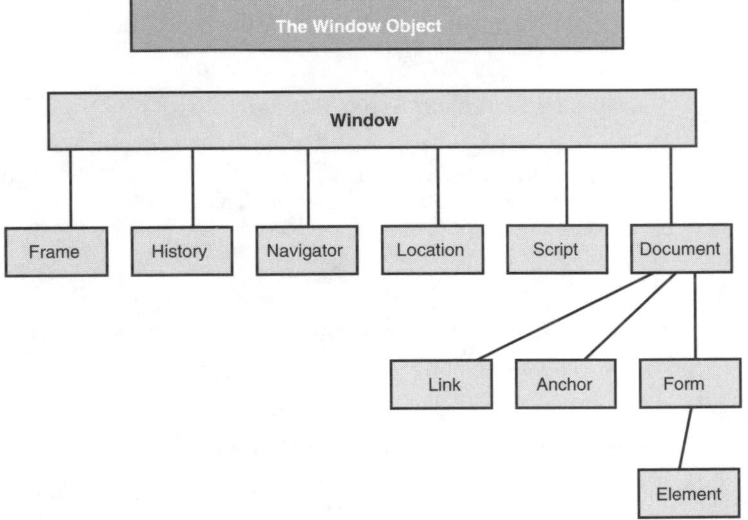

FIG. 18.1
Internet Explorer Object Model.

Window Object Events The `Window` object has two events: `OnLoad`. and `OnUnload` `OnLoad` fires when a page is loaded. Inline code (VBS code that is contained within `<Script>` blocks but outside any procedures) executes before the `OnLoad` event occurs, and may be a pseudo-event mimicking the `Initialize` event in VB. All inline code is affected, regardless of position. If multiple blocks of inline code exist in different locations within the page, they are executed first to last. After the last inline block finishes executing, the `OnLoad` event fires, and any associated code executes.

There is a significant distinction between inline code and `OnLoad` event code. Operations that change the content on the page, such as `document.write` method invocations, can *only* be performed with inline code because this code is executed as the page is being loaded, whereas the `OnLoad` event fires after the page has been loaded and formatted.

The `OnUnload` event is the counterpart to the `OnLoad` event. It is fired when the page is about to be unloaded.

Frame Object The `Frame` object is an array of windows. It is covered in Chapter 2, "Review of HTML."

History Object The `History` object exposes the Internet Explorer's History list (previous locations). It has no events.

Navigator Object The `Navigator` object contains information about the browser, similar to the `App` object in Visual Basic. It has no events.

Location Object The `Location` object has no events. However, changing its properties results in events being fired by the `Window` object as pages are unloaded and loaded.

Script Object The `Script` object is a collection of all scripts in the page. Because scripts are contained in the object hierarchy, they can be called from different windows by prefacing them with the name of the window that contains them, similarly to prefacing a procedure with a form or module name in VB. They expose no events.

Document Object The `Document` object provides no events. However, it serves as a container for other objects that do fire events. (The `Link`, `Anchor`, and `Form` objects are contained in the `Document` object, and are described in the following sections.)

Form Object The `Form` object has one event: `OnSubmit`. When a form is submitted, the contents of the controls in the form are sent to the server. Immediately prior to sending them, the `OnSubmit` event fires, and can be used to perform whatever validation is required, and cancel the submission if required. Unfortunately, at the time this book is going to press, `OnSubmit` is not yet functional using the pre-release tools available. This should be resolved by the time Internet Explorer 3.0 and VBScript are released.

Link Object The `Link` object contains a collection of all link-type anchors on the page. It provides `MouseMove`, `OnMouseOver`, and `OnClick` events for each link. The example in Listing 18.3 (`LinkEvent.htm` on the CD), demonstrates how to trap the `MouseMove` and `OnClick Link` events.

Listing 18.3 LINKEVENTS.HTM—*Link* Events Example

```
<A HREF="http://www.microsoft.com" NAME="MSLink">Microsoft Main Web Site</A>
<p>
<Input Type=Text ID="txtStatus" Size=35>

<OBJECT ID="tmrStoppedMoving" WIDTH=39 HEIGHT=39
 CLASSID="CLSID:59CCB4A0-727D-11CF-AC36-00AA00A47DD2">
   <PARAM NAME="Interval" VALUE="100">
```

continues

Listing 18.3 Continued

```
</OBJECT>

<SCRIPT LANGUAGE="VBScript">

    Sub MSLink_OnClick
       Confirmation=MsgBox("Really go to MS?", 4)
       If Confirmation=7 then          '7 = "No" button pressed
          MsgBox "That's unfortunate, since the Link can't be cancelled!"
       end if
    End Sub

    Sub MSLink_MouseMove(Button, Shift, X, Y)
       txtStatus.Value="You ARE moving over a link!"  'Update the display
       tmrStoppedMoving.Interval=0    'Stop the clock
       tmrStoppedMoving.Interval=250 'Start timing, 250 msec.
    End Sub

    Sub tmrStoppedMoving_Timer
       txtStatus.Value="You're NOT moving over a link!"
   'Time ran out, update display
    End Sub

</SCRIPT>
```

The LinkEvents example contains one Link, one Text control, one Timer, and a script. The Link is given a NAME property (*MSLink*), so that its events can be trapped by the event routines in the script.

The `MSLink_OnClick` event procedure will execute if the on-screen link is clicked. When it executes, it first displays a messagebox asking for confirmation. If you click the "No" button, you'll see another messagebox informing you that the Link can't be cancelled. The browser will then take you to the URL contained in the link. *C'est la vie.* (This event *is* actually useful—for cases where you need to perform "cleanup" code before leaving for the new URL.)

The `MSLink_MouseMove` event fires repeatedly as the mouse travels over the link. Three things are done here in this example: the Value property of the Text control is updated to reflect the fact that the mouse is moving over the `Link`, the Interval property of the Timer control is set to 0 to disable it, and then immediately reset to 250.

By setting the Interval to 0 and then 250, the Timer is stopped, and another 250 millisecond period begins; as long as the mouse keeps moving over the `Link`, the Timer will be continuously reset, and never fire its event. If the mouse stops moving, or moves off the Link, the `MouseMove` event will stop firing, and the Timer will time out, and fire its Timer event. At that point, the code in the `tmrStoppedMoving_Timer` event procedure will execute.

NOTE As this book goes to press, the `OnMouseOver` event is documented, but not implemented. If implemented, it will provide a simplified form of the `MouseMove` event—it will be invoked the same way, but without any parameters. ■

Listing 18.4 IMGAST.HTM—ImageMap Assistant Example

```
<HTML>
<TITLE>ImageMap Assistant</TITLE>

<HEAD>
<CENTER><H1>VBScript ImageMap Assistant</H1></CENTER>

<SCRIPT LANGUAGE="VBScript">

Dim ClickCount
Dim HotspotCoords

      Sub picXY_MouseMove(Shift, Button, X, Y)
          txtX.Value = X
          txtY.Value = Y
      End Sub

      Sub picXY_OnClick
          If ClickCount = 0 Then
             ClickCount = 1
                HotspotCoords = txtX.Value & ", " & txtY.Value & ", "
          Else
              ClickCount = 0
                HotspotCoords = HotspotCoords & txtX.Value & ", " & _
                   txtY.Value
          End If
          txtHotspot.Value = HotspotCoords
      End Sub

</SCRIPT>
</HEAD>
<BODY>

<p>
<center>
<a id="picXY" href=href><img src="events.bmp"></a>
<p>
CurrentX: <input type="text" name="txtX" size=10>
        CurrentY: <input type="text" name="txtY" size=10>
<p>
Hotspot: <input type="text" name="txtHotspot" size=20>
</center>

Position the mouse at the upper left corner of your desired hotspot,
and click. Then, move to the lower right corner of the hotspot, and
click again. The "Hotspot:" textbox will contain your X, Y, X1, Y1
```

continues

Listing 18.4 Continued

```
coordinates.

</BODY>
</HTML>
```

The ImageMap Assistant is a useful VBS application. Although it only uses 16 lines of VBS code, it solves a problem that vexes anyone creating image maps—how to determine coordinates for hotspots.

NOTE To use the ImageMap Assistant with your bitmaps, find the line

```
<a id="picXY" href=href><img src="events.bmp"></a>
```

Then, replace `events.bmp` with the name of your actual bitmap.

The `MouseMove` event is repeatedly fired as the mouse is moved over the link. The ImageMap Assistant example uses this event to periodically update the `CurrentX` and `CurrentY` textboxes.

The `MouseMove` event passes four parameters: `Shift`, `Button`, `X`, and `Y`. The `Shift` parameter returns a value indicating the state of the Shift, Ctrl, and Alt keys, according to the following table:

Key	Shift Parameter Value
Shift	1
Ctrl	2
Alt	4

You can test for a condition of multiple shift keys by "ANDing" the values. The following example code evaluates whether or not the Shift and Ctrl keys are pressed at the time the event occurs. (If none of the Shift keys are pressed, the Shift parameter returns 0.)

▶ **See** "Logical Operators," for information on AND and other logical operators. **p. 301**

```
If ((Shift And 1) > 0) And ((Shift And 2) > 0) Then
End If
```

The `Button` parameter is similar in behavior to the `Shift` parameter; it returns a value indicating which, if any, mouse buttons were pressed when the event occurred. The following table lists the values it can return:

Button	Button Parameter Value
Left	1
Right	2
Middle	4

You can test for multiple button press conditions using the same formula used with the `MouseMove` event, substituting the `Button` parameter for the `Shift` parameter.

The `X` and `Y` parameters return the position of the mouse pointer relative to the upper-left corner of the object. In the ImageMap Assistant example (this code fragment from `IMGAST.HTM` on the CD is shown in Listing 18.5), they are used to populate the `CurrentX` and `CurrentY` textboxes and to create the coordinate list. (The coordinate list is the list of the four numbers—starting XY and ending XY—contained in the txtHotspot Text control.)

The `OnClick` event occurs when the user clicks the left mouse button while the mouse pointer is over the object. It's a simple event, but is probably used more than all others combined. In the ImageMap Assistant, it's used to update the hotspot coordinates list.

Listing 18.5 IMGAST.HTM—*OnClick* Event Code

```
Sub picXY_OnClick
    If ClickCount = 0 Then
        ClickCount = 1
               HotspotCoords = txtX.Value & ", " & txtY.Value & ", "
    Else
        ClickCount = 0
               HotspotCoords = HotspotCoords & txtX.Value & ", " & txtY.Value
    End If
    txtHotspot.Value = HotspotCoords
End Sub
```

In this event `Sub`, you check to see if this is the first time the mouse is clicked. If it is, you replace anything in the hotspot coordinates textbox (`txtHotspot`) with the current `X` and `Y` values. Otherwise, you append them to the existing contents. After two clicks you have four values, which can be copied to the Clipboard and pasted into a VBS script. (You need to write additional VBS code to deal with the lists of hotspot coordinates, but that's the easy part—the ImageMap Assistant code eliminates the tedium of trial and error guess-work when creating image maps.)

Figure 18.2 shows how the ImageMap Assistant will look when you load it into Internet Explorer.

FIG. 18.2
ImageMap Assistant.

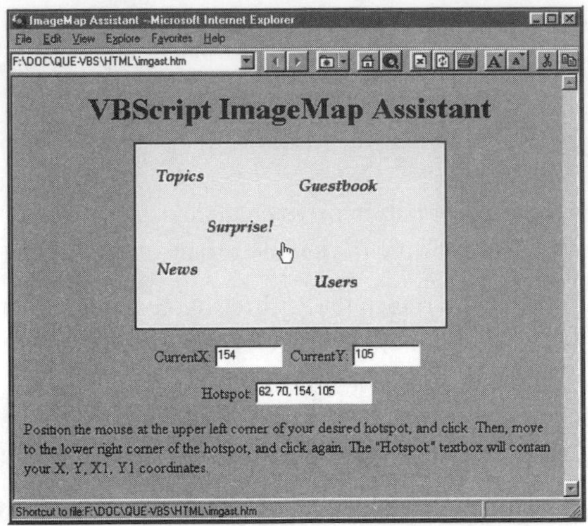

The ImageMap Assistant will be invaluable when you're creating hotspots in imagemaps. For more information on imagemap issues, check out Chapter 11, "Designing VBScript Applications."

Anchor Object The `Anchor` Object has no events. It's mentioned here in passing, since it's part of the Object Model. For full coverage of the Object Model, see "The Internet Explorer Object Model," in Chapter 10, "Embedding Internet Explorer into Your Application."

Form Object The `Form` Object contains one event: `OnSubmit`. The `OnSubmit` event fires when a form (an HTML form, not to be confused with a VB form) is submitted. There are two ways to submit a form—the form's `Submit` method, and the use of a Submit HTML Intrinsic control. (As this book goes to press, the `OnSubmit` method is documented insofar as it is known that it will be available in the final release of IE 3.0, however, it is not yet implemented in the pre-release version, nor is VBScript syntax available.)

Element Object The `Element` Object is an array of all controls—HTML and OBJECT (such as ActiveX)—on a page. It's similar in concept to the Control Collection in Visual Basic. Because it's really just a series of pointers to "real" objects, it has no events of its own. For a full discussion of the Element Object, see "The Internet Explorer Object Model," in Chapter 10, "Embedding Internet Explorer into your Application."

Control Events

VBS is able to detect events fired by the Intrinsic HTML and ActiveX controls. The main differences between using HTML controls and ActiveX controls involve declaration conventions and event names. (Control declaration issues are covered in other chapters.)

Hammers, Nails, and Platforms

Apart from usage differences, you may notice that HTML controls have a dearth of events when compared to most ActiveX controls. HTML, even when VBS-enabled, is not a full-fledged program development platform. VBS scripts are not complete applications. Automating Web pages is not the same as creating Visual Basic applications.

This is not by any means derogatory toward VBS. It's just a different animal. The axiom that says, "To a man with a hammer, everything looks like a nail," is something you need to keep in mind when developing script-enabled Web pages.

The ability to create HTML Layout Pages by using the ActiveX Control Pad does indeed make it possible to create real programs with VBS. Still, trying to do some things, such as accessing INI files or the registry, and using API calls require severe work-arounds in VBS.

So, sooner or later, you'll find a situation where what you really need is a comprehensive solution best provided by a Visual Basic application. Ideally, you'll make that discovery *before* you commit massive amounts of time and/or money developing Web pages for the project. And, there will be times when you'll experience the reciprocal of this principle—a simple Web page, brought to life with some concise, effective VBS code, is a life-saver.

The moral: Use the appropriate tool for each job.

If you use VB, you are familiar with the `Click` event; with HTML controls, it's the `OnClick` event. Similar differences with other event names are detailed in the following sections.

Button Control Events The Button control has one event: `OnClick`. This is functionally identical to the `Click` event in VB. When the user clicks the button, the event fires, and any associated event code is executed. The following example demonstrates use of the `OnClick` event with a Button control.

```
Sub cmdCalculate_OnClick
     Total = LastMonth + Current
End Sub
```

Checkbox Control Events Like the Button control, the Checkbox control also has `OnClick` as its sole event. Checkboxes, like option buttons (called radio controls in

HTML-speak), are frequently used without requirements for active processing at click-time. In many, if not most, cases, they are checked as the user requires, and when ready to proceed, a button is clicked telling the application to process the controls. At that point, all options are parsed and whatever action is required is taken.

However, there are also many situations in which you may need to perform processing when the user clicks an option. For instance, you may have mutually-exclusive or interlocking combinations of options. By testing at click-time, you can deal with input dynamically rather than all at once in a type of "batch mode."

Listing 18.6 (available on the CD as CHKEVENTS.HTM) demonstrates one such hypothetical example.

Listing 18.6 CHKEVENTS.HTM—Checkbox Events Example

```
<HTML>

<HEAD>
<TITLE>VBScript Events</TITLE>

<SCRIPT LANGUAGE="VBS">

   Sub DoAll
      If chkAll.Checked Then 'If the "All" box is checked
         chkTest1.Checked = True
         chkTest2.Checked = True
         chkTest3.Checked = True
      End If
   End Sub

</SCRIPT>
</HEAD>

<body>
<INPUT TYPE=CheckBox NAME="chkTest1" size=10> Oranges<p>
<INPUT TYPE=CheckBox NAME="chkTest2" size=10> Peaches<p>
<INPUT TYPE=CheckBox NAME="chkTest3" size=10> Pears<p>
<INPUT TYPE=CheckBox NAME="chkAll" size=10 OnClick="DoAll">All

</body>
</HTML>
```

Listing 18.6 demonstrates use of the `CheckBox` control's `OnClick` event. In this example, the user sees a list of four items, which can be selected in any combination. If the last item (`All`) is clicked, the `DoAll` routine in the VBS script checks all of the options.

The declaration for the `chkAll` HTML CheckBox control contains an `OnClick="DoAll"` clause. This causes the DoAll Sub procedure to replace the default (`chkAll_OnClick`, which is not used) event handler. This syntax can be useful when you want to have several controls use the same event handler.

The DoAll routine first tests whether or not the chkAll CheckBox is checked. If it is checked, the routine proceeds to check all three of the other CheckBoxes.

Password Control Events The Password Control is a specialized form of the Text control. It's used when you want the user to enter text without having the characters entered echo on screen. When a character is typed into a Password control, an asterisk (*) is displayed.

The Password control has `OnFocus` and `OnBlur` events, like the Text control, but does not have `OnChange` or `OnSelect` events. For usage of the `OnFocus` and `OnBlur` events, see "Text and TextArea Control Events" earlier in this chapter.

NOTE At the time of this writing, the `OnFocus` and `OnBlur` events are documented, but not implemented for the Password control.

Radio Control Events Radio Controls (hereinafter referred to by their "VB name" of `OptionButtons`), have one event: `OnClick`. Generally, you won't need to trap this event, as `OptionButtons` tend to be used for the purpose of determining one of a number of fixed selections. However, there are situations in which you may want to perform an action at the time a button is clicked. One example would be a quiz, where you want the victim (er, "student") to be unable to test the answer unless an answer was first selected. To accomplish this, it's necessary to be able to tell whether or not an `OptionButton` has been clicked. The example in Listing 18.7 (`OptionEvents.htm` on the CD) demonstrates such a situation.

Listing 18.7 OPTIONEVENTS.HTM—*OptionButton* Event Example

```
<HTML>

<HEAD>
<TITLE>VBScript OptionButton Events</TITLE>
</HEAD>

<SCRIPT LANGUAGE="VBScript">

   Dim OkToTest, c

   Sub Window_OnLoad     'Can't set controls before page created
      optNum.Item(0).Value = False 'Clear default selection
      txtStatus.Value = "Your answer please!"
```

continues

Listing 18.7 Continued

```
    End Sub

    Sub CanTest
       OkToTest = True
       For c = 0 To 2  'Walk through all buttons
          If optNum.Item(c).Checked Then  'If we've found the selection
             Exit For   'Answer found, stored in c
          End If
       Next
       txtStatus.Value = "Answer "  & c + 1 & " Selected"  'Add 1 because
    End Sub                                               'buttons start at 0

    Sub cmdTest_OnClick
       If OkToTest Then
          FindAns
       Else
          txtStatus.Value = "Must Select an Answer!"
       End If
    End Sub

    Sub FindAns
       Select Case c  'Test if it's the right answer
          Case 0, 2
             txtStatus.Value = "Wrong!"
          Case 1
             txtStatus.Value = "Correct!"
          End Select
    End Sub
</SCRIPT>

<BODY>
One Plus One Equals:<P><P>

<INPUT TYPE="Radio" NAME="optNum" size=10 OnClick="CanTest">One<P>
<INPUT TYPE="Radio" NAME="optNum" size=10 OnClick="CanTest">Two<P>
<INPUT TYPE="Radio" NAME="optNum" size=10 OnClick="CanTest">Three<P><P>
<INPUT TYPE="Button" NAME="cmdTest" VALUE="Test"><P>
<INPUT TYPE=TEXT NAME="txtStatus" size=20>

</BODY>
</HTML>
```

The example in Listing 18.7 uses four controls—three `OptionButtons`, a `CommandButton`, and `Text`:

```
<INPUT TYPE="Radio" NAME="optNum" size=10 OnClick="CanTest">One<P>
<INPUT TYPE="Radio" NAME="optNum" size=10 OnClick="CanTest">Two<P>
<INPUT TYPE="Radio" NAME="optNum" size=10 OnClick="CanTest">Three<P><P>
<INPUT TYPE="Button" NAME="cmdTest" VALUE="Test"><P>
<INPUT TYPE=TEXT NAME="txtStatus" size=20>
```

The OptionButtons are all given the same name (optNum), which is what associates them as a group. In this example, they all use the same event handler (CanTest) although you can use different handlers for each of them if you require. (You can also use the default handlers, which for this example *would* have been optNum_OnClick.)

The CommandButton is named cmdTest, and the Text control is named txtStatus.

The script begins with a declaration of two Public variables:

```
Dim OkToTest, c
```

It's necessary to make these variables Public because they're used in more than one procedure. By declaring them outside of any procedure, they're automatically available to all procedures.

The first procedure is the Window_OnLoad event handler:

```
Sub Window_OnLoad    'Can't set controls before page created
   optNum.Item(0).Value = False 'Clear default selection
   txtStatus.Value = "Your answer please!"
End Sub
```


Before you can set properties of a control, the control has to be loaded. And, if you want to set control properties during the initialization phase (such as, only once, when the page loads) you'll have to do so in the Window_OnLoad event, because if you execute them outside
of any procedure, they'll be executed during the parse phase, before any controls are created.

To address a specific OptionButton in code, you need to use the Item property. The code in the Window_OnLoad event sets the Value property of the first OptionButton to False. Because OptionButtons begin with 0, that's the one that's set here. This code clears the first button. (By default, the first button in a group is selected, and because this example needs to have *none* selected, the first one has to be explicitly cleared.)

Before the procedure ends, it places "Your answer please!" into the Text control, so that the user will know to click one of the OptionButtons.

The CanTest event serves as the event handler for the OptionButtons:

```
Sub CanTest
   OkToTest = True
   For c = 0 To 2  'Walk through all buttons
      If optNum.Item(c).Checked Then  'If we've found the selection
         Exit For   'Answer found, stored in c
      End If
   Next
   txtStatus.Value = "Answer "  & c + 1 & " Selected"
'Add 1 because buttons start at 0
End Sub
```

The first thing this routine does is set the `OkToTest` variable to True. This variable is used in the `cmdTest_OnClick` event handler to determine whether or not an answer has been provided. (The `CanTest` procedure isn't called *unless* an `OptionButton` has been clicked. Because an `OptionButton` has been clicked, it's "OkToTest" the answer when the Test button is clicked.)

▶ **See** *"For...Next,"* **p. 312**, for information on *For...Next* loops.

After setting the `OkToTest` variable, a `For...Next` loop counts through the `OptionButtons`, looking for the one that was selected. Because `OptionButtons` start with an *Item* of 0, the loop counts from 0 to 2. When it finds the selected `OptionButton`, it executes an `Exit For` statement to escape the loop. Because the loop counter (*c*) reflects the current `OptionButton` at the time it's found, it stores its number. For instance, if the second `OptionButton` (`.Item(1)`) has its `.Checked` property set to True, then the value of *c* will be 1.

After the loop finds the number of the selected `OptionButton`, the status string (the `.Value` property of `txtStatus`) is set to a string composed of the word "Answer," the number of the `OptionButton`, and the word "Selected."

Because `OptionButtons` start at 0, but answers on a quiz start at 1, the number in the string is offset by one (by adding c + 1).

After an answer is selected, the user will have to click the Test button to see if it's correct. The `OnClick` event for the `cmdTest` button directs the script to the `FindAns` routine to determine if the right answer was provided:

```
Sub cmdTest_OnClick
   If OkToTest Then
      FindAns
   Else
      txtStatus.Value = "Must Select an Answer!"
   End If
End Sub
```

Before handing control over to the `FindAns` routine, `cmdTest_OnClick` checks the value of `OkToTest`. (This is the variable that is only set if the user first clicks an `OptionButton`.) If it's indeed ok to test, `FindAns` is called. If not, `txtStatus` is loaded with a warning to select an answer.

The `FindAns` routine does the actual testing:

```
Sub FindAns
   Select Case c  'Test if it's the right answer
      Case 0, 2
         txtStatus.Value = "Wrong!"
      Case 1
         txtStatus.Value = "Correct!"
      End Select
End Sub
```

A `Select Case` block tests the value of *c* against 0 and 2 (the incorrect answers), and 1 (the correct answer), and displays the appropriate message in the status `Text` control.

▶ **See** "Programming Structures in VBScript," **p. 308**

Reset Control Events The Reset control is a special type of button control. When it's clicked, it clears the contents of the other controls. At the time this book goes to press, it has one event implemented: the `OnClick` event. (An `OnFocus` event is documented, but not working.)

Submit Control Events The Submit control has one event: `OnSubmit`, which is covered under "Form Object" earlier in this chapter.

Text and TextArea Control Events The Text and TextArea controls have `OnFocus` and `OnBlur` events. These correspond to `GotFocus` and `LostFocus` events in VB. Because the TextArea control can be considered a functional equivalent of a VB TextBox control with a `Multiline` property set to True, we examine the two of them together here.

Part IV Ch 18

NOTE At the time of this writing, the `OnChange` and `OnSelect` events are documented, but not implemented for the Text, TextArea, and Password controls. The `OnChange` event will fire when the contents of the control change, and the `OnSelect` event will fire when text is selected within the control.

Listing 18.8 Text and TextArea Events Example

```
Sub txaTest_OnFocus
    txtTest.Value ="OnFocus"
End Sub
Sub txaTest_OnBlur
    txtTest.Value ="OnBlur"
End Sub
```

The code in Listing 18.8 updates the display in a Text control (`txtTest`) whenever the `OnFocus` or `OnBlur` events occur in a TextArea control (`txaTest`).

ActiveX Control Event Issues

In many situations, the HTML Intrinsic controls provide all the interactivity your applications require. For certain situations, however, you need features they do not provide. ActiveX controls provide specialized functionality that is not available via the Intrinsic controls.

When an Intrinsic control does the job, use it. The Intrinsic controls are general-purpose input and display controls; ActiveX controls are specialized controls. Each ActiveX control is unique, and is created with a specific purpose in mind. Many of them are quite complex, and require quite a bit of detailed study to use effectively—some of them are essentially major applications disguised as "tools" that can be embedded in a container such as an HTML Layout Web page. Their power and flexibility aside, they require no less attention to detail and study than does a standalone program of a similar nature. Those developers who choose to learn the details of their tools are able to leverage them to great effect.

ActiveX controls are supplied by numerous vendors. Remember, the main usage distinction between ActiveX controls and HTML Intrinsic controls deal with declaration and naming of properties and events; the actual *use* in your script blocks is the same (in regards to event handling). The information provided earlier in this chapter for HTML controls also equally applies to ActiveX controls.

From Here...

An understanding of event handling is necessary to make real use of VBS. The material presented in this chapter provides you with the mechanics involved in using event routines. The information presented in Part 4 of this book presumes an understanding of the material presented here, and goes on to teach you how to use that knowledge to create powerful script-enabled Internet applications.

- See Chapter 2, "Review of HTML," for general HTML programming information.
- See Chapter 4, "Creating a Standard HTML Page," for more coverage of HTML control programming issues.
- See Chapter 9, "An Introduction to Distributed Objects," for cutting edge information on controls.

- See Chapter 11, "Designing VBScript Applications," for information on putting this chapter's material to work.
- See Chapter 20, "VBScript Forms, Controls, and Managing Transactions," which covers data validation and transactions.
- See Que's *Special Edition Using HTML.*

CHAPTER 19

VBScript Procedures

by Ibrahim Malluf

In this chapter, we discuss the processes involved in creating procedures in Visual Basic Script, along with different strategies in arranging those procedures. In an earlier chapter, I discussed the concept of limiting the scope of data and encapsulating functionality as much as possible. Here, I take the discussion a little further by developing strategies in the decisions that involve making procedures in what constitutes a well designed routine hierarchy. When you are finished with this chapter, you will have learned some new approaches to application design and perhaps even been stimulated to develop these ideas even further.

Constructing procedures

Why break up your code into function and subroutine procedures? Here's the scoop on how to create them and why.

Calling procedures

Look here to learn how to use those procedures in your scripts.

Exiting procedures

Things to consider when terminating a procedure.

Procedure parameters

Passing information between procedures, the how and why of procedure parameters.

Strategies for good code design

Discusses how to break up your VBScripts into managable sections.

Applying structured techniques

Constructing Procedures

If you are coming entirely from an HTML background with little experience in a structured programming environment, like Visual Basic Script, this is the chapter for you. A procedure in Visual Basic Script is a structure with a single entry point and one or more exit points containing a series of statements that perform a particular task. Procedures are called by other lines of code to perform a given task and return the program flow back to the line that the procedure was called from. In most cases, procedures can look just like keywords and intrinsic functions when used and, in fact, work the same way.

The process of creating a procedure starts with identifying the reasons for a procedure. A procedure's primary purpose is to reduce the complexity of your program. Procedures should hide the detail information so you don't have think about those details when you are actually using those procedures. Other reasons for a procedure include code reuse, maintainability, and accuracy. You decide how the procedure will actually go about performing the task assigned to it, write the code for that procedure, and thoroughly test it for accuracy and volatility. The accuracy of the results derived from your procedure should be checked using the extreme ranges of your expected data. Find out what breaks your procedure, and then devise ways to prevent that procedure from being broken.

The following are good candidates for a procedure:

- A process that involves multiple lines of code
- A process that can be reused by other areas
- A process subject to later modification
- A process that includes complex logic

Declaring Procedures

In Visual Basic Script, you declare a procedure by declaring it as a `Sub` or `Function`, and provide a unique name for the procedure, as well as any arguments that should be included. The basic syntax for declaring a procedure is:

```
[Private¦Public] Sub¦Function name (arg1, arg2,...)
...procedure code
End [Sub¦Function}
```

The `[Private¦Public]` arguments are scope arguments. A public procedure can be seen by all procedures in all script modules. A private procedure's scope is limited to the script module that it is declared in. Both arguments are optional and the default is a public procedure.

The Sub¦Function keywords define the type of procedure it is. Note that in Visual Basic Script there are no property procedures as in Visual Basic. The (arg1,arg2,...) portion is where you declare the arguments that are to be passed to your procedure. Here is a good place to talk about variable scope again. Global variables should be used as little as possible. It is much better programming practice to pass values to other procedures through the argument list. This way you know what data the procedure requires and what data the procedure modifies. Global variables, on the other hand, can be modified in any procedure anywhere in your code.

Many programmers like the convenience of global variables because they are easily accessible. Others, like myself, prefer to minimize the scope of a variable as much as possible so their purpose can be maintained and readily understood. When they are globally available you no longer have that maintainability and do not easily understand all the complexities that can be involved with that data. The End Sub or End Function statements mark the limits of the procedure.

Function Procedures

A function type procedure is a block of code that takes arguments, processes those arguments, and then returns a value as part of its call. A function can also be used as part of an expression. Functions are mostly used to process information in a specified manner and return a result on the basis of the information. A function can return any of the data subtypes supported by the variant. Also, by default, arguments passed to a function are passed by reference so that if you change the value contained in an argument those changes are available to the procedure that called it. If you do not want the function to make changes to an argument that is passed back to the calling procedure then you have to declare the argument as ByVal. In this case, the argument is passed as a value rather than a pointer to the location where the data is stored (see Listing 19.1).

Listing 19.1 The Syntax for Declaring a Function Procedure

```
[Private¦Public] Function name ([arg1, arg2,...)
...Code block
End Function
'explanation:
'Private¦Public are optional scope declarations. The default is public.
'name is a string expression that identifies the subroutine
'arg1,arg2,.. are optional arguments passed to the subroutine

'code block is where you enter the code to be executed by the procedure
'example declaration
Public Function WhatDayIsToday(DateValue)
```

continues

Listing 19.1 Continued

```
If not IsDate(DateValue) then
WhatDayIsToday = "Invalid Date"
Else
Dim MyResult
            MyResult = WeekDay(DateValue)
WhatDayIsToday = MyDayArray(MyResult)
End If
End function
'example use of function
Label1.caption = WhatDayIsToday(Now)
```

In the function example provided in Listing 19.1, you may notice there is some simple error trapping that checks to make sure the `DateValue` argument is, in fact, a date value. Another point you may notice is that when reading the function you learn exactly what the function does. This is an important feature to strive for. Name your procedures and variables with names that fully describe what they do or what they contain. You may understand your code when you write it, but when you come back to maintain it in a week, month, or even a year, you'll appreciate being able to instantly recognize your intended logic thanks to adequate naming conventions.

Subroutine Procedures

A Subroutine (`Sub`) procedure differs from a function in that it does not return a value and cannot be used as part of an expression. Like the function procedure, it is a discrete block of code that is called from another procedure, and, when it is done, immediately returns to the next operation after the line that called it. The syntax of a `Sub` is as shown in Listing 19.2:

Listing 19.2 Syntax for Declaring a Subroutine

```
[Private¦Public] Sub name ([arg1, arg2,...])
...code block
End Sub
'explanation:
'Private¦Public are optional scope declarations. The default is public.
 'name is a string expression that identifies the subroutine
'arg1,arg2,... are optional arguments passed to the subroutine
 'code block is where you enter the code to be executed by the procedure
'example of Sub declaration:
Private Sub DisplayDay(DateValue)
Label1.caption = MyDayArray(WeekDay(DateValue))
End Sub
'using the sub
DisplayDay Now
Call DisplayDay(Now)
```

In Listing 19.2, you see two ways to invoke a subroutine. If you just use the `Sub`'s name you pass the argument without the parentheseses. If you use the `Call` keyword then you must surround the arguments with parenthesis. Again, you may notice that the naming convention of the `Subroutine` describes exactly what it does.

Calling Procedures

Calling procedures in Visual Basic Script work exactly the same as in Visual Basic. Functions are usually used as part of expressions, since they can return a value, and subroutines are used as statements.

To call a function procedure, you can either use it as part of an expression or use it like a subroutine ignoring the return value. If you use it as part of an expression, you must include the parentheses whether there are parameters to pass or not. If you do not use it as part of an expression then you must leave off the parentheses. Examples of both types of calls are given in Listing 19.3.

Listing 19.3 Using a Function in an Expression

```
'CheckSpeed() is used in an expression to set a value
lngRotation = CheckSpeed(txtDegrees.Value)
'here, CheckSpeed() is used without regard for a return value
CheckSpeed txtDegrees.Value
```


Call

`Call` is an optional argument used to transfer control to a subroutine or function. When used, it requires you to wrap the argument list in parentheses. When the `Call` statement is used with a function, the return value is discarded using the call statement would look like this: `Call ChangeRotation()`.

Exiting Procedures

You may not think exiting procedures the subject of much discussion at first glance, but I have had some interesting discussions on this subject that revolve around the proper way to exit a procedure. I am a strong advocate of the single-entry, Single Exit rule that states there should only be a single point of entry in a procedure and a single point of exit. In Visual Basic, the single entry is enforced for all types of procedures. The single exit point, however, is another matter.

In Visual Basic, labels and the much-maligned `GoTo` statement allow a programmer to easily construct procedures that follow the single exit point rule. Visual Basic Script, however, does not utilize labels or `GoTo`. You can still have your procedures follow the single exit point, but this involves more complex logic in certain situations. I like having procedures that follow a consistent pattern with distinct logic, exit, and error handling sections. Visual Basic Script makes this a little difficult since error handling has to be inline; and if an error cannot be rectified in your procedure logic, you must provide your error exit code immediately after the error or concoct some unique and probably convoluted logic to delay the need to exit the procedure. If there is a way to correct an error in line, there is no way to repeat the line that caused the error except to add additional logic to duplicate the line if the error can be corrected. I sincerely hope that future versions of Visual Basic Script address this shortcoming.

Exit Function

The `Exit` function can be placed anywhere within your procedure to immediately exit the function and return control to the line that invoked it. The `Exit Function` statement is not required since once reaching the `End Function` line, the function is exited anyway. The `Exit Function`'s most likely use would be to exit the function after an error had occurred or if some other special condition occured where you would want to immediately exit the Function.

Procedure Parameters

Procedure parameters are values that are passed to a procedure for processing by that procedure. Procedure parameters are also where a large portion of all program errors occur. The fact that Visual Basic Script is a weakly typed language makes the interface between procedures even more error prone since you can pass a string where a long is expected. There is no built-in parameter type checking when passing a value to a procedure. So the first order is to make sure that the actual parameters passed to the procedure match the formal parameters of the procedure declaration. Fortunately, Visual Basic Script comes equipped with a set of functions that checks the subtype of the parameter being passed. Table 19.1 enumerates those functions and describes what they do. To use them, you simply place the variant as an argument to the function and check for a true or false.

Table 19.1 Functions that Verify a Variable's Subtype

Name	Description
`IsArray()`	Returns a Boolean indicating if variant is an array
`IsDate()`	Returns a Boolean indicating if variant contains a date
`IsEmpty()`	Returns a Boolean indicating if variant is uninitialized
`IsNull()`	Returns a Boolean indicating if variant contains a Null
`IsNumeric()`	Returns a Boolean indicating if variant contains a number
`IsObject()`	Returns a Boolean indicating if variant contains an object

In Listing 19.4, you may notice that I wrapped the functionality of the procedure in an `If...Then...Else` statement. This ensures that the procedure's code logic is run only if the parameter passed to the function is of a valid type. If the procedure is also sensitive to range values then you should also check for a valid range of values before proceeding with procedure logic. There's no sense in allowing a divide by zero or overflow error to stop your code. The type checking doesn't include checking for a string or for a long, double, or other specific number type. The number types automatically adjust to the values they contain. If you want to coerce a value to a particular type, you can do so using the conversion functions. If you really need to confirm that a variant contains a string, you have to do it through a process of eliminating the other possible types so that the only possible type left is a string.

Listing 19.4 Checking the Sub Type of a Variant

```
General Syntax:
boolean = IsNumeric(variable)
boolean:  value returned indicating if it is the required type
variable: name of the variable to check
Public Function Foo(MyParameter)
      If IsNumeric(MyParameter) Then
            'do whatever the procedure
      'is supposed to do
      'and return the expected value
      Foo = ResultValue
      Else
      'oops, wrong type passed
      'tell the calling procedure
      'we have an error here so
      'return an error value
Foo = CVErr(INVALID_SUB_TYPE)
End If
End Function
```

When declaring the procedure's parameters, use a consistent method of ordering them. Many of the experts, like Steve McConnel of Code Complete fame (Microsoft Press 1993), suggest the use of the input-modify-output order of arranging your parameter declarations. You can use an alphabetical, datatype, or other arrangement, but be consistent in your choice. The input-modify-output order implies that you place input only parameters first, modifiable parameters second, and output only parameters last. Also, if you are using the same parameters in several different procedures, make sure they are consistently placed in the same order so you don't get confused between them. Don't include arguments that are not going to be used by your procedure. If you decide that the parameter is not needed, then remove it from the declaration.

Strategies for Good Code Design

Visual Basic Script is a structured programming language with many weak parts in its design. Among the most obvious drawbacks is weakly typed variables. Another is the very limited options for error handling. If this was a full-blown programming environment it would be a nightmare to work with; but its target audience is the limited environment of a scripting language for Web browsers, servers, and other applications that require limited scripting capability. With that in mind, I'll discuss some programming strategies using Visual Basic Script.

Encapsulation of Your Code

Encapsulation of your code and data as much as possible has the effect of containing logic and programming errors into discrete areas that can be more easily diagnosed and corrected. This is one of the main driving forces behind the OOP programming paradigm that has been permeating almost every aspect of the industry. Unfortunately, Visual Basic Script does not include the class/object creation capabilities of Visual Basic itself. Even more dangerous is that you can write code that runs outside of a procedure definition. This has the effect of letting you write a set of code that works every time you load the page, but can open the door to writing large inline code blocks without any structure at all. HTML is like this as well, but, with HTML, you have a very limited ability to do anything on the client side. With the introduction of scripting languages like Java, JavaScript, and Visual Basic Script, the limitations are rapidly disappearing.

For those coming from an HTML background and limited programming experience, you should begin adopting habits right now that make your scripts more readable and maintainable. Some of the key concepts of encapsulated code follow.

Limiting Information Hiding the internal workings of a procedure as much as possible from the rest of your application helps prevent you from abusing the purpose of that procedure and introducing errors. Once you design, debug, and test a procedure to produce a given result, leave it alone. If you need added functionality then write another procedure to produce that functionality. You can even wrap the original procedure within another procedure and modify its results to get the added functionality, but don't modify the original procedure itself if it is already being called by other procedures.

Loose Coupled Code Another aid to encapsulation is loose coupling between procedures. This means that procedures should have a minimal dependency upon each other. A procedure should be entirely self dependent for its results and not rely on another procedure's validity. Don't assume that a procedure you are calling will always work. Later modifications to another procedure can introduce errors in your procedure. If your procedure requires arguments then check those arguments for proper value range and type, and introduce a graceful exit for that procedure if the arguments do not meet specification. Conversely, if you are calling a procedure whose results your procedure depends upon, then include code that protects your procedure should the procedures you are calling fail. If you are calling functions that are returning values then also check those values for proper range and type. If your procedure is supposed to supply a value then make sure that it returns a value of some sort regardless of whether it succeeds or fails in its purpose. In Visual Basic Script, you can convert a function's return value to an error value to indicate that an error has occurred in your procedure.

Naming Conventions Another, very important aspect of design for your Visual Basic Scripts is using naming conventions that clearly explain what your code does. As an example, look at Listing 19.5. Obviously, this procedure is the click event of a control. The two lines of code contained in the procedure don't do much in the way of explaining themselves. Can you recognize their purpose?

On the CD

Listing 19.5 CH19_1.HTM—Poor Procedure Naming Practices

```
Sub sprlbl1_Click
ChgLblDrctn
ChgLblClr
End Sub
```

Okay, if you can't be sure what these lines of code do then maybe we should look at the underlying code within these two procedure calls. Listing 19.6 contains the code for both procedures. The first procedure, `ChgLblDrctn` doesn't tell you much except that it reverses a value from a positive to a negative and back again. There is no indication of what the value is used for, though looking at the next procedure, upon seeing the `lbl`, you can deduce that it changes the forecolor of a label.

Well, that's what the procedure does all right, but can you tell me what colors it changes the forecolor to? This procedure is using what many programmers refer to as magic numbers! Magic numbers are literal values that magically accomplish a purpose without you knowing what or how. If you understand the RGB palette system that Windows uses then you recognize that these magic numbers are the three primary colors of red, green, blue, and also black. Even if you figure out the procedure's entire purpose and the meanings of the parameters it uses, you must interrupt your reading of the code to think about it. Now imagine having to debug several hundred lines of code written in this style.

Listing 19.6 CH9_1.HTM—More Poor Naming Practices

```
Sub ChgLblDrctn
lngRtn = lngRtn * -1
End Sub
Sub ChgLblClr
If SPRLBL1.Forecolor = &HFF Then
SPRLBL1.Forecolor = &HFF0000
ElseIf SPRLBL1.Forecolor=&HFF0000 Then
SPRLBL1.Forecolor = &HFF00
ElseIf SPRLBL1.Forecolor=&HFF00 Then
SPRLBL1.Forecolor=&H0
Else
SPRLBL1.Forecolor=&HFF
END IF
End Sub
```

Now let's look at the same procedures done with informative names and naming conventions. Listing 19.7 shows the label's click event calling procedures with informative names. The first procedure changes the direction of the label. The second procedure leaves no doubt that its purpose is to change the label's color.

Listing 19.7 CH9_1.HTM—The Right Way to Name Procedures

```
Sub sprlbl1_Click
ChangeLabelDirection
ChangeLabelColor
End Sub
```

Okay, we really don't need to look any further because we already know what the procedures do to a fair degree. But I want to know what colors it changes to and what direction is being changed (see Listing 19.8).

Listing 19.8 CH19_1.HTM—More Self Documenting Code!

```
Sub ChangLabelDirection
    lngRotation = lngRotation * -1
End Sub
Sub ChangeLabelColor
    If Sprlbl.Forecolor = CLR_RED THEN
       Sprlbl.Forecolor = CLR_BLUE
    ElseIf Sprlbl.Forecolor=CLR_BLUE THEN
       Sprlbl.Forecolor = CLR_GREEN
    ElseIf Sprlbl.Forecolor=CLR_GREEN THEN
       Sprlbl.Forecolor=CLR_BLACK
    Else
       Sprlbl.Forecolor=CLR_RED
    END IF
End Sub
```

Looking at the `ChangeLabelDirection` procedure I see a variable named `lblRotation`, which leaves me with no doubt that the purpose of the procedure is to change the rotation direction of the label. The second procedure lets me know what colors are being used because the magic numbers are replaced with descriptive constants. Notice that the constants are all uppercase with an underscore between the prefix and the color name. Altogether, this is what you call self documenting code. This is part of a naming convention that I use and is similar to the one that Microsoft suggests.

You can use any convention you want including one you devise on your own. Just use it consistently and document the rules of your naming conventions so that others using your code can understand what you are doing. Listing 19.9 shows a code header in a script module that explains to the reader what conventions are being used in the accompanying code.

Listing 19.9 CH19_1.HTM—Documenting Your Naming Conventions

```
'================================================
'This Script Module Contains all Constant and
'Global Variables as well as Initialization code
'constants should be all upper case with
'underscores between words: MY_CONSTANT
'other variables should use identity prefixes
'Prefix    Meaning
'bln       Boolean
'byt       Byte
'dtm       Date/Time
'dbl       Double
'Err       Error
```

continues

Listing 19.9 Continued

```
'int      Integer
'lng      Long
'obj      Object
'sng      Single
'str      String
'==================================================
'make all declarations explicitly declared
'==============Constant Declarations============
'instead of using literals for values that are
'repeatedly used, setup constants with names
'that fully explain what they do
DIM CLR_WHITE
CLR_WHITE = &HFFFFFF
DIM CLR_BLACK
CLR_BLACK = &H000000
DIM CLR_RED
CLR_RED = &H0000FF
DIM CLR_GREEN
CLR_GREEN = &H00FF00
DIM CLR_BLUE
CLR_BLUE = &HFF0000
```

What Is a Good Reason for a Procedure?

When deciding where to place a certain functionality into a procedure you first must understand what a procedure is or should be. A procedure should be a block of code that is called upon for a single purpose. That procedure may call several other procedures to accomplish its purpose, but its very existence should only be for that single purpose. When you have recognized the need for a discrete procedure, then you have the justification for a procedure. A discrete procedure can be identified as any purpose that includes one of more of the following items:

Functionality involves more than one line of code.

Functionality can be used by more than one other procedure.

Functionality can introduce errors into a program.

Functionality can be self-contained.

Functionality involves complex calculations.

Functionality can return a value.

Some might argue the preceding list, but these have usually been the best arguments for creating a discrete function or subroutine. Your procedures should act like a black box in that the calling procedure should only know what it does, not how it does it. If you go back to Listing 19.7 and look at the `sprlbl1_Click` event, you not only fully understand what each of the contained procedures do, you are not confronted with any complex logic either. The complexity is kept within the procedures that actually do the discrete tasks required. From that, you build the next layer that controls the order and circumstances that these discrete tasks are called. Even further up the ladder of the hierarchy might be the user interface that responds to user events.

In the case of this example of Visual Basic Script being used with an HTML document, the HTML code actually provides the upper hierarchy portion of this design. You can design your Visual Basic Scripts to interact as a single layer under the HTML code but you soon find the more complex pages become near impossible to maintain. Design your VBScript scripts to take full advantage of the encapsulation techniques available and break discrete functionality into maintainable procedures.

FIG. 19.1
The black box procedure.

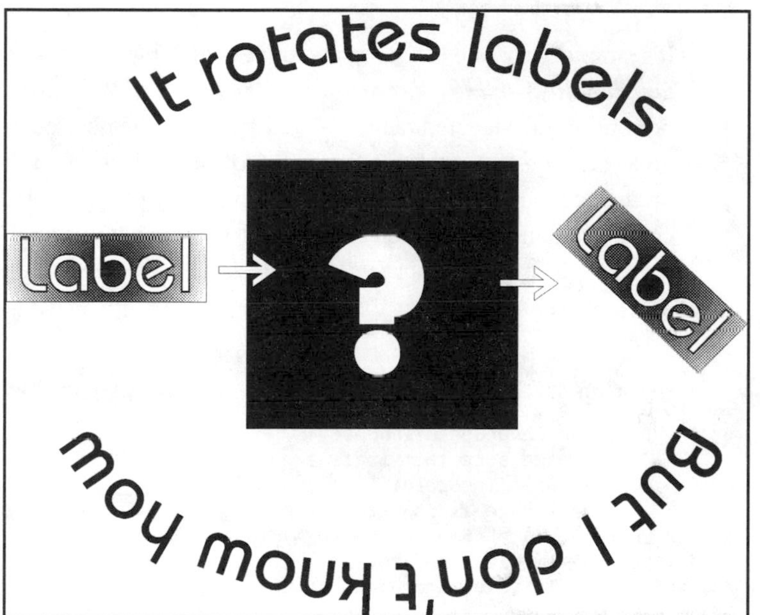

Should It Be a Sub or a Function?

I started to say that you should use functions when a return value is expected and subroutines when no return value is expected. While true enough, it begs a much more precise response. Whether your procedure should be a subroutine or function can be directly tied to whether the calling procedure is dependent on the success or failure of the procedure it's calling. That is to say, if the procedure's failure does not adversely affect the calling procedure's purpose, then a subroutine is adequate. But if the calling procedure requires the procedure to succeed in order for itself to succeed then it must be a function.

Let's add another functionality to our rotating label project. I want to control the speed of the rotation by entering a number that represents the degrees of rotation with every clock tick. I need a textbox in which to enter the desired speed and a button control to register the speed change. I call the textbox `txtDegrees` and the button `btnSpeed`. The idea is that I enter some value into the textbox, click the button, and, in the click event, I change the value of `lngRotate` to reflect that new value (see Listing 19.10).

Listing 19.10 CH19_1.HTM—Should This Be a Discrete Procedure?

```
Sub btnSpeed_OnClick
lngRotation = txtDegrees.Value
End Sub
```

It's simple, only one line long, and understandable. So what is wrong with this code? *The functionality can introduce errors into the program!* What happens if the user enters a number out of the accepted range? What happens if the user enters a non-numeric value? You generate an error and bring the script to a halt. Now remember, you don't want to clutter up the second layer of code with the complexity of a discrete process so you create a procedure to handle this. I don't want to pass too much information to the procedure so I limit it to just the value of the `txtDegrees` and expect it to return a valid value for `lblRotation` (see Listing 19.11).

Listing 19.11 CH19_1.HTM—Moving Things to a Discrete Procedure

```
Function CheckSpeed(lngSpeed)
'first make sure that it is a number
If IsNumeric(lngSpeed) Then
'now make sure it is within range
If lngSpeed > 45 Or lngSpeed <1 then
'if not within range return
'a default value and warn the user
alert "Speed Must be between 1 & 45"
CheckSpeed = 5
Else
'it's a valid entry so return it
CheckSpeed = lngSpeed
End If
Else
'it's not a number so complain
'about it and return a default value
alert "Must be a numeric value"
CheckSpeed = 5
End If
End Function
```

This function procedure first checks to see if the argument is of the right data type and, if it is, checks to see if the value of the argument is within a specified range. In essence, no matter what the user enters into the textbox this function returns a valid value that allows the purpose of the application to continue. The possible errors are contained within this procedure and not allowed to percolate upwards in the hierarchy. You now have a function procedure that performs the required process. Do you know what the process it performs is? It's not the changing of the rotation speed. That's the purpose of the click event. The purpose is to validate the user's data entry. Listing 19.12 shows the click event using our function procedure.

Listing 19.12 CH19_1—Click Event with Validated User Input

```
Sub BtnSpeed_OnClick
lngRotation = CheckSpeed(txtDegrees.Value)
End sub
```

Once again you can see the effects of self-documenting code. At a glance, you can see that the click event sets the rotation speed of the label after checking the validity of the value in `txtDegrees`. The idea is to design your procedures so they are as bulletproof as possible and completely safe from external circumstances crashing them. The modified Label rotation example is illustrated in Figure 19.2.

FIG. 19.2 The rotating label example with the speed modification.

Applying Structured Techniques

Tired of rotating labels yet? Okay, let's move on to some serious application development. In Chapters 12 and 13 we develop a database application that allows the user to browse or search a catalog of products and make an order.

We can start to lay out the overall design for the product catalog here. I base this example on a database model that has equivalents in both Access and SQL Server 6.5, but I refer to the publishers demo database example in SQL Server 6. If you only have VB4 or Access then you have to use the BIBLIO.MDB database and modify the table names accordingly as this project takes shape.

The HTML Document

An HTML document already has clearly defined divisions within it. There is the head, body, or frames. The head section of an HTML document is used to describe that document. The body contains the active content of the document such as forms, objects, and VBScript. How to use these areas is explained in Chapter 3. The Visual Basic Script area of the document is usually the last group of sections in the document. There are no hard coded rules that require this, but good organization of your HTML document probably causes you to gravitate towards this convention anyway. You'll also see that I further divide the scripting area into three functional sections that help to make your code more understandable by subsequent editors (see fig. 19.3). Remember, you just might be one of those subsequent editors that is trying to remember why you did what you did.

FIG. 19.3
Organizing your application's Visual Basic Scripts.

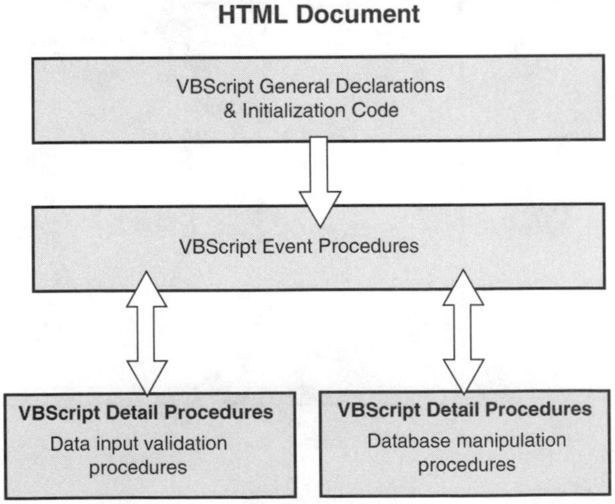

In any case, coming from a Visual Basic background, I've become accustomed to the way things are organized in that environment, and it is heavily influencing the suggestions I make here. As your scripts become more involved the initial organization presented here will go a long way towards helping you keep a handle on things.

The General Declarations Area

In Visual Basic, the General Declarations area is where all module-wide variables, DLL declarations, and object references are declared. In Visual Basic Script, I am suggesting that this practice also be followed. You may also want to provide a header that describes your naming conventions, as shown in Listing 19.13. While Visual Basic Script only has the variant type available, it is still a good idea to identify the subtype of the value it contains by using meaningful prefixes. Visual Basic Script does not directly support constants, but you can create and clearly identify constants using one of two conventions. The first is to use all uppercase characters and separate words with an underscore, which is the convention I use in this book. Another valid convention is to use the prefix `cst` to identify constants. What is important is that you do adopt a consistent method of documentation.

Besides using this area as the place for declarations, you can also define initialization code. Unlike Visual Basic, where you must place all code within a defined procedure, Visual Basic Script allows you to place code outside of procedures. The code you place outside of a procedure runs every time the document is loaded into the browser (see Listing 19.13). If you need to utilize this feature, it is best to place that code in the General Declarations area script so its presence is immediately recognized later by you or someone else who might need to understand or edit the document. Another advantage to consider is you can develop a declarations area script that is generic and can be used in all your projects with slight modification.

Listing 19.13 SCRIPTTEMPLATE.TXT—Suggested Outline of a Declarations Area Script

```
<SCRIPT LANGUAGE="VBS">
<!--
'======================================
'    General Declarations Area
'======================================
'
'=========Prefix Conventions==========
'Data Types
'ary = Array  bln = Boolean
'byt = Byte  cur = Currency
'dbl = Double  dte = Date
'err = Error  int = Integer
'lng = Long  obj = Object
```

continues

Listing 19.13 Continued

```
'sng = single  str = String
'
'Controls
'btn = Command Button cmb = ComboBox
'cht = Chart Control lbl = Label Control
'lst = List control txt = TextBox
'
'=============Constants===============
'declare constants here with explanation

'=========Public Variables============
'declare variables here with explanation


'=====Inititialization Procedures=======
'

'place code here that you want to run
'every time the page is loaded
-->
</SCRIPT>
```

The Event Procedures Area

Event procedures are usually called through the actions of the user such as clicking a button, selecting an item from a combo box, or entering text into a text field. There are also other events like the `Timer_Time` event that is program controlled or the VRML collision event; these are independent of user interaction. Regardless of what the event is, they should be placed in a script whose purpose is to only contain events. Within the event procedures you can call the user defined procedures that produce the desired reaction to those events. Very little actual computational code should be placed at this level. Think of the Event level scripts as the medium for controlling logic flow, not as the place for the actual computational logic.

An observer should be able to look at your event procedures and understand exactly what they do without having to spend time figuring out the arcane logic of your computational code. Listing 19.10 shows an event procedure with one line of code that simply sets the value of rotation according to the checked value of a textbox. There is underlying logic that checks the value of that textbox for type and range, and returns a safe value for the `lngRotation` value; but all of that is hidden in a detail procedure that you don't need to see to understand the event procedure's purpose. Its purpose is to change the value of the rotation rate according to what is in the textbox.

The Detail Procedures Area

This section should contain all the detail procedures that actually perform calculations, control graphic renderings, submit forms, and all other detail logic of your document's program. You should not include any event procedures here at all. Your procedures at this level should provide for error trapping and handling to make sure that generated errors do not percolate upward enough to lock up the browser or even stop the document's functionality. This is a very important concept to consider.

Many of the HTML documents you author will be used by people who are not very computer literate. The computer and the Internet are rapidly becoming a household commodity with the inherent lack of computer experience many of these new users have. A lockup or even a non-responsive Web page frustrates and even upsets many who are not at all cognizant of what is going on. That's not a fault of the user, it's a fault of the technology that didn't insulate them from these potential problems.

Write your detail procedures so they are capable of handling any logic or user error. Design into your logic a way to degrade gracefully without unduly alarming the user of your page. And, finally, if there is no other alternative, then inform him that an error has occurred through a message box and suggest to him how to recover.

Procedures that return a value should always check to ensure that the value they return is within reasonable limits given their purpose.

From Here...

In this chapter I went over the syntax of creating function and subroutine procedures. If you are an experienced programmer, you will immediately miss the ability to alter the values of arguments passed to a procedure. It seems that the only workaround to this is to allow your variables a wider scope that crosses procedure boundaries. Be sure to incorporate adequate type and bounds checking within your procedures to account for this.

The proposal to arrange your code into four levels of Script, Initialization, Event, and Utility is not a hard wired rule that you must follow. It is more a suggestion that you adopt or develop an organizational and naming convention that helps to make your scripts easier to understand and maintain.

CHAPTER 20

VBScript Forms, Controls, and Managing Transactions

by Ron Schwarz

Designing Forms Using the ActiveX Control Pad

Create input and presentation forms that behave like real programs.

Sending Data to a Server

Learn how to send information to the Web server.

Receiving Data from a Server

Sending data is fairly easy, but receiving data—especially when you want to avoid replacing the current page with a query results page—is decidedly non-trivial.

Updating the Existing Page

Standard HTML pages cannot be updated once they're displayed. To show new data when received from a server, it's necessary to replace the whole page. VBScript and HTML Layout Page technology make it possible to receive and display new data without replacing the current page.

The new HTML Layout Page features, combined with VBScript techniques, make it possible to do the hitherto unthinkable—create a web page that behaves like a real *program*, rather than a "souped-up" *document*. Although there's a fair amount of work involved, and several layers of interlocked logic are required, it's definitely something you should consider using if you want your work to appear as professional as possible.

The example in this chapter demonstrates everything you'll need to know to accomplish this on the client end. You'll also need to provide something on the server end to supply the data you're requesting. That's covered in Chapter 21, "Accessing Data."

▶ **See** " Using Client Side Data," **p. 411**

The discussion of the project in this chapter assumes that you've loaded the project from the CD into your copy of the ActiveX Control Pad. To do this, right-click the icon for the Validation.htm file. When the pop-up menu appears, select the entry to load it into the ActiveX Control Pad. ■

Creating a Web Application

The example presented in this chapter uses the sample Publishers database supplied with Microsoft SQL Server 6.5. The principles involved in sending, receiving, and presenting data can be used with whatever type of system you're using, as long as it can be configured to return its data in the form of an HTML page based on a template you design.

The steps involved in creating an application such as this example are these:

1. Define the nature of the transactions (such as what data was sent, and what data was received).
2. Create the database on the server.
3. Design the form with the ActiveX Control Pad.
4. Write supporting code for data transfer and control handling.

Hiding Data in a Frame

Due to the reluctance of HTML to support true two-way interactivity, retrieving data into the current screen requires some fancy footwork. The approach taken in this chapter consists of a bit of apparent deception; we "trick" Internet Explorer into thinking it's receiving a new page by using a near-hidden frame as a type of data buffer. The reason it's "near" hidden is because it's not possible to completely hide a frame; however, by sizing it to one pixel by one pixel, it will be a light gray spot on a gray background. Even if you know what you're looking for, and where on the screen to look, you'll have a hard time finding it.

By hiding incoming data in this frame, you make it available to your script, and you can extract, manipulate, and display it any way you choose. You are no longer at the mercy of HTML.

Handling Queries

After you've created your database, you'll need to have code on the server to respond to queries and create HTML content. Two queries are used in this example. One creates a list of Publishers, and one returns a list of books. Each query consists of two files: an .IDC file, which contains the actual SQL statement, and an .HTX file, which contains an HTML template. This example uses the Internet Data Control (IDC), which is described in Chapter 21, "Accessing Data."

Listing 20.1 shows the SQL statement used to create the query that returns a list of all publishers in the database. It's not necessary for you to understand SQL to create applications like the example in this chapter, *if* you have someone available to handle that end of the job. This is feasible because the client and server ends of the project are completely separate. The one line you need to pay attention to defines the .HTX template file that the query uses for output. In this case, it's pub.htx, as shown in the third line.

Listing 20.1 pub.idc—Publishers SQL Statement File

```
Datasource: Publishers
Username: sa
Template: pub.htx
SQLStatement:
+SELECT Publishers.Pub_ID,
+Publishers.Pub_Name,
+HighPrice = Max(price),
+LowPrice = Min(price)
+FROM Publishers,
+Titles
+WHERE Publishers.pub_id =
+Titles.Pub_ID
+GROUP BY Publishers.pub_id, Pub_Name
```

Listing 20.2 appears at first glance to be fairly standard HTML, with the addition of an ActiveX ListBox control (lstPublishers), contained in an `<OBJECT>` tag, and a short script at the end of the file. One thing you should notice is the inclusion of a series of placeholders in the script, such as "`<%Pub_Name%>`". These contain instructions for the Internet Data Control, telling it what data to insert. The inserted data will replace the placeholders in the HTML file that is sent to your buffer frame. Everything between the `<%begindetail%>` and `<%enddetail%>` placeholder will be duplicated one time for each record in the result set created by the query.

Listing 20.2 pub.htx—Publishers HTML Template File

```
<HTML>
<HEAD><TITLE>Publishers List</TITLE></HEAD>
<BODY>
<BODY BGCOLOR="FFFFFF">
<OBJECT ID="lstPublishers" WIDTH=90 HEIGHT=90
 CLASSID="CLSID:8BD21D20-EC42-11CE-9E0D-00AA006002F3">
    <PARAM NAME="ScrollBars" VALUE="3">
    <PARAM NAME="DisplayStyle" VALUE="2">
    <PARAM NAME="Size" VALUE="5151;811">
    <PARAM NAME="MatchEntry" VALUE="0">
    <PARAM NAME="FontCharSet" VALUE="0">
    <PARAM NAME="FontPitchAndFamily" VALUE="2">
    <PARAM NAME="FontWeight" VALUE="0">
```

continues

Listing 20.2 Continued

```
</OBJECT>

<Script Language="VBScript">

<%begindetail%>
lstPublishers.AddItem "<%Pub_Name%>" & ";" & _
"<%Pub_ID%>" & ";" & _
"<%HighPrice%>" & ";" & _
"<%LowPrice%>"
<%enddetail%>

Top.TriggerPub

</script>

</BODY>
</HTML>
```

Right after the result definition, you'll see a VBScript statement of `Top.TriggerPub`. This is a call to a procedure in the application that tells it that the data is loaded into the buffer, and it's OK to proceed to display it in the form.

This file is typical of those you'll encounter when using Microsoft SQL Server 6.5 and the IDC. If you're using different server-end software, your queries will have to be handled accordingly. The server-end details are irrelevant to your work with VBScript and the ActiveX Control Pad, as long as the server is able to accept a query and return an HTML page.

Listing 20.3 contains the Titles query, which returns a list of books via the Titles.htx template. The same rules described for Listing 20.1 also apply here.

Listing 20.3 titles.idc—Titles SQL Statement File

```
Datasource: Publishers
Username: sa
Template: Titles.htx
SQLStatement:
+SELECT Distinct Titles.*,
+Publishers.*,
+titleAuthor.*,
+Authors.*
+FROM Titles Join Publishers
+on titles.Pub_ID = publishers.Pub_ID
+Left Join titleauthor on
+Titles.title_id = titleauthor.title_id
+Join Authors on titleauthor.au_id = authors.au_id
+WHERE Titles.Price >= Convert(money, '%LowPrice%')
+AND Titles.Price <= Convert(Money, '%HighPrice%')
```

```
+AND Publishers.Pub_id ='%PubID%'
```

Listing 20.4 is similar in concept to the file in Listing 20.2, and the same rules apply. As in that file, the script ends with a VBScript call to a procedure in your project; in this case, it's a procedure named `Top.TriggerTitle`.

Listing 20.4 titles.htx—Titles HTML Template File

```
<HTML>
<HEAD><TITLE>Authors and YTD Sales</TITLE></HEAD>
<BODY>
<BODY BGCOLOR="FFFFFF">
<OBJECT ID="lstBooks" WIDTH=100 HEIGHT=100
 CLASSID="CLSID:8BD21D20-EC42-11CE-9E0D-00AA006002F3">
    <PARAM NAME="ScrollBars" VALUE="3">
    <PARAM NAME="DisplayStyle" VALUE="2">
    <PARAM NAME="Size" VALUE="5151;811">
    <PARAM NAME="MatchEntry" VALUE="0">
    <PARAM NAME="FontCharSet" VALUE="0">
    <PARAM NAME="FontPitchAndFamily" VALUE="2">
    <PARAM NAME="FontWeight" VALUE="0">
</OBJECT>

<Script Language="VBScript">
Dim strBuffer
On Error Resume Next
<%begindetail%>
lstBooks.AddItem "<%title%>" & ", " & "<%au_fname%>" & " " & _
 "<%au_lname%>" & ", " & "<%Price%>"
<%enddetail%>
<%Query_String%>
<%Remote_User%>
<%request_Method%>
Top.TriggerTitle
</Script>
</BODY>
</HTML>
```


In Listings 20.2 and 20.4, the script created by the query exists solely for the purpose of loading a ListBox with the results of the query. This forms the basis of the buffer. Once your application is notified that the buffer is loaded, it can proceed to extract the data from the ListBox and perform whatever processing is required.

Using HTML Layout Page Forms

The client end of the project consists of two files—an HTML file and an .ALX file. The HTML file contains a small amount of standard HTML code and a reference to the .ALX

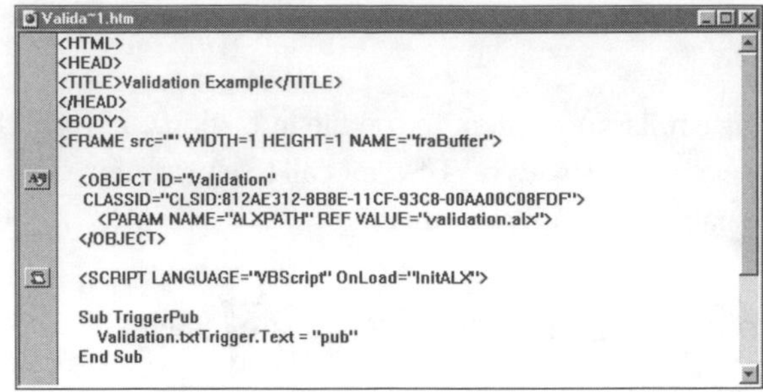

FIG. 20.1
Validation.htm is loaded into ActiveX Control Pad.

NOTE file. The actual Layout Page is contained in the .ALX file. Figure 20.1 shows the HTML file loaded into the ActiveX Control Pad.

As this book goes to press, HTML Layout Pages must reside in separate .ALX files. Microsoft plans to make it possible for them to reside in the same file as the HTML portion of a project as soon as the World Wide Web Consortium standards committees settle on the syntax.

Listing 20.5 contains three significant sections (apart from the usual HTML tags such as, `<HTML>`, `<HEAD>`, `<BODY>`, and so on). The `<iFRAME>` tag defines the nearly hidden buffer frame, named frmBuffer. As mentioned, it has a width and height of 1, which makes it, for all intents and purposes, invisible. Because it's in the main HTML file (it's not possible to place it in an HTML Layout Page), it's declared here, and its one-pixel display will appear outside the Layout Page.

On the CD

Listing 20.5 validation.htm—Main HTML form for Validation Example

```
<HTML>
<HEAD>
<TITLE>Validation Example</TITLE>
</HEAD>
<BODY>
<iFRAME src="" WIDTH=1 HEIGHT=1 NAME="fraBuffer" OnLoad = "Foo">
<FRAME src="" WIDTH=1 HEIGHT=1 NAME="fraBuffer" OnLoad = "Foo">
</iFRAME>

    <OBJECT ID="Validation"
     CLASSID="CLSID:812AE312-8B8E-11CF-93C8-00AA00C08FDF">
        <PARAM NAME="ALXPATH" REF VALUE="validation.alx">
    </OBJECT>

    <SCRIPT LANGUAGE="VBScript" OnLoad="InitALX">

    Sub TriggerPub
        Validation.txtTrigger.Text = "pub"
    End Sub
```

```
    Sub TriggerTitle
        Validation.txtTrigger.Text = "title"
    End Sub
    </SCRIPT>

</BODY>
</HTML>
```

The second section to observe is the declaration beginning with `<OBJECT ID="Validation"`. This is the declaration for the HTML Layout Page, which is named Validation, and is contained in the validation.alx file.

The script is notable because it contains an OnLoad="InitALX" parameter in its declaration. This assures that the script is linked to the HTML Layout Pad. Without that parameter, procedures in the script would not be able to communicate with objects in the Layout Page.

The actual script contains two simple procedures, used to create a link between the buffer frame and the Layout Page. The first, TriggerPub, is called by the `Top.TriggerPub` statement in the page returned by the server when requesting a list of publishers.

```
Sub TriggerPub
    Validation.txtTrigger.Text = "pub"
End Sub
```

The one line of code in the routine sets the value of a hidden TextBox (`txtTrigger` in the `Validation` Layout Page) to "pub". Because of limitations in the current version of VBScript, this is the easiest way to invoke a routine in a Layout Page. When the contents of the control change, an event is fired, which the script intercepts and uses as notification that the data is loaded in the buffer and ready to go.

```
Sub TriggerTitle
    Validation.txtTrigger.Text = "title"
End Sub
```

The TriggerTitle procedure is identical to the TriggerPub procedure, except that it sets the value of the TextBox to "title", indicating that the list of book titles is received and ready for processing.

This small HTML page is all that's required to create a foundation for the HTML Layout Page and provide a means to move data in dynamically.

Using ActiveX Controls on Layout Page Forms

The ActiveX Control Pad provides an ideal environment for creating data input and display forms. This project uses a number of visible and hidden controls. The complete form, with the hidden controls exposed in the Layout editor, is shown in Figure 20.2. See Chapters 3,

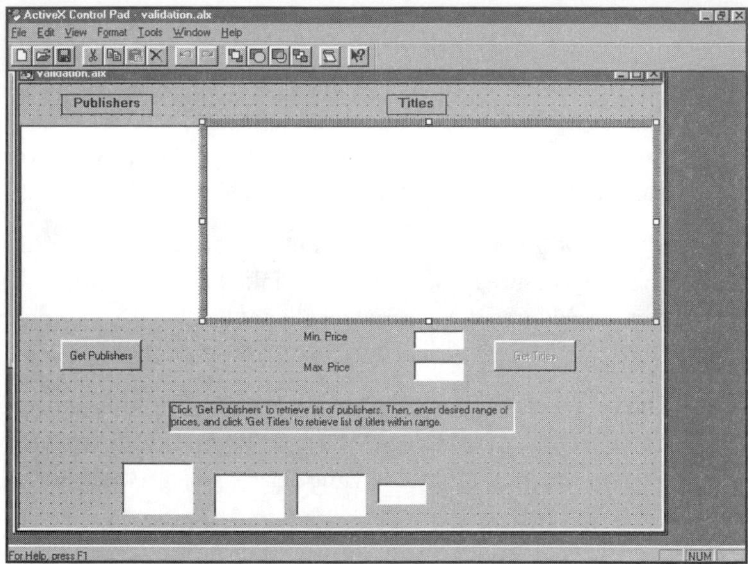

FIG. 20.2
Here's the complete form with all controls visible.

NOTE "Introducing the ActiveX Control Pad," and 4, "Creating a Standard HTML Page," for more on this subject.

The controls at the bottom of Figure 20.2 are three ListBoxes and one TextBox.

The pre-release version of VBScript available as this book goes to press does not provide reliable use of arrays; therefore, hidden ListBoxes are used in their place. Sometimes you will want to use ListBoxes instead of arrays even after the final release versions of Internet Explorer and VBS are available. For instance, you can sort the contents of a ListBox by simply setting the value of a property, which is quite a bit easier than writing your own sort routine in VBS. You can also insert or remove specific elements from a ListBox with one method call, also much easier than doing the same work in VBS code.

Because there's quite a bit going on here, it's necessary to hopscotch around in the script in order to adequately describe it. Bear with the discussion, because once you understand the principles involved, you'll be able to create knock-'em-dead presentations; the payoff will be well worth the effort.

Debugging Tip

When you're using hidden controls, you may want to make them visible during your initial testing, so that you can see what's going on in them. This can save you hours of frustration, as

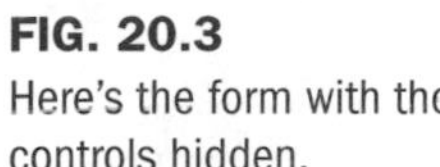

FIG. 20.3
Here's the form with the controls hidden.

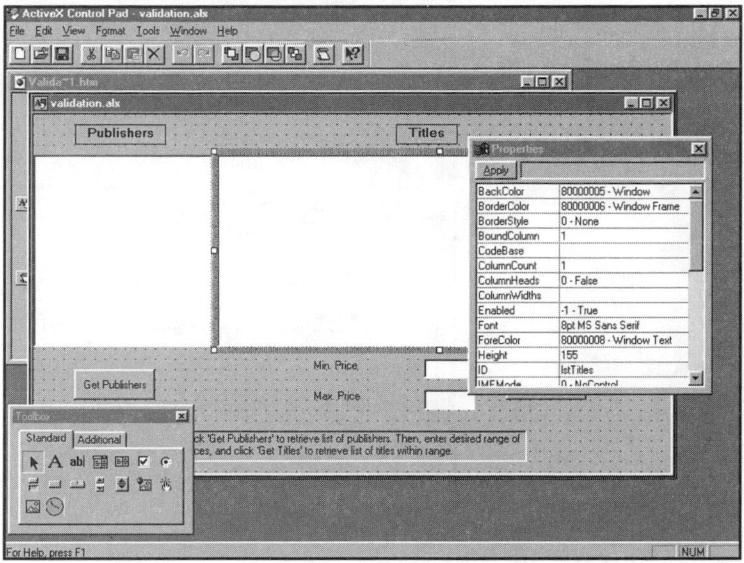

well as eliminate the need to salt your code with numerous MsgBox statements to report on the status of variables. After testing, be sure to use the Properties window (shown in fig. 20.3) to set the Visible property of your hidden controls to False—and, for good measure, move the border of your form to cover them (also shown in fig. 20.3).

When you want to edit your Layout code in the ActiveX Control Pad, you have two choices: You can load it into Notepad (via the View Source Code selection available when right-clicking over the form in the Layout Page editor), or you can use the Script Wizard (also available via the right-click pop-up menu).

You may choose to do a little of each. It's very convenient to have the Script Wizard create event and procedure headers and insert method calls (see fig. 20.4). It's also very handy to be able to navigate the object trees, if for no other reason than to have ready access to a visible representation of the structure.

CAUTION

Once you've entered the bulk of your code, you may find it easier to hop back and forth by loading the entire file into Notepad. Be careful to avoid having dual versions of the same file.

For instance, let's say you have the project loaded into the Control Pad and decide to load the file into Notepad. After doing some work in Notepad, you decide to browse the object trees in the Control Pad to check out the spelling of a certain object you want to add. While there, you get a phone call, and fifteen minutes later you say, "Hmm, now where was I?" You look at your monitor, find your place in the object tree, and remember that you were looking for a property event. You find the event, and without

FIG. 20.4
This is the ActiveX Control Pad Script Wizard.

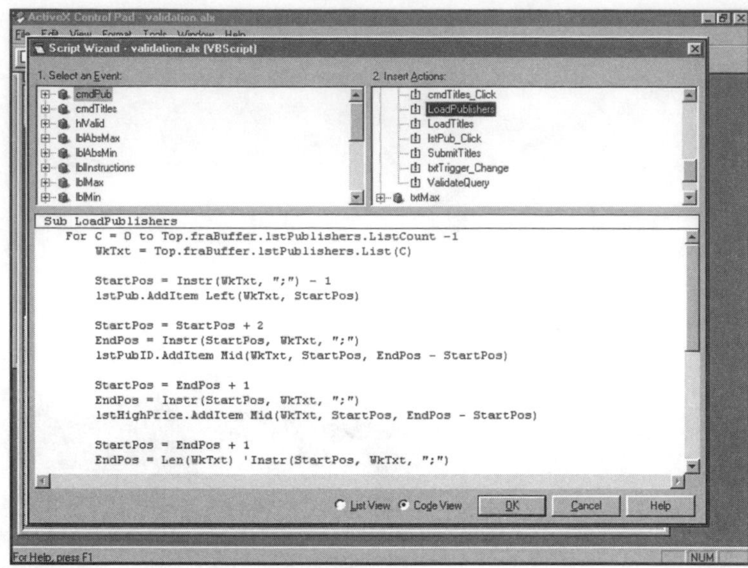

giving it a second thought, click it, enter your code into the Control Pad, and then save the file. At this point, you have one set of changes in the copy in Notepad and a different set of changes in the Control Pad. Reconciling them will be tedious at best, and the potential for disaster is high—if you make significant changes in one medium and overwrite them with the other after exiting the first.

The complete code for the Layout Page in this project is contained in Listing 20.9. Although the Control Pad creates multiple scripts, and the actual placement of procedures within them is immaterial to actual order of execution, the procedures in this file have been moved around by hand into more or less their order of execution, to facilitate explanation in this book. VBScript is an event-driven language, which means that not all things *have* to happen in any specific order. The code of your real-world applications doesn't have to adhere to any specific order.

Creating a Sample Form

The process of creating a form is fairly straightforward, if not entirely obvious at a glance. The example program starts out in Internet Explorer with an empty form, as shown in Figure 20.5.

The user sees two ListBoxes, two TextBoxes (both TextBoxes are disabled but visible), and two CommandButtons (one of which is disabled). A Label control contains instructions on how to proceed. The ListBox on the left is titled Publishers, and the button be-

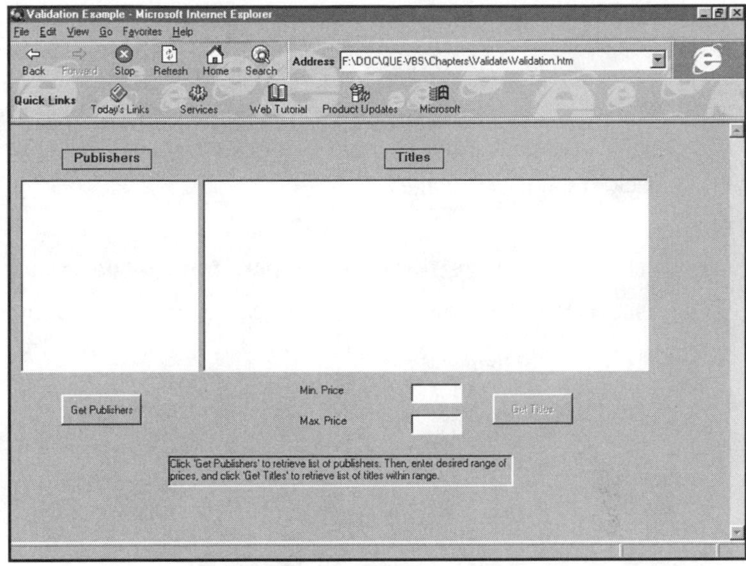

FIG. 20.5
Here's the beginning of the example project in Internet Explorer.

NOTE neath it is captioned Get Publishers.

When the user clicks Get Publishers, the application sends a simple command to the server:

```
Top.window.document.fraBuffer.location = "http://iymalluf.rt66.com/jftproot/
➥pub.idc?"
```

The examples in this chapter use the address of the test server the authors used for development purposes. If you're setting these examples up on your own server, be sure to insert the correct URL in your code.

This statement tells the server to execute the `pub.idc` query and send the HTML page it creates to the buffer frame (fraBuffer) located on the main HTML page. The `Top.window.document.` prefix specifies that the fraBuffer frame is to be found at the "top" level of the project—the document part of the object hierarchy on the main HTML page.

At this point, the program does nothing. But as soon as the page is loaded into the frame, the `Top.TriggerPub` statement in the returned page is executed, which invokes the

TriggerPub procedure in the main HTML page. TriggerPub contains one line of code:

```
Validation.txtTrigger.Text = "pub"
```

which sets the contents of the txtTrigger control (on the Layout Page) to "pub". This causes the txtTrigger_Change event (see Listing 20.6) to fire, which brings execution back to the Layout Page.

Listing 20.6 txtTrigger Procedure from validation.alx

```
Sub txtTrigger_Change() 'Called by kludge routine in main HTML

If Working Then
   Exit Sub
End If

Working = True

    Select Case txtTrigger.Text
        Case "pub"
            txtTrigger = ""
            Working = False
            LoadPublishers  'to provide ersatz load event for frame
        Case "title"
            txtTrigger = ""
            Working = False
            LoadTitles      'to provide ersatz load event for frame
        Case Else
            MsgBox "Illegal call!: " & txtTrigger.Text
            txtTrigger = ""
            Working = False
    End Select
end sub
```

The txtTrigger_Change event contains a Select Case block.

This block contains three options. One runs the LoadPublishers procedure, if the hidden TextBox contains "pub", one runs LoadTitles if the TextBox contains "title", and the third one is a catch-all that returns an error message via a MessageBox if anything else is in the control.

You'll notice some seemingly extraneous code here. The procedure begins with three lines apparently unrelated to the task at hand:

```
If Working Then
   Exit Sub
End If
```

The code also contains the lines

```
txtTrigger = ""
Working = False
```

in each Case block.

This brings up a problem endemic to all event-driven code. When you change the contents of a TextBox, you trigger the TextBox's Change event. That's not necessarily a bad thing; in fact, it's the very "trick" we used to get here in the first place.

However, because we want to be able to call this procedure more than once, we have to clear the contents of the TextBox after we use them. But, if we try to arrive here with "title" twice in a row, we'll be replacing "title" with "title", which means there's no change, and hence, no Change event!

The solution seems obvious: Clear the contents of the TextBox as soon as we've used them. But there's a catch: When you clear the contents of the TextBox, you're changing it. This, in turn, fires off *another* Change event. Because the event occurs while you're still *in* the Change event, you invoke what's called *cascading events*, which *is* generally considered a *very* bad thing. In fact, it can quickly crash your program by consuming all stack space, as it repeatedly calls itself.

In this example, the event would not cascade too far. In fact, it would only cascade once; the moment it double-fired, the Select Case block would fall through to the third test and report an error because the empty TextBox does not match either of the two valid options.

The solution is an old trick: You use a variable (in this case, one called "Working") to track whether you're in the procedure the first time or are in a cascaded invocation. When the procedure is first run, it checks whether the value of "Working" is True. If it is, the procedure recognizes that it is already executing, and it immediately exits. If it's not, it proceeds. After the TextBox is set to "" to empty it, "Working" is restored to False, to allow the procedure to run the next time it's invoked.

Because VBScript does not at this time provide a means to create static variables (a *static variable*, legal in Visual Basic, will retain its value between successive invocations of a procedure) it's necessary to declare "Working" outside of any procedure, to give it global scope.

Returning to the development of the example program, the LoadPublishers procedure does as its name implies—it loads the list of publishers from the ListBox contained in the invisible frame. The procedure is shown in Listing 20.7.

Listing 20.7 LoadPublishers Procedure from validation.alx

```
Sub LoadPublishers
```

continues

Listing 20.7 Continued

```
    For C = 0 to Top.window.document.fraBuffer.lstPublishers.ListCount -1
        WkTxt = Top.window.document.fraBuffer.lstPublishers.List(C)

        StartPos = Instr(WkTxt, ";")—1
        lstPub.AddItem Left(WkTxt, StartPos)

        StartPos = StartPos + 2
        EndPos = Instr(StartPos, WkTxt, ";")
        lstPubID.AddItem Mid(WkTxt, StartPos, EndPos—StartPos)

        StartPos = EndPos + 1
        EndPos = Instr(StartPos, WkTxt, ";")
        lstHighPrice.AddItem Mid(WkTxt, StartPos, EndPos—StartPos)

        StartPos = EndPos + 1
        EndPos = Len(WkTxt)
        lstLowPrice.AddItem Mid(WkTxt, StartPos, EndPos—StartPos)
    Next

    lstPub.ListIndex = 0     'Select first item.

    PubID = lstPubID.List(0)      'publisher ID
    PubMin = CDbl(lstLowPrice.List(0))  'publisher minumum
    PubMax = CDbl(lstHighPrice.List(0)) 'publisher maximum

    lblAbsMin = "(" & PubMin & ")"
    lblAbsMax = "(" & PubMax & ")"

    txtMin.Enabled=True      'Allow user to proceed to set Min
    txtMax.Enabled=True      'Allow user to proceed to set Max
    cmdTitles.Enabled=True   'Allow user to proceed to get Titles
end sub
```

The LoadPublishers procedure takes each entry in the `Top.window.document.fraBuffer.lstPublishers` ListBox using the following line:

```
For C = 0 to Top.window.document.fraBuffer.lstPublishers.ListCount -1
```

to count through them. Because the first entry in a ListBox is 0, the count starts at 0 and continues to one less than the value in the ListBox's ListCount property. (ListCount contains the number of items in the list, *not* the number of the highest item.)

The items in the ListBox contain four pieces of data: the publisher's name, the publisher's ID number, the price of the publisher's most expensive book, and the price of its least expensive book. The pieces of data are separated by semicolons.

This data is separated into four ListBoxes (the large one on the left of the form and the three hidden ones on the bottom). The publisher's name goes into the visible ListBox, and the other three bits of information are used by the program to validate entry and construct queries.

To separate this data, it's first put into a string named "WkTxt" (which stands for *work text)*:

```
WkTxt = Top.window.document.fraBuffer.lstPublishers.List(C)
```

The `.List(C)` property returns the value of the item at the position represented by C, which is the variable created by the For-Next loop.

▶ **See** section on "For... Next" loops, **p. 312**

```
StartPos = Instr(WkTxt, ";")-1
lstPub.AddItem Left(WkTxt, StartPos)
```

"StartPos", a numeric variable, is set to contain a value representing a position one character before the position of the first semicolon in the string, using the Instr function, which searches one string for a match with a smaller string. Then "lstPub" (the visible ListBox) is set to the "Left" part of the string (up to but not including the semicolon).

▶ **See** "String Handling", **p. 427**

```
StartPos = StartPos + 2
EndPos = Instr(StartPos, WkTxt, ";")
lstPubID.AddItem Mid(WkTxt, StartPos, EndPos-StartPos)
```

The process is repeated above for the second part of the string. In this case, it's modified, since it's not at the start of the string; therefore, the Left function can't be used. Instead, the Mid function is used to extract characters from within the string. The first line sets StartPos to point one character *after* the semicolon. The second line creates a new variable, EndPos, which points to the second semicolon. (Instr is invoked here using the optional first parameter, which tells it where in the string to start searching.)

Then, the Mid function returns the second item by fetching the characters between the two semicolons. The first parameter in the Mid function ("WkTxt") is the string containing all the bits of data in the item. The second ("StartPos") tells Mid where to start copying characters, and the third parameter contains an expression; the result of "EndPos - StartPos" contains the number of characters to copy.

The characters are copied into the invisible lstPubID ListBox, for use later on with the query to the server.

```
StartPos = EndPos + 1
EndPos = Instr(StartPos, WkTxt, ";")
lstHighPrice.AddItem Mid(WkTxt, StartPos, EndPos-StartPos)
```

The third bit of data is extracted using the identical process as that used for the second, except this time, the retrieved information is loaded into the lstHighPrice invisible ListBox.

```
StartPos = EndPos + 1
EndPos = Len(WkTxt)
```

```
lstLowPrice.AddItem Mid(WkTxt, StartPos, EndPos-StartPos)
```

Finally, the last part of the item is retrieved. This time, EndPos is simply set to the length of "WkTxt" by use of the Len string handling function. Because there's no closing semicolon, the length of the string marks the last character that's required here.

This process is repeated for each item in the ListBox contained in the buffer frame. Then, a few global variables are set:

```
PubID = lstPubID.List(0)          'publisher ID
PubMin = CDbl(lstLowPrice.List(0))  'publisher minumum
PubMax = CDbl(lstHighPrice.List(0)) 'publisher maximum
```

PubID, PubMin, and PubMax are described in the comments at the end of each line. PubID is used for the queries of book titles, and the PubMin and PubMax variables are used in data validation.

▶ **See** "Using Data Validation", **p. 391**

```
lblAbsMin = "(" & PubMin & ")"
lblAbsMax = "(" & PubMax & ")"
```

Two labels on the form are set to display the absolute minimum and maximum prices of all books the current publisher carries. (The "current publisher" is whichever one is highlighted in the Publishers ListBox.)

NOTE

```
txtMin.Enabled=True        'Allow user to proceed to set Min
txtMax.Enabled=True        'Allow user to proceed to set Max
cmdTitles.Enabled=True     'Allow user to proceed to get Titles
```

Finally, the three disabled controls are enabled, allowing the user to proceed. Now the

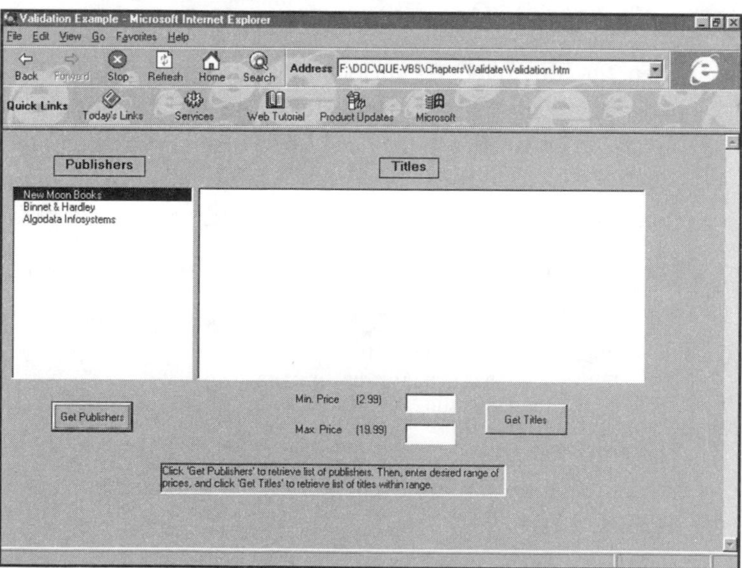

FIG. 20.6
Here's the example project after getting publisher data.

program waits for something to happen.

One of the simplest and most effective methods of data validation is preventing entry of invalid data. Intentionally disabling controls when they are not supposed to be used is one effective method of prevention.

At this point, the example will appear as shown in Figure 20.6.

Using Data Validation

You can't always prevent bad data by disabling controls. In this example, the user is expected to select a publisher, then enter a desired range of prices and submit a query. You can prevent the user fairly easily from entering prices or sending a query before publisher data is loaded—just disable the relevant controls. But what of the situation *after* the data is loaded? What happens if the user enters a low price that is lower than the publisher's least expensive title or a high price that is higher than the most expensive?

In this case, you could rely on the server to trap the error. But it could take a long time, and it might not even trap it! One of the features of VBScript is the ability to validate data

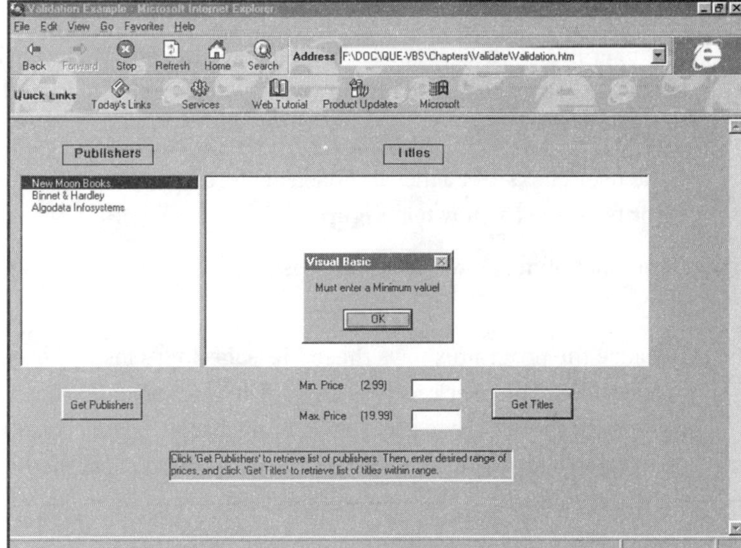

FIG. 20.7
In this error example, no minimum value was specified.

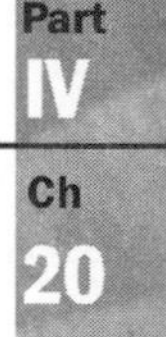

locally, *before* sending it to the server.

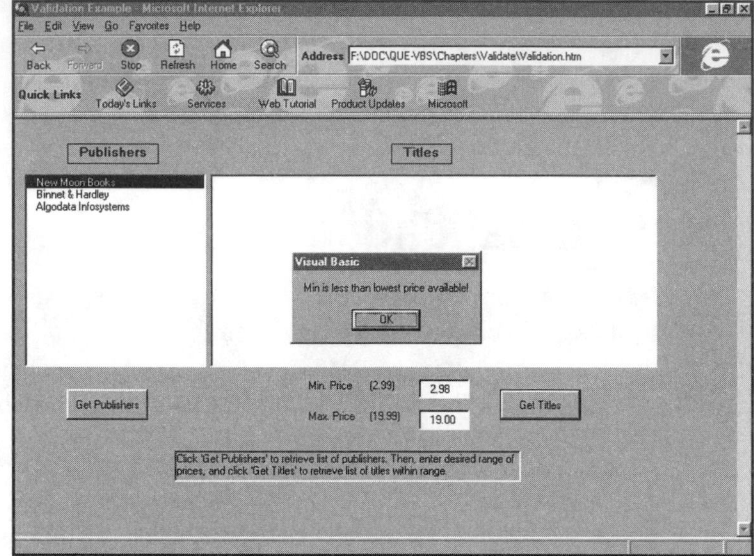

FIG. 20.8
In this error example, the minimum value specified was too low.

In this example, the values entered by the user are validated using a simple set of rules: The user has to enter *both* numbers; the lowest can't be lower than the least expensive book, the highest can't be higher than the most expensive, and the highest can't be lower than the lowest.

If the user clicks Get Titles but hasn't entered any numbers, the application displays an error message as shown in Figure 20.7

If the minimum is lower than the least expensive book, the message in Figure 20.8 is shown.

Because the program shows these MessageBoxes instead of simply passing bad data on to the server, the user receives immediate feedback and can correct the situation without waiting for the server to process and pass back its data. This kind of entry-error-prevention also makes it easier for the program to parse incoming data, as it's not necessary to test for these errors when processing query results.

When the user clicks Get Titles, the code in the ValidateQuery procedure (shown in Listing 20.8) executes and performs the tests necessary to trap for these errors.

Listing 20.8 ValidateQuery Procedure from validation.alx

```
Sub ValidateQuery()
    Min = Trim(txtMin.Text) 'Store values to variables
    Max = Trim(txtMax.Text)

    If Min = "" Then
        MsgBox "Must enter a Minimum value!"
        Exit Sub
    End If

    If Max = "" Then
        MsgBox "Must enter a Maximum value!"
        Exit Sub
    End If

    Min = CDbl(Min)            'Convert variables to numeric
    Max = CDbl(Max)

    ErStr = ""       'initialize to empty string
    If Min > 0 then
        If Max > Min Then
            If Min >= PubMin Then
                If Max <= PubMax Then
                    SubmitTitles
                Else
                    ErStr = "Max is greater than highest price available!"
                End If
            Else
                ErStr = "Min is less than lowest price available!"
            End If
        Else
            ErStr = "Max must be greater than Min!"
        End If
    Else
        ErStr = "Min must be greater than 0!"
    End If

    If ErStr > "" then MsgBox ErStr

end sub
```

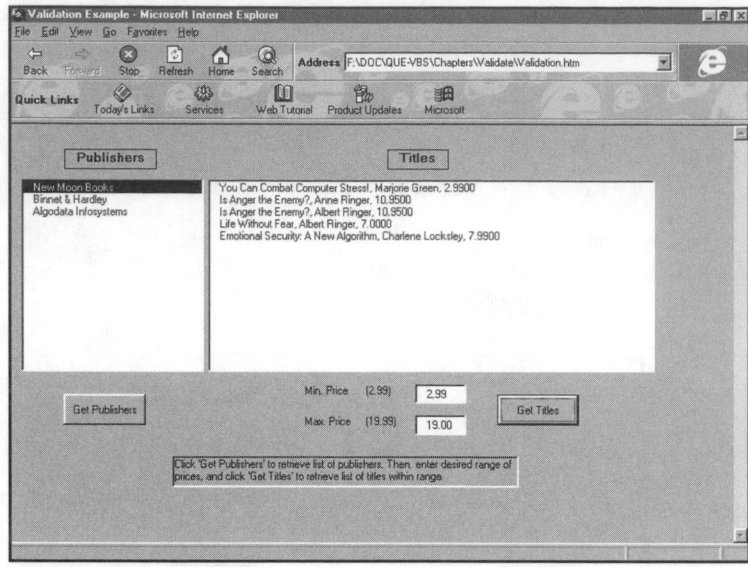

FIG. 20.9
Titles are returned when data is validated.

The code in Listing 20.8 is fairly straightforward and fairly self-documenting. It first checks to make sure the user has entered values; then it tests for all possible error conditions, using a series of nested If-Then blocks. By properly indenting the If-Then tests, you can tell at a glance where each block starts and ends.

After all data is accepted as valid, the procedure passes control to the SubmitTitles procedure, which constructs a string containing the query and sends it on its way to the server (see fig. 20.9).

▶ **See** "Handling Data Transactions," **p. 394**

Handling Data Transactions

The SubmitTitles procedure is elegant in its simplicity. All the data having been accepted and validated prior to arrival here, it's relatively trivial to combine it into a query string and send it to the server. The string consists of the URL of the server, which is comprised of the machine address ("http://iymalluf.rt66.com"), the path containing the query file ("/jftproot/"), the name of the query file ("titles.idc"), a question mark, which indicates that it's a query to execute rather than a file to fetch, and the query itself: "pubID=" & PubID & "&HighPrice=" & Max & "&LowPrice=" & Min". The query consists of names in the format required by the server ("pubID=", "&HighPrice=", "&LowPrice=") concatenated with the names of the VBScript variables containing the actual data:

```
Sub SubmitTitles()   'query server
    lstTitles.Clear
    Top.window.document.fraBuffer.location="http://iymalluf.rt66.com/
jftproot/➥titles.idc? pubID=" & PubID & "&HighPrice=" & Max & "&LowPrice="
& Min
end sub
```

After this query is sent, the application does nothing until notified that the result file is waiting in the buffer frame, exactly as with the Publishers query. When the result file is received, LoadTitles is executed, and the Titles ListBox is populated with the results. Because the list of book titles doesn't need to be separated into discrete elements, placing it into the ListBox is simple:

On the CD

```
Sub LoadTitles
    For C = 0 to Top.window.document.fraBuffer.lstBooks.ListCount -1
        lstTitles.AddItem Top.window.document.fraBuffer.lstBooks.List(C)
    Next
end sub
```

The LoadTitles procedure counts through the list of items and adds them, one at a time, to the lstTitles ListBox.

Understanding the Layout Page Source Listing

Listing 20.9 contains the entire source for the HTML Layout Page used in this example. The section after the final script contains declarations for the controls used in the project.

Listing 20.9 validation.alx—Layout Page Code for Validation Example

```
<SCRIPT LANGUAGE="VBScript">
<!--
Dim PubID, PubMin, PubMax, Min, Max, Working

Sub txtTrigger_Change() 'Called by kludge routine in main HTML

If Working Then
   Exit Sub
End If

Working = True

    Select Case txtTrigger.Text
        Case "pub"
            txtTrigger = ""
            Working = False
            LoadPublishers  'to provide ersatz load event for frame
        Case "title"
```

continued

Listing 20.9 Continued

```
            txtTrigger = ""
            Working = False
            LoadTitles      'to provide ersatz load event for frame
        Case Else
            MsgBox "Illegal call!: " & txtTrigger.Text
            txtTrigger = ""
            Working = False
    End Select
end sub

Sub ClearPubLists
     lstPub.Clear
     lstPubID.Clear
     lstLowPrice.Clear
     lstHighPrice.Clear
End Sub
-->
</SCRIPT>
<SCRIPT LANGUAGE="VBScript">
<!--
Sub cmdPub_Click()
    ClearPubLists
    lstTitles.Clear
REM query server, load hidden listbox into lstPub
    Top.window.document.fraBuffer.location="http://iymalluf.rt66.com/jftproot/
➥pub.idc?"
end sub

Sub LoadPublishers
    For C = 0 to Top.window.document.fraBuffer.lstPublishers.ListCount -1
        WkTxt = Top.window.document.fraBuffer.lstPublishers.List(C)

        StartPos = Instr(WkTxt, ";")-1
        lstPub.AddItem Left(WkTxt, StartPos)

        StartPos = StartPos + 2
        EndPos = Instr(StartPos, WkTxt, ";")
        lstPubID.AddItem Mid(WkTxt, StartPos, EndPos-StartPos)

        StartPos = EndPos + 1
        EndPos = Instr(StartPos, WkTxt, ";")
        lstHighPrice.AddItem Mid(WkTxt, StartPos, EndPos-StartPos)

        StartPos = EndPos + 1
        EndPos = Len(WkTxt)
        lstLowPrice.AddItem Mid(WkTxt, StartPos, EndPos-StartPos)
    Next

    lstPub.ListIndex = 0     'Select first item.

    PubID = lstPubID.List(0)      'publisher ID
    PubMin = CDbl(lstLowPrice.List(0))  'publisher minumum
    PubMax = CDbl(lstHighPrice.List(0)) 'publisher maximum
```

```
    lblAbsMin = "(" & PubMin & ")"
    lblAbsMax = "(" & PubMax & ")"

    txtMin.Enabled=True      'Allow user to proceed to set Min
    txtMax.Enabled=True      'Allow user to proceed to set Max
    cmdTitles.Enabled=True   'Allow user to proceed to get Titles
end sub
-->
</SCRIPT>
<SCRIPT LANGUAGE="VBScript">
<!--
Sub cmdTitles_Click()
    ValidateQuery
end sub

Sub ValidateQuery()
    Min = Trim(txtMin.Text)  'Value)   'Store values to variables
    Max = Trim(txtMax.Text)  'Value)

    If Min = "" Then
        MsgBox "Must enter a Minimum value!"
        Exit Sub
    End If

    If Max = "" Then
        MsgBox "Must enter a Maximum value!"
        Exit Sub
    End If

    Min = CDbl(Min)            'Convert variables to numeric
    Max = CDbl(Max)

    ErStr = ""       'initialize to empty string
    If Min > 0 then
        If Max > Min Then
            If Min >= PubMin Then
                If Max <= PubMax Then
                    SubmitTitles
                Else
                    ErStr = "Max is greater than highest price available!"
                End If
            Else
                ErStr = "Min is less than lowest price available!"
            End If
        Else
            ErStr = "Max must be greater than Min!"
        End If
    Else
        ErStr = "Min must be greater than 0!"
    End If

    If ErStr > "" then MsgBox ErStr
```


continued

Listing 20.9 Continued

```
end sub

Sub SubmitTitles()   'query server
    lstTitles.Clear
    Top.window.document.fraBuffer.location="http://iymalluf.rt66.com/jftproot/
➥titles.idc? pubID=" & PubID & "&HighPrice=" & Max & "&LowPrice=" & Min
end sub

Sub LoadTitles
    For C = 0 to Top.window.document.fraBuffer.lstBooks.ListCount -1
        lstTitles.AddItem Top.window.document.fraBuffer.lstBooks.List(C)
    Next
end sub
-->
</SCRIPT>
<SCRIPT LANGUAGE="VBScript">
<!--
Sub lstPub_Click()
    PubID = lstPubID.list(lstPub.ListIndex)      'publisher ID
    PubMin = CDbl(lstLowPrice.list(lstPub.ListIndex))  'publisher minumum
    PubMax = CDbl(lstHighPrice.list(lstPub.ListIndex)) 'publisher maximum

    lblAbsMin = "(" & PubMin & ")"
    lblAbsMax = "(" & PubMax & ")"

End Sub
-->
</SCRIPT>
<DIV ID="hlValid" STYLE="LAYOUT:FIXED;WIDTH:519pt;HEIGHT:290pt;">
    <OBJECT ID="cmdPub"
     CLASSID="CLSID:D7053240-CE69-11CD-A777-00DD01143C57"
➥STYLE="TOP:206pt;LEFT:33pt;WIDTH:66pt;HEIGHT:25pt;TABINDEX:0;ZINDEX:0;">
        <PARAM NAME="Caption" VALUE="Get Publishers">
        <PARAM NAME="Size" VALUE="2328;882">
        <PARAM NAME="FontCharSet" VALUE="0">
        <PARAM NAME="FontPitchAndFamily" VALUE="2">
        <PARAM NAME="ParagraphAlign" VALUE="3">
        <PARAM NAME="FontWeight" VALUE="0">
    </OBJECT>
    <OBJECT ID="cmdTitles"
     CLASSID="CLSID:D7053240-CE69-11CD-A777-00DD01143C57"
➥STYLE="TOP:206pt;LEFT:385pt;WIDTH:66pt;HEIGHT:25pt;TABINDEX:1;ZINDEX:1;">
        <PARAM NAME="VariousPropertyBits" VALUE="25">
        <PARAM NAME="Caption" VALUE="Get Titles">
        <PARAM NAME="Size" VALUE="2328;882">
        <PARAM NAME="FontEffects" VALUE="1073750016">
        <PARAM NAME="FontCharSet" VALUE="0">
        <PARAM NAME="FontPitchAndFamily" VALUE="2">
        <PARAM NAME="ParagraphAlign" VALUE="3">
        <PARAM NAME="FontWeight" VALUE="0">
    </OBJECT>
    <OBJECT ID="lblPublishers"
     CLASSID="CLSID:978C9E23-D4B0-11CE-BF2D-00AA003F40D0"
```

```
➥STYLE="TOP:8pt;LEFT:34pt;WIDTH:74pt;HEIGHT:17pt;ZINDEX:2;">
        <PARAM NAME="Caption" VALUE="Publishers">
        <PARAM NAME="PicturePosition" VALUE="393216">
        <PARAM NAME="Size" VALUE="2611;600">
        <PARAM NAME="BorderStyle" VALUE="1">
        <PARAM NAME="FontEffects" VALUE="1073741825">
        <PARAM NAME="FontHeight" VALUE="240">
        <PARAM NAME="FontCharSet" VALUE="0">
        <PARAM NAME="FontPitchAndFamily" VALUE="2">
        <PARAM NAME="ParagraphAlign" VALUE="3">
        <PARAM NAME="FontWeight" VALUE="700">
    </OBJECT>
    <OBJECT ID="lblTitles"
     CLASSID="CLSID:978C9E23-D4B0-11CE-BF2D-00AA003F40D0"
➥STYLE="TOP:8pt;LEFT:296pt;WIDTH:50pt;HEIGHT:17pt;ZINDEX:3;">
        <PARAM NAME="Caption" VALUE="Titles">
        <PARAM NAME="Size" VALUE="1764;600">
        <PARAM NAME="BorderStyle" VALUE="1">
        <PARAM NAME="FontEffects" VALUE="1073741825">
        <PARAM NAME="FontHeight" VALUE="240">
        <PARAM NAME="FontCharSet" VALUE="0">
        <PARAM NAME="FontPitchAndFamily" VALUE="2">
        <PARAM NAME="ParagraphAlign" VALUE="3">
        <PARAM NAME="FontWeight" VALUE="700">
    </OBJECT>
    <OBJECT ID="txtMin"
     CLASSID="CLSID:8BD21D10-EC42-11CE-9E0D-00AA006002F3"
➥STYLE="TOP:198pt;LEFT:319pt;WIDTH:41pt;HEIGHT:16pt;TABINDEX:5;ZINDEX:4;">
        <PARAM NAME="VariousPropertyBits" VALUE="746604569">
        <PARAM NAME="Size" VALUE="1446;564">
        <PARAM NAME="FontEffects" VALUE="1073750016">
        <PARAM NAME="FontCharSet" VALUE="0">
        <PARAM NAME="FontPitchAndFamily" VALUE="2">
        <PARAM NAME="FontWeight" VALUE="0">
    </OBJECT>
    <OBJECT ID="txtMax"
     CLASSID="CLSID:8BD21D10-EC42-11CE-9E0D-00AA006002F3"
➥STYLE="TOP:223pt;LEFT:319pt;WIDTH:41pt;HEIGHT:16pt;TABINDEX:6;ZINDEX:5;">
        <PARAM NAME="VariousPropertyBits" VALUE="746604569">
        <PARAM NAME="Size" VALUE="1446;564">
        <PARAM NAME="FontEffects" VALUE="1073750016">
        <PARAM NAME="FontCharSet" VALUE="0">
        <PARAM NAME="FontPitchAndFamily" VALUE="2">
        <PARAM NAME="FontWeight" VALUE="0">
    </OBJECT>
    <OBJECT ID="lblMin"
     CLASSID="CLSID:978C9E23-D4B0-11CE-BF2D-00AA003F40D0"
➥STYLE="TOP:198pt;LEFT:229pt;WIDTH:41pt;HEIGHT:8pt;ZINDEX:6;">
        <PARAM NAME="Caption" VALUE="Min. Price">
        <PARAM NAME="Size" VALUE="1446;282">
        <PARAM NAME="FontCharSet" VALUE="0">
        <PARAM NAME="FontPitchAndFamily" VALUE="2">
        <PARAM NAME="FontWeight" VALUE="0">
    </OBJECT>
```


continued

Listing 20.9 Continued

```
    <OBJECT ID="lblMax"
     CLASSID="CLSID:978C9E23-D4B0-11CE-BF2D-00AA003F40D0"
➥STYLE="TOP:223pt;LEFT:229pt;WIDTH:41pt;HEIGHT:8pt;ZINDEX:7;">
        <PARAM NAME="Caption" VALUE="Max. Price">
        <PARAM NAME="Size" VALUE="1446;282">
        <PARAM NAME="FontCharSet" VALUE="0">
        <PARAM NAME="FontPitchAndFamily" VALUE="2">
        <PARAM NAME="FontWeight" VALUE="0">
    </OBJECT>
    <OBJECT ID="lblInstructions"
     CLASSID="CLSID:978C9E23-D4B0-11CE-BF2D-00AA003F40D0"
➥STYLE="TOP:256pt;LEFT:121pt;WIDTH:281pt;HEIGHT:25pt;ZINDEX:8;">
        <PARAM NAME="Caption" VALUE="Click 'Get Publishers' to
➥ retrieve list of publishers. Then, enter desired range
➥ of prices, and click 'Get Titles' to retrieve list of
➥ titles within range.">
        <PARAM NAME="Size" VALUE="9913;882">
        <PARAM NAME="SpecialEffect" VALUE="2">
        <PARAM NAME="FontCharSet" VALUE="0">
        <PARAM NAME="FontPitchAndFamily" VALUE="2">
        <PARAM NAME="FontWeight" VALUE="0">
    </OBJECT>
    <OBJECT ID="txtTrigger"
     CLASSID="CLSID:8BD21D10-EC42-11CE-9E0D-00AA006002F3"
➥STYLE="TOP:322pt;LEFT:289pt;WIDTH:40pt;HEIGHT:17pt;TABINDEX:10;
➥DISPLAY:NONEZINDEX:9;">
        <PARAM NAME="VariousPropertyBits" VALUE="746604571">
        <PARAM NAME="Size" VALUE="1411;600">
        <PARAM NAME="FontCharSet" VALUE="0">
        <PARAM NAME="FontPitchAndFamily" VALUE="2">
        <PARAM NAME="FontWeight" VALUE="0">
    </OBJECT>
    <OBJECT ID="lblAbsMin"
     CLASSID="CLSID:978C9E23-D4B0-11CE-BF2D-00AA003F40D0"
➥STYLE="TOP:198pt;LEFT:278pt;WIDTH:26pt;HEIGHT:17pt;ZINDEX:10;">
        <PARAM NAME="Size" VALUE="917;600">
        <PARAM NAME="FontCharSet" VALUE="0">
        <PARAM NAME="FontPitchAndFamily" VALUE="2">
        <PARAM NAME="FontWeight" VALUE="0">
    </OBJECT>
    <OBJECT ID="lblAbsMax"
     CLASSID="CLSID:978C9E23-D4B0-11CE-BF2D-00AA003F40D0"
➥STYLE="TOP:223pt;LEFT:278pt;WIDTH:26pt;HEIGHT:17pt;ZINDEX:11;">
        <PARAM NAME="Size" VALUE="917;600">
        <PARAM NAME="FontCharSet" VALUE="0">
        <PARAM NAME="FontPitchAndFamily" VALUE="2">
        <PARAM NAME="FontWeight" VALUE="0">
    </OBJECT>
    <OBJECT ID="lstTitles"
     CLASSID="CLSID:8BD21D20-EC42-11CE-9E0D-00AA006002F3"
➥STYLE="TOP:33pt;LEFT:150pt;WIDTH:362pt;HEIGHT:155pt;TABINDEX:13;
➥ZINDEX:12;">
        <PARAM NAME="VariousPropertyBits" VALUE="746586139">
```

```
        <PARAM NAME="ScrollBars" VALUE="3">
        <PARAM NAME="DisplayStyle" VALUE="2">
        <PARAM NAME="Size" VALUE="12771;5468">
        <PARAM NAME="MatchEntry" VALUE="0">
        <PARAM NAME="FontCharSet" VALUE="0">
        <PARAM NAME="FontPitchAndFamily" VALUE="2">
        <PARAM NAME="FontWeight" VALUE="0">
    </OBJECT>
    <OBJECT ID="lstPubID"
     CLASSID="CLSID:8BD21D20-EC42-11CE-9E0D-00AA006002F3"
➥STYLE="TOP:305pt;LEFT:83pt;WIDTH:57pt;HEIGHT:42pt;TABINDEX:16;
➥DISPLAY:NONEZINDEX:13;">
        <PARAM NAME="ScrollBars" VALUE="3">
        <PARAM NAME="DisplayStyle" VALUE="2">
        <PARAM NAME="Size" VALUE="2011;1482">
        <PARAM NAME="MatchEntry" VALUE="0">
        <PARAM NAME="FontCharSet" VALUE="0">
        <PARAM NAME="FontPitchAndFamily" VALUE="2">
        <PARAM NAME="FontWeight" VALUE="0">
    </OBJECT>
    <OBJECT ID="lstPub"
     CLASSID="CLSID:8BD21D20-EC42-11CE-9E0D-00AA006002F3"
➥STYLE="TOP:33pt;LEFT:0pt;WIDTH:146pt;HEIGHT:155pt;TABINDEX:2;
➥ZINDEX:14;">
        <PARAM NAME="VariousPropertyBits" VALUE="746586139">
        <PARAM NAME="ScrollBars" VALUE="3">
        <PARAM NAME="DisplayStyle" VALUE="2">
        <PARAM NAME="Size" VALUE="5151;5468">
        <PARAM NAME="MatchEntry" VALUE="0">
        <PARAM NAME="FontCharSet" VALUE="0">
        <PARAM NAME="FontPitchAndFamily" VALUE="2">
        <PARAM NAME="FontWeight" VALUE="0">
    </OBJECT>
    <OBJECT ID="lstHighPrice"
     CLASSID="CLSID:8BD21D20-EC42-11CE-9E0D-00AA006002F3"
➥STYLE="TOP:314pt;LEFT:157pt;WIDTH:57pt;HEIGHT:36pt;TABINDEX:14;DISPLAY:
➥NONEZINDEX:15;">
        <PARAM NAME="ScrollBars" VALUE="3">
        <PARAM NAME="DisplayStyle" VALUE="2">
        <PARAM NAME="Size" VALUE="2011;1270">
        <PARAM NAME="MatchEntry" VALUE="0">
        <PARAM NAME="FontCharSet" VALUE="0">
        <PARAM NAME="FontPitchAndFamily" VALUE="2">
        <PARAM NAME="FontWeight" VALUE="0">
    </OBJECT>
    <OBJECT ID="lstLowPrice"
     CLASSID="CLSID:8BD21D20-EC42-11CE-9E0D-00AA006002F3"
➥STYLE="TOP:314pt;LEFT:223pt;WIDTH:57pt;HEIGHT:35pt;TABINDEX:15;
➥DISPLAY:NONEZINDEX:16;">
        <PARAM NAME="ScrollBars" VALUE="3">
        <PARAM NAME="DisplayStyle" VALUE="2">
        <PARAM NAME="Size" VALUE="2011;1235">
        <PARAM NAME="MatchEntry" VALUE="0">
```

```
            <PARAM NAME="FontCharSet" VALUE="0">
            <PARAM NAME="FontPitchAndFamily" VALUE="2">
            <PARAM NAME="FontWeight" VALUE="0">
        </OBJECT>
    </DIV>
```

From Here...

The exciting possibilities shown in this chapter require a working knowledge of the HTML Control Pad, HTML Layout Pages, and the VBScript language. To a lesser extent, an understanding of HTML is important.

- See Chapters 3, "Introducing the ActiveX Control Pad," and 4, "Creating a Standard HTML Page," for information about using the ActiveX Control Pad.
- See Chapter 6, "Creating an HTML Layout Page," for more information on using .ALX files with the ActiveX Control Pad.
- See Chapters 11–20 for details on the VBScript language implementation.
- See Chapter 21, "Accessing Data," for information on creating the server-side logic required to provide data to the client.

PART V

Advanced Techniques, Tactics, and Pitfalls

CHAPTER 21

Accessing Data

by Ibrahim Malluf

- **Using data sources**
- **Using server side data**

  The Internet Database Connector (IDC) provides a simple, direct method for accessing data.
- **Using client side data**
- **Building query pages**

One of the most exiting aspects of recent developments in Web servers is the ability to access Open Database Connectivity (ODBC) data sources directly through interactive queries. Microsoft's Internet Information Server (MSIIS), for example, provides the IDC interface that automatically queries the database and returns a result page based on the specifics of an HTX file that describes how the output should be formatted. The process involves three steps: the user submits a request for data to the Web server, the request is processed, and a results page is created and returned to the user's browser. Traditionally this has been done through CGI scripts with all processing being done on the server side of things. With VBScript, you can validate the query data and determine what type of query should be submitted and even what the return data should look like.

ODBC data sources cover a very wide range of RDBMS from Syquest and Oracle to Microsoft SQL Server and even ISAM databases through the Jet DBEngine. Microsoft Internet Information Server directly accesses these databases using a very simple interface. While you can still develop CGI scripts and use them for data access, the rest of this chapter is about the IDC interface provided by Microsoft's Internet Information Server. ■

Using Data Sources

With the Microsoft Internet Information Server (MSIIS), you can access any ODBC-compliant data source. This includes Access, SQL Server, Oracle, DB2, and many others. This book uses SQL Server and Access for its database examples. When using the ODBC databases in conjunction with the MSIIS, you have to create the datasource as a DSN entry:

1. Select the ODBC icon from the control panel (NT351).
2. Select the System DSN command button.
3. At this point you should see the dialogs shown in Figure 21.1. Fill in the required information including the database name in the options section.

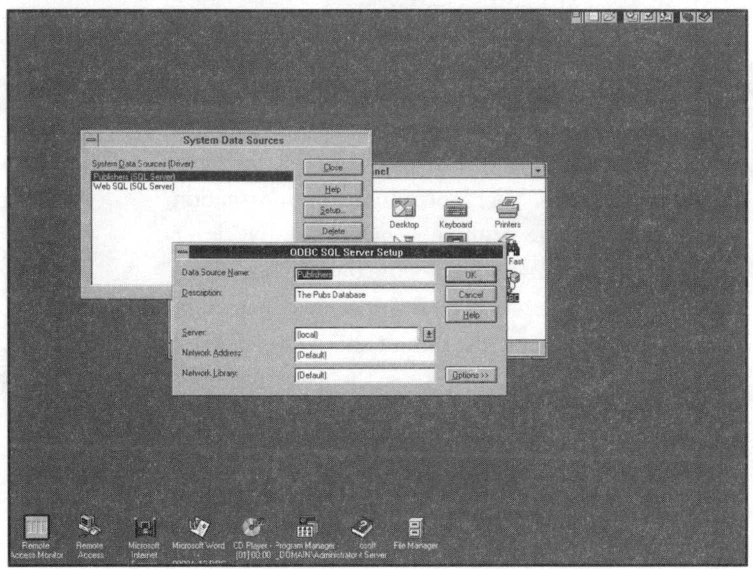

FIG. 21.1
Add a DSN datasource to the system.

Using Server Side Data

On the server side of things, an array of methods is available for processing data. Depending on your platform, you can use CGI, perl, Java, Visual Basic, and many other tools. Our focus here is on the Microsoft Internet Information Server, so our examples discuss the main tool made available for database operations: the Internet Database Connector.

The Internet Database Connector (IDC) is an interface between the MSIIS Web server and ODBC data sources. If you are looking for a simple, direct method for accessing data, this is an outstanding choice. It requires three files to produce an HTML results page. The IDC file structure contains the components shown in Table 21.1.

Table 21.1 Components of the IDC File

Field	Required	Description
DataSource	Yes	The name of the ODBC Data Source
Template	Yes	The name of an HTX file that contains the format for the returned data in HTML
SQLStatement	Yes	The SQL statement to be executed
DefaultParameters	No	The default values for parameters if the client did not specify any
Expires	No	Specifies how long a cached page will remain before being refreshed by the IDC
MaxFieldSize	No	The maximum size of a returned field
MaxRecords	No	The maximum number of rows to return
Password	No	The Client's Password (see MIIS Manual)
RequiredParameters	No	Specifies required parameters; returns an error to the client if parameters are not provided
Username	No	A valid user name
ContentType	No	Any valid Mime Type to be returned to the client

The DataSource, Template, and SQLStatement must be present in every IDC file. The DataSource specifies the ODBC datasource that contains the desired database. When you set this data source up, you must set it up as a SystemDSN.

The Template specifies the name of the .HTX file that contains the formatting information for the recordset returned from the query. The file looks just like an HTML file but contains special formatting instructions that modify the output HTML file with special keywords and values. Here are some of those keywords and values with examples of their use.

<%begindetail%>...<%enddetail%> These two keywords mark the beginning and end of a merged data row. For each row returned, the details included between them will be repeated (see Listing 21.1).

Listing 21.1 Inserting the Data Returned from the IDC into a Web Page

```
<SELECT NAME="AuthorList">
<%begindetail%>
<OPTION VALUE = <%au_fname%> <%au_lname%>
<%enddetail%>
</SELECT>
```

This code would add the name of every author returned in the recordset into a dropdown box on the resultant HTML form.

<%if...%>...<%Else%>...<%EndIf%> Conditional keywords are provided so that you can include some branching logic in the creation of your HTML page. This `If…Else…EndIf` structure should be familiar to most BASIC programmers. The conditional statement is contained within the If statement: `<%If Conditional%>`. There is no Then statement after it (see Listing 21.2).

Listing 21.2 Using Conditional Statements in a Template File

```
<%IF CurrentRecord EQ 0%>
      There are no Authors matching your criteria!
<%Else%>
<SELECT NAME="AuthorList">
<%begindetail%>
<OPTION VALUE = <%au_fname%> <%au_lname%>
<%enddetai%>
</SELECT>
<%EndIf%>
```

Listing 21.2 is a variation on the previous example that creates a dropdown box and adds data to it only if there are rows returned in the rowset. The EQ operator and CurrentRecord value used in this example is explained below.

***EQ, LT, GT, CONTAINS* Operators** Along with the keywords, the IDC provides some operators to use with .HTX pages to further increase the flexibility of your page templates. Their meanings are pretty straightforward (see Table 21.2).

Table 21.2 HTX Operator Descriptions

Name	Description
EQ	Equals operator. Returns True if both arguments are equal to each other
LT	Less Than operator. Returns True if the left argument's value is less than the right argument's value
GT	Greater Than operator. Returns True if left argument's value is greater than the right argument's value
CONTAINS	Returns True if the string arguement on the left contains the string arguement on the right

In the example for the `<%If%>...<%Else%>...<%EdnIf%>` statement, you saw the EQ operator used. The LT and GT operators work pretty much the same. The CONTAINS operator is a string searching tool that provides a means for you to check for specific values.

***CurrentRecord, MaxRecords* Built-In Variables** The CurrentRecord intrinsic variable contains the row number being processed. It is incremented every iteration of the `<%begindetail%>...<%enddetail%>` pair.

The MaxRecords is the value of the MaxRecords field set in the IDC file. If no value was set, it will return 0.

Both of these variables only work within the `<%If...%><%Else%><%EndIf%>` conditional statement.

IDC Parameters Your .HTX file can access the parameters originally passed to the .IDX file by the HTML Query page. If one of the criteria parameters was named `%lName%` you could access the value of `%lName%` by using the construct: IDC.lName

HTTP Variables HTTP variables contain information about the client sending the request. The complete header is contained in the ALL_HTTP variable. In addition there are HTTP variables that contain specific information. All of these variables must be prefaced with the HTTP_ prefix and must be all uppercase characters. Table 21.3 gives a list of some of them. For a more comprehensive list, see the MSIIS Server documentation.

Table 21.3 Some HTTP Variables

Variable	Description
ACCEPT	Describes the type of data the client will accept
USER_AGENT	Client browser information
REFERER	Name of HTML file that called this operation
AUTH_TYPE	Type of authorization in effect
QUERY_STRING	Information following the '?' in a URL
REMOTE_ADDR	IP address of the client
REMOTE_HOST	The host name of the client
REMOTE_USER	The username supplied by the client

Suppose you had to know what kind of browser client was requesting data, in order to use, or not use, certain features. The IDC provides access to HTTP variables that include that name of the browser. The ALL_HTTP variable contains a header that has the browser type within the string. To check to see whether you were using Explorer 3.0, for example, you might do something like what's shown in Listing 21.3.

Listing 21.3 Other Conditionals Based on the HTTP Variables

```
<%IF HTTP_USER_AGENT CONTAINS "Explorer/3.0"%>
      ...do something
<%Else%>
      ...do somthein else
<%EndIf%>
```

To see exactly how the IDC works, try a simple page using Microsoft Internet Information Server. Looking at Figure 21.2, you can see the steps involved in retrieving data. The first HTML page provides the user with a method of specifying criteria for the search. When the user is done specifying criteria, the criteria are submitted to an .IDC file that gets the resultset and submits it to an .HTX file that formats the data into an HTML page and returns it to the browser. This process can be repeated as many times as you wish, creating a drill-down search with each query returned building a new set of search options. For now, we'll try a simple query page that will give you a working example of how things fit together.

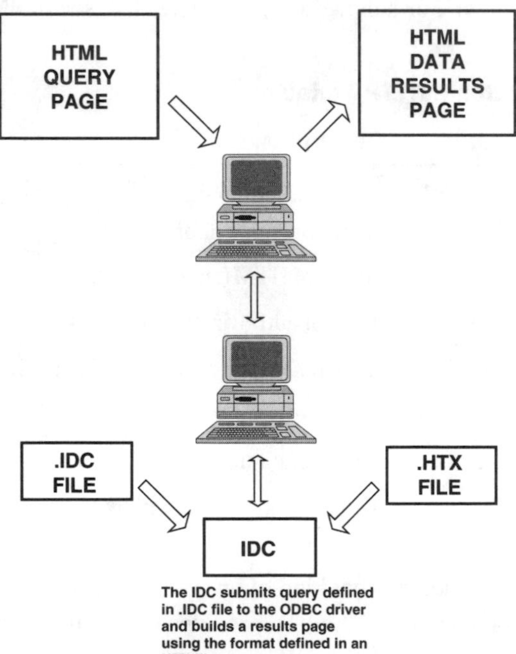
HTML QUERY PAGE
HTML DATA RESULTS PAGE
.IDC FILE
.HTX FILE
IDC
The IDC submits query defined in .IDC file to the ODBC driver and builds a results page using the format defined in an HTX file

FIG. 21.2
The Internet Database Connector in action, step by step.

Using Client Side Data

Client side data includes search criteria, data entry, and returned rows from a query. Search criteria uses the input from a user to build a query to submit to the data server. What you most commonly see in Web pages are single-entry searches or searches that allow multiple fields with little control over whether it's an *or* or an *and* type of relationship. They also don't allow for sophisticated pattern matching queries.

Data entry is part of client side data. In the past, Web pages have just passed the entered data back to the server as entered by the user without any qualifications. If there was invalid or incomplete data, this could not be checked until the server passed had the data to the program that was responsible for the response to the query. Errors would be detected there, and the appropriate response would then be sent back to the source of the query. Because there are situations involving bandwidth, server load, and other factors that could really slow down the interaction between the client and the server, it is paramount to have the ability to screen data before sending it. VBScript gives you that ability.

Building Query Pages

The current limitations of the Web server/browser interface even with VBScript dictate limitations on your interface design. Perhaps the most limiting condition when using the IDC is that the way the data is returned must be already defined and formatted in a preexisting .HTX document. The .HTX format allows you considerable formatting options, but the basic document must preexist. This means is that users are going to be limited to the query structures that you provide. Ad-hoc queries simply won't work using the IDC.

As an introduction into building SQL queries for submission, consider this simple scenario. This page will allow the user to select one of three tables from the PUBS sample database in SQL Server 6. In order for this example to work, you have to have MIIS and SQL Server 6 up and running. You must also create an ODBC datasource on your server using the ODBC utility in the control panel of NT 3.51 with service pak4 or from NT4.0. The ODBC source must be set up as a DNS datasource. Use the name 'Publishers' as the name of the datasource and set 'Pubs' as the database name. Using Notepad as your text editor, create the file shown in Listing 21.4. Alternatively, you could retrieve the file from the companion CD. This is an .IDX file that receives the query string from your page and submits it to SQL Server.

Listing 21.4 quepub1.idc—An .IDX File that Requests a Rowset from SQL Server

```
quepub1.idx
Datasource: Web SQL
Username: sa
Template: quepub1.htx
SQLStatement:
+SELECT *FROM authors
+WHERE au_lname LIKE '%lname%'
+AND au_fname LIKE '%fname%'
```

This .IDX file takes two arguments, %lname% and %fname%, as parameters for the query. It passes the query to SQL Server and then takes the resultset and sends it to the quepub1.htx file that will format the results into a HTML page and give it to the Web server to return it to the client browser. The .HTX file that is being called by this example is in Listing 21.5.

Listing 21.5 quepub1.htx—Template File Used in the Creation of a Return Page that Contains the Requested Data

```
<HTML>
<HEAD><TITLE>Authors and YTD Sales</TITLE></HEAD>
<BODY BACKGROUND="/samples/images/backgrnd.gif">
<BODY BGCOLOR="FFFFFF">
<OBJECT ID="ieList" WIDTH=350 HEIGHT=80
CLASSID="CLSID:8BD21D20-EC42-11CE-9E0D-00AA006002F3">
<PARAM NAME="ScrollBars" VALUE="3">
<PARAM NAME="DisplayStyle" VALUE="2">
<PARAM NAME="Size" VALUE="5151;811">
<PARAM NAME="MatchEntry" VALUE="0">
<PARAM NAME="FontCharSet" VALUE="0">
<PARAM NAME="FontPitchAndFamily" VALUE="2">
<PARAM NAME="FontWeight" VALUE="0">
</OBJECT>
<br>
<br>
<%http_all_http%>
<br>
<!--
The table is not needed for a floating frame but I used it
to provide the frame with a more distinctive border
-->
<TABLE WIDTH=500 HEIGHT=300 BORDER=5>
<TR WIDTH=600><TD>
<!--
This is what creates the floating frame. I used fixed pixels for width
and height so that the frame would fit the table exactly. If you want
the frame to size proportionately to the browser winf, don't use a table
and specify the width and height parameters with percentages: Width=80%
-->
```

```
<FRAME WIDTH=500 HEIGHT=300 ID= "FLOATER" SRC="foo.htm">
</TD></TR>
</Table>
<%QUERY_STRING%>
<Script Language="VBScript" OnLoad>
<%begindetail%>
ieList.addItem "<%au_fname%>" & " " & "<%au_lname%>" & ":" & "<%au_id%>"
<%enddetail%>
Sub ielist_click
Dim buffer
Buffer = "http://iymalluf.rt66.com/eftproot/QuePub2.idc?authid=" &
right(ieList.List(ielist.listindex),11)
Floater.Location = buffer
End Sub
</Script>

</BODY>
</HTML>
```

The key part of this .HTX listing is between the `%begindetail%...%enddetail%` pair. These two keywords constitute a loop that will iterate through all of the rows returned in the recordset. In this application, the author's first and last names will be added to a dropdown list on the returned Web page.

Finally, the HTML page that calls all of this is presented in Listing 21.6.

Listing 21.6 datacc1.htm—Initial HTML File that Accepts the Query Parameters and Requests Data from the Server

```
<HTML>
<HEAD>
<TITLE>VBS Query1</TITLE>
</HEAD>

Enter search criteria in either the First Name or Last Name Boxes
Standard SQL Server Wild Cards are accepted.
<br>
"First Name"
<Input type=text id=txtFName Value="">
"Last name"
<Input type=text id=txtLName Value="">
<br><br>

<input type=button name="btnGetData" Value="Click to Send Query">

<BODY>
<script Language="VBScript">
<!--
Dim MyQuery
Sub btnGetData_OnClick
```

continues

Listing 21.6 Continued

```
Location = "Quepub1.idc?fname=" & FixEntry(txtFName.Value) _
& "&lname=" & FixEntry(txtLName.Value)
End sub
Function FixEntry(MyText)
Dim lngStart
Dim lngEnd
Dim Buffer
lngStart = 1
Do While lngStart > 0
lngEnd = Instr(lngStart, MyText, "%")
If lngEnd > 0 then
Buffer = Buffer & Mid(mytext, lngStart, lngEnd - lngStart)
Buffer = Buffer & "%25"
lngStart = lngEnd + 1
Else
if len(buffer)>0 then
buffer=buffer & right(mytext,len(mytext)-lngstart+1)
End if
lngstart = 0
End If
Loop
If len(myText) = 0 then buffer = "%25"
If len(buffer) > 0 then
FixEntry = buffer
Else
FixEntry = MyText
End If
End Function
-->
</script>
</BODY>
</HTML>
```

Listing 21.6 is a simple form that allows the user to enter any characters into the text boxes and then submits that data to the .IDX file. To try this application, type in a character or two with a trailing %. This is SQL Server's wildcard character. In Listing 21.6, you will find a VBScript procedure called FixEntry(). The purpose of this function is to search the string passed to it for any '%' wildcard characters, strip them out, and replace them with an HTML equivalent that can be passed through an HTML argument to a server. The resulting Web page from this document is illustrated in Figure 21.3.

In the example in Figure 21.3, let's run a query that will accept any first name, by using only a % character in the first name field and any last name that starts with *Gr* by entering **Gr%** into the last name field. Press the "click to send query" button, and the two parameter fields are sent to the Microsoft Internet Information Server's IDC component. Using the quepub1.idc and quepub1.htx files along with these parameters produces the Web page illustrated in Figure 21.4.

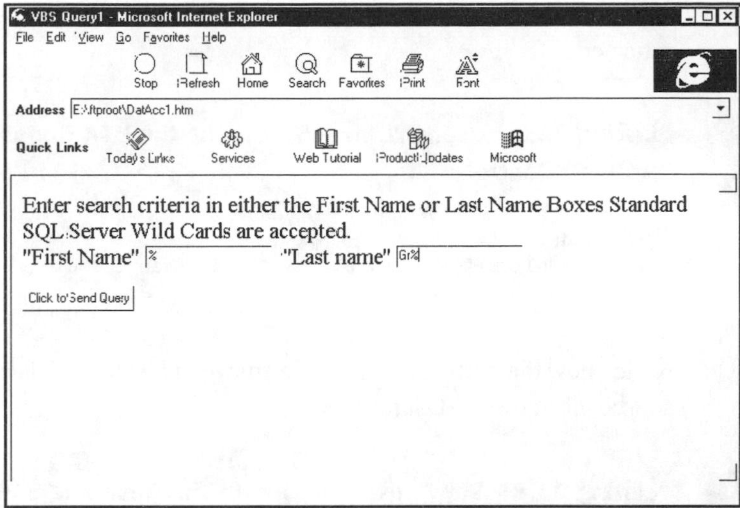

FIG. 21.3
The DacAcc1.htm screen looks like this.

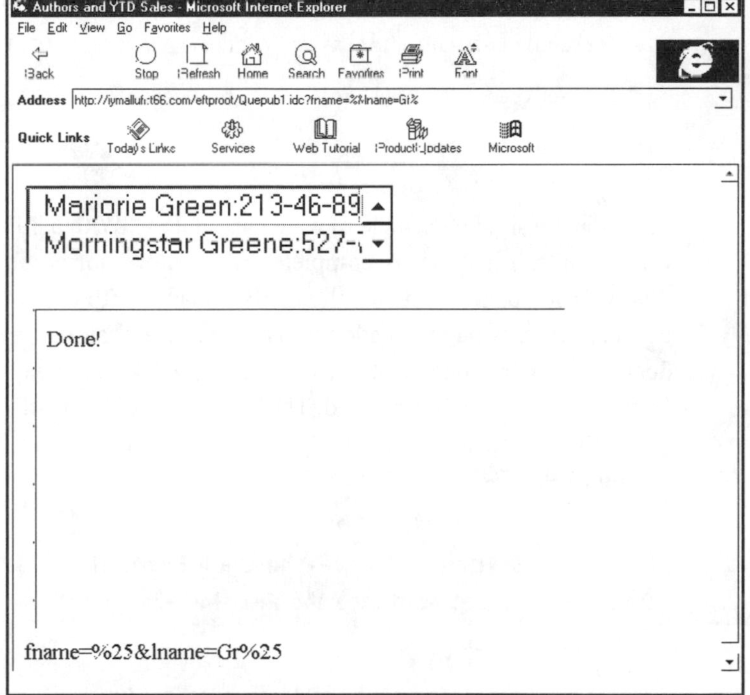

FIG. 21.4
This Web page results from the datacc1.htm to quepub1.idc to quepub1.htx interaction.

The page you see in Figure 21.4 is the result of the quepub1.htx file (refer to Listing 21.5) being fed data from the rowset created through the quepub1.idc file (refer to Listing 21.4). We used an ActiveX ListBox as the container for the data being returned so that users could scroll through the list and easily select the author they seek from the resultset returned.

Listing 21.7 quepub1.htx—Setting up the HTX Code to Load Data into an ActiveX Control

```
<Script Language="VBScript" OnLoad>
<%begindetail%>
ieList.addItem "<%au_fname%>" & " " & "<%au_lname%>" & ":" & "<%au_id%>"
<%enddetail%>
```

Notice how the section of HTX code shown in Listing 21.7 is converted to a final output source file shown in Listing 21.8

Listing 21.8 View Source of Query: The Resulting Source Code from the quepub1.htx Showing the ieList additem Detail

```
<Script Language="VBScript" OnLoad>

ieList.addItem "Marjorie" & " " & "Green" & ":" & "213-46-8915"

ieList.addItem "Morningstar" & " " & "Greene" & ":" & "527-72-3246"

ieList.addItem "Burt" & " " & "Gringlesby" & ":" & "472-27-2349"
```

This is just a simple example of what can be done. With a little imagination, you can create very complex result pages, complete with whatever formatting is needed. Included with this returned page is not only the ListBox loaded with the query results but also a floating frame. A dummy page is loaded into it initially, so that the frame can later accept other documents being loaded into it. When a user clicks on one of the authors returned in the ListBox, another query is called. The click event of the ListBox is used to send another query to the IDC containing the au_id data from the list box. That click event is shown in Listing 21.9.

Listing 21.9 quepub1.htx—The Click Event of the List Box Calling Another Query and Targeting it into the Floating Frame

```
Sub ielist_click
Dim buffer
Buffer = "http://iymalluf.rt66.com/eftproot/QuePub2.idc?authid=" _
& right(ieList.List(ielist.listindex),11)
Floater.Location = buffer
End Sub
```

All we had to do was create a string that included the file path to the .IDC file, a question mark character, and the expected parameter for this query. Continuing with this example, click the 'Marjorie Green' data row, and the resulting parameter is sent to the quepub2.idc file through the MIIS. That file is shown in Listing 21.10, which includes a three-table join.

Listing 21.10 quepub2.idc—The Qupub2.idc File with the Three-Table Join

```
Datasource: Publishers
Username: sa
Template: quepub2.htx
SQLStatement:
+SELECT titles.*,titleauthor.*,Authors.*
+FROM titles LEFT JOIN titleauthor
+ON titles.title_id = titleauthor.title_id
+LEFT JOIN authors
+ON titleauthor.au_id = authors.au_id
+Where authors.au_id ='%authid%'
```

By now you are probably beginning to see that the .IDC files are fairly straightforward, requiring only a datasource, username, template path, and the query that requests rows from the database. The quepub2.idc, while simple, returns many columns of data. In the .HTX file shown in Listing 21.11, we added a few extras in addition to the returning of rows.

Listing 21.11 quepub2.htx—The Template File with Additional HTTP Variable Information

```
<HTML>
<HEAD><TITLE>Authors and YTD Sales</TITLE></HEAD>
<BODY BACKGROUND="/samples/images/backgrnd.gif">
<BODY BGCOLOR="FFFFFF">
<%QUERY_STRING%>
<%ALL_HTTP%>
<br>
<hr>
<%begindetail%>
TITLE: <%title%>
<br>
TYPE: <%type%>
<br>
PRICE: <%price%>
<br>
PUBLISHED: <%pubdate%>
<br>
YTD SALES: <%ytd_sales%>
<br>
NOTES: <%notes%>
<hr>
<br>
```


continues

Listing 21.11 Continued

```
<%enddetail%>
<%IF CurrentRecord EQ 0%>
      There are no publications matching this author
<%EndIf%>
<Script Language="VBScript">
</Script>
</BODY>
</HTML>
```

In the first part of Listing 21.11, we use two variables that are not part of the rowset returned. The `<%Query_String%>` variable returns the parameters sent to the .IDC file by the client page, in this case quepub1.htx. The `<%ALL_HTTP%>` variable returns all of the known information about the current transaction, including the server address, the client address, and the client browser. This information is detailed in Table 21.3. Clicking any name in the ListBox fills the floating frame with the data related to the author selected. Figure 21.5 shows the result of clicking a name.

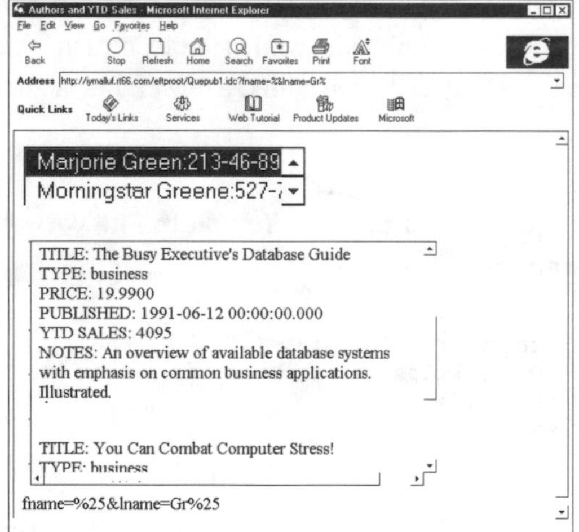

FIG. 21.5 The author information is loaded into the floating frame.

From Here...

The subject of the Miscrosoft Internet Information Server's Internet Database Connector could take a whole book by itself. The intention here was to give you an idea of what can be done using the IDC to build Web pages during runtime on the server side that included VBScript as part of the package. If anything, this chapter hopefully gives you some ideas of your own to try out. You can build very sophisticated VBScript-based template files using the IDC.

CHAPTER 22

VBScript Language Elements

by Ron Schwarz

- **Language features**

  Various language elements make up VBScript.

- **Programming elements by group**

  Programming elements are grouped by category. Learn which statements and functions work together.

- **Tying it all together**

  Learn to use different parts of the language with each other.

- **Make the language work for you**

  Use this chapter as a roadmap to the parts of this book that focus on specific parts of the VBScript language. Copious cross-references make it easy.

This chapter describes VBScript language features. If you're familiar with Visual Basic, you can use this chapter, as well as Chapter 13, "Comparing VBScript, VBA, and Visual Basic," to apprise yourself of the differences you'll run into with VBScript. Many of the language elements named in this chapter are discussed in-depth in other chapters (references to these are provided) and are therefore given light coverage here.

If you're new to Visual Basic programming in general, this chapter will give you a good understanding of the language and capabilities of VB/VBS code. Other chapters in this book focus on structural aspects of scripting and event handling, specific language topics, visual program design using the ActiveX Control Pad and HTML Layout features, and other programming issues; this chapter covers the language and syntax as a whole, and points you to places in the book where specific features are discussed in-depth.

Language elements are covered in groups of topically related methods, statements, functions, and keywords. This chapter is more of a guide than a reference; it presents each group of language features in the context of similarly related features, and the groups are presented in order of typical frequency of use.

Each section contains a table listing related features (with a short description of each) and tutorial information describing the commonly used language elements in each category. ■

Declaration and Array Handling

VBScript contains a variety of language elements pertaining to variable and procedure declarations, and array handling. Table 22.1 lists them.

Table 22.1 Declaration and Array Handling Elements

Keyword	Description
Option Explicit	Requires all variables to be declared before they can be used
Sub	Declaration keyword for Sub procedures
Function	Declaration keyword for Function procedures
Public	Declares a variable or array to be available to all procedures regardless of where it is declared
Private	Declares a variable or array to be local to the script in which it is declared
Dim	Declares a variable or array; scope is determined by placement of Dim statement
ReDim	Resizes an array; can only be used with dynamic arrays
Erase	Clears contents of an array
IsArray	Reports whether a variable is or is not an array
Lbound	Returns lowest element of an array (always 0 in VBScript)
Ubound	Returns highest element of an array

▶ **See** Chapter 15, "VBScript Data Types and Variables," **p. 281** for further discussion of arrays.

▶ **See** Chapter 19, "VBScript Procedures," **p. 355** for in-depth coverage of declaration and procedure-calling issues.

Option

Unlike Visual Basic (which provides options for array base subscript, string comparison modes, and variable declaration scope), the only option implemented in VBScript is Option Explicit. When Option Explicit is selected, a variable must be declared before it can be used, or an error will occur. When Option Explicit is *not* used, a variable will be automatically created the first time it is referenced. (This does not apply to arrays, however; they *must* be explicitly dimensioned prior to use, regardless of Option Explicit settings.)

To use Option Explicit, simply place it as the first statement in your script, before any code or procedures.

While it may seem tempting to avoid using Option Explicit, it's recommended that you include it in anything beyond the simplest of scripts. The safety net it provides more than compensates for the slight inconvenience of having to explicitly declare each variable before use. Remember, VBScript doesn't have the sophisticated analysis and debugging tools that makes Visual Basic development so effortless; with VBScript you need every advantage you can get. Being able to flag bugs caused by simple typos in variable names can save you hours of grief in a single project, and Option Explicit provides that ability.

Procedure Declarations

Sub and Function are used to declare Sub procedures and Functions. A *Sub procedure* is a block of code that is invoked by using its name (as if it were a built-in statement, or method) and following it with any parameters that are declared in the actual Sub.

To declare a Sub procedure, use this syntax:

```
Sub ProcedureName (Arg1, Arg2, Arg3, ...)
```

A procedure named ChangeURL, which accepted one argument named NewURL, would be declared as:

```
Sub ChangeURL (NewURL)
```

To invoke it and pass it a value of "www.microsoft.com", you'd use:

```
ChangeURL "www.microsoft.com"
```

A complete routine might look like Listing 22.1.

Listing 22.1 Example *Sub* Procedure Invocation

```
Sub ChangeURL (NewURL)
   NewURL = Trim(NewURL)
   If NewURL = "" then
      Exit Sub
```

continues

Listing 22.1 Continued

```
    Else
        Location.href = "HTTP://" & NewUrl
    Endif
End Sub
```

In the example in Listing 22.1, we first use Trim to remove any leading and trailing spaces from the NewURL variable. Then we test to see if it's got anything left in it. If the result is " " (an empty string), we exit the Sub procedure.

If the variable is greater than an empty string, we create a new .href for the Location object by combining the "HTTP://" prefix with the contents of NewURL.

The Sub procedure ends with an "End Sub" statement.

While you normally invoke a Sub procedure by typing its name and any required arguments (separated by commas), you may encounter an alternate syntax. The Call statement can be used, in this form:

```
Call AnySubProcedure (arg1, arg2, arg3)
```

The main difference here (apart from the actual inclusion of the *Call* keyword, of course) is the fact that the argument list *must* be surrounded by parentheses. When invoking a Sub procedure *without* the Call statement, you cannot use the parentheses. (The *Call* syntax is included for backward compatibility with versions of the BASIC language that predate the current procedure-name-only invocation style.)

Functions are declared in a similar manner as Sub procedures:

```
Function FunctionName (Arg1, Arg2, Arg3, ...)
```

Invoking a Function is a bit different, however; unlike a Sub procedure, a Function returns a value in its name. Here's a typical Function procedure:

```
Function BuildURL (NewURL)
      BuildURL = "HTTP://" & NewUrl
End Function
```

In this example, we build a URL by passing an address to the function and returning "HTTP://" with the address concatenated. To return the value, we assign it to the function, just as if we were assigning it to a variable. We can combine the preceding two examples and use a Sub and Function procedure to modularize our code, as shown in Listing 22.2.

Listing 22.2 Using *Sub* and *Function* Procedures

```
Sub ChangeURL (NewURL)
   NewURL = Trim(NewURL)
   If NewURL = "" then
      Exit Sub
   Else
      Location.href = BuildURL (NewUrl)
   Endif
End Sub

Function BuildURL (NewURL)
      BuildURL = "HTTP://" & NewUrl
End Function
```

The ChangeURL Sub procedure in Listing 22.2 calls BuildURL and passes the result to the Location.href property. The code is invoked exactly as in the prior ChangeURL example:

```
ChangeURL "www.microsoft.com"
```

Variable Declarations

Three keywords deal with variable declaration: Dim, Public, and Private. Once a variable is declared, the result is identical. The only difference is scope. (*Scope* determines in which context(s) a variable will exist.) When declared Public, a variable will be available in all procedures. When declared Private, it will be limited to the script in which it appears. When declared with Dim, scope is determined by context; if you Dim a variable at the script level (outside a procedure), it will be available to all procedures in that script. If you Dim it within a procedure, it will be local to that procedure.

Here's an example of the three forms of variable declaration:

```
<SCRIPT LANGUAGE=VBScript>
Public UserName
Private Tally

Sub RefreshInfo
   Dim ItemCount
   ...
```

The Public *UserName* variable will be available in all scripts, the Private *Tally* variable will only be available in the script in which it's used, and the *ItemCount* variable will only be available in the *RefreshInfo* procedure.

NOTE As this book goes to press, Public and Private keywords are documented but not yet implemented in the prerelease version of Internet Explorer that is available for testing.

Array Declarations

Arrays are lists of variables. They are created with the same three declaration keywords as variables and are subject to the same scoping rules. Here is a typical array declaration:

```
Dim Age(10)
```

This creates an array named *Age*, with 11 elements (arrays begin with 0). To access a specific element of an array, use it as you would any other variable but include its subscript in parentheses; for example, `Age(5) = YourAge` will assign the value in the variable named YourAge to element 5 of the Age array.

You can create multidimensional arrays. `Dim Phone(100, 4)` will create an array with 101 elements and 5 subelements. For each subscript of the first part, you will be able to have 5 subelements (remember, the first element is 0). So, `Phone(1,3)` will return the fourth phone number for the second "record."

The ReDim keyword can be used to change the size of an array after it's created. There are a couple of caveats:

- You can't change the number of dimensions. (For example, you can't change `Phone(100,4)` to `Phone(100)`.)
- You can only redimension a dynamic array. (A *dynamic array* is dimensioned with empty parentheses—like `Dim Users()`. An array declared with a specific number is known as a *static array*; it can't be fully erased, or resized.)
- Before you can use a dynamic array for the first time, you have to ReDim it.

ReDim uses the same syntax as Dim. It does have one option, however. You can use the Preserve keyword to retain any preexisting contents of the array. (If you make the array smaller, of course, you'll lose anything in the elements that are removed.) To increase the size of an array named Count by 10, you'd use this code:

```
ReDim Count(Ubound(Count) + 10) Preserve
```

The Ubound function returns the number of the highest subscript in an array. So if the array was previously ReDimmed to 100, `Ubound(Count)` would return 100, and `Ubound(Count) + 10` would equal 110, which is what the array would be ReDimmed to in this example.

NOTE VBScript also has an Lbound function, which returns the lowest subscript in an array. However, since all VBScript arrays begin with element 0, it's not of much use.

You can remove a dynamic array with the Erase statement. The following syntax demonstrates how to create and erase a dynamic array:

```
Dim ScratchVars()
ReDim ScratchVars(25)
Erase ScratchVars
```

You *can* use Erase with static arrays; however, it won't remove the array—it will only clear the contents of the elements it contains.

The IsArray function will return True if tested with a variable name, so `IsArray(NameList)` will return True if NameList is an array and False if it's a simple variable.

Comments

Comments are not executed. They are only for human eyes. By commenting your code, you make it easier to understand when you look at it later on. While it's easy to understand your code as you write it, it's amazingly easy to forget what's going on a month or two later when you revisit it. You can place comments in your code by using either Rem or `'` (see Table 22.2).

Table 22.2 Comments

Keyword	Description
Rem	Used at beginning of line to create comment ("Remark")
'	Used anywhere in line, everything beyond is comment

Rem is generally used when entering comments alone on a line, and `'` is used when placing comments at the end of a line of code. (*Rem* is shorthand for *remark*.) Both are shown in the following example:

```
Rem This routine accepts a number and adds it to the running tally.
For C = 1 to Total     'Count through the list
```

The first line is a comment; it has no executable code. The second line consists of a line of code with a comment appended to the end.

Constants

Unlike Visual Basic, VBScript doesn't provide a way to use true Constants. If you need to define a constant, you'll have to use a variable as a pseudo-constant and be very careful to avoid changing it in code. There are, however, some built-in constants, such as *True* and *False*, and the *Empty*, *Nothing*, and *Null* keywords which exhibit constant-like behavior.

True and False contain the values -1 and 0, respectively. They're used when you're testing conditions returned by expressions and various functions. (Throughout this book, you'll see frequent reference to True and False as returned values.)

Empty is a special value used with variables. An Empty variable is one that has been created, but not yet assigned a value. With a numeric value, it is 0; with strings, it's `""`.

Null is another type of special value. It indicates that the variable is not valid. It is not equal to any value, therefore, it's not equal to 0 in a numeric variable nor is it equal to `""` in a string. If any part of an expression is Null, the Null will propagate throughout the expression, and the result will be Null.

Nothing removes an object reference. If you create an object reference with

```
Set Handy=LongFormName.LongControlName
```

you'll be able to refer to `LongFormName.LongControlName` properties by using the `Handy.`*`Property`* format. To remove the Handy reference, use

```
Set Handy=Nothing
```

Assignment

VBScript Assignment Operators are listed in Table 22.3. (The equals sign (=) and the *Let* keyword are fully discussed in Chapter 16, "VBScript Operators," in the "Equality" section.)

Table 22.3 Assignment Operators

Keyword	Description
=	Assigns an expression to a variable
Let	Obsolete statement used at start of assignment
Set	Creates an Object Reference; useful for creating shortcuts to items in the Internet Explorer object hierarchy

Set can be used to assign an object to a variable. The example in Listing 22.3 demonstrates one use of the Set keyword.

On the CD

Listing 22.3 set.htm—Example of Set Operator

```
<HTML>

<TITLE>Set Example</TITLE>
<p>
<FORM NAME="LongFormName">
<INPUT TYPE="TEXT" NAME="LongControlName" SIZE="10">
</FORM>

<SCRIPT language="VBScript">
   Sub Window_OnLoad
      Set Handy=LongFormName.LongControlName
      Handy.Value="It Works!"
   End Sub
</SCRIPT>

</HTML>
```

In Listing 22.3, a Form named *LongFormName* contains a Text control named *LongControlName*. To access the control's Value property, you can either use `LongFormName.LongControlName.Value` or use Set to assign it to a variable. After the Set statement above creates the variable *Handy*, you can use it instead of the longer `LongFormName.LongControlName`, as demonstrated in the example.

It's important to note that you're not creating a new instance of the original object; you're simply assigning a type of alias to it. When you use the variable named Handy in the example, you're really using the actual control in `LongFormName.LongControlName`. When you run the example, you'll see `It works!` in the Text control, indicating that by setting `Handy.Value`, you're really working with the control.

String Handling

Microsoft's Basic language implementations have always been noted for a rich set of string handling features. VBScript carries on with this tradition. Table 22.4 lists the string handling functions implemented in VBScript.

Table 22.4 String Handling Functions

Function	Description
Asc, AscB, AscW	Returns the ASCII value of the first character in the string being evaluated
Chr, ChrB, ChrW	Returns a one-character string representing the numeric value being evaluated

continues

Table 22.4 Continued

Function	Description
Instr, InStrB	Returns the position of a search string within a target string
Len, LenB	Returns the length of a string
LCase	Returns a lowercase representation of a string
UCase	Returns an uppercase representation of a string
Left, LeftB	Returns a specified number of leftmost characters in a string
Right, RightB	Returns a specified number of rightmost characters in a string
Mid, MidB	Returns a specified number of characters from a specified position in a string
Space	Returns a string containing a specified series of space characters
String	Returns a string containing a specified series of any specified character
Ltrim	Returns a string that is a copy of the target string, with all leading spaces removed
Rtrim	Returns a string that is a copy of the target string, with all trailing spaces removed
Trim	Returns a string that is a copy of the target string, with all leading and trailing spaces removed
CStr	Converts number to string
StrComp	Performs a case-sensitive, or case-insensitive comparison on two strings

NOTE Some string functions end with *B* or *W*. These functions are *byte* and *wide* equivalents for the corresponding functions without a suffixed letter. For instance, Len returns the length of a string in characters, but LenB returns the length in bytes. Asc returns a numeric value of a character, and AscW returns the numeric value of a Unicode character.

You'll probably be using the string handling functions extensively in your scripting work.

Asc and *Chr*

Asc and Chr are the inverse of each other. Asc returns the ASCII numeric value of a one-character string, and Chr returns a one-character string representing a numeric ASCII value. (ASCII means American Standard Code for Information Interchange.)

The syntax for Asc is `NumericValue = Asc("A")`, which returns "65." `StringValue = Chr(65)` returns "A."

Instr

To search a string for a sub-string, use the Instr function:

```
Source = "This is a test"
Search = "test"
Found = Instr(Source, Search)
```

Found will contain the position of Search within Source. So if Source contains "This is a test" and Search contains "test", Found will contain "11."

NOTE As this book goes to press, Microsoft documents a third optional parameter for Instr. If Found = Instr(Source, Search, 1) is used, the test will be case-insignificant. However, this option was not functional with the preliminary versions of software available for testing. ■

Len

The Len function returns the length of a string. The syntax is this:

```
StringLength = Len(TestString)
```

LCase and UCase

LCase and UCase are used to respectively return a lowercase or uppercase representation of a target string. So, `UCase("fubar")` will return `FUBAR`.

Left and Right

Left and Right will return a specified number of the leftmost or rightmost characters of a string. For example, `Left(Source, 10)` will return the first 10 characters of Source.

Mid

If you're a Visual Basic programmer, you know that Mid is unique in that it can be used as a function or a statement. VBScript, however, only provides the Function implementation of Mid.

Mid returns a specified numbers of characters of a string, just like Left and Right; however, unlike those functions, it accepts a starting position. So, `Fragment = Mid(Source, 5, 2)` will return the two characters starting with the fifth character of Source.

Space

Space returns a string containing the specified number of space characters. `Space(10)` returns a string consisting of ten spaces.

String

String is similar to Space, but it allows you to specify which character to return. You supply a string or a literal, and a number. So, `String(25, "*")` will return a string consisting of 25 "*" characters. You can alternatively supply an ASCII number instead of a string for the second argument. In that case, `String(10, 32)` will return ten spaces. (32 is the ASCII code for the space character.)

Ltrim, *Rtrim*, and *Trim*

Ltrim, Rtrim, and Trim remove leading, trailing, or leading and trailing spaces from a string. `Ltrim(User)` will return the contents of User, with any leading spaces removed. Rtrim works the same way for trailing spaces, and Trim removes leading *and* trailing spaces.

CStr

CStr returns a string representation of a number. `CStr(5)` will return a string containing "5". CStr is aware of international conversion issues, such as different style decimal separators. Additionally, it will convert Boolean (True/False), Date, and Error values to strings.

StrComp

StrComp is used to compare one string against another. If you know that both strings being compared are of the same case, you can simply use an equal sign to compare. Thus, if `String1 = "Cantaloupe"` and `String2 = "CANTALOUPE"`, testing `If String1 = String2` will fail. StrComp can be used to perform case-significant or case-insignificant tests, by using the syntax: `Test = StrComp(String1, String2, CompareMode)`. If CompareMode is 0 (or, if CompareMode is absent) the test will be case-significant, just like an equal sign test. But if CompareMode is 1, the test will be case-insignificant.

▶ **See** "String Operators," **p. 297**

Control Flow Statements

Table 22.5 presents the control flow statements and their descriptions.

Table 22.5 Control Flow Statements

Statement	Description
Do...Loop	Executes code block while or until a test condition is met
While...Wend	Executes code block while test condition is met
For...Next	Executes code block a specified number of times
If...Then...Else	Executes code block(s) depending on results of test
Select Case	Tests for multiple conditions, executes corresponding Space blocks of code

▶ **See** "Looping Structures," **p. 308** for more about looping and testing structures.

Variant Management/SubTypes

Table 22.6 shows the various variant subtypes.

Table 22.6 Variant Subtypes

Subtype	Description
IsArray	Tests if subtype of variable is Array
IsDate	Tests if variable or expression returns a Date
IsEmpty	Tests if variable is uninitialized
IsNull	Tests if variable is initialized, but does not contain data
IsNumeric	Tests if variable or expression returns a valid number
IsObject	Tests if variable refers an OLE automation object
VarType	Returns a String containing the subtype of a specified variable

VBScript does not have true variable typing; all variables are of the Variant type. However, Variants can contain any variable type as a subtype. When a type (such as String, Date, and so on) is mentioned, it should be understood to refer to a Variant subtype (refer to Table 22.6).

▶ **See** "The Variant's Data Sub-Types," **p. 282**, for a full discussion of data types and programming issues. [Chapter 15, "VBScript Data Types and Variables"]

Math Functions

The math functions provide a variety of trigonometric, logarithmic, and other mathematical capabilities. Table 22.7 lists these functions.

Table 22.7 Math Functions

Function	Description
Atn	Returns the arctangent of a number or expression
Cos	Returns the cosine of a number or expression
Sin	Returns the sine of a number or expression
Tan	Returns the tangent of a number or expression
Exp	Returns e raised to a power from a number or expression
Log	Returns the natural (base e) logarithm of a number or expression
Sqr	Returns the square root of a number or expression
Randomize	Seeds the random number generator
Rnd	Returns a random number

The Atn, Cos, Sin, and Tan trigonometric functions all use the same simple syntax (`keyword(number)`) to return their respective value:

```
Atn(35)
```

The Exp and Log logarithmic functions also use that syntax to return their results, as does the Sqr square root function.

Randomize and Rnd are used for seeding the random number generator and for generating a random number. Using Randomize by itself causes the random number generator to be seeded with the current value in the system timer. You can also place a number or numeric argument after Randomize and use that value as a seed, such as `Randomize 7365`.

To retrieve a random number, use this syntax:

```
RandomNumber = Rnd
```

The variable (in this case, RandomNumber) will contain a random number within the range of 0–1. The Rnd function will accept a number as an optional argument. If you supply one, the following rules are used:

< 0	Always returns the same value, seeded by the supplied number
> 0	The next random number in the sequence created by the random number generator
0	The last random number created by the random number generator

Random Number Trivia

The numbers returned by the random number generator (a built-in part of VBScript) are not *truly* random. Technically, they are referred to as *pseudo-random numbers*. Each time the random number generator is started, it produces a sequence of random numbers. By using Rnd with a negative argument one time before calling Randomize with a seed, you can produce identical "runs" of pseudo-random numbers. (Remember to use the same seed value for Randomize each time also when doing this.)

Even though the number returned by Rnd is limited to the range of 0–1, you can convert this to other ranges. By using the formula `Int((HighRange - LowRange + 1) * Rnd + LowRange)`, you can produce random numbers in any range. (Assign your lowest and highest desired numbers to LowRange and HighRange before calling this formula, and it will return a result in the desired range.)

The following expression returns a random number between 10 and 20:

```
Int((20 - 11) * Rnd + 10)
```

Date and Time Functions

`VBScript` has a wealth of Date and Time functions. Table 22.8 lists those functions.

Table 22.8 Date and Time Functions

Function	Description
Now	Returns the current Date and Time
CDate	Returns a Date type representation of a number or expression
Date	Returns the current Date
DateSerial	Returns a Date type variable (containing the date) representing the Date of a specified Year, Month, and Day

continues

Table 22.8 Continued

Function	Description
DateValue	Returns a Date type variable(containing the date) from a string variable or expression containing text representing a date
Day	Returns the day of month for a specified date
Month	Returns the number of the month for a specified date
Weekday	Returns a number representing the day of the week for a specified date (1 = Sunday, 2 = Monday, and so on)
Year	Returns the year part of a specified date
Time	Returns the current Time
TimeSerial	Returns a Date type variable (containing the time) when provided a specfied time in parameters containing the hour, minute, and second
TimeValue	Returns a Date type variable (containing the time) from a string variable or expression containing text representing a time
Hour	Returns a number representing the Hour of a specified time
Minute	Returns a number representing the Minute of a specified time
Second	Returns a number representing the Second of a specified time

Date returns the current date as a string in the form of `1/1/97`. Time likewise returns the current time, in the form of a string like `12:00:00 PM`. Now returns both date and time in one string, such as `1/1/97 12:00:00 PM`. All three of these functions are used without arguments. Like all functions, you can assign them anywhere it's legal to accept a value, such as a variable or the Value property of a Text control.

DateSerial returns a Date sub-typed variant when passed three arguments (for Year, Month, and Day). `DateSerial(1997, 1, 1)` will return a variable containing the date for `1/1/97`. You can do simple date math by adding (or subtracting) a value to any of these three parameters. So, `DateSerial(1997, 1-5, 3)` will return `8/3/96`.

DateValue also returns a Date sub-typed variant, but it accepts a single string, using many common date formats, such as `4/16/1975` and `11/16/76`. It can also recognize text representations of dates, such as `October 23, 1949` (common abbreviations such as `Oct` are also accepted).

TimeSerial is identical in use to DateSerial, but uses Hour, Minute, and Second in place of Year, Month, and Date. It returns a variable containing the time represented by the combined parameters.

TimeValue is likewise identical in form to DateValue but accepts common time formats (such as `8:00PM` or `20:00`) in its single parameter. It returns a variable containing the time as interpreted from the string supplied in the parameter.

Year, Month, and Day return their respective values when passed a Date. You can use common forms of date, so `Year("Dec 25, 1997")` will return `1997`, for instance.

Hour, Minute, and Second are the time counterparts to the Year, Month, and Day functions, and use the same syntax. They return their respective values when passed any valid time in their parameter.

Conversion Functions

In VBScript, all variables are of Variant type. A variant can hold any type of data. VBScript assigns a subtype to a variant depending on content, context, and by using conversion functions (listed in Table 22.9). In most cases, conversion is automatic and transparent. When you want to override the settings created by the content of a variable, or the context in which it is assigned a value, you can use the conversion functions.

Table 22.9 Conversion Functions

Function	Description
Abs	Returns the Absolute value of a number or expression
Asc	(Described in String Functions)
Chr	(Described in String Functions)
CBool	Evaluates an expression and returns either True or False (if non-zero, True; otherwise, False)
CByte	Returns a Byte type representation of a number or expression
CDate	(Described in Date and Time Functions)
CDbl	Returns a Double precision type representation of a number or expression
CInt	Returns an Integer type representation of a number or expression
CLng	Returns a Long type representation of a number or expression
CSng	Returns a Single precision type representation of a number or expression
CStr	(Described in String Functions)

continues

Table 22.9 Continued

Function	Description
DateSerial	(Described in Date and Time Functions)
DateValue	(Described in Date and Time Functions)
Fix	Same as Int for positive values, but returns next lower whole negative number for negative values
Hex	Returns a String containing a Hexadecimal (base 16) representation of a specified number or expression (the opposite can be accomplished by prefixing a hex number with &H; for instance, &HFF equals 255)
Int	Returns next lower whole number value for positive values, next higher whole negative number for negative values
Oct	Returns a String containing an Octal (base 8) representation of a specified number or expression (the opposite can be accomplished by prefixing a hex number with &O (that is the letter *O*, not a zero); in other words, &O77 equals 63 decimal)
Sgn	Returns the sign of a number or expression; 1 if positive value, -1 if negative value
TimeSerial	(Described in Date and Time Functions)
TimeValue	(Described in Date and Time Functions)

Int, CInt, and Fix are related functions that return integers. For positive numbers, Int and Fix round down to the next lowest integer, and CInt rounds up. For negative numbers, CInt and Fix round up toward zero, and Int rounds down to the next highest negative number. (So, `CInt(-1.6)` returns -2, but `Fix(-1.6)` returns -1, while `Int(-1.4)` returns -2, and `Fix(-1.4)` returns -1.)

Abs returns the Absolute Value (the number without its sign) of a variable. `Abs(1.23)` and `Abs(-1.23)` will both return 1.23.

CBool, CByte, CDbl, CLng, and CSng convert a number to their respective sub-types as described in Table 22.9. They all use the `Result = Keyword(Value)` syntax. So, in the expression `Answer = CBool("True")`, Answer will contain -1.

Hex and Oct return strings containing Hexadecimal and Octal equivalents for decimal arguments. `Hex(255)` returns FF, and `Oct(255)` returns 377 (&hff and &o377 both return 255, as described in Table 22.9).

The Sgn function accepts a single argument and returns either 1 or -1 depending on the sign of the value passed. `Sgn(25)` will return 1, and `Sgn(-25)` will return -1.

Input/Output

The two built-in modal dialogs—InputBox and MsgBox (see Table 22.10)—are useful for times when you need to either notify the user of something out of the ordinary or to obtain a short bit of information via keyboard input.

NOTE *Modal* means that the rest of the application is suspended while the dialog is visible.

Table 22.10 Input/Output

Keyword	Description
MsgBox	Displays short messages and optionally returns a value indicating which of a series of buttons was clicked
InputBox	Accepts text entry and returns it as a String value

MsgBox

MsgBox creates a MessageBox and takes two forms: it can be used as a statement or as a function. In its simplest form, it takes a single string argument and waits until OK is clicked. The following statement:

```
MsgBox "Click me!"
```

will result in a MessageBox with `Visual Basic` in the title bar, `Click me!` in the center, and a single button labeled `OK`. The underlying script that invokes the MessageBox will pause until the user clicks OK.

MsgBox can also be used as a function. When placed on the right side of an equal sign, it will return a value to the variable on the left side. When used as a function, the parameters have to be enclosed in parentheses, as is the case with all function calls.

Optional parameters are available for Buttons, Title, HelpFile, and HelpContext. (For information on creating your own Windows help files, see Que's *Designing Windows Help Systems.*)

This is the MsgBox syntax:

```
MsgBox(Prompt, Buttons, Title, Helpfile, HelpContext)
```

This is a typical invocation of the MsgBox function:

```
Value = MsgBox("Click me!", 4, "A Test", "C:\MyDir\MyApp.hlp", 123)
```

Figure 22.1 shows the MessageBox the preceding expression creates.

Whatever you enter for the Title parameter will appear on top of the MessageBox when it's displayed. It's similar to a form's Caption property in Visual Basic.

Using the Buttons parameter can be a bit tricky. The number you enter determines how many buttons are displayed, how they're labeled, which (if any) icon is displayed on the MessageBox, the default button, and the level of modality. The following tables (22.11 through 22.14) will help you make sense of it.

FIG. 22.1
A MessageBox.

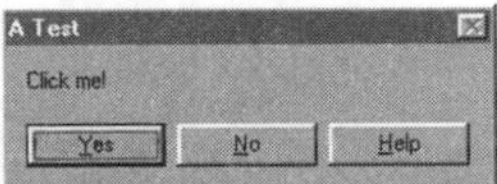

Table 22.11 MessageBox Button Options: Buttons

Value	Button(s)
0	OK
1	OK, Cancel
2	Abort, Retry, Ignore
3	Yes, No, Cancel
4	Yes, No
5	Retry, Cancel

If the value of the Button parameter is 0, or if it's missing, only the OK button will be displayed. Otherwise, the five other options are available.

Table 22.12 MessageBox Button Options: Icons

Value	Icon
16	Critical Message (red circle/"X")
32	Warning Query (Question Mark)
48	Warning Message (Exclamation Mark)
64	Information Message (Small "i")

When the Button value is 0, or is missing, no icon will be displayed.

Table 22.13 MessageBox Button Options: Defaults

Value	Default Button
0	First
256	Second
512	Third
768	Fourth

When only one button is displayed, it will be the default.

Table 22.14 MessageBox Button Options: Modality

Value	Modality
0	Application (Internet Explorer is suspended while MessageBox is displayed)
4096	System (All applications are suspended while MessageBox is displayed)

NOTE System modality is essentially imaginary in 32-bit Windows. It's accepted as part of the API but has no modal effect. Other programs can continue to be accessed, even though the system modal flag is set. It will, however, be an "always on top" window, which means that even though you can continue to interact with other applications, the system-modal MessageBox will always float on top of any other windows on your screen.

You may be wondering how to combine this mess of information spread over several tables into *one* variable. Actually, it's quite simple—you just add them all together! Take one selection from each table, add them together, and you'll have *all* the effects you specified. So, `Value = MsgBox("Click me!", 2 + 32 + 256 + 4096)` will result in a system-modal MessageBox, with three buttons (Abort, Retry, Ignore), the second (Retry) button as the default, and a question-mark icon.

Once you're able to create the type of MessageBox you need, you're most of the way home. The only remaining issue is how to determine which button was clicked after the MsgBox function executes. The answer is always returned by the function, according to Table 22.15.

Table 22.15 MessageBox Return Values

Value	Button
1	OK
2	Cancel
3	Abort
4	Retry
5	Ignore
6	Yes
7	No

If the user presses Enter, the effect will be the same as if the default button was clicked. And pressing Esc will have the same result as clicking Cancel (if present).

InputBox

The InputBox function displays an application-modal dialog and contains a single TextBox that can accept keyboard entry. The syntax is generally similar to MsgBox, with a few differences. Unlike MsgBox, InputBox has no confusing proliferation of numeric options for buttons, icons, and modality. InputBox is pretty straightforward in that regard. The user sees one TextBox, two buttons (OK and Cancel, with OK always the default), and optionally a title and prompt. When OK is clicked, or Enter is pressed, any text contained in the TextBox is returned by the InputBox. When Cancel is clicked, or Esc is pressed, InputBox returns an empty string (`""`).

In addition to the absence of a Buttons parameter, the InputBox function has Default, Xpos, and Ypos parameters. The syntax for InputBox is this:

```
InputBox(Prompt, Title, Default, Xpos, Ypos, Helpfile, HelpContext)
```

You must have at least the Prompt parameter. All others are optional. If you skip a parameter, you need to include a comma in its place. Also, if you use Xpos, you must use Ypos, and vice versa. Similarly, HelpFile, and HelpContext must also be used with each other.

If you want the InputBox to contain any preexisting text when it appears, place the text in the Default parameter. If the Default parameter is absent, the TextBox will be empty when the user first sees it.

Xpos and Ypos determine where the InputBox will appear on the user's screen. You can either enter a value in Twips for each of them, or leave them empty. Xpos determines the distance from the left edge of the screen, and Ypos determines placement relative to the top of the screen. If you do not provide Xpos and Ypos parameters, the InputBox will appear horizontally centered and about 1/3 of the way down from the top of the screen.

NOTE A *Twip* is a typesetting unit of measurement, equal to 1/1440 of an inch.

The following expression creates an input box with a title of *Flavor Entry,* and a prompt asking *Which flavor?* If the user just clicks OK without entering anything, the default value of `Vanilla` will be returned to the `Flavor` variable.

```
Flavor = InputBox("Which flavor?", "Flavor Entry", "Vanilla")
```

Error Object

Error handling in VBScript is a simplified version of that which VB provides. Most of the *On Error* and *Resume* options are unimplemented. On *Error Resume Next,* which forces the code to continue execution when an error occurs, and *On Error Goto 0,* which turns off error handling, are the only error handling statements. The Error Object contains several properties which are set when an error occurs; testing it after an operation that is suspected of causing an error is your only available means of error trapping.

▶ **See** "Error Handling," **p. 317**, for more information on the Error Object.

Operators

Functions and values are useless without a means of assigning, testing, and otherwise accessing them. VBScript implements a rich set of Operators, which provide the ability to assign, compare, combine, and perform math on variables and expressions.

VBScript Operators, (+ - * /\ > < = and so on) are covered in Chapter 16, "VBScript Operators."

Objects

Traditional object management is essentially nonexistent in VBScript. The CreateObject and IsObject keywords are supported, but you cannot create objects when your scripts are used in Internet Explorer, due to security considerations. If you are writing your own script object server (a non-trivial task, unrelated to the subject of Web page automation), you can use these features.

You can include objects written in other languages, such as Visual Basic, if they are properly registered. The <OBJECT> tag provides the means for this.

From Here...

VBScript's implementation of the Basic language is very powerful. Even though it's a subset of the full VB language, its features merit attention and study. The following resources will prove invaluable in helping you to learn the language.

- See Que's *Special Edition Using Visual Basic 4*, and *Visual Basic 4 Expert Solutions*, for extensive information on the Visual Basic language.
- Refer to the *Microsoft Visual Basic Scripting Edition Language Reference,* for exhaustive syntax descriptions and requirements of all statements, functions, and methods.
- See Chapter 11, "Designing VBScript Applications," to see how to use the language elements to create script-enabled pages.
- See Chapter 15, "VBScript Data Types and Variables," for information on variant sub-type issues.
- See Chapter 16, "VBScript Operators," for coverage of Arithmetic, String, Comparison, and Logical operators.
- See Chapter 17, "VBScript Control of Flow and Error Handling," which delves into the looping and testing structures, and the Error Object.
- See Chapter 19, "VBScript Procedures," for more information on declarations and procedures.

CHAPTER 23

Microsoft SQL Server Web Extensions

by Ibrahim Malluf

About the new Web extensions to SQL Server 6.5

These extensions come in the form of three stored procedures; sp_makewebvtask, sp_dropwedtask, and sp_runwebtask.

About using the Web Assistant, a new wizard supplied with SQL Server 6.6

The wizard enables you to create static web pages from your SQL Server databases.

How to create custom template files for the SQL Server 6.5 Web extensions

These extensions include VBScript as part of those templates.

Microsoft has embraced the Internet with enthusiasm, as witnessed by the explosion of new products directly targeted at the Internet and by the revamping of existing products to accommodate the Internet. SQL Server is no exception to this drive by Microsoft to place its product line in the forefront of Internet development. Besides the MS Internet Information Server's IDC, which allows for interactive data operations, Microsoft has added a set of extensions to SQL-Server itself that provide a means for easily publishing your data on the Internet. They are called the SQL Server 6.5 Web Extensions. ■

Introducing the SQL Server 6.5 Web Extensions

The core of this Web publishing capability is the addition of three new stored procedures: sp_dropwebtask, sp_makewebtask, and sp_runwebtask. By using these three new stored procedures, you can generate HTML Web pages. You can generate these pages on demand, at regular timed intervals, or from triggers designed to react to the changes of critical data. There is even a Web Assistant tool to help you create these pages, which I will discuss later in the chapter. For now let's go over each of these new procedures.

Creating Web Tasks by Using *sp_makewebtask*

The sp_makewebtask creates a task in SQL Server that makes HTML pages from a set of properties described in the procedures syntax. Listing 23.1 shows this syntax. I am expecting that most of you reading this chapter have a fair knowledge of SQL Server's stored procedure syntax; so I'll just go over the parts that are really HTML page specific. More detailed information is available using the SQL Server's Books Online or the What's New In SQL Server 6.5 manual. The parameter specifications I am showing here come from there. I added additional comments and modifications when I found things to be a little more flexible than described in the original documentation.

Listing 23.1 The *sp_makewebtask* Syntax

```
sp_makewebtask {@outputfile = 'outputfile', @query = 'query'}
[, [@fixedfont = fixedfont,] [@bold = bold,] [@italic = italic,]
[@colheaders = colheaders,] [@lastupdated = lastupdated,]
[@HTMLHeader = HTMLHeader,] [@username = username,]
[@dbname = dbname,] [@templatefile = 'templatefile',]
[@webpagetitle = 'webpagetitle',] [@resultstitle = 'resultstitle',]
[[@URL = 'URL', @reftext = 'reftext'] ¦
[@table_urls = table_urls, @url_query = 'url_query',]]
[@whentype = whentype,] [@targetdate = targetdate,]
[@targettime = targettime,]
[@dayflags = dayflags,] [@numunits = numunits,] [@unittype = unittype,]
[@procname = procname, ] [@maketask = maketask,] [@rowcnt = rowcnt,]
[@tabborder = tabborder,] [@singlerow = singlerow,] [@blobfmt = blobfmt]]
```

The following list explains the parameters in more detail:

- @outputfile is the path where the generated HTML file should be stored. This can be a UNC name if the file is to be created on a remote computer. This parameter is required and must be unique for each task created with sp_makewebtask. The *outputfile* variable is of *varchar* datatype and has a maximum of 255 characters.

- `@query` specifies the query to be run and is a required parameter. The results of the query will be displayed in the HTML document in a table format when the task is run with `sp_runwebtask` unless your template file uses a different scheme. Multiple SELECT queries can be specified and will result in multiple rowsets returned to the `@outputfile`. The *`@query`* parameter is of *`text`* datatype.
- `@colheaders` determines whether the query results are displayed with column headers (1) or no column headers (0). Column headers (1) is the default. The *`colheaders`* variable is of *`tinyint`* datatype.
- `@lastupdated` determines whether the generated HTML document displays a Last Updated: timestamp indicating the last updated date and time (1) or no timestamp (0). Timestamp (1) is the default. The timestamp appears one line before the query results in the HTML document. The *lastupdated* variable is of *tinyint* datatype.
- `@HTMLHeader` specifies the HTML formatting code for displaying the text contained in the `@resultstitle` variable. The *HTMLHeader* variable is of *tinyint* datatype. These are the values.

Value	HTML Formatting Code
1	H1
2	H2
3	H3
4	H4
5	H5
6	H6

- `@templatefile`, an optional parameter, specifies the path of the template file used to generate the HTML document. This is also where the VBScript programmer can really provide powerful adaptions to the standard output usually generated by SQL Server 6.5. While I am including the description of output here that Microsoft uses, I show you later in the chapter how to bypass the need to display the row data in tables and instead use that data in other ways. The template file contains information about formatting characteristics for HTML documents and contains the tag `<%insert_data_here%>`, which indicates the position to add the query results in an HTML table. The *templatefile* variable is of *varchar* datatype and has a maximum of 255 characters If `@templatefile` is specified, the following parameters are ignored when the HTML file is generated; `@bold`, `@singlerow`, `@fixedfont`, `@tabborder`, `@HTMLHeader`, `@table_url`, `@italic`, `@URL`, `@lastupdated`, `@url_quer`, `@reftext`, `@webpagetitl`, and `@resultstitle`. There are two ways to specify the location of the results of a query in a template file:

Include the tag `<%insert_data_here%>`, which indicates the position to add the query results in an HTML table. There are no spaces between the less than sign (<) and the "%i" of `%insert` or between the "e%" of `here%` and the greater than sign (>).

Specify a complete row format between the keywords `<%begindetail%>` and `<%enddetail%>` including `<TR>`, `</TR>`, `<TD>`, and `</TD>` HTML tags. For each column to display in the results set, include the tag `<%insert_data_here%>` inside the row format keywords. Specifying the complete row format produces a more precise layout of the results set. When used with this complete row format, `@colheaders` is ignored.

- `@webpagetitle` is the title of the HTML document which is place between the `<TITLE>...</TITLE>` tags. The default is SQL Server Web Assistant. The *`webpagetitle`* variable is of *`varchar`* datatype and has a maximum of 255 characters.
- `@resultstitle` specifies the title displayed above the query results in the HTML document. The default title is Query Results. The *`resultstitle`* variable is of *`varchar`* datatype and has a maximum of 255 characters.
- `@URL` provides a hyperlink to another HTML document. The hyperlink is placed after the query results and at the end of the HTML document. This parameter is used to provide links from your document to other documents. If this parameter is specified, `@reftext` must also be specified, and `@table_urls` and `@url_query` cannot be specified. The *`URL`* variable is of *`varchar`* datatype and has a maximum of 255 characters. If `@table_urls = 1`, then `@url_query` must be included to specify the query to be executed for retrieving hyperlink information, and `@URL` and `@reftext` cannot be specified. Information is specified either in `@URL` and `@reftext`, or in `@url_query` and `@table_urls`.
- `@reftext` is the the hyperlink text that describes to what HTML document the hyperlink should take the user. The hyperlink text describes the destination and the hyperlink address comes from the URL in the `@URL` parameter. The *`reftext`* variable is of *`varchar`* datatype and has a maximum of 255 characters.
- `@table_urls` determines whether hyperlinks are be included on the HTML document and whether the hyperlinks will come from a SELECT statement executed on Microsoft SQL Server. A value of 0 (the default) indicates that there is no query that will generate hyperlinks for the HTML. `@URL` and `@reftext` may still be specified for a single hyperlink. A value of 1 indicates that a list of hyperlinks will be created by using `@url_query`. The *`table_urls`* variable is of *`tinyint`* datatype. If `@table_urls = 1`, then `@url_query` must be included to specify the query to be executed for retrieving hyperlink information, and `@URL` and `@reftext` cannot be specified. Information is specified either in `@URL` and `@reftext`, or in `@url_query` and `@table_urls`.

- @url_query is the SELECT statement used to create the URL and its hyperlink text. URLs and hyperlink text come from a SQL Server table. With this parameter, it is possible to generate multiple URLs with associated hyperlinks. Use @url_query with @table_urls. The *url_query* variable is of *varchar* datatype with a maximum of 255 characters. The *url_query* variable must return a results set containing two columns: The first column is the address of a hyperlink and the second column describes the hyperlink. The number of hyperlinks inserted into the HTML document equals the number of rows returned by executing @url_query.
- @whentypen is a required parameter that specifies when to run the task that creates the HTML document. The *whentype* variable is of *tinyint* datatype. The possible values are described in Table 23.1.

Table 23.1 The Values and Their Meanings of the *@whentypen* Parameter

Value	Description
1	Create page now. The web task will be created, executed immediately, and deleted immediately after execution. This is the default.
2	Create page later. The stored procedure for creating the HTML document will be created immediately, but execution of the web task is deferred until the date and time specified by @targetdate and @targettime (optional). If no @targettime is specified, the web task will be executed at 12:00 a.m. @targetdate is required when @whentype = 2. This web task will be deleted automatically after the targeted date and time has passed.
3	Create page every *n* day(s) of the week. The HTML document will be created on day(s) specified in @dayflags and at the time specified by @targettime (optional), beginning with the date in @targetdate. If no @targettime value is specified, the default is 12:00 A.M. The @targetdate parameter is required when @whentype = 3. The day(s) of the week are specified in the @dayflags parameter. More than one day of the week can be specified with the @dayflags parameter. Web tasks created with @whentype = 3 will not be deleted automatically and continue to run on the specified day(s) of the week until the user deletes them by using sp_dropwebtask.
4	Create page every *n* minutes, hours, days, or weeks. The HTML document is created every *n* time period beginning with the date and time specified in @targetdate and @targettime (optional). If no @targettime is specified, the Web task will be executed at 12:00 A.M. The @targetdate parameter is required in this case. The task will run automatically every *n* minutes, hours, days, or weeks as specified by the @numunits and @unittype parameters. The tasks will run until the user deletes them by using sp_dropwebtask.

continues

Table 23.1 Continued

Value	Description
5	Create page upon request. The procedure is created without automatic scheduling. The user creates a HTML document by running `sp_runwebtask` and deletes it only by using `sp_dropwebtask`.
6	Create page now and later. The HTML document is created immediately and re-created according to `@whentype` = 2.
7	Create page now and every *n* day(s) of the week. The HTML document is created immediately and re-created according to `@whentype` = 3, except no `@targetdate` is required.
8	Create page now and periodically thereafter. The HTML document is created immediately and re-created according to `@whentype` = 4, except no `@targetdate` is required.
9	Create page now and upon request. The HTML document is created immediately and re-created according to `@whentype` = 5. The task must be deleted manually.

While not a comprehensive description of the `sp_makewebtask`, it is enough to get us started with the examples that will be provided later. I would like to make note of the fact that a `whentype()` other than 1 will result in a task being stored as a repeatable task within your database that will be called according to the specified `@whentyen`. To remove this task you will need to use the `sp_dropwebtask` stored procedure or directly delete it from the tasks list.

Using the *sp_dropwebtask* to Remove Webtasks

The `sp_dropwebtask` is a much simpler stored procedure than the preceding one. Its purpose is simpler as well. It merely deletes a previously defined Web task that was created by the `sp_makewebtask` stored procedure. The syntax is shown in Listing 23.2.

```
sp_dropwebtask {@procname = procname ¦ @outputfile = outputfile
➥¦ @procname = procname, @outputfile = outputfile}
```

Parameter	Definition
`@outputfile`	Specifies the name of the web task to be deleted. The *`outputfile`* variable is of *`varchar`* datatype and has a maximum of 255 characters.

@procname	Specifies the name of the web task procedure to delete. The named procedure describes the query for the web task. The *procname* variable is of *varchar* datatype and has a maximum of 28 characters.

Using *sp_runwebtask* to Specifically Run a Previously Created Web Task

```
sp_runwebtask {@procname = procname ¦ @outputfile = outputfile ¦
```

Parameter	Definition
@procname = *procname*, @outputfile = *outputfile*} where @outputfile	Specifies the name of the web task to run. The outputfile variable is of varchar datatype and has a maximum of 255 characters.
@procname	Specifies the name of the web task procedure to run. The named procedure defines the query for the web task. The procname variable is of varchar datatype and has a maximum of 28 characters.

Using the SQL Server Web Assistant—for the Faint of Heart

Does the prospect of directly using the sp_makewebtask stored procedure intimidate you? Relax! The Web Assistant is a wizard-type program that provides a step-by-step interface for creating standard HTML pages from your database. The Web Assistant uses Transact-SQL queries, stored procedures, and extended stored procedures as the foundation for the generated HTML pages. You can let the Web Assistant design an HTML page that includes a table containing all the data in standard table rows for you. The alternative is to provide a template file that contains a custom format for the creation of your HTML pages. Figure 23.1 shows the opening screen of the Web Assistant. In order to use the Web Assistant, you need to have sufficient privileges to create procedures, files, and select privileges on columns. To run Web Assistant double-click the Web Assistant icon in the SQL Server program group.

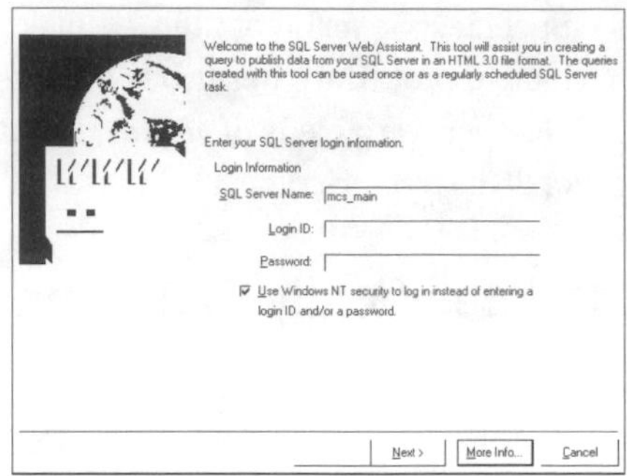

FIG. 23.1
The opening screen for the Web Assistant.

When starting the Web Assistant, specify the server that contains the database and provide either a logon id, and password, or alternatively select the logon security of NT itself. In Figure 23.1, you can see that I chose the latter. Like all other Wizards, you select the Next button to proceed on to the next step. The Web assistant logs on to the server and presents you with a window that gives you a choice of three different ways to construct your HTML pages.

Interactively Creating a Query

To interactively create a query from which your HTML page will be built, follow these steps:

1. From the query screen, select "Build a Query" from a Database Hierarchy option.
2. From the database treeview at the bottom of the window, select and expand your database to get to the tables and columns you want to include. To expand a database object, click the plus sign (+) next to it.
3. From the expanded database list, select the table(s) to use in your query. This option is equivalent to a SELECT * FROM *table_name* statement.
4. To select individual columns, expand the table selection. All columns are selected by default. To cancel a selection, clear the column(s).
5. In the Do You Want Any Additional Criteria… box, type additional clauses for the query, such as WHERE or ORDER BY.
6. To continue, choose the Next button. To exit, choose the Cancel button.

While this method works and is real easy to use for those who are novices with Transact-SQL, I found it to be an awkward and limiting interface for those who are competent in writing their own SQL queries. The Build a Query from a Database Hierarchy window is shown in Figure 23.2.

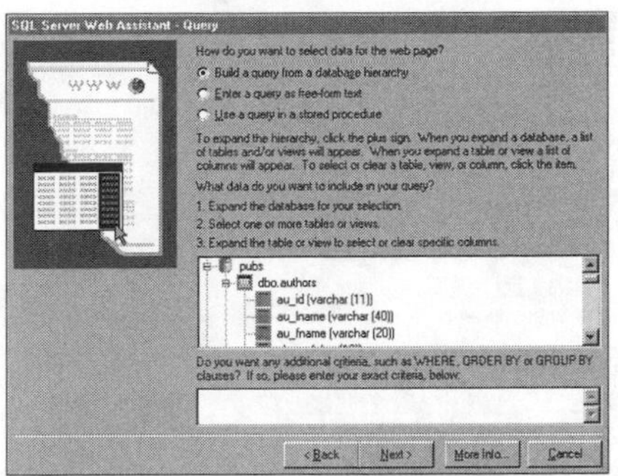

FIG. 23.2
Using the Web Assistant's Build A Query from a Database Hierarchy option.

Entering a Query as Freeform Text Option

With this option, there are no training wheels; you have to create your query as you see fit and make sure that it will act as you desire. Of course, with this option you can create a rowset that can be as complicated as your needs require, without restraints. In the example I am going to use here, I developed and tested the queries in ISQL/w, a utility program that comes with SQLServer (see fig. 23.3).

Looking at the Query window in Figure 23.3, you can see that I have two Select type queries in the window. The Web Assistant treats these as two table sets in the resulting HTML page. All I need to do is cut and paste the perfected query into the Web Assistant's Freeform Query text window, as shown in Figure 23.4. Listing 23.2 shows the query that I developed for this chapter.

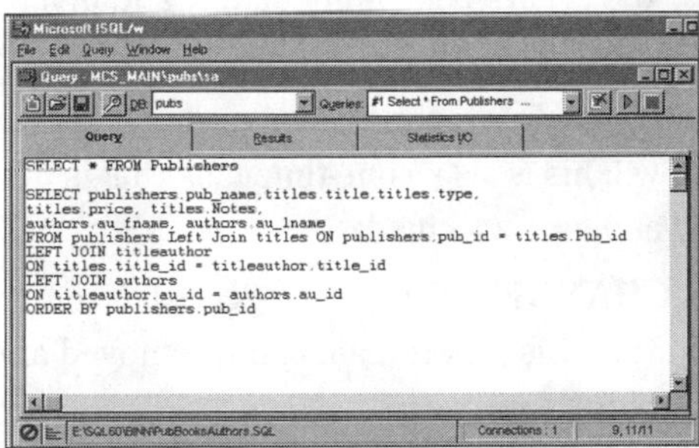

FIG. 23.3
Using ISQL/w to create queries.

Listing 23.2 Multi Select Query that Results in Two Rowsets Being Returned

```
SELECT * FROM Publishers

SELECT publishers.pub_name,titles.title,titles.type,
titles.price, authors.au_fname, authors.au_lname
```

continues

Listing 23.2 Continued

```
FROM publishers Left Join titles ON publishers.pub_id = titles.Pub_id
LEFT JOIN titleauthor
ON titles.title_id = titleauthor.title_id
LEFT JOIN authors
ON titleauthor.au_id = authors.au_id
ORDER BY publishers.pub_id
```

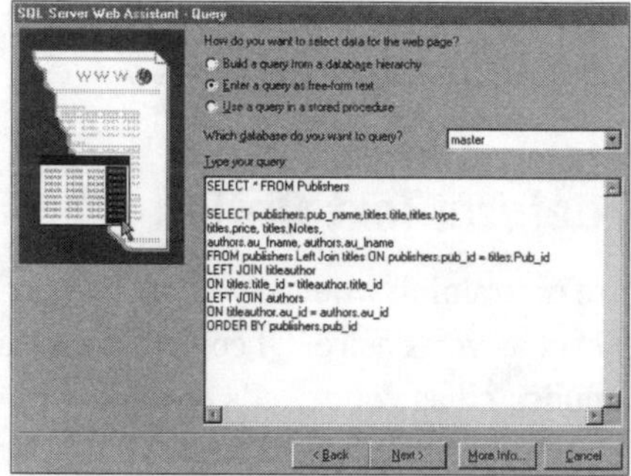

FIG. 23.4
The perfected Transact-Sql Query pasted from ISQL/w into the Web Assistant.

Scheduling a Web Page Task

With the query now pasted into the Web Assistant, I move on to the next window, which includes a single drop down box titled Scheduling Options. There are five choices that determine the life span of your Web page task; they are described in the following list:

- **NOW** Creates the HTML page immediately and deletes the task from the database when finished. This is a one-time task.
- **LATER** Creates the HTML page at a later date & time that you specify in an argument window. This is also a one-time task that is deleted immediately after it runs on the day and time specified.
- **WHEN DATA CHANGES** Creates triggers based on your selection of tables or columns to monitor. This task remains until removed and repeats every time that one of the triggers is called.
- **ON CERTAIN DAY OF THE WEEK** The task executes on the specified days of the week until the task is dropped.
- **ON A REGULAR BASIS** The task repeats on a regular schedule of *n* minutes, hours, days, or weeks. The task repeats until dropped from the task list.

This is a very flexible system for scheduling Web page updates. You can schedule one-time tasks, triggered tasks, or regular timed schedules. Figure 23.5 shows the Web Assistant window in the When Data Changes mode. The format of this window changes depending on your selection of a scheduling option.

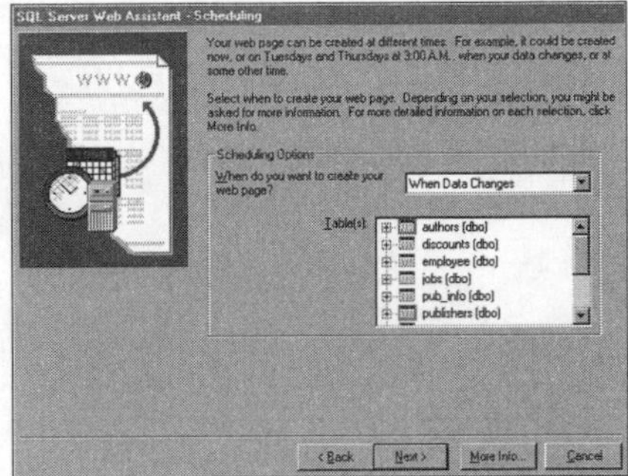

FIG. 23.5
Setting a scheduling option in the Web Assistant.

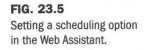

Using File Options with the Web Assistant

The next Web Assistant page, after scheduling, is the Files Options page. Of course the first option is the final location path of the HTML page to be generated. You need to provide a fully qualified path, or a UNC path for the page to which you are writing. In the next option, you decide if you want to use a template file. I will go into more detail on this option in the "Building a VBScript-Based Web Page" later in this chapter. For now I'll leave it unchecked and the Web Assistant will progress on to some basic page customizations. On the File Options page, there is also an option for including one URL link, or several links from a table in the database. Using this option places one or more URL links at the bottom of the resulting Web page. You can view the File Options page in Figure 23.6.

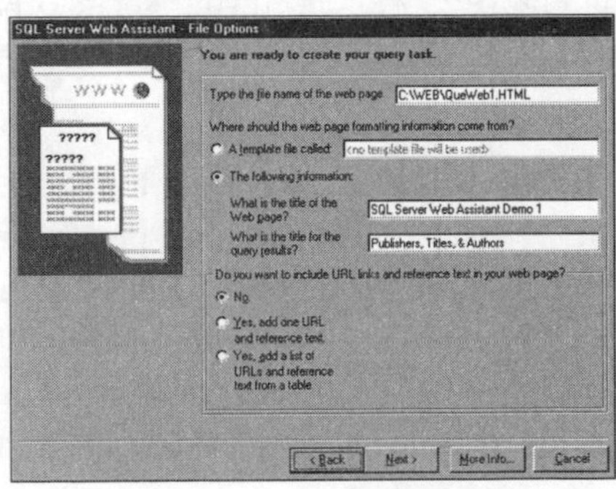

FIG. 23.6
Filling in the File Options of the Web Assistant.

Formatting the Page with the Web Assistant

Don't get excited; there are not a lot of options here. You can select a header type for the page title from a drop down list that includes H1 to H6. You can also select a fixed or proportional font, and bold or italic text for the output data. You can also add a date-time stamp to the top of the page and allow column names for the data tables. Figure 23.7 shows the resulting HTML page from the supplied query.

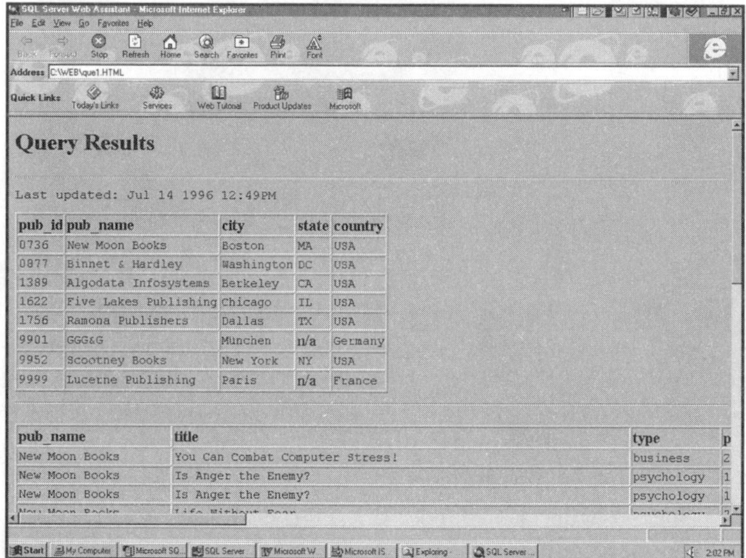

FIG. 23.7
The HTML page made by the Web Assistant shown in Explorer 3.0b1.

Building a VBScript-Based Web Page

If the Web page shown in Figure 23.7 knocked your socks off and met with your ideas of what a Web page should look like, move on to the next chapter because you are done here.

Still reading? Okay, let's build a real Web page using the Web Assistant. There are only two things you have to do: write a template file, and specify that file in the File Options page. In this example, I want to have a ComboBox loaded with publisher names. When I select a publisher from the ComboBox, I want a book printed by that publisher to appear in the text boxes below. The first thing we have to do is create the query that drives the page. That query is in Listing 23.2 shown earlier in the chapter. The next step is to create a template that the Web Assistant will use to make this page. The first part of the template's code populates the template with the ActiveX controls that will contain the data and lay out the visible part of the HTML page. This part is contained in Listing 24.3.

On the CD

Listing 23.3 QUEWEB2.TPL—The Layout Portion of the Template File Including the ActiveX Control Declarations

```
<HTML>

<HEAD>

<TITLE>SQL Server Web Assistant Demo 2</TITLE>

</HEAD>

<BODY>
<OBJECT ID="ieList" WIDTH=1 HEIGHT=1
 CLASSID="CLSID:8BD21D20-EC42-11CE-9E0D-00AA006002F3">
    <PARAM NAME="ScrollBars" VALUE="3">
    <PARAM NAME="DisplayStyle" VALUE="2">
    <PARAM NAME="Size" VALUE="5151;811">
    <PARAM NAME="MatchEntry" VALUE="0">
    <PARAM NAME="FontCharSet" VALUE="0">
    <PARAM NAME="FontPitchAndFamily" VALUE="2">
    <PARAM NAME="FontWeight" VALUE="0">
</OBJECT>
<OBJECT ID="ieCombo" WIDTH=391 HEIGHT=24
 CLASSID="CLSID:8BD21D30-EC42-11CE-9E0D-00AA006002F3">
    <PARAM NAME="VariousPropertyBits" VALUE="746604571">
    <PARAM NAME="DisplayStyle" VALUE="3">
    <PARAM NAME="Size" VALUE="10336;635">
    <PARAM NAME="MatchEntry" VALUE="1">
    <PARAM NAME="ShowDropButtonWhen" VALUE="2">
    <PARAM NAME="FontHeight" VALUE="200">
    <PARAM NAME="FontCharSet" VALUE="0">
    <PARAM NAME="FontPitchAndFamily" VALUE="2">
    <PARAM NAME="FontWeight" VALUE="0">
</OBJECT>
<br>
<br>
TITLE:
<BR>
<INPUT TYPE=TEXT NAME="txtTitle" Size=100>
<BR>
TYPE:
<BR>
<INPUT TYPE=TEXT NAME="txtType" Size=100>
<BR>
PRICE:
<BR>
<INPUT TYPE=TEXT NAME="txtPrice" Size = 100>
<BR>
AUTHOR:
<BR>
<INPUT TYPE=TEXT NAME="txtName" Size = 100>
```

The ComboBox and ListBox need to be populated with the rowsets returned from the query. I should note here that a ListBox is being used to receive data in place of a data array. At the time of writing this book, arrays were not yet working in VBScript. By the time you read this, they should be working, which will make some of the contortions being performed here unnecessary. Anyway, what I do is load all of the query results into these two controls separating the fields with a semicolon. Use the `<%insert_data_here%>` placeholder to mark where the data fields should be placed. The fields will be filled in the order that the query requests them in the `Select` part of the query. Take a look at that code now in Listing 23.4.

Listing 23.4 QUEWEB2.TPL—The Code that Inserts the Query's Data into the ActiveX Controls

```
<SCRIPT LANGUAGE="VBSCRIPT">
Dim Pubname
Dim AllData
<%begindetail%>
PubName = "<%insert_data_here%>" & ";" & "<%insert_data_here%>"
ieCombo.additem PubName
<%enddetail%>
<%begindetail%>
ielist.additem "<%insert_data_here%>" & ";" & "<%insert_data_here%>"  _
& ";" & "<%insert_data_here%>" & ";" & "<%insert_data_here%>"  _
& ";" & "<%insert_data_here%>" & ";" & "<%insert_data_here%>"
<%enddetail%>
```

The `<%begindetail%><%enddetail%>` pair mark off the boundaries of a given rowset. That means that the procedure will iterate through all of the rows returned and place the data in that rowset repeatedly, along with what ever other code is between those markers, in the resulting file. To understand what I mean, look at the corresponding section in the resulting HTML page in Listing 23.5.

Listing 23.5 QUEWEB2.HTML—The Resulting Section of Code Returned by the *sp_makeweb* Procedure

```
<SCRIPT LANGUAGE="VBSCRIPT">
ieCombo.additem "0736" & ";" & "New Moon Books"

ieCombo.additem "0877" & ";" & "Binnet & Hardley"

ieCombo.additem "1389" & ";" & "Algodata Infosystems"

ieCombo.additem "1622" & ";" & "Five Lakes Publishing"
```

```
ieCombo.additem "1756" & ";" & "Ramona Publishers"

ieCombo.additem "9901" & ";" & "GGG&G"

ieCombo.additem "9952" & ";" & "Scootney Books"

ieCombo.additem "9999" & ";" & "Lucerne Publishing"
...
...
```

What you see in Listing 23.5 are the results of the first `<%begindetail%><%enddetail%>` pair. Finally to complete our template file, add the VBScript code that parses the data into its component parts and loads those parts into the TextBoxes. There is also a click event of the `ieCombo` that calls the parsing procedure. It's all in Listing 23.6.

Listing 23.6 QUEWEB2.TPL—The *click* Event and Parsing Procedures

```
Sub ieCombo_Onclick
    SeparateData
End sub

Sub SeparateData
Dim lngStart
Dim lngEnd
Dim strItems
Dim strName
strItems = ielist.list(ieCombo.ListIndex)
lngStart = 1
   lngEnd = instr(lngStart,strItems,";")
   txtTitle.Value = mid(strItems,lngStart,lngEnd-lngStart)
   lngStart=lngEnd + 1

   lngEnd = instr(lngStart,strItems,";")
   txtType.Value = mid(strItems,lngStart,lngEnd-lngStart)
   lngStart=lngEnd + 1

   lngEnd = instr(lngStart,strItems,";")
   txtPrice.Value = mid(strItems,lngStart,lngEnd-lngStart)
   lngStart=lngEnd + 1

   lngEnd = instr(lngStart,strItems,";")
   strName = mid(strItems,lngStart,lngEnd-lngStart)
   lngStart=lngEnd + 1
   lngEnd = instr(lngStart,strItems,";")
   strName = strName & " " & mid(strItems,lngStart,lngEnd-lngStart)
   lngStart=lngEnd + 1
   txtName = strName
End Sub
</SCRIPT>
</BODY>
</HTML>
```

After this template file is stored include the template file in the Web Assistant's Option page by specifying the fully qualified path to it. After completing the remaining steps of the Web Assistant's process, the page will be created by SQL Server. That page will look like the one in Figure 23.8.

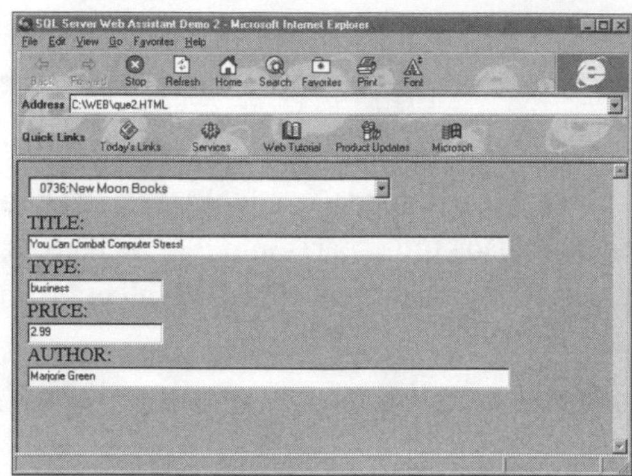

FIG. 23.8
The queweb2.html page displayed in Explorer 3.0b1.

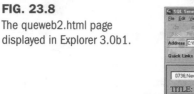

The above example shows how the Web Assistant can help you to create your Web pages. As another example, using only the `sp_makewebtask` procedure, I'll show how you can construct procedures that will do the same thing without the Web Assistant. First I'll make a slightly prettier template file that uses a table to contain the detail `TextBoxes`. The code in Listing 23.7 shows that template file.

Listing 23.7 SQL6WEB.TPL—A Template File Using a Table and Text Box Combination to Display Data

```
<HTML>

<HEAD>

<TITLE>SQL Server Multiple Queries with Template Web Sample</TITLE>

<BODY>

<H1>Books For Sale</H1>
<HR>
<OBJECT ID="ieList" WIDTH=1 HEIGHT=1
 CLASSID="CLSID:8BD21D20-EC42-11CE-9E0D-00AA006002F3">
    <PARAM NAME="ScrollBars" VALUE="3">
    <PARAM NAME="DisplayStyle" VALUE="2">
    <PARAM NAME="Size" VALUE="5151;811">
    <PARAM NAME="MatchEntry" VALUE="0">
    <PARAM NAME="FontCharSet" VALUE="0">
    <PARAM NAME="FontPitchAndFamily" VALUE="2">
    <PARAM NAME="FontWeight" VALUE="0">
</OBJECT>
```

```
<OBJECT ID="ieCombo" WIDTH=391 HEIGHT=24
 CLASSID="CLSID:8BD21D30-EC42-11CE-9E0D-00AA006002F3">
    <PARAM NAME="VariousPropertyBits" VALUE="746604571">
    <PARAM NAME="DisplayStyle" VALUE="3">
    <PARAM NAME="Size" VALUE="10336;635">
    <PARAM NAME="MatchEntry" VALUE="1">
    <PARAM NAME="ShowDropButtonWhen" VALUE="2">
    <PARAM NAME="FontHeight" VALUE="200">
    <PARAM NAME="FontCharSet" VALUE="0">
    <PARAM NAME="FontPitchAndFamily" VALUE="2">
    <PARAM NAME="FontWeight" VALUE="0">
</OBJECT>

<br>
<br>
<TABLE BORDER=5>
<TR BGCOLOR="YELLOW">
<TH Size = 35>Table Name</TH>
<TH Size = 35>Table Data</TH>
</TR>
<TR>
<TD BGCOLOR="TAN">AUTHOR ORDER</TD>
<TD>
<Input Type=Text Size=30 ID="AUTHORD" VALUE="TEST">
</TD></TR>
<TR>
<TD BGCOLOR="TAN">AUTHOR NAME</TD>
<TD>
<Input Type=Text Size=30 ID="AuthName" VALUE="TEST">
</TD></TR>
<TR>
<TD BGCOLOR="TAN">PRICE OF BOOK</TD>
<TD>
<Input Type=Text Size=30 ID="AUTHPrice" VALUE="TEST">
</TD></TR>
<TR>
<TD BGCOLOR="TAN">GROSS SALES</TD>
<TD>
<Input Type=Text Size=30 ID="AUTHSales" VALUE="TEST">
</TD></TR>
<TR>
<TD BGCOLOR="TAN">PUBLISHER ID</TD>
<TD>
<Input Type=Text Size=30 ID="AUTHPubID" VALUE="TEST">
</TD></TR>
</TABLE>
<P>
<Script Language="VBScript">
blnLoading = True
<%begindetail%>
ieCombo.additem "<%insert_data_here%>"
ieList.addItem "<%insert_data_here%>"  _
& ";" & "<%insert_data_here%>"  _
& " " & "<%insert_data_here%>"  _
```

continues

Listing 23.7 Continued

```
& ";" & "<%insert_data_here%>" _
& ";" & "<%insert_data_here%>" _
& ";" & "<%insert_data_here%>"
<%enddetail%>
blnLoading = False

Sub ieCombo_Click()
    dim lngItem
    If blnLoading then Exit Sub
    SeparateData
End Sub

Sub SeparateData
Dim lngStart
Dim lngEnd
Dim strItems
strItems = ielist.list(ieCombo.ListIndex)
lngStart = 1
   lngEnd = instr(lngStart,strItems,";")
   AuthOrd.Value=mid(strItems,lngStart,lngEnd-lngStart)
   lngStart=lngEnd + 1

   lngEnd = instr(lngStart,strItems,";")
   AuthName.Value=mid(strItems,lngStart,lngEnd-lngStart)
   lngStart=lngEnd + 1

   lngEnd = instr(lngStart,strItems,";")
   AuthPrice.Value=mid(strItems,lngStart,lngEnd-lngStart)
   lngStart=lngEnd + 1

   lngEnd = instr(lngStart,strItems,";")
   AuthSales.Value=mid(strItems,lngStart,lngEnd-lngStart)
   lngStart=lngEnd + 1
End Sub
</Script>
<P>

<A HREF = "http://www.w3.org.pub/WWW/">The World Wide Web Consortium</A><P>
<A HREF = "http://www.w3.org/hypertext/WWW/MarkUp/html3/contents.html">HTML 3
➥specs</A><P>
<A HREF = "http://www.microsoft.com">MICROSOFT</A><P>
</BODY>
</HTML>
```

To use this template in conjunction with the `sp_makewebtask` stored procedure we'll call up the ISQL/w file and enter the text shown in Listing 23.9. The ISQL/w query screen looks like Figure 23.8.

FIG. 23.9
Using the ISQL/w program to execute the sp_makewebtask procedure.

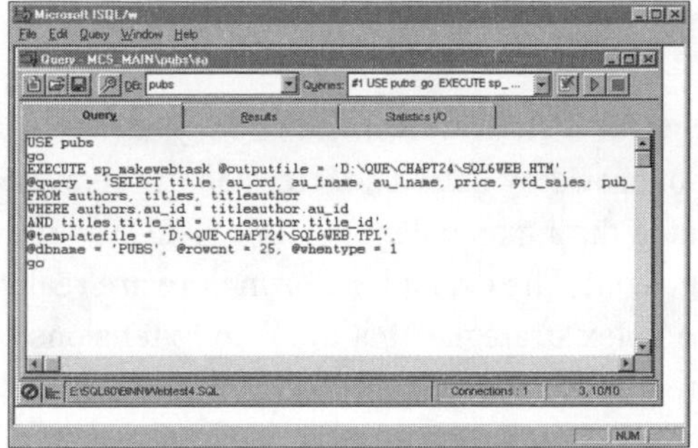

Listing 23.8 WEBTEST4.SQL—A Typical *sp_makewebtask* Procedure

```
USE pubs
go
EXECUTE sp_makewebtask @outputfile = 'D:\QUE\CHAPT24\SQL6WEB.HTM',
@query = 'SELECT title, au_ord, au_fname, au_lname, price, ytd_sales, pub_id
FROM authors, titles, titleauthor
WHERE authors.au_id = titleauthor.au_id
AND titles.title_id = titleauthor.title_id',
@templatefile = 'D:\QUE\CHAPT24\SQL6WEB.TPL',
@dbname = 'PUBS', @rowcnt = 25, @whentype = 1
go
```

Just by executing this query the Web page shown in Figure 23.10 will be created.

FIG. 23.10
The Web page created by the query in Listing 23.8.

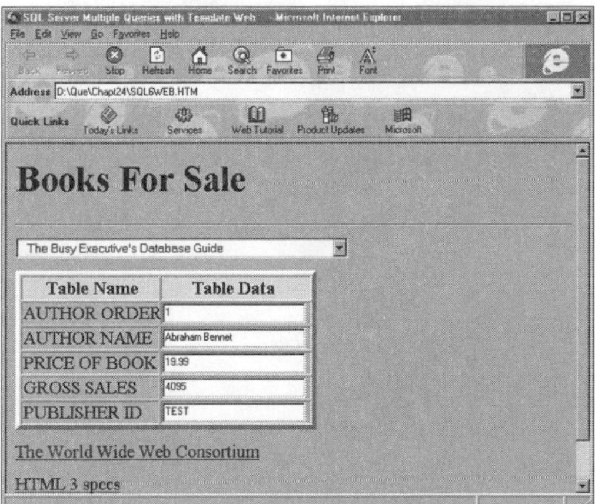

From Here...

The Web extensions for SQL Server provide a very attractive alternative to the more complex IDC method of providing data. The stress on the server is also minimized since the pages are not created during user demand time. The Web server merely sends the already existing pages out. The examples shown here are really simple and do not touch too deeply on more complex strategies that the Web Extensions could be targeted towards. What was presented here was really intended to show you how you could use VBScript to enhance the Web pagers produced through the use of customized template files.

CHAPTER 24

Building Internet Rating Applications

by William R. Beem

- **Evaluating the content**

  The material is clearly inappropriate for children.

- **Evaluating the appropriateness of use**

  Corporate users accessing these sites on company time waste productivity.

- **Evaluating the usefulness of the information**

  Some people simply don't want this material in their life.

As mainstream consumers converge upon the Internet, they bring with them a collection of baggage accumulated over the past few decades. The Internet was once the playground of academics and government agencies. For the most part, your average person off the street would have considered the content listless and dull. The content today is quite a bit more diverse. As consumers move into the Internet, they bring along the things that interest them most. While Madison Avenue types try to sell us everything from Pepsi to the latest movie, other parts of the Internet aren't quite as wholesome. One of the most pervasive items in the consumer world is sex. For good or bad, it's on the Internet and the Web. ■

How did the Internet move from boring technical diatribes to sex-for-sale? It's not that hard to imagine. Back in the 1980s, parents wanted to provide their college-bound youth with computers. The universities complied with the idea by providing network connections to each dorm room, and sometimes requiring a personal computer for admission. The next part is a simple matter of human nature. What happens when you provide a bunch of college educated people with raging youthful hormones access to an enormous network? You get creative ways to distribute sex-related material around the world in the blink of an eye.

As you can see, the influence of sex permeated the Internet before the average consumer jumped on board in the 1990s. In fact, sex-related topics probably helped drive Internet acceptance, just as sexy movies spurred VCR sales in the 1980s. While some of the prudish among us may wish to eradicate sexual content completely, that simply isn't going to happen. There's too much interest among some users and that means someone will always be around to provide material for them to use.

Content Issues

The chief concern right now is how easy it is for anyone to access sexually related Internet sites, whether intentionally or not. In other areas of life, we have safeguards to prevent children from accessing adult entertainment clubs, movies, and magazines. With a broader range of people using the Internet, it seems appropriate that we devise similar safeguards for online access to similar adult material.

Although many people never consider corporate users wasting time at work, the problem is very real. Some corporate studies estimate that employees waste as much as 40 percent of their time on the Web viewing sites unrelated to their work. Interestingly, not all of them are looking for sexual content. One major aerospace firm has a tremendous problem with employees spending more time looking at current sports scores than reviewing the less exciting technical publications on the Web.

It's Not Censorship

Not everyone is trying to prevent someone else from accessing inappropriate material. Some people just want to protect themselves from unwanted images. It's quite easy to run across sexual content while surfing from one link to another, or by performing searches on seemingly harmless topics. For example, not everyone who enjoys photography wants to follow links to some of the adult subjects often associated with the profession. A person interested in building models may find unanticipated consequences in the results from a search query. While investigating the topic for this chapter, I discovered far more adult links than links to Internet Ratings material.

Each of these scenarios provides incentive for some measure of content selection. Although the government recently passed an intrusive Communications Decency Act (CDA), the reality is that many of these sites are still online and do nothing to prevent access by those who shouldn't be there. Fortunately, the Internet is a community unto itself, and it responds when a need arises.

A free market economy tends to rise up and meet demand. In this case, we have several new software packages on the market that enable parents and supervisors to control which Internet sites their children and users may access. Some of these packages include SurfWatch and CyberPatrol. Online services, such as CompuServe and America Online, are also providing parental control features with their user software.

The Platform for Internet Content Selection (PICS) Standard

In August of 1995 representatives from 23 organizations gathered with MIT's World Wide Web Consortium to discuss content labeling for use with content selection software. The attendees had the following two major considerations in mind:

- Allowing parents, schools, and employers to control what computer users under their care can or cannot access
- Providing a positive, self-regulating method as an alternative to government intervention

The result of the conference was PICS, the Platform for Internet Content Selection. PICS design allows a supervisor to block access to certain Internet sites. The key difference between PICS and the CDA is censorship. While the government bill seeks to eradicate anything it considers inappropriate, the PICS standard allows the user to merely avoid that which it doesn't want to see without imposing the same restrictions on other Internet users. The PICS standard facilitates the following:

- *Self-rating:* It enables content providers to voluntarily label the content they create and distribute.
- *Third-party rating:* It enables multiple, independent labeling services to associate additional labels with content created and distributed by others. Services can devise their own labeling systems, and the same content can receive different labels from different services. This does not require the cooperation of the content provider.

- *Ease of use:* It allows supervisors to use ratings and labels from diverse sources to control information presented to users under their control.

NOTE A *supervisor* is someone responsible for setting the blocking criteria for Internet users. A supervisor can be a parent, teacher, employer, or anyone else who takes responsibility for the user's Internet access.

It Takes Two

PICS requires action on both the client and server side of the connection. Content providers apply labels in their HTML code that describe the rating level of the material on their site. The users require software that detects these labels and acts upon them based upon permission settings that a parent or supervisor defines for the user. If both parties adhere to the same rating system, a user does not need to actually see the material to know that he or she wants to block it from view.

How do we define that which is or isn't appropriate? There are three factors at work here, as follow:

- *The supervisor's style or choice of content:* Some people, particularly parents and employers, are responsible for the actions of others.
- *The recipient:* The same rules may not apply to all users across the board.
- *The context:* Something completely appropriate at home may have no place at school or work.

These three factors present a need for a flexible method of blocking content. They also present a problem, since different people disagree upon which content is or isn't harmful. Consider television programming as an example. In accordance with FCC regulations, broadcast television stations restrict nudity and sexual content in programs. Nevertheless, television is rife with blood and guts violence. Suggestively sexual programming comes on late in the evening, presumably when parents are home to supervise their children's watching habits, yet Saturday afternoons are often filled with war movies. There's a growing movement objecting to television violence.

The PICS standard tackles this problem by defining a mechanism for implementing rating structures, and then allowing others to implement the ratings system. Prior to PICS, a cottage industry came forth to fill the need. Instead of determining the ratings structure themselves, supervisors subscribed to services that catered to their needs. Different entities defined these subscription-based rating services, such as selection software business entities CyberPatrol and SurfWatch.

The Old Way

The selection software positions itself between the user and the online services, and uses a predetermined list of URLs known as unacceptable, or at least questionable, sites (see fig. 24.1). The software also uses a list of labels and keywords to determine if an unknown site is acceptable given the supervisor's criteria. Unfortunately, none of these products could process labels provided by competitors. This left content providers with a dilemma: how to provide adequate warning for selection software without spending an inordinate amount of time complying with an ever increasing number of conflicting products. There was a clear and present need for a content selection standard.

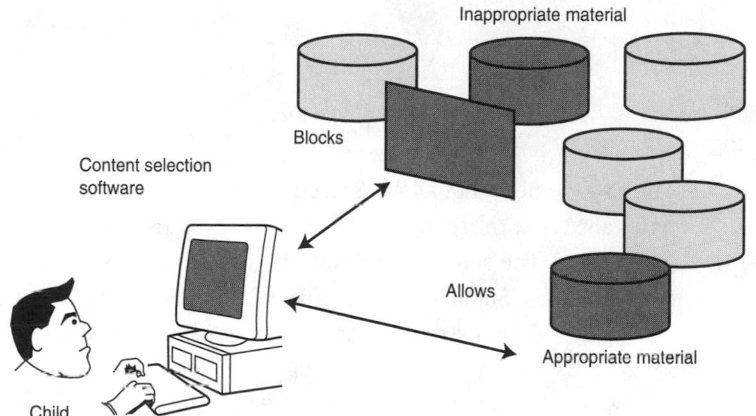

FIG. 24.1
Content selection software before PICS could block some pre-defined sites but not others.

The PICS Way

PICS separates the software from the labels. Any PICS-compatible selection software product can read PICS-compliant labels implemented on a server. This means the content providers can implement one set of labels, and users can choose the selection software they desire (see fig. 24.2).

The PICS standard does not provide selection software or a specific rating system. It merely establishes the conventions for describing rating systems and label formats. The open nature of the PICS standard allows different rating systems for use by the same PICS-compliant software product. These ratings aren't restricted to adult-oriented material. As previously mentioned, the aerospace employer whose employees are addicted to sports scores may seek to block ESPN's Web site. A corporate intranet may use labels as a measure of security to access confidential materials published on the internal network.

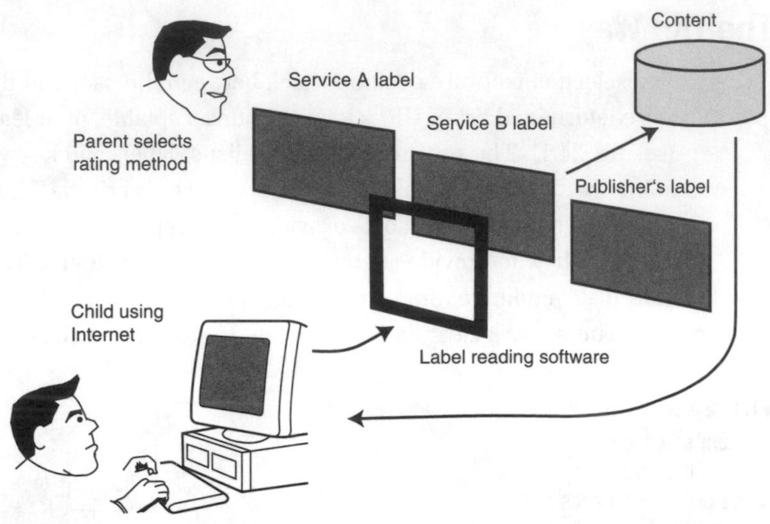

FIG. 24.2
PICS-compliant selection software uses labels provided by publishers and ratings services, as well as the supervisor's criteria, to provide more accurate content blocking.

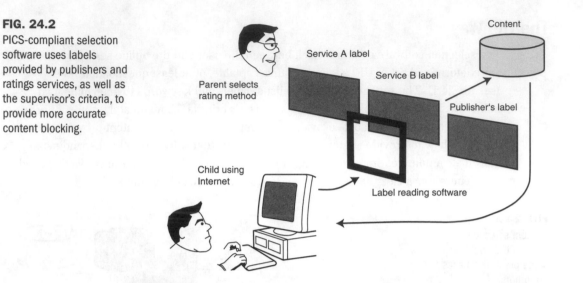

The key element that allows selection software to read any set of labels is a new MIME type (`application/pics-service`) that specifies a standard format for describing a labeling service. The selection software reads service descriptions in this format to determine content labels. Supervisors use this information to configure their selection software. Listing 24.1 demonstrates a sample rating service based upon the MPAA movie rating scale.

Listing 24.1 Setting Up a Rating Service

```
((PICS-version 1.0)
   (rating-system "http://moviescale.org/Ratings/Description/")
   (rating-service "http://moveiscale.org/v1.0")
   (icon "icons/moviescale.gif")
   (name "The Movies Rating Service")
   (description "A rating service based upon the MPAA's movie rating scale")

   (category
     (transmit-as "r")
     (name "Rating")
     (label (name "G") (value 0) (icon "icons/G.gif")
     (label (name "PG") (value 1) (icon "icons/PG.gif")
     (label (name "PG-13") (value 2) (icon "icons/PG-13.gif")
     (label (name "R") (value 3) (icon "icons/R.gif")
     (label (name "NC-17") (value 4) (icon "icons/NC-17.gif"))))
```

The initial section points to a URL that describes the labeling system and criteria for assigning ratings, an icon, a name, and a longer description of the service. Referring to resources by their URLs makes it possible to match a label with its associated resource, even if distributed separately. This separation is important, since it allows a ratings service to define labels for sites that may not wish to cooperate with the service. Anything named by a URL can have a label attached to it, including resources accessed by FTP, Gopher, HTTP, or Usenet. The PICS standard also defined a URL naming system for IRC so that supervisors can also restrict access to unacceptable chat rooms.

The latter section of Listing 24.1 describes the categories and their dimensions. In this case, there is only one category. Another example may have categories based upon Sex, Violence, and Language, each with its own series of levels. A supervisor creating a definition for a user, or group of users, must choose the level at which the selection software blocks content. If a user has a PG level clearance, the software denies access to PG-13 (value 2) and higher content pages.

The following are two optional security features that labels can include:

- Message integrity check
- Digital signatures

▶ **See** "Secure Electronic Transactions," **p. 146**, for a discussion about Message Digests and Digital Signatures.

The message integrity check, in the form of an MD5 message digest, enables the software to detect whether or not something changed the resource after creating the label. A digital signature on the contents of the label itself allows the selection software to guarantee that a label was really created by the service it references. Think of this as a seal of approval. If you subscribe to a service that provides ratings, it can create a unique, unforgeable digital signature to associate with its labels. If a label claims to represent this service provider, a quick check of its signature verifies whether it's authentic or not.

Rate that URL

As previously mentioned, PICS provides an open platform for multiple, independent rating services. A rating service is an individual, group, or organization that provides content labels for information provided on the Internet. The new MIME type, `application/pics-service`, is the base type for defining a label. Each label has a rating system that defines it.

A rating system specifies the dimensions used for labeling, the scale of allowable values on each dimension, and a description of the criteria used to assign values. The Movie Scale used in Listing 24.1 is a single dimension rating system with five allowable values, G through NC-17. Other rating systems may have multiple dimensions.

Each rating system is identified by a valid URL. By doing so, several services can use the same rating system and refer to it by its unique identifier (the URL). Using a URL to name a rating system allows users to access it and obtain a human-readable description of the rating system. Although the format for this description is unspecified, it should provide a supervisor with enough information about the rating system to allow for an accurate decision on whether the system fits the supervisor's needs or not.

A content label, or rating, has the following three parts that contain information about a document:

- The URL naming the rating service that produced the label
- A set of PICS-defined attribute value pairs, which provide information about the rating (date the rating was assigned, date it expires, and so on)
- A set of rating-system-defined attribute pairs, which actually rates the item along various dimensions or categories

Describing the *application/pics-service* Type Listing 24.1 shows the general format of a MIME `application/pics-label` type. Unfortunately, it's not a complete example. As mentioned previously, a rating system can have more than one category. Likewise, these categories can have different options than the ones displayed in the sample. This section displays a few more examples in HTML code. Web page designers who wish to provide their own PICS ratings transmissions implement these HTML tags in their Web page design. Clients using PICS-compliant software will translate these tags and allow or deny access to the site based upon how the client's rules and preferences interpret the information presented by these tags.

```
(category
   (transmit-as "Value")
   (name "Value Index")
   (min 0.0)
   (max 1.0))
```

This category tag still defines a transmission name and a longer name value. Notice there are some differences, though. Notably, this category does not provide any labels. Instead, it defines this category with a rating range of 0.0 to 1.0. A rating service can choose a value in between for the content, and supervisors can also choose a value inside the range to block content.

```
(category
   (transmit-as "Subject")
   (name "Document subject")
   (multivalue true)
   (unordered true)
   (label (name "Sex") (value 0))
   (label (name "Violence") (value 1)
   (label (name "Language") (value 2))
   (label-only))
```

The preceding category sample demonstrates a rating system for a document that contains multiple subjects. A supervisor may choose to deny access based upon any one of these labels, or perhaps a combination of labels.

```
(category
   (transmit-as "Color")
   (name "Picture color")
   (integer)

   (category
      (transmit-as "Hue")
      (label (name "Blue") (value 0))
      (label (name "Red") (value 1))
      (label (name "Green") (value 2)))

   (category
      (transmist-as "Intensity")
      (min 0)
      (max 255))))
```


This sample demonstrates that a category can also have sub-categories that make up its properties. Note the flexibility that this combination allows. The `Hue` category provides three attributes, multiplied by an `Intensity` category range of 256 values.

Some Semantic Issues There are always rules for any kind of code, and the syntax of `application/pics-service` attributes is no exception. This section describes some of the syntax rules you must observe when creating your `application/pics-service` attributes.

- `application/pics-service` attributes ignore white space, except in quoted strings. Multiple white space characters are treated as a single white space character.
- Transmitted names and quoted strings are case sensitive. Option names and other tokens are case insensitive.
- The extension attribute allows PICS to add more attributes at a later time. Each extension requires a quoted URL to avoid duplication of extension names. The URL provides a human-readable description of the extension. Extensions can be optional or mandatory. Selection software can disregard optional extensions if it doesn't understand how to implement them. Selection software should reject any mandatory extensions that it doesn't understand.
- The PICS specification requires US-ASCII so that it can transmit over Internet lines to computers on multiple platforms.
- Any options defined in a particular service-info construct apply to all labels within that construct, unless an option in a specific label overrides it.
- Numbers in PICS labels can be integers or fractions with no greater range or precision than that provided by IEEE single-precision floating point numbers.

- You must use the multi-value syntax when the value of a particular scale has either zero or more than one value. Additionally, you can use it for a single or multi-value field when there is exactly one value.
- The only options that can occur more than once in a particular *single-label* or *service-info* are `comment` and `extension`. For each instance of the `extension` option, you must provide a unique quoted URL to define the extension.

Labels and Label Lists

The PICS specification uses a *labellist* to transmit a set of PICS labels. The format is the same `application/pics-labels` MIME type discussed previously. The format transmits labels, as well as reasons why a label may be unavailable, along with a document. The *labellist* is always surrounded by parentheses and begins with the PICS version number. The following fragment displays a sample label list:

```
labellist :: '(' version service-info+ ')'
```

Label lists either specify that there are no labels available or they are separated into sections of labels for each rating service. The URL of each service is specified as the *serviceID*. Following the URL is either an error message indicating why no labels are available from that service, or an overall set of optional information followed by the keyword labels and the *labels* from the service. The optional information applies to every label from the service, unless an a specific label has its own option to override the general service option.

Embedding Labels in HTML

You can imbed PICS labels in HTML files as meta-information using the HTML `META` element. Use the HTTP header equivalence, as in the following example:

```
<META http-equiv="PICS-Label" content='labellist'>
```

NOTE Note that the content attribute uses single quotation marks, since the PICS label syntax uses double quotation marks.

PICS includes an extension to HTML that allows a client to request one or more labels be included in a header along with a document. HTTP servers should only include PICS label headers if requested by the client, and then only include labels from services requested by the client. Including unrequested labels adds unnecessary burden on the bandwidth and serves no purpose, since the client ignores those labels.

NOTE The PICS extension to HTML only works with HTTP protocol. It's possible that later revisions of the PICS standard will incorporate extensions for other protocols.

An example PICS client request appears as follows:

```
GET some.html HTTP/1.0
Protocol-Reqest: (PICS-1.0 {params full
               {services "http://www.someplace.org/v1.0"}}}
```

Here's what has happened so far. First, the client sends a request for `some.html`—a document on a Web server. The client's request asks for the full label of the document from the rating service at **http://www.someplace.org**. A client interested in examining a rating before retrieving the full document can substitute the word `HEAD` instead of `GET` in the request. The server responds with the header shown in the following listing, but not the document itself. This provides the user an opportunity to check ahead to see if the document has a suitable rating before spending the time to retrieve the document.

The server's response to the client appears as follows:

```
HTTP/1.0 200 OK
Date: Tuesday, 07-May-96 13:35:34 GMT
MIME-version: 1.0
Last-modified: Thursday, 07-May-96 05:12:47 GMT
Protocol: {PICS-1.0 {headers PICS-Label}}
PICS-Label:
     (PICS-1.0 "http://www.someplace.org/v1.0" labels
     on "1994.11.05T08:15-0500"
     exp "1995.12.31T23:50-0000"
     for "http:/www.website.com/some.html"
     by "William Beem"
     ratings (value 0.7 intensity 0 color/hue 1))
Content-type: text/html
...contents of some.html...
```

The server responds by sending back the label in a `PICS-Label` header, and also the requested document. The format of the `PICS-Label` headers field (labellist) allows the server to reply with either a label or an explanation of why the label isn't available. It's inappropriate for a server to generate an HTTP error status if the document is available, but the labels are unavailable.

Selection software can also request PICS labels separately from the documents to which they refer. In order to do this, a client contacts a label bureau. Label bureaus are HTTP servers that understand a particular type of query syntax. They provide labels for documents on other servers and for documents available through other protocols than HTTP. These label bureaus are most likely run by rating services, and may charge a fee for label queries. In fact, the PICS standards documentation encourages rating services to act as label bureaus.

Suppose a ratings service has a URL on the Web called **http://www.ratem.org/Ratings**. It decides to run a label bureau to dispense labels for its own documents. The following sample requests the URL to send a single label that applies to everything in the `/images` directory of another URL titled **http://www.nasty.net**.

```
GET /Ratings?opt=generic&
     u="http%3A%2F%2www.nasty.net%2Fimages"&
     s="http%3A%2F%2Fwww.ratem.org"&
     HTTP/1.0
```

NOTE Notice the use of `%3` to represent a colon (:) and `%2` to represent a forward slash (/). This is necessary for encoding characters within a URL. RFC-1738 has more complete details on this topic. ■

Upon receiving this query, the server sends back a MIME `application/pics-label` type document. The document should be complete, containing all options contained within the label. From this information, the client can decide whether to proceed into the `/images` directory or not.

Digital Signatures

As discussed in Chapter 8, "Security," digital signatures provide a mechanism to determine whether the contents of a data file or document were altered. The PICS standard makes use of this technology to determine whether a document changed since it was last labeled. This is quite a frequent occurrence since Web pages tend to change on a regular basis. It's possible that a change can happen due to some unauthorized access, but PICS labels have three option fields intended to identify and deter such events. These fields are as follows:

- *At:* Assuming that the Web page owner accurately identifies the last modification time, this field detects updates to the document made after the label was created.
- *Until or exp:* This is an expiration date for the document. The label becomes invalid if something changes the contents prior to this date.
- *MD5:* Message Digest 5 is a well-known checksum algorithm used in many encryption methods. It creates a message digest based upon the contents of the document. When a user retrieves the document, an algorithm compares its contents to the message digest using the same algorithm. It is very unlikely that the results will be the same if something changed the document. This technique is perhaps the best of the three, since it prevents even knowledgeable criminals from making undetected document changes. Since it's possible to embed PICS labels inside the document,

take care to ensure that the message digest computation does not include the PICS label itself. It's best to compute the message digest after removing all META elements and white space in HTML documents.

The next problem is to ensure that the labels received from a rating service are indeed coming from that service, and that they haven't been altered during transmission. PICS uses digital signatures to address both problems.

The rating service signs its labels with a public key pair. The service keeps its private key secret and distributes the public key to anyone who wishes to use the service. Upon creating the label, the service computes a message digest of the label using the MD5 algorithm and then encrypts it with the service's private key. The result of this process is the digital signature. The signature gets converted to US-ASCII using a base64 encoding technique and is then stored in the **signature-rsa-md5** option of the label it transmits to the client.

After receiving the label, the client can verify the signature by converting the label back to binary form and re-computing the message digest. The client must also convert the contents of the **signature-rsa-md5** option back to binary and decrypt it using the service's public key. Finally, a comparison of the new message digest and the decrypted message digest should provide an exact match if the document is authentic. While this sounds like a lot of work for the user, that's not really the case. It's a lot of work for the programmer, since that is who should automate all of these steps when a user receives a label.

PICS specifically requires the use of RSA signature algorithm with the MD5 message digest. This may change in the future. Such a change only requires a new label option that supports a different algorithm pair. PICS does not specify the key length necessary for encryption. This detail is left to the users and rating services to decide.

SafeSurf—A Ratings Example

SafeSurf is a company that provides content selection software and a rating service targeted at parents who want to protect their children from inappropriate content on the Internet. Parents using the SafeSurf Rating Standard can activate several layers of blocking based upon what the parents approve. Something parents find unsuitable for a small child may perhaps be less restricted for a teenager. SafeSurf maintains a master database of categories and updates new categories in as timely a manner possible. This section illustrates a rating scheme using SafeSurf's published categories and their associated levels.

Table 24.1 is a guide that relates to the numbered items presented in the lists that follow. Parents can choose any level they want, regardless of title.

Table 24.1 SafeSurf Ratings Scheme

Adult Themes with Caution Levels

Caution Level	Description
0	Age Range
1	All Ages
2	Older Children
3	Teens
4	Older Teens
5	Adult Supervision Recommended
6	Adults
7	Limited to Adults
8	Adults Only
9	Explicitly for Adults

Profanity

Rating Number	Rating Name	Description
1	Subtle Innuendo	Subtly implied through the use of slang
2	Explicit Innuendo	Explicitly implied through the use of slang
3	Technical Reference	Dictionary, encyclopedia, news, technical references
4	Non-Graphic-Artistic	Limited non-sexual expletives used in an artistic fashion
5	Graphic-Artistic	Non-sexual expletives used in an artistic fashion
6	Graphic	Limited use of expletives and obscene gestures
7	Detailed Graphic	Casual use of expletives and obscene gestures
8	Explicit Vulgarity	Heavy use of vulgar language and obscene gestures. Unsupervised Chat Rooms
9	Explicit and Crude	Saturated with crude sexual references and gestures. Unsupervised Chat Rooms

Heterosexual Themes

Rating Number	Rating Name	Description
1	Subtle Innuendo	Subtly implied through the use of a metaphor
2	Explicit Innuendo	Explicitly implied (not described) through the use of a metaphor
3	Technical Reference	Dictionary, encyclopedia, news, technical references
4	Non-Graphic-Artistic	Limited metaphoric descriptions used in an artistic fashion
5	Graphic-Artistic	Metaphoric descriptions used in an artistic fashion
6	Graphic	Descriptions of intimate sexual acts
7	Detailed Graphic	Descriptions of intimate details of sexual acts
8	Explicitly Graphic or Inviting Participation	Explicit descriptions of intimate details of sexual acts designed to arouse. Inviting interactive sexual participation. Unsupervised Sexual Chat Rooms or Newsgroups
9	Explicit and Crude or Explicitly Inviting Participation	Profane graphic descriptions of intimate details of sexual acts designed to arouse. Inviting interactive sexual participation. Unsupervised Sexual Chat Rooms or Newsgroups

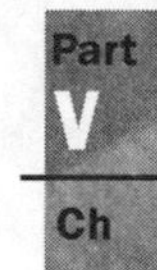

Homosexual Themes

Rating Number	Rating Name	Description
1	Subtle Innuendo	Subtly implied through the use of a metaphor
2	Explicit Innuendo	Explicitly implied (not described) through the use of a metaphor
3	Technical Reference	Dictionary, encyclopedia, news, technical references
4	Non-Graphic-Artistic	Limited metaphoric descriptions used in an artistic fashion
5	Graphic-Artistic	Metaphoric descriptions used in an artistic fashion
6	Graphic	Descriptions of intimate sexual acts

continues

Table 24.1 Continued

Homosexual Themes

Rating Number	Rating Name	Description
7	Detailed Graphic	Descriptions of intimate details of sexual acts
8	Explicitly Graphic or Inviting Participation	Explicit descriptions of intimate details of sexual acts designed to arouse. Inviting interactive sexual participation. Unsupervised Sexual Chat Rooms or Newsgroups
9	Explicit and Crude or Explicitly Inviting Participation	Profane graphic descriptions of intimate details of sexual acts designed to arouse. Inviting interactive sexual participation. Unsupervised Sexual Chat Rooms or Newsgroups

Nudity

Rating Number	Rating Name	Description
1	Subtle Innuendo	
2	Explicit Innuendo	
3	Technical Reference	
4	Non-Graphic Artistic	
5	Graphic Artistic	
6	Graphic	
7	Detailed Graphic	
8	Explicit Vulgarity	
9	Explicit and Crude	

Violence

Rating Number	Rating Name	Description
1	Subtle Innuendo	
2	Explicit Innuendo	
3	Technical Reference	
4	Non-Graphic-Artistic	
5	Graphic-Artistic	

Violence

Rating Number	Rating Name	Description
6	Graphic	
7	Detailed Graphic	
8	Inviting Participation in Graphic Interactive Format	
9	Encouraging Personal Participation, Weapon Making	

Sex, Violence, and Profanity

Rating Number	Rating Name	Description
1	Subtle Innuendo	
2	Explicit Innuendo	
3	Technical Reference	
4	Non-Graphic-Artistic	
5	Graphic-Artistic	
6	Graphic	
7	Detailed Graphic	
8	Explicit Vulgarity	
9	Explicit and Crude	

Intolerance

Rating Number	Rating Name	Description
1	Subtle Innuendo	
2	Explicit Innuendo	
3	Technical Reference	
4	Non-Graphic-Literary	
5	Graphic-Literary	
6	Graphic Discussions	
7	Endorsing Hatred	

continues

Table 24.1 Continued

Intolerance

Rating Number	Rating Name	Description
8	Endorsing Violent or Hateful Action	
9	Advocating Violent or Hateful Action	

Glorifying Drug Use

Rating Number	Rating Name	Description
1	Subtle Innuendo	
2	Explicit Innuendo	
3	Technical Reference	
4	Non-Graphic-Artistic	
5	Graphic-Artistic	
6	Graphic	
7	Detailed Graphic	
8	Simulated Interactive Participation	
9	Soliciting Personal Participation	

Other Adult Themes

Rating Number	Rating Name	Description
1	Subtle Innuendo	
2	Explicit Innuendo	
3	Technical Reference	
4	Non-Graphic-Artistic	
5	Graphic-Artistic	
6	Graphic	
7	Detailed Graphic	
8	Explicit Vulgarity	
9	Explicit and Crude	

Gambling

Rating Number	Rating Name	Description
1	Subtle Innuendo	
2	Explicit Innuendo	
3	Technical Discussion	
4	Non-Graphic-Artistic, Advertising	
5	Graphic-Artistic, Advertising	
6	Simulated Gambling	
7	Real Life Gambling without Stakes	
8	Encouraging Interactive Real Life Participation with Stakes	
9	Providing Means with Stakes	

From Here...

Content controls provide a means for parents and employers to decide what is acceptable for their users to access. The key element is that supervisors have a choice in what they allow, rather than a government body dictating standards for everyone. Content controls provide enough flexibility that different users can have customized views of the Internet, and they allow a child to grow and access a larger variety of content as some restrictions become unnecessary.

This chapter provided an overview of a topic in its infancy. The PICS standard is a version 1.0 release, which suggests that it will undergo more changes in the coming months. To help you keep abreast of the most current information, we suggest you access the following Web sites for more information. Don't worry; they're all safe.

- CyberPatrol at **http://www.cyberpatrol.com/**
- CyberAngels at **http://www.safesurf.com/cyberangels/**

- Parental Control Page at **http://www.worldvillage.com/wv/school/html/control.htm**
- PICS Standard at **http://www.w3.org/pub/WWW/PICS/**
- SafeSurf at **http://www.safesurf.com/index.html**
- Internet LifeGuard at **http://www.safesurf.com/ss_aol.html**

PART VI

Appendixes

APPENDIX A

History of the Internet

Rather than plow into a long, boring dissertation on dates (it all started in 1969) and names (Defense Advanced Research Projects Agency started it all, and it's been know as, and comprised of, DARPANET, ARPANET, MILNET, NSFNET, and Merit at one time or another), let's take a look at what the Internet was, is, and will become.

When it all began, the idea was simple: Create a very fault-tolerant network of military computers. By completely decentralizing administration and control, and by providing automatic routing over multiple paths, the system would be able to withstand everything from minor localized outages all the way up to nuclear war.

From that humble beginning (there were initially only a handful of large computers "on the Net"), today we have a massive network-of-networks, growing at such a phenomenal rate that providing any usage figures would be meaningless by the time you read this book.

Originally, the network was used to transfer data from one large facility to others. Personal computers would not be available for a decade, and widespread usage would take even longer. The Internet was the playground of the lucky few and the elite. Mere mortals need not apply.

Those of us on "the outside" would occasionally see tantalizing glimmers of it in magazine articles, or hear words like "UseNet" and "e-mail" from friends with accounts on large university mainframes. However, getting "on the Net" was simply not possible for most of us.

One of the first avenues of Net access for non-insiders was a system called "The Cleveland Free-Net," which was created by CWRU (Case Western Reserve University) using Freeport software that they developed. Within a few years, numerous "Free-Nets" appeared all over the country, providing local residents basic access to the Internet. They could use e-mail, browse Gophers, access UseNet newsgroups, local community news and events, and more.

Other providers also bcgan offering Internet access, but by and large, users faced an intimidating obstacle: However nifty the concept was, it never got far from its UNIX roots. Users worked with character-based shells that ran over the UNIX operating system. This meant no graphics, no buttons to click, scrollbars to slide, boxes to check, or menus to pull down. Creating e-mail required use of a UNIX text editor and complex commands. In short, it was not for the faint of heart.

For this type of access, users dialed up with a terminal program, and whichever Internet host they dialed behaved like a sort of super-BBS system. As great as it all was, there were sufficient built-in limitations to restrict it to the few brave souls who were willing to put up with the difficulties.

Two things brought us where we are today: the Winsock API and the WWW. Winsock is a protocol stack that provides a layer that creates a link between Internet applications and the Internet itself. Before the creation of Winsock, there were a few approaches to TCP/IP access on PCs, but they were difficult to use, and installation and setup was tantamount to a black art. Winsock provided a consistent platform that developers could write for, and write they did.

Applications like Telnet, FTP, Finger, e-mail, IRC and talk programs, newsreaders, and so forth were quickly made available for free download at FTP sites all over the world. These programs, when run over a Winsock link, made each user's computer a station on the Internet, just like any other site. Suddenly, dial-up UNIX hosts became functionally obsolete; users could send e-mail by clicking a button and typing in a convenient Windows text box, rather than learning a crude remote UNIX editor. They could browse newsgroups while downloading files, and receive e-mail at the same time. (Winsock allows multitasking, in effect, giving each running application its own virtual modem.)

About this time (the early '90s), the WWW started taking off. Applications like Mosaic created the capability to "browse the Web" and see a mix of text and graphics, all tied together with hypertext style links. This created the current wave of interest in the Internet, and the demand for access spurred numerous small companies to start provider services.

You Are Here

At this point in the rapidly developing history of the Internet, the "big boys" are getting into the ISP (Internet Service Provider) game. Everyone from CompuServe to telephone companies to cable TV operators are becoming ISPs. Internet access is rapidly becoming a commodity, and nearly everyone is within a local call of a dial-up modem pool at a reasonable price.

Today, access is ubiquitous. The Internet is no longer the exclusive province of the pro peller-beanie and pocket-protecter crowd. The next wave will not be one of access, but of content. For all its popularity, the WWW is essentially a one-way, static medium. It's sort of like television for computers. Now, with tools like VBScript, Web pages can easily be provided with active content. The personal communications systems that have been predicted for years might very well arrive on the scene as little more than wireless browsers of an active-content-rich WWW.

Learning the concepts presented in this book will place you in the right place at the right time to position yourself to capitalize on the next major growth stage of the Internet. It's a good time to know Visual Basic. ●

APPENDIX B

HTML Appendix

This appendix covers all the HTML elements (or tags) supported by the current version of Internet Explorer (3.0 beta 1). This appendix is loosely based on the HTML 3.2 Standard and the Internet Explorer 3.0 documentation available with the Internet Software Development Kit (SDK). Examples demonstrating the syntax of the HTML tags are shown at the end of each section. Several of the elements are standard HTML, while others are not and may change considerably in subsequent versions of Internet Explorer.

The appendix is organized into four major sections. The first contains elements that are used with the header portion of an HTML page. The second section contains elements that are used with the body portion of an HTML page; the third section contains miscellaneous tags and a brief glossary on HTML terminology. The final section contains a full list of supported color names used by Internet Explorer. Special sections are given to client-side image maps, lists, frames, tables, forms, and objects since they contain several sub-attributes and elements. ■

Header Tags

The <HEAD> Tag

Purpose The <HEAD> tag is what specifies the header portion of the document. It is within the <HEAD> tags that all the information describing the document should be placed. A header should exist if you plan to give your document a title, using external style sheets, or incorporating other bits of miscellaneous information that doesn't relate to the content of the page.

NOTE The New HTML 3.2 Standard implies that the header section does not necessarily have to exist for header information, scripts, and style formats.

Syntax

```
<HEAD>...</HEAD>
```

Attributes None.

Example

```
<HEAD>
<TITLE>This is the title of the document and appears in the
➥ title. bar...</TITLE>
</HEAD>
```

The <LINK> Tag

Purpose The <LINK> tag provides information about what references or what is referenced by an HTML document, in terms of information that is not usually included in the document. The <LINK> tag is treated very loosely in these cases and there can be several possible attributes for this tag. The major purpose for the LINK element in Microsoft Internet Explorer 3.0 is for style sheet purposes and possibly for Visual Basic Script. Use of the <LINK> tag with style sheets is covered in the Style Sheets section (see Chapter 2, "Review of HTML"). The <LINK> tag does not have a closing tag.

Syntax `<LINK>`

Attributes

Attribute	Required	Purpose
REL	✔	Specifies a relationship to the document, for instance the value, Made, would relate to the person who made the document.

Attribute	Required	Purpose
REV	✔	Specifies a reverse relationship, something that references the document the link tag is in. This is not commonly used.
TITLE		Specifies a title of the item the link references or is referenced by.
HREF	✔	Specifies a URL for the referenced or referencing item.
TYPE	✔	Specifies what MIME type the referencing or referenced item is. In the case of style sheets, this would be, style/css.

Example

```
<LINK REL="style" TYPE="text/css" HREF="http://www.styles.org/formal.css">
```

The <META> Tag

Purpose The <META> tag allows meta-information to exist in the document. Special information that further describes the document can be included as well.

Syntax

```
<META>
```

Attributes

Attribute	Required	Purpose
HTTP-EQUIV	✔	Specifies what function or task to perform on the document. Internet Explorer has only one value for this: "refresh."
TYPE		Specifies what the purpose of the meta information.
CONTENT		Specifies the CONTENT of HTTP-EQUIV, or TYPE.

The value, "refresh," for the HTTP-EQUIV attribute implies that the document should be refreshed after the amount of time specified by the VALUE attribute. Additionally, the VALUE attribute can specify another URL to load after a given time in the form of:

```
VALUE = "n URL"
```

where, n is the number of seconds to load the document and URL is the location of the document to load.

Example

```
<META HTTP-EQUIV="refresh" CONTENT="10 http://www.yahoo.com">
```

The <*TITLE*> Tag

Purpose

The <TITLE> tag specifies the title of the document it is in. The value that is encapsulated in the title tag is displayed in the title bar of Internet Explorer.

Syntax

```
<TITLE>...</TITLE>
```

Attributes

None.

Example

```
<HEAD>
<TITLE>This is an HTML document</TITLE>
</HEAD>
```

Body Tags

The <*A*> Tag

Purpose The <A>, or anchor tag, specifies a hyperlink, which is used for accessing other documents and resources. Whatever is encapsulated by the anchor tag is either an anchor, which is accessed by other resources, or a link, which accesses other anchors and resources.

Syntax

```
<A>...</A>
```

Attributes

Attribute	Required	Purpose
HREF	✔	Specifies the resource to hyperlink to, this can be in the form or a URL or a filename.
NAME		Identifies the anchor or hyperlink
TARGET		Specifies the window or frame in which the resource is loaded.

Example

```
<A HREF="http://www.rt66.com/iymalluf">Go To Malluf Consulting
➥ Services Homepage</A>
```

The <*ADDRESS*> Tag

Purpose The <ADDRESS> tag renders the text it surrounds in *italics* to represent an e-mail, postal, or other contact address.

Syntax

```
<ADDRESS>...</ADDRESS>
```

Attributes None.

Example

```
<ADDRESS>123 Main Street<BR>
         Anytown, USA
         87743-0123 </ADDRESS>
```

The <*B*> Tag

Purpose The <B> tag renders the text it encapsulates in bold.

Syntax

```
<B>...</B>
```

Attributes None.

Example

```
The text at the end of this line is in <B>bold</B>.
```

The <*BIG*> Tag

Purpose The <BIG> tag increases the size of the text it encapsulates. The size of this text is slightly larger than normal paragraph text.

Syntax

```
<BIG>...</BIG>
```

Attributes None.

Example

```
We want you to notice <BIG>this text</BIG>.
```

The <*BLOCKQUOTE*> Tag

Purpose The <BLOCKQUOTE> tag is used in citing references, or other material. The text that is surrounded by the <BLOCKQUOTE> tags is indented .5 inches to the right.

Syntax

```
<BLOCKQUOTE>...</BLOCKQUOTE>
```

Attributes None.

Example

```
<BLOCKQUOTE>This sentence of words is indented - can't you see???
➥</BLOCKQUOTE>
```

The <*BODY*> Tag

Purpose The <BODY> tag specifies the beginning and the end of the Content portion of the document, or of the document that is actually displayed.

Syntax

```
<BODY>...</BODY>
```

Attributes

Attribute	Required	Purpose
BACKGROUND		Specifies an image that is tiled across the back of the screen.
BGCOLOR		Specifies a background color. This color can be in the form of one of several colors names, or a hexa-decimal value in the form of

Attribute	Required	Purpose
		#rrggbb where rr is the hexadecimal value for red on the 0–255 color palette, gg and bb are the hexadecimal value for green and blue on the 0 -255 color palette, respectively. The 16 standard colors and their hexadecimal equivalents are listed in the table at the end of the section. Refer to the last section of this appendix for a full list of supported color names.
BGPROPERTIES		Specifies the properties of the BACKGROUND attribute. The only valid value for BGPROPERTIES now is fixed, which indicates that the graphic specified by BACKGROUND will not be tiled but rendered as a watermark.
LEFTMARGIN		Specifies the width of the left margin of the page (values are in pixels).
LINK		Specifies the color of an unvisited link in the same manner as BGCOLOR.
TEXT		Specifies the color of the foreground text in the same manner as BGCOLOR.
TOPMARGIN		Specifies the width of the top margin of the page (values are in pixels).
VLINK		Specifies the color of visited links in the same manner as BGCOLOR.

Color Name	Hexadecimal Equivalent
"Aqua"	"#00FFFF"
"Black"	"#FFFFFF"
"Blue"	"#0000FF"
"Fuchsia"	"#FF00FF"
"Gray"	"#808080"
"Green"	"#008000"
"Lime"	"#00FF00"
"Maroon"	"#800000"
"Navy"	"#000080"
"Olive"	"#808000"
"Purple"	"#800080"
"Red"	"#FF0000"
"Silver"	"#C0C0C0"
"Teal"	"#808000"
"White"	"#FFFFFF"
"Yellow"	"#FFFF00"

Example

```
<BODY>
<H1>This</H1>
<B>This</B><BR>
<P>And this are in the body</P>
</BODY>
```

The <*BR*> Tag

Purpose The <BR> tag inserts line breaks in HTML. Normally, there are no line breaks in HTML; text continues to flow until it reaches the end of the browser, then a line break occurs.

Syntax

```
<BR>
```

Attributes

Attribute	Required	Purpose
CLEAR		Causes all the text following the to be aligned with the margin specified by

Attribute	Required	Purpose
		the CLEAR attribute. For instance, if there were a left aligned image tag, and a tag following some text had the attribute: CLEAR="left," then the text would be left aligned with the left-hand margin right below the image. The "right" value does the for the right side. The "all" value causes the text following the tag to be placed past all floating images.

Example

```
This line has no breaks in it
This <BR> line does <BR> have brea<BR>ks.<BR>
<IMG SRC="test.gif" ALIGN="left">Some text is here
<BR CLEAR="left"> and some text is just below the image, on the left side.
```

The <*CENTER*> Tag

Purpose The <CENTER> tag centers any text, pictures, or other entities it surrounds.

Syntax

```
<CENTER>...</CENTER>
```

Attributes None.

Example

```
This text is left aligned.
<CENTER>This text is centered</CENTER>
```

The <*CITE*> Tag

Purpose The <CITE> tag renders text in *italics* and also has the same purpose as the <BLOCKQUOTE> tag: to cite references, or other material.

Syntax

```
<CITE>...</CITE>
```

Attributes None.

Example

```
<CITE>"He didn't do it"</CITE> the reporter said.
```

Client-Side Image Maps

This section covers client-side image maps and how to implement them. Currently, Microsoft Internet Explorer and Netscape Navigator support client-side image maps. The USEMAP attribute of the image tag accesses client side image maps. The USEMAP attribute indicates which map it should bind to (or in essence, which map it should use). The map contains coordinate-defined areas (polygons, circles, rectangles), which outline hotspots. When the user clicks a hotspot in the image, the coordinates are compared to the area regions specified by the map and the appropriate action specified by the HREF attribute is made.

Syntax

```
<MAP>
<AREA>
...
</MAP>
```

Attributes

Attribute	Required	Purpose
NAME	✔	Gives the map a name, which is referenced by the USEMAP attribute of the `<IMG>` tag.

The *<AREA>* Tag The `<AREA>` tag is used to specify the various hotspots on an image. The `<AREA>` tag is encapsulated inside the `<MAP>` tag and is the only tag allowed in the `<MAP>` tag. The table below lists the attributes of the `<MAP>` tag.

Attribute	Required	Purpose
COORDS	✔	Specifies the coordinates of a hotspot area specified by the SHAPE attribute. The coordinates are specified in (x,y) pairs until the coordinates cover an area. For example, a polygon would have the value: COORDS="x1,y1,x2,y2,..." and so on.
HREF	✔	Indicates where the user will go (in the form of a URL) if they click in a region that is specified by the corresponding COORDS attribute.
NOHREF	✔	Indicates that if the user clicks in a region specified by the corresponding COORD tag, then no action will

Attribute	Required	Purpose
		occur. This attribute is required if the HREF attribute is not used.
SHAPE	✔	Specifies the shape of the hotspot region. The valid values are: circle, rectangle, and polygon. With a circle you must specify the center point of the circle (x,y), then the radius of the circle, in that order. (COORDS="center.x,center.y,radius") With a rectangle, you must specify the coordinates of two adjacent end-points of the rectangle (COORDS= "x1,y1,adjacent.x2,adjacent.y2"). With a polygon, you specify multiple sets of (x,y) coordinates that do not overlap (COORDS="x1,y1,x2,y2,x3,y3,...").

NOTE The values "polygon", "circle," and "rectangle" can be shortened to "poly", "circ", and "rect", respectively, for the SHAPE attribute of the AREA tag.

Example See Listing B.3 in the Frames section for an example.

The *<CODE>* Tag

Purpose The <CODE> tag renders its encapsulated text in a fixed-width font, similar to that of a code listing.

Syntax

```
<CODE>...</CODE>
```

Attributes None.

Example

```
<H2>The code for a simple C program</H2>

<CODE>
#include<stdio.h> <BR>
main() <BR>
{<BR>
printf("This is a test");<BR>
}<BR></CODE>
```

The <*DFN*> Tag

Purpose The <DFN> tag is one of the many tags that renders text in italics.

Syntax

```
<DFN>...</DFN>
```

Attributes None.

Example

```
This is an example of the <DFN>&lt;DFN&gt;</DFN> tag.
```

The <*EM*>Tag

Purpose The <EM> tag, is used to emphasize a particular group of words it surrounds. The text it surrounds is in italics. The only difference between the <EM> tag and other italic rendering tags is that <EM> is used in a logical sense.

Syntax

```
<EM>...</EM>
```

Attributes None.

Example

```
You <EM>must</EM> turn on the computer to get anything done.
```

The <*FONT*> Tag

Purpose The <FONT> tag is used for changing the size, color, and face of the text it surrounds.

Syntax

```
<FONT>...</FONT>
```

Attributes

Attribute	Required	Purpose
COLOR		Specifies the new color of the text. The color is specified by one of several color names (noted in the <BODY> tag section) or by a hexadecimal value, in the form of #RRGGBB (where RR, GG, and BB is a hexadecimal number from 0 to FF (255) in red, green and blue respectively).

Attribute	Required	Purpose
FACE		Specifies the new font for the text being encapsulated. Whether the font is shown or not, depends on whether it is available on the user's system. Some common fonts are listed in the following table. Also, you can specify multiple font names in case the user does not have the first specified font (in other words, if FACE ="Times, Arial, Bahamas," the Times font will be used, if it's not available, the Arial font will be used and so on.) There is technically no limit to the number of alternate fonts one can specify.
SIZE		Specifies the size of the text surrounded. This can be a size relative to the base size (1 by default) or a new size (from 1–7). A relative size to the default size (3), or to the default size specified by `<BASEFONT>`, can also be used (such as, SIZE ="+2" means two sizes larger than the default size or "5" and SIZE="-1" is one size smaller than the default size of "2".)

Common Font Names
Arial
Courier
Courier New
Comic Sans Ms
Dingbats
Expo
FrankfurtGothic
Script
Times New Roman
Wingdings

NOTE The listed fonts only work on a user's system if they are available (if the font is installed). The listed fonts are fonts that are most likely to be on a user's Windows operating system.

Example

```
The following text is the largest size:<BR>
<FONT SIZE="7">The Largest Size</FONT><BR>
The following text is one size bigger that the current text<BR>
<FONT SIZE="+1">One Size Bigger</FONT><BR>
<FONT SIZE="2" COLOR="blue" FACE="Arial">
This text is one size larger than the normal text,
blue and is rendered in the Arial FONT </FONT>
```

Forms

This section is devoted to forms and how to implement them. Forms are an important tool for Visual Basic Script and they can provide more interactive Web pages. The syntax expressed in the next section is the syntax for forms in general and all the form controls or elements are encapsulated inside the form.

Form Syntax

```
<FORM>...</FORM>
```

Form Attributes The following are attributes that forms use to specify how and where to send its data:

Attribute	Purpose
ACTION	Specifies the URL of where the data should be submitted when the user submits the form. The URL is usually a CGI (common gateway interface) program, which processes the data.
METHOD	Specifies how the data should be submitted. There are two valid values for METHOD. These include: "get", and "post". The Get METHOD should be used when most of the data the user submits is not going to be permanently stored (as in a search). The Post METHOD is used when all the data the user submits is intended to be kept (as in a guestbook). Also, when the Get METHOD is used, all the data in the form is appended to the URL. When the Post METHOD is used, all the data is sent via a set of variables and arrays, called the HTTP post transaction.

NOTE When using just Visual Basic Script with forms (the form is not going to be further processed), the previous attributes are unneeded. Internet Explorer 3.0 also allows for form controls (`<INPUT>` and `<SELECT>` tags) to be used without specifying a parent form. ■

Form Controls There are two actual tags for specifying all the form controls. These tags are the `<INPUT>` tag, and the `<SELECT>` tag. The `<INPUT>` tag specifies most of the form's controls, while the `<SELECT>` tag is used for providing list boxes and drop-down lists.

The <INPUT> Tag The `<INPUT>` tag is a single tag used for specifying various form controls including the: button, text, radio, and checkbox controls. The table in this section specifies all the attributes of the `<INPUT>` tag and the controls you can specify.

Syntax

```
<INPUT>
```

Attributes

Attribute	Required	Purpose
ALIGN		Specifies the alignment of the image (used with the image control). Valid values are middle, bottom, and top.
CHECKED		Indicates whether a checkbox or a radio button is selected or checked (used with radio buttons and checkboxes). CHECKED is a valueless attribute and its presence inside the checkbox, or radio input tag indicates that the button is selected.
MAXLENGTH		Specifies the maximum amount of characters that can be entered into a text control.
NAME		Identifies the form control.
SIZE		Specifies the size of the control (text box or text area). For a text box, the width in characters is given SIZE ="width". For a text-area, the width and the height are specified with the characters, SIZE ="width,height."
SRC		Used with the image control to specify the location of the image (either by URL or filename).

continues

continued

Attribute	Required	Purpose
TYPE		Specifies the type of form control. See the next table for the types of form controls available and how to implement them.
VALUE		Gives a default value for the form control. For buttons, this gives the button a name.

TYPE (control)	Value	Function
"button"		Makes a clickable button control that has no special function (see the "submit" and "reset" values.)
"checkbox"		Indicates a square box that can be checked on and off. A group of checkboxes with related data should be given the same name. The default submitted value, if none is specified, is "on." Values are submitted only if the checkboxes are checked.
"hidden"		Indicates a hidden input control (the control is not seen by the user and is commonly used for values that the user does not need to see).
"image"		Specifies a clickable image in the form which submits the coordinates of the user's click in the form of image-name.x and image-name.y. Image-name is the name of the image assigned by the NAME attribute and the appended .x and .y values are the x and y coordinates respectively where the origin (where x and y both equal zero) is at the top left-hand corner of the image.
"password"		Specifies a text box in which all the input is hidden by *s.

TYPE (control)	Value	Function
"radio"		Specifies a radio button that remains selected when clicked. If several radio buttons are given the same name, only one of the collection remains selected when clicked.
"reset"		Specifies a button that resets the entire form when clicked.
"submit"		Specifies a button that submits the form to the URL specified by the ACTION attribute of the <FORM> tag.
"text"		Specifies a plain text box that can accept text characters and strings.
"textarea"		Similar to a text box but it can span several lines and it enables the user to input multiple lines of text.

The <SELECT> Tag The `<SELECT>` tag is used for specifying drop-down, or list box controls. For items in these controls, the `<SELECT>` tag uses the `<OPTION>` tag to specify these items.

Syntax

```
<SELECT>...</SELECT>
```

Attributes

Attribute	Purpose
MULTIPLE	Specifies that multiple items can be selected from the drop-down or list box.
NAME	Identifies the name of the drop-down or list box.
SIZE	Specifies how many entries of the `<SELECT>` tag should be displayed. As a rule of thumb, the SIZE determines whether the `<SELECT>` tag is a drop-down, or list box. If the SIZE="1" (by default it does) then the `<SELECT>` tag becomes a drop-down box. If the value for SIZE is any other positive number, then the `<SELECT>` tag becomes a list box displaying (vertically) the items in the box. If there are more items in the list box than those displayed, then the box becomes scrollable.

The *<OPTION>* Tag The `<OPTION>` tag is what specifies the entries, or list items in the `<SE-LECT>` tag. The general syntax for the option tag is: `<OPTION>`. All the words that follow the option tag become the text that is displayed on screen. The following table specifies the attributes of the `<OPTION>` tag.

Attribute	Purpose
SELECTED	Is a valueless attribute. Its purpose is to set one of the options as selected (the item is highlighted). If no SELECT attribute exists in any of the option tags, then the first attribute is selected by default.
VALUE	Gives a value to the option tag. This value is submitted with the form if the option is selected.

Example The code in Listing B.1 can also be referenced off the accompanying CD.

Listing B.1 FORMD1.HTM—A Demonstration of All the Form Controls

```
<HTML>
<HEAD>
<TITLE>Sample Form</TITLE>
</HEAD>
<BODY BGCOLOR="#44AC55">
<FORM NAME="formme">
<FONT COLOR="blue" SIZE="+2">Checkboxes</FONT><BR>
Small:<INPUT TYPE="checkbox" NAME="ch1"><BR>
Medium:<INPUT TYPE="checkbox" NAME="ch1"><BR>
Large:<INPUT TYPE="checkbox" NAME="ch1"><BR>
<FONT COLOR="navy" SIZE="+2">Buttons</FONT><BR>
<INPUT TYPE="button" NAME="b1" VALUE="click-me I">
<INPUT TYPE="button" NAME="b2" VALUE="click-me II">
<INPUT TYPE="button" NAME="b3" VALUE="click-me III"><BR>
<FONT COLOR="tan" SIZE="+2">Hidden Fields</FONT><BR>
<INPUT TYPE="hidden" VALUE="I am clickmeone" NAME="ha">
<INPUT TYPE="hidden" VALUE="I am clickmetoo" NAME="hb">
<INPUT TYPE="hidden" VALUE="I am clickmethree" NAME="hc">
<FONT COLOR="yellow" SIZE="+2">Image Controls</FONT><BR>
<INPUT TYPE="image" NAME="im1" SRC="natback.gif"><BR CLEAR="all">
<FONT COLOR="aqua" SIZE="+2">Password Box</FONT><BR>
<INPUT TYPE="password" NAME="p1" VALUE="fdgdgd"><BR>
<FONT COLOR="fuchsia" SIZE="+2">Radio Buttons</FONT><BR>
Yes <INPUT TYPE="radio" name="r1"> No <INPUT TYPE="radio" name="r1">
Maybe <INPUT TYPE="radio" name="r1"><BR>
<FONT COLOR="maroon" SIZE="+2">Submit and Reset</FONT><BR>
<INPUT TYPE="submit" NAME="haha" VALUE="submit me">
<INPUT TYPE="reset" NAME="boowho" VALUE="reset me">
<BR>
<FONT COLOR="teal" SIZE="+2">Text box</FONT><BR>
<INPUT TYPE="text" NAME="t1" VALUE="default value">
<BR></FORM></BODY></HTML>
```

Frames

Frames provide an efficient, convenient, and sharp way of presenting information in HTML documents. There are two frame systems: a collection of frames in a frameset, which replace normal HTML pages, and floating frames, which exist in normal HTML documents.

Frame Sets Frame sets are used to replace normal HTML documents. With a frame set, a collection of frames that display different documents are displayed the browser screen. The <FRAMESET> tag is used to initiate and end the frame collection. The only tags that are allowed to be encapsulated in the <FRAMESET> tag is the <FRAME> tag and other <FRAMESET> tags. The <FRAME> tag specifies the properties for each individual frame.

Frameset Syntax

```
<FRAMESET>
<FRAME>
...
</FRAMESET>
```

Attributes for *<FRAMESET>*

Attribute	Required	Purpose
COLS	✔	Specifies the number of columns in a frame set and their width, separated by commas. The column's length can be specified either by pixels, a relative size, or as a percentage of a screen. For example, COLS="200,20%,*" specifies three columns. The first is 200 pixels wide, the second takes 20 percent of the leftover space on the screen, and the last takes the rest of the screen.
FRAMEBORDER		Indicates whether a border for the frames should be present or not. Valid values for this attribute are Yes (specifying that a border is present), and No (specifying no border). The default value, if none is used is Yes.
FRAMESPACING		Specifies the length between each of the frames. This length also specifies

continues

continued

Attribute	Required	Purpose
		the uniform length of the border (if one is present)
ROWS	✔	Specifies the number of rows in a frame set and their height, separated by commas. The row's height can be specified in the same manner as columns (in pixels, screen percentage or a relative size). For example, ROWS="*,2*", specifies two rows. Thc first row is half the size of the second row, or takes 1/3 of the available space while, the second takes 2/3 of the space.

NOTE Either the attribute COLS or ROWS is specified when defining a frame set, but not both. Frame sets can be nested; which means one `<FRAMESET>...</FRAMESET>` can exist in another. The nested `<FRAMESET>` element can be defined differently as well (if the first was defined by COLS the second could be defined by COLS or ROWS making dynamic, richer looking pages (see the example section).

Attributes for *<FRAME>*

Attribute	Required	Purpose
FRAMEBORDER		Indicates whether a border for the individual frame is present, or not. This attribute is identical to the attribute in the <FRAMESET> attribute table.
MARGINHEIGHT		Specifies the margin height of the frame in pixels.
MARGINWIDTH		Specifies the margin width of the frame in pixels.
NAME		Identifies the frame so it can be accessed by other elements in HTML.

Attribute	Required	Purpose
NORESIZE		An attribute without a specified value, that indicates that the frame will not be resizable by the user.
SCROLLING		Specifies whether the frames should be scrollable, or not (a scroll bar is on the right and bottom sides if the item is scrollable).
SRC	✔	Specifies the URL the frame should load and display.

The TARGET attribute

The TARGET attribute is the attribute that other HTML entities use to display their content (or hyper-references) in different frames on the page. If a frame is named frame1, then the TARGET attribute would access that frame by TARGET="frame1". The TARGET attribute works for the tags listed in the following table.

Tag	TARGET's Function
<A>	When the TARGET attribute is specified in an <A> tag, the link in the <A> tag is loaded in the specified window. If the <A> tag is in a frame and no TARGET is specified, the page is just loaded into the frame the link resides in.
<AREA>	When an image's area, specified by the area tag, is clicked, the URL is loaded into the window specified. If no window is specified, the URL is loaded into the frame with the image map that requested it.
<BASE>	When the TARGET attribute is specified in the <BASE> tag, all the links on a page are directed to the frame specified by the TARGET attribute. This is a quick and short way of directing all the links on a page to a specified frame instead of having to add the TARGET attribute to each one. If a tag does contain a different TARGET attribute, however, then the frame that the TARGET attribute references will receive that data.
<FORM>	When the TARGET attribute is in the <FORM> tag, the results returned by submitting the form will be sent to the frame specified by TARGET.

There are also special reserved names that can be used by the TARGET attribute to reference different frames on the screen. The following table shows the reserved names that can be used with the TARGET attribute.

TARGET Special Value	Function
"blank"	This value for the TARGET attribute specifies that the content requested by the tag, which contains the TARGET attribute, be loaded in a new window (new browser).
"parent"	This value indicates that the content, referenced by the element containing the TARGET attribute, is to be loaded into the frame's parent window.
"self"	This value indicates that the content should be loaded into its own window.
"top"	This value indicates that the content should be loaded into the topmost frame. The "_top" value is not functioning properly in the beta 1 version of Internet Explorer 3.0

NOTE If a name specified by the target attribute does not exist, or is not one of the special names, a new browser with the URL specified by the tag with the TARGET attribute is loaded. ■

Examples The examples in Listings B.2 through B.6 demonstrate how frames are used, these files can also be found on the accompanying CD under their respective name. All these files should be in the same directory to work properly.

Listing B.2 QAB.HTM—The Main Frames Page

```
<HTML>
<HEAD>
<TITLE>Demonstrations of Frames</TITLE>
</HEAD>
<BODY BGCOLOR="cornsilk">
<FRAMESET COLS="*,350" FRAMESPACING="5">
<FRAME SRC="default1.htm" SCROLLING="no" NAME="left1">
<FRAMESET ROWS="*,100">
<FRAME SRC="default2.htm" SCROLLING="no" NAME="right1">
<FRAME SRC="menu.htm" SCROLLING="no" NAME="right2">
</FRAMESET>
</FRAMESET>
</BODY></HTML>
```

Listing B.3 MENU.HTM—The Main Menu-Navigation Bar

```
<BODY BGCOLOR="slateblue" TOPMARGIN="0" LEFTMARGIN="0">
<IMG SRC="map.jpg" HEIGHT="100" WIDTH="350" USEMAP="#mapone">
<MAP NAME="mapone">
<AREA SHAPE="poly" COORDS="0,0,0,99,128,99,66,0" HREF="default1.htm"
target="right1">
<AREA SHAPE="poly" COORDS="70,0,185,0,258,99,132,99" HREF="default2.htm"
TARGET="left1">
<AREA SHAPE="circ" COORDS="302,53,33" HREF="default3.htm"
TARGET="left1">
</MAP>
</BODY>
```

Listing B.4 DEFAULT1.HTM—The Default Screen for the "left1" Frame

```
<BODY BGCOLOR="gold" TEXT="chocolate">
<FONT SIZE="+3" COLOR="violet">This is the default page for the first
frame. Note the diversity of color names</FONT> in the source.</BODY>
```

Listing B.5 DEFAULT2.HTM—Default for the "right1" Frame

```
<BODY BGCOLOR="seagreen" TEXT="moccasin">
This is another frame.
<A HREF="blank.htm" TARGET="right2">This link clears the menu</A><BR>
<A HREF="menu.htm" TARGET="right2">This brings it back</A>
<HR>
</BODY>
```

Listing B.6 DEFAULT3.HTM—The Default Screen 3, When the User Clicks Item 3 in the Navigation Bar

```
<BODY BGCOLOR="midnightblue" TEXT="mistyrose">
<H1>
This is another test frames. How does it look??
</H1>
</BODY>
```

The <*Hn*> Tag

Purpose The <H*n*> tags are tags that specify headings for an HTML page, where n is a number between 1 and 7 (7 being the smallest).

Syntax

```
<H1>...</H1>
<H2>...</H2>
```

```
<H3>...</H3>
<H4>...</H4>
<H5>...</H5>
<H6>...</H6>
<H7>...</H7>
```

Attributes

Attribute	Required	Purpose
ALIGN		Specifies the alignment of the Header. ALIGN can have the values, "left", "right", and "center".

Example

```
<H1 ALIGN="center">Outline</H1>
<H2>Introduction</H2>
<H3>Purpose</H3>
<H3>Doscussion</H3>
<H2>Methods</H2>
<H3>Resourse</H3>
<H3>Procedure</H3>
<H2>Results</H2>
<H2>Conclusions</H2>
```

The <*HR*> Tag

Purpose The <HR> tag is used to specify a horizontal rule, or divider across the page.

Syntax

```
<HR>
```

Attributes

Attribute	Required	Purpose
ALIGN		Specifies the alignment of the horizontal rule. The value for ALIGN can be either "right", "left", or "center". The horizontal rule is centered by default.
COLOR		Specifies the color of the horizontal line. The color can be one of several supported color names, or a hexadecimal value. Refer to the <BODY> section of this appendix for more information on colors and color names.

NOSHADE	Specifies that the rule does not have any shading (or 3-D look). This attribute does not have a value.
SIZE	Specifies the height of the horizontal rule. The value for this attribute is in pixels.
WIDTH	Specifies the length of the horizontal rule. The value for WIDTH can either be in pixels, or a percentage of the screen (for example, SIZE="50%" would be 50 percent of the screen.)

Example

```
<HR WIDTH="20%" COLOR="red" NOSHADE>
<HR>
<HR SIZE="25" COLOR="LIME">
```

The <I> Tag

Purpose The `<I>` tag renders text in italics and functions the same as the `<DFN>`, `<EM>`, and other tags.

Syntax

```
<I>...</I>
```

Attributes None.

Example

```
<I>This text is in Italics</I><BR>
<EM>So is this.</EM>
```

The <IMG> Tag

Purpose The `<IMG>` tag allows the insertion of graphics images, animations, and animated GIF images.

Syntax

```
<IMG>
```

Attributes

Attribute	Required	Purpose
ALIGN		Specifies the alignment of text relative to the image or vice versa, depending on the value. The

continues

continued

Attribute	Required	Purpose
		values "bottom", "middle", or "top" specify the alignment of text respective to the name of the value. The values right or left specify the alignment of the image on the page. The latter two values also permit text to flow around the image.
ALT		Specifies an alternative text to display if the user chooses not to display graphics. Also, the string contained as a value in the ALT attribute is what gets displayed when a user points at a picture.
BORDER		Draws a uniform border around the image. The values for the BORDER are measured in pixels.
CONTROLS		Is a valueless attribute. This attribute can be used when an animation (.AVI) file is displayed. When the CONTROLS attribute is used, a set of video controls is displayed under the animation.
DYNSRC	✔	Used to display an animation on-screen usually with the .AVI extension. The value for this attribute can be the name of a file, or a URL of a file.
HEIGHT		Specifies the height of the image in pixels. If the height specified is not the original height of the image, then Internet Explorer scales the image to the specified height.
HSPACE		Specifies the horizontal spacing, or offset of the image on its right and left sides.
ISMAP		Specifies that the image is a clickable imagemap. It sends the coordinates the user clicks to the server, where the program is specified that handles these coordinates
LOOP		Specifies how many times the animation should loop. The values for this attribute can be a number or infinite, meaning a continuous loop.
SRC	✔	Specifies the name of the image to be displayed. Several formats are supported by explorer. Some are .BMP, .GIF, and .JPG also proposed is the

Attribute	Required	Purpose
		.PNG format. The specified location can either be a filename, or a URL pointing to a file.
START		Specifies when the animation should start after the image is loaded. The values for this attribute are fileopen, or mouseover. Fileopen indicates that the animation should start playing when the animation is done loading. Mouseover indicates that the image will start playing when the user points the mouse at the animation. Both attributes can be used together.
USEMAP		Specifies the location (name) of a client-side imagemap to use with the image. The image map is usually in the same document and is called by the value "#name" where name is the name of the image map (see the client side image map section for more information.)
VSPACE		Specifies, in pixels, the top and bottom offset space of the image. This is similar to the HSPACE attribute except it specifies widths for the top and the bottom of the image.
WIDTH		Specifies the width, in pixels, of the image. If the width specified is not the original size of the image, then it is scaled to the size specified.

NOTE Either the DYNSRC, or the SRC attribute is required but not both. However, both can be used simultaneously. ■

Example

```
<P>The following displays a normal image:</P><BR>
<IMG SRC="test.gif" SIZE="100" HEIGHT="100"><BR>
<P>The following image is the same image but half the size:</P>
<IMG SRC="test.gif" SIZE="50" HEIGHT="50"><BR>
<P>Text is flowed around <IMG SRC="hi.gif" ALIGN="left">
this image if you get what I am saying</P>
<BR><P>This is an animation with controls that will
start when it is finished downloading and will start
afterwards when you move the mouse over it:</P><BR>
<IMG DYNSRC="ball.avi" START="fileopen,mouseover">
```

The <ISINDEX> Tag

Purpose The <ISINDEX> tag is used to create a simple input box, which serves the purpose of being a search engine powered by some program.

Syntax

```
<ISINDEX>
```

Attributes

Attribute	Required	Purpose
ACTION		Specifies the location of the program used to process the information entered into ISINDEX box.
PROMPT		Specifies what prompt name should be given to the <ISINDEX> input box. If no name is specified, then the prompt "You can search this index. Type the keyword(s)you want to search for:" appears by default.

Example

```
<ISINDEX ACTION="http://www.place.com/cgi-bin/myengine.cgi"
PROMPT="Enter Words to search for:">
```

The <KBD>Tag

Purpose The <KBD> tag is used to logically represent what one would type on a keyboard (instructional). Text encapsulated by this tag is rendered in a fixed-width font and is in bold.

Syntax

```
<KBD>...</KBD>
```

Attributes None.

Example

```
You type the words: <KBD>cd ..</KBD> then enter.
```

The <LISTING> Tag

Purpose The <LISTING> tag is used to render text in a small, fixed-width font that resembles a code listing. No tags are recognized within the context of the <LISTING> tag and line breaks are natural (no special tags are required to insert line breaks).

Syntax

```
<LISTING>...</LISTING>
```

Attributes None.

Example

```
An example FORTRAN 77 program:
<LISTING>
       program test
       print*,'This is a test'
       end
</LISTING>
```


Lists

Definition Lists Definition lists are used to define a list of terms. There are three parts to a definition list. These are shown in the following syntax. The <DT> tag is used to specify the terms in the definition list, and the <DD> tag is the Definition Data or the defining of the term specified by <DT>. The definition terms are put on one line and the definition is on the next line, slightly indented.

Syntax

```
<DL>
<DT>...</DT><DD>...</DD>
...
</DL>
```

Attributes None.

Although the </DT> and the </DD> tags are not required for encapsulating their respective text, it is a good idea to include them for clarity and to avoid confusion.

Directory Lists The <DIR> tag is used to specify a directory of items. Each entry is displayed in a single column. The <LI> tag is used for specifying the entries in the directory list.

Syntax

```
<DIR>
<LI>...</LI>
...
</DIR>
```

Attributes None.

Menu Lists The menu lists create lists similar to the <DIR> lists except there is no limit on characters. The <LI> tag is used to indicate the individual entries inside the <MENU> tag. Technically, there is no difference between <MENU> and <DIR> lists.

Syntax

```
<MENU>
<LI>...</LI>
...
</MENU>
```

Attributes None.

Ordered Lists Ordered lists are lists whose entries are preceded with numbers, letters, or Roman Numerals whose list number (or what have you) increases when subsequent entries are specified. The `<LI>` tag is used to specify each of the entries in the ordered list.

Syntax

```
<OL>
<LI>...</LI>
...
</OL>
```

Attributes

Attribute	Required	Purpose
START		Specifies a start number where the list should start. If the type of list is not a number, then the list starts out with the nth item in order (where n is the start value specified). For example, if the number type was a roman numeral, and START="3", the value that would be displayed in the list for the first item is III.
TYPE		Specifies what type of numbering system to use. The following table lists the listing types.

TYPE Value	Renders As
"1"	Renders the list entries as normal Arabic numerals (1, 2, 3, and so on).
"A"	Renders the list entries as capital letters (if there are more than 26 entries, then the value goes to AA, AB and so forth. but if the value for START exceeds 702 then the items are rendered as a digit again).

"a"	Renders list entries as lowercase letters. The same situation for number limits is the same as uppercase letters.
"I"	Renders list entries as uppercase Roman numerals. If the value for uppercase Roman numerals exceeds 3999 (MMMCXCIX), then the style resumes as digits.
"i"	Renders list entries as lowercase Roman numerals. The situation for number limits is the same as uppercase Roman numerals.

Attributes for *<LI>*

Attribute	Required	Purpose
TYPE		Specifies which type of list-number should be used (valid values are in the previous table.)
VALUE		Specifies the starting value of the list item. The value that is initially specified in the list and the value that is set in the `<LI>` tag are independent. The `<LI>` tag's value has precedence over the `<OL>`'s START value. Also, the list proceeds from the value specified by the `<LI>` tag.

Unordered Lists Unordered lists are lists, preceded by bullets and used when order is of no particular importance. The `<LI>` tags are used in the `<UL>` list to denote the different entries.

Syntax

```
<UL>
<LI>...</LI>
...
</UL>
```

Attributes None.

Example

```
<HTML>
<HEAD>
<TITLE>Demo 2 of Body demonstration</TITLE>
</HEAD>
<BODY BACKGROUND="natback.gif" TEXT="#0000FF" >
<H1 ALIGN="CENTER">Demo of ordered lists</H1>
<H3>This is a definition list</H3>
<DL>
<DT>Hydrogen</DT><DD>Earth's lightest gas. A proton in ionized form</DD>
<DT>Helium</DT><DD>A noble gas, second lightest</DD>
<DT>Clorine</DT><DD>A Halide. Very reactive with alkaline metals</DD>
```

```
<DT>Carbon</DT><DD>A non-metal whose presence indicates an organic material.
</DD>
</DL>
<H3>This is a directory list</H3>
<DIR>
<LI>Sam Smith</LI><LI>Joe Jones</LI>
<LI>Al Able</LI>
<LI>Billy Bob</LI>
<LI>dsdsdsdsdsdsdsdsdsdsdsds this has more than 20 chars.</LI>
</DIR>
<H3>This is a menu list</H3>
<MENU>
<LI>Soup</LI>
<LI>Beef</LI>
<LI>Veggies</LI>
<LI>Milk</LI>
</MENU>
<H3>This is an ordered list with Uppercase letters</H3>
<OL TYPE="A" START="698">
<LI>This the first entry starting at 698</LI>
<LI>Second (699)</LI>
<LI>Third (700)</LI>
<LI>Fourth (701)</LI>
<LI>Fifth (702)</LI>
<LI>What did I tell you?</LI>
</OL>
<H3>This is an unordered list</H3>
<UL>
<LI>Strawberries</LI>
<LI>Tires</LI>
<LI>Baseball gloves</LI>
<LI>Scissors</LI>
<LI>Pillows</LI>
</UL>
</BODY></HTML>
```

The *<MARQUEE>* Tag

Purpose The <MARQUEE> tag enables the user to create a text marquee that is scrollable across the screen. This is one of the "elegant" tags of the Internet Explorer 3.0 HTML collection.

Syntax

```
<MARQUEE>...</MARQUEE>
```

Attributes

Attribute	Required	Purpose
ALIGN		Specifies the alignment of the text in the marquee. The "top" value aligns the text of the marquee with the top of the marquee

Attribute	Required	Purpose
		container (where the text of the marquee is.) The "bottom" value aligns the marquee with the bottom of the container and the "middle" value aligns the text with the middle. The text is middle aligned by default.
BEHAVIOR		Indicates how the text of the marquee should behave. The value "scroll" (also the default behavior) makes the text repeatedly scroll on and off the screen. The value "slide" causes the text to scroll in on one side and stay. The value "alternate" causes the text to bounce back and forth within the marquee.
BGCOLOR		Specifies the background color of the marquee. The value for BGCOLOR is specified the same way as the BGCOLOR attribute for the <BODY> tag (see the <BODY> tag).
DIRECTION		Specifies the direction the marquee scrolls. Valid values are RIGHT and LEFT. The default value is LEFT (from left to right).
HEIGHT		Specifies the height of the marquee area, in pixels, or a percentage of the screen (such as HEIGHT="500" for pixels or HEIGHT="20%" for percentage.
HSPACE		Indicates the left and right marginal distance, or offset of the marquee.
LOOP		Specifies the number of times the marquee perform whatever action specified by behavior. Valid values are numbers specifying how many times the marquee should loop, or the word "infinite" specifying that there is no end to the looping.
SCROLLAMOUNT		Specifies the number of pixels between each successive draw of marquee text. Values are in pixels.

continues

Attribute	Required	Purpose
SCROLLDELAY		Specifies the time of each successive draw of the marquee text in milliseconds.
VSPACE		Specifies the top and bottom marginal distance or offset of the marquee's area. Values are in pixels.
WIDTH		Specifies the width of the marquee, in pixels, or as a percentage of the screen (similar to height).

You can make symbol type graphics scroll in a marquee by using a symbol font, such as Wingdings, for the text scrolling in a marquee. For example: `<FONT FACE="wingdings"><MARQUEE SCROLL="left">Q</MARQUEE></FONT>`.

CAUTION

It is not a good idea to encapsulate tags inside the marquee tag. It's best to nest the marquee in the different rendering tags you use. For instance: `<I><MARQUEE>Hi Y'all</MARQUEE></I>` is preferable. Some tags cause the marquee not to scroll when they are used. For information about putting graphics and other elegant items in marquees, read about the ActiveX Marquee which will be covered in Chapters 2 and 11.

Example

```
<MARQUEE DIRECTION="right" BEHAVIOR="slide" SCROLLAMOUNT="45"
➥ SCROLLDELAY="4" BGCOLOR="blue"><FONT COLOR="white">This text
➥ scrolls fast.</MARQUEE>
```

The <*NOBR*> Tag

Purpose The `<NOBR>` is used to force a line to remain together without breaking (where a break would normally occur).

Syntax

```
<NOBR>...</NOBR>
```

Attributes None.

Example

```
<NOBR> All of this text will remain on one line, regardless of the
➥ size of the browser.</NOBR>
```

Objects

For a detailed explanation of Microsoft Internet Explorer's object model, see Chapter 11.

The <P> Tag

Purpose The <P> tag is used to separate paragraphs of text. A line break also occurs between every use of the <P> tag.

Syntax

```
<P>...</P>
```

or just

```
<P>
```

Attributes

Attribute	Required	Purpose
ALIGN		Specifies the alignment of the paragraph text. Valid values are "right", or "left".

Example

```
<P ALIGN="left"> This text is left aligned</P>
<P ALIGN="right"> This test is right aligned </P>
```

The <PLAINTEXT> Tag

Purpose The <PLAINTEXT> tag renders text similar to the <LISTING> and <XMP> tags. All the text that is surrounded by the <PLAINTEXT> tag is rendered in a fixed-width font and no tags are recognized inside the <PLAINTEXT> tag.

Syntax

```
<PLAINTEXT>...</PLAINTEXT>
```

Attributes None.

Example

```
<PLAINTEXT> This is plain text</PLAINTEXT>
```

The <PRE> Tag

Purpose The <PRE> tag renders the text it surrounds in a fixed-width font. Additionally, natural line breaks are allowed and some tags (such as the <A> tag) are allowed to be used within the <PRE> tag.

Syntax

```
<PRE>...</PRE>
```

Attributes None.

Example

```
<PRE>
This is line one
.
.
.
This is line #x
This is line #<A HREF="three.html">x + 1</A>
</PRE>
```

The <*S*> Tag

Purpose The <S> tag renders the text it surrounds in a strike-out style, in which a line is run through the middle of the encapsulated text.

Syntax

```
<S>...</S>
```

Attributes None.

Example

```
<S>not needed</S>
```

The <*SAMP*> Tag

Purpose The <SAMP> tag is used to make the text it surrounds look like a code listing.

Syntax

```
<SAMP>...</SAMP>
```

Attributes None.

Example

```
<SAMP>print "A test"</SAMP>
```

The <*SCRIPT*> tag

The <SCRIPT> tag is fully covered in Chapters 2 and 11.

The <SMALL> Tag

Purpose The <SMALL> tag is used to render the text it encapsulates in a size smaller then the normal text.

Syntax

```
<SMALL>...</SMALL>
```

Attributes None.

Example

```
<SMALL>This is the fine print.</SMALL>
```

The <STRIKE> Tag

Purpose The <STRIKE> tag does the exact same thing the <S> tag does. See the previous <S> tag entry.

Example

```
<STRIKE>this works the same as the &lt;S&gt; tag. </STRIKE>
```

The <STRONG> Tag

Purpose The <STRONG> tag is another tag that renders the text it surrounds in bold. It is used to logically represent a strong emphasis.

Syntax

```
<STRONG>...</STRONG>
```

Attributes None.

Example

```
The victim is <STRONG>her</STRONG>.
```

The <SUB> Tag

Purpose The <SUB> tag is used to render the text it encapsulates as a subscript.

Syntax

```
<SUB>...</SUB>
```

Attributes None.

Example

```
The chemical formula for the combustion of octane is:
C<SUB>3</SUB>H<SUB>8</SUB> + 5O<SUB>2</SUB> = 4H<SUB>2</SUB>O
➥ + 3CO<SUB>2</SUB>
```

The <*SUP*> Tag

Purpose The <SUP> tag renders the text it surrounds as a superscript.

Syntax

```
<SUP>...</SUP>
```

Attributes None.

Example

```
x<SUP>y</SUP> = y<SUP>x</SUP> <BR>
for how many values of x and y?
```

Tables

Tables are one of the extensions to HTML that have been around the longest. Although tables are still not a standard, they are quite close and probably will not change in regards to syntax. Tables were first implemented by Netscape Navigator and since then improved upon by Internet Explorer (support for background and frame colors and stricter support for the HTML 3.0 Table Model). There are two different methods for making a table. The first uses basic tags defining rows and columns. The second method uses rows and columns but also treats the table as three parts: the header, the body, and the footer.

The Simple Table This section is an overview of the basic tags and attributes for tables, excluding the additional attributes covered in the new HTML 3 table model. These table extensions and additional tags and attributes will be covered in the next section. The simple table consists of a group of rows that can contain several cells. The table's content is defined by rows and then by all the cells on that row.

Syntax

```
<TABLE>
<CAPTION>...</CAPTION>
<TR><TH>...</TH><TD>...</TD>...</TR>
...
</TABLE>
```

The <TABLE> Tag The <TABLE> tag is what specifies the beginning and end of a table. All the information about rows, columns, and other information must be inside the table tags. Below are the attributes for the <TABLE> tag. These attributes can also be used for the <TD>, <TH>, and <TR> (except for the BORDER attribute). These attributes are inheritable, which means that if the attribute is specified in the <TABLE> tag, it is also used by the <TR>, <TD>, and <TH> tags unless they have a different value for that attribute. If the <TR>, <TD>, and <TH> tags have attribute values different from their parent (higher) tags, then that attribute is used instead.

Attribute	Required	Purpose
ALIGN		Specifies the alignment of the text in the table cells. Valid values are "left", "right," and "center". By default, the <TABLE>, <TD>, and <TR> tags have left aligned text and the <TH> tag's text is centered.
BACKGROUND		Specifies a background image to be displayed in the table's cells. Valid values are filenames, or URLs that point to a displayable image.
BGCOLOR		Specifies a background color for the table cells. Valid values are one of several color names or a color defined in hexadecimal (see the <BODY> tag for more information).
BORDERCOLOR		Specifies the border color to be used. When this attribute is used, the table's border and the border between the cells become the specified color and are no longer 3-D. Valid colors are one of the supported color names, or a hexadecimal #rrggbb value (see the <BODY> tag for more details).
BORDERCOLORDARK		Sets the color for the upper-right-hand border of a frame. Colors are specified the same way as in BORDERCOLOR.
BORDERCOLORLIGHT		Sets the color for the lower left-hand border of the frame. Colors are specified the same way as in BORDERCOLOR.
VALIGN		Specifies the vertical alignment of a table/cell/cell group. Valid values are "top", and "bottom". The value, "top" aligns the cell text with the topmost portion of the cell

continues

continued

Attribute	Required	Purpose
		and the “bottom” value aligns the cell’s text with the bottom most portion of the cell.

The following table contains attributes that are specific to the <TABLE> tag:

Attribute	Required	Purpose
BORDER		Specifies the uniform width of the table’s outer border in pixels. If this attribute is not present, the value is “0” (no border). If the attribute is present but has no value, the width of the border becomes on pixel. Any other value for the border is in pixels (for example, BORDER=“3” sets a border that has a uniform width of 3 pixels).
CELLPADDING		Specifies the amount of uniform margin space (space separating the cell text from its borders) in pixels.
CELLSPACING		Specifies the uniform spacing of the individual cells, in pixels. If there is a border present, the value for this attribute is the uniform size of the border between the cells, and between the cells and the border.
HEIGHT		Specifies the total screen height the table takes up. This value can be in pixels but values using percentages of the screen are more useful (in other words, HEIGHT =“88%” would take up 88 percent of a screen lengthwise).
WIDTH		Specifies the total screen width the table should take up. This value can be in pixels but is more useful as a percentage of the screen (such as, WIDTH=“90%” would take up 90 percent of the horizontal screen space).

The <*CAPTION*> tag The caption tag is used to specify a caption for the table. The <CAPTION> tag has only one attribute, ALIGN, used to specify the alignment of the caption text. Valid values are "top", "bottom", "left", and "right". Each value indicates its respective location to the table.

The <*TR*> tag The <TR> tag defines a row group. All the cells in the row group are placed horizontally (side-by-side) on the screen. The tag's cell data, and the cell tags (<TD> and <TH>) go inside the <TR> tag.

The <*TD*> and <*TH*> Tags The <TD> and <TH> tags are used to specify the cells in a table; they are encapsulated in the <TR> tags. The <TD> is a normal table data cell and is rendered in normal text, by default. The <TH> tag is a table-cell header tag and is rendered in bold and centered, by default. There are several attributes specific to the <TD> and <TH> tags and they are listed in the following table.

Attribute	Required	Purpose
ALIGN		ALIGN specifies the alignment of the text in the cell. Valid values are "right", "left", and "center".
COLSPAN		COLSPAN specifies the amount of columns a cell should span (for example, COLSPAN="2" would make the cell span over two columns).
HEIGHT		HEIGHT specifies the height of a table's cell in pixels. All cells on the same row will be stretched to the height specified (if there is more than one height attribute on a row, the largest height will be used as the height of all the cells in the same row).
NOWRAP		NOWRAP indicates all the text in the cell should remain on one line (this attribute requires no value).
ROWSPAN		ROWSPAN specifies the number of rows a cell should span (in other words, ROWSPAN="3" would make a cell span over three rows).
VALIGN		VALIGN specifies the vertical alignment of the text in the cell relative to the cell.

continues

continued

Attribute	Required	Purpose
		Valid values are Top (text is aligned with the top of the cell), Bottom (text is aligned with the bottom of the cell), Middle (text is aligned with the middle of the cell), and Baseline (text is aligned with the baseline of the cell, all the text in a row of cells is on a straight line).
WIDTH		WIDTH specifies the width of a table's cell, and incidentally, the width of its entire column (the column stretches to the longest width specified).

NOTE The VALIGN attribute can be used in both the <TR>, <TD>, and <TH> attributes.

Advanced Table Layouts This section covers the more in-depth tags of the HTML 3.0 table model covered by Internet Explorer 3.0. These elements include table header, body, and footer elements, as well as attributes for frame and border layout, and control over column groups instead of row groups.

Header-Body-Footer Based Layout It's possible to design a table with Header/Body/ Footer sections in mind. To do this three tags are introduced: <THEAD>, <TBODY>, and <TFOOT>. These improve upon the simple table model. All the original cell and row tags can be encapsulated in the <THEAD>, <TFOOT>, and <TBODY> tags. There are also two new attributes introduced to the <TABLE> tag: FRAME, and RULING. These will be discussed in the attributes section.

Syntax

```
<TABLE>
<THEAD>...</THEAD>
<TBODY>...</TBODY>
<TFOOT>...</TFOOT>
</TABLE>
```

Using this method, if no sections (header, body , footer) are specified, just a table body exists. However, if <THEAD> or <TFOOT> are used to define their respective sections, then <TBODY> must be included.

The FRAME and RULES Attributes for <TABLE> The FRAME attribute for the <TABLE> specifies which sides of the border (if any) are to be rendered. The following table shows all the valid values for specifying which border frames to render.

FRAME Value	Function
"void"	No outside borders of the table are displayed if this value is used
"above"	Only the top side of the border is rendered
"below"	Only the bottom side of the border is rendered
"hsides"	Only the left and right sides of the frame are rendered
"lhs"	Only the left side of the border is displayed
"rhs"	Only the right hand of the table's border is displayed
"vsides"	Only the top and bottom borders are displayed
"box"	All four sides of the frame are displayed
"border"	The same as "box"

The RULES attribute for the <TABLE> tag specifies which interior borders (borders between cells and the major sections of the table) should be rendered. The table below shows all the valid values for designating which interior rulings to render.

RULES Value	Function
"all"	All interior rules are displayed.
"groups"	Interior rules are placed between each row group and each column group. The three row groups are specified by the <THEAD>, <TBODY>, and <TFOOT> tags (see the next section for column groups).
"none"	No interior rules are drawn.
"cols"	This functions similarly to the "groups" value except vertical rules are drawn for all columns.
"rows"	This functions similarly to the "rows" value except horizontal rules are drawn between every row.

NOTE The <TBODY>-<THEAD>-<TFOOT> style must be used for RULES and FRAMES to work.

Controlling Alignment by Columns In addition to having properties for groups of rows in tables, you can also have column groups in tables that can change the alignment and size of groups of columns. The <COLGROUP> tag is used to encapsulate a collection of column groups which are indicated by <COL>.

Syntax

```
<TABLE>
<COLGROUP>
<COL>
...
</COLGROUP>
...
<THEAD>...</THEAD>
...
</TABLE>
```

The <COLGROUP> can be used to set alignments on column groups, or the <COL> tag, according to the attributes listed below. The <COL> tags have inheritance and override the attributes specified by its parent <COLGROUP> tag. The <COL> tag inside the <COLGROUP> tag is not required, because the spanning for a column group can be specified in the <COLGROUP> tag; the <COL> tag is used for control of individual column groups, for alignment, and width. Both the <COLGROUP> and the <COL> tags support the attributes in the following table.

Attributes for *<COLGROUP>* and *<COLS>*

Attribute	Required	Purpose
ALIGN		Specifies the alignment of the text in a column group. Valid values are "left" aligned, "right" aligned, and "center" aligned.
SPAN		Indicates how may columns the <COLGROUP> or <COL> spans. For instance, if SPAN="2" then the column group consists of two columns.
WIDTH		Specifies the width of the column group (this attribute is apparently not implemented in the beta 1 version of Internet Explorer 3.0).

NOTE <COL> tags and <COLGROUP> tags are cumulative. For example, if a column group had a column span of 2 (`<COLGROUP SPAN="2">`) and another column group had two <COL> elements with a span of 1 (`<COLGROUP><COL SPAN=1><COL SPAN=1></COLGROUP>`), then four columns have been used already. If a column group has a SPAN value and it also contains <COL> elements with a SPAN value, then the SPAN values for the <COL> tag are used and the value for the <COLGROUP> is ignored.

Examples Listing B.7 invokes both the methods of simple tables and tables with column groups, frames and rules. This example can be found on the accompanying CD.

Listing B.7 TABLESTF1.HTM—This is an Example of Two Tables

```
<HTML>
<HEAD>
<TITLE>A Demonstration of tables</TITLE>
</HEAD>
<BODY BGCOLOR="#345678">
<H2>A simple table using various alignment, formatting and coloring tags.</H2>
<!-- This is table 1 -->
<TABLE BORDER="1" BGCOLOR="tan">
<TR>
<TD ROWSPAN=2 BGCOLOR="black"></TD>
<TH COLSPAN="4" BGCOLOR="white">Revenue (in 10<SUP>6</SUP> $'s)</TH>
</TR>
<TR>
<TH COLSPAN=2 BGCOLOR="yellow">First Half</TH>
<TH COLSPAN=2 BGCOLOR="yellow">Second Half</TH>
</TR>
<TR><TH WIDTH="100" BGCOLOR="goldenrod">Year</TD>
<TH BGCOLOR="gold">First Quarter</TH>
<TH BGCOLOR="gold">Second Quarter</TH>
<TH BGCOLOR="gold">Third Quarter</TH>
<TH BGCOLOR="gold">Fourth Quarter</TH>
</TR>
<TD BGCOLOR="green">1994</TD>
<TD BGCOLOR="#3737373"><I>30</I></TD>
<TD BGCOLOR="#3737373"><I>30</I></TD>
<TD BGCOLOR="#3737373"><I>23</I></TD>
<TD BGCOLOR="#3737373"><I>44</I></TD>
</TR>
<TR>
<TD BGCOLOR="green">1995</TD>
<TD BGCOLOR="#3737373"><I>31</I></TD>
<TD BGCOLOR="#3737373"><I>33</I></TD>
<TD BGCOLOR="#3737373"><I>23</I></TD>
<TD BGCOLOR="#3737373"><I>45</I></TD>
</TR>
<TR>
<TD BGCOLOR="green">1996</TD>
<TD BGCOLOR="#3737373"><I>29</I></TD>
<TD BGCOLOR="#3737373"><I>33</I></TD>
<TD BGCOLOR="#3737373"><I>23</I></TD>
<TD BGCOLOR="#3737373"><I>56</I></TD>
</TR>
</TABLE>
<!-- This is end of table 1 -->
<BR CLEAR="all">
<HR>
```

continues

Listing B.7 Continued

```
<TABLE BORDER="3" CELLSPACING=2 CELLPADDING=3" RULES="groups"
➥ BGCOLOR="lightblue" WIDTH="100%">
<CAPTION ALIGN="top">
<FONT SIZE="-1" FACE="Comic Sans MS" COLOR="red">
A more complex table utilizing the RULES, FRAME, &lt;COLGROUP&gt;
, &lt;COL&gt;, and other entities of a table.</FONT>
</CAPTION>
<COLGROUP SPAN="1" ALIGN="center">
<COLGROUP>
<COL SPAN="3" ALIGN="center">
</COLGROUP>
<COLGROUP SPAN="1">
<COLGROUP SPAN="2" ALIGN="center">
<THEAD>
<TR BGCOLOR="aquamarine">
<TH>Product #</TH>
<TH>Department A</TH>
<TH>Department B</TH>
<TH>Department C</TH>
<TH>Total #</TH>
<TH WIDTH="100">Good</TH>
<TH WIDTH="100">Defective</TH>
</TR>
</THEAD>
<TBODY>
<TR>
<TD BGCOLOR="aqua" BORDERCOLOR="aqua">225A</TD>
<TD BGCOLOR="lightblue">5</TD>
<TD BGCOLOR="lightblue">6</TD>
<TD BGCOLOR="lightblue">7</TD>
<TD BGCOLOR="lightblue">18</TD>
<TD BGCOLOR="lightblue">10</TD>
<TD BGCOLOR="lightblue">8</TD>
</TR>
<TR>
<TD BGCOLOR="aqua" BORDERCOLOR="aqua">761C</TD>
<TD BGCOLOR="lightblue">2</TD>
<TD BGCOLOR="lightblue">4</TD>
<TD BGCOLOR="lightblue">5</TD>
<TD BGCOLOR="lightblue">11</TD>
<TD BGCOLOR="lightblue">10</TD>
<TD BGCOLOR="lightblue">1</TD>
</TR>
<TR>
<TD BGCOLOR="aqua" BORDERCOLOR="aqua">3999</TD>
<TD BGCOLOR="lightblue">1</TD>
<TD BGCOLOR="lightblue">0</TD>
<TD BGCOLOR="lightblue">1</TD>
<TD BGCOLOR="lightblue">2</TD>
<TD BGCOLOR="lightblue">1</TD>
<TD BGCOLOR="lightblue">1</TD>
</TR>
<TR>
```

```
<TD BGCOLOR="aqua" BORDERCOLOR="aqua">702</TD>
<TD BGCOLOR="lightblue">5</TD>
<TD BGCOLOR="lightblue">5</TD>
<TD BGCOLOR="lightblue">5</TD>
<TD BGCOLOR="lightblue">15</TD>
<TD BGCOLOR="lightblue">5</TD>
<TD BGCOLOR="lightblue">10</TD>
</TR>
<TR>
<TD BGCOLOR="aqua" BORDERCOLOR="aqua">56</TD>
<TD BGCOLOR="lightblue">25</TD>
<TD BGCOLOR="lightblue">25</TD>
<TD BGCOLOR="lightblue">6</TD>
<TD BGCOLOR="lightblue">56</TD>
<TD BGCOLOR="lightblue">50</TD>
<TD BGCOLOR="lightblue">6</TD>
</TR>
<TR>
<TD BGCOLOR="aqua" BORDERCOLOR="aqua">1123</TD>
<TD BGCOLOR="lightblue">11</TD>
<TD BGCOLOR="lightblue">23</TD>
<TD BGCOLOR="lightblue">0</TD>
<TD BGCOLOR="lightblue">34</TD>
<TD BGCOLOR="lightblue">30</TD>
<TD BGCOLOR="lightblue">4</TD>
</TR>
</TBODY></TABLE></BODY></HTML>
```


The <TT> Tag

Purpose The <TT> tag renders encapsulated text in a typewriter type font.

Syntax

```
<TT>...</TT>
```

Attributes None.

Example

```
<TT>Demonstration of the &lt;TT&gt; tag.</TT>
```

The <U> Tag

Purpose The <U> tag is used to underline the text it encapsulates.

Syntax

```
<U>...</U>
```

Attributes None.

Example

```
<U>This is not a link</U>
```

The <*VAR*> Tag

Purpose The <VAR> tag is used to surround text that logically represents a variable. The text rendered is in italics.

Syntax

```
<VAR>...</VAR>
```

Attributes None.

Example

The <*WBR*> Tag

Purpose The <WBR> tag is used to insert a soft word break inside a <NOBR> tag.

Syntax

```
<WBR>
```

Attributes None.

Example

```
<NOBR> This line will not break. Except, <WBR> here.</NOBR>
```

The <*XMP*> Tag

Purpose The <XMP> tag is used to render text in a fixed-width font. This tag is similar to the <LISTING> tag.

NOTE The <XMP>, <LISTING>, and <PLAINTEXT> tags are considered legacy tags and probably will not be included in future versions of the HTML draft or in Internet Explorer 3.0. ■

Syntax

```
<XMP>...</XMP>
```

Attributes None.

Example

```
<XMP>
This is MyPoem()
first line here;
second line here;
third line here;
End MyPoem
</XMP>
```


Miscellaneous Tags

The <BASE> Tag

Purpose The `<BASE>` tag is used to specify the base URL of the document in which the tag resides. This mechanism is especially useful when the file that contains the `<BASE>` tag is taken out of context.

Syntax

```
<BASE>
```

Attributes

Attribute	Required	Purpose
HREF	✔	Specifies the URL of the document in which the `<BASE>` tag resides. The full URL is used.

Example A file called welcome.html located at www.nm.org would have the following base tag:

```
<BASE HREF="http://www.nm.org/welcome.html">
```

The <BASEFONT> Tag

Purpose The `<BASEFONT>` tag is used to specify the base, or normal, size of the text that is normally used on-screen.

Syntax

```
<BASEFONT>
```

Attributes

Attribute	Required	Purpose
COLOR		Specifies the new color of the text. The color is specified by one of several color names (noted in the <BODY> tag section), or by a hexadecimal value in the form of #RRGGBB (where RR, GG, and BB is a hexadecimal number from 0 to FF (255) in red, green and blue, respectively).
FACE		Specifies the new font for the text being encapsulated. Whether the font is shown or not depends on whether it is available on the user's system. Some common fonts are listed in the next table. You can specify multiple font names in case the user does not have the first specified font (for example, if FACE="Times, Arial, Bahamas" the Times font will be used, if it's not available, the Arial font can be used, and so on). There is technically no limit to the number of alternative fonts you can specify.
SIZE		Specifies the size of the text surrounded. This can be a size relative to the base size (1 by default) or a new size (from 1–7). A relative size to the default size (3) can also be used (in other words, SIZE="+2" means two sizes larger than the default size or "5" and SIZE="-1" is one size smaller than the default size of "2").

Example This size specified by the following <BASEFONT> is size 4.

```
<BASEFONT SIZE="4" FACE="Sans">
```

The size specified by <BASEFONT> below is also 4 but with a relative size.

```
<BASEFONT SIZE="+1" COLOR="pink">
```

The *<BGSOUND>* Tag

Purpose The <BGSOUND> tag is used to specify a background sound, or soundtrack, that will play when the page is loaded.

Syntax

```
<BGSOUND>
```

Attributes

Attribute	Required	Purpose
SRC	✔	Specifies the source of the sound in the form of a URL, or a file.

Example

```
<BGSOUND SRC="tada.wav">
```

The <*COMMENT*> Tag

Purpose The <COMMENT> tag is used to insert remarks, which are not displayed, into an HTML document. Any text that is surrounded by the <COMMENT> tag is not displayed on the screen. The <COMMENT> can also take the one-tag form of: <!--......-->.

Syntax

```
<COMMENT>...</COMMENT>
```

or

```
<!-- ... -->
```

Attributes None.

Example

```
<COMMENT>Version: 3</COMMENT>

<!-- This is version 3 -->
```

The <*HTML*> Tag

Purpose The <HTML> tag is used to specify the beginning and end of an HTML document. Everything that is related to HTML, including the <HEAD> and <BODY> tags, should fall within the <HTML> tags.

Syntax

```
<HTML>...</HTML>
```

Attributes None.

Example

```
<HTML>
<HEAD>
<TITLE>This is a test</TITLE>
</HEAD>
<BODY BGCOLOR="C0C0C0">
<H1> This is a test</H1>
</BODY>
</HTML>
```

HTML Terminology

This section defines some general HTML terms and some Internet terminology that can help you read this appendix.

- *Attribute:* Usually refers to a property of an HTML tag that the user can change. For example, the HREF property is an attribute of the `<A>` tag.
- *Encapsulation:* Refers to when the start and ending (`<TAG>` and `</TAG>`) tags surround text and other tags for rendering, or other purposes.
- *Element:* Refers to the tags (such as `<EM>`). An element may also refer to the key word without the angle brackets (EM instead of `<EM>`).
- *Entity:* An entity, in HTML, is a tag, or a group of tags that have common purpose. The `<B>` tag renders text as bold, while client side image maps are used for making clickable maps.
- *HTML:* This stands for Hypertext Markup Language.
- *Value:* A value is what the user can assign an attribute of an HTML tag, if it requires a value. Some attributes do not require a value. The presence of a valueless attribute in a tag indicates some change.
- *URL:* This stands for Uniform Resource Locater, which is the standard means for referencing information over the Internet. For example: http://www.microsoft.com/ie/ie.htm is a URL, http:// is the type of resource that is being requested by the URL (in this case its hypertext transfer protocol). www.microsoft.com is the address (domain name) from where to get this resource and /ie/ie.htm is the location and name of the resource.

Color Names Supported by Internet Explorer 3.0 Beta 1

This section covers all the colors supported in Internet Explorer 3.0 and their corresponding hexadecimal value in the form of #RRGGBB. RR is the color intensity of red of the color (a hexadecimal number from 0-FF), GG is the color intensity of green of the color (a hexadecimal number from 0-FF), and BB is the blue color intensity of the color (a hexadecimal number from 0-FF).

Color Name	Hexadecimal Value
"aliceblue"	"#F0F8FF"
"antiquewhite"	"#FAEBD7"
"aqua"	"#00FFFF"
"aquamarine"	"#7FFFD4"
"azure"	"#F0FFFF"
"beige"	"#F5F5DC"
"brisque"	"#FFE4C4"
"black"	"#000000"
"blanchedalmond"	"#FFEBCD"
"blue"	"#0000FF"
"blueviolet"	"#8A2BE2"
"brown"	"#A52A2A"
"burlywood"	"#DEB887"
"cadetblue"	"#5F9EA0"
"chartreuse"	"#007FFF"
"chocolate"	"#D2691E"
"coral"	"#FF7F50"
"cornflowerblue"	"#6495ED"
"cornsilk"	"#FFF8DC"
"crimson"	"#DC143C"
"cyan"	"#00FFFF"
"darkblue"	"#00008B"
"darkcyan"	"#008B8B"

continues

continued

Color Name	Hexadecimal Value
"darkgoldenrod"	"#B8860B"
"darkgray"	"#A9A9A9"
"darkgreen"	"#006400"
"darkkahki"	"#BDB76B"
"darkmagenta"	"#8B008B"
"darkolivegreen"	"#556B2F"
"darkorange"	"#FF8C00"
"darkorchid"	"#9932CC"
"darkred"	"#8B0000"
"darksalmon"	"#E9967A"
"darkseagreen"	"#8FBC8F"
"darkslateblue"	"#483D8B"
"darkslategray"	"#2F4F4F"
"darkturquoise"	"#00CED1"
"darkviolet"	"#9400D3"
"deeppink"	"#FF1493"
"deepskyblue"	"#00BFFF"
"dimgray"	"#696969"
"dodgerblue"	"#1E90FF"
"floralwhite"	"#FFFAF0"
"forestgreen"	"#228B22"
"fuchsia"	"#FFFF00"
"gainsboro"	"#DCDCDC"
"ghostwhite"	"#F8F8FF"
"gold"	"#FFD700"
"goldenrod"	"#DAA520"
"gray"	"#808080"
"green"	"#008000"
"greenyellow"	"#ADFF2F"
"honeydew"	"#F0FFF0"

Color Name	Hexadecimal Value
"hotpink"	"#FF69B4"
"indianred"	"#CD5C5C"
"indigo"	"#4B0082"
"ivory"	"#FFFFF0"
"khaki"	"#F0E68C"
"lavender"	"#E6E6FA"
"lavenderblush"	"#FFF0F5"
"lawngreen"	"#7CFC00"
"lemonchiffon"	"#FFFACD"
"lightblue"	"#ADD8E6"
"lightcoral"	"#F08080"
"lightcyan"	"#E0FFFF"
"lightgoldenrodyellow"	"#FAFAD2"
"lightgreen"	"#90EE90"
"lightgrey"	"#D3D3D3"
"lightpink"	"#FFB6C1"
"lightsalmon"	"#FFA07A"
"lightseagreen"	"#20B2AA"
"lightskyblue"	"#87CEFA"
"lightslategray"	"#778899"
"lightsteelblue"	"#B0C4DE"
"lightyellow"	"#FFFFE0"
"lime"	"#0000FF"
"limegreen"	"#32CD32"
"linen"	"#FAF0E6"
"magenta"	"#FF00FF"
"maroon"	"#800000"
"mediumaquamarine"	"#66CDAA"
"mediumblue"	"#0000CD"
"mediumorchid"	"#BA55D3"
"mediumpurple"	"#9370DB"

continues

continued

Color Name	Hexadecimal Value
"mediumseagreen"	"#3CB371"
"mediumslateblue"	"#7B68EE"
"mediumspringgreen"	"#00FA9A"
"mediumturquoise"	"#48D1CC"
"mediumvioletred"	"#C71585"
"midnightblue"	"#191970"
"mintcream"	"#F5FFFA"
"mistyrose"	"#FFE4E1"
"moccasin"	"#FFE4B5"
"navajowhite"	"#FFDEAD"
"navy"	"#000080"
"oldlace"	"#FDF5E6"
"olive"	"#808000"
"olivedrab"	"#6B8E23"
"orange"	"#FFA500"
"orangered"	"#FF4500"
"orchid"	"#DA70D6"
"palegoldenrod"	"#EEE8AA"
"palegreen"	"#98FB98"
"paleturquoise"	"#AFEEEE"
"palevioletred"	"#DB7093"
"papayawhip"	"#FFEFD5"
"peachpuff"	"#FFDAB9"
"peru"	"#CD853F"
"pink"	"#FFC0CB"
"plum"	"#DDA0DD"
"powderblue"	"#B0E0E6"
"purple"	"#800080"
"red"	"#FF0000"
"rosybrown"	"#BC8F8F"

Color Name	Hexadecimal Value
“royalblue”	“#4169E1”
“saddlebrown”	“#8B4513”
“salmon”	“#FA8072”
“sandybrown”	“#F4A460”
“seagreen”	“#2E8B57”
“seashell”	“#FFF5EE”
“sienna”	“#A0522D”
“silver”	“#C0C0C0”
“skyblue”	“#87CEEB”
“slateblue”	“#6A5ACD”
“slategray”	“#708090”
“snow”	“#FFFAFA”
“springgreen”	“#00FF7F”
“steelblue”	“#4682B4”
“tan”	“#D2B48C”
“teal”	“#008080”
“thistle”	“#D8BFD8”
“tomato”	“#FF6347”
“turquoise”	“#40E0D0”
“violet”	“#EE82EE”
“wheat”	“#F5DEB3”
“white”	“#FFFFFF”
“whitesmoke”	“#F5F5F5”
“yellow”	“#FFFF00”
“yellowgreen”	“#9ACD32”

APPENDIX C

VBScript Coding Conventions

Coding conventions are nothing more than a set of rules pertaining to good programming practice. A computer can understand "spaghetti code" (convoluted, messy code that makes no sense at all to a human who tries to understand it) and other types of gobbledygook that would drive any sane person over the edge. By adhering to some simple guidelines, your code will not only be understandable to the next person who needs to maintain it, but, even you will be able to understand it six months after you wrote it.

These guidelines are based on commonly accepted rules of good programming practice, but they are not carved in stone. Pick what you like, modify what you don't like, and create your own set of rules that you can understand and communicate to others should the need arise. But, by all means, once you've determined which set of rules to use, use them, and use them rigorously and consistently. ■

Controls

When you create a control using a tool such as the VB IDE, or the ActiveX Control Pad, the control is created with a default name, such as *Frame1*. While any name can be used, it's good practice to replace the default with a more meaningful name. It's also extremely helpful to use a prefix, so you will know what *type* of control it is when looking at code it pertains to. For example, *Frame1* tells you that the object in question is a Frame control, *Options* gives you a clue about what the control pertains to, and *fraOptions* lets you know that you're dealing with a Frame control that has something to do with Options.

Since the inception of Visual Basic, common usage has resulted in a widely-accepted collection of control name prefixes. If you use these prefixes, there will never be any confusion as to exactly what type of controls you're using.

There are literally thousands of ActiveX controls available. Obviously, somewhere along the line, you'll either have to use the same three-letter prefix for two different types of controls, or, apply a longer (or shorter) prefix to distinguish between them.

Table C.1 lists some typical prefixes suggested by Microsoft.

Table C.1 Typical ActiveX Control Prefixes

Control Type	Prefix
3D Panel	pnl
Animated Button	ani
CheckBox	chk
ComboBox	cbo
Command Button	cmd
CommonDialog	dlg
Frame	fra
Horizontal ScrollBar	hsb
Image	img
Label	lbl
Line	lin
ListBox	lst

Control Type	Prefix
Spin	spn
TextBox	txt
Vertical ScrollBar	vsb
Slider	sld

Variables and Constants

Like controls, variables should also be given prefixes that identify their type. In addition to documenting a variable's type, you should consider adding an additional prefix to describe its scope if it's not a global variable. Microsoft suggests prefixing a variable name with an *s* if it's a Script-level variable. Thus, using the suggested prefix from Table C.1 for a Script-level Integer variable, a typical example would be *sintUserID*.

Remember, these prefixes are strictly for the benefit of people (including you, of course) who read the code—giving a String a prefix of "*byt*" will *not* change it into a Byte!

NOTE Functions (in addition to executing code) return values. Therefore, you should also use these prefixes in your Function declarations.

Table C.2 contains the variable type prefixes Microsoft recommends.

Table C.2 Variable Name Prefixes

Variable Type	Prefix
Boolean	bln
Byte	byt
Date/Time	dtm
Double	dbl
Error	err
Integer	int
Long	lng
Object	obj
Single	sng
String	str

Procedures

Procedure names, like variable names, should be given descriptive names. Functions, like variables, should be given a type prefix according to the examples in Table C.2, because they return a value; subprocedures, on the other hand, don't return any value, and therefore require no prefix.

Loops, Blocks, and White Space

Just as judicious use of white space makes text easier to read, a well-formatted code listing is easy to understand at a glance. When loops and other structures are properly indented, it's immediately apparent how the program is intended to flow. It's *much* easier to debug a program where each nested If/Then is indented a few spaces more than the preceding level. Placing all code flush left may be a little easier when you first type it in, but doing so guarantees you a maintenance nightmare.

If you simply indent each level of a loop and block by three or four spaces, you'll do well.

Here's how some typical code *should* look:

```
Sub CheckOrder
    For intC = intStart to intFinish
        If intRequired(intC) <= intOnHand Then
            Select Case intOnHand
                Case intReorderLevel
                   GeneratePO
                   ProcessOrder
                Case Is < intReorderLevel
                   ProcessOrder
            End Select

        Else
            NotifyReceiving
        EndIf
    Next
End Sub
```

Compare the preceding section of code with the following, and see which *you* would rather work with:

```
Sub CheckOrder
For intC = intStart to intFinish
If intRequired(intC) <= intOnHand Then
Select Case intOnHand
Case intReorderLevel
GeneratePO
ProcessOrder
Case Is < intReorderLevel
```

```
ProcessOrder
End Select
Else
NotifyReceiving
EndIf
Next
End Sub
```

In addition to using white space for indentation within a block of code, major sections of code (such as scripts, and major sections within scripts)should also have a blank line between them, to visually separate them.

Comments

It's important to comment every significant thing your program does and contains. Put blocks of indented comments at the start of every procedure (and every major section within a procedure), describing the purpose of the code that follows and providing meaningful information about how it accomplishes its task. Describe which variables it uses, which ones it modifies, and which it returns.

You should also place in-line comments at the end of significant lines of code, explaining what's being done.

HTML Considerations

As this book goes to press, recommended placement for scripts within HTML pages is uncertain. Some sources within Microsoft suggest placing them within the `<HEAD>` section, and others recommend putting them at the end of the `<BODY>` section. This is largely a style consideration, inasmuch as execution is unaffected by placement.

Regardless of where you put them, you should consider surrounding your scripts in HTML Comment tags (`<!--......-->`) to prevent them from appearing as text when viewed by non-ActiveX-enabled browsers.

Also, even though they won't actually *do* anything in browsers that don't support ActiveX, HTML controls will be visible in them if you place them within `<FORM>` blocks. ●

APPENDIX D

Porting Visual Basic Applications

When VBScript first appeared on the scene, it seemed unlikely that any effort to port VB programs to VBS scripts was even remotely feasible. Even apart from language limitations (such as no file I/O, no Typed structures, no Class modules, no Collections, and so on), the overriding reality was that VBS "applications" were HTML-bound. As has oft been noted, HTML—basically an upper-left to lower-right text-flow formatter—is ill-suited in situations that vector off from its original mission.

The recent appearance of HTML Layout Page functionality, combined with the productivity-enhancing ActiveX Control Pad, has changed this assessment to the degree that it is no longer unthinkable to port *some* VB applications to the Web.

If you are willing to do a fair amount of work dealing with the limitations and differences that remain, you will be able to bring certain VB applications to VBScript. At the very least, you should be able to duplicate most, if not all, of your user interface elements.

Even so, there are some show stoppers you need to be aware of from the start. If your program depends on any of them, you'll need to seriously consider whether you want to proceed. ■

Considering a Few Caveats

HTML Layout Pages, for all their similarity to VB Forms, are severely lacking in terms of properties, methods, events, and behavior. Essentially, they are dumb containers of controls; if you need to do anything at the form level (VB form, not HTML form), it won't happen, at least at this stage of the game. This includes such things as using the Print method to place text directly on a form, graphics methods (Line, Circle, and so on) to draw on a form, hiding, showing, or unloading a form, and trapping any events (such as mouse clicks or keystrokes).

You won't be able to do anything with Typed records. You might be able to get around this limitation by using multidimensional arrays, or, groups of arrays. You can't create Collections. Again, you might be able to use arrays—this was SOP prior to VB4, so it's definitely within the realm of "doability."

Class modules don't exist in VBScript. Nor, for that matter, do standard .BAS modules. You can deal with the latter omission by placing your procedures in the same file as your controls, or the HTML file that holds points to it. (At the time this book goes to press, HTML Layout Pages must reside in .ALX files, and an `<OBJECT...>` reference to the .ALX file must be placed in an HTML file. Microsoft has announced that when IE 3.0 is released, it is expected to support the use of HTML Layout Pages within an .HTM page.) As to Class modules, you might be able to duplicate their functionality by using procedures. Clearly, if you have a heavy investment in Class modules that you want to port over to Web applications, it might be in your interest to wait a while. See "Sweeping the Horizon" in this appendix for what might be a glimmer of hope.

Other features that you're "protected" from include the Printer Object, communications ports, and API (or other .DLL) calls.

File I/O is a real problem. You *can* write Class wrappers in VB4, and compile them to in-process .DLLs (for information on this topic, check out Que's *Special Edition Using VB4*), but, you should realize that it's an exercise that's not for the faint of heart. In addition to heavy VB coding, you'll need to embed `<OBJECT>` tags at the HTML level, using ClassID references, and at this time, it's impossible to use them with HTML Layout Pages, as the ActiveX Control Pad won't work with anything that doesn't meet the new ActiveX qualifications.

If you get that far, you'll still be faced with a security issue. The creators of the Internet Explorer have not simply relied on VBScript's lack of native file I/O for protection from malicious programmers. Attempting to use an object that does not contain a valid digital signature from a certificate agency, will result in warning boxes being displayed each time the page is loaded, unless security in the Internet Explorer is shut down. Shutting down security is definitely *not* recommended unless you are absolutely certain that the browsers in question will *never* wander off the safety of a corporate Intranet.

Sweeping the Horizon

If you do require language and/or object functionality that is not available in VBScript, you should remember that VBScript, VB, Internet Explorer, Windows, and even the Internet, are all moving targets. The only time something stands still is when it's dead in the water. It's not unreasonable to hope that later versions of the platform will include functionality that is missing now. Right now, VBScript is in its first generation. Windows is poised to undergo a major transformation, as the desktop blends into the Internet. No one outside the inner sanctums at Microsoft can say exactly *where* things will end up, although we do know that in general, we'll be getting better tools, more robust language implementations, and easier means for accomplishing tasks.

Microsoft has been dropping teasers in the press regarding the next major release of Visual Basic. Some of what they've publicly made known has a direct bearing on the things you'll be doing with VBScript and HTML Layout Pages.

For instance, you'll be able to write your own ActiveX controls, and roll in whatever functionality you require. Because Visual Basic is a full-featured language, this means that you should be able to supply much of the functionality that is currently missing from VBScript.

In the majority of cases, if you have a VB application that you want to port to VBS, you'll be looking at a complete rewrite. You should, however, be able to preserve the "look and feel" of your applications, assuming you can avoid use of graphics methods and form events. Many specific procedures, and much of your existing event code routines, can be carried over to VBScript, in some cases with little or no change. However, the structural aspects of your code—Modules, Classes, and data structures—will need to be redesigned, or rewritten.

If, after you assess the situation, you realize that the law of diminishing returns has been invoked, you'll need to make the hard choice to either scrap the project, or come up with a workable alternative. No amount of advice or counsel can protect you from situations like this, and although they test your mettle, they can also provide opportunity. Take the resources at hand, reason out the situation, and present a solution. That's what sets *you* apart from the pack. ●

Index

Symbols

A

B

C

E

F

M

N

P

Q

R

T

W

X-Z

Complete and Return this Card for a *FREE* Computer Book Catalog

Thank you for purchasing this book! You have purchased a superior computer book written expressly for your needs. To continue to provide the kind of up-to-date, pertinent coverage you've come to expect from us, we need to hear from you. Please take a minute to complete and return this self-addressed, postage-paid form. In return, we'll send you a free catalog of all our computer books on topics ranging from word processing to programming and the internet.

Mr. ☐ Mrs. ☐ Ms. ☐ Dr. ☐

Name (first) ________ (M.I.) ___ (last) ________

Address ________

____

City ________ State ___ Zip ________ ____

Phone ___ ___ ____ Fax ___ ___ ____

Company Name ________

E-mail address ________

1. Please check at least (3) influencing factors for purchasing this book.

- Front or back cover information on book ☐
- Special approach to the content ☐
- Completeness of content ☐
- Author's reputation ☐
- Publisher's reputation ☐
- Book cover design or layout ☐
- Index or table of contents of book ☐
- Price of book ☐
- Special effects, graphics, illustrations ☐
- Other (Please specify): ________ ☐

2. How did you first learn about this book?

- Saw in Macmillan Computer Publishing catalog ☐
- Recommended by store personnel ☐
- Saw the book on bookshelf at store ☐
- Recommended by a friend ☐
- Received advertisement in the mail ☐
- Saw an advertisement in: ________ ☐
- Read book review in: ________ ☐
- Other (Please specify): ________ ☐

3. How many computer books have you purchased in the last six months?

- This book only ☐
- 2 books ☐
- 3 to 5 books ☐
- More than 5 ☐

4. Where did you purchase this book?

- Bookstore ☐
- Computer Store ☐
- Consumer Electronics Store ☐
- Department Store ☐
- Office Club ☐
- Warehouse Club ☐
- Mail Order ☐
- Direct from Publisher ☐
- Internet site ☐
- Other (Please specify): ________ ☐

5. How long have you been using a computer?

- ☐ Less than 6 months
- ☐ 6 months to a year
- ☐ 1 to 3 years
- ☐ More than 3 years

6. What is your level of experience with personal computers and with the subject of this book?

	With PCs	With subject of book
New	☐	☐
Casual	☐	☐
Accomplished	☐	☐
Expert	☐	☐

Source Code ISBN: 0-7897-0809-4

7. Which of the following best describes your job title?

Administrative Assistant ☐
Coordinator ☐
Manager/Supervisor ☐
Director ☐
Vice President ☐
President/CEO/COO ☐
Lawyer/Doctor/Medical Professional ☐
Teacher/Educator/Trainer ☐
Engineer/Technician ☐
Consultant ☐
Not employed/Student/Retired ☐
Other (Please specify): ______________ ☐

8. Which of the following best describes the area of the company your job title falls under?

Accounting ☐
Engineering ☐
Manufacturing ☐
Operations ☐
Marketing ☐
Sales ☐
Other (Please specify): ______________ ☐

9. What is your age?

Under 20 ☐
21-29 ☐
30-39 ☐
40-49 ☐
50-59 ☐
60-over ☐

10. Are you:

Male ☐
Female ☐

11. Which computer publications do you read regularly? (Please list)

____

____

____

____

____

____

____

____

***Comments*:** ______________________________

____

____

Fold here and scotch-tape to mail.

NO POSTAGE
NECESSARY
IF MAILED
IN THE
UNITED STATES

BUSINESS REPLY MAIL
FIRST-CLASS MAIL PERMIT NO. 9918 INDIANAPOLIS IN

POSTAGE WILL BE PAID BY THE ADDRESSEE

ATTN MARKETING
MACMILLAN COMPUTER PUBLISHING
MACMILLAN PUBLISHING USA
201 W 103RD ST
INDIANAPOLIS IN 46290-9042

License Agreement

By opening this package, you are agreeing to be bound by the following: